ENCYCLOPEDIA OF WORLD WRITERS

BEGINNINGS THROUGH THE 13TH CENTURY

ENCYCLOPEDIA OF WORLD WRITERS
BEGINNINGS THROUGH THE 13TH CENTURY

Dr. Thierry Boucquey

GENERAL EDITOR
Department of French
Scripps College
Claremont University Consortium

Dr. Gary Johnson

ADVISER
Department of English
University of Findlay

Dr. Nina Chordas

ADVISER
Academic Programs
University of Alaska Southwest

☑®
Facts On File, Inc.

Encyclopedia of World Writers: Beginnings through the 13th Century

Written and developed by BOOK BUILDERS LLC
Copyright © 2005 by BOOK BUILDERS LLC

Facts On File, Inc.
132 West 31st Street
New York NY 10001

Library of Congress Cataloging-in-Publication Data

Encyclopedia of world writers, beginnings to the twentieth century / Thierry Boucquey, general editor ; Gary Johnson, advisor ; Nina Chordas advisor ; [written and developed by Book Builders LLC].
    p. cm.
    General editor for v. 3: Marie Josephine Diamond; advisors, Maria DiBattista and Julian Wolfreys.
    Vol. 3 previously published as: Encyclopedia of 19th- and 20th- century world writers / Marie Josephine Diamond, general editor.
    Includes bibliographical references and index.
    ISBN 0-8160-6143-2 (set : alk. paper) — ISBN 0-8160-5190-9 (v. 1 : alk. paper) — ISBN 0-8160-5191-7 (v. 2 : alk. paper) — ISBN 0-8160-4675-1 (v. 3 : alk. paper) 1. Authors—Biography—Dictionaries. 2. Literature—Bio-bibliography—Dictionaries. I. Boucquey, Thierry. II. Diamond, Marie Josephine. III. Book Builders LLC. IV. Encyclopedia of 19th- and 20th- century world writers.
    PN451.E55 2005
    809'.003--dc22

                                                                    2004020551

Text design by Rachel L. Berlin
Cover illustration by Smart Graphics

Printed in the United States of America

VB FOF 10 9 8 7 6 5 4 3 2 1

This book is printed on acid-free paper.

CONTENTS

Preface   vii

Introduction   ix

Timeline of Authors and Works   xi

Writers and Works Covered, by
   Geographical Area   xv

Entries A to Z   1

Selected Bibliography   342

Index   377

PREFACE

From the beginning of time, stories have fascinated humans in every society. Because storytellers grasp certain social and psychological phenomena within their societies which others do not, and are able to interpret those phenomena and bring them to life, their status is unique.

Encyclopedia of World Writers, Beginnings through the 13th Century presents a list of the world's visionaries and their masterpieces, covering many centuries from the earliest recorded writings to the year 1300. Entries include discussions of poetry, fiction, religious writings, drama, epics, history, political science, maxims, biography, philosophy, and nonfiction. Each entry is followed by the suggestion of a translation in English

of the original work whenever available. The main considerations that ruled the selection of writers and works were their intrinsic value, their interest for young contemporary scholars, and their geographic and linguistic diversity.

We wish the readers a pleasant and exciting voyage into the realm of the world's masters and their literature. It is our hope that this volume will stimulate readers to further explore the masterpieces for the essence and exquisiteness that in this work can only be suggested.

Thierry Boucquey
General Editor

INTRODUCTION

Encyclopedia of World Writers, Beginnings through the 13th Century offers a comprehensive yet accessible overview of early world literature, covering the period from the first vestiges of human literary activity to the year 1300. The survey spans the globe, covering 12 main geographic domains: Africa, the Americas, Britain-Ireland, Classical Greece and Rome, East Asia, Francophone Europe, Germany-Netherlands-Scandinavia, the Middle East, the Iberian Peninsula, India, Italy, and Russia-eastern Europe.

The nearly 300 entries in this volume naturally include the giants of the classical Greco-Roman canon, such as Plato, Homer, and Ovid, in addition to anonymous great Western literary works such as *Beowulf,* the *Song of Roland,* and the *Nibelungenlied,* as well as well-known medieval figures such as Dante, Marco Polo, and Chrétien de Troyes. However, a particular effort has been made to include a significant number of entries representing language domains that are traditionally less studied in Western institutions. Our aim has been to include not only texts and authors sanctioned by academic tradition—canonized one might say—but also writers and works often excluded from the traditional curriculum for reasons that are not always clear or convincing. Often literary encyclopedias apply a strict definition of

literature and limit themselves to poetry, prose, and theater but omit, for example, religious writers, chroniclers, mystics, artists, or philosophers. In our view, however, these writers and their works are often carriers of literary significance in that they have strongly influenced their era and the more traditional authors of their time.

In this volume, therefore, major figures that have dominated the East Asian canon, such as Confucius or Murasaki Shikibu, appear alongside the Middle Eastern *Gilgamesh* and *The Thousand and One Nights,* the Indian *Bhagavad Gita* and *Ramayana,* and the Native American *tuuwutsi* narratives. The entries also include a significant number of lesser-known but nonetheless notable authors and works—from all domains—which have influenced global literary traditions and generated renewed scholarly research as of late. Because a parallel encyclopedia on British writers is available, entries regarding British writers have been kept to a minimum.

A few words must also be said concerning oral literature. In certain genres, such as the epic, the folk tale, or the love song, literary traditions have been transmitted orally for centuries and still remain in vogue in certain areas of the world. In fact, today in the United States and lately in France as well, a strong revival of the storytelling tradition is taking place. Alas, some civilizations never embraced writing, therefore dooming their literary production to extinction. The concept of oral literature itself may be a contradiction in terms, for we can only know it as it becomes written, which is also when it fundamentally changes. This dilemma, however, could not dissuade us from recognizing the importance of the oral tradition in world literature and incorporating it into the encyclopedia. Furthermore, the particular performative style of oral literature tends to blur the lines between recitation, song, dance, and even religious liturgy, adding yet another distinctive interdisciplinary layer to our entries.

The volume further incorporates definitions of important literary movements and phenomena, such as mystery plays, mythology, or troubadours, as well as literary terminology, such as epic, Purana, and *deus ex machina*. Some historical terms and events that are closely associated with the literary output of certain epochs, such as the Crusades, are also included in the hope that they will assist the reader in a more complete evaluation and understanding of works from bygone eras.

Aimed at both high school and college-level students, this encyclopedia endeavors to encour-age and motivate the aspiring scholar to explore the literary wealth of world writers and their masterpieces. Tools at the students' disposal include biographical information, critical analyses of major works, appropriate cross-references, and the inclusion of the titles of translated editions as well as suitable critical texts. Whenever possible, English translations of works written in other languages have been included.

Readers, then, will be able to stroll through space and time from Egypt's and China's ancient literary beginnings to the romances of late medieval Europe. They may continue their journey through Incan and Aztec lands to the sacred Native American world and on to Africa's wealth of oral traditions. It was impossible to include everything here, but it is our sincere hope that, in reviving the old ideal of the Renaissance, this volume will pique its readers' curiosity and stimulate their interest by suggesting intriguing avenues and tools for research that may direct them to many genres in numerous unfamiliar literatures.

Thierry Boucquey
Huntington Beach, California

TIMELINE OF AUTHORS AND WORKS

Because there is no way to date the entries on Native American and African works (they all originated from the oral tradition, and most were not put into written form until after 1800), we have
listed them as having no date ("n.d.").

Dates	Entry	Dates	Entry
n.d.	African proverbs	ca. 1500–600 B.C.	Rig-Veda
n.d.	Nahuatl poetry, ancient	ca. 1400 B.C.–ca. A.D. 200	Book of the Dead
n.d.	Chinook myths and tales		
n.d.	Coyote tales	1125–570 B.C.	*Book of Songs*
n.d.	creation myths, Native American	ca. 900s–100s B.C.	Bible, Hebrew
		700s B.C.	Homer
n.d.	Navajo Nightway Ceremony songs	700s B.C.	Hesiod
		ca. 620–565 B.C.	Aesop
n.d.	Ojibway myths and legends	fl. ca. 610–ca. 580 B.C.	Sappho of Lesbos
n.d.	Oklahoma Cherokee folktales	600s–500s B.C.	Alcaeus
n.d.	*O'othham Hoho'ok A'agitha*	551–479 B.C.	Confucius
n.d.	*telapnaawe* narratives	fl. ca. 550 B.C.	Valmiki, Maharishi
n.d.	*tuuwutsi* narratives	ca. 528–483 B.C.	Zen parables
n.d.	*waikan* narratives	ca. 525–456 B.C.	Aeschylus
n.d.	White Mountain Apache myths and tales	ca. 522–ca. 438 B.C.	Pindar
		500s B.C.	Anacreon
n.d.	*worak* narratives	500s B.C.	Laozi (Lao Tzu)
n.d.	Yaqui deer songs	late 500s B.C.	Sunzi (Sun Tzu)
n.d.	Zuni narrative poetry	ca. 496–ca. 405 B.C.	Sophocles
ca. 2500–1300 B.C.	*Gilgamesh*	ca. 484–406 B.C.	Euripides

Dates	Entry
ca. 480–425 B.C.	Herodotus
ca. 469–399 B.C.	Socrates
ca. 460–ca. 400 B.C.	Thucydides
ca. 460–ca. 377 B.C.	Hippocrates
459–380 B.C.	Lysias
ca. 450–385 B.C.	Aristophanes
436–338 B.C.	Isocrates
ca. 431–ca. 352 B.C.	Xenophon
ca. 428–ca. 348 B.C.	Plato
400s B.C.	Bacchylides
400s–300s B.C.	Attic orators
400s B.C.–A.D. 1849	*Kalevala*
ca. 400 B.C.–ca. A.D. 400	*Mahabharata*
384–322 B.C.	Aristotle
384–322 B.C.	Demosthenes
ca. 372–ca. 287 B.C.	Theophrastus
ca. 342–292 B.C.	Menander
341–270 B.C.	Epicurus
332–296 B.C.	Qu Yuan (Ch'ü Yüan)
ca. 305–ca. 240 B.C.	Callimachus
300s B.C.	*Qu Elegies*
300s B.C.	Isaeus
fl. ca. 300 B.C.	Euclid
ca. 295–ca. 247 B.C.	Apollonius of Rhodes
254–184 B.C.	Plautus, Titus Maccius
239–169 B.C.	Ennius, Quintus
ca. 200 B.C.–A.D. 135	Dead Sea Scrolls
ca. 185–159 B.C.	Terence
106–43 B.C.	Cicero, Marcus Tullius
100–44 B.C.	Caesar, Julius
ca. 100s B.C.	*Panchatantra*
ca. 99–ca. 55 B.C.	Lucretius
ca. 90–43 B.C.	Hirtius
ca. 90–21 B.C.	Diodorus
86–35 B.C.	Sallust
84–54 B.C.	Catullus, Gaius Valerius
70–19 B.C.	Virgil
65–8 B.C.	Horace
63 B.C.–A.D. 14	Augustus
ca. 63 B.C.–ca. A.D. 24	Strabo
59 B.C.–A.D. 17	Livy

Dates	Entry
ca. 50–ca. 15 B.C.	Propertius, Sextus
43 B.C.–ca. A.D. 18	Ovid
ca. 10–90s B.C.	Apollodorus
ca. 10–90s B.C.	Bhagavad Gita
ca. 10–90s B.C.	Dionysius of Halicarnassus
ca. 4 B.C.–A.D. 65	Seneca
ca. 10–90s	Longinus
ca. 10s–90s	Phaedrus
10s–1400s	*purana*
23–79	Pliny the Elder
27–66	Petronius
ca. 37–ca. 101	Josephus, Flavius
39–65	Lucan
ca. 40–ca. 96	Quintilian
ca. 40–ca. 104	Martial
ca. 50–ca. 125	Plutarch
ca. 50–ca. 127	Juvenal
55–135	Epictetus
ca. 56–ca. 120	Tacitus, Cornelius
ca. 61–ca. 112	Pliny the Younger
78–139	Zhang Heng (Chang Heng)
ca. 115–ca. 180	Lucian
115–180	Pausanias
121–180	Marcus Aurelius Antoninus
ca. 125–after 170	Apuleius
129–ca. 199	Galen
ca. 150–ca. 225	Sextus Empiricus
192–232	Cao Zhi (Ts'ao Chih)
200s	Longus
ca. 200–ca. 550	Talmud
205–270	Plotinus
210–263	Ruan Ji (Juan Chi)
ca. 232–ca. 303	Porphyry
300s	*Kama Sutra*
ca. 340–397	Ambrose, Saint
ca. 340–420	Jerome, Saint
354–430	Augustine, Saint
365–427	Tao Yuanming (Tao Ch'ien)
385–433	Xie Lingyun (Hsieh Ling-yün)
400s	Jataka
400s	Kalidasa
ca. 410–485	Proclus

Dates	Entry	Dates	Entry
ca. 450–ca. 1450	Middle Ages	ca. 935–1020 or 1026	Firdawsī (Abū ol-Qāsem Mansūr)
468–533	Fulgentius, Saint		
ca. 480–524	Boethius	936–995	Mother of Fujiwara Michitsuna
500s	ʿAmr ibn Kulthum		
500s	*Hanged Poems*	ca. 965–unknown	Sei Shōnagon
500s–1200s	bardic poetry	ca. 970–1030	Izumi Shikibu
513–581	Yu Xin (Yü Hsin)	973–1058	Maʿarrī, Abū al-ʿAlāʾ, al-
543–ca. 569	Tarafah ʿAmr ibn al-ʿAbd	ca. 978–ca. 1016	Murasaki Shikibu
		980–1037	Avicenna
d. ca. 550	Imruʾ al-Qays	1007–1072	Ouyang Xiu (Ou-yang Hsiu)
ca. 560–661	Labid		
ca. 570–632	Muhammad	ca. 1021–1058	Ibn Gabirol, Solomon ben Yehuda
575–ca. 661	ʿAlī ibn Abī Tālib		
575–ca. 645	Khansāʾ, al-	1021–1086	Wang Anshi (Wang An-shih)
600s	Caedmon		
fl. 600s	Nukada, Princess	ca. 1030–1070	*Song of Roland*
ca. 610–632	Koran	1037–1101	Su Shi (Su Shih)
ca. 640–728	Farazdaq, al-	ca. 1043–1099	Cid, El
673–735	Bede	ca. 1048–1131	Omar Khayyám
699–759	Wang Wei	ca. 1057	*Ostromir Gospel*
701–762	Li Bai (Li Bo)	before 1075–after 1141	Halevi, Judah
712	*Kojiki*		
718–785	Otomo Yakamochi	1083–ca. 1141	Li Qingzhao (Li Ch'ing-chao)
fl. 750–800	Han Shan		
768–824	Han Yu (Han Yü)	1083–ca. 1154	Anna Comnena
772–846	Bai Juyi (Po Chü-i)	1098–1179	Hildegard von Bingen
776–868	Jāhiz, al-	1100s	Abélard and Héloïse
791–817	Li He (Li Ho)	early 1100s	Jaufré Rudel
800s–1200s	*Thousand and One Nights, The*	1100s	*Nibelungenlied*
		1100s–1200s	*Tristan and Iseult*
ca. 800–ca. 1250	*Edda*	ca. 1100–1155	Geoffrey of Monmouth
ca. 805–845	Abū Tammām	1126–1193	Fan Chengda (Fan Ch'eng-t'a)
ca. 813–858	Li Shangyin (Li Shang-yin)		
ca. 834–910	Wei Zhuang (Wei Chuang)	1126–1198	Averroës
		1127–1206	Yang Wanli
849–899	Alfred the Great	1135–1204	Maimonides, Moses
fl. ca. 850	Ono no Komachi	ca. 1140–ca. 1210	Heinrich von Veldeke
ca. 872–946	Ki no Tsurayuki	ca. 1141–ca. 1203	Nezāmī
891–1154	Anglo-Saxon Chronicle	ca. 1142–ca. 1220	ʿAttār, Farīd od-Dīn
900s	*Beowulf*	fl. ca. 1147–ca. 1170	Bernard de Ventadour
900s	*Shahnameh*	ca. 1150–ca. 1200	Marie de France
900s–1100s	*David of Sassoun*	ca. 1150–ca. 1213	Villehardouin, Geoffroi de
ca. 915–965	Mutanabbī, al-	ca. 1155–1216	Komo no Chomei

Dates	Entry	Dates	Entry
fl. 1160–1185	Chrétien de Troyes	d. 1201	Shikishi, Princess
ca. 1160–1200	Hartmann von Aue	1207–1283	Rumi, Jalaloddin
1162–1241	Fujiwara no Teika	ca. 1210–ca. 1290	Saadi
ca. 1170–ca. 1225	Wolfram von Eschenbach	ca. 1212–ca. 1294	Būsīrī, al-
ca. 1170–ca. 1230	Walther von der Vogelweide	ca. 1212–ca. 1294	Latini, Brunetto
		ca. 1215–ca. 1237	Guillaume de Lorris
ca. 1175–1250	*Roman de Renart*	ca. 1224–1274	Thomas Aquinas, Saint
1179–1241	Sturluson, Snorri	ca. 1225–1277	*Romance of the Rose*
fl. 1180–1200	Arnaut Daniel	ca. 1230–1306	Jacopone da Todi
ca. 1180–ca. 1225	Gottfried von Strassburg	ca. 1235–ca. 1280	Davanzati, Chiaro
ca. 1181–1226	Francis of Assissi, Saint	ca. 1240–ca. 1305	Jean de Meun
fl. ca. 1183–ca. 1204	Vidal, Peire	fl. 1245–1285	Rutebeuf
1185–1196	*Song of Igor, The*	fl. mid-1200s	Hadewijch
ca. 1190–1249	Vigne, Pier delle	ca. 1250–ca. 1306	Adam de la Halle
1200s	*Aucassin et Nicolette*	ca. 1250–1337	Wang Shifu (Wang Shih-fu)
1200s	Daibu, Lady		
1200s	Donzella, Compiuta	1254–1324	Marco Polo
1200s	*Epic of Son-Jara*	1260–ca. 1312	Angiolieri, Cecco
1200s	*Kebra Nagast Chronicles*	1265–1321	Dante Alighieri
1200s	*Sundiata, an Epic of Old Mali*	ca. 1280	*Njal's Saga*
		1283–1352	Yoshida Kenkō
ca. 1200–ca. 1544	myth of Manco Capac	1305–ca. 1370	Gao Ming (Kao Ming)
1200–1268	Beatrice of Nazareth		

Writers and Works Covered, by Geographical Area

AFRICA

African proverbs
Book of the Dead
Epic of Son-Jara
Kebra Nagast Chronicles
Sundiata, an Epic of Old Mali

ASIA

China

Bai Juyi (Po Chü-i)
Book of Songs
Cao Zhi (Ts'ao Chih)
Confucius
Fan Chengda (Fan Ch'eng-t'a)
Han Shan
Han Yu (Han Yü)
Gao Ming (Kao Ming)
Laozi (Lao Tzu)
Li Bai (Li Bo)
Li He (Li Ho)
Li Qingzhao (Li Ch'ing-chao)
Li Shangyin (Li Shang-yin)
mythology, Oceanic
Ouyang Xiu (Ou-yang Hsiu)
Qu Elegies
Qu Yuan (Ch'ü Yüan)
Ruan Ji (Juan Chi)

Sunzi (Sun Tzu)
Su Shi (Su Shih)
Tao Yuanming (Tao Ch'ien)
Wang Anshi (Wang An-shih)
Wang Shifu (Wang Shih-fu)
Wang Wei
Wei Zhuang (Wei Chuang)
Xie Lingyun (Hsieh Ling-yün)
Yang Wanli
Yu Xin (Yü Hsin)
Zen parables
Zhang Heng (Chang Heng)

India

Bhagavad Gita
Kalidasa
Kama Sutra
Mahabharata
Panchatantra
purana
Rig-Veda
Valmiki, Maharishi

Japan

Daibu, Lady
Fujiwara no Teika
Izumi Shikibu
Kamo no Chomei

Ki no Tsurayuki
Kojiki
Mother of Fujiwara Michitsuna
Murasaki Shikibu
Nukada, Princess
Ono no Komachi
Otomo Yakamochi
Sei Shōnagon
Shikishi, Princess
tanka
Yoshida Kenkō

Thailand
Jataka

EUROPE

Britain and Ireland
Alfred the Great
Anglo-Saxon Chronicle
bardic poetry
Bede
Beowulf
Geoffrey of Monmouth
mythology, Celtic

French-Speaking Europe
Abélard and Héloïse
Adam de la Halle
Arnaut Daniel
Aucassin et Nicolette
Bernard de Ventadour
Chrétien de Troyes
Guillaume de Lorris
Jaufré Rudel
Jean de Meun
Marie de France
Old English poetry
Romance of the Rose
Roman de Renart
Rutebeuf
Song of Roland
Tristan and Iseult
troubadours

Vidal, Peire
Villehardouin, Geoffroi de

German-Speaking Europe, Scandinavia, and the Netherlands
Beatrice of Nazareth
Edda
Gottfried von Strassburg
Hadewijch
Hartmann von Aue
Heinrich von Veldeke
Hildegard von Bingen
Kalevala
mythology, Norse
Nibelungenlied
Njal's Saga
Snorri Sturluson
Walther von der Vogelweide
Wolfram von Eschenbach

Greece/Rome
Aeschylus
Aesop
Alcaeus
Ambrose, Saint
Anacreon
Apollodorus
Apollonius of Rhodes
Apuleius
Aristophanes
Aristotle
Attic orators
Augustine, Saint
Augustus
Bacchylides
Boethius
Caesar, Julius
Callimachus
Catullus, Gaius Valerius
Cicero, Marcus Tullius
Demosthenes
Diodorus
Dionysius of Halicarnassus
Ennius, Quintus

Epictetus
Epicurus
Euclid
Euripides
Fulgentius, Saint
Galen
Herodotus
Hesiod
Hippocrates
Hirtius, Aulus
Homer
Horace
Isaeus
Isocrates
Jerome, Saint
Josephus, Flavius
Juvenal
Livy
Longinus
Longus
Lucan
Lucian
Lucretius
Lysias
Marcus Aurelius Antoninus
Martial
Menander
mythology, Greek and Roman
Ovid
Pausanias
Petronius
Phaedrus
Pindar
Plato
Plautus, Titus Maccius
Pliny the Elder
Pliny the Younger
Plotinus
Plutarch
Porphyry
Proclus
Propertius, Sextus
Quintilian
Sallust

Sappho of Lesbos
Seneca
Sextus Empiricus
Socrates
Sophocles
Strabo
Tacitus, Cornelius
Terence
Theophrastus
Thucydides
Virgil
Xenophon

Italy
Angiolieri, Cecco
Dante Alighieri
Davanzati, Chiaro
Donzella, Compiuta
Francis of Assisi, Saint
Jacopone da Todi
Latini, Brunetto
Polo, Marco
Thomas Aquinas, Saint
Vigne, Pier delle

Russia/Eastern Europe
Ostromir Gospel
Song of Igor, The

Spain and Portugal
Cid, El
Maimonides, Moses

MIDDLE EAST

Abū Tammām
'Alī ibn Abī Tālib
'Amr ibu Kulthum
Anna Comnena
'Attār, Farīd od-Dīn
Averroës
Avicenna
Bible, Hebrew
Būsīrī, al-

Caedmon
David of Sassoun
Dead Sea Scrolls
Farazdaq, al-
Firdawsī (Abū ol-Qāsem Mansūr)
Gilgamesh
Halevi, Judah
Hanged Poems
Ibn Gabirol, Solomon ben Yehuda
Imru' al-Qays
Jāhiz, al-
Khansā', al-
Koran
Labid
Ma'arrī, Abū al-'Alā', al-
Muhammad
Mutanabbī, al-
Nezāmī
Omar Khayyám
Rumi, Jalaloddin
Saadī
Shahnameh

Talmud
Tarafah 'Amr ibn al- 'Abd
Thousand and One Nights, The

THE AMERICAS

Chinook myths and tales
Coyote tales
creation myths, Native American
myth of Manco Capac
Nahuatl poetry, ancient
Navajo Nightway Ceremony songs
O'othham Hoho'ok A'agitha
Ojibway myths and legends
Oklahoma Cherokee folktales
telapnaawe narratives
tuuwutsi narratives
waikan
White Mountain Apache myths and tales
worak narratives
Yaqui deer songs
Zuni narrative poetry

Abélard and Héloïse (12th century)
theologian, philosopher, poet; student, abbess

Pierre Abélard (1079–1142) is remembered as the most important philosopher and logician of 12th-century France, and Héloïse as his most famous student. Abélard was born to a noble Breton family but gave up the life of a knight for the life of a scholar, devoting himself to the study of philosophy, rhetoric, and logic, or dialectic. Education in Abélard's day was administered by the Church, and he most likely studied PLATO and ARISTOTLE through the work of BOETHIUS. He was an enormously popular teacher due to his technique of *disputatio,* or argumentation, and he traveled widely, attracting students from all over the world.

Around 1113, Abélard decided to study theology under Anselm of Laon, then returned to the school at Notre Dame to teach. For Abélard, logic was the only way to reach understanding. Around 1105 he began writing his *Glosses on Logic,* which were separated into Greater and Lesser volumes and completed about 1130. In Paris he began working on two of his most influential treatises, *Sic et Non* (Yes and No) and *Theologica Summi Boni* (On the Divine Unity), written between 1118 and 1120. *Sic et Non,* structured as a list of questions with both yes and no answers, outlines Abélard's scholastic method and its tools of argumentation, inquiry, and example.

The years following Abélard's entry into St. Denis were his most productive in terms of writing; he published several commentaries, *Treatise on Understandings* (1122–25), *Introduction to Theology* (1125–30), and a disposition on *Dialectic,* which he worked on continuously between 1130 and 1140. During this time, Abélard, always a controversial figure, came under suspicion of heresy for certain points in his *Theologica.* The public condemnation and the burning of his books proved to be the second most calamitous event of Abélard's life.

The three most important works of his later life were his *Theologica Christiana* (Christian Theology, 1134–38); *Dialogue between a Philosopher, a Christian, and a Jew;* and his *Ethics, or Know Thyself,* both written between 1138 and 1142. While the later *Theologica* shows Abélard's intimacy with Christian doctrine, the *Dialogue,* structured as a discussion between three voices on the nature of good and the necessity of virtue to happiness, shows his familiarity with Judaism and Islam. In *Ethics,* he daringly proposes that virtue or sin lie in the intention behind an act and not in the act itself. This ethic of intention, which he shared with Héloïse, unsettled traditional theologians but has kindled the imagination of many subsequent scholars.

Abélard's contributions as a teacher and logician are frequently overshadowed by his doomed love affair with Héloïse, whom he began to tutor at Paris sometime before 1119. She had been previously educated at the convent of Argenteuil and had developed a reputation for intelligence and beauty, and the two quickly began a passionate affair. At the insistence of her uncle, they married, but when Héloïse returned to Argenteuil, her uncle, believing she had been abandoned, had Abélard beaten and castrated. The assault prompted Héloïse to take vows as a nun, and in 1128 she became prioress of the Paraclete, the religious institution that Abélard had founded.

The surviving correspondence between Abélard and Héloïse begins in 1132, after she had read his *History of My Calamities.* The first four letters of the collection, called the "personal letters," discuss their love affair from all angles and reveal Héloïse as a passionate and highly intelligent woman as skilled in the art of rhetoric as her teacher. Within these letters, both lovers cite the BIBLE as often as they quote scholars like AUGUSTINE or Latin writers like OVID, and they logically analyze their beliefs on marriage, human and divine love, and spirituality. The "letters of direction," which complete the collection, include deeply philosophical contemplation, outlines for a reformed religious order, and poems and prayers Abélard writes that the nuns may say on his behalf.

Despite Abélard and Héloïse's rhetorical sophistication and philosophical skills, later writers JEAN DE MEUN and Petrarch remembered them as doomed lovers similar to Anthony and Cleopatra of Julius CAESAR's time or Shakespeare's Romeo and Juliet. Yet Héloïse's service as prioress made her widely beloved in her community, and Abélard has been called the first modern thinker, whose philosophy formed the basis of empiricism.

English Versions of Works by Abélard and Héloïse

Abélard, Peter. *Ethical Writings.* Translated by Paul Vincent Spade. Indianapolis: Hackett Publishing Company, 1995.

Abélard and Héloïse. *The Letters of Abélard and Héloïse.* Translated by Betty Radice. New York: Penguin, 1974.

Works about Abélard and Héloïse

Clanchy, M. T. *Abelard: A Medieval Life.* Oxford: Blackwell Publishers, 1999.

Marenbon, John. *The Philosophy of Peter Abelard.* Cambridge, U.K.: Cambridge University Press, 1999.

Meade, Marion. *Stealing Heaven: The Love Story of Heloise and Abelard.* New York: Soho Press, 1994.

Abū al-ʿAlāʾ al-Maʿarrī

See MAʿARRĪ, ABŪ AL-ʿALĀ, AL-.

Abū Tammām (Abū Tammām Habīb ibn Aws al-Taʾi) (ca. 805–845) *poet, anthologist*

Abū Tammām was a prime exponent of the *badi,* or new school of Arab poetry that emerged in the Abbasid period. He was also one of the first to assemble an anthology of pre-Islamic and other early Arabic poetry.

Born in Syria to a Christian family, Abū Tammām converted to Islam in his youth, changed his name to indicate descent from a noble Arab tribe, and moved to Cairo to study Arabic poetry. He specialized in panegyrics, poems extolling leading figures of the day, from the Abbasid caliphs (rulers) al-Maʾmun and al-Muʿtasim to provincial governors who would pay for the service.

The most famous of Abū Tammām's panegyrics is his ode "Amorium," which celebrates al-Muʿtasim's victory over the Byzantines in 838: "O day of the Battle of ʿAmmuriya, [our] hopes have returned from you overflowing with honey-sweet milk; / You have left the fortunes of the sons of

Islam in the ascendant, and the polytheists and the abode of polytheism in decline."

Abū Tammām's innovative style aroused criticism in his day and from later commentators. His use of archaic words, far-fetched similes, and homonyms was often considered mannered, abstract, and overly sophisticated. His poems were unfavorably compared with the supposed naturalism of earlier poets, and the debate became an important stimulus to the tradition of Arab linguistic and literary criticism.

As an anthologist, Abū Tammām put together several *diwans,* or poetry collections, the most famous of which is *al-Hamasa* (Heroism), consisting of hundreds of poems from pre-Mohammed Arabia down to his own time, mostly by less famous poets. Unlike his own poetry, the works he collected and thus helped preserve have been universally celebrated as among the purist models of classic Arabic form.

English Versions of Works by Abū Tammām

"Amorium." In *Night and Horses and The Desert.* Edited by Robert Irwin. Woodstock, N.Y.: Overlook Press, 2000, 132–135.

Arberry, A. J., ed. *Arabic Poetry: A Primer for Students.* Cambridge, U.K.: Cambridge University Press, 1965.

A Work about Abū Tammām

Stetkevych, Suzanne Pinckney. *Abu Tammam and the Poetics of the Abbasid Age.* Boston: Brill Academic Publishers, 1991.

Adam de la Halle (ca. 1250–ca. 1306)
musician, playwright

Adam de la Halle was born in Arras, France, and spent most of his life there. He was educated in the church but did not take holy orders. Because of his writing talent and connections in literate and cultural circles, Adam became a spokesman for a group of local men who criticized the corrupt aristocratic government of Arras. In 1283, he traveled as court musician to Robert II, Count of Artois, in Naples, where he died around 1287.

Adam de la Halle was a gifted composer whose surviving body of work includes motets and chansons for single and multiple voices. He was not only talented enough to contribute to medieval music but also wrote two plays that are some of the most frequently anthologized pieces of medieval drama. Both *The Play of Madness* (Le Jeu de la Feuillée, ca. 1276) and *The Play of Robin and Marion* (Le Jeu de Robin et Marion, ca. 1283) are secular comedies that are fresh, charming (and in *The Play of Madness*'s case, raunchy and absurdist) glimpses into the medieval mind and society.

The Play of Robin and Marion is a pastoral in which the title characters court each other and entertain their fellow shepherds with songs and dances. There is some dramatic tension when a knight becomes infatuated with Marion and tries to abduct her, but Robin and his friends recover her and they celebrate with a picnic and games. The piece charms readers and spectators because of its playfulness and light touches of humor and realism; when Marion asks Robin to dance the farandole, a lively court dance, he excuses himself because his leggings are torn. The picnic consists of water, bread, apples, and cheese, and the partygoers are extravagant in their delight; one wonders if a courtly audience laughed condescendingly at the rustic characters' simple pleasures or recognized themselves in some of the games and songs the characters play. *The Play of Robin and Marion* has been recorded by several contemporary early-music groups and could still entertain a contemporary audience.

The Play of Madness, however, more closely resembles 20th-century experimental theater than the morality plays and farces of the time period. Adam's characters are himself and his friends from his Arras circle mingling with fairies, and there are stock comic characters such as an old woman, a doctor, and a village idiot. Nothing is sacred in this piece; Adam mocks his own desire to leave Arras for Paris, as well as his distaste for his aging wife.

The humor in the play is often bawdy and insensitive; male characters complain about their wives' shrewishness, the idiot spouts obscene jokes, and characters mock church politics and the public's gullibility when it comes to worshipping saints' relics. Political and social satire intertwine with physical comedy. There is no plot per se; characters shift from center stage to background, from participant to observer of what takes place center stage. The play's in-jokes about the well-to-do townsmen of Arras indicate its original audience may have been the literate burghers of this prosperous northern French city. The specific details of medieval life and the fresh direct language of both plays make Adam de la Halle's surviving plays not only significant artistic contributions to European drama but also intriguing glimpses into his world.

English Versions of Works by Adam de la Halle

Le Jeu de Robin et Marion. Translated by Shira I. Schwam-Baird. New York: Garland, 1994.

Medieval French Plays. Translated by Richard Axton and John Stevens. New York: Barnes & Noble, 1971.

Works about Adam de la Halle

Baltzer, Rebecca A., Thomas Cable, and James I. Wimsatt, eds. *The Union of Words and Music in Medieval Poetry.* Austin: University of Texas Press, 1991.

Dane, Joseph A. *Res/Verba: A Study in Medieval French Drama.* Leiden, Netherlands: E.J. Brill, 1985.

Aeschylus (ca. 525–456 B.C.) *tragedian*

Aeschylus was born in Eleusis, a Greek coastal city not far from Athens that was the center for the worship of Demeter, goddess of the harvest. His father, Euphorion, was descended from nobility, but little else is known about Aeschylus's family and early years.

In 499 B.C., Aeschylus began competing in Athenian dramatic contests, which were popular at the time. His initial victory was achieved in 484 B.C., and he went on to win first prize in a dozen more contests during his career. In 490 B.C., Aeschylus fought at Marathon against the Persian Empire in its attempt to conquer Greece, a battle that claimed his brother, Cynegirus. Aeschylus also fought the Persians at Salamis, Plataea, and other battles. Military valor had such a cachet in Aeschylus's day that his self-written epitaph, according to Greek scholar Edith Hamilton, describes his "glorious courage [on the] hallowed field of Marathon" but makes no mention of his stunning achievements as a playwright.

Aeschylus twice visited the court of Hieron of Syracuse, who was also patron of the poet PINDAR, in Sicily. Several of Aeschylus's productions were performed there. In 476 B.C., Aeschylus composed a play commemorating the king's founding of the new city of Aetna; he died during his second visit. An official Greek ruling later honored Aeschylus by providing that the city of Athens would fund the revival of any of his plays.

Some critics would profess that the art of tragedy is Aeschylus's creation. His plays incorporate genuine dramatic power and tension, startling and profoundly poetic imagery, and grand, eloquent language. His subject matter, always lofty, particularly explores the relationship between humans and God. Aeschylus was the first tragedian to supplement the chorus, a group of singers and dancers who performed the drama, with dialogue and interaction between individual actors. He was also the first playwright to enhance the spectacle with elaborate costumes and stage sets.

Aeschylus penned some 90 plays, of which only seven remain. His work was powerfully influenced by the Persian conflict, in which Greece challenged the ruling world power in order to become a cultural and political empire in its own right. Accordingly, *The Persians,* which won first prize at the Great Dionysia festival of 472 B.C., dramatizes the defeat of Athens's bitter enemy. It is a tribute to the humanity of the playwright that he portrays the characters, including Xerxes, king of the Persian

Empire, in a sympathetic light. In *The Persians,* he also gives voice to the universal hopes and fears that characterize life during wartime. The play is one of the few surviving Greek tragedies based on contemporary rather than mythological or historical events.

Seven Against Thebes, part of a trilogy that has not survived, was awarded first prize in the dramatic contests in 467 B.C. In it, Eteocles, king of the ancient Greek city of Thebes, thwarts an attempt by his brother Polyneices and six warriors to seize the throne. Both brothers are killed, and order is restored.

The Suppliant Maidens, written in the 460s B.C., is the first play of a lost trilogy in which the 50 daughters of Danaus have escaped from the 50 sons of Egypt who want to marry them against their wishes. The maidens have no right to refuse their suitors under Egyptian law, so they flee to Argos. There, King Pelasgus, after a democratic conference with his people, agrees that the State will provide sanctuary. The play ends with a prayer and a depiction of the god Zeus as the ultimate guardian of justice, highlighting the conflict between human, natural, and divine law.

Aeschylus's final triumph at the Great Dionysia took place in 458 B.C. with the *Oresteia,* a tale of a familial curse upon an aristocratic household. Each of the three plays that comprise it—*Agamemnon, The Choephori* (also called *The Libation Bearers*), and *The Eumenides*—can be seen as one great act of a complete drama.

Prometheus Bound, produced after the playwright's death, was an early part of a trilogy featuring the ancient hero Prometheus. Prometheus was the divine being who stole fire from the gods to give it to man and was therefore condemned by Zeus to be shackled to a cliff. In Richmond Lattimore's translation, Prometheus laments this error he made on behalf of humankind: "You see me a wretched God in chains, the enemy of Zeus, hated of all the Gods that enter Zeus's palace hall, because of my excessive love for Man." But he is ever rebellious and defiant, and the play concludes with

an aggravated Zeus plunging Prometheus into the underworld amid a splendid display of thunder and lightning.

Critical Analysis

The *Oresteia* trilogy is today the most-studied of Aeschylus's works. Several important historical events take place before the first play opens. Aeschylus's audience was familiar with the legend of the ancestral curse upon the noble House of Atreus, which impelled generation after generation to perform unspeakable acts. King Pelops's sons Atreus and Thyestes quarreled over the kingdom and became enemies; Thyestes seduced and betrayed Atreus's wife; and, in retaliation, Atreus fed Thyestes' own children to him in a grisly feast. This was the legacy inherited by Atreus's sons Menelaus and Agamemnon, who became king. When Menelaus's wife, the beautiful Helen, fled to Troy with Paris, Agamemnon coordinated an expedition to retrieve her. Before sailing, Agamemnon was forced to sacrifice his daughter Iphigenia to appease the gods and cause favorable winds to blow. The mission to fetch Helen escalated into the Trojan War. After 10 years of combat, Troy was captured and the Greeks began to make their way home. This is where the *Oresteia* begins.

In *Agamemnon,* the first play of the trilogy, the king's wife Clytaemnestra, aggrieved by the sacrifice of her daughter Iphigenia, takes as her lover Aegisthus, son of Thyestes. Together they plot to assassinate Agamemnon upon his return from Troy, and they succeed. In the second play, *The Libation Bearers,* Orestes and Electra, son and daughter of Agamemnon and Clytaemnestra, slay their mother and Aegisthus to avenge their father's murder. Orestes states that his was an act of justice, but when he spies the spirits of retribution known as the Furies, he knows there is more anguish to come.

In *The Eumenides,* the third and final play, Orestes is besieged by the Furies. They are determined to avenge the crime of matricide whether or not it was justifiable. Orestes seeks refuge with the god Apollo, who purifies him of his misdeed, but the Furies are not appeased. Orestes is then tried and absolved by a jury in a court set up by the goddess Athena, but the Furies are enraged that their authority has been usurped. Lattimore translates their lamentation:

> Gods of the younger generation, you have ridden down the laws of the elder time, torn them out of my hands. I, disinherited, suffering, heavy with anger shall let loose upon the land the vindictive poison dripping deadly out of my heart upon the ground.

To mollify the Furies, Athena offers them honorable positions as tutelary goddesses. "No household shall be prosperous without your will," she promises. "So we shall straighten the lives of all who worship us." Thus, the curse on the House of Atreus is no more.

The *Oresteia* dramatizes both the conflict between barbarian ways, represented by the curse and the Furies, and Hellenism, or the civilization and culture of ancient Greece that developed and flourished over Aeschylus's lifetime. Only Athena, who represents wisdom and reason as well as the city of Athens, can persuade the bloodthirsty, ruthless, and childish Furies to relinquish their ancient system of punishment in favor of one in which the law is the instrument of justice.

Aeschylus portrays ordinary men as heroic, with indomitable spirit, and life itself as a peculiar combination of suffering and joy, misery, and optimism. He presents conflicts between and within individuals that are universal and enduringly relevant. The Romantic poets Lord Byron, Percy Bysshe Shelley, and Samuel Taylor Coleridge all wrote about Aeschylus's Prometheus in the 19th century. The 20th-century playwrights Eugene O'Neill and T. S. Eliot recast Orestes' tragedy in *Mourning Becomes Electra* and *The Family Reunion,* respectively.

"The strange power tragedy has to present suffering and death in such a way as to exalt and not depress is to be felt in Aeschylus's plays as in those of no other tragic poet," writes Edith Hamilton in *The Greek Way.* "He was the first tragedian; tragedy was his creation, and he set upon it the stamp of his own spirit."

English Versions of Works by Aeschylus

Aeschylus I: Oresteia. Edited by David Grene and Richmond Lattimore. Chicago: University of Chicago Press, 1983.

Aeschylus II: The Complete Greek Tragedies. Edited by David Grene and Richmond Lattimore. Chicago: University of Chicago Press, 1992.

Aeschylus: Prometheus Bound. Translated by Paul Roche. Wauconda, Ill.: Bolchazy-Carducci, 1997.

Orestes Plays of Aeschylus. Translated by Paul Roche. New York: New American Library, 1962.

Works about Aeschylus

Hamilton, Edith. *The Greek Way.* New York: W.W. Norton, 1983.

Herington, John. *Aeschylus.* New Haven, Conn.: Yale University Press, 1986.

Rosenmeyer, Thomas G. *The Art of Aeschylus.* Berkeley: University of California Press, 1983.

Spatz, Lois. *Aeschylus.* Boston: Twayne Publishers, 1982.

Aesop (ca. 620–565 B.C.) *storyteller, fabulist, orator*

Aesop was born in Phrygia, an ancient country in the center of what is now Turkey. He may have been taken prisoner by one of his homeland's many conquering invaders; it is known he was enslaved and eventually sold to a man called Iadmon. On Samos, a Greek island in the Aegean Sea where the prosperous landowner took him, Aesop established a reputation as a masterful storyteller and fabulist (maker of fables). Aesop so impressed Iadmon with his gifts that his master freed him so he might tell his humorous animal tales throughout Greece. Aesop was later retained by King Croesus of Lydia as a diplomat and ambassador.

Aesop successfully represented his various employers in legal matters and other negotiations by telling instructive, lively stories featuring animals with very human traits. The great Greek philosopher ARISTOTLE tells the following story of Aesop in *Rhetoric,* a treatise on the art of persuasion: While defending a popular political leader of Samos who had swindled the public, Aesop recounted "The Vixen and the Hedgehog." In this story, Aristotle explains, a fox who becomes trapped in a gully and tormented by fleas is offered help by a passing hedgehog. The fox declines the offer, explaining that the fleas clinging to her skin had had their fill of her, but if the fleas were taken away they would be replaced by another set of parasites that would drain the rest of her blood.

"So, men of Samos," Aesop concluded, according to Aristotle, "my client will do you no further harm; he is wealthy already. But if you put him to death," he explained, other ambitious politicians will assume the position the man has vacated, "and their peculations will empty your treasury completely."

Aesop died while on a diplomatic mission to the sacred site of Delphi, where he found the residents to be not holy, but arrogant and greedy. Fearful that Aesop would use his powers of oratory to discredit them, the Delphians enacted a conspiracy to frame him with theft. In his defense, the already legendary fabulist told of "The Rat and the Frog" and "The Eagle and the Beetle," tales cautioning that oppressors of the innocent will be subjected to divine vengeance. Notwithstanding his warnings, Aesop was found guilty and executed by being flung from the cliffs at Delphi.

There are hundreds of fables attributed to Aesop, but it is uncertain how many he actually composed, if any. He did not write any down, and some of the stories in the body of work known as "Aesop's Fables" are known to have originated well before his birth or after his death. He may merely have been a brilliant raconteur of oft-told tales that were then recited in the "Aesopic" manner. They were written down for the first time around 300 B.C., probably by storytellers and other fabulists.

Critical Analysis

In Aesop's *Fables,* talking moles, swallows, monkeys, and a host of other animals demonstrate all-too-human flaws, virtues, and desires. Accordingly, they are taught lessons that humans might do well to mind. Like all fables, those attributed to Aesop are both brief—sometimes as short as two sentences—and fanciful, and are designed to teach a lesson about such themes as modesty, honesty, and industriousness.

Perhaps the best-known tale is "The Hare and the Tortoise," in which the speedy hare challenges the sluggish tortoise to a race. The confident hare, thinking he has all the time in the world, takes a nap, while the tortoise trudges laboriously to the finish line, teaching that slow and steady wins the race.

In "The Fox and the Grapes," another popular favorite, a ravenous fox spies a bunch of the fruit hanging from a trellis. Unable to reach them, he tells himself they weren't ripe, anyway, giving rise to the term *sour grapes.*

Aesop also relates the story of a shepherd boy who falsely "cries wolf" so often that when a real wolf appears and threatens the herd, nobody heeds his pleas for help; and of a mule who boasts of his racehorse mother but is compelled to acknowledge that his father is a jackass ("There are two sides to every story"). Another narrative tells of a fox happening upon a lion for the very first time and nearly dying of fright. The fox becomes bolder upon each encounter until one day he strolls up to the lion with a cheeky greeting, because "familiarity breeds contempt."

In "The Dairy Maid and Her Milk Can," a milkmaid is carrying a pail of milk on her head daydreaming about what she will do with the money she will earn from selling it. She imagines increasing her stock of eggs, which will produce a certain number of chicks that she will sell at a certain price. She'll have enough money for a new gown, and her beauty will attract many suitors, but she will just toss her head at the lot of them. At that, she tosses her head and the pail of milk crashes to the ground—along with her fantasy. The moral: Do not count your chickens before they hatch.

The greedy owner of "The Goose with the Golden Eggs" squanders an even greater windfall than that of the milkmaid. He cuts the goose open, hoping to find a large gold nugget inside. Thus, when referring to people whose impatience for great riches causes them to lose what little they do have, we may say they "killed the goose that laid the golden egg."

Another familiar expression comes from "The Fishes and the Frying Pan." Some live fish are placed in a skillet over a flame to cook. As the pan heats up, the fish find the high temperature intolerable, so they leap from the pan, landing in the flames. Today, we use the expression "out of the frying pan and into the fire" to mean a choice that exchanges one unpleasant situation for one that is worse.

Our very language owes a debt to Aesop's fantastical universe, insofar as everyday speech is populated with animals who have the human traits Aesop ascribed to them. We speak of wily foxes, wolves in sheep's clothing, vain peacocks, rapacious vultures, and hardworking ants.

The lessons Aesop's fables teach are very much in evidence in contemporary expressions, too, and in the way civic and ethical matters are framed and judged in modern society. "The Country Mouse and the City Mouse" is an exceptionally popular fable that is no less relevant today than in ancient times, and it aptly illustrates the benefits and drawbacks of rural and urban living. As the Country Mouse sums up: "You can dine in this way and grow fat, if you like; jolly good luck to you if you can enjoy feasting sumptuously in the midst of danger. For my part, I shall not abandon my frugal home under ground, where I can eat coarse food in safety."

Aesop is generally credited with introducing the fantastical animals who made the tales and their characters so beloved, keeping the tales simple and providing a "moral of the story" tagline that made them so unforgettable. The fables have been translated and augmented many times over, perhaps most famously by the 17th century French poet Jean de La Fontaine, and they have retained their straightforward appeal for more than 2,000 years.

In many ways, it is irrelevant whether Aesop was, in fact, the author of the fables. He was the storyteller who brought them to vivid life and made them, and himself, universal and timeless. *See also* PHAEDRUS.

English Versions of Works by Aesop

Aesop: The Complete Fables. Translated by Olivia and Robert Temple. New York: Penguin, 1998.

Aesop's Fables: With a Life of Aesop. Edited by John Esten Keller. Lexington: University Press of Kentucky, 1993.

Works about Aesop

Bader, Barbara. *Aesop and Company: With Scenes from His Legendary Life.* New York: Houghton Mifflin/Walter Lorraine Books, 1999.

Lewis, Jayne Elizabeth. *English Fable: Aesop and Literary Culture, 1651–1740.* Cambridge, U.K.: Cambridge University Press, 1996.

Wheatley, Edward. *Mastering Aesop: Medieval Education, Chaucer, and His Followers.* Gainesville: University Press of Florida, 2000.

African proverbs

Proverbs distinguish themselves from other forms of ORAL LITERATURE by their brevity, consistency (their word order rarely changes over time), and widespread acceptance within a community. Some African cultures, such as that of the Bushmen, have few proverbs, while others have hundreds. One recent collection contains approximately 3,000 proverbs from 64 Nigerian peoples. Researchers have recorded 4,000 proverbs in the Rundi language alone, and the Chaga people claim they "have four big possessions: land, cattle, water and proverbs."

In many African cultures, speakers use proverbs as a way to catch their audience's attention, display intelligence and learning, lend authority to their words, settle legal disputes, provide entertainment, and resolve moral or ethical dilemmas. As one Igbo puts it, "The proverb makes somebody think twice. If you use a proverb people might be more likely to take your advice."

The writer Ruth Finnegan points out that African maxims use rhythm, striking imagery (many involving comparisons with animals or household objects), and exaggeration to make their points clear.

Proverbs appear in stories, poems, art, and songs. The Ashanti even make brass weights depicting figures from proverbs. In addition, proverbs are usually short (from a few words to a sentence), allowing the speaker to wittily communicate complicated ideas or concepts. This, in turn, makes the ideas easier to learn.

The themes of African proverbs include power, death, marriage, wealth, foolishness, fate, and the importance of community. A particular culture's choice of proverbs tells something about that culture. Americans and Europeans know that the term *sour grapes* refers to one of AESOP's fables; similarly, the Yoruba and other African peoples believe that "Half a word will do for an intelligent boy." And the proverbs of Bantu-speaking peoples reveal that they raise livestock. Their saying, "Don't throw away the milk pails," is their way of saying people should keep hope.

Because some proverbs are often incomprehensible to listeners unfamiliar with African cultures, they are sometimes used as a secretive type of language to keep "outsiders" from understanding. As one Igbo saying goes, "Proverbs are used to confuse stupid people." In addition, because some proverbs are indirect, they can be used in situations when more direct speech might be insulting. For instance, one might speak the Yoruba proverb "Children are a man's clothes" in the presence of a father with misbehaving young children. The children would not understand the reference, but their father would. The phrasing of the proverb would allow him the chance to curb his children's actions without taking offense. This is similar to proverbs that encourage appropriate behavior. "Those who eat together shouldn't eat each other," say the Igbo, reminding friends and family to respect each other. The Longuda emphasize the importance of keeping promises by saying, "A promise is not just a knot which you can simply untie with your hands." Finally, a Tswanan saying, "To give is to put away for yourself," encourages generosity by implying it will someday be returned.

There are also numerous ambiguous proverbs that can be used in different situations. For example, the Boko saying, "A sheep does not give birth to a goat" (or the Ga's "A crab does not beget a bird") can humiliate a thief's child, but it can also reassure a woman that her child will be as healthy and intelligent as she is.

Such lessons, advice, and compliments were passed down for centuries in African cultures. They are part of the same oral tradition that created and preserved stories like the EPIC OF SON-JARA. It has been only in recent centuries that Europeans and Africans themselves have written down these sayings. The explorer Richard Burton's collection *Wit and Wisdom from West Africa* (1865) was one of the first of its kind. This and other works reveal the proverbs' archaic words and grammatical constructions, but this seems almost irrelevant when compared to the African proverbs' versatility, authority, rhythm, and imagery, for it is these elements that give the proverbs their universal and lasting appeal.

See also ZEN PARABLES.

English Collections of African Proverbs

Ibekwe, Patrick, ed. *Wit & Wisdom of Africa: Proverbs from Africa & the Caribbean.* Trenton, N.J.: Africa World Press, 1999.

Pachocinski, Ryszard. *Proverbs of Africa: Human Nature in the Nigerian Oral Tradition.* St. Paul, Minn.: Professors World Peace Academy, 1996.

Zona, Guy, ed. *The House of the Heart Is Never Full and Other Proverbs of Africa.* New York: Touchstone, 1993.

A Work about African Proverbs

Finnegan, Ruth. "Proverbs in Africa." In *The Wisdom of Many: Essays on the Proverb.* Edited by Wolfgang Mieder and Alan Dundes, 10–42. New York: Garland, 1981.

al-Būsīrī
See BŪSĪRĪ, AL-.

Alcaeus (seventh century–sixth century B.C.)
poet

During the centuries before the Persian Wars, the Greeks produced a number of outstanding literary figures whose works later inspired the more famous Greek poets and playwrights. Among these early figures of Greek literature was the poet Alcaeus.

Alcaeus was a native of the city of Mytilene, which was on the island of Lesbos, off the coast of modern-day Turkey in what was then known as Ionia. During Alcaeus's lifetime, the Greek islands of Ionia were in a state of almost continuous disorder, suffering invasion from outsiders, constant infighting between city-states, and bitter internal quarrels. Alcaeus involved himself in the political disputes in Mytilene and was forced into exile as a result.

Most of Alcaeus's work has been lost, but some survives. His poetry reflects the turmoil of the time in which he lived. Editor Kenneth Atchity says of him: "Extroverted and aggressive, better at hating than loving, Alcaeus lived, drank hard, and wrote primarily of wine, women, and war." Poems such as "To the Baseborn Tyrant" express his bitter hatred toward the idea of tyranny and praise the brave men who fight for honorable causes. He feels only hostility toward those who betray their city-state, since traitors had torn his own city apart. Several surviving poems extol the beauty of women, and many express Alcaeus's favorite theme of being happy in spite of troubled times. In "Winter Evening," after cursing the cold, the poet urges men to nurture friendship and conviviality to keep despair at bay:

> *Pile up the burning logs*
> *and water the great flagons of red wine;*
> *place feather pillows by your head, and*
> *   drink.*
> *Let us not brood about hard times.*

Alcaeus had a large influence on Greek and Roman poets who came after him. The Roman poet HORACE claimed Alcaeus as one of his great models for metrical style (Alcaeus invented the Alcaic meter) and poetic inspiration, as his *Odes* demonstrate. The rhetorician QUINTILIAN approved of Alcaeus in "his work where he assails tyrants; his ethical value is also great; his style is concise, magnificent, exact, very much like HOMER's; but he stoops to humor and love when better suited for higher themes."

An English Version of a Work by Alcaeus
Alkaiou Mele: The Fragments of the Lyrical Poems of Alcaeus. Edited by Edgar Lobel. Oxford, U.K.: The Clarendon Press, 1927.

A Work about Alcaeus
Martin, Hubert. *Alcaeus.* New York: Twayne Publishers, 1972.

al-Farazdaq
See FARAZDAQ, AL-.

Alfred the Great (849–899) *king, scholar, translator, educator*

King Alfred of Wessex, present-day southern England, is known in history as a strong military and political strategist and cultural and scholarly leader. He is credited with having developed an Old English prose style through his translations of well-known works from Latin.

Until the time of Alfred's reign (871–899) there was no prose in Old English. With the exception of laws and charters, all prose was in Latin. By the ninth century, England was in a cultural and intellectual decline, and the people understood only Old English. Alfred was the first to realize the need for educating the people, and he set about translating works he deemed suitable. As Alfred himself said, "Without wisdom no faculty can be fully brought out. . . ."

Alfred was tireless in his devotion to preserving Anglo-Saxon literature by copying and translating important pieces of his times into Old English. He himself did some of the translating and also supervised scribes and monks, influencing them to follow his example. Some of the important works he translated include *Consolation of Philosophy* by BOETHIUS, a philosophical work from the sixth century that had an important influence on much of the literature of the MIDDLE AGES; *Cura Pastoralis (Pastoral Care),* a handbook by Gregory describing the responsibilities of a bishop; and *Soliloquies* by St. AUGUSTINE, an ecclesiastical manual.

Two of the works that Alfred translated and compiled, BEDE's *Ecclesiastical History of the English People* and the ANGLO-SAXON CHRONICLE, have generated a storm of arguments among scholars through the ages. Most of the debates are based on the style of writing in these works, as it differs from the style in works soundly attributed to Alfred's hand. Thus, whether Alfred directly contributed to the works or not, it is established that the translation of the works was accomplished during and inspired by his reign.

Knowledge of Alfred's early years is based on a biography by John Asser, who was Alfred's companion. Alfred had no schooling in his childhood and could read neither Latin nor Old English until after his 12th year; however, once he started learning, there was no stopping him.

He came to the throne of England in 871, following the death of his brother, King Aethelred I. His early years as a monarch were spent organizing successful campaigns against the Danish Vikings, forcing them north back into the Danelaw, where many became Christians. This saved England from becoming part of the Norse empire. The rest of England accepted Alfred as their national leader.

Alfred acutely felt the pressures of being a monarch and of constantly having to fight to defend his land. His infirm health was also a continual source of aggravation to him. Despite all of this, he continued to ably administer his kingdom; bestow alms and largesse on natives and foreigners; practice hunting; instruct his goldsmiths, falconers, and dog-keepers; design and build majestic houses; attend Mass twice a day; memorize poems and psalms; translate works of literature into his native tongue; participate in discussions and debates with scholars from all over Britain and Europe; and, above all, pursue the education of the people of his kingdom.

English Versions of Works by Alfred the Great

Schreiber, Carolin, trans. *King Alfred's Old English Translation of Pope Gregory the Great's Regula Pastoralis and its Cultural Context.* New York: Peter Lang Publishing, 2003.

Waite, Greg, trans. *Old English Prose Translations of King Alfred's Reign.* Suffolk, U.K.: Boydell & Brewer, 2000.

Works about Alfred the Great

Asser, John. *The Medieval Life of King Alfred the Great.* Translated by Alfred P. Smythe. London: Palgrave Macmillan, 2001.

Harrison, Frederick. *The Writings of King Alfred.* New York: M.S.G. Haskell House, 1970.

Peddie, John. *Alfred: Warrior King.* Gloucestershire, U.K.: Sutton Publishing, 2001.

Plummer, Charles. *The Life and Times of Alfred the Great.* New York: Haskell House, 1970.

Smyth, Alfred P. *King Alfred the Great.* Oxford: Oxford University Press, 1995.

Alighieri, Dante
See DANTE ALIGHIERI.

'Alī ibn Abī Tālib (Imam 'Alī) (575–ca. 661) *poet, homilist*
Born in Mecca, 'Alī ibn Abī Tālib was the son-in-law of MUHAMMAD. He is venerated by Shi'ite Muslims as the prophet's rightful successor. The poems, sermons, lectures, and sayings that are attributed to Ali are esteemed by Shi'ites to this day.

'Alī was a cousin and foster brother of Muhammad, the founder of Islam. He was among Muhammad's supporters, serving as his secretary and marrying his daughter Fātima. After Muhammad's death, a faction of Muslims supported 'Alī as his rightful heir. 'Alī did become the fourth Caliph, or leader of the faithful, in 656, only to be murdered five years later; his sons Hasan and Huseyn were later murdered as well.

'Alī is considered the first great writer of sermons and an eloquent writer of aphorisms. As caliph, he was patron of moralistic poetry and of the first systematic Arabic grammarians, and he was also known as an expert calligrapher.

'Alī's sermons and other prose works were collected in the 11th century by al-Sayyid al-Sharif ar-Radi, an Islamic scholar, in *Nahj al Balagha* (Peak of Eloquence). Al-Sharif divided 'Alī's works into three categories: sermons, letters, and short sayings. In the first section, 'Alī stresses spirituality, justice, ethics, and worship. The second section consists of letters 'Alī wrote to friends and enemies, as well as his instructions as Caliph to government officials, stressing their role as servants and protectors of the people. Finally, the third section is a collection of 'Alī's aphorisms, which serves as a set of instructions on how to live "purely" and prosper. It is the emotional depth and wisdom of these works that have given 'Alī a place in world literature.

An English Version of a Work by 'Alī ibn Abī Tālib

Peak of Eloquence: Nahjul Balagha. Translated by Askari Jafery. New York: Tahrike Tarsile Qur'an, 1996.

Works about 'Alī ibn Abī Tālib

Ahmad, Abdul Basit. *Ali Bin Ali Talib: The Fourth Caliph of Islam.* Houston, Tex.: Dar-Us-Salam Publications. No publication date given.

Chirri, Mohamad Jawad. *The Brother of the Prophet Mohammad (the Imam Ali).* Qum, Iran: Ansariyan Publications, 1996.

al-Mutanabbī

See MUTANABBĪ, AL-.

Ambrose, Saint (ca. 340–397) *religious writer*

Ambrose was born to an ancient noble family of the Roman Empire. His father was Prefect of Gallia. He had a younger brother, Satyrus, and an older sister, Marcellina, who influenced Ambrose's dedication to the virtue of virginity.

Ambrose received a brilliant liberal and legal education, acquiring a thorough mastery of Greek language and literature. He also studied law, and his eloquent speeches attracted the attention of Emperor Valentinian, who named him consular governor of Liguria and Æmilia. In 374, Ambrose became the bishop of Milan and occupied this position until his death. He became famous as one of the most illustrious of the Four Doctors of the Church, which included St. AUGUSTINE, St. JEROME, and St. Gregory.

From his lifetime to the present day, Ambrose is known for the exceptional clarity and piety with which he expressed the Church's teachings. Most of his writings are homilies, or commentaries, on the Old and New Testaments. His education allowed him to engage in scholarly and spiritual studies of authors, such as VIRGIL, Origen, CICERO, St. Basil, and others, which he did primarily to learn how to teach.

Some scholars divide Ambrose's surviving texts into four groups: scripture-commentaries, moral texts (referred to as ascetico-moral writings), dogmatic texts (concerning the divinity of Jesus, the Holy Ghost, and the sacraments), and occasional texts. His most influential piece, *De Officiis ministrorum,* belongs to the moral texts and, as such, is a treatise of Christian morality. Also belonging to this group are his "On Virgins," which he addressed to his sister.

Of his dogmatic texts, his *De Mysteriis* (a treatise on baptism, confirmation, and the Eucharist) is extant, as are many of his occasional texts (mostly letters, official notes, and reports). From these and other of Ambrose's writings, much social, religious, and cultural information of ancient Milan and Rome has been preserved.

English Versions of Works by Saint Ambrose

De Officiis. Edited with an introduction, translation, and commentary by Ivor J. Davidson. Oxford: Oxford University Press, 2001.

On Abraham. Translated by Theodosia Tomkinson. Chrysostomos of Etna: Center for Traditionalist Orthodox Studies, 2000.

Works about Saint Ambrose

McLynn, Neil B. *Ambrose of Milan: Church and Court in a Christian Capital.* Berkeley: University of California Press, 1994.

Theresa, Sister M. *Nature-Imagery in the Works of Saint Ambrose* (1931). Whitefish, Mont.: Kessinger Publishing, 2003.

Vasey, Vincent R. *The Social Ideas in the Works of St. Ambrose: A Study on De Nabuthe.* Rome, Italy: Institutum Patristicum "Augustinianum," 1982.

Williams. Daniel H. *Ambrose of Milan and the End of the Nicene-Arian Conflicts.* Oxford: Oxford University Press, 1995.

'Amr ibn Kulthum (sixth century) *poet*

'Amr ibn Kulthum was among the classic Arabic poets who flourished in the century before MUHAMMAD. Though not considered a great innovator, his inclusion in the *Mu'allaqāt* (The Seven Odes), the standard collection of pre-Islamic poetry, has given him a place in literary history.

Like many of the pre-Islamic poets, 'Amr was of high birth and a chief of the Taghlib tribe that lived in the mid-Euphrates River area of Iraq. He was the grandson of al-Muhalhil, himself a celebrated Taghlib chief and poet. Little is known of 'Amr's life, but some of the feats alluded to in his poems were later accepted as facts. For example, one legend has 'Amr beheading the powerful Lakhmid king 'Amr ibn Hind (ca. 568) for allowing the poet's mother to be insulted. Within a century of his death, reputedly by drinking too much unmixed wine, he had become a legendary hero in Arabic tales.

There are not many surviving examples of 'Amr's poetry, but one of his longer poems (untitled) was included in the *Mu'allaqāt* when it was assembled in the late eighth century. In his *qasidah* (ode), 'Amr fiercely extols the strength, courage, and cruelty of his tribe, and hurls threats against its foes:

> *Ours the right of the wells, of the springs
>   untroubled;*
> *theirs the dregs of the plain, the rain-pools
>   trampled.*

This type of writing is a classic example of the *fakhr* (boasting) often found in Arabic poetry of the time. 'Amr's poem became so popular among his Taghlib tribesmen that they expanded it in the retelling from 100 to 1,000 lines, and the ode has since influenced subsequent generations of Arabic poets.

See also HANGED POEMS, THE.

An English Version of a Work by 'Amr ibn Kulthum

Untitled Ode in *The Seven Odes: The First Chapter in Arabic Literature.* Translated by A. J. Arberry. New York: Macmillan, 1957.

A Work about 'Amr ibn Kulthum

Nicholson, R. A. *A Literary History of the Arabs.* Cambridge, U.K.: Cambridge University Press, 1966, 109–113.

Anacreon (sixth century B.C.) *poet, composer*

Anacreon was one of the most influential and famous Greek literary and musical figures who flourished during the time before the Persian Wars and the Golden Age of Athens. Greek writers continued to imitate him long after his death, and his impact on Greek culture was profound.

Anacreon was born in the Ionian Greek city of Teos, on the eastern coast of the Aegean Sea.

Throughout his life, he was never able to remain in the same place for very long, being continually forced to relocate because of political turmoil. After Teos fell to the Persians, the poet became a guest of Polycrates, the tyrant-ruler of the island of Samos. According to the historian HERODOTUS, Anacreon may have been dining with Polycrates when the latter was assassinated. Following this event, Anacreon moved again, this time to Athens. When another political friend was assassinated, Anacreon again fled, this time to Thessaly, but was later recalled to Athens. He died there, according to legend, by choking on a raisin.

Anacreon was best known for his brilliant and bawdy feasting songs. They glorified the enjoyment of life, the subjects generally being wine, women, and pleasure. The chief theme of his work is that people should strive to enjoy life while they have the chance. People throughout the Greek world enjoyed these songs, and Anacreon was extremely popular. He also wrote satirical pieces that were well received. Greek and Roman writers continued to imitate his style for many centuries, and the tradition of popular "drinking songs" owes much to Anacreon.

In the 16th century, a large collection of Anacreon's works was published in Paris for the first time. It influenced writers such as Ben Jonson, Richard Lovelace, and Robert Herrick. An English translation by Thomas Moore, titled *Odes of Anacreon*, appeared in 1800.

An English Version of Works by Anacreon

"If you can count the number" and other untitled
    poems in *The Norton Book of Classical Literature.*
    Edited by Bernard Knox. New York: W. W. Norton,
    1993, 243–246.

Works about Anacreon

Greek Songs in the Manner of Anacreon. Translated by
    Richard Aldington. London: The Egoist Ltd., 1919.
Rosenmeyer, Patricia. *The Poetics of Imitation:
    Anacreon and the Anacreontic Tradition.* Cambridge, U.K.: Cambridge University Press, 1992.

Angiolieri, Cecco (1260–ca. 1312) *poet*

Cecco Angiolieri was born in Siena to parents Angioliero degli Angelioleri and Lisa Salimbeni. As a youth he entered military service, where he was reprimanded several times for unauthorized absences and once for making noise after curfew. In 1288 he served in a military campaign where he is thought to have met fellow poet DANTE. Angiolieri's later history is equally colorful: In 1291 he was accused but not convicted of stabbing a man, and sometime in the next decade he was banished from Siena. In 1302 he sold a vineyard to a neighbor for a tidy profit, but in 1313, after his death, his five children renounced their claims to his estate to avoid the huge debts placed upon it.

Of Angiolieri's poetry, 150 sonnets survive. He wrote in a realistic and burlesque style, and translator Thomas Caldecot Chubb says that "his is the best and the most vivid writing of this interesting school." Angiolieri often introduces a comedic touch into the conventional depictions of love and lovers. His sonnets to Becchina, the shoemaker's daughter, show him using the tropes of love with laudable skill:

> Whatever good is naturally done
> Is born of Love as fruit is born of flowers:
> By Love all good is brought to its full power.

In other sonnets, he parodies those who are slaves to love and celebrates his freedom, as in this playful verse in which the poet says,

> Love is no lord of mine, I'm proud to vouch.
> So let no woman who is born conceive
> That I'll be her liege slave. . . .

Angiolieri also wrote three bantering poems to his friend Dante, one of which respectfully points out how Dante appears to contradict himself in the last sonnet of his *New Life.* Angiolieri's contemporaries spared him no less in their own literary works; Boccaccio portrays him as a gambler and prankster in the *Decameron,* which no doubt contributed to Angiolieri's reputation, in Chubb's terms, as a handsome and well-mannered rogue.

An English Version of Works by Cecco Angiolieri

Cecco, As I Am and Was: The Poems of Cecco Angiolieri. Translated by Tracy Barrett. Boston: Branden Publishing Co., 1994.

A Work about Cecco Angiolieri

Alfie, Fabian. *Comedy and Culture: Cecco Angiolieri's Poetry and Late Medieval Society.* Leeds, U.K.: Northern Universities Press, 2001.

Anglo-Saxon Chronicle (891–1154)

The Anglo-Saxon Chronicle is a collection of manuscripts detailing British history from the beginning of the Christian era to A.D. 1154. Translator M. J. Swanton speculates that "the Chronicle, as we know it, had its origins towards the end of the ninth century: a reflection of both the 'revival of learning' and revival of English national awareness during the reign of King Alfred" (ALFRED THE GREAT, 849–899). For information on events beginning with Julius CAESAR's first Roman invasion, the clerics in charge of the work drew their material from documents already in circulation, such as *Ecclesiastical History of the English People* written by The Venerable BEDE. The Chronicle was maintained and added to by generations of anonymous scribes until the middle of the 12th century. The final entry in 1154 describes the death of Stephen and the coronation of Henry II:

> In this year died the King Stephen; and he was buried where his wife and his son were buried, at Faversham . . . Then when he [Henry] came to England, he was received with great honour and was blessed as king in London on the Sunday before midwinter day, and there held a great court.

Four distinct manuscripts exist, named by the religious houses where they were kept: Winchester, Abingdon, Worcester, and Peterborough. The Winchester manuscript is the oldest, while the Peterborough manuscript was the longest maintained and is considered the most complete. Variations between the individual manuscripts show that they circulated among religious houses, and recorders made note not only of national events but also doings of more local concern.

The Chronicle remains a crucial historical document, not only because it dates from a time when few other records exist, but it is also significant, as Swanton observes, "that so fundamental a cultural document of English history should have been composed in English." In addition to their historical importance, the Chronicle serves as a literary text. Several passages contain vivid prose, and in the 937 entry, the account of the Battle of Brunanburh stands as one of the finer examples of Anglo-Saxon poetry, reminiscent of the heroic motifs in the epic poem BEOWULF.

See also OLD ENGLISH POETRY.

A Modern Version of the Anglo-Saxon Chronicle

The Anglo-Saxon Chronicle. Translated and edited by M. J. Swanton. London: J. M. Dent, 1996.

A Work about the Anglo-Saxon Chronicle

Bredehoft, Thomas A. *Textual Histories: Readings in the Anglo-Saxon Chronicle.* Toronto: University of Toronto Press, 2001.

Anna Comnena (1083–ca. 1154) *historian*

Anna Comnena was born in Constantinople, the eldest daughter of an aristocratic general who later, as Alexius I, became one of the greatest emperors of Byzantium (the Eastern Roman Empire). Nevertheless, Comnena spent the latter half of her life in exile, where she wrote a remarkable history book, perhaps the first written by a woman.

Anna was betrothed at age five to Constantine, son of then-emperor Michael VII. Her royal ambitions were thwarted, however, due to her husband's early death and the birth of a son and heir to her parents, who had since become the imperial couple.

Anna enjoyed major influence in affairs of state via her mother, the empress Irene. They conspired together to obtain the succession to the throne for Anna's husband—in effect for Anna herself. After the death in 1118 of her father, Alexius I, Anna plotted with her second husband to overthrow her brother, the new emperor John II. When the plot was discovered, Anna's properties were confiscated, and she was banished from the capital for life. She retired to the convent of Kecharitomene, built by her mother, where she spent her remaining 35 years as a patron of scholarships and the arts as well as the center of a literary and political faction opposed to Emperor Manuel I. She died in exile, becoming a nun on her deathbed.

Before her death, Anna composed a long history of her father's glorious career, the *Alexiad*, covering the years from 1169 through his death. Later translated into spoken Greek, her book gained wide popularity. It is still celebrated for its forceful, vivid writing; its thoughtful if biased analysis; and its wealth of information on contemporary literature, society, religion, internal politics, and international affairs.

In her writing, Comnena tried to emulate the language and spirit of classical Greece, whose pedigree was as ancient and authentic as the Christian scriptures. The title *Alexiad* was a deliberate tribute to HOMER's *Iliad*. Not that Anna had any tolerance for rationalistic heresies. Her conservative outlook found expression in her distaste for frivolity, astrology, and gambling, and in the heroic language and conventions she used for her protagonists.

The *Alexiad* is in some ways a traditional imperial enconium, in which the emperor emerges as wise, brave, and tirelessly devoted, the very model of *mesotes* (the middle way). But Anna added depth to her portrayals, even of her father, whom she described as frequently depressed by temporary setbacks or guilt. She gives even the villains motives and recognizes their strong qualities.

Anna was a master of emotionally powerful descriptions, both of people and events. Describing

John Italos, a leading philosopher denounced for heresy, she wrote in the *Alexiad:* "His writings wore a frown and in general reeked of bitterness, full of dialectic aggression, and his tongue was loaded with arguments. . . . The man was no more in control of his hands than his tongue."

Anna's career shows that the social status of women improved in Byzantium in her era, at least among the elite. The characters she describes in her writing provide further evidence. For example, according to the *Alexiad,* her father appointed his own mother, Anna Dalassena, as coruler. Anna writes: "One might say that he was indeed the instrument of her power—he was not emperor, for all the decisions and ordinances of his mother satisfied him, not merely as an obedient son, but as an attentive listener to her instruction in the art of ruling."

Anna's importance was twofold: Her book was the first great product of a Greek renaissance that lasted until the last days of the Byzantine Empire, three centuries later, and it is the primary original source of information for the era of the First Crusade.

An English Version of a Work by Anna Comnena

The Alexiad of Anna Comnena. Translated by E. R. A. Sewter. Baltimore: Penguin, 1969.

Works about Anna Comnena

Dalven, Rae. *Anna Comnena.* New York: Twayne, 1972.

Kazhdan, A. P. and Ann Wharton Epstein. *Change in Byzantine Culture in the Eleventh and Twelfth Centuries.* Berkeley: University of California Press, 1985.

Apollodorus (first century B.C.) *mythologist*

Apollodorus is largely responsible for the information modern scholars possess concerning the religion and mythology of ancient Greece. Very little is known about his life, and the dates of his birth and death cannot be established with any certainty. It is known that he studied in the city of Alexandria, which in the first century was the intellectual heart of the classical world, under the tutelage of the astronomer Aristarchus and the philosopher Panaetius. He spent most of his life in his native Athens.

Apollodorus is best known for his work *Bibliotheke* (Library). In essence, this work is a summary and description of the identities and activities of the Greek gods. It discusses famous events in Greek mythology, such as the war between the Titans and Olympians and Prometheus's gift of fire to humanity. It is a straightforward story that Apollodorus tells uncritically and without digressions. From this compilation comes much of the modern knowledge of Greek mythology, although only fragments of the work survive to the present day.

Apollodorus also wrote a work entitled *Chronicle,* a historical reference covering Greek history from the time of the Trojan War to Apollodorus's own time. Again, only fragments of this work remain. Apollodorus wrote other works, some dealing with geography, which is said to have influenced the geographer STRABO, and grammar, but it is his works on mythology that are of greatest importance and that have influenced such writers as John Milton and Ben Jonson.

English Versions of Works by Apollodorus

Apollodorus: Library, Volume 1, Books 1 & 3 (9). Loeb Classical Library. Translated by J. G. Frazer. Cambridge, Mass.: Harvard University Press, 1992.

Church, Alfred Jr., ed. *Stories from the Greek Comedians: Aristophanes, Philenon, Diphilus, Menander and Apollodorus.* Cheshire, Conn.: Biblo and Tanner Booksellers, 1998.

The Library of Greek Mythology. Translated by Keith Aldrich. Lawrence, Kans.: Coronado Press, 1974.

Works about Apollodorus

Carey, Christopher. *Greek Orators: Apollodorus against Nesira.* Vol. 6. Oakville, Conn.: David Brown Book Co., 1992.

Ireland, S., ed. *Apollodorus: "Argonauts and Heracles."* London: Bristol Classical Press, 1992.

Apollonius of Rhodes (ca. 295–ca. 247 B.C.) *epic poet*

Apollonius of Rhodes is one of the great literary figures of the Hellenistic Age. He was born in the city of Alexandria, a Greek community founded in Egypt when Alexander the Great conquered that country. During Apollonius's lifetime, Alexandria was the greatest city of the Hellenistic world, not only a hub of economic and political activity but also the center of scholarly life for the Greeks. Apollonius spent many years in Rhodes, another city noted for its civilization and learning, working as both a writer and a teacher. Eventually he returned to Alexandria, called there by the great Library, one of the famed intellectual institutions of the ancient world and the pride and joy of the city. After a period of serving as tutor to the ruling family, the Ptolemies, Apollonius was made head of the Library, where he wrote his only surviving work, *Argonautica,* or "The voyage of the *Argo.*"

This piece tells the famous story of Jason and the Argonauts, as they make their way through dangers and adventures in search of the legendary Golden Fleece, which some historians believe is based on real expeditions into the Black Sea dating from the fourth or third millennium. As a well-known legend, the story made an appealing subject for epic poetry; moreover, as far as audiences of the time were concerned, the legend was true. As scholar Green observes, the Greeks felt that tales such as the expedition of the Argonauts and the fall of Troy were datable, if distant, events. To them, "the mythic past was rooted in historical time, its legends treated as fact, its heroic protagonists seen as links between the 'age or origins' and the mortal, everyday world that succeeded it." Both HERODOTUS and PINDAR, writing centuries before Apollonius, make references to the story as though it were actual fact.

The *Argonautica* differs from traditional Greek epic poems in many ways. Like his contemporary and sometime-friend CALLIMACHUS, Apollonius dared to experiment with the traditional epic form as shaped by HOMER. Jason, the hero of the poem, is portrayed as reluctant and not entirely confident in his abilities, which stands in stark contrast to the valiant and superhuman portrayals of such figures as Achilles and Hercules in other Greek works. Furthermore, despite being an adventurous story, the main theme of the poem is not the quest of heroic achievement, but rather the romantic love between Jason and Medea. Apollonius's achievement in the poem is the psychological depth given to the character of Jason's spurned wife. She is portrayed as having complex feelings, as in the passage from Book III where she waits in worried anticipation for Jason to appear. In a passage rich with poetic tension and epic similes, Apollonius writes, "Medeia could not remove her thoughts to other matters / whatever games she might play," and instead was continually "looking round up the road, peering into the distance":

> The times her heart snapped in her breast,
>   when she
> couldn't be sure
> if the sound that scampered by her was
>   wind or
> footfall!
> But soon enough he appeared to her in her
>   longing
> like Seirios, spring high into heaven out of
>   Ocean,
> a star most bright and splendid to
>   observe . . .

Thus, the writing of Apollonius, with ideas of the reluctant hero and romantic love, stands as a predecessor for much of the Western literature that followed it.

Disagreements over the use and function of the epic genre led Apollonius to argue bitterly and ultimately break with Callimachus. In his lifetime he saw the Alexandrians warm to his work and welcome him as a great poet. Though the Callimachean fashion was to treat poetry with intellectualism and self-conscious irony, Apollonius's explorations of the human heart and the numinous mystery of the Golden Fleece made his poem enduringly popular. Apollonius's lasting impression on the tradition of Greek epic poetry eventually passed on to the Roman world, where echoes of Apollonius would resound in the Latin epics, particularly in the *Aeneid* of VIRGIL.

English Versions of Works by Apollonius of Rhodes

The Argonautika. Translated by Peter Green. Berkeley: University of California Press, 1997.

Jason and the Golden Fleece (The Argonautica). Translated by Richard Hunter. Oxford: Oxford University Press, 1993.

Works about Apollonius of Rhodes

Albis, Robert. *Poet and Audience in the Argonautica of Apollonius.* Lanham, Md.: Rowman and Littlefield Publishers, 1996.

Beye, Charles Rowan. *Epic and Romance in the Argonautica of Apollonius.* Carbondale: Southern Illinois University Press, 1982.

Harder, M. A, R. F. Regtuit and G. C. Wakker, eds. *Apollonius Rhodius.* Sterling, Va.: Peeters, 2000.

Apuleius (Lucius Apuleius, Apuleius of Madaura) (ca. 125–after 170) *novelist, philosopher, rhetorician*

Apuleius was born in Madaura, a Roman city in North Africa. His father was a *duumvir*, or provincial magistrate. Apuleius attended the University of Carthage and then studied philosophy in Athens, where he followed the teachings of PLATO. In 155 he married Pudentilla, a wealthy widow, but was brought to court and accused of seducing her by magic to acquire her money. Apuleius freed himself from the charge by giving a speech, known today as *Apologia*, in his own defense. He then settled in the African city of Carthage, where he wrote and gave lectures, but nothing is known about his later life.

Though Apuleius wrote a number of philosophical works, he is best known as the author of the *Metamorphoses*, or *Transformations* (also called *The Golden Ass*), the only complete Roman novel to survive from antiquity.

The novel relates the adventures of a young man named Lucius, who engages in a love affair with a slave girl to persuade her to show him the forbidden magical practices by which her mistress transforms herself into an owl. Lucius tries to transform himself but turns into a donkey instead. He then goes through a series of bizarre, dangerous, and humiliating adventures under different masters. Finally he prays to the Egyptian goddess Isis, "the loftiest of deities, queen of departed spirits, foremost of heavenly dwellers, the single embodiment of all gods and goddesses." Isis appears to him and changes him back to his human form, and he devotes himself to her as a priest.

For a long time, it was thought that the *Metamorphoses* was autobiographical, but it is actually based on an earlier novel by LUCIAN, *Lucius, or the Ass.* Apuleius embedded some other stories within the narrative and changed the ending to reflect the hero's salvation by Isis. Most of the embedded stories are in the style of the "Milesian tales," the bawdy stories, written in extravagant language, told by Egyptian street-corner storytellers.

Since Apuleius's novel is largely comic, many critics have believed it was intended as simple entertainment without any moral message. Others see it as a serious story of religious conversion. Carl Schlamm describes the novel as "a work of narrative entertainment . . . [A]mong the pleasures it offers is the reinforcement of moral, philosophic and religious values shared by the author and his audience." In this sense, the story is allegorical. It also gives readers an excellent picture of the lives of people in the second century, especially of the popularity of the mystery religion of Isis.

One of the embedded stories in the *Metamorphoses* has become much better known than the novel itself—the myth of Cupid and Psyche, for which Apuleius is the earliest source. The character Lucius listens to the myth when he is in his donkey form. Psyche is so beautiful that people worship her instead of the goddess Venus, and the jealous Venus arranges to have Psyche exposed on a mountain as prey for a monster. But Venus's son Cupid (Love) falls in love with Psyche. He rescues her and visits her by night as her husband, but forbids her to see his face. Urged by her jealous sisters, Psyche looks on her husband's face one night with a lamp, but he awakens, rebukes her for her lack of faith, and deserts her. The grieving Psyche wanders far and wide and must perform many labors assigned her by Venus, but she finally wins back her husband and becomes a goddess.

This story contains the themes of the entire novel. Both Lucius and Psyche are led by curiosity to try to see forbidden secrets of the gods, for which they both pay dearly. Both stories illustrate Plato's conception of the striving of the soul (*psyche* in Greek) for union with God.

Apuleius's philosophical works *The God of Socrates, Plato and his Doctrines,* and *On the World,* helped transmit knowledge of the teaching of Plato and his followers to the MIDDLE AGES. The *Florida* is made up of excerpts from Apuleius's lectures in Carthage.

The *Metamorphoses* has had a great influence on world literature since it was rediscovered in the RENAISSANCE. Boccaccio and a host of successive writers have analyzed, been influenced by, and retold the tale of Cupid and Psyche, as can be seen in William Shakespeare's *Midsummer Night's Dream* and John Keats's "Ode to Psyche."

An English Version of a Work by Apuleius

Apuleius: The Golden Ass. Translated by P. G. Walsh. Oxford, U.K.: Clarendon Press, 1994.

A Work about Apuleius

Schlamm, Carl C. *The Metamorphoses of Apuleius: On Making an Ass of Oneself.* Chapel Hill: University of North Carolina Press, 1992.

Aquinas, Saint Thomas

See THOMAS AQUINAS, SAINT.

Arabian Nights

See THOUSAND AND ONE NIGHTS, THE.

Aristophanes (ca. 450–385 B.C.) *playwright*
Born in Attica near Athens, Aristophanes became a playwright as a fairly young man; his first play, *Banqueters* (now lost), was staged in 427 B.C., and he penned approximately 40 comedies throughout his life. He was profoundly influenced by the Peloponnesian War between Athens and Sparta, which erupted in 431 B.C. and lasted more than 25 years.

Precious little is known about Aristophanes' life; what can be gleaned comes mainly from his 11 surviving plays, in which he attempts to cultivate the self-image of a brilliant but underappreciated artist. However, in his dialogue *The Symposium,* the philosopher PLATO portrays Aristophanes as a rascal. In Plato's work, Aristophanes gathers with other erudite and prominent Athenians at the home of tragic poet Agathon and admits to having spent the previous day carousing. After attempting various tactics to cure a violent case of the hiccups, Aristophanes narrates an entertaining and fanciful account of the origins of sexual desire that nevertheless manages to reveal his sophisticated intellect, learnedness, and familiarity with the scholarly theories of the day.

Critics defer to Aristophanes as a satirist of the highest order, and his work represents the only extant examples of Old Comedy, which is characterized, in part, by farcical plots, satire, and social and political commentary. Aristophanes caricatures self-important individuals as being dim-witted and foolish. He indiscriminately mocks theories of education, intellectuals, poets, women's suffrage, religion, and political systems, including democracy. In addition, he criticizes the affectations of civil society by alluding to bodily functions, indelicate acts, and parts of the anatomy usually not discussed in polite company. No fantasy was too outrageous for Aristophanes to imagine, and no subject was immune to his brutal, bawdy, and often vulgar wit. Yet his poetic dialogue at times reveals a tender, sympathetic soul. His protagonists are often underdogs, such as rural farmers and women, who have no real power or influence but who, in the world of the play, realize fantastic dreams.

Part of Aristophanes' breadth can be understood in context: Athenians enjoyed absolute freedom of speech during most of Aristophanes' life. Nevertheless, when *Babylonians* (426 B.C.) was presented at the Great Dionysia, an annual festival held to honor the god Dionysus, the demogogue Cleon denounced Aristophanes for ridiculing the city's elected magistrates before numerous foreign visitors.

Though Cleon's charge was serious, Aristophanes was not prosecuted, and he exacted revenge in his next two productions. In the *Acharnians* (425 B.C.), in which the farmer Dikaipolos arranges a one-man truce with Sparta to end the Peloponnesian War, one scene shows Aristophanes' version of the indictment. Worse, *Knights* (424 B.C.) depicts Cleon as the grasping and unscrupulous slave of a foolish old man, Demos, who symbolizes the Athenian people. When Demos plans to replace him, Cleon attempts to curry favor in an uproarious display of self-abasement. Both plays were awarded first prize in the theatrical contests at Lenaia.

Clouds, first produced in 423 B.C. and later revised, spoofs intellectuals, modern theories of education, and even the great philosopher SOCRATES, who is suspended in air, suggesting he is less than firmly rooted in reality. Aristophanes returns to political satire in *Wasps* (422 B.C.), wherein the democratic jury system, which the Athenians held in high esteem, becomes the target of his comic savagery. The play features an old man with a consuming passion for jury service because it allows him to wield irresponsible power and deliver harsh punishments. His son argues that the power belongs to the prosecutors who use the jurors to exact revenge on enemies. Father and son set up a mock court in which a dog prosecutes another dog for stealing some cheese, and the old man is tricked into voting for acquittal. The singers and dancers of the chorus dress as wasps to suggest that those who would spend their days on jury duty are peevish and predisposed to find fault.

Peace won second prize at the Great Dionysia in 421 B.C., when the Peace of Nicias was being negotiated between Athens and Sparta. Like Dikaipolos of *Acharnians,* Trygaios is a war-weary farmer who takes matters into his own hands. He fattens up a dung-beetle to immense proportions and then flies it to Mount Olympus to appeal to the gods for peace. The next surviving play, *Birds,* received the second prize at the Great Dionysia in 414 B.C. Three years later, the renewed conflict between Athens and Sparta provided the subject matter for *Lysistrata* (411 B.C.). In this play, the women of Athens and Sparta go on strike, withholding conjugal relations to force their warrior husbands to reconcile with their enemies. To this day, *Lysistrata* is performed to express antiwar sentiment.

Like his other plays, *Frogs* (405 B.C.) shows Aristophanes using comedy for a serious purpose. On the surface, the action parodies Greece's eminent poets and the gods themselves. The playwrights SOPHOCLES and EURIPIDES have died, leaving Athens with no important living tragedian, so Dionysus travels to the underworld to retrieve Euripides. To the latter's indignation, Dionysus returns instead with AESCHYLUS, whose poetry had been weighed on a scale like so much cheese and found to be more substantial, weighted, Aristophanes suggests, by ponderous language and overelaborate syntax. In reality, Aristophanes took seriously the poet's ability to sway public opinion, and *Frogs* reached its audience at a time when Athenian morale was flagging and the preservation of the city was at stake.

The Peloponnesian War came to an end in 404 B.C. when the people of Athens surrendered to Sparta. The conquerors installed an oligarchy, a form of government in which power is in the hands of a few, to replace democracy. This greatly impeded free speech. As a result, Aristophanes' final comedies lack the bite of his earlier plays and feature few direct references to current events.

Critical Analysis

Birds (414 B.C.) is considered Aristophanes' utopian tour de force, boasting a fantastical plot, splendid costumes, exuberant dialogue, and graceful lyric poetry. Wearied by the constant taxation and litigation that are part of Athenian life, two citizens, Peisetairos and a companion, seek a more suitable place to live. They visit the mythical hoopoe bird in the hopes that he has spied an appealing metropolis from the air but decide instead to build their own utopia in the sky from which they can reign over all humankind. The hoopoe gives the Athenians a potion that causes them to sprout awkward wings, and the new city is dubbed "Cloudcukooland." Immediately, the self-serving opportunists appear: a priest who attempts to ingratiate himself by reciting a list of bird-gods; a fortune-teller who offers his services for a fee; and officials who threaten legal action if the new city doesn't comply with various regulations.

The gods are furthermore enraged by the Athenians' presumption, and a battle ensues. At last, a divine embassy arrives in Cloudcukooland to resolve the conflict, and Peisetairos arranges a luncheon consisting of birds "condemned for revolting against the democratic birds." The gluttonous gods agree to a truce. In the end, the utopian city is no less politically corrupt, imperialistic, or bureaucratic than Athens; and Peisetairos is no less arrogant and ineffectual than any of the demagogues whose government he was fleeing.

Contemporary audiences continue to enjoy *Birds* for many reasons, not the least of which is its spectacle: the magnificently arrayed chorus of birds, each with a distinctive call; the appearance of a messenger goddess via theatrical crane; and the final battle between the Athenians and the birds, in which the men's weapons consist of cooking utensils. The action of the play aptly illustrates the qualities which continue to make Aristophanes' work accessible and appealing: His conflicts are relevant, his characters have complex personalities, and his ideals always suffer tragic defeat when meeting with the real world.

The New Comedy introduced with MENANDER eventually replaced the Old, but Aristophanes continued to fascinate audiences, perhaps because ARISTOTLE included him in his widely influential *Poetics.* Eugene O'Neill, Jr., in *Seven Famous Greek*

Plays, credits the playwright with a timeless appeal, saying, "There has never been anything quite like the comic drama of Aristophanes, and regrettably there will never be anything quite like it again." His "exceptionally high intellect and inexhaustibly fertile imagination" are expressed in "concentrations of splendid and dazzling conceits which follow one another in breathless abundance," while the "soft side of his personality expresses itself in his lyrics," which astound and delight. His plays seek to instruct as well as entertain, and with this blend of motives, Aristophanes set a standard by which all great art is judged.

English Versions of Works by Aristophanes

Aristophanes 1. 3 vols. Edited by David R. Slavitt and Palmer Bovie. Philadelphia: University of Pennsylvania Press, 1998.

Four Plays by Aristophanes: Clouds, Birds, Lysistrata, Frogs. Translated by William Arrowsmith, Richmond Lattimore, and Douglass Parker. New American Library, 1984.

Works about Aristophanes

Dover, K. J. *Aristophanic Comedy.* Berkeley: University of California Press, 1972.

MacDowell, Douglas M. *Aristophanes and Athens.* Oxford, U.K.: Oxford University Press, 1995.

Spatz, Lois. *Aristophanes.* Boston: Twayne Publishers, 1978.

Aristotle (384–322 B.C.) *philosopher, scholar, teacher, treatise writer*

Aristotle was born in the small Greek town of Stagirus (now Stagira). His father, Nicomachus, spent some time serving as personal physician to Amyntas II, king of Macedonia, at the kingdom's capital of Pella. Aristotle's mother and father died when he was a boy, and he was reared by other family members in the town of Atarneus in Asia Minor. In his late teens, Aristotle moved to Athens and enrolled in PLATO's famed Academy to study philosophy, mathematics, and the sciences. There he remained until Plato's death 20 years later. Aristotle and some fellow scholars soon relocated to settle in Atarneus, which was ruled by another Academy alumnus, Hermias, whose niece, Pythias, Aristotle married.

Around 343 B.C., Aristotle was invited by Philip of Macedonia, son of Amyntas II, to come to Pella and tutor his 13-year-old son, the future Alexander the Great. The tutorship lasted only three years, for the young man was obliged to take a more active role in Macedonian affairs; he would become one of the most brilliant military leaders of all time. In 335 B.C., Aristotle returned to Athens to establish his own institution of higher learning, the Lyceum, where he taught and wrote. His surviving works, or treatises, were probably lecture notes or textbooks for his classes. Upon Alexander's death in 323 B.C., anti-Macedonian sentiment in Athens became violent, and Aristotle, with his ties to the erstwhile royal family, was forced to flee for his own safety. He and his family sought refuge at Chalcis, where he died shortly thereafter.

Aristotle mastered every field of learning known to the Greeks, as demonstrated by the breadth of his treatises, which cover subjects ranging from biology to public speaking to literary criticism. Indeed, he assumed the task of identifying the distinguishing characteristics of each of the scholarly disciplines. Because humans are the only animals that possess the faculty of reason, Aristotle believed that to behave as a human being is to behave rationally. Furthermore, he defined three areas that comprise all possible human knowledge and activity in which the power of reason is expressed: theoretical, productive, and practical.

Theoretical is the purest form of rational knowledge, since it seeks truth only for its own sake. The person who pursues theoretical knowledge has no ulterior motive beyond understanding and insight. Examples of the theoretical branches of learning are natural sciences such as physics (bodies at rest and in motion), abstract mathematics, and metaphysics (the nature of being and reality).

The productive sciences, such as the arts, use reason for a specific purpose: to generate an end product. Practical sciences employ rational abilities to organize life within society, such as in the practices of ethics and politics. Living an honorable and productive life is the goal of the practical sciences.

Aristotle's *Physics* is a logical and methodical inquiry into such questions as how things come into being and how they are changed, and the difference between the fundamental nature of a thing and its incidental characteristics.

Metaphysics begins by stating that all people, by their very nature, desire knowledge. After all, Aristotle argues, that is why we value our senses so highly and our eyesight the most; they help us gather the information we desire. The knowledge Aristotle seeks in this treatise is the very nature of being, the basic and eternal principles of reality itself. Because God is depicted as the quintessential eternal and unchanging being and the primary cause of all that is, *Metaphysics* is also a theological tract.

In *Nicomachean Ethics* (named for Aristotle's son, who edited it after the philosopher's death), he states that "Every art of applied science and every systematic investigation, and similarly every action and choice, seem to aim at some good; the good, therefore, has been well defined as that at which all things aim." Happiness is the "good" toward which human activity aims, and people cannot be happy unless they live and act in a virtuous manner. Moral behavior is learned and becomes habitual as it is practiced, according to Aristotle. However, actions are considered virtuous only if they are intentional and take place within the context of human society. Ultimately, Aristotle conceded that ethics was an imprecise science.

In the category of the practical sciences, Aristotle wrote on such topics as ethics, politics, and rhetoric. In *Rhetoric* he offers, after careful observation of human behavior, a practical psychology for teaching the art of persuasive public speaking. The first book outlines the nature of rhetoric and the second its means and ends and the ways rhetoric can influence decisions, while the third book analyzes techniques of successful rhetorical style. The practical analysis of thought and conduct contained in these three books influenced Latin rhetoricians like CICERO and QUINTILIAN and thereafter swayed thinkers in the MIDDLE AGES, Renaissance, and beyond.

Politics contains a discussion of the role of the individual in the government of the city-state. Aristotle describes humans as political and social beings; some individuals are meant to lead, and others must be led. He condoned slavery as a natural state of affairs because he believed that those who became slaves were not capable of rational thought; otherwise, they would be rulers instead of servants. This, of course, is a circular argument; the fact that a phenomenon can be observed does not, by necessity, make it appropriate.

Aristotle was one of the great philosophers, but not all of his ideas have borne the tests of time and scrutiny. *Poetics* is the outstanding exception.

Critical Analysis

Poetics is a pioneering work that identifies the criteria and establishes the standards for excellence in literature, particularly tragic drama. Aristotle introduces such enduring concepts as unity of plot and action; catharsis, or a cleansing of the audience's emotions; and HUBRIS, arrogance that leads to a hero's downfall, which is itself an example of *hamartia*, a tragic flaw or catastrophic misjudgment.

Human beings are possessed of a natural ability to imitate, Aristotle says, and enjoy both viewing and producing imitative works of art. The basic ingredients of tragedy are, in order of importance, plot, character, thought, diction, song, and spectacle; and each element plays a part in artistic imitation.

According to Aristotle, drama is superior to EPIC poetry because it is enhanced by song and spectacle, the plot is more unified, and it achieves its artistic goal in a shorter period of time because the episodes are short. In an epic poem, the episodes are longer, even if there is not much to the story. As an example, he says, HOMER's epic poem the *Odyssey,* which is composed of over 12,000 lines, can be summed up as follows:

A certain man has been away from home for many years, kept that way by [sea god] Poseidon, and he ends up being alone. Meanwhile, his affairs at home are in such a state that his wife's suitors are squandering his property and are plotting against his son. Tempest-tossed, he arrives home; he reveals himself to some; he attacks and destroys his enemies and is saved. That is the essence of the *Odyssey;* the rest is made up of episodes.

Poetics instructs its readers that the best tragedies feature a protagonist who possesses virtue and is prosperous. The transformation of his good fortune to misfortune is caused not by his wickedness or indulgence in some vile practice, but by hamartia: "an error from ignorance or bad judgment or some other such cause."

The finest plots present events that follow one another of necessity as a matter of cause and effect. The fear and pity aroused in the audience should not be achieved by spectacle, Aristotle says, but rather by the structure of the events themselves, as was practiced by the better tragedians such as SOPHOCLES.

Aristotle criticizes the use of artificial dramatic devices. For instance, scenes of recognition between long-lost loved ones should occur as a consequence of events, he says, not through contrivances such as signs from the heavens, the detection of physical scars, or the recollection of keepsakes. He particularly disliked the practice of DEUS EX MACHINA ("god from the machine"), a device used frequently in the plays of EURIPIDES.

Only a fragment of *Poetics* remains for contemporary readers to enjoy. Nevertheless, scholar Sheldon P. Zitner rightly calls it "the most influential work of literary criticism in Western culture." Says he, "from the Renaissance on, the *Poetics* has been the foundation of both literary theory and 'practical' criticism, and it has been translated and retranslated, interpreted, applied, and cited in polemics as the final authority."

English Versions of Works by Aristotle

Aristotle's Poetics. Translated by Hippocrates G. Apostle, Elizabeth A. Dobbs, and Morris A. Parslow. Grinnell, Iowa: The Peripatetic Press, 1990.

Nicomachean Ethics. Translated by Martin Ostwald. New York: Macmillan Publishing Company, 1962.

Works about Aristotle

Bradshaw, David. *Aristotle East and West: Metaphysics and the Division of Christendom.* New York: Cambridge University Press, 2004.

Creed, J. L. and A. E. Wardman, translators. *The Philosophy of Aristotle.* Commentaries by Renford Bambrough. New York: Signet Classics, 2003.

Granger, Herbert. *Aristotle's Idea of the Soul.* Hingham, Mass.: Kluwer Academic Publishers, 2004.

Hintikka, Jaakko. *Analyses of Aristotle.* Hingham, Mass.: Kluwer Academic Publishers, 2004.

Rubenstein, Richard E. *Aristotle's Children: How Christians, Muslims, and Jews Rediscovered Ancient Wisdom and Illuminated the Dark Ages.* New York: Harcourt, 2003.

Arnaut Daniel   (Arnaud Daniel)
(fl. 1180–1200)   *poet, troubadour*

Arnaut Daniel was born into a noble family at the castle of Riberac in Perigord, France. He was a member of the court of Richard Coeur de Lion and was highly regarded as a Provençal poet and TROUBADOUR. Troubadours flourished from the late-11th to the late-13th century in southern France and in northern Spain and Italy, and they acquired a social influence unprecedented in the history of medieval poetry. They generally employed complex poetic structures to explore the theme of love, as Arnaut does in his poem "Anc ieu non l'aic, mas elha m'a" ("I don't hold it, but it holds me"):

> . . . *I tell a little of what's in my heart:*
> *fear makes me silent and scared;*
> *tongue hides but heart wants*
> *what on which, in pain, so broods*

I languish, but I do not complain
because so far
as the sea embraces the earth
there's none so kind,
actually
as the chosen one
for whom I long. . . .

This, like many troubadour songs, would have been set to music and performed in noble dining halls.

The poetic style of Arnaut's poems is called the *trobar clus,* which used intricate rhymes and complex metrics. Words of the *trobar clus* were chosen more for their rhythmic and rhyming functions than for their meaning. In terms of form, Arnaut wrote most of his poems in sestinas, six unrhymed stanzas of six lines each that involved elaborate word repetition. He was, in fact, credited with inventing the sestina.

Arnaut was admired by Petrarch and greatly influenced DANTE, who imitated his sestina form, dubbed him the "best crafter of the mother tongue," and gave him a prominent place in the *Divine Comedy.* In the 20th century, interest in his work was revived by T. S. Eliot and Ezra Pound, who translated several of his sestinas.

Only about 18 of Arnaut's poems survive, and they are among the best examples of troubadour poetry. Arnaut is remembered for his ability to write of love in language that was also flavored by religion, eroticism, and humor, and to set all of his words to music that gave his songs complex metrical schemes.

An English Version of Works by Arnaut Daniel

The Poetry of Arnaut Daniel. Translated by James J. Wilhelm. London: Taylor & Francis, 1983.

A Work about Arnaut Daniel

Wilhelm, James J. *Miglior Fabbro: The Cult of the Difficult in Daniel, Dante, and Pound.* Orono, Maine: National Poetry Foundation, 1982.

'Attār, Farīd od-Dīn (Farīd od-Dīn Mohammad ebn Ebrāhīm 'Attār)
(ca. 1142–ca. 1220) *poet, philosopher*

Farīd od-Dīn 'Attār was one of the greatest mystical writers and poets of the Muslim tradition. His works strongly influenced later Persian and other Islamic literature in both subject matter and style. Farīd od-Dīn was born in Nishapur, in northeastern Iran. Not much is known about his life, but the name 'Attār (perfumer or druggist) may indicate his family's line of work. As a young man he traveled extensively throughout most of the Muslim world, from Egypt to Central Asia and India, then returned to his hometown to pursue his writing. Apart from writing his many poems (over 45,000 couplets) and mystical prose works, he was a diligent collector of the sayings and writings of the great Sufi saints and masters who, in the previous two centuries, profoundly influenced the civilization of Persia.

Farīd od-Dīn's most celebrated work is his long allegorical or didactic epic, *The Conference of the Birds.* The poem follows the birds as they search for the Simurgh, or Phoenix, whom they want to make their ruler. Passing through the philosophical trials and tribulations of the seven valleys of inner perfection, most of them die through a fatal attachment to the self: the nightingale cannot give up the rose, nor the parrot its cage; the wagtail decides it is too small, the peacock too large. The remaining 30 birds (*si murgh*) find the king's palace at last, only to see themselves reflected in the phoenix's face.

The searchers, representing aspiring Sufis, are thus identified with the divine beloved they have been seeking all their lives. The beloved tells them:

Since you came here as thirty birds, you
appeared thirty in the mirror.
But We are altogether far superior: We are
Simurgh, the One Reality.
Known by a hundred glorious Names. Be
annihilated, so that you may find
yourselves in us.

Farīd od-Dīn's *divan,* or poetry anthology, is suffused with many more such verses of mystical and philosophical exploration. Two examples are *Book of Affliction,* in which Farīd od-Dīn traces the progress of a soul through 40 stages of isolation; and *Elahinama,* in which a king instructs his six sons on how to attain perfection of the self and, through that, all their other desires.

One of Farīd od-Dīn's prose works, *Muslim Saints and Mystics,* is a thorough account of the early Sufi movement that has served as a source book for historians of the era. Among his most popular works is *Book of Secrets,* a collection of edifying short stories.

Some 30 of 'Attār's 100 books have survived. The poet had a great influence on all subsequent Persian mystics, including the great mystic poet RUMI.

English Versions of Works by Farīd od-Dīn 'Attār

Attar Stories for Young Adults. Translated by Muhammad Nur Salam. Chicago: Kazi Publications, 2000.

Conference of the Birds: The Selected Sufi Poetry of Farid Ud-Din Attar. Translated by Raficq Abdulla. Northampton, Mass.: Interlink Publishing Group, 2003.

Works about Farīd od-Dīn 'Attār

Levy, Reuben. *An Introduction to Persian Literature.* New York: Columbia University Press, 1969.

Ritter, Hellmut. *Ocean of the Soul: Men, the World and God in the Stories of Farid Al-Din 'Attar.* Leiden, Netherlands: Brill Academic Publishers, 2003.

Thackston, Wheeler M. *A Millennium of Classical Persian Poetry.* Bethesda, Md.: Iranbooks, 1994.

Attic orators   (fifth century–fourth century B.C.)

During the Golden Age of ancient Greece, many of the Greek city-states began experimenting with representative forms of government. Rather than being ruled by kings or tyrants, the citizens of these city-states attempted to rule themselves in the name of the common good. It was the birth of democracy.

One of the keys to this new form of government was the assembly, where the citizens of a city would come together to debate and discuss political and social issues. Differences of opinion were freely aired, and each speaker was allowed the opportunity to convince the audience to agree with his argument. This gave birth to oratory (also know as rhetoric), the art of speaking well and persuasively. In addition to political matters, oratory was used by lawyers to persuade the courts to find in favor of their clients.

The city-state of Athens, which controlled the region known as Attica (from which the Attic orators take their name), was indisputably the most powerful democracy in Greece, and the influence of the Athenian Assembly was tremendous. The fact that Athens was deeply involved in all the great political, military, and diplomatic events of the day meant there was a great deal for Athenian politicians to discuss. The two centuries between 500 and 300 B.C. saw two Persian invasions of Greece, the rise and fall of Athenian power, the disastrous Peloponnesian War, the conquest of Greece by Macedonia, and the astonishing career of Alexander the Great. Through all these years, the politicians and orators of Athens constantly debated and discussed these events, attempting to decide what to do. It is no surprise that many eminent orators lived and worked in Athens during this time.

One of the first of the great Athenian orators was Antiphon (ca. 480–411 B.C.), who was a lawyer interested in murder cases. He did not take much of an interest in politics until near the end of his life, when he organized a revolt by oligarchs, wealthy men who distrusted democracy. The revolt failed, and Antiphon was executed for treason against Athens. His most famous works are the *Tetrologies,* four hypothetical paired speeches, and surviving fragments of his speeches on law and justice.

Another orator who favored the oligarchs was Andocides (ca. 440–391 B.C.). He wrote his speeches *On the Mysteries, On His Return, On the*

Peace with Sparta, and *Against Alcibiades* in defense of charges brought against him for his involvement in the defacing of the statues of *Hermes* (considered religious monuments) and another religious scandal relating to the revelation of the Eleusinian Mysteries during the Sparta peace mission, for which he was exiled once from 415 to 403, and again in 392.

Not all the orators favored the oligarchs, however. One such democrat was LYSIAS (459–380 B.C.), who lived and worked mostly in the aftermath of the Athenian defeat in the Peloponnesian War. During this time, a continual struggle was being waged between the oligarchs and the democrats. Lysias, who was a foreigner, was granted Athenian citizenship for his assistance in helping democracy return to Athens. He was regarded as an outstanding speaker and was knowledgeable on a wide variety of subjects. His speech *On the Murder of Eratosthenes,* about a peasant who murders Eratosthenes, is perhaps his best-known work, but he also wrote a speech in defense of SOCRATES that is known for its simplicity and clarity.

During the fourth century B.C., as King Philip of Macedonia began to encroach upon Greek independence, the Athenians constantly debated how to respond. One orator who favored accommodating Philip was Aeschines (389–314 B.C.), who, as DEMOSTHENES' rival, spoke in favor of peace and against opposing Macedonia. Three of Aeschines' speeches survive: *Against Timarchus,* a sanction against Timarchus for his homosexuality; *On the Embassy,* a defense against Demosthenes' charge that he was accepting bribes; and *Against Ctesiphon,* his opposition to Ctesiphon's claim that Demosthenes should be awarded the golden crown. In the matter of King Philip's rule, Aeschines accepted the point of view of ISOCRATES (436–338 B.C.), who states in his speech *Philip* that he wanted King Philip to unite all of Greece under a strong ruler. Isocrates is also known for having trained many of the great Athenian orators of his day, including Hyperides, ISAEUS, and Lycurgus.

Other orators, however, were bitterly opposed to Macedonia and spoke out in favor of continued resistance. One of these men was Hyperides (ca. 390–322 B.C.), who spoke out repeatedly against King Philip, even after Athens had been defeated by Macedonia at the Battle of Chaeronea. He is believed to have written more than 70 speeches, all of which were lost until the latter half of the 19th century, when six were discovered in Egypt. In the debate over Macedonia's rule of Athens, Hyperides was an ally of Demosthenes (384–322 B.C.), who was bitterly opposed to peace with Macedonia, as can be seen in his eloquent speeches known as *Philippics.* Demosthenes is still regarded by many as the greatest orator Athens has ever produced. He is believed to have been a student of the Attic orator Isaeus (fourth century B.C.), whose speeches are valued for the legal, social, and cultural information they provide on ancient Greece.

After Macedonia had ended Greek independence, Athens's political and military power declined. Nevertheless, debates continued in the Athenian assembly. An orator named Lycurgus (ca. 390–324 B.C.) sought to persuade the citizens of Athens to become more religious and moral and also attempted to make the city government more efficient. He studied the art of rhetoric under PLATO and Isocrates, but he is most remembered for his efforts as a financier in increasing Athens's wealth.

The last of the great Athenian orators was Dinarchus (ca. 360–after 292 B.C.), who actually came to Athens from the city-state of Corinth, and who wrote speeches seeking to prosecute many distinguished Athenians for corruption, including Demosthenes. His works mark the decline of Attic oration in ancient Greece.

The Athenian tradition of oratory has had a tremendous influence on history and the art of debate. Today, in places like the United States Congress, the British Parliament, the Sansad of India, and the Diet of Japan, politicians debate and discuss the great issues facing their nations, and in city councils and town hall meetings across the world, ordinary citizens do the same regarding local issues facing their communities. But it was in the city-states of ancient Greece, and in Athens in particular, that the art of oratory first came into being through the efforts and skills of the Attic orators.

English Versions of Works by the Attic Orators

Aeschines. *Aeschines: Speeches.* Translated by C. D. Adams. Cambridge, Mass.: Harvard University Press, 1992.

Andocides. *On the Mysteries.* Edited by Douglas M. MacDowell. Oxford: Oxford University Press, 1989.

Antiphon and Andocides. Translated by Michael Gagarin and Douglass M. MacDowell. Austin: University of Texas Press, 1998.

Demosthenes. *Demosthenes: On the Crown.* Edited by Harvey E. Yunis. New York: Cambridge University Press, 2001.

Dinarchus, Hyperides, and Lycurgus. Translated by Ian Worthington, et. al. Austin: University of Texas Press, 2001.

Isaeus. Loeb Classical Library. Translated by Edward S. Forster. Cambridge, Mass.: Harvard University Press, 1992.

Lysias. The Oratory of Classical Greece Series. Translated by S. C. Todd. Austin: University of Texas Press, 1999.

Selections from the Attic Orators. Edited by E. E. Genner. Oxford, U.K.: Clarendon Press, 1955.

Works about the Attic Orators

Edwards, Michael. *The Attic Orators.* London: Bristol Classical Press, 1994.

Gagarin, Michael. *Antiphon the Athenian: Oratory, Law, and Justice in the Age of the Sophists.* Austin: University of Texas Press, 2002.

Harris, Edward Monroe. *Aeschines and Athenian Politics.* Oxford: Oxford University Press, 1994.

Jebb, Richard Claverhouse. *The Attic Orators from Antiphon to Isaeus.* Chicago: The University of Chicago Press, 2003.

Too, Yun Lee. *Rhetoric of Identity in Isocrates: Text, Power, Pedagogy.* New York: Cambridge University Press, 1995.

Worthington, Ian. *Demosthenes: Statesman and Orator.* London: Taylor & Francis, 2001.

———. *Historical Commentary on Dinarchus.* Ann Arbor: University of Michigan Press, 1993.

Aucassin et Nicolette   (13th century)
French tale

Aucassin et Nicolette is the only surviving example of the genre of the French *chantefable,* a medieval tale told in alternating sections of prose and verse. The word *chantefable* is from Old French and literally means "(it) sings (it) recites." The term may have been coined by the author of *Aucassin et Nicolette,* for he says in the work's concluding lines, "No chantefable prent fin" ("Our chantefable draws to a close"). Nothing is known of the author of this work except that he may have been a professional minstrel from northeastern France, as the work is written in this dialect.

Aucassin et Nicolette is a tale of adventure revolving around the romance of Aucassin, the son of the Count of Beaucaire, and Nicolette, a captive Saracen woman recently converted to Christianity. The work shares much in common with an earlier French romance titled *Floire et Blancheflor* (ca. 1170): both works share common Moorish and Greco-Byzantine sources and use similar themes of separation and reunion (the lovers endure many complications, including flight, capture, and shipwreck before they are finally able to marry).

The author of *Aucassin and Nicolette* skillfully depicts the ardor of the characters' young love, yet he also mocks the EPIC and romance forms by inverting the roles of the two lovers. Nicolette is portrayed as an intelligent, resourceful young woman (in fact, she proves to be the daughter of the King of Carthage) who disguises herself as a minstrel in order to be reunited with her love. Aucassin, however, is depicted as a pathetic lovesick swain:

> *He made his way to the palace*
> *Climbed the step*
> *And entered the chamber*
> *Where he began to cry*
> *And give vent to his grief*
> *And mourn his beloved*

He lacks initiative, is ungrateful to his parents, and must ultimately be bribed to uphold his duties as a knight. Only under the threat of death does he rise to the task of defending his honor. Aucassin is also shown to be a poor Christian when he states he would prefer to be in hell with his love rather than in heaven.

The verse and musical portions of the work are considered to be more finely wrought than the prose narrative, in which the author displays comparatively less skill. The only surviving manuscript of *Aucassin et Nicolette* is housed in France's Bibliothèque Nationale. It is valued for its mixture of prose and verse, reversal of gender roles, and subtle mocking of courtly fiction.

An English Version of *Aucassin et Nicolette*

Of Aucassin and Nicolette: A Translation in Prose and Verse from the Old French. Translated by Laurence Housman. New York: Dial Press, 1930.

Works about *Aucassin et Nicolette*

Cobby, Anne Elizabeth. *Ambivalent Conventions: Formula and Parody in Old French.* Amsterdam: Rodopi BV Editions, 1995.

Pensom, Roger. *Aucassin et Nicolette: The Poetry of Gender and Growing up in the French Middle Ages.* New York: Peter Lang, 1999.

Stedman, Edmund Clarence. "Aucassin and Nicolette." In *Yale Book of American Verse.* Edited by Thomas Lounsbury. New Haven, Conn.: Yale University Press, 1912.

Aue, Hartmann von

See HARTMANN VON AUE.

Augustine, Saint (Augustine of Hippo, Aurelius Augustinus) (354–430)

memoirist, theologian, philosopher, essayist

Saint Augustine was born in Thagaste, the site of modern Souk Ahras, Algeria. His father, Patricius, was a pagan who died while Augustine was still in his teens. His mother Monica was a devout Christian who profoundly influenced Augustine's way of thinking in his later years.

Much of what we know about Augustine's life comes directly from his *Confessions.* He was educated in Thagaste and Madaura and then sent to Carthage to study rhetoric. There, abandoning the Christian Church and its teachings, he took a mistress with whom he had a son, Adeodatus, and began to dabble in Manichaeism, a Persian religious philosophy that held a dualistic view of good and evil.

Augustine taught rhetoric in Carthage, Rome, and finally Milan, where he fell under the influence of Bishop Ambrose, whose sermons inspired him to read the Epistles of Saint Paul. In 386, Augustine converted to Christianity and devoted himself to scholarly and literary pursuits. He was ordained as a priest in 391 and established a new monastery near Hippo in northwest Africa. He was consecrated assistant bishop there by the ailing Valerius in 396 and spent the remainder of his life caring for the diocese. He died while Hippo was under siege from the invading Vandals.

Augustine's literary output was phenomenal. He produced tracts against heretics and enemies of the church, including the Manichaeans; philosophical and literary essays in a dialogue form inspired by the works of PLATO; scriptural exegeses; religious instruction and pastoral works; and a prodigious quantity of personal correspondence. Among his most important earlier works are *Contra academicos* (Against the Skeptics), which counters the academic skepticism of the followers of CICERO; *De beata vita* (On the Happy Life), in which he argues that enduring happiness is to be found only in the love of God; *De ordine* (On Order), an attempt to explain how evil can exist when God is both omnipotent and completely good; *De immortalitate animae* (On the Immortality of the Soul, 386/387); and *De animae quantitate* (On the Greatness of the Soul, 387/388), inquiries into the nature of the soul and its aspects. He also wrote *De musica* (On Music, 387/391), in which he addresses time and number in the abstract and treats music as a matter of rhythm; *De libero arbitrio*

(On Free Will, 388–395), in which he argues that "willing" in the appropriate way will bring about happiness; and *De magistro* (The Teacher, 389), a dialogue between Augustine and Adeodatus on how knowledge is obtained and transferred.

City of God, written between 413 and 426 and composed of 22 books, is Augustine's most well-known work besides *Confessions*. Following the sack of Rome by the Goths in 410, the Christian Church was widely blamed for the loss of faith in the pagan gods and the subsequent fall of the Roman Empire. Augustine answered these charges with *City of God*, a refutation of the idea that in order to flourish people must appease a diverse and sundry assortment of gods, as well as an interpretation of the development of contemporary society and Western thought in the context of the struggle between good and evil.

Critical Analysis

Confessions, written in 397–398, is both a memoir and a testament of faith. Even as a child, Augustine constantly faced temptation in an environment characterized by powerful pagan influences, as was typical of the time and place of his youth. He disobeys his parents and teachers, participates in sporting events or attends theatrical productions when he is supposed to be studying, and resists Monica's attempts to expose him to the teachings of the Christian Church. "I was a great sinner for so small a boy," he writes.

As an adolescent, he finds that he derives genuine pleasure from doing things that are forbidden simply because they are forbidden, and when he goes to Carthage to study rhetoric, he lands "in the midst of a hissing cauldron of lust." In this hedonistic environment, he soon finds a suitable object of his affection, although his joy is tempered by "the cruel, fiery rods of jealousy and suspicion, fear, anger, and quarrels." Nevertheless, Augustine joins the other sensualists of Carthage in their endless pursuit of pleasure. "Give me chastity and continence," he prays, "but not yet."

At age 19, Augustine's ambition is "to be a good speaker, for the unhallowed and inane purpose of gratifying human vanity." As part of his studies, he is assigned CICERO's *Hortensius*, which arouses in him a love of philosophy. "It altered my outlook on life. . . . All my empty dreams suddenly lost their charm and my heart began to throb with a bewildering passion for the eternal truth. . . . In Greek the word 'philosophy' means 'love of wisdom,' and it was with this love that the *Hortensius* inflamed me." In his quest, he joins the Manichees, whose dualistic and materialistic approach to good and evil appeals to him: Blame for the sin is cast not on the sinner, but elsewhere. For nine years, to his mother's great distress, Augustine is "led astray . . . and [leads] others astray" by his affiliation with the Manichees.

When Faustus, a bishop of the Manichees, comes to Carthage, Augustine is disappointed that the bishop cannot resolve the discrepancies between the tenets of the Manichees and known scientific facts. "The Manichaean books are full of the most tedious fictions about the sky and the stars, the sun and the moon," he writes. "I badly wanted Faustus to compare these with the mathematical calculations which I had studied in other books . . . but I now began to realize that he could not give me a detailed explanation."

Augustine's final rejection of the Manichaean doctrines would come in Milan when, listening to the sermons of AMBROSE, he recognizes his prior misconceptions about Christian doctrine. Scripture may be understood metaphorically, not literally, he realizes. Evil is not a material substance, as the Manichees would have it, but a distortion of free will. He also acknowledges the factors that are preventing him from embracing Christianity wholeheartedly. They include his worldly ambitions, his reluctance to relinquish his mistress, and his difficulty conceiving of God as a spiritual entity. Nevertheless, he wishes with increasing agitation and desperation to convert to the faith.

One day he is weeping bitter tears in the garden of his house, asking for the grace to "make an end of my ugly sins," when he hears a child's voice saying, "'Take it and read, take it and read.'" Taking this as a divine message, Augustine opens Paul's

Epistles and reads the first passage his eyes land upon: "'Not in revelling and drunkenness, not in lust and wantonness, not in quarrels and rivalries. Rather, arm yourselves with the Lord Jesus Christ; spend no more thought on nature and nature's appetites.'"

"I had no wish to read more and no need to do so," Augustine recalls. "For in an instant, as I came to the end of the sentence, it was as though the light of confidence flooded into my heart and all the darkness of doubt was dispelled."

He relates his conversion to Monica, who is overjoyed, and the following year (387), Augustine is baptized on Easter Sunday.

Thus concludes the autobiographical portion of *Confessions*. In the remainder of the book, Augustine variously examines his ability to master temptation and expounds upon the first chapter of Genesis, discussing the nature of time with respect to God (i.e., there was no "time" as we know it before God created the heavens and the Earth).

"The life of Augustine has a special appeal because he was a great sinner who became a great saint and greatness is all the more admirable if it is achieved against odds," writes the translator of *Confessions*, R. S. Pine-Coffin. "He hinges on the incidents of his life such considerations as tend to elevate the mind and heart of the reader." Pine-Coffin adds, "The *Confessions* and the *City of God* rightly belong to the great literature of the world."

Moreover, Augustine's theories of sin, forgiveness, and free will have provided the foundation for basic Roman Catholic tenets as well as those of Calvinism, Lutheranism, and other religions.

English Versions of Works by Saint Augustine

City of God. Translated by Marcus Dods. New York: Random House, 2000.

Confessions. Translated by R. S. Pine-Coffin. Middlesex, U.K.: Penguin Books, 1961.

Monastic Rules. Commentaries by Gerald Bonner. Foreword by George Lawless. New York: New City Press, 2004.

Works about Saint Augustine

Barry, Sister M. *St. Augustine, the Orator: A Study of the Rhetorical Qualities of St. Augustine's Sermons Ad Populum (1924).* Whitefish, Mont.: Kessinger Publishing, 2003.

Chadwick, Henry. *Saint Augustine, Bishop of Hippo.* Oxford, U.K. : Oxford University Press, 1986.

O'Meara, John Joseph. *The Young Augustine: The Growth of St. Augustine's Mind up to His Conversion,* rev. ed. Staten Island, N.Y.: Alba House, 2001.

Augustus (Gaius Octavius) (63 B.C.– 14 A.D.) *emperor, patron of writers*

Augustus was the first and perhaps the greatest of the Roman emperors, rising to power in the aftermath of the fall of the Roman Republic. The adopted son and successor of Julius CAESAR, Augustus brought stability and peace to Rome, ushering in an era of tranquillity known as the *Pax Romana,* or "Roman Peace." Augustus was also a writer of some talent, but his most important contributions to the world of literature came from his support and encouragement of some of the greatest writers the Western world has ever produced.

Born Gaius Octavius, Augustus came from a distinguished family and received an excellent education. He was fascinated by philosophy and literature and initially possessed a rather introverted personality. As a young man, he served with his great-uncle, Caesar, although his political and military roles were limited. When Caesar was assassinated in 44 B.C., Augustus was surprised to discover that he had been made Caesar's heir, after which he became Gaius Julius Caesar.

Over the next several years, Augustus was engaged in a bitter political and military struggle, first with Caesar's assassins, then with his rival for power, Marcus Antony. In 31 B.C., at the decisive Battle of Actium, the forces of Antony were defeated and Augustus had emerged as the single most powerful man in the Roman world.

In 27 B.C., the Roman Senate surrendered virtually all its power to Augustus, who thereafter ruled as emperor. This is the traditional date for the end of the Roman Republic and the beginning of the Roman Empire. For the remaining four decades of his life, Augustus would use his power to reform the government of the Empire and bring order to the entire Mediterranean region. He launched a sweeping program of construction that beautified the city of Rome itself, improved the transportation and communication systems in the Imperial provinces, developed the economy, and reformed the military. By the time of his death, the Roman Empire was peaceful and prosperous.

Augustus was deeply interested in literature and commissioned several writers to produce works that glorified Roman achievement. By far the most famous of these works was the *Aeniad,* written by Rome's greatest poet, VIRGIL. The author had left instructions that the epic poem be destroyed when he died, but Augustus ordered that it be preserved, thus saving one of the great works of classical literature.

Augustus also supported the work of LIVY and HORACE. Most writers found Augustus to be an extremely positive influence and welcomed the gift of peace he had brought to their world. For reasons which remain unclear, the emperor quarreled with the writer OVID, but the general attitude of Augustus toward the great authors of his day was one of encouragement and assistance. This greatly furthered the literary arts of Rome, which has deeply influenced Western literature to the present day.

Augustus was himself a writer, although most of the work he produced has been lost. He penned an autobiography and at least one poem and one play. His only extant work is *Res Gestae Divi Augusti,* or "Acts of the Divine Augustus." This was his last will and testament, in which he described for posterity what he believed his greatest achievements were. It is in this work that he makes the celebrated remark that he found Rome a city of bricks and left it a city of marble.

An English Version of a Work by Augustus

Res Gestae Divi Augusti: English and Latin. Translated by P. A. Brunt and J. M. Moore. London: Oxford University Press, 1967.

Works about Augustus

Forsyth, Fiona. *Augustus: The First Emperor.* New York: The Rosen Publishing Group, 2003.

Severy, Beth. *Augustus and the Family at the Birth of the Roman Empire.* New York: Routledge, 2003.

Southern, Pat. *Augustus.* New York: Routledge, 1998.

Aurelius, Marcus

See MARCUS AURELIUS ANTONINUS.

Averroës (Abū al-Walīd Muhammad ibn Ahmad ibn Muhammad ibn Rushd)
(1126–1198) *philosopher*

Averroës was the last in a great line of medieval Arabic philosophers. The author of many books in all fields of knowledge, he was particularly known as an interpreter of the Greek philosopher ARISTOTLE and a defender of philosophy in a religious, Muslim civilization. His greatest influence was in Europe, where his works inspired Christian scholars for hundreds of years.

Averroës was born into a prominent family of scholars and public servants in Córdoba, the ancient capital of Muslim Spain. His grandfather and father served as *qadis,* or chief judges and administrators; he himself rose to that position, first in Seville (1169) and then in Córdoba (1171). He studied with prominent scholars, and took advantage of Córdoba's famed library of some 500,000 volumes.

Around 1160, Averroës was introduced to the caliph, Abu Yaqub Yusuf, himself an accomplished scholar. The ruler was so impressed with his guest that he asked him to write a commentary on all of Aristotle, a task that Averroës devoted much of his life to completing. Despite moral support from the caliph, the philosopher had to contend with a public mood that was hostile to Greek philosophy and to any learning outside the confines of traditional Muslim theology and law. (Spain and Morocco were then ruled by the North African Almohad Dynasty, which had been founded as an austere Muslim reformist movement.)

Sometime in the 1170s, the caliph brought Averroës to Marrakesh in Morocco to be court physician. There, under the caliph's protection, Averroës wrote his greatest works in defense of philosophy. Yaqub's son, al-Mansūr, confirmed the appointment on his succession to the throne in 1184. However, in 1195, al-Mansūr banished Averroës to a village in Spain and had his philosophical book burned. Historians claim the caliph had acted to gain wider support for a *jihad,* or holy war, against Christian Spain. Three years later, he forgave Averroës and invited him back to Marrakesh, where the philosopher died.

Critical Analysis

When the Arabs conquered the ancient civilizations of the Middle East in the seventh century, they discovered Greek philosophy, which dominated intellectual life at that time. Many of the works of Aristotle and some of PLATO were translated from Syriac translations of the Greek into Arabic.

The new Muslim civilization gave pride of place to theology and law, but Greek philosophy was also developed, though not without the criticism of the leaders of other fields of study. Averroës devoted much of his life and writings to an attempt to reconcile Aristotelian philosophy with Muslim law and theology. Over the course of several decades (1169–95), he wrote commentaries on most of Aristotle's known works and on Plato's *Republic.* Each commentary had three sections: the *Jami,* a brief summary or simple paraphrase of the original; the *Talkhis,* a more elaborate exposition of the text; and the long *Tafsir,* which included extensive elaborations and many of Averroës's own contributions, often relating the material to Islamic thought and society.

Apart from these commentaries, Averroës wrote three great works that established his reputation as a literary scholar and philosopher, especially in Europe. *On the Harmony of Religion and Philosophy (Fasl al-Maqal), Examination of the Methods of Proof Concerning the Doctrines of Religion (Kashf al-Manahij),* and *The Incoherence of The Incoher-*ence *(Tahafat al-Tahafat)* were all written in Marrakesh between 1179 and 1180.

The first two works describe the exalted role of philosophy. According to Averroës, only philosophers, armed with the logical techniques provided by Aristotle, could understand the true inner meaning of the laws as revealed to the prophet MUHAMMAD. In addition, theologians could only reach a certain level of understanding, while the masses must be content with the stories and metaphors provided in the Koran and other religious works. Averroës conceded, however, that some revealed truths were beyond rational understanding and must be accepted on faith, even by philosophers. In the third book in the trilogy, Averroës refutes al-Ghazali's condemnation of rational philosophy, as presented in al-Ghazali's book *The Incoherence of the Philosophers.*

Nearly all of Averroës's books survive only in Hebrew and Latin translation (with the Latin usually translated from Hebrew) or in Arabic written in Hebrew characters. This may reflect the philosopher's greater reputation in the non-Muslim world.

Averroës, in Latin translation, was probably the most important source of Greek philosophy for Christian religious and secular scholars of the Middle Ages. His works helped spark a revolution in learning throughout Europe, which historians often say laid the groundwork for modern science. Freethinkers were often called "Averroists," but this was not considered to be a good thing. Some Christian religious authorities considered Averroës to be a threat to the church because he advocated a "double truth" in which theology and philosophy held different, opposing views.

Averroës was also known for a major medical treatise (ca. 1162), known in its Latin translation as the *Colliget.* European universities continued to use the book for hundreds of years.

On another issue—the role of women—Averroës's position was very unusual for his time and place. In his view, confining women to the sole function of childbirth and raising children betrayed women's true potential. It also deprived society of a major economic resource.

As a bridge between the ancient Greeks and modern European civilization, Averroës had an enormous impact. His attempts to reconcile Islamic and secular philosophy made him an ideal model for many later Christian thinkers.

English Versions of Works by Averroës

Averroës' De substantia orbis: Critical Edition of the Hebrew Text. Translated and edited by Arthur Hyman. Cambridge, Mass.: Medieval Academy of America, 1986.

Averroës on Plato's Republic. Translated and edited by Ralph Lerner. Ithaca, N.Y.: Cornell University Press, 1974.

Averroës' Three Short Commentaries on Aristotle's Topics, Rhetoric, and Poetics. Translated and edited by Charles E. Butterworth. Albany: State University of New York Press, 1977.

The Book of the Decisive Treatise Determining the Connection Between the Law and Wisdom, and Epistle Dedicatory. Translated and edited by Charles E. Butterworth. Provo, Utah: Brigham Young University Press, 2001.

Works about Averroës

Leaman, Oliver. Averroës and His Philosophy. Richmond, U.K.: Curzon, 1998.

Streight, David. Averroës: A Rationalist in Islam. Notre Dame, Ind.: University of Notre Dame Press, 2000.

Avicenna (nickname of Ibn Sīnā, Abū 'Alī al-Husayn ibn 'Abd Allah ibn Sīnā)
(980–1037) philosopher, scientist, nonfiction writer

Avicenna was one of the most respected philosophers and scientists in the history of Islam. For hundreds of years, his works influenced philosophy and the teaching and practice of medicine in the Christian and Muslim worlds.

Avicenna was born in the village of Afshana near Bukhara, in present-day Uzbekistan. His father was a local governor under the Samanid rulers, the first independent Iranian dynasty since the Arab conquest 300 years before. Avicenna was given the best education available in all fields of knowledge. A brilliant student, he had learned the KORAN (Qur'an) and memorized much Arabic poetry by the time he was 10. He also became very adept at medicine, a skill that would eventually make his career. At age 17, he cured Nuh Ibn Mansur, the Samanid ruler at Bukhara (a feat he would later repeat with other rulers when political turmoil forced him to move). He was rewarded with access to the royal library, one of the best of the time, where he began to write some of his major works.

The death of his father and the defeat of the Samanids at the hand of new Turkish rulers forced Avicenna to begin several years of travel, working as physician, local administrator, and jurist. He was known as a hard worker, and he devoted his evenings to continued learning and writing, surrounded by a convivial group of scholars and students.

Wherever Avicenna went, he always found the time to write, eventually producing an astounding body of some books and treatises, some of them encyclopedic in length, on an unusually wide range of subjects. About 200 of these works survive. He wrote most of his works in Arabic, the dominant scholarly language of the Muslim world. He also wrote a few works in Persian, including the first book of Aristotelian philosophy in that language.

After several years of travel, in 1015 Avicenna won an appointment as court doctor to Shams ad-Dawlah, the Buyid prince of Hamadan in northwestern Iran, whom he cured of a severe colic. The prince eventually named him vizier (prime minister), though political troubles forced him to spend a few months in prison and longer spells hiding in exile. At Hamadan Avicenna completed his monumental medical treatise, The Canon of Medicine (al-Qanun fi al Thibb).

Forced by the death of the ruler in 1022 to flee Hamadan, Avicenna found refuge two years later at Isfahan, at the court of another Buyid ruler, 'Ala' ad-Dawlah, where he lived the last 13 years of his life in peace, accompanying the prince in all his military campaigns and journeys. He died in Hamadan during one of these trips.

Avicenna eventually wrote an autobiographical sketch. It is the main source of information pertaining to his life, together with a biography, *The Life of Avicenna,* written by his lifetime companion Juzjani, which was included in Latin translations of Avicenna's major works.

Critical Analysis

Avicenna's *Canon of Medicine* may be the most influential medical textbook in history; at more than 1 million words, it is certainly one of the longest written by one person. The book relied to a certain degree on the works of the great Greek physicians, including GALEN, but it also incorporated knowledge gained by many Muslim doctors and scientists, as well as through Persian and Indian lore. Avicenna was able to add to this bulk of knowledge a great deal of insight he had personally acquired through his long medical practice. His discoveries included an understanding that tuberculosis and other diseases were contagious, that some diseases could spread via environmental factors like water, and that psychology affected health.

The Muslim world soon recognized the book as a major step forward in medical science. It was translated into Latin in the 12th century, and it soon became the chief medical textbook in all European universities, maintaining that status until after 1600.

The book contains five volumes: treating physiology and hygiene; simple drugs; pathology (two volumes covering fevers, tumors, rashes, and poisons); and drug combinations. In addition, Avicenna's descriptions of the many hundreds of herbs, powders, tablets, leeches, ointments, and other remedies constituted the most complete and accurate listing of remedies ever assembled. During his lifetime he wrote some 40 other medical works, most of them specialized treatises.

Like most Muslim philosophers of his day, Avicenna worked in the Aristotelian tradition handed down from ancient Greece, with a substantial influence of Neoplatonism from the Roman period. Many of his ideas were developed in *The Book of Healing,* which was in effect an encyclopedic summation of knowledge in almost every scientific and philosophical field.

Avicenna's central philosophic idea is that God exists as the "first cause"; everything else in the universe emanates from that cause. The first things to emanate are pure ideas, perfect and unchanging, which can be understood through intelligence. Souls emanate next; they can move matter in the heavens and on earth. Then come the physical laws of nature, followed by matter, which is by itself incapable of motion.

One of the four sections of *The Book of Healing* was devoted to mathematics, under which Avicenna included music and astronomy. He also wrote works on psychology, geology, and physics, in some cases adding his own original insights, theories, and proofs, such as his designs for equipment for measuring the exact coordinates of stars (their location on the heavenly sphere or sky).

Like many Persian writers, Avicenna was also influenced by mystical thought. He elaborated his mystical ideas in one of the main works of his later years, *Oriental Philosophy,* which was apparently lost during an attack on Isfahan in 1043. However, some of these ideas survive in his personal testimony, *The Book of Directives and Remarks,* in which he describes a spiritual journey from the start of faith to an eventual direct vision of God.

After Avicenna's death, prominent orthodox Sunni Muslim writers criticized him for denying that God can directly influence events in the world. Nevertheless, his philosophy remained influential for centuries in both the Muslim and Christian worlds.

English Versions of Works by Avicenna

A Treatise on the Canon of Medicine of Avicenna, Incorporating a Translation of the First Book. Translated by O. Cameron Gruner. London: Luzac & Co., 1930.

Avicenna's Poem on Medicine. Edited by Haven C. Krueger. Springfield, Ill.: Thomas, 1963.

Ibn Sīnā and Mysticism: Remarks and Admonitions, Part Four. Edited by Shams Constantine Inati. New York: Kegan Paul International, 1996.

Works about Avicenna

Burrell, David B. *Knowing the Unknowable God: Ibn-Sina, Maimonides, Aquinas.* Notre Dame, Ind.: University of Notre Dame Press, 1986.

Chishti, Hakim G. M. *The Traditional Healer's Handbook: A Classic Guide to the Medicine of Avicenna.* Rochester, Vt.: Healing Arts Press, 1991.

Gohlman, William E. trans. and ed. *The Life of Ibn Sina; A Critical Edition and Annotated Translation.* Albany: State University of New York Press, 1974.

Goodman, Lenn Evan. *Avicenna.* New York: Routledge, 1992.

Parviz, Morewedge. *The Mystical Philosophy of Avicenna.* Binghamton, N.Y.: Global Publications, 2001.

Siraisi, Nancy G. *Avicenna in Renaissance Italy: The Canon and Medical Teaching in Italian Universities after 1500.* Princeton, N.J.: Princeton University Press, 1987.

Wisnovsky, Robert, ed. *Aspects of Avicenna.* Princeton, N.J.: Markus Wiener, 2001.

Bacchylides (fifth century B.C.) *lyric poet*

During the Golden Age of ancient Greece, all forms of literature reached new heights. The writing style known as lyric poetry, which was designed to be sung by a performer, was of particular importance. One of the most important Greek lyric poets of this era was Bacchylides.

The nephew of the lyric poet Simonides, Bacchylides was born in the town of Ceon but later emigrated to the city-state of Syracuse, on the island of Sicily. Syracuse was then controlled by the powerful ruler Hieron, who was a great patron of the arts. During his time in Syracuse, Bacchylides was a rival of the more famous poet PINDAR.

Bacchylides' works were almost unknown to historians until the late 19th century. Fortunately, a collection of works was discovered in the Egyptian desert in 1897, preserved in writing on papyrus. Nineteen poems were recovered, including dithyrambs (lyric poems written in a lofty style) and epinician odes (poems written to honor Greek athletes who won victories in the Olympic Games). In one of his dithyrambs, Bacchylides memorializes the legendary Greek hero Theseus. The poem takes the form of a dramatic dialogue between King Aegeus and a chorus of Athenians. The dialogue describes a young man (Theseus) and his epic defeat of a host of monsters.

Bacchylides' works are important in the details they provide of ancient Greek culture and traditions, as well as for the insight they give to changes taking place in the formation and purpose of Greek poetry.

English Versions of Works by Bacchylides

Complete poems. Translated by Robert Fagles. New Haven, Conn.: Yale University Press, 1961.
Bacchylides: A Selection. Edited by Herwig Maekler. New York: Cambridge University Press, 2004.

Works about Bacchylides

Burnett, Anne Pippin. *The Art of Bacchylides.* Cambridge, Mass.: Harvard University Press, 1985.
Pfeijffer, Ilja Leonard and Simon R. Slings, eds. *One Hundred Years of Bacchylides: Proceedings of a Colloquim Held at the Virje Universeieit Amsterdam.* Amsterdam: VU Boekhandel/Uitgeverij, 2004.

Bai Juyi (Po Chü-i) (772–846) *poet*

Bai Juyi, the son of a minor government official, was born in Hsin-cheng, China. Though his family was poor, Bai received a good education that prepared him for his government service examinations in 800 and 803. After passing his examinations, he was assigned to a job in Ch'ang-an, the Tang dynasty capital. His experiences in the capital influenced his early poems, which were mostly political and social commentaries, known as the "New Ballads." His poetry is known for its clear, simple style and its reflection of Confucian thought. The autobiographical nature of his poems also reveals that he was influenced by the poet Tu Fu.

Despite Bai's popularity, in 815 his political commentary caused him to be demoted to a post outside the capital, in Chiang-chou on the Yangtze River. While there, he began to address more spiritual concerns in his poetry. While studying and meditating at the Buddhist temples on Mount Lu, he became interested in the work of TAO YUANMING (365–427), a Buddhist poet whose work extolled nature and the virtues of idleness and serenity.

Bai's most powerful poetry reflects everyday events and the effect they had on his inner thoughts. Some of these poems include "Watching the Reapers," in which the poet compares the sparseness of the reapers' lives to his own well-to-do life; "Golden Bells," in which he philosophizes on the joy and burden of having a baby daughter; and "Pruning Trees," in which the act of pruning trees symbolizes clearing one's vision to find the important things in life.

One of the most famous groups of letters in Chinese literature is Bai's extensive literary correspondence with his friend, fellow poet and government official Yuan Zhen, who compiled Bai's poetry and prose into a volume for which he wrote the preface. Through its distribution to Buddhist temples throughout China, the work preserved more than 2,800 of Bai's poems.

Bai Juyi retired from public service in 833. He spent the remaining 13 years of his life studying Buddhism and adding poetry and essays to his collected works. He is widely regarded as one of the Tang Dynasty's greatest poets.

English Versions of Works by Bai Juyi

Po Chü-i: Selected Poems. Translated by Burton Watson. New York: Columbia University Press, 2000.
The Selected Poems of Po Chü-i. Translated by David Hinton. New York: New Directions, 1999.

A Work about Bai Juyi

Waley, Arthur. *The Life and Times of Po Chü-i.* London: Allen & Unwin, 1949.

bardic poetry (sixth–13th centuries)

Bardic poetry refers to an oral tradition of verse composition and performance largely associated with the Celtic cultures of Anglo-Saxon England, Scotland, Ireland, and Wales. The forms of bardic poetry followed precise metrical and alliterative patterns since the word-music, made from the sounds of the language itself, was considered as important as the music of the accompanying instrument. To meet the demands of a strict meter, bards drew on a repertoire of stock phrases and metaphors, and when necessary they used adjectives or kennings to fill out a line. A kenning is typically a compound descriptor using an innovative image or metaphor to convey the qualities of a person or thing. For instance, a person might be called "strong arm," "steady glance," or "bright cheek." Unfortunately for modern listeners, not only does little of the bards' music survive, but the word-music itself is often lost in translation.

Documentation on early bards is scarce and obscure. The bulk of the early lyrics remain anonymous, and some authorial attributions are apocryphal. Manuscript fragments attempt to capture works that could have been composed centuries before. Part of the literary style was to use intentional archaisms to make the language sound older and therefore superior. Most bards were rigorously educated, well-respected members of the aristocratic classes who could boast of a long poetic heritage. Some traveled, performing their works, while others had patrons. Celtic culture accorded great esteem to bards, and noble Celtic families, who attached great importance to having honor of "face," often feared to provoke a poet to slander. Women could be bards as well as men, and several surviving Irish lyric love poems are attributed to female authors.

Since it was composed and sung in the vernacular or native language, much bardic poetry retains a flavor of the Celtic culture prior to Christianity, which brought literacy in the form of Latin. The forms and subject matter of bardic poetry can often be traced to pre-Christian influences. In addition to nature poems, devotional lyrics, and encomiums of praise or protest directed at rulers, the bards preserved their culture's native history in saga or chronicle poems populated with gods, heroes, and other mythical creatures. Anglo-Saxon bards were as revered as warriors, since their ability to describe a warrior's feats after his death, thus elevating him to hero status, was often the only consolation a warrior had to achieve enduring fame. Such an achievement was based in the concept of the heroic ideal: Kings and their retainers sought perfection in battle, honor, and chivalry. This heroic ideal is aptly portrayed in the Old English EPIC poem *Beowulf.*

Much of Irish bardic poetry features the legendary figures Finn MacCool; Cuchulain; Cano, the Irish version of Tristan (*see TRISTAN AND ISEULT*); and Oisín, remembered in the Ossianic or Fenian cycles. Welsh poets often sang of Arthur and his warriors.

Anglo-Saxon and Irish bardic poetry spans the Old, Middle, and Early Modern English periods; Old Irish turns into Middle Irish around the 12th century, whereupon the tradition changes from a mainly oral legacy to a documented practice of literary composition maintained by clerics and court poets. The early Irish tradition distinguished between a bard who sang and played the poems and a *file* who composed the poetry and functioned as a historian, genealogist, seer, and social satirist as well as an artisan. *Fili* (the plural of *file*) trained at bardic schools. In its earliest uses the word suggests someone who is a master poet and also initiated in spiritual practices such as divination. This may reflect the status and service held by the druids, who were, for the pre-Christian Celts, poets, prophets, lawmakers, guardians of traditional knowledge, and practitioners of the occult.

Many *fili* liked to preserve a sense of mystery around their work and perpetuated the romantic myth that the best poets created under very spe-cial circumstances, specifically in a dark room, lying down, with no outside noise or distractions. Thereafter, the bard would offer a recitation and musical performance. Though at one point bards received about half the pay that a *file* did, later the terms *bard* and *file* became interchangeable. Some of the best-remembered Irish bards are Donnchadh Mór, Gofraidh Fionn, Eochaidh Ó hEoghusa, Fear Flatha, Fearghal Óg, and Tadhg Mac Dáire.

Though the Irish and Welsh embraced Christianity well before the Anglo-Saxons did, early Welsh poetry escapes Latin influence. The sixth-century Welsh bards are themselves figures of legend: Taliesin; Llywarch Hen; and Anerin, who is credited with the battle poem "Gododdin," the earliest reference to King Arthur. Manuscripts of their works date to the 12th century. Other Welsh bards from the 12th and 13th centuries are Meilyr; his son Gwalchmai; Owain prince of Powys; Owain's court bard Cynddlew; and the greatest of the medieval Welsh bards, Dafydd ap Gwilym (1340–1400), who lived at the same time as the English poet Geoffrey Chaucer.

See also MYTHOLOGY, CELTIC; ORAL LITERATURE/ TRADITION.

English Versions of Bardic Poetry

Gurney, Robert, ed. *Bardic Heritage: A Selection of Welsh Poetry in Free English Translation.* London: Chatto & Windus, 1969.
Medieval Irish Lyrics. Translated by James Carney. Dublin: Dolmen Press, 1999.

Works about Bardic Poetry

Lofmark, Carl. *Bards and Heroes: An Introduction to Bardic Poetry.* Cribyn, Wales: Llanerch Press, 1989.
Matthews, John, ed. *The Bardic Source Book: Inspirational Legacy and Teachings of the Ancient Celts.* Poole, Dorset, U.K.: Blandford Press, 1999.

Beatrice of Nazareth (1200–1268) *mystic, diarist, treatise writer*

Beatrice of Nazareth was born to a merchant family of Tienen, near Brussels, Belgium. As a very young child she showed an aptitude for scholarship, and at age seven, upon the death of her mother, her father sent her to live for a year with a group of beguines. The beguines were laywomen in the Low Countries who chose to lead spiritual lives without taking vows at a religious institution. When Beatrice discovered her vocation for monastic life, her father allowed her to enter the Cistercian convent at Bloemendaal.

In 1216 Beatrice officially became a novice, and in 1217 she traveled to the convent at Rameya to study with Ida of Nivelles. Under her tutelage Beatrice had her first mystical experience in January 1217. In 1221 she returned to Bloemendaal, where the visions continued, and the esteem with which she was treated troubled this very modest woman. In 1236 she joined the Cistercian community at Nazareth, near Antwerp, where she was made prioress and where she remained until her death.

The anonymous *Life of Beatrice* was composed from a private diary Beatrice kept, recording her experiences. She also wrote several treatises on the spiritual life. The only one to survive, called *Seven Modes of Sacred Love,* is considered the first vernacular work exploring the soul's ascent to God. For Beatrice, sacred love, *minne* in Flemish, is the pinnacle of the soul's existence. In *Seven Modes* she writes: "love strives only for the purity, the nobility and the highest excellence which she herself is . . . and it is this same striving which love teaches to those who seek to follow her." Beatrice shares her belief that experience of God is a personal interaction mediated by love with other women mystics, such as Mechthild of Magdeburg, Julian of Norwich, and Hadewijch, as well as the later Belgian theologian Jan van Ruusbroec.

An English Version of a Work by Beatrice of Nazareth

Bowie, Fiona, ed. *Beguine Spirituality: Mystical Writings of Mechthild of Magdeburg, Beatrice of Nazareth, and Hadewijch of Brabant.* Translated by Oliver Davies. New York: Spiritual Classics, 1990.

Works about Beatrice of Nazareth

De Ganck, Roger. *Beatrice of Nazareth in Her Context.* 3 vols. Kalamazoo, Mich.: Cistercian Publications, 1991.
———. *The Life of Beatrice of Nazareth.* Kalamazoo, Mich.: Cistercian Publications, 1991.

Bede (Baeda, The Venerable Bede)
(673–735) *historian, scholar, commentator, biographer, treatise writer, poet*

Bede was born in a small village in the vicinity of Jarrow in Northumbria, near the present-day city of Newcastle in northern England. In 679, at age seven, as was the culture in those times, Bede was fostered at the monastery in Wearmouth in the care of Abbot Benedict Biscop, and later at the monastery in Jarrow under Abbot Ceolfrith. In addition to his theological studies, he was educated in literature, grammar, rhetoric, history, philosophy, arithmetic, geometry, astronomy, law, and music. He was ordained deacon in 691 and priest in 702 by Bishop John of Hexham.

From his extensive readings, his own observations, and the stories he gathered from travelers visiting the monasteries, Bede wrote scores of books: Biblical exegeses (commentaries, explanations, and critical interpretations of texts); hagiographies (biographies of saints and venerated people); treatises on astronomy, botany, and meteorology; hymns; and poems. The 60 volumes and 950 manuscripts that Bede produced over a period of some 30 years make him one of the most prolific and greatest of English writers.

In recognition of his piety and contribution to theological writing, historians of the ninth century conferred the title of "Venerable" upon him. He was canonized in 1899 by Pope Leo XIII, who conferred the title of "Doctor of the Church" upon him for being "an ecclesiastical writer of great learning and sanctity." His feast day is celebrated on May 25.

Writers throughout history have attempted translations of Bede's works. In 1910, J. A. Giles published an English version of *Historia abbatum* (Lives of the Abbots), which Bede wrote ca. 725 as a compilation of biographies of the lives of abbots and saints. In addition, C. W. Jones published a translation of Bede's *De natura rerum liber* (On Nature, ca. 691), a scientific text on nature and astronomy, in 1975.

However, no single work written by Bede has been more frequently copied in longhand, from the date of its completion in 731 until the printed book was published in 1475, than his *Historia ecclesiastica gentis Anglorum* (The Ecclesiastical History of the English People). It has never ceased to be read, and more than 150 manuscript copies of it survive to this day. This celebrated work served as the guiding model for historians throughout the Middle Ages, and it is the work for which Bede is remembered as the "Father of English History."

Bede himself modestly described the work as "the history of the Church of our island and race." Composed entirely in medieval Latin, this indispensable source of early Anglo-Saxon history is a continuous narrative of five books that spans a period of almost eight centuries, from Julius Caesar's invasion of Britain to 731. It is, in effect, a depiction of a saint's life with the English nation as hero, and it highlights the rapid conversion of the Anglo-Saxons by missionaries from Rome and Ireland. In addition, the work serves as an authority on the early English Church, daily monastic and secular life, and major historical events of the period.

Passionate in his support of orthodoxy and in condemnation of heresy, Bede was a traditionalist whose prime concern was the spread of the accepted beliefs of the Catholic Church. Such commitment led him to write most of his works, including an exposition of the Great Cycle of 532 years that was of fundamental value to the Roman Church in calculating the date of Easter. He also introduced the custom of *anno Domini*, dating events from the birth of Christ.

In addition to writing, reciting written works to the accompaniment of music was one of Bede's great delights. He was skilled in the recitation of the music of the liturgy, vernacular English poetry, and songs of Anglo-Saxon Britain. Despite being grievously ill the day he died, the dedication and diligence he brought to his teaching duties is best reflected in his cheerful reminders to his students throughout that day to learn their lessons quickly since he might not be there long to instruct them.

Bede is best described by the words of Peter Hunter Blair in *The World of Bede* (1970):

> The scholar who never spared himself in the search for truth, the monk who loved music and was deeply moved by the beauty of his church all brightly lit for a festal day, the teacher whose last thought was for the pupils of his school, and the endearingly humble man who chose the image of griddle, frying-pan and oven to illustrate stages in the growth of spiritual understanding.

English Versions of Works by Bede

De natura rerum liber (On Nature). Edited by C. W. Jones. Turnhout, Belgium: Brepols 1975.

The Ecclesiastical History of the English People. Edited and translated by B. Colgrave and R. A. B. Mynors. Oxford, U.K.: Clarendon Press, 1969.

Historia abbatum (The Lives of the Holy Abbots of Wearmouth and Jarrow). Translated by J. A. Giles. London: J. M. Dent, 1910.

Works about Bede

Blair, Peter Hunter. *The World of Bede.* New York: St. Martin's Press, 1970.

Brown, George Hardin. *Bede the Venerable.* Boston: Twayne Publishers, 1987.

Beowulf (10th century) *epic poem*

One of the finest EPIC poems of Anglo-Saxon literature, *Beowulf* is a stirring adventure story and a deeply serious commentary on human life. It tells the story of the life and death of the legendary hero

Beowulf in his great battles with supernatural monsters and in his reign as a cultured and popular monarch. Beowulf is a model of heroic spirit at its finest, the ideal Anglo-Saxon image of warrior-aristocrat.

Cyclical in movement and unified by striking contrasts of youth and old age, success and failure, bravery and cowardice, *Beowulf* is a sophisticated poem following CAEDMON's style of poetry, with a Germanic hero-warrior code of honor coupled with Christian religious underpinnings. The poem is written in the unrhymed four-beat alliterative meter of OLD ENGLISH POETRY. The author is unknown. There is much debate about when the poem was written, but it was most likely composed sometime between the middle of the seventh and the end of the 10th centuries. As such, it is the longest surviving poem in Old English, containing more than 3,100 lines. While the poem was written in Anglo-Saxon England in the Old English language, the events it describes are set in Denmark, Sweden, and Geatland (now southern Sweden).

Critical Analysis

The epic opens, as it ends, with a funeral, the sea burial of the founder of the Danish royal line. Then the scene changes to King Hrothgar's court in Heorot, Denmark, where the huge demon Grendel kills and eats warriors every night. Beowulf, prince of the Geats and strongest man of his time, hears of the troubles and journeys there with his troop of men to win his fame by challenging the giant monster. He conquers Grendel barehanded, ripping off the monster's arm at the shoulder:

> . . . *No Dane doubted*
> *The victory, for the proof, hanging high*
> *From the rafters where Beowulf had hung*
> *it, was the monster's*
> *Arm, claw and shoulder and all.*
>
> (ll. 833–836)

There is much rejoicing at the royal banquet the next day. Many heroic tales are told in Beowulf's

honor, and a bard sings the lay of the Finnsburg episode, a tragic feud from the Danish past.

Later that night, Grendel's mother attacks the royal hall to avenge her son. Beowulf dives down to the bottom of the haunted lake where she dwells. At first she nearly kills him, but he manages to slay her with the help of a strange, magical sword. When he resurfaces, the onlookers, who had given him up for dead, rejoice in his victory.

Beowulf has thus succeeded in cleansing Denmark of the evil monsters. In a moving sermon of exceptional poetic force, the king, who is very fond of young Beowulf, warns him of the dangers of pride and weeps as Beowulf returns to Geatland.

Part I of the epic ends with Beowulf's recounting of his adventures in Denmark and of the political state of affairs there to his uncle, King Hygelac of the Geats. Beowulf bestows Hrothgar's gifts on Hygelac, who in turn rewards Beowulf with treasure and lands.

Part II takes up the last thousand lines of the poem and deals with a Beowulf of mature years, when he comes to the Geatish throne upon the death of Hygelac and his son. Beowulf rules wisely and peacefully for 50 years, a remarkable feat in those troubled times. Then one day, a robber accidentally disturbs a sleeping dragon that guards a treasure hidden in a grave mound. The dragon awakens and starts wreaking havoc in the surrounding villages by burning down houses.

Beowulf decides to meet the fire-breathing dragon in combat. Upon seeing the dragon, his troops flee in terror, but his kinsman Wiglaf refuses to leave his side. Together they kill the dragon, but Beowulf receives a fatal wound in his neck. Knowing his end is near, he rejoices over the life he has led and is at peace with his conscience. His only regret is that he leaves behind no heirs. Wiglaf grieves as Beowulf breathes his last. When the cowardly troops return, Wiglaf heaps scorn upon their heads.

Wiglaf then sends a messenger to the king's household informing them of the tragedy. The messenger's speech is a prophecy of the doom for the Geats at the hands of their enemies, the Swedes, now that their hero-protector is dead.

Beowulf is cremated on a great funeral pyre. All the Geats, warriors and common folk alike, gather around in despair, and the poem ends as the treasure from the grave mound that the dragon was guarding and Beowulf's ashes are buried together in a monumental barrow on a headland by the sea.

Beowulf's importance and value lie in its details, which give us a glimpse of the warrior-hero's spirit and code of honor and of the attitudes and beliefs of the monk who transcribed the oral story, thus giving the poem a Christian influence and reflecting pagan England during its transition to Christianity.

English Versions of Beowulf

Beowulf. Translated by Howell D. Chickering, Jr. New York: Doubleday, 1977.
Beowulf. Translated by Seamus Heaney. New York: W.W. Norton, 2000.

Works about Beowulf

Bjork, Robert E. and John D. Niles, eds. A Beowulf Handbook. Lincoln: University of Nebraska Press, 1998.
Cook, Albert Stanburrough. The Possible Begetter of the Old English Beowulf and Widsith. New York: M.S.G. Haskell House, 1970.
Tolkien, J. R. R. Beowulf and the Critics. Edited by Michael Drout. Phoenix: Arizona State University, 2002.

Bernard de Ventadour (Bernart de Ventadorn) (fl. ca. 1147–ca. 1170)
troubadour

Bernard de Ventadour was born in the province of Limousin in south-central France. One biographer, writing long after his subject's death, claimed that Bernard was a lowly servant in charge of heating the ovens at the viscount of Ventadorn's castle. According to this biographer, Bernard fell in love with the viscount's wife and addressed his love songs to her. The viscount discovered the affair, and Bernard moved to Normandy, where he had a love affair with Eleanor of Aquitaine. When she left to marry Henry II of England, Bernard joined the court of Count Raymond V of Toulouse. Finally, when Raymond died, Bernard became a monk.

In reality, we know little of Bernard's life apart from what we can glean from his songs. Although he was probably not a menial servant, he almost definitely grew up in the castle of Ventadorn (or Ventadour). In the vida (a biographical portion of verse found in most TROUBADOUR songs) of one song, he claims to be the son of a man-at-arms and a relative of the viscount of Ventadorn. He was acquainted with Eleanor of Aquitaine, and it is certain that he knew Henry II of England. Because 12th-century Ventadour was a hotbed of troubadour activity, Bernard must have been acquainted with the works of earlier composers like JAUFRÉ RUDEL and with the more popular MEDIEVAL ROMANCE.

Bernard's songs are remarkable expressions of courtly love (see CHIVALRY AND COURTLY LOVE) and, more specifically, of fin'amor (expressions of the impact of love on the individual), of which he is credited as being the creator. Unlike the works of some of his contemporaries, they are neither too complicated nor difficult to understand, nor too polished or simple. "It is no wonder if I sing better than any other singer," begins one song, "for my heart draws me more towards love and I am better made for its commands." In another song, which begins with the line "I have a heart so full of love," Bernard declares himself to be so happy "That the ice appears to me a flower, / And the snow lies green." Later in the poem, however, he complains that he is suffering even more than Tristan did when trying to win Iseult (see TRISTAN AND ISEULT). Scholar James Wilhelm notes that Bernard's reasoning thus "follows the rather helter-skelter pattern of the somewhat crazed, moon-bewitched lover."

At times, Bernard implicitly and wittily compares his secular love for a woman to a pious love for the Virgin Mary. (The Provençal language in which he wrote derived from Latin, the language of the Church.) Mentions of paradise, grace, and a lady whom the poet hopes will grant his pleas all were sure to remind medieval listeners of religion, even as the poet wished for a reward that was decidedly secular.

Several of Bernard's contemporaries enjoyed more popularity in the 12th century, but 20th-century readers and critics esteem Bernard's work far above that of rival troubadours. Wilhelm believes that Bernard

> has one of the best senses of humor in medieval literature. Furthermore, he is diversified: his stanzas constantly surprise with their sudden, sometimes illogical shifts of tone that keep the reader's wits on edge. He has the same kind of brittle, inexhaustible melodic quality that crackles in Mozart's sonatas.

Approximately 40 of Bernard's songs still survive, and scholars rank his verses above those of fellow troubadours Rudel and Marcabru for their sensuality and freedom of expression.

See also MIDDLE AGES.

English Versions of Works by Bernard de Ventadour

Bilingual Edition of the Love Songs of Bernart de Ventadorn in Occitan and English: Sugar and Salt. Translated by Ronnie Apter and Mark Herman. Lewiston, N.Y.: Edwin Mellen, 1999.

"I have a heart so full of love." In *Seven Troubadours: The Creators of Modern Verse.* Edited by James J. Wilhelm. University Park, Pa.: Penn State University Press, 1970.

"It is no wonder if I sing better than any other singer" and "When I see the lark moving its wings against the sun's rays." In *The Courtly Love Tradition.* Edited by Bernard O'Donoghue. Totowa, N.J.: Barnes & Noble, 1982.

A Work about Bernard de Ventadour

Merwin, W. S. *The Mays of Ventadorn.* Washington, D.C.: National Geographic Society, 2002.

bestiary *medieval literary genre*

The bestiary is a literary genre of the European MIDDLE AGES generally consisting of a collection of stories, each detailing the qualities of an animal, plant, or even stone. These stories were often presented in the form of Christian allegories for moral enlightenment.

The bestiaries are derived from the Greek text *Physiologus,* compiled between the second and fourth centuries by an unknown author and consisting of 48 sections, each linking a creature, plant, or stone to a Biblical text. Translations and adaptations of this and other bestiaries spread throughout Europe in the 12th and 13th centuries and were very popular in France.

Many of the medieval bestiaries, such as "The Panther" and "The Whale," were also lavishly illustrated with pictures of sometimes-fabulous beasts. Creatures in other tales included a gryphon, a lion/eagle hybrid; a basilisk, a half-bird, half-reptile so poisonous that its glance could kill; and an aphibaena, a two-headed reptile. In addition, many traditional attributes of real and mythical creatures, such as the phoenix and the unicorn, derive from the bestiaries. These attributes, again intended to help teach a moral tale, have since been absorbed into folklore, literature, and art.

A 14th-century tale titled *Bestiare d'amour* applies the allegorical structure of a bestiary to courtly love, but the intent of most bestiaries was to elaborate on the virtues of abstinence and chastity and to warn against heresy. Some of the animals in the tales symbolize religious virtues or characters from the BIBLE. The lion, for example, is portrayed in one bestiary as an animal that can revive its dead offspring, reminiscent of God's resurrection of the Christ. In another tale, goats were used to symbolize sinners who strayed from God's path.

The power of using animals to teach lessons about friendship and honesty can still be seen today in tales such as those about Winnie the Pooh and Hank the Cowdog. The ancient tales and their medieval translations and adaptations, however, found their place in world literature by illustrating how the written word was used to transfer religious teachings and concepts to the illiterate masses.

English Versions of Bestiaries

Bestiaries In Mediaeval Latin And French. Translated by Florence McCulloch. Chapel Hill, N.C.: University of North Carolina Press, 1956.

The Book of Beasts. Edited by T. H. White. Mineola, N.Y.: Dover, 1984.

Medieval Latin and French Bestiaries. Translated by F. McCulloch. Chapel Hill: University of North Carolina Press, 1960.

Works about Bestiaries

Baxter, Ron. *Bestiaries and their Users in the Middle Ages.* Phoenix Mill, U.K.: Sutton Publishing, 1998.

Davis, Norman. "Notes on the Middle English Bestiary." *Medium Aevum* 19, Oxford, U.K.: The Society for the Study of Medieval Languages and Literature, 1950: 56–59.

Hallbeck, Einar S. *The Language of the Middle English Bestiary.* Cristianstad, Virg. Is.: Länstidning Press, 1905.

Bhagavad Gita (Bhagavad–gita, Bhagavadgita) (first century B.C.)
Sanskrit text

The Bhagavad Gita is a philosophical poem that summarizes and explains the key concepts underlying Hindu religious belief and practice. The poem is staged as a dialogue between the warrior Arjuna, one of the five Pandava brothers, and his charioteer Krisna, an engaging and remarkable young man. In these conversations, Arjuna ostensibly asks for advice on how to regain his composure and courage to fight against the evil Kurowas, his half-cousins. Krisna, who is an incarnation of the Hindu god Vishnu, answers with a series of instructions that coherently unify and communicate the foundational tenets of Hindu beliefs, and also, in the guidance Krisna gives his pupil on how to

conduct himself in war and life, provides a spiritual manual for daily living.

The setting of the work is the battlefield of Kurukshetra, where the two armies led by the Pandavas and Kurowas gather for battle—also the setting of the greatest and most elaborate of Indian epic poems, the MAHABHARATA, of which the Bhagavad Gita forms the sixth chapter. The essential teachings of the Gita most likely existed long before the *Mahabharata* was composed, transmitted through oral teachings in the manner of the Upanishads and the four Vedas, the oldest known Sanskrit scriptures. The actual events of the *Mahabharata* are thought to have transpired between 1000 and 700 B.C. The Bhagavad Gita contains the outlines of a spiritual practice that may date to the earliest indigenous settlers in the Indus valley, around 3000 B.C.

Unlike other important works of Indian literature, like the *Ramayana,* the author of the Bhagavad Gita remains unknown. Early Indian commentators have suggested that the Gita may have been written by the Hindu god Krisna or by the seer Vyasa, who is considered the author of the *Mahabharata* and the PURANA.

Critical Analysis

The dramatic beauty of the Gita is that, in appearing in the midst of a physical battle, the war between good and evil provides a metaphorical parallel to the Bhagavad Gita's true topic. As translator Eknath Easwaran says, "the Gita's subject is the war within, the struggle for self-mastery that every human being must wage if he or she is to emerge from life victorious."

The poem opens with a metaphysical dialogue between Dhritarashtra, the blind king of Kurukshetra and father of the Kurowas, and his courtier sage, Sanjaya. Worried about the course of the war, Dhritarashtra asks Sanjaya (who is blessed with the ability to see all that transpires in the past, present, and future) to relate to him every detail of the war. Sanjaya first tells of the conversation that takes place between Duryodhana, Dhritarashtra's son, and his teacher, Drona, in which Duryodhana boasts of his great number of forces and his confidence in securing victory. This sets the scene for the long dialogue between Arjuna and Krisna in which Krisna instructs Arjuna that it is the latter's duty to fight and win the war. The Greek idea of hubris, or exaggerated pride, is exemplified in the contrast between the haughtiness of Duryodhana and the unwillingness of Arjuna to engage in a war in which his teachers and kin will be killed.

Given this background of war, in the poem, Arjuna becomes concerned with the universal questions of life and death. Seeing that his courage wavers, Krisna proceeds to explain to him the nature of the soul, the soul's relation to God, the laws that govern the natural world, and the laws that govern consciousness and reality. In the end, Krisna reveals himself as an *avatar,* or incarnation of Vishnu, one of the faces of the Infinite God, the lord of life and death. Arjuna goes on to engage in battle because it is his duty; as the remainder of the *Mahabharata* describes, he will, with Krisna's help, be victorious, and the proper rulers will be restored. The heart of the Bhagavad Gita, however, is its essential teachings about living with love and compassion toward others. The Indian political and spiritual leader Mahatma Gandhi, who based his life on the tenets of the Gita, found its instructions incompatible with harming others. In learning how to transcend mortal consciousness and attain spiritual union with God, Arjuna learns how to enter his *atman,* or essential self, which transcends life and death. He learns the profound Hindu concepts of karma and dharma, which govern human life, and he understands that the demands of duty and consequence must be fulfilled.

Briefly, the ultimate goal of samsara, the cycle of birth and death, is *moksha,* or spiritual liberation, also called nirvana. Spiritual liberation is achieved through a combination of three things: *jnana,* or knowledge; *bhakti,* or devotion; and yoga, or spiritual discipline and practice. Union with the Brahman, or Infinite God, is the highest good, as Krisna explains in passage 6:30–32 of Eknath Easwaran's translation:

I am ever present to those to have realized me in every creature. Seeing all life as my manifestation, they are never separated from me. They worship me in the hearts of all, and all their actions proceed from me. Wherever they may live, they abide in me.

The challenges of human life, Krisna explains, are the result of karma and dharma. Karma, which literally means "something that is done," is often translated as "deed" or "action" and basically states that every event contains both a cause and an effect. The consequences of each action engender another act, with similar consequences, and so on in a potentially unending series of events. An individual acts out karma until he or she learns how to act in harmony with dharma. Dharma, often translated as "duty," can be thought of as the master plan to which each living thing in the universe is connected. When one learns not to pursue selfish interests but rather contributes to the welfare of the whole, the karmic debt is discharged.

One learns and understands one's duty through yoga, the disciplined practice through which one heals the splintered, unconscious self and learns how to come in contact with the *atman,* the higher self, and through that the Brahman or divine. Meditation and yoga bring one to essential truths, as Krisna instructs Arjuna in passages 6:19–21:

When meditation is mastered, the mind is unwavering like the flame of a lamp in a windless place. In the still mind, in the depths of meditation, the Self reveals itself. Beholding the Self by means of the Self, an aspirant knows the joy and peace of complete fulfillment. Having attained that abiding joy beyond the senses, revealed in the stilled mind, he never swerves from the eternal truth.

The surrounding environment of imminent war serves, in the poem, to highlight the importance of the spiritual path, transcendence, and union with the divine. Krisna's explanation of the relationships among the ideas of death, sacrifice, and devotion exemplify the Hindu belief that transcendental truth can only be experienced and grasped when one heroically faces death and fulfills one's duty. Hence, the path to liberation lies not in the avoidance of action but through action performed simultaneously with detachment to consequences and with devotion to the divine God. Krisna teaches Arjuna that he is not being asked to commit indiscriminate violence but instead has a mortal duty to restore the legitimate rulers, who have been given their authority by the gods.

Through disciplined action combined with knowledge, committed with a detachment from selfish interest in the outcome and an interest in the greater welfare, Arjuna will be led not only to mortal victory but also to an understanding of his essential connection to the higher order. Thus, the Bhagavad Gita dramatically portrays Arjuna's inward journey and also shows in human form the possibility of union with the divine. Arjuna's recognition of his destiny, coinciding with Krisna's revelation of his divinity, is the climax of the poem.

As a document of Hindu culture and belief, the Bhagavad Gita has had a profound impact. Barbara Stoler Miller says the "Bhagavad-gita has been the exemplary text of Hindu culture for centuries, both in India and in the West." The true value of the Gita, Easwaran believes, is in the philosophical truths it contains: "Like [Jesus'] Sermon on the Mount, it has an immediacy that sweeps away time, place, and circumstance. Addressed to everyone, of whatever background or status, the Gita distills the loftiest truths of India's ancient wisdom into simple, memorable poetry that haunts the mind and informs the affairs of everyday life."

English Versions of the Bhagavad Gita

The Bhagavad Gita. Translated by Eknath Easwaran. New York: Vintage Books, 2000.

The Bhagavad-gita: Krishna's Counsel in Time of War. Translated by Barbara Stoler Miller. New York: Bantam Books, 1986.

The Bhagavad-Gita: Translated and Interpreted. 2 vols. Translated by Franklin Edgerton. Cambridge, Mass.: Harvard University Press, 1952.

Works about the Bhavagad Gita

Minor, Robert N. *Bhagavad-Gita: An Exegetical Commentary.* Columbia, Mo.: South Asia Books, 1982.

Van Buitenen, J. A. B. *Ramanuja on the Bhagavadgita.* Delhi: Motilal Banarsidass, 1968.

Zaehner, R. C. *The Bhagavad-Gita: With a Commentary Based on the Original Sources.* London: Oxford University Press, 1969.

Bible, Hebrew (ca. 10th–first centuries B.C.)

The Hebrew Bible is a collection of 24 different books of history, poetry, stories, and moral instruction, compiled toward the end of the first millennium B.C. It is the most sacred book of the Jewish religion and also forms the largest part of the Christian Bible. As such, it is one of the most widely read and influential books ever written.

Standard printed editions of the Hebrew Bible divide the books into three sections: Five Books of Moses (Pentateuch in Latin, *Torah* in Hebrew); the Prophets (*Nevi'im* in Hebrew); and the Writings (*Ketuvim* in Hebrew). The initials of the three Hebrew titles form the acronym *Tanach*, which is how the Bible is known in Hebrew.

Critical Analysis

The Torah part of the Hebrew Bible consists of five books. Genesis begins with a majestic account of the creation of the universe. Out of chaos, God creates light, fashions the heavenly bodies and the physical world, makes plants and animals, and finally shapes man and woman.

Compared with the florid creation myths of other ancient cultures, this work is a tightly written poetic account of the making of the world. God creates human beings as stewards of his work, and they are expected to abide by moral laws or face the consequences.

The book continues with a history of the first humans, leading to the gradual emergence of the different nations after a great flood. Most of the book is devoted to the life stories of the first Hebrews—Abraham, Sarah, and their descendants, especially their son Isaac, grandson Jacob (also known as Israel), and great-grandson Joseph.

God leads Abraham to the land of Canaan and promises to give it to his descendants, who are expected to obey God's laws in return. The Jews of ancient times, who compiled the Bible and claimed to live by its laws, considered this promise as their deed to the land of Israel.

The book of Exodus recounts the tribulations of the Children of Israel in Egypt, their liberation from slavery under the leadership of Moses, and their receiving of the Ten Commandments at Mount Sinai. Scholars disagree as to whether the story has factual basis.

The rest of the Torah is largely devoted to a discussion of God's laws—criminal, economic, moral, and ritual. These passages eventually formed the basis of the laws in the TALMUD and of all subsequent Jewish ethical and legal thought.

Prophets, despite its name, starts off with six history books. Joshua describes the conquest of the Land of Canaan by the Children of Israel. Judges is a collection of stories about heroes and heroines, both military and spiritual, who lived in the era following Joshua; they include such famous figures as Samson, Gideon, and Deborah.

Samuel I and II tell of the first kings of Israel—Saul, David, and Solomon—describing their victories, defeats, family struggles, and moral challenges. Kings I and II take the story from the death of Solomon, through the breakup into two kingdoms—Israel in the north and Judah in the south—to the final conquest and destruction of both kingdoms.

More than a century of archeological research has confirmed the overall historical accuracy of Kings I and II. Of course, God's role in the events and their moral significance are questions of faith rather than history. In the Bible's viewpoint, good kings and law-abiding citizens ensure prosperity, success, and peace, while injustice and idol-worship bring about national disaster and suffering.

The rest of Prophets is devoted to the words of Isaiah, Jeremiah, Ezekiel, and the 12 "minor" prophets, so called because of the brevity of their statements. Each book records the visions and inspired sermons of a different holy man, all of them active in the era of the kingdoms and their immediate aftermath.

The prophets explore the purpose of life, for humans in general and the Hebrews in particular. In very powerful language, they chastise wrongdoers and mourn the calamities God has inflicted on the nation. They call on individuals and society to return to the ways of righteousness, promising God's pardon if they do. In Jonah, this message is explicitly aimed at all the peoples of the world. But even in despair, the prophets keep faith with their inspiring vision of eventual redemption and peace, when "The wolf also shall dwell with the lamb, and the leopard shall lie down with the kid" (Isaiah 11:6).

The Writings section of the Bible begins with the book of Psalms, a collection of 150 religious poems said to have been written by King David. Some of the psalms were apparently sung by the Levites at the Temple in Jerusalem. Others are more personal in tone, heartfelt missives to God from an individual, often in trouble, expressing faith in God's ultimate justice and mercy.

The Writings contain two examples of ancient Near Eastern "wisdom literature," Proverbs and Ecclesiastes. They are full of worldly advice written in a tone of disillusion, at least concerning human behavior. The Writings also include Song of Songs, a series of lyrical love poems set in idyllic natural settings; Job, a tale that explores the question of why good people suffer; Lamentations, a sad dirge about the destruction of Jerusalem by the Babylonians; Esther, about a Jewish queen of Persia who saves her people from the threat of genocide; Ruth, about a Moabite woman who refuses to abandon her bereaved mother-in-law, throws in her lot with the Hebrew people, and becomes the ancestor of King David; and Daniel, a series of miracle tales and strange prophesies set during the Babylonian exile.

Finally, the last two books of the Writings, and thus of the Hebrew Bible, are Ezra-Nehemiah, which describes the return of the Jews to Judea under the Persians; and Chronicles, a retelling of the royal histories first recounted in Samuel and Kings.

Nearly all the Bible is written in ancient Hebrew, a West Semitic language, though some sections of Daniel are written in Aramaic, a related tongue. The narrative sections, if not the poetry, are easily read and understood by modern Hebrew speakers in Israel, though there are some obscure words and short passages that even scholars do not understand.

The first translation of the Bible was the *Septuagint,* a Greek rendition composed in Alexandria, Egypt, in the second century B.C. by a committee of 70 scholars; this became the basis of the texts used by Christians. Together with two ancient translations into Aramaic (the spoken language of Judea in Roman times), the *Septuagint* is often used to illuminate unclear passages in the Hebrew and to resolve minor differences that exist in the earliest existing Hebrew manuscripts.

Printed versions of the Hebrew Bible have been around for hundreds of years, but the traditional format is still in use in synagogues. One long parchment scroll contains the Pentateuch, handwritten in ancient calligraphy. There are no titles and no chapter-and-verse indications, which were a later addition.

Printed Hebrew Bibles traditionally include commentaries from various medieval or modern sages. They also include musical notation marks above and below each line of text, as a guide for those who chant the text during worship services. Each week on the Sabbath, a portion of the Torah is read; the entire volume is read in the course of a year (or three years, in some communities), as are sections of Prophets and several entire books of the Writings.

Traditionally, Jews believed that Moses wrote the entire Torah at one time, although they always knew of small variations in the text. But most scholars now believe, on the basis of textual analysis, that the Torah was gradually assembled by different editors from written and oral fragments over the course of hundreds of years.

Modern archeology has discovered parallels in ancient Egyptian, Mesopotamian, and Syrian writings to certain elements of the Hebrew Bible. They include poetic imagery, stories in Genesis, legal provisions, and even some pronouncements of the prophets. But the discovery of the DEAD SEA SCROLLS in the mid-20th century demonstrated that whatever the ultimate sources, the overall text had been largely standardized by Roman days, around the first century B.C.

In addition to the 24 books of the Hebrew Bible, several other "apocryphal" books, in Hebrew and Aramaic, were also considered sacred by many ancient Jews but were not included in the "canon," or standard collection. Some of them, like Maccabees, Judith, and Ecclesiasticus, are included in various Christian Bibles.

Once Christianity began to spread in the western Roman Empire, it became necessary to translate the Bible, including the Greek books of the New Testament, into Latin. Since that time, the Hebrew Bible has been translated into several hundred languages. It has inspired thousands of books of commentary and interpretation, as well as a wealth of poetry, music, plays, and films. Its themes have influenced the culture and religion of nations around the world, becoming part of the cultural heritage of all humankind.

English Versions of the Hebrew Bible

JPS Hebrew-English Tanakh. Pocket Edition. Philadelphia: Jewish Publication Society, 2003.

Tanach: The Torah/Prophets/Writings. Edited by Nossn Sherman. Brooklyn, N.Y.: Mesorah Publications, 1996.

The Jewish Study Bible, College Edition: Tanakh Translation. Edited by Marc Zvi Brettler. Oxford: Oxford University Press, 2003.

Works about the Hebrew Bible

Alter, Robert. *The Art of Biblical Poetry.* New York: Basic Books, 1985.

Collins, John F. *Introduction to the Hebrew Bible with CD-ROM.* Minneapolis, Minn.: Augsburg Fortress Publishers, 2004.

Davies, Eryl W. *The Dissenting Reader: Feminist Approaches to the Hebrew Bible.* Aldershot, Hampshire, U.K.: Ashgate Publishing, 2003.

Exum, J. Cheryl and H. G. M. Williamson, eds. *Reading from Right to Left: Essays on the Hebrew Bible in Honor of David J. A. Clines.* London: Continuum International Publishing Group, 2003.

Friedman, Richard Elliott. *Who Wrote the Bible?* San Francisco: Harper, 1997.

Bingen, Hildegard von

See HILDEGARD VON BINGEN.

Boethius (Anicius Manlius Severinus Boethius) (ca. 480–524) *philosopher, translator, treatise writer*

Boethius was a Roman of noble ancestry. His father served under the Roman king Odovacar, and his very name, Anicius Manlius Severinus Boethius, reflects his patrician heritage as well as his relationship to some of the most eminent aristocratic families of the Western Roman Empire.

Orphaned as a boy, Boethius became the ward of Quintus Aurelius Memmius Symmachus, who would later become his father-in-law. Symmachus oversaw Boethius's education, and by the time the young man was in his 20s, he was being celebrated for his accomplishments in Greek scholarship. One of his goals was to translate and interpret the works of PLATO and ARISTOTLE to demonstrate that the Greek philosophers were fundamentally in agreement with one another.

Boethius's first published work was *De institutione arithmetica* (Principles of Arithmetic, ca. 503), followed by *De institutione musica* (Principles of Music). For centuries, this treatise was considered the foremost authority on ancient music and was an important teaching text. Boethius also wrote several theological treatises in the form of correspondence to friends.

Boethius's masterpiece is his *De consolatione philosophiae* (The Consolation of Philosophy), written in 524 after his fortunes had undergone a reversal. In 500 he began an illustrious political career in the employ of Theodoric, king of the Ostrogoths, who deposed Odovacar and became ruler of Italy. Boethius counseled Theodoric on matters ranging from the building of a water clock to the employment of a harpist. In 510, he became Consul of Rome, and in 523, Theodoric named him *magister officiorum* (Master of the Offices), which made Boethius one of the king's closest advisers.

In 524, Theodoric became aware of a conspiracy in Rome to overthrow his rule. When Boethius defended one of the implicated parties, he himself was charged with treason and sentenced to death. Imprisoned in a dungeon near Milan awaiting execution, Boethius penned *The Consolation of Philosophy* as a dialogue between himself and Lady Philosophy. In this exchange, the character of Boethius bemoans his fate, claiming he was unjustly convicted with false evidence. He asserts that he went into public service in order to practice his philosophical principles, that he opposed abuses of power, and that he protected the oppressed in the service of what was right. Yet when Lady Philosophy first appears, Boethius is too full of self-pity to see her.

Lady Philosophy speaks of the capriciousness of human affairs and the fleeting nature of worldly achievements such as fame and wealth. For true happiness, she claims, people must free themselves from earthly concerns; otherwise, they will be enslaved by false desires. She goes on to enlighten Boethius on such complex subjects as the role of evil in the world, the fickle course of fate, the unpredictable nature of chance, the mind of God, predestination, and free will. Lady Philosophy explains that what humans call "chance" is actually part of God's plan; humans perceive certain events as unexpected or accidental because they fail to understand the grand design.

How, then, Boethius asks, is it possible to reconcile God's foreknowledge with the human perception of free will? If the choices people make do not determine the outcome of events, then rewards and punishments are meaningless and unfair. This is an age-old problem, according to Lady Philosophy. But, she reasons, the inelegant mechanism of human intelligence simply cannot compare with the immediacy of divine knowledge, which exists outside of the concept of time.

Boethius's "consolation" lies in the ultimate understanding that good and evil will indeed be met with a divine and universal justice and that all that happens is for the best. We cannot know God's plan. But we can desire and love what God desires, and this leads to the greatest freedom and the greatest happiness. The contemplation of God reconciles humans to ill fortune on earth.

As translator Edmund Reiss writes in *Boethius:*

The Consolation of Philosophy is without a doubt one of the greatest books ever written. It possesses that certain timeless quality which marks all great works of literature, and it gives the impression that it can never be used up. The more one reads the work, the more one finds in it, and the more one comes to admire the artistry and genius of the public administrator-scientist-philosopher-theologian-poet who was its author.

This seems an accurate assessment of Boethius's work, for his use of allegory, his blend of poetry and prose, and his dialogue-debate framework profoundly influenced medieval, Renaissance, and romantic literature for centuries to come.

English Versions of a Work by Boethius
The Consolation of Philosophy. Translated by P. G. Walsh. Oxford, U.K.: Clarendon Press, 1999.
The Consolation of Philosophy. Translated by Victor Watts. New York: Penguin, 2000.

Works about Boethius
Chadwick, Henry. *Boethius, the Consolations of Music, Logic, Theology and Philosophy.* Oxford, U.K.: Clarendon Press, 1990.
Marenbon, John. *Boethius.* Oxford: Oxford University Press, 2003.
Reiss, Edmund. *Boethius.* Boston: Twayne Publishers, 1982.

Book of Songs (*Shijing, Shih Ching*)
(1125–570 B.C.)

The *Book of Songs,* an anthology comprising 305 odes sung to the accompaniment of music and dance, is the earliest collection of Chinese poems. The actual date of its composition remains undetermined, even though two traditions account for the origin and survival of the songs.

The first tradition asserts that CONFUCIUS selected the songs from an earlier corpus of over 3,000 songs. He chose only songs that best exemplified his ideas about statecraft and harmonious human relations and revised the musical scores before placing them in order. The second tradition, currently held by Chinese scholars, believes that the Zhou (Chou) dynasty ruler sent out court officials to collect folk songs in the feudal states of his kingdom. The feudal lords collected the songs and forwarded them to the ruler, who would listen to them and ascertain whether his subjects lived happily under his reign. The songs also enabled the officials in the royal court to gather information regarding the prevailing customs of the vassal states. Despite these differing traditions, Confucius was, in both cases, credited with the selection and editing of the collection now known to us as the *Book of Songs.*

The songs are generally written in four-syllabic verses with occasional irregular meter. This restrictive structural style was later abandoned in favor of the freer and variant five- and seven-syllabic verses.

The anthology is divided into three unequal sections: 160 *feng,* or folk songs; 105 *ya,* or court songs; and 40 *song* (*sung*), or sacrificial songs. The *feng* ("air of the states") songs collectively represent each of the 15 feudal states in ancient China. The stylistic uniformity among them suggests that the songs have been reworked. Simple in style and spontaneous in expression, often about courtship and love, the *feng* songs look at the lives of common people, examining their hardship, joys, misgivings, and work. Since they make the common people their protagonist, the *feng* poems are read as social commentaries and protests at the state of

Chinese society. Scholars suspect these may be the latest poems in the book, dating to the period of chaos and disorder following the decline of the Chou dynasty.

The section of the *Book of Songs* containing the *ya,* or "courtly" songs, is divided into two main parts: 74 *xiao ya* (*hsiao ya;* "Lesser Courtly Songs") and 31 *da ya* (*ta ya;* "Greater Courtly Songs"). The *hsiao ya* contain songs devoted to praises of the king and deal with concerns of courtly or royal life, such as ceremonies, feasts, and hunting expeditions. The *da ya* section, whose poems are considerably longer, discusses the legendary heroes and myths of the Zhou dynasty. The *ya* poems, which celebrate the pleasures of the world, were most likely written by aristocrats at the Chinese court.

The *song* odes are hymns of praise and ritual songs describing religious ceremonies and celebrating a particular dynasty's victories in military campaigns. This section contains 40 religious and sacrificial hymns divided into three parts on the basis of geographical origin. Thirty-one odes are attributed to the Zhou court, four to the Lu court, and five to the Shang dynasty. These songs, accompanied by music and dancing, were performed while the king worshipped his ancestors and celebrated their heroic deeds. The *song* odes are believed to be the earliest of the songs collected in the book, and their religious character and pompous style suggest they were commissioned by the kings and written to glorify the glory of the Chinese state.

By the time of the Han dynasty, the *Book of Songs* had entered the Chinese canon of literary texts. Confucius's interest in the book played an important part in its survival. In addition, his advice to his disciples best summarizes the importance of the work in Chinese literary tradition:

> Young men, why do you not study the *Songs*? They can be used to inspire, to make you fit for company, to express grievances; near at hand they will teach you how to serve your fathers, and, looking further, how to serve your sovereign; they also enable you to learn the names of many birds, beasts, plants, and trees.

English Versions of the *Book of Songs*
Legge, James. *The Chinese Classics, with a translation, critical and exegetical notes, prolegomena, and copious indexes.* Hong Kong: Hong Kong University Press, 1960.
The Book of Songs. Translated by Arthur Waley. New York: Grove Press, 1996.

Works about the *Book of Songs*
Hu, Patricia Pin-ching. "The Book of Odes." In *Random Talks on Classical Chinese Poetry.* Hong Kong: Joint Sun Publishing Co., 1990.
Lynn, Richard J. "Introduction." In *Guide to Chinese Poetry and Drama.* Boston: G. K. Hall, 1984.

Book of the Dead (The Chapters of Coming Forth by Day) (ca. 1400 B.C.– ca. A.D. 200) *religious writings*
The Chapters of Coming Forth by Day, commonly known as the Book of the Dead, is a collection of hymns and incantations taken from the papyri buried with ancient Egyptians to help deceased souls navigate the afterlife. Altogether, the Book of the Dead consists of 189 chapters that describe Egyptian religious beliefs about life and death. The Book of the Dead not only describes the pathways, laws, and guardians of the gates of the afterlife but also contains the essential truths that would admit a soul to heaven. Knowledge was the way the soul became eternal, as texts from the sixth dynasty suggest with their simple advice: "Live your life and you will never die."

The Book of the Dead was never a single entity or text but rather a template of prayers, hymns, incantations, instructions, and addresses to the divine. Scribes kept a principal copy, which they were commissioned to selectively reproduce and personalize for the person who had died. Those preparing in advance could select the chapters and illustrations they wished to be included. Texts that have been recovered from Egyptian burials give scholars an idea of the chapters that composed the original Book of the Dead, as well as an understanding of how Egyptian funerary practices and religious beliefs developed over time.

The ancient Egyptians believed that the Book of the Dead was written about 50,000 B.C. by Tehuty, one of the first created beings, who brought language and speech into the world. The written language of the ancient Egyptians consisted of pictorial characters or symbols called hieroglyphs. A cursive form of hieroglyphics, called hieratic, was also used. Certain versions of the Book of the Dead are composed entirely in hieroglyphics and some in a combination of hieroglyphs and hieratic.

The earliest Egyptian funerary texts, called the Pyramid Texts, appear as inscriptions on chamber walls and passages of the pyramid of Wenis, the last ruler of the fifth dynasty, ca. 2345 B.C. The language of the texts suggests that these burial inscriptions had already been in use for centuries. In later dynasties, these standard inscriptions were copied onto many other pyramids and monuments, even sarcophagi, and are collected and printed as the Coffin Texts. The Pyramid and Coffin Texts precede the papyrus copies of the Book of the Dead, the earliest of which date to the mid-15th century B.C.

The oldest papyri, such as those of Nu, Userhat, Kha, and Yuya, tend to be brief, with a small number of chapters and few illustrations. The Papyrus of Hunefer, discovered at Thebes in 1852 and named for the man it was written for (and perhaps by), the chief scribe of Pharaoh Seti I, dates to 1400 B.C. It is perhaps the shortest text of the Book of the Dead, containing only three chapters, but it is one of the most beautifully illustrated. The chapters of the Book of the Dead known today are an arrangement imposed by Egyptologists, which provides a unified and comprehensive view of the Egyptian afterlife but sometimes fails to capture the unique beauty and distinct style of the individual papyri.

Critical Analysis

Egyptian belief sometimes varied slightly by city or dynasty, but on the whole they believed that the world was divided into three realms: Ta, which was earth or the world of the living; Nut, the world above, a spiritual realm or heaven; and Dwat, the netherworld, or the world between. This passage from the Papyrus of Ani best summarizes the essential belief regarding the eternal nature of the soul:

> Men do not live once, in order to vanish forever. They live several lives in different places but not always in this world, and between each life there is a veil of shadows.

Since the soul was able to move between varying states of being, death was simply a passageway to the Dwat, the world of shadows. Reciting and reenacting the directions of the Book of the Dead, it was believed, guided souls through the Dwat and led them to the Garden of Reeds, a place of everlasting peace inhabited by perfected souls. Those souls who were not perfected reincarnated into living forms and might return to Ta or earth as humans, animals, or insects, there to continue acquiring the knowledge that would help them succeed at their next judgment.

The Egyptians called the collection The Chapters of Coming Forth by Day because these writings represented the beginning of a new phase of life. During the time of the Old Kingdom, as the Pyramid Texts suggest, departed souls perambulated at will among the stars. Later, during the Middle Kingdom, Osiris emerged as the king of the underworld. Prayers in the Book of the Dead largely address him for protection and guidance, and most copies open with a hymn addressed to Osiris, as do these lines from the Papyrus of Hunefer:

> Maker of heaven and earth, adoration to you!
> O, you are embraced by Maat at the two seasons. You are striding over heaven with joy.
> (1.4–5, trans. by Ramses Seleen)

While the earliest funerary inscriptions addressed a single divine being called Amen-Ra, as beliefs evolved over the span of several centuries, other names and divine personifications developed, among them Isis, the patroness of fertility and love; Horus, the redeemer of good deeds, and Anubis; the guardian of secret knowledge. Part of the complexity of Egyptian spirituality is its ability to absorb and contain its own history without apparent contradiction. Chapters of the Book of the Dead simply expanded to address evolving beliefs.

Praises in homage to Osiris were part of the protective function of the Book of the Dead, to help the traveling soul reach its destination safely. There were dangers in the otherworld, one of them being that the soul could die again. Chapter 135 contains a spell to be said when the moon is new on the first day of the month. The prayer is essentially for illumination, and has enormous benefits, as Raymond Faulkner translates:

> As for him who knows this spell, he will be a worthy spirit in the realm of the dead, and he will not die again in the realm of the dead, and he will eat in the presence of Osiris. As for him who knows it on earth, he will be like Thoth, he will be worshipped by the living, he will not fall to the power of the king or the hot rage of Bastet, and he will proceed to a very happy old age.

As this passage suggests, chapters from the Book of the Dead could be studied by the living to ensure a fruitful life on earth and equip oneself in advance for the journey beyond. The Egyptians imagined this further journey to be much like life on earth. One was required to eat, rest, and also work. Therefore, the practice developed of including clay figurines or other images in the burial chamber; in the shadow realms, these spirit figures could be recruited to do hard labor.

Part of the spirit's progress involved a judgment at which one had to account for the deeds done in life. The judgment took place immediately on arrival in the afterlife, and the outcome determined whether the soul would progress to the Garden of Reeds or return to earth. Therefore, many papyri contain confessions or declarations of activities its owner has or has not engaged in, which, it is hoped, will help the judges reach a favorable decision. The confessions show what behaviors hold the soul in ignorance, among them lying, quarreling, blaspheming, or being hot-tempered, quarrelsome, or deaf to words of truth.

The chapters specify when and sometimes where incantations should be performed for maximum effect. Most are in favor of a speedy progress to the realms of bliss, while some are a safeguard against tricks or punishments. Some translators refer to the chapters as spells or magical charms, which reflects a certain long-held bias that ancient Egyptian beliefs were primitive, barbaric, confused, and often corrupt. In reality, the civilization and learning of ancient Egypt had an enormous influence on other developing cultures, particularly those of the Greeks and Romans, and the Tibetans also have a Book of the Dead. The philosophical tenets of reincarnation and the perfection of the soul are also found in the beliefs of the Taoists, the ancient Celts (see MYTHOLOGY, CELTIC), the Jewish Kabbalah, the writings of Zoroaster, the teachings of Buddha, and the Hindu *Vedas* of India.

English Versions of the Book of the Dead

The Ancient Egyptian Book of the Dead. Edited by Carol Andrews. Translated by R. O. Faulkner. New York: Macmillan, 1985.
The Book of the Dead. Translated by E. A. Wallis Budge. Mineola, N.Y.: Dover Publications, 1996.

Works about the Book of the Dead

Karenga, Maulana. *The Book of Coming Forth by Day: the Ethics of the Declarations of Innocence.* Los Angeles: University of Sankore Press, 1990.
Seleem, Ramses. *Egyptian Book of the Dead.* New York: Sterling Publishing Co., 2001.

Buddha parables

See ZEN PARABLES.

Būsīrī, al- (Sharaf ad-Dīn Muhammad ibn Sa'īd al-Būsīrī as-Sanhājī)
(ca. 1212–ca. 1294) *poet*

Al-Būsīrī was the author of one of the most famous poems in the world of Islam, the "Qasidat al-Burda," or "Ode to the Mantle," a panegyric (poem of praise) to the prophet MUHAMMAD.

Born in the village of Abusir in Egypt, al-Būsīrī made a modest living in Alexandria copying manuscripts. He studied under a mystic Sufi master and was affected by the atmosphere of Sunni religiosity cultivated by the Ayyubid sultans. As a result, he produced a body of poems praising Muhammad that continue to be read by Muslims today. These poems, like others of the period, ascribe miracles and prodigies to the prophet.

By far his most famous work was the "Burda" (also called "Luminous Stars in Praise of the Best of Mankind"), which critics have celebrated and other poets have attempted to imitate. Admirers have learned its verses by heart and have had them inscribed in gold letters on public buildings. The poem has even been venerated as a charm against evil.

According to legend, al-Būsīrī began to compose the "Burda" after praying for a cure for a stroke, which had paralyzed half of his body. Falling asleep, he dreamed that Muhammad touched his body and threw his mantle over him—a mantle celebrated in another poem from the prophet's day. The poet was instantly cured, and he penned his adoring poem in gratitude. The tone of pious love can be seen in these lines:

> The merits of God's Prophet are limitless;
> No human speech can encompass them.
>
> If his miracles in their greatness were equal
>   to his rank
> Dry bones would revive at the mention of
>   his name.

Such is the power of al-Būsīrī's imagery and expressions of love for Muhammad that his poem continues to influence Arabic poetry to the present day.

An English Version of a Work by al-Būsīrī
"Burda." Translated by Stefan Sperl and Christopher Shackle. Reproduced in *Night and Horses and the Desert,* edited by Robert Irwin, 334–45. Woodstock, N.Y.: Overlook Press, 2000.

Works about al-Būsīrī
Huart, Clement. *A History of Arabic Literature.* Beirut: Khayats, 1966.
Nicholson, R. A. *A Literary History of the Arabs.* New York: Kegan Paul International, 1998.

Caedmon (seventh century) *poet*

Caedmon was a layman from Northumbria whose one surviving poem, "Caedmon's Hymn" (658–680), had a revolutionary influence on Anglo-Saxon poetry. His application of the Germanic technique of heroic poetry to Christian themes and edification set the standards for vocabulary, style, method, and diction that were mimed by Anglo-Saxon poets for centuries thereafter.

In the monastery of the Abbess St. Hild, Caedmon was said to be distinguished by divine grace because he took what he learned from Latin scriptures and effortlessly composed poetic words of the greatest sweetness in the language of the Angles of Northumbria. His moving poetry inspired many of his listeners to despise the earthly world and long for heavenly life.

What we know of "Caedmon's Hymn" comes from BEDE's descriptions in his *Ecclesiastical History of the English People* (731). Bede tells us that in his youth, Caedmon had settled down to a secular life of an illiterate herdsman. Sometimes at feasts, the hosts decided that their guests would provide entertainment by reciting verses to the accompaniment of a harp. Whenever Caedmon saw the harp coming close to him, he would leave the feast and walk back to his house with a feeling of shame for his lack of skill in reciting poetry.

One day, upon leaving such a party, he went to the cattle pens to check on the cattle. He then fell asleep and dreamed that a man was standing by him and calling his name: "Caedmon, sing me something." Caedmon replied that he did not know how to sing and that is why he had departed so precipitously from the feast earlier that evening. But the man insisted: "Yet you shall sing to me." Caedmon decided to humor the man and asked him what he should sing about. The man replied: "Sing of the beginning of created things."

Caedmon immediately began singing in praise of God the creator. That nine-line song became known as "Caedmon's Hymn": "Now let me praise the keeper of Heaven's Kingdom, / the might of the Creator, and his thought, / The work of the Father of glory. . . ."

Caedmon is said to have composed hundreds of religious poems in his lifetime. However, despite Bede's research and recording efforts, only the "Hymn" can be authentically attributed to Caedmon. Nevertheless, his place in history is assured by the stylistic revolution in poetry that he set in motion. As Bede tells us:

[Caedmon] made many compositions concerning divine blessings and judgments, by all of which he sought to turn men's minds from delight in wickednesses, and indeed to stir them to the love and skilful practice of good deeds. He was a most religious man who subjected himself with humility to the disciplines of monastic rule. But against others who wished to act otherwise he was aflame with fervid zeal. Hence it was that he closed his life with a beautiful ending.

See also OLD ENGLISH POETRY.

An English Version of a Work by Caedmon
In *Anglo-Saxon Spirituality: Selected Writings.* Translated by Robert Boenig. Mahwah, N.J.: Paulist Press, 2001, 168.

Works about Caedmon
Gaskin, Robert T. *Caedmon: The First English Poet.* M.S.G. Haskell House, 1990.

Gurteen, Stephen H. V. *Epic of the Fall of Man: A Comparative Study of Caedmon, Dante, and Milton.* Murieta, Calif.: Classic Books, 1996.

Morehouse, Ward and Gregory A. Minahan. *The Caedmon School: An Anecdotal History and Appreciation.* Philadelphia: Xlibris, 2003.

Caesar, Julius (100 B.C.–44 B.C.) *statesman, general, writer*

Julius Caesar is arguably the most famous historical figure of ancient Rome and one of the most famous men of all time. He had an indelible influence on the political, social, and military events of his time, and his life story has become one of history's great epics, as his actions caused the downfall of the Roman Republic and the rise of the Roman Empire. In addition, he was a writer of no little talent, and his works set the standard for a unique literary genre, the military memoir.

Julius Caesar's family was aristocratic but not particularly distinguished. At the time of Caesar's birth, Rome was by far the strongest power in the Mediterranean region and was engaged in nearly continuous warfare with numerous enemies; it would be through service in these wars that Caesar would first come to prominence.

Though still a republic at the time of Caesar's birth, the governmental structure of Rome had been designed when it was a small city-state, and the republican foundations were beginning to break down under the stress of gaining and controlling a far-reaching empire. In his early years, Caesar served the government in various military, political, and diplomatic posts. As time passed, he gradually worked his way up through the Roman hierarchy. He served as the chief financial officer of Roman-controlled Spain and later became responsible for public entertainment and religious functions in Rome. In 61 B.C., he became governor of a province in Spain, and he used the position to enrich himself and gain influence. Caesar was a gifted politician, being both shrewd and indomitable. He had no particular political ideology and strove entirely to satisfy his personal ambitions. Intellectually gifted, he followed the philosophy of EPICURUS and his own highly developed sense of honor.

In 60 B.C., Caesar was elected consul, the highest office in the Roman Republic. Now one of the most powerful men in Rome, he formed a partnership with two other politicians, Crassus and Pompey, creating what was called the "First Triumvirate." In 58 B.C., hoping to raise his prestige through military victories, Caesar took command of the Roman armies in Gaul, now modern France. Over several years and numerous campaigns, Caesar's armies waged relentless war on the Gallic tribes and fought several battles against native settlements in Germany and Britain. Caesar displayed a cunning military genius and a ruthless command of strategy. In 52 B.C., at the Siege of Alesia, the Gauls still resisting Roman rule were crushed.

During lulls in the fighting, Caesar began writing his famous *Commentary on the War in Gaul.* He wanted his achievements to be recorded so he could use them as political propaganda and as justification for his decisions. His was the first true military memoir.

Political leaders in Rome became increasingly fearful of Caesar's growing power. Crassus had been killed, leaving Pompey and Caesar as rivals. After Caesar completed the conquest of Gaul, he turned his attention once more to political matters in Rome. In 49 B.C., the Senate demanded that Caesar turn over the command of his army. He refused to do so and instead marched his forces toward Rome, beginning a civil war that would topple the Roman Republic. Over the next several years, Caesar fought Pompey and his allies in numerous campaigns throughout the Mediterranean. By the time the war was over in 45 B.C., Caesar had emerged victorious and was completely in control of Rome and all its territory.

Caesar's writings during the time of the civil war were produced mainly to increase his support among the people and damage his enemies' reputations. He penned a bitter denunciation of his deceased rival Cato, named the *Anticato,* and also wrote *Commentary on the Civil Wars,* which was very similar to the work he had written on the war in Gaul. In his clear and straightforward style, Caesar gives accounts of the military and political events of the conflict. He writes in the third person, and his prose resembles that of a newspaper reporter, giving a simple and clear description of what is happening. Nevertheless, these accounts served primarily as propaganda to embellish Caesar's achievements at the expense of his opposition.

Once in possession of Rome, Caesar made himself dictator and thereby became the unchallenged ruler of the Roman world. He began a program of ambitious reforms designed to improve life for average Roman citizens and ensure his popularity. Many people, however, feared Caesar would attempt to make himself king and thus completely destroy whatever was left of the Roman Republic. On March 15, 44 B.C., Caesar was assassinated by a group of senators. The circumstances surrounding Caesar's assassination have fascinated people for 2,000 years and serve as the subject matter for one of the greatest plays in English history, William Shakespeare's *The Tragedy of Julius Caesar* (1623).

Caesar was one of the most influential figures of Western history. His political, military, and literary skills were remarkable, and his personality, willpower, and amazing abilities continue to fascinate people to the present day. He is remembered as one of the most capable men of ancient times.

Critical Analysis

Caesar is best known for his political and military achievements, but it is also acknowledged that he was a writer of considerable ability. The most famous piece of literature he produced was *Commentary on the War in Gaul,* a firsthand account of his campaigns in that region. The *Commentary's* seven books describe the campaigns from 58 to 52 B.C. Sometime later, a former staff officer of Caesar's named Aulus HIRTIUS added an eighth book, which completes the narrative.

Caesar writes in the third person, referring to himself as Caesar, though he makes occasional references to "our" troops. His commentary describes battles and sieges not dramatically but rather dispassionately, seemingly striving for accuracy instead of excitement. Yet his prose contains its own dynamic energy, as in this description in S. A. Hanford's translation of a turn in the battle against the Nervii:

> . . . the Roman cavalry and light-armed troops, routed by the first attack, were in the act of retreating into the camp, when they found themselves face to face with the Nervii . . . The servants . . . on looking back and seeing the enemy in the camp immediately ran for their lives. Meanwhile shouting and din arose from the drivers coming up with the baggage, who rushed panic-stricken in every direction.

For the most part Caesar strives to portray himself as a determined man performing a necessary mission, but at times he likes to add a touch of the dashing hero, for instance in this passage where he describes how he turned the Nervii battle with a heroic gesture:

> As the situation was critical and no reserves were available, Caesar snatched a shield from a soldier in the rear . . . made his way to the front

line, addressed each centurion by name, and shouted encouragement to the rest of the troops. . . . His coming gave them fresh heart and hope; each man wanted to do his best under the eyes of his commander-in-chief, however desperate the peril.

Caesar also describes himself as a merciful man and uses such opportunities to remind his readers how grateful they should be to him. After sending word to Rome of his victory against the Atuatuci, he observes that "a public thanksgiving of fifteen days was decreed to celebrate his achievements—a greater honour than had previously been granted to anyone."

Despite the ostensibly objective tone of the *Gallic Wars*, it focuses more on Caesar's successes and less on his failures, glossing over many of the serious setbacks and atrocities committed by his men. He intended that this work, like his *Commentary on the Civil War*, would serve first as political propaganda and later as a record of achievements that would elevate his reputation well after his death. Caesar presents himself as a traditional soldier, serving the interests of Rome, and nowhere in the narrative does one find any hint of the ambitious and unscrupulous politician that Caesar truly was.

Caesar's *Commentary on the War in Gaul* has become the classic military memoir, which has evolved into a unique literary genre. Like the records of Cornelius TACITUS, Caesar's account is a valuable source of historical information as well as an admirable piece of Latin prose.

English Versions of Works by Julius Caesar

Caesar. Translated by A. G. Peskett. Cambridge, Mass.: Harvard University Press, 1984.

The Civil War. Translated by Jane F. Gardner. New York: Viking Press, 1976.

The Conquest of Gaul. Translated by S. A. Hanford. New York: Viking Press, 1983.

The Gallic War. Translated by Carolyn Hammond. Oxford: Oxford University Press, 1999.

Works about Julius Caesar

Gelzer, Matthias. *Caesar: Politician and Statesman.* Translated by Peter Needham. Cambridge, Mass.: Harvard University Press, 1985.

Meier, Christian. *Caesar: A Biography.* Translated by David McLintock. New York: Basic Books, 1982.

Shakespeare, William. *The Tragedy of Julius Caesar.* New York: Washington Square Press, 2004.

Suetonius. *The Twelve Caesars.* Translated by Robert Graves. New York: Penguin, 2003.

Callimachus (ca. 305–ca. 240 B.C.) *poet, scholar*

Callimachus was born in Cyrene (in present-day Libya) and received his education in Athens. A distinguished scholar and poet, he opened his own school in the suburbs of Alexandria, where many distinguished grammarians and poets, including ARISTOPHANES, attended.

Since it was customary at the time to assign library work to scribes and scholars, Ptolemy II of Egypt employed Callimachus as the chief librarian of the Alexandrian Library. Callimachus occupied this position for the rest of his life, and his outstanding achievements in the field of librarianship earned him the title "Founding Father" of librarians. He created the chronological subject catalog called *Pinakes,* consisting of 120 volumes and containing critical information on the library's holdings, as well as biographical information on all the authors. *Pinakes* is not only the first catalog of the largest library in the ancient world but also the first complete literary history of Greek literature.

It is Callimachus's witty and elegant poetry, however, that brought him fame. He is said to have written about 800 works, of which only six hymns, 64 epigrams, and some fragments of longer poems are extant.

Callimachus's hymns are written in an extremely learned, intricate language. His "Bath of Pallas" is a story about the bathing ritual of Athena's statue in Argos, and "The Blinding of Tiresias" refers to Athena's retaliation against Tiresias, who saw her bathing in a stream. These and Callimachus's hymns are known for their lyric quality.

Callimachus's elegies and epigrams were among his greatest achievements. He was referred to by his contemporaries as the chief of the elegiac poets, and Roman poets used his elegies as models for their erotic poetry. History tells us that Callimachus once engaged in a literary dispute with APOLLONIUS OF RHODES, arguing that well-crafted short poems of quality are superior to long ones of quantity. He wrote of this dispute in *Ibis,* in response to the long, epic poems of Apollonius's *Argonautica.*

Callimachus's most famous work, written ca. 270 B.C., was the *Aetia* (also *Aitia,* meaning "causes"), a four-book collection of legend-like, narrative elegies (totaling 7,000 lines) that explore the causes (or origins) of the foundation of cities, religious ceremonies, and other customs. OVID used the *Aetia* as a model for his *Metamorphoses.*

Of Callimachus' epigrams, the scholar Kathryn J. Gutzwiller says that they "formed the most famous and admired of Greek epigram collections" and that they "belonged to the canon of works read by boys in school." These works were praised not only for their perfect literary form but also "for their charm and human feeling, their sweetness, expressiveness, and wit." In one epigram, Callimachus praises Ptolemy II's wife: "Blest, radiant Berenĭkê, / Without whom the very Graces are graceless." And in another epigram, Callimachus honors a fellow poet:

> They told me, Heraclitus, they told me you
>   were dead,
> They brought me bitter news to hear and
>   bitter tears to shed.
> I wept as I remember'd how often you and I
> Had tired the sun with talking and sent
>   him down the sky. . . .

Callimachus's longer works include *Hecale,* an EPIC in which the old woman Hecale shelters the hero Theseus from a storm; and *Iambi,* a collection of 13 poems written in iambic form and covering various themes such as criticism, fables, and poetic voice.

Callimachus recognized literature as a powerful means for expressing and sharing knowledge and wisdom. His works influenced later Greek and Roman poets, including Ovid, CATULLUS, HORACE, and PROPERTIUS.

English Versions of Works by Callimachus

Callimachus (Musaeus: Aetia, Iambi, Lyric Poems, Hecale, Minor Epic & Elegiac Poems & Other Fragments). Loeb Classical Library. Translated by C. A. Trypanis. Edited by Thomas Gelzer and Cedric Whitman. Cambridge, Mass.: Harvard University Press, 1992.

Callimachus: Hymn to Demeter. Edited by Neil Hopkinson. Cambridge, Mass.: Cambridge University Press, 2004.

The Poems of Callimachus. Translated by Frank Nisetich. Oxford, U.K.: Oxford University Press, 2001.

Works about Callimachus

Acosta-Hughes, Benjamin. *Polyeideia: The Iambi of Callimachus and the Archaic Iambic Tradition.* Berkeley: University of California Press, 2002.

Coffta, David Joseph. *Influences of Callimachean Aesthetics on the Satires and Odes of Horace.* Lewiston, N.Y.: Edwin Mellen, 2002.

Gutzwiller, Kathryn J. *Poetic Garlands: Hellenistic Epigrams in Context.* Berkeley: University of California Press, 1998, 183–213.

Cao Zhi (Ts'ao Chih) (192–232) *poet*

Cao Zhi is considered to be one of China's greatest early lyric poets. The son of a famous northern Chinese ruler and general, he showed great literary promise at an early age. Though the young poet had an easygoing personality, he also liked to drink heavily and was thought to be undignified. Because of this reputation and the tradition of primogeniture, his father named Cao Zhi's older brother and poet, Cao Bi, as his sole heir, which led to a lifelong rift between the two brothers. After Cao Bi's ascension to the throne in 220, Cao Zhi was exiled by his brother to a number of minor provincial areas, where he served as a feudal lord until his death.

Cao Zhi's poetry is highly personal, reflecting his feelings about his political situation, his lack of leadership skills, and his strained relationship with his brother. The following untitled poem, for example, serves as a metaphor for Cao Bi (the stalks) and his torture of Cao Zhi (the beans):

> Frying beans with bean stalks as fuel.
> Beans weep sadly in the pan
> From the same root we both grew.
> Why is the hurry in the grill?

In "Dew upon Grass," Cao Zhi offers an ambiguous lament—sorrow that his talents do not serve to protect his homeland against invasion, or sorrow that his country's leader, his brother, is not "enlightened":

> Man's lifetime in this world goes by
> as quickly as the wind upon the dust
> Would I be able to employ my talents
> To exert myself in the service
> Of the enlightened ruler!

Cao Zhi is recognized as one of the first Chinese poets to put himself at the center of his poetry, which he uses as both a reflection of his inner thoughts and a means by which he could achieve immortality. By the time of his death, he had written hundreds of highly regarded poems and prose works.

Works about Cao Zhi

Dunn, Hugh. *Cao Zhi: The Life of a Princely Chinese Poet.* Tenn.: University Press of the Pacific/Ingram, 2000.

Zong-qi Cai. *The Matrix of Lyric Transformation: Poetic Modes and Self-Presentation in Early Chinese Pentasyllabic Poetry.* Ann Arbor, Mich.: Center for Chinese Studies, 1996.

carpe diem   *term*

Carpe diem, Latin for "seize the day," is a popular motif in love poetry. In such lyrics, the speaker exhorts the listener to grasp and enjoy the immediate pleasures of youth and everyday life, particularly love, because the future is uncertain and time is fleeting.

The theme of seizing and making the most of the moment appears in the earliest of poetry. In the Sumerian *Epic of Gilgamesh*, dated to 3000 B.C., Gilgamesh's heroic quest to recover his lost friend Enkidu leads to his learning he must make the most of mortal life. The teachings of the Greek philosopher EPICURUS (fourth century B.C.) encourages the pursuit of pleasure as an antidote to pain caused by human frailty and the inevitable recognition of mortality. The carpe diem motif appears frequently in early Greek poetry, particularly in the poems of ALCAEUS, who advocates drinking and other pleasures as a salve for despair caused by brutal events, and SAPPHO, as well as the lyric poems of HOMER.

The term *carpe diem* first appeared in the 11th poem of Book One of Horace's *Odes* (23 B.C.) in a slightly less romantic context. Affixed with the title "Enjoy the Passing Hour," by translator C. E. Bennett, the verse urges:

> Busy thyself with household tasks; and since life is brief, cut short far-reaching hopes! Even while we speak, envious Time has sped. Reap the harvest of today, putting as little trust as may be in the morrow!

Book I, Ode IX, conveys a similar injunction:

> Cease to ask what the morrow will bring forth, and set down as gain each day that Fortune grants! Nor in thy youth neglect sweet love nor dances, whilst life is still in its bloom and crabbed age is far away!

In Book II of the Odes, Horace continues this theme, observing "Fresh youth and beauty are speeding fast away behind us . . . Why not rather quaff the wine?"

Due in part to the frequency with which Horace was read in the MIDDLE AGES and later, and also in part to its broad human appeal, the theme frequently appears in poetry of the Renaissance and beyond. The French poet Pierre Ronsard (1524–85) famously uses the passing seasons in his sonnets addressed to Hélène to introduce a wistful, poignant tone into the consummation of their love; all is in bloom on May 1, but when fall winds blow and winter storms rage, the only solace they may have is in each other.

Carpe diem was a favorite theme among the English lyric poets as well. The sonnets and plays of William Shakespeare take up this motif, most notably the comedy *Twelfth Night* and Sonnet 73, where he entreats his reader to "love that well, which thou must leave ere long." The "cavalier" poets of the 17th century made a jaunty use of the theme as a means of persuading their sweethearts to yield to their demands. In "To the Virgins, to Make Much of Time" (1648), Robert Herrick writes:

> *Gather ye Rose-buds while ye may,*
> *Old Time is still a flying;*
> *And this same flower that smiles to day,*
> *To morrow will be dying. . . .*

Similarly, in "Corinna's Going A Maying" (1648), Herrick urges his love to join him on a pleasure outing, since "[o]ur life is short, and our dayes run / As fast away as does the Sunne." Andrew Marvell employs the carpe diem motif in "To His Coy Mistress" (1681) with the resonant line, "Had we but world enough, and time." In contrast to Herrick's somewhat joyous and reckless tone, Marvell moans that "at my back I always hear / Times winged Chariot hurrying near," lamenting the transience of life.

Eastern poetry also employs the carpe diem theme to observe a lament on the inevitable passage of time and to encourage the pursuit of pleasure. In the 11th-century Persian collection of verses called the *Rubáiyát*, as translated by Ahmad Saidi, the poet muses:

> *Why worry whether wealth I have or not,*
> *And life in happiness shall end or not—*

> *Come, fill the cup; for 'tis unknown to me*
> *The breath inhaled shall be exhaled or not.*

The carpe diem motif continues to appeal to modern poets and appears particularly in the poetry of Robert Frost and W. B. Yeats as well as the novels of Saul Bellow and Bruno Francés.

Works Employing the Carpe Diem Motif

Bellow, Saul. *Seize the Day.* New York: Penguin USA, 1996.

Fitzgerald, Edward, trans. *Rubáiyát of Omar Khayyám.* Edited by Christopher Decker. Charlottesville: University Press of Virginia, 1997.

Horace. *Horace: The Odes and Epodes.* Translated by C. E. Bennett. Cambridge, Mass.: Harvard University Press, 1964.

Shakespeare, William. *The Complete Sonnets and Poems.* Edited by Colin Burrow. Oxford, U.K.: Oxford University Press, 2002.

White, Helen C., et al., eds. *Seventeenth-Century Verse and Prose.* Vol. 1, 2d ed. New York: Macmillan, 1971.

Catullus, Gaius Valerius (84–54 B.C.) *poet*

Gaius Valerius Catullus was born in Verona to an elite family; his father was a close friend of Julius CAESAR's. In his early youth Catullus moved with his family to Rome. He was expected to have a brilliant political career and traveled in Asia in the entourage of the governor of Bithynia Memmius to satisfy the requirement of all politicians to spend time in the army. In spite of his training and his father's influential connections, though, Catullus devoted himself to writing poetry.

In his poetry, Catullus is as daring as he was in his personal life. He was educated in the classical tradition and translated the works of many of the old masters, including CALLIMACHUS and SAPPHO. He also became one of the first "neoteric poets," who used colloquialisms and even obscene words in their works.

Catullus's poetry was unique for the period, because he made good use of his education, combining the conversational language with the learned one and using elaborate sentence structure and subtle allusions. His successors gave him the name *doctus,* which recognized his mastery in the skill of literary technical perfection, known as the ideal of Alexandrianism.

Another of Catullus's revolutionary innovations was to employ poetry to express his personal feelings and reflect on his unique experiences. Thus, in some of his early poems, Catullus mocks the established custom of networking among the elite, which was practiced by his family: "So much for running after powerful friends!"

The majority of Catullus's poems, however, reflect his personal feeling toward the two loves of his life: Juventius, his unfaithful boyfriend; and Clodia, an older, married woman from high society who was accused of poisoning her husband during her affair with Catullus. Under the name *Lesbia,* Clodia became the inspiration and the heroine for 26 of Catullus's poems. These poems not only describe his feelings for Clodia but also provide a lively account of the lovers' passionate quarrels, including Catullus's criticism of his lover's immorality and his disappointment of and anger about her infidelity.

Other themes in Catullus's poetry are his sadness over the death of his brother, who died at Troy; the life of the young elite of the Roman Empire; and his friendship with Gaius Julius Caesar. Catullus is often critical of Caesar, this criticism, however, is not political, but very personal, characteristic of most of his poetry. In one poem, he even says, "I HAVE no very great desire to make myself agreeable to you, Caesar," to emphasize that he believed himself to be independent of Caesar's patronage.

Catullus's influence is apparent in the lyrics of VIRGIL, who often openly expressed his admiration for Catullus, and of HORACE. In the century following Catullus's death, he was mostly remembered for his epigrams in which he attacked his rivals and enemies and which the first-century poet MARTIAL once described as masterpieces. Today Catullus is considered to be one of the most effective lyric poets of ancient Roman literature.

English Versions of Works by Gaius Valerius Catullus

Catullus. Translated by Charles Martin. New Haven, Conn.: Yale University Press, 1992.
Works: With Commentary. Edited by C. J. Fordyce. Oxford: Oxford University Press, 1990.

Works about Gaius Valerius Catullus

Fitzgerald, William. *Catullan Provocations: Lyric Poetry and the Drama of Position.* Berkeley: University of California Press, 1996.
Wiseman, T. P. *Catullus and His World: A Reappraisal.* Cambridge, U.K.: Cambridge University Press, 1986.

Celtic mythology
See MYTHOLOGY, CELTIC.

Chang Heng
See ZHANG HENG.

Chanson de Roland
See SONG OF ROLAND.

Chinook myths and tales   *folklore*
As with most Native American tribes, the Chinook did not have a written history; rather, their history was passed down generation to generation through oral tradition. Many of their tales were formulated from their surrounding area. Located in the Pacific Northwest, near the mouth of the Columbia River and the Pacific Ocean, the Chinook relied primarily on the influence of the ocean, river, and land.

One creation myth of the Chinook is about the first Chinook people. According to Chinook legend, Old Man South Wind was traveling north along the Pacific Coast when he met Giant Woman near the mouth of the Columbia River. There she taught him how to fish and gave him a net. Old Man South Wind used the net and pulled a whale out of the ocean. When he tried to cut the whale, though, it turned into a large Thunderbird that flew to the top of a great mountain and nested. As the legend goes,

> Atop Saddle Mountain, Thunderbird built a large nest and laid several eggs in it. One day when Thunderbird flew away, Giant Woman climbed high to the bird's nest. She mischievously cracked an egg, but it was bad, and she threw it down the mountain. She cracked another and another until she had broken them all and hurled them from the peak. Each time an egg landed at the base of the mountain, it became an Indian. This was how the first Chinook men, women, and children came to be.

This myth is very important to the Chinook and is still told to their children to this day.

Another important aspect of Chinook history was their belief that the coyote, or Italapas, was a cocreator with Ikanam, the creator. According to Chinook belief, Italapas waited in the tree for floodwaters to subside after a great flood. While waiting, he threw sand into the water and created land. Italapas then helped Ikanam create humans and taught them to hunt and weave.

Yet another Chinook tale is about the first "white man." An important part of the Chinook oral literary tradition, this was retold for many generations. The tale starts with a Chinook woman mourning the death of her son. While on a walk for the first time in more than a year, she went to the ocean where she saw something in the water coming to shore:

> When it landed on the beach it appeared to be a monster with two giant spruces planted in its body and sprung with many ropes that evidently sprouted out of the monster's back. Also on the back of the monster stood two hairy animals, probably bears, although their faces seemed to be human.

The tale continues with the woman getting two Chinook to look at the creature. The two Chinook men boarded the boat where they met two friendly white traders. The story of how the Chinook met the "white man" was very important to the Chinook because for some time they had a good trade relationship with the "white man."

An English Version of Chinook Myths and Tales
Myths and Legends of the Pacific Northwest. Edited by Katharine Berry Judson. Introduction by Jay Miller. Lincoln: University of Nebraska Press, 1997. 93–95, 102–104.

A Work about Chinook Myths and Tales
Content and Style of an Oral Literature: Clackamas Chinook Myths and Tales. Translated by Melville Jacobs. Chicago: University of Chicago Press, 1959.

chivalry and courtly love
Chivalry and courtly love are social concepts that strongly influenced the literature of western Europe during the later MIDDLE AGES. Both concepts attempted to describe the rules for polite behavior for the aristocrats of a feudal society. Feudalism bound all classes of society in mutual oaths of loyalty in exchange for patronage or service.

The code of chivalry dictated a knight's behavior in battle and in relationships with his overlord and his own servants, while the code of courtly love dictated how the knight should behave at court, particularly in his amorous addresses to the court's ladies. Portrayals of chivalry and courtly love in the literature, however, suggest that these artificial modes of behavior were difficult to actually practice, and even in their fictionalized versions, characters adhering to the standards of chivalry and courtly love do not find them free of contradictions.

Chivalry required knights and nobles to swear loyalty to their superiors and show compassion and mercy to the weak and socially inferior. The ideal chivalric knight was brave, loyal, and determined as well as compassionate, just, and helpful to those in distress—an exemplar of Christian virtue. As the CRUSADES into the Holy Land began, many knights took vows of chastity and poverty to give their exploits a more spiritual dimension.

The beginnings of the code of chivalry in the MEDIEVAL ROMANCE can be traced to the French *Le Chanson de Roland* (SONG OF ROLAND), which dates to the late 10th century. The narrative retells the story of an actual battle in 778 when a group of Basques attacked the rearguard of Charlemagne's army as he withdrew from Spain. The *Roland* poet, composing near the end of the 11th century, turns the attacking party into Saracens (Moors, who were Muslims from the Moroccan coast), making a central issue of the poem a defense of Christianity. He also turns Charlemagne's army into a set of feudal nobles governed by feudal attitudes and bonds of loyalty. Roland and his warriors refuse to abandon one another even though it appears they will all likely die. In addition, Roland hesitates to blow the horn that will summon reinforcements, since this act, suggesting that he is not heroic enough, would shame his and his family's honor. Roland's tragic death and the vengeance of Charlemagne valorize the behavior of the hero in war, a theme that would continue into other French *chansons de geste,* or songs of adventure. In addition, as literature elaborated on the conduct of the hero in war, it also elaborated on the conduct of the hero in love. In love, poetically imagined as a type of polite warfare, hearts were at stake instead of lives. Thus, the concepts of chivalry and courtly love develop simultaneously in the romantic literature.

The practice of courtly love developed around the 11th century. C. S. Lewis, in his classic study *The Allegory of Love,* claimed that courtly love developed suddenly and spontaneously in the lyrics of the Provençal TROUBADOURS of southern France. Other scholars, like Denis de Rougemont, suspect that the troubadours drew inspiration from the Arabic and Hebrew lyric poems circulating in the courts of Muslim Spain. For example, the system of love described in the Arabic work *The Dove's Necklace* by Ibn Hazm (1022) closely resembles Andreas Capellanus's *The Art of Courtly Love* (1174), a Latin text that codifies the practice of courtly love along the lines of OVID's first-century *Art of Love.* Thus, courtly love as a literary device had its roots in both a Latin and a vernacular poetic tradition.

The elements of courtly love, according to Lewis, are humility, courtesy, adultery, and the religion of love. In this religion, Cupid, or Amor, and Venus preside as god and goddess. Courtly convention requires that the lover be hopelessly devoted to a lady who is his social superior; most often, she is married to his overlord, and he refers to himself, in feudal terms, as her servant and she his master. She is universally described as beautiful, graceful, and refined. The lover puts himself through grueling tests to prove the extent of his devotion. He suffers torments of the heart and spirit; often, he has a rival for the lady's love (never her husband), and just as often, the lady is cold or indifferent to him. The lover describes himself as wounded by love's arrows, near death with despair. Frequent plot devices include a springtime setting, an image of the court and all the ladies dancing, and a debate wherein the lover must defend himself.

Using the elements established by the troubadours and by Capellanus, the French romances of the 12th century refined the concept of courtly love in such works as the ROMANCE OF THE ROSE by GUILLAUME DE LORRIS and Jean de Meun. Courtly conventions also appear in the *Lais* of MARIE DE FRANCE and the Arthurian romances of CHRÉTIEN DE TROYES. The characters from the Arthurian legends, called "the matter of Britain," were popularly recast as feudal heroes and made models of chivalric conduct. Later incorporated with the story TRISTAN AND ISEULT and legends of the HOLY GRAIL, Arthurian tales by GOTTFRIED VON STRASSBURG, WOLFRAM VON ESCHENBACH, and others repeatedly returned to the themes of chivalry and courtly love. Chrétien's *Erec and Enide* shows the hero experiencing a crisis of reputation when his absorption in love makes him neglect deeds of chivalry, and he is thus thought to be losing his touch. The English poem *Sir Gawain and the Green Knight* explores the demands of the chivalric code as it governs behavior at court, behavior at love-play, and the necessity of keeping one's promises and preserving one's honor.

Love as a noble and ennobling concept reached its finest expression in the poetry of DANTE ALIGHEIRI and his contemporaries in Italy. Dante, along with Petrarch, elevated the worship of a distant lady to its highest degree. Later authors working in this tradition, including Geoffrey Chaucer, Charles d'Orléans, and Jean Froissart, borrowed images from Dante and Petrarch to describe their own adventures in love.

Almost as soon as the literature of courtly love developed, it began to satirize itself. The concept contained inherent contradictions, not least being that a hero was required to be a ferocious killer as well as a courteous lover. In actual practice the application of chivalric codes could be dangerous as well as absurd, as demonstrated by the conflicted hero of Miguel de Cervantes' *Don Quixote*. Arguably, Ovid and Capellanus were writing tongue-in-cheek, suggesting that that taking love seriously was, itself, a joke. Capellanus's insistence that courtly love could only exist between an adulterous couple, and that marriage prohibited romance, was certainly a morally troubling stance for a cleric to take. Chrétien's romances, while articulating the concepts of fine love or *fin amor,* also made gentle fun of them, as in the episode from *The Knight of the Cart* where Guinevere shuns Lancelot for hesitating to use a criminal's cart as a means to come to her rescue.

Also, the practice of courtly love, while appearing to elevate women to near-sacred status, did very little to ameliorate the positions of actual medieval women. Critics have argued that the code of chivalry more correctly governed male social relations than it described or governed male-female romantic relations. Moreover, courtly literature frequently objectified or even maligned women, as Christine de Pisan pointed out in her querulous response to the *Romance of the Rose.*

Nevertheless, the concepts of chivalry and courtly love persisted into literature of the later MIDDLE AGES and the Renaissance, in the Arthurian romances of Thomas Malory, the poetry of Edmund Spenser and Philip Sidney, and the sonnets of William Shakespeare and Pierre de Ronsard. The idea of suffering for love marks romantic literature from Abbe Prévost's *Manon Lescaut* to Samuel Richardson's *Clarissa.* C. S. Lewis observes that the code of chivalry and courtly love "have made the background of European literature for eight hundred years . . . They effected a change which has left no corner of our ethics, or imagination, or our daily life untouched."

English Versions of Works of Chivalry and Courtly Love

Andreas Capelanus. *The Art of Courtly Love.* Translated by John Jay Parry. New York: Columbia University Press, 1941.

Chrétien de Troyes. *Arthurian Romances.* Translated by D. D. R. Owen. Rutland, Vt: Charles E. Tuttle, 1997.

Lorris, Guillaume de. *The Romance of the Rose: Guillaume de Lorris and Jean de Meun.* Translated by Frances Horgan. Oxford: Oxford University Press, 1994.

Works about Chivalry and Courtly Love

Allen, Peter L. *The Art of Love: Amatory Fiction from Ovid to Romance of the Rose.* Philadelphia: University of Pennsylvania Press, 1992.

Boase, Roger. *The Origin and Meaning of Courtly Love: a Critical Study of European Scholarship.* Manchester, U.K.: Manchester University Press, 1977.

O'Donoghue, Bernard. *The Courtly Love Tradition.* Manchester, U.K.: Manchester University Press, 1982.

Rougemont, Denis de. *Love in the Western World.* Translated by Montgomery Belgion. New York: Pantheon Books, 1956.

Topsfield, L. T. *Troubadors and Love.* London: Cambridge University Press, 1975.

Chrétien de Troyes (fl. 1160–1185) *poet*

As scholar D. D. R. Owen observes, Chrétien de Troyes has been called one of the great figures of world literature, the father of Arthurian romance, precursor to the modern novel, and a brilliant chronicler of French chivalry. But biographical information on Chrétien is scarce. In his writings he gives his name as Chrétien de [of] Troyes and says he studied under Peter of Beauvais. Chrétien was trained as a cleric, but he may not have taken orders in the priesthood and instead made his living as a court poet. His dedications show that he had wealthy patrons; he began *The Knight of the Cart* at the prompting of Marie de Champagne, the daughter of Eleanor of Aquitaine, and he wrote *The Story of the Grail* for Count Philip of Flanders.

Troyes, France, functioned as a center for trade, financial business, and the court of Champagne. Chrétien was thus exposed to two traditions of literature: the antique EPIC style, which focused on the deeds of great heroes, and the resurgence of French or vernacular literature. In his lifetime, the MEDIEVAL ROMANCE had begun to flower, writers were inspired by the codes of CHIVALRY AND COURTLY LOVE, and the TROUBADOURS were developing a new style of poetry. Chrétien's early works follow in the footsteps of the Latin tradition. He translated three of OVID's works, though only the story of Philomela survives. He then began to write poems, such as *The Bitten Shoulder* and *King Mark and Iseult the White,* in the more current courtly style. These early efforts are also lost.

Another poem, *William of England,* gives its author's name as Chrétien, but scholars disagree whether this is the same Chrétien who composed the Arthurian romances. Though Chrétien was not a common name in 12th-century France, some scholars, like Jean Frappier, believe that *William of England* "lacks the turn of mind, style, and subtlety of the author of *Lancelot, Yvain,* and *Perceval.*" The five poems involving characters from the King Arthur legends, which are collectively referred to as the *Arthurian Romances,* are considered Chrétien's greatest achievement.

Critical Analysis

Chrétien is not the father of Arthurian romance in the sense that he invented King Arthur; those legends had long existed in the popular imagination of both England and France, originating as Celtic or Breton tales told about a warrior who resisted the Anglo-Saxon invasions. In the medieval period, Arthur became a fashionable topic for chronicle and romance. GEOFFREY OF MONMOUTH gave a legendary history of Arthur in his *History of the Kings of Britain,* translated into French by the poet Wace. The legend of TRISTAN AND ISEULT and the *Lais* of MARIE DE FRANCE refashioned the folkloric material into matter worthy of courtly attention. These lines from the opening of *The Knight with the Lion* suggest that Chrétien found Arthur the ideal character around which to structure his romances:

> So it is my pleasure to relate a story worth listening to about the king whose fame spreads near and far. And I do agree with the belief of so many Bretons that his renown will last forever. Thanks to him, people will recall his chosen knights, fine men who strove for honor.

Chrétien re-creates in the court of Arthur all the attitudes and structures that prevailed in 12th-century France: its nobility of knights and ladies, its staged battles in the form of jousts, and its oaths of loyalty as demanded by the structure of feudalism. In his hands, the fierce warriors from the Celtic legends become courteous, highly trained knights devoted to honor, loyalty, and the service of ladies, and the tales of their quests explore ideals of love and chivalry during the story of each knight's quest for adventure, fame, recognition, and the love of his lady fair.

The first of Chrétien's Arthurian romances, *Erec and Enide,* describes the romance of the two title characters. After their marriage, Erec is in danger of losing his reputation for prowess because he spends all of his time with his lovely wife. She does not want to see his reputation damaged, and so together they go on a series of adventures which proves the valor of the knight and the strength of love.

The second romance, *Cligés,* blends British history with legends of Constantinople, as Cligés is born of both Greek and British cultures. Though the story has magical elements, it is realistic in the ways in which Chrétien explores the motives, conflicts, and struggles of his main characters.

Chrétien worked on *Yvain, or the Knight with the Lion* the same time as he worked on *Lancelot, or The Knight of the Cart.* Both tales abound with heroic idealizations, fantastic adventures, mystical events, and psychological challenges. Both tales also focus at some length on Gawain. The tale of Yvain frequently introduces comic and sentimental elements, while Lancelot is the most reflective and inwardly torn of Chrétien's characters. *The Knight of the Cart* was finished, so the manuscript says, by one Godfrey of Lagny, who took up the tale at Chrétien's request.

The last and most complex of the tales, *Perceval, or the Story of the Grail,* was never completed.

A distinct characteristic of Chrétien's style is his use of the conventions of courtly love and his depictions of beautiful if somewhat remorseless women. His narratives are also marked by frequent battles. Chrétien takes great delight in describing fight scenes, as in this description of a joust in *The Knight of the Cart:*

> After the swearing of the oaths, their horses, fair and fine in every way, were led forward. Each knight mounted his and charged at the other as fast as his horse could carry him. With their horses galloping at top speed, the vassals struck each other so hard that there was nothing left of their two lances except the shafts they held in their hands.

Like many poets composing in Old French, Chrétien writes in octosyllabic couplets, meaning his lines are rhymed and contain eight syllables. English translators most often translate his poetry into prose, sacrificing the structure in favor of preserving the sense. Chrétien did not use any archaisms or colloquialisms in his language, but instead wrote in a direct, accessible style. He incorporates dialogue and makes frequent use of humor. His individual approach and flexible voice had an enormous impact on later romance writers. As translator David Staines writes, Chrétien "reshaped his Arthurian inheritance, and created a design that would serve as the standard and an essential source for all subsequent Arthurian literature."

One chief contribution Chrétien made to the Arthurian legends was the introduction of the story of the HOLY GRAIL, which translator Urban Holmes calls "a mystery so vast that men have never ceased to be intrigued by it." Topsfield calls Chrétien's story "the imaginative high point" of the author's Arthurian romances and "the zenith of his literary achievement." Readers have endlessly speculated on Chrétien's vision for the remainder of the poem, and several have tried to write continuations.

Chrétien had a permanent effect on the body of Arthurian legend and thus influenced all Arthurian writers who followed. The romances of the German WOLFRAM VAN ESCHENBACH borrow from Chrétien, and in France the Merlin romances of Robert de Boron and the *Prose Lancelot* continued to elaborate on the subject. "The Wife of Bath's Tale" in Geoffrey Chaucer's *The Canterbury Tales,* the alliterative Sir Gawain and the Green Knight, and Sir Thomas Malory's *The Death of Arthur* are all set in Arthurian times. Edmund Spenser in *The Faerie Queene* and Alfred Tennyson in *The Idylls of the King* wrote their own versions of the Arthurian romance. John Milton considered writing about Arthur before choosing the biblical book of Genesis as the subject matter for his epic *Paradise Lost.* Modern masterpieces such as T. H. White's *The Once and Future King* and Marion Zimmer Bradley's *The Mists of Avalon* also contain echoes of the tales of Chrétien. As Jean Frappier says, Chrétien "raised a still new and uncertain genre to a high degree of excellence," and he succeeded in "the classic task of endowing old materials with a more exquisite flavor, a clearer meaning, and broader human values."

English Versions of Works by Chrétien de Troyes

Chrétien de Troyes: Arthurian Romances. Translated by D. D. R. Owen. Rutland, Vermont: Charles E. Tuttle, 1997.

The Complete Romances of Chrétien de Troyes. Translated by David Staines. Bloomington: Indiana University Press, 1990.

Works about Chrétien de Troyes

Frappier, Jean. *Chrétien de Troyes: The Man and His Work.* Translated by Raymond J. Cormier. Athens: Ohio University Press, 1982.

Topsfield, L. T. *Chrétien de Troyes: A Study of the Arthurian Romances.* Cambridge, U.K.: Cambridge University Press, 1981.

Ch'u Elegies

See QU ELEGIES.

Ch'u Yuan

See QU YUAN.

Cicero, Marcus Tullius (106–43 B.C.)

orator, statesman, writer

Cicero was born in the village of Arpinum in the Volscian hills near Rome. Cicero's family was of the equestrian order, which denoted some degree of privilege and social standing. Caius Marius, a relative, dominated Roman politics and military affairs for the first two decades of Cicero's life, which influenced the aspirations Cicero's father would have for his own sons. The family took advantage of connections with distinguished Romans to secure the brilliant young Cicero a first-rate education in rhetoric (the art of persuasion) and law.

Although Cicero desired a career in politics, he decided first to make a name for himself as a public advocate. Many of his existing writings are from speeches he made on behalf of his clients in the courtroom. He proved to be a captivating public speaker with an exceptional gift for oratory. His talent, connections, and an advantageous marriage to a moneyed woman named Terentia all contributed to his successful candidacy for quaestor in 75 B.C., the lowest ranking of the magistrate positions. Ultimately, Cicero was elected to the supreme magistrate seats, that of praetor in 66 B.C. and consul in 63 B.C., an extraordinary achievement for a nonaristocrat.

Cicero enjoyed his greatest professional triumph in 63 B.C. when he single-handedly thwarted a conspiracy organized by the politician Lucius Catiline. Because he summarily executed some of the conspirators without benefit of trial, however, Cicero was briefly exiled from Rome in 58 B.C.

His last years were ones of despair and bitterness. He and Terentia divorced; his beloved daughter Tullia died in childbirth; his son Marcus was a hopeless underachiever; and, as Classics scholar Jasper Griffin writes in the *New York Review of Books:*

> The Republic that he loved, in which he had won his spectacular successes, the Republic which had conquered the world, had crashed to defeat at the hands of one of its own generals, the invincible Julius Caesar, who was in the process of establishing a monarchy, with himself as its king.

Nevertheless, Cicero's literary output during these last years was prodigious, since he viewed writing as an occupation to distract him from his sorrows.

After Caesar was assassinated, Cicero collaborated with his killers to restore the Republic and delivered a series of scathing denunciations of Mark Antony, head of the Caesarian faction. The *Philippics,* as the 14 orations were known, portray Antony as despicable in personal appearance, lifestyle, ancestry, background, morals, and political skills. The vindictive Antony drew up a proscription list with Cicero's name on it. Cicero was slain by bounty hunters on December 7, 43 B.C., and his head and hands were displayed over the public speaking platform in the Forum.

Cicero's best-known speeches as an advocate include *Pro Murena* (63 B.C.), a successful defense of the politician Lucius Murena against charges of bribery, in which Cicero deflected the accusation by satirizing lawyers' nitpicking ways; *Pro Sulla* (63 B.C.), which helped acquit Publius Sulla of conspiracy even though, due to an obscure law, the prosecutor hand-picked the jury; *Pro Archia* (62 B.C.), which appealed to Roman self-satisfaction and patriotism in a petition to gain citizenship for the poet Archias; and *Pro Flacco* (59 B.C.), which argued that a person of the defendant Lucius Flaccus's character and achievement was incapable of committing the malfeasance with which he was charged.

In *De oratore* (*On the Orator,* 55 B.C.), Cicero provided instruction in the art of speaking to arouse, persuade, or entertain an audience and included vivid examples of the tricks of his trade. In 46 B.C., he composed two additional treatises on public speaking: *Brutus,* which discusses the history of the art as well as the role of the audience; and *Orator,* a depiction of the ideal speaker.

In his later years, Cicero's work became increasingly philosophical in nature. *De re Publica* (On the Commonwealth, 51 B.C.), an homage to the Greek philosopher PLATO's *Republic,* is an account in dialogue form of different types of government and how they degenerate. He presents the Roman Republic as the ideal state.

In 45 B.C., the year Tullia died, a heartbroken Cicero produced *Disputationes Tusculanae* (Discussions in my villa at Tusculum), which undertakes to demonstrate that widely held notions, such as that death is evil, are false; and *De natura Deorum* (The Nature of the Gods), a theological discussion from the viewpoints of various philosophical schools.

The following year saw the publication of the dialogues *De Divinatione* (On Divination), *De Senectute* (On Old Age), and *De Amicitia* (On Friendship), as well as *de Officiis* (On Duties), an essay to Cicero's son providing principles of proper conduct for those who aspire to political office.

Cicero was also an avid and accomplished correspondent, and hundreds of his letters survive.

The conspiracy of Lucius Catiline inspired some of Cicero's greatest orations. Catiline came from an aristocratic but rather dissipated family. A reckless opportunist with a conspicuously self-indulgent and decadent lifestyle, he held several public offices in Rome, but the consulship eluded him year after year and he did not have the financial resources to run indefinitely.

A desperate Catiline decided to organize a revolt. He began soliciting support from disgruntled and volatile citizens, both destitute and patrician, whose treatment by previous governments had left them facing financial ruin. Catiline promised them the cancellation of debts, and a scheme was devised to seize the government by wreaking havoc in Rome with arson and the massacre of aristocrats and senators, and by instigating armed insurrection in Etruria. The murder of Cicero was another item on the agenda.

Cicero was politically shrewd. He had many well-placed observers and became aware of Catiline's plot. The day after Cicero thwarted his would-be assassins, he arranged an emergency meeting of the senate and delivered an impassioned speech, the first oration of *In Catilinam.* As translated by Louis E. Lord, it begins with great vehemence and endless rhetorical questions:

> In heaven's name, Catiline, how long will you abuse our patience? How long will that madness of yours mock us? To what limit will your unbridled audacity vaunt itself? Is it nothing to you that the Palatine has its garrison by night, nothing to you that the city is full of patrols, nothing that the populace is in a panic, nothing that all honest men have joined forces, nothing that the senate is convened in this stronghold, is it nothing to see the looks on all these faces? Do you not know that your plans are disclosed? Do you not see that your conspiracy is bound hand and foot by the knowledge of these men? Who of us do you think is ignorant of what you did last night, what you did the night before, where you were, whom you called together, what plan you took?

In the second, third, and fourth orations against Catiline, Cicero describes the measures being taken to protect the city, reveals how the evidence against the conspirators was obtained, and argues that the penalty for the crimes against Rome should be death. Cicero also states that, as consul, if a senatorial decree empowering him to order an execution of the conspirators were passed, he would do so. The decree was passed.

"This was the proudest moment of Cicero's life," writes Olivia Coolidge in *Lives of Famous Romans:*

> He had saved the State he loved and had also shown himself as prompt as those who called themselves men of action. Perhaps he had even surprised himself on this occasion, for he never allowed anyone to forget it. He even wrote a long poem on his own consulship, most of which has unhappily vanished except for one crashing line of self-admiration: "Oh lucky Rome that I was consul then!"

Cicero was a master of Latin prose, which served his purposes as a philosopher, politician, or persuader. His use of the language transformed Latin from a rough and serviceable tongue suitable for military or commercial use to a supple, melodious means of expressing the range of human thoughts and emotions. Scholar Jasper Griffin calls him "incomparably the greatest stylist and the greatest writer that the Latin language had ever seen."

English Versions of Works by Cicero

Cicero: The Speeches. Translated by Louis E. Lord. Cambridge, Mass.: Harvard University Press, 1959.
Cicero: Volume XXVIII. Letters to Quintus and Brutus. Translated by D. R. Shackleton Bailey. Cambridge, Mass.: Harvard University Press, 2002.

Works about Cicero

Coolidge, Olivia. *Lives of Famous Romans.* Boston: Houghton Mifflin Company, 1965.
Everitt, Anthony. *Cicero: The Life and Times of Rome's Greatest Politician.* New York: Random House, 2002.

Cid, El (Rodrigo Díaz de Vivar) (ca. 1043–1099) *legendary Spanish warrior*

"El Cid" was the name given to the 11th-century Spanish warrior who was one of the greatest sources for legend and poems of the MIDDLE AGES and later centuries. Though often depicted in literature as a hero of the Spanish Reconquest, the Cid of history often fought alongside Muslims. The name *Cid* came from his Muslim vassals and allies, who called him *Sayyid*, or "My Lord." He is also known as the Cid Campeador, which means "doctor (or master) of the battlefield."

Historical records reveal that Rodrigo Díaz was probably born around 1043 in the village of Vivar near Burgos in the kingdom of Castile. His father, Diego Laínez, belonged to the *infanzones*, or lesser landowning aristocracy under Fernando I of Castile, but his mother was of a more distinguished lineage. Rodrigo entered the service of Fernando's son, Sancho II, and was probably knighted when he was 18 or 20. He quickly distinguished himself on military campaigns. After Sancho was killed in 1072 by supporters of his brother, who became Alfonso VI, Rodrigo entered the new king's service. In 1074, when he was about 30, Rodrigo married a relative of Alfonso, Doña Jimena, the daughter of Diego, the count of Oviedo. They had two daughters, María and Cristina, and a son, Diego. However, in 1081, Rodrigo fell out of favor with the king and was exiled.

At the time, about two-thirds of Spain was made up of small Muslim taifa kingdoms. El Cid's campaigns were sometimes directed against the Muslims and sometimes in alliance with them. At one time he fought in the service of the Muslim ruler of Zaragoza (Saragossa). He was reconciled with King Alfonso in 1087 but was exiled again from 1089 until 1092. In 1084, he captured the Muslim-held city of Valencia and successfully held it against attacks by the Almoravid. He died on July 10 and was buried in the monastery of San Pedro in Cardeña, near Burgos. Jimena, who probably died around 1116, was buried there as well.

Historians disagree about whether El Cid was a Christian knight or a self-serving mercenary, but the Cid most loved by poets was the devout Christian warrior and ever-loyal vassal to an ungrateful lord. In early medieval Spain, few people other than kings and saintly monks attracted the notice of chroniclers and biographers. El Cid was the first to break with this tradition. He appears in two Muslim chronicles of Spain, written shortly after his death. One is by Ibn 'Alqama, called the *Eloquent Testimony of the Great Calamity* (ca. 1110), which describes the Cid's conquest of Valencia. The other is ibn Bassam's *Treasury of the Excellencies of the Spaniards.* Though the tone of these works is understandably hostile, they both show that El Cid was a formidable warrior.

The earliest poem about El Cid is an incomplete work called the "Carmen Campidoctoris," or the "Song of the Campeador," which may have been written in his lifetime. The author, perhaps a learned cleric, describes in vigorous Latin verses some of Rodrigo's early campaigns. The earliest biography of the hero, also written in Latin, is the *Historia Roderici* (History of Rodrigo, ca. 1150). It is extraordinarily detailed in some instances and may have been written by someone involved in Rodrigo's campaigns.

The legend of El Cid soon found its way into the Spanish vernacular. A Latin poem from 1147 says that the story of "Meo Cid" was celebrated in song. Some believe this song may actually have been the later famous "Cantar de mío Cid," while others believe it refers to a simple popular song. Another Spanish work, the *Lineaje del Cid* (ca. 1197), is a genealogy with an account of the hero's life that gives him a royal pedigree.

The culmination of this early development of El Cid's legend was the EPIC poem *El Cantar de mío Cid.* It omits the campaigns in which Rodrigo fought for the Muslims, instead characterizing him as a devout Christian warrior fighting against them.

A further development of the legend appears in a work by the monks of Cardeña, El Cid's burial place, called the *Estoria del Cid.* Later, a team of writers working under Alfonso X (1221–84) incorporated the *Estoria* into their *Crónica de veinte reyes;* they also took much of the *Cantar de mío Cid* into their *Primera Crónica General.*

Later works include a series of *romanceros,* which began around 1300. The ballads they contained were translated as *Ancient Spanish Ballads* by Lockhart Scott, the son of Sir Walter Scott. These romances give the legendary account of El Cid's romance with Jimena, in which he kills her father in a duel but later wins her love and marries her.

Many works of later centuries drew on these *romanceros,* including Guillén de Castro's play *Mocedades del Cid* (1618) and French dramatist Pierre Corneille's masterpiece *Le Cid* (1637).

Critical Analysis

The most famous medieval work about El Cid is *Cantar de mío Cid,* also known as *Poema de mío Cid.* It is the only complete epic poem in Spanish surviving from the Middle Ages. Early scholar Ramón Menéndez Pidal believed it had its origins, like the French *chansons de geste,* in the song of a minstrel and that it was written down before 1140. Most scholars now believe the poem is a purely literary work, written around 1207, the date found in the only surviving manuscript from a nunnery in Vivar.

The manuscript says that Per Abad wrote the work, but it is unclear whether he is the actual author or the copyist. He was probably associated in some way with the monastery of San Pedro de Cardeña, which plays an important role in the story. According to scholar and author Colin Smith, the details of the *Poema* (poem) show that the author had an interest in genealogical and legal matters. He knew the SONG OF ROLAND and possibly other 12th-century French epics. He also may have had access to documents about El Cid contained in Spanish archives in Salamanca, which enabled him to fill the poem with the names of people who appear in historical records of the time.

The *Poema* is divided into three parts, or *Cantars.* The first recounts El Cid's departure into exile after his second dismissal by Alfonso VI and his subsequent military campaigns, through which he gains wealth and a number of followers. It incorporates some adventures that actually took place during Rodrigo's earlier life. The second part tells of El Cid's conquest of Valencia, where he is joined by his wife and daughters. After winning back his honor in military glory, he is pardoned by King Alfonso and marries his daughters to two Leonese noblemen. In the third part, El Cid's cowardly sons-in-law abuse their young brides, and El Cid wins redress for their dishonor in Alfonso's court through judicial duels.

The poem is written in lines with a caesura (pause) in the middle and an irregular number of syllables in each line. It also makes use of assonance, or similar vowel sounds in the lines.

The description, dialogue, and characterization are vivid. El Cid is an attractive hero, a man of military prowess, stoic endurance, and gravity but also good humor. He is not only brave but generous to his men and honorable. He is an exemplary husband and father, but most importantly, he is loyal to his feudal lord, Alfonso, even when the king rejects and exiles him. In the poem's most thrilling passage, the conquest of Valencia, the poet evokes greatly varied moods. When El Cid's young daughters hear the drums of the Muslim army, for example, the hero comforts them:

> He strokes his beard calmly, the good Cid
>   Campeador.
> "Don't be afraid, everything's in your favor;
> Before fifteen days are up, if it please the
>   Creator
> We'll have those drums in the house [for
>   you to play with]."
>
>   (11.1663–1666)

This image of El Cid contrasts nicely with images of him during the heat of battle:

> Using his lance first, the Cid got his hand
>   on the sword,
> He killed so many Moors you could not
>   have counted them,
> The blood was streaming from his arm
>   above the elbow.
>
>   (11.1722–1724)

In his introduction to *The Poem of the Cid*, scholar Ian Michael compares the poem to the *Song of Roland*, suggesting that the Cid's character is "an amalgam of the poetic Roland's youthful boldness and Charlemagne's elderly caution." While *Cantar de mío Cid* lacks the tragic grandeur of the *Song of Roland*, it is a stirring work that illustrates the virtues the medieval Spanish most admired in a man and a warrior. It is a vision of heroism that many other cultures respond to as well.

English Versions of Works about El Cid

Poem of the Cid. Translated by Paul Blackburn. Norman: University of Oklahoma Press, 1998.

The Poem of the Cid. Translated by Rita Hamilton and Janet Perry. Introduction by Ian Michael. New York: Penguin, 1984.

The World of El Cid: Chronicles of the Spanish Reconquest. Edited by Simon Barton and Richard Fletcher. Manchester, U.K.: Manchester University Press, 2001.

Works about El Cid

Clissold, Stephen. *In Search of the Cid*. New York: Barnes & Noble, 1994.

Smith, Colin. *The Making of the Poema de mio Cid*. Cambridge, U.K.: Cambridge University Press, 1983.

Confucius (Kong Qiu [K'ung Ch'iu], Kongfuzi [K'ung Fu-tzu]) (551–479 B.C.)
philosopher

Kong Qiu (K'ung Ch'iu) is best known in the West as Confucius, the Latinized form of Kongfui (K'ung Fu-tzu; "the master Kong"). Confucius was born in Nishan, Qufu (Ch'ü-fu), a town in central China in what was then the state of Lu. During his lifetime, the Zhou (or Chou) dynasty (11th–third century B.C.) no longer wielded the authority it once had enjoyed. China was experiencing a period of feudalism, during which power essentially rested with the leaders of a number of small states. Struggles for influence often occurred within individual states and between neighboring leader-warlords. In his philosophy, Confucius would look back to a supposed golden age earlier in the Zhou dynasty, a time when order reigned and when rulers and subjects behaved as befitted their roles in society.

Confucius's father, who held a minor government post, died when his son was three, leaving the boy to grow up under his mother's influence. Married at age 18, Confucius had children and worked at a number of menial jobs. Despite his love of learning and desire to serve the state, Confucius was unable to obtain a meaningful government position until, in his late 40s or early 50s, the duke of Lu appointed him minister of public works, then minister of justice. He soon left office, however. Tradition says he was disgusted with government corruption, but he may also have offended important members of the nobility. He spent some years traveling outside of Lu and in 484 B.C. returned to his home state, where he died five years later.

History credits Confucius with editing the BOOK OF SONGS, from which he often quoted, as well as the *Book of Documents* and Lu court chronicles. Most important, about 520 B.C. he established a school to teach others how to govern. The curriculum focused on writing, mathematics, music, ritual, archery, and chariot driving. Confucius emphasized morality over practical skills, and he cultivated an informal teaching style that seems to have included many question-and-answer sessions.

Confucius's answers to his pupils' questions often came in the form of brief but memorable sayings. Like SOCRATES, to whom Western readers have often compared him, Confucius never recorded his teachings. It was his pupils who later recorded a number of his sayings and comments in the *Lun Yu* (*Analects*), a book that became the basis for his later fame as a philosopher. His reputation grew greatly after his death. A later philosopher, Mencius (ca. 371–298 B.C.), claimed, "Ever since man came into this world, there has never been one greater than Confucius."

In the third century B.C., the first Qin (Ch'in) dynasty emperor ordered massive book burnings that consigned many ancient texts to oblivion. The state also buried Confucian scholars alive. Nevertheless, the *Analects* lived on, and Confucius's life took on an aura of legend. The historian Sima Qian (Ssu-ma Ch'ien, ca. 185–145 B.C.) claimed that Confucius's impoverished family descended from an imperial dynasty and that Confucius was acquainted with LAOZI (Lao Tsu). Beginning in the second century B.C., Confucianism was required knowledge for government officials, and every government examination given between A.D. 960 and 1905 (except during the Yuan (Mongol) dynasty, 1271–1368) required would-be civil servants to display extensive familiarity with Confucian texts.

Later philosophers criticized and revised Confuciun texts. In the 10th century, scholars, including WANG ANSHIH (Wang An-Shih), drew on the *Analects* in developing their philosophies, collectively called Neo-Confucianism.

Critical Analysis

The *Analects* are divided up into 20 sections, or "books," that contain approximately 500 brief subsections, or "chapters." Each chapter consists of a snippet of dialogue, a comment, or an anecdote, including some of Confucius's jokes and occasional complaints about his life, as well his more profound thoughts. Other chapters included the recorded sayings of his disciples.

Rather than being composed all at once, the *Analects* came together gradually, as various individuals added their memories of Confucius or other Confucian teachers. It probably did not coalesce into the book we know today until sometime around the second century B.C. Scholars have concluded that books three through nine and 11 through 15 are most likely genuine stories from Confucius's life rather than additions from writers in later centuries.

The cornerstone of Confucius's philosophy is *ren,* a word that appears more than 100 times in the *Analects.* It means "showing magnanimity, compassion, and humaneness in one's thoughts and actions." To exhibit humaneness is the epitome of virtue. In one passage, Confucius asserts that "the humane man, wishing himself to be established, sees that others are established, and wishing himself to be successful, sees that others are successful. To be able to take one's own familiar feelings as a guide may definitely be called the method of humaneness." Elsewhere, Confucius reiterates this idea: "Zigong asked: 'Is there a single word such that one could practise it throughout one's life?' The Master [Confucius] said: 'Reciprocity perhaps? Do not inflict on others what you yourself would not wish done to you.'"

The *Analects* also stress the importance of loyalty, filial piety, and harmony. Individuals prove they are fit to govern others by exhibiting these qualities, observing traditional rituals, and showing humaneness. They should concern themselves with their own virtue rather than with pleasing those in power or attempting to obtain a salary. According to Confucius, "One is not worried about not holding position; one is worried about how one may fit oneself for appointment."

Confucius does not believe that everyone can exhibit true virtue and humaneness. He comments, "the people may be made to follow something, but not to understand it." It is for this reason that the "gentleman" must provide others with an example to follow. "To govern," he says, "means to correct. If you take the lead by being correct, who will dare not to be corrected?"

Confucius developed the philosophical and ethical concept of *ren*, and he was the first to describe his ideal method of behavior as the Way. Translator Raymond Dawson notes that many of the *Analects's* chapters "may be seen as seminal expressions of some of the typical ideas of Chinese civilization." He adds: "The earliest parts of the Analects are the earliest [Chinese] writings . . . which deal primarily with ethical matters for their own sake and feature [people's] inclination to act for ethical reasons rather than for reasons of practical advantage. This is an important breakthrough in the history of Chinese thought." Thus, the *Analects* are a key to understanding not only Chinese philosophy but also human nature and behavior.

English Versions of Works by Confucius

The Analects. Edited and translated by Raymond Dawson. New York: Oxford University Press, 1993.

Wisdom of Confucius. New York: Kensington Publishing, 2001.

Works about Confucius

Brown, Brian, ed. *The Story of Confucius: His Life and Sayings (1927).* Introduction by Ly Yu Sang. Whitefish, Mont.: Kessinger Publishing, 2003.

Creel, H. G. *Confucius and the Chinese Way.* New York: Harper & Row, 1975.

Dawson, Raymond. *Confucius.* Oxford: Oxford University Press, 1981.

Schwartz, B. I. *The World of Thought in Ancient China.* Cambridge, Mass.: Harvard University Press, 1985.

Stover, Leon. *Imperial China and the State Cult of Confucius.* Jefferson, N.C.: McFarland & Co., 2004.

courtly love

See CHIVALRY AND COURTLY LOVE.

Coyote tales (Hopi)

In the ORAL LITERATURE of the Hopi, who originally settled in the southwestern regions of the United States, the coyote features prominently as a trickster figure that possesses qualities both animal and human, and sometimes divine. Coyotes appear frequently in the folklore, myths, legends, and sacred teachings of many Native American tribes. Scholars of tribal religions believe that the coyote and other animals represent the First People of the Native American CREATION MYTHS and therefore serve as prototypes for human life and culture. In these tales, wherein divine figures are given human personalities, stories about the coyote serve many purposes. Intended for audiences of all ages, these stories combine sacred and spiritual teachings, moral instruction, and humorous entertainment in the form of the character Coyote's adventures.

Scholars like Ekkehart Malotki and Michael Lomatuway'ma, who have dedicated their careers to the preservation and understanding of Hopi tales, believe that the function of the coyote in the stories reflects the impact of the coyote on Hopi life. To a tribe whose livelihood consisted mostly of agricultural practices, the coyote was sometimes a dangerous predator, but most often a nuisance and a useless creature that provided neither pelt nor meat. In Hopi literature, the coyote is not given the status of *kachina,* a powerful spirit in animal form that protects and benefits humans. The tales most often portray Coyote as a trickster figure whose inquisitive and highly gullible nature always gets him into trouble.

In Malotki and Lomatuway'ma's *Hopi Coyote Tales,* for instance, many of Coyote's interactions with other animals end with his defeat. Grasshopper confounds Coyote's efforts to eat him and leaves him starving; both Badger and Porcupine trick Coyote into bleeding himself to death. The tales can be taken as a lesson about gullibility; Porcupine, when he finds his friend's corpse on the hearth, yells at him: "Why do you have to believe everything? What I told you had to be a lie!" Badger's tale serves a moral purpose, for Coyote's death is his punishment for lechery, gluttony, mayhem, and disobedience to Badger, who is the medicine man of their village and therefore a wise and powerful being who ought to be obeyed. Badger, too, berates Coyote's corpse, telling him, "It's your own fault that you are so wicked."

A characteristic of the Hopi Coyote tales is that they make little attempt to drive home a moral point; rather, they simply end the narratives with "and here the story ends." What the audience makes of the Coyote tales is left to their own discretion. Close readers can find a wealth of information about life among the Hopi, everything from social relations, etiquette, and advice for raising children to detailed descriptions of spiritual practices, village ethics, geographical descriptions, and tasty menus. Many of the tales contain etio-logical elements or explanations on how something came to be; the story of Coyote and the turkeys, for instance, tells why no turkeys are found in a Hopi village.

Coyote's flexibility, however, makes him more than a simple buffoon character or lampoon. Coyote can take the form of a male or female, a hunter or mother, a boy or a girl, and can roam through any landscape, including the underworld and the sky. Some tales show Coyote engaging in the more sinister side of witchcraft and sorcery, but these tales, too, always end in disaster. In "Coyote Learns Sorcery" in Malotki and Lomatuway'ma's collection, Coyote gets turned into a jackrabbit and goes home to some very hungry children.

Other tales show a better side to Coyote's nature. In "Coyote and So'yoko," Coyote saves the children of the Orayri village from being eaten by an ogre. Later he defends his village from the Korowiste Kachinas. Coyote even experiences romance, falling in love with and marrying a girl from Musangnuvi.

As a literary tradition, the coyote tales function as more than other animal fables like those of AESOP in European literature. Like the folklore of all cultures, these tales, as Malotki observes in *Hopi Animal Stories,* are "an important way of expressing culturally shared values, attitudes, and concerns." In this way the Hopi Coyote tales have something in common with literatures of many other cultures, from the PANCHATANTRA of India to the German fairy tales of the Grimm brothers.

English Versions of Coyote Tales

Hopi Animal Stories. Edited by Ekkehart Malotki. Lincoln: University of Nebraska Press, 2001.

Malotki, Ekkehart. *Gullible Coyote: Una'ihu.* Tucson: University of Arizona Press, 1985.

Malotki, Ekkehart and Michael Lomatuway'ma. *Hopi Coyote Tales: Istutuwutsi.* Lincoln: University of Nebraska Press, 1984.

Works about Coyote Tales

Bright, William. *A Coyote Reader.* Berkeley: University of California Press, 1993.

Haile, Berard, O.F.M. *Navajo Coyote Tales.* Edited by Karl W. Luckert. Lincoln: University of Nebraska Press, 1984.

Waters, Frank and Oswald White Bear Fredericks. *Book of the Hopi.* New York: Viking Press, 1977.

creation myths, Native American

Each of the cultures that inhabited the continents of North and South America before the arrival of the first European settlers had a unique and distinct explanation for the creation and ordering of the world as they knew it. As part of the ORAL LITERATURE that was handed down through generation after generation, the origin stories explained how the world had come to exist, how humans were formed, how and why plants and animals were given their functions, and why such natural cycles as sunrise, sunset, and the seasons governed the world. These creation myths might explain anything from why the landscape appeared as it did to how a tribe had gotten its name, and from the explanation of the deer's antlers to the origins of corn.

As a whole, the creation myths take place in a prehistoric time when the same natural laws did not apply. Animals could speak and reason, elements had personalities and could communicate with each other, and humans were created not to rule the world but simply to be one of an infinite variety of creatures who lived in it. These mythic First Beings, who brought forth by one means or another the world as it was known to listeners of the story, were often regarded as still having an interest in the business of human life. Therefore many Native American religions regarded the elements, the heavenly bodies, and the spirits of animals to have the supernatural ability to understand and participate in human affairs. Plants, animals, insects, and even aspects of the landscape were frequently treated as sentient beings that could either provide assistance if appropriately addressed or might cause harm if scorned or offended. Many ceremonies, rituals, daily practices, and even whole systems of thought in Native American life acknowledged and celebrated the gifts that had been given humans by their divine predecessors, and in this way, the creation myths played an intimate and ongoing role in the daily life of the tribe.

The creation stories are more than just literature. As David Martinez observes in *The Legends and Lands of Native North Americans,* "they are the foundation of culture itself, stemming from the most basic and fundamental experiences required for founding a people."

Critical Analysis

Many of the creation myths told by different cultures share similarities, not just with each other, but with cultures from other parts of the world. In the Hopi tradition, like the creation story in the Hebrew BIBLE, the earth was originally covered with water. The Lakota tell of a great flood that wiped out humans except for one girl, who was saved by Spotted Eagle. Later she married him and bore children, thus repopulating the new earth with the Lakota people. Aside from the story of the Bible, a worldwide flood is also described in the Sumerian epic GILGAMESH, set in an entirely different hemisphere.

The creation myths traditionally describe how, in the dawn of the world, before humans were created, the earth was populated with creatures that had animal, human, and divine qualities. Different cultures account for the creation of humans in different ways, but many share the common theme that humans were created out of a natural substance—earth, or sometimes corn—that was animated by one of the First Beings, perhaps the Wind, Old Spider Woman, or Old Badger Man. Several Native American tribes regard the sun as the first generative being. The Aztecs in the ancient NAHUATL POETRY and the Inca in the MYTH OF MANCO CAPAC recount stories of how their tribal ancestors were descendants of the sun, and the Navajo also tell a story of how the sun fathered a child with the First Woman.

Often the prehuman world was inhabited by water monsters, giants, or other creatures that needed to be defeated so that humans could survive. Most of the stories account, in some way, for the progression from a prehistoric time when humans and animals could communicate with one another, when all existed in harmony and balance, to a fallen state where violence and conflict exist in the world, humans experience strife with one another as well as the natural elements, and animals have lost the power of speech, though they might retain powers of another type.

Many cultures also preserve creation myths that explain how humans came to possess certain skills. In the OKLAHOMA CHEROKEE FOLKTALES, Selu provided humans with the first corn, and set the example for women to plant, harvest, and prepare it as food, while her husband, Kana'ti, showed the first men how to be hunters. In the creation myths of the Crow, Old Man Coyote is responsible for fashioning the first humans; it was he who decreed the functions of the animals, and he who created the separate tribes with different languages, which, for the Crow, explained why there was warfare, tribal rivalries, and the practice of wife stealing. In the creation myths of the Sanpoil, Coyote was the one who taught the first humans how to catch and prepare salmon, a staple of the Sanpoil diet.

The stories of creation and of the first interaction between humans and the divine beings who instruct them serve as more than entertaining stories; they convey the wisdom that ancestors of native peoples have deemed important for the preservation and satisfaction of life. The NAVAJO NIGHTWAY CEREMONY SONGS might call it *hózhó*, the ZUNI INDIAN NARRATIVE POETRY might call it the Pollen Way, and the YAQUI DEER SONGS might refer to it as the "flower world," but in all cases, the songs, poems, and stories that furnish the creation myths of a people preserve directions for a way of life lived in harmony with the divine things of the world and their plan for human survival. As Jeremiah Curtin explains in *Creation Myths of Primitive America*: "Every act of an Indian in peace or in war, as an individual or as a member of a tribe, had its only sanction in the world of the first people, the American divinities." Part of the responsibility

of the listening audience, it was understood, was to remember and continue to observe the wisdom that the First People had brought to humans.

Particularly in cultures that do not make use of written language, stories become a way to preserving and communicating cultural memory. In each retelling, with the contributions of each storyteller and the reception of the audience, the story inherits something. In this way, stories, like the lands they describe, become living things with a history of their own. Creation myths from many Native American cultures share a common belief that a territory, with its sacred features, its provisions, and its abundance, is not given to people to own but is given rather as a trust, a gift that must be cared for and preserved. Scholars who understand the value that the creation myths hold in preserving and communicating cultural foundations and ancient wisdom have made efforts, in the past century, to capture tales in writing and translate them into English so their knowledge might be communicated to a broader audience. The settlement of Europeans in the Americas irrevocably changed the conditions under which the native tribes lived, and our contemporary world, which depends on written media and print culture, has made traditions of oral communication such as storytelling seem quaint, old-fashioned, and obsolete. It requires care and attention on the part of present-day scholars to preserve the language, history, and mythologies of the Native American creation myths and thus ensure that entire cultures do not become extinct.

English Versions of Native American Creation Myths

Curtin, Jeremiah. *Creation Myths of Primitive America*. Whitefish, Mont.: Kessinger Publishing Company, 2003.

Cushing, Frank Hamilton. *Outlines of Zuni Creation Myths*. New York: AMS Press, 1996.

Erdoes, Richard and Alfonso Ortiz, eds. *American Indian Myths and Legends*. New York: Pantheon Books, 1985.

Feldmann, Susan, ed. *The Storytelling Stone: Traditional Native American Myths and Tales.* New York: Delta, 1999.

McNeese, Tim, ed. *Myths of Native America.* New York: Four Walls Eight Windows, 2003.

Works about Native American Creation Myths

Brown, Joseph Epes and Emily Cousins. *Teaching Spirits: Understanding Native American Religious Traditions.* Oxford: Oxford University Press, 2001.

Page, Jake and David Adams Leeming. *The Mythology of Native North America.* Norman: University of Oklahoma Press, 2000.

Crusades (ca. 1095–ca. 1291) *historic event*

The Crusades were a series of wars fought by European Christians between 1095 and 1291 to recover the Holy Land, especially Jerusalem, from the followers of Islam, known as Muslims. In the first century A.D., Christianity spread through the Roman Empire, including the Middle Eastern lands of Palestine, Syria, and Jerusalem. By the end of the fourth century, the Romans' vast empire was officially Christian. It remained so until the seventh century, when the religion of Islam rose out of Arabia. While Islam officially condemned the use of force as a means of conversion, states often found the use of force necessary. Arab armies of Muslims began conquering the Middle East, beginning with Persia (now Iraq) and Byzantium. By A.D. 638, the city of Jerusalem, considered by Christians the holiest of cities, was under Muslim control.

Though the Holy Land was under Islamic rule, Christians who came to worship at the holy places were, for the most part, tolerated. One exception was "Mad" Caliph Hakim (996–1021), who destroyed the Church of the Holy Sepulcher, Jesus' tomb, and persecuted both Christians and Jews. After his death, relations between Muslims and other religious groups became more and more strained. In the middle of the 11th century, the Arabs were displaced as leaders of Islam by the Turks, who disapproved of Christian pilgrims. When Byzantine emperor Alexius I found his empire overrun by the Seljuk Turks, he appealed to the West for help. In 1095, Pope Urban II, speaking at the Council of Clermont, urged all of Christendom to go to war to end Muslim rule of the Holy Land.

The result of Urban's speech was the first Crusade (1095–99). Combatants called themselves "crusaders" because they took as their emblem the Christian cross. The crusaders reached Jerusalem in the summer of 1099, took it back from the Muslims, and established four Latin states in the Middle East: Edessa, Antioch, Tripoli, and the Kingdom of Jerusalem.

The second Crusade (1147–49) transpired after the Turks took Edessa. This attempt by the Christian soldiers to regain the country ended in failure, and by 1187 most of the four Latin states set up during the first Crusade had again fallen back under Muslim control.

In 1187 the Kurdish Muslim military leader Salah ad-Din Yusuf (1138–93), or Saladin as he was known in the West, captured Jerusalem. Pope Gregory VIII called on Christians to embark upon a third Crusade (1189–92). For the next 100 years, crusades continued to be fought by Christians hoping to overturn Muslim rule over the Holy Land. The ninth and final crusade (1271–72) was led by Prince Edward of England, later Edward I. Edward landed in Acre, near Jerusalem, but retired after negotiating a truce. In 1289 Tripoli fell to the Muslims, and in 1291, Acre, the last Christian stronghold, followed. Conflicts between the Eastern and Western cultures did not end at that point, but after the loss of Acre, crusades were discussed but not launched.

The causes for the Crusades are deep and varied, and their consequences infinitely complex. Author Jean Richard, as translated by Jean Birrell, suggests that the "crusade poses a problem that is still present in the human consciousness, that of the legitimacy of war." Divine law for the Christians demanded the preservation of human life, but the business of government often required defense or aggression. The code of CHIVALRY in Western Europe evolved as a way to reconcile Christian virtues with life in violent times. Richard speculates that "when the barbarian monarchies settled in the old Roman Empire, warlike societies replaced a civil society, and this led to an exaltation of war." Literature of the Charlemagne cycle depicted the emperor's battles against the "Saracens" of Italy and Spain as a holy war, particularly in the SONG OF ROLAND. The concept of the "just war" evolved as Western Europe after Charlemagne found itself besieged on virtually all sides: Scandinavian tribes attacked from the north, Hungarian cavalry invaded from the east, and Saracen (the medieval Christian appellation for adherents of the Islamic faith) armies waged war from the south. The papacy felt that the defense of the "patrimony of St. Peter" was imperative, and the Crusades, as they developed, had dual aims: to defend Christian lands against Turkish invasion, and to secure Christian possession of the ancient Holy Land, where Christ had lived and died.

Contemporary accounts reveal that, from the start, the questions surrounding the Crusades have received different answers at the hands of different authors. Several writers of the early 12th century preserve Pope Urban II's speech at the Council of Clermont, among them Baldric, archbishop of Dol, and Robert and Monk, who wrote *History of Jerusalem*. The eyewitness accounts of the First Crusade such as *The Deeds of the Franks* (ca. 1100–01), written by an anonymous crusader who followed Bohemund of Antioch, reveal the complex maze of motivations and consequences of events. Fulcher of Chartres, who was also close to the action, began his chronicle in 1101, which is commonly held to be the most reliable of contemporary sources for the First Crusade. Raymond of Aguilers, Odo of Deuil, and Oliver of Paderborn were also clerics in close association with leaders of various crusades.

The Fourth Crusade was memorably observed and chronicled by Geoffroi de VILLEHARDOUIN, whose account is remembered and read as much for its historical value as for its lively prose. Villehardouin (ca. 1160–1213) deals with the facts of the Crusade rather than its deeper historical implications, and while he writes from a strong belief in the rightness of his cause, his narrative makes clear the internal opposition and debate among the crusaders. Robert of Clari, a knight who fought under Pierre of Amiens, also wrote of the Fourth Crusade in his *Conquest of Constantinople* (ca. 1216), though his account has been overshadowed in popularity by Villehardouin's.

Jean de Joinville (1224–1317) completed his *Chronicle* in 1309, describing his activities on crusade under Louis IV. Translator Frank Marzials observes that while Villehardouin writes "soberly, with an eye on important events . . . Joinville writes as an old man looking lovingly, lingeringly, at the past—garrulous, discursive, glad of a listener." Joinville's account shows keenly the conviction and idealism that motivated the men and women who gave up their familiar lives to go on a holy crusade.

The above chronicles were written by either combatants or clerics who had a stake in the success of the Christian armies. A thorough evaluation of the Crusades requires looking at the viewpoint of the other side. Fortunately, accounts of contemporary Arab historians and studies of the Crusades' effect on the Eastern states are becoming increasingly available to English audiences.

In the West, literature following the Crusades tended to glorify the accomplishments and valorize the heroes. The French *chansons de geste* (literally, "songs of adventure") frequently embellished actual events with legendary material, as in the *Song of Antioch* by Richard the Pilgrim or the anonymous *Song of Jerusalem*. These verse narratives preceded other chivalric romances like Torquato Tasso's *Jerusalem Delivered*, which portrays Godfrey of Bouillon as an EPIC hero. Likewise, Western historians up until the Enlightenment tended to exalt heroism and faith. However, Denis Diderot, and Jean d'Alembert, authors of the massive *Encyclopedia*, described the Crusades as "a time of the deepest darkness and of the greatest folly." Voltaire, too, referred to the Crusades as "that epidemic fury . . . marked by every cruelty, every perfidy, every debauchery, and every folly of which human nature is capable."

The Crusades have been viewed, positively, as bringing the West in contact with the East and revealing a whole new continent, Asia, which could then be explored (as Marco POLO proceeded to do). But they have also been blamed for deepening gulfs between Christians and Muslims. Some histories have argued that these wars were no less bloody than any other wars in human history; others see them as a tragic and destructive episode, "nothing more," as Steven Runciman writes in his *History of the Crusades,* "than a long act of intolerance in the name of God."

English Versions of Crusade Chronicles

Allen, S. J. and Emilie Amt, eds. *Crusades: A Reader.* Peterborough, Ontario: Broadview Press, 2003.

Clari, Robert de. *The Conquest of Constantinople.* Translated by Edgar Holmes McNeal. Medieval Academy Reprints for Teaching, 36. Toronto: University of Toronto Press, 1996.

Gabrieli, Francesco, ed. *Arab Historians of the Crusades.* Berkeley: University of California Press, 1984.

Villehardouin, Geoffrey de and Jean de Joinville. *Chronicles of the Crusades.* Translated by Margaret R. Shaw. New York: Viking Press, 1963.

Works about the Crusades

Maalouf, Amin. *The Crusades through Arab Eyes.* New York: Schocken Books, 1989.

Madden, Thomas F. *A Concise History of the Crusades.* Lanham, Md.: Rowman & Littlefield Publishing, 1999.

Peters, Edward M., ed. *The First Crusade.* Philadelphia: University of Pennsylvania Press, 1998.

Richard, Jean. *The Crusades, c.1071–c.1291.* Translated by Jean Birrell. Cambridge, U.K.: Cambridge University Press, 1999.

Vallejo, Yli Remo. *The Crusades.* Edited by Thor Johnson. Great Falls, Va.: AeroArt International, Inc., 2002.

D

Daibu, Lady (Kenreimon-in Ukyo no Daibu) (13th century) *poet, memoirist*

Lady Daibu lived during the decline of the Heian court in Japan, between the 12th and 13th century. Like most female writers of the Heian court, little is known of her life, including her real name. The first part of her name, Kenreimon-in, comes from the name of the empress she served as a lady-in-waiting. The second part of her name is the name of her male sponsor at court. Several of Lady Daibu's poems appeared in the imperial anthology *Shinchokusenshu* (1232), but she is mostly known for her memoirs, the *Kenrei Mon'in Ukyo no Daibu shu* (The Journal of Kenreimon-in Ukyo no Daibu, ca. 1233). Her writing can be studied in relation to other Japanese female court writers. The most famous of these writers is MURASAKI SHIKIBU, author of *The Tale of Genji* (ca. 1000).

Lady Daibu is not considered a first-rate writer by most critics, but her writing contains vivid descriptions of court life and moving reflections on her tragic affair with the imperial regent Taira no Sukemori. Although she never writes directly about political events, her words reflect the tumultuous times she lived in, particularly when she describes her despair at the death of her lover in battle. Her memoirs describe her personal experiences, interspersed with the poetry that these events inspired. She also includes poetry that she used to privately communicate with other members of court. She wrote short lyrical poems that used images from nature to express her emotions:

> *Unforgettable!*
> *That time I gazed*
> *At the morning glory,*
> *With the dawn moon in the sky—*
> *But would I had some way to forget!*

The sincerity of Lady Daibu's writing, together with her portrayal of life in uncertain times and her use of imagery to convey emotion, has given her a place in the history of world literature.

An English Version of a Work by Lady Daibu

The Poetic Memoirs of Lady Daibu. Edited and translated by Phillip Tudor Harries. Stanford, Calif.: Stanford University Press, 1980.

Daniel, Arnaut

See ARNAUT DANIEL.

Dante Alighieri (1265–1321) *poet, philosopher*

Dante Alighieri, known simply as Dante, was born in Florence, Italy, to Alighirro di Bellincione d'Alighiero, a notary, and his wife, Donna Bella, who died during her son's childhood. Although details of Dante's youth in Florence are scarce, it is likely that during his early years he received a standard Latin education, including schooling in the *Trivium* (grammar, logic, and rhetoric) and the *Quadrivium* (arithmetic, music, geometry, and astronomy). Dante eventually engaged in the advanced study of grammar and rhetoric under the tutelage of Brunetto LATINI, a renowned philosopher, poet, and politician.

Among his most well-known works are *La vita nuova* (*The New Life*, ca. 1292), *Convivio* (*Banquet*, 1304–1308), *Monarchia* (*Monarchy*, 1309–1312), and *La Divina Commedia* (*The Divine Comedy*, completed in 1321). *Banquet* was a philosophical piece comprised of 14 treatises containing the author's opinions on his own works. *Monarchy*, another Latin treatise, concerned Dante's views on the Roman Empire, the emperor, and the pope. Dante's greatest works, however, were *The New Life* and *The Divine Comedy*, the first of which was inspired by a childhood event.

When he was nine years old, he met a young girl named Beatrice Portinari (1266–90). This meeting would prove to be one of the two most important events in Dante's life—and an equally important event in the history of world literature. In an early collection of autobiographical poems and prose commentary entitled *The New Life* Dante describes the profound impact that meeting Beatrice had on him. "[From] that time forward," Dante reflects in that work's opening prose section, "Love ruled over my soul. . . ." Dante's love for Beatrice became a guiding force in his life and is considered the inspiration for his greatest sonnets and odes.

Dante and Beatrice were not destined to be together, however. On January 9, 1277, when Dante was only 11 years old, his father arranged for him to marry a nobleman's daughter, Gemma Donati, whose considerable dowry Dante's family received when the marriage ceremony finally took place, probably around 1285.

In 1290, when Dante was 25, Beatrice died. Despite having met her only twice, Beatrice's death propelled Dante into a state of profound despair. In *The New Life* the poet laments:

> To weep in pain and sigh in anguish
> destroys my heart wherever I find myself
>   alone,
> so that it would pain whoever heard me:
> and what my life has been, since
> my lady went to the new world,
> there is not a tongue that knows how to
>   tell it.

In a way, the remainder of Dante's life as a poet would be devoted to finding the "tongue" to describe both the impact that Beatrice had on his life and the state of his soul after she died. Although *The New Life* ends on a note of failure, because it closes with Dante's decision "to write no more of this blessed one until [he] could more worthily treat of her," he ultimately finds the language worthy of his subject in his greatest poetic achievement, *The Divine Comedy*.

Before writing *The Divine Comedy*, however, Dante endured a second life-altering loss, this time losing his status as a citizen of his beloved Florence. Dante belonged to the Guelphs, the party that controlled Florence at the time, but it was divided into two factions, the Blacks and the Whites, who constantly battled for political control. Dante was a member of the Whites, and in 1301 he went to Rome as part of a delegation to regain the support of Pope Boniface VIII. While Dante was away, the Blacks regained power in Florence and subsequently banished many of the Whites (including Dante) from the city. When the Blacks decreed that he would be executed if he returned to Florence, Dante went into permanent exile, leaving his wife, his four children, and his birthplace behind. He spent the rest of his life in different cities in Italy and other countries, and he died at Ravenna.

Critical Analysis

As scholar Robert Hollander notes, the premise on which Dante's poetic masterpiece *The Divine Comedy* is founded would be a difficult one to sell to a publisher today: "Take a not-very-successful (though respected), soon-to-be exiled civic leader and poet, then send him off to the afterworld for a week." Yet this is, succinctly put, the plot of *The Divine Comedy.* Dante's great poem is the fantastic story of his journey through Hell, Purgatory, and Paradise. And while Hollander's plot summary makes it sound like an unlikely candidate for inclusion among the world's greatest works of literature, *The Divine Comedy* is a poem of such power and beauty that critic Harold Bloom has been moved to rank Dante second only to Shakespeare among the Western world's literary figures: "When you read Dante or Shakespeare you experience the limits of art, and then you discover that the limits are extended or broken."

Dante's ability to transcend the traditional limits of art derives from his strength in three areas. First, as the *The Divine Comedy* illustrates, Dante is a master storyteller. The poem, divided into 100 cantos, takes the reader on a journey through Hell (*Inferno*), Purgatory (*Purgatorio*), and Paradise (*Paradiso*). The reader encounters various figures from the Christian religious tradition, history, literature, and Dante's own life, all of whom are woven into a compelling narrative structure. Even if a reader chooses to interpret *The Divine Comedy* primarily as a Christian allegory, he or she can hardly deny the allure of the literal level of the story. On this level, the poem is a spellbinding journey that rivals the great epics of HOMER in plot, characterization, and imagery. All of these narrative elements come together at the end of "The Inferno," as readers find themselves climbing with the poet and his guide, a shadow of the poet VIRGIL, through the afterworld, over the disgusting body of Satan. To escape Hell and enter Purgatory, Dante

and Virgil must literally and figuratively surmount the beast who

> . . . wept with six eyes, and the tears
>   beneath
> Over three chins with bloody slaver dropt.
> At each mouth he was tearing with his teeth
> A sinner, as is flax by heckle frayed.
>   (Canto XXXIV)

This vivid description is just one example of Dante's power as a poet. Not only is his language rich and vivid but he also maintains an elegant and challenging poetic structure throughout his long poem. Dante composed his verse in *terza rima,* an interlocking rhyme scheme in which the last word of the second line of each tercet (a group of three lines) rhymes with the first and third lines of the preceding tercet. In the original Italian, the opening lines of *The Divine Comedy* read:

> Nel mezzo del cammin di nostra vita
> mi ritrovai per una selva oscura
> ché la diritta via era smarrita.
> Ahi quanto a dir qual era è cosa dura
> esta selva selveggia e aspra e forte
> che nel pensier rinolva la paura!
>   (Canto I)

According to Robert Hollander, "Dante's invention of *terza rima* was, as Erich Auerbach observed, a brilliant solution for a narrative poem, for it both 'looses and binds,' at once bringing the verse to momentary conclusion and propelling it forward."

In addition to the poem's structure, Dante's use of an Italian vernacular (as opposed to Latin) was a significant poetic achievement because he demonstrated that a vernacular language could be a suitable vehicle for great literature. He makes this argument more completely in an unfinished work entitled *De vulgari eloquentia* (Eloquence in the Vernacular, 1303–07). The fact that he did use an Italian vernacular is one of the reasons that Dante called his work a "comedy"; this term distinguishes the poem from the tragic literature generally composed in Latin.

The third distinguishing strength of Dante's masterpiece is its spiritual vision. This is without question a Christian (specifically a Catholic) poem, and any reader must be impressed by the power of Dante's faith. The work opens with Dante lost in a dark wood at the midpoint of his life's journey, and it is ultimately Virgil and Beatrice (who takes over as his guide in Purgatory) who lead him from darkness and despair to the light and hope offered by God. (This upward, positive trajectory is the second reason the poem is called a "comedy.") The journey to salvation—in both a literal and an allegorical reading of the poem—is an arduous one that takes great strength, determination, and conviction. By the end of the poem, however, we, as readers, are thankful that Dante had the courage to undertake it and to allow us to share his experience. It is a testament to his brilliance as a poet that even those who do not share his religious convictions can appreciate the power and the beauty of his *Divine Comedy,* a work that is truly one of the landmarks of Western and world literature.

English Versions of Works by Dante Alighieri

Dante Alighieri's Divine Comedy. 6 vols. Translated by Mark Musa. Bloomington: Indiana University Press, 1997–2003.

The Divine Comedy: The Inferno, The Purgatorio, The Paradiso. Translated by John Ciardi. New York: New American Library, 2003.

The Portable Dante. Edited by Paolo Milano. New York: Penguin, 1975.

Works about Dante Alighieri

Auerbach, Erich. *Dante: Poet of the Secular World.* Chicago: University of Chicago Press, 1961.

Hollander, Robert. *Dante: A Life in Works.* New Haven, Conn.: Yale University Press, 2001.

O'Cuilleanain, Cormac, et al., eds. *Patterns in Dante.* Dublin: Four Courts Press, 2004.

Quinones, Ricardo J. *Dante Alighieri.* Boston: Twayne Publishers, 1979.

Daodejing

See LAOZI.

Daphnis and Chloë

See LONGUS.

Davanzati, Chiaro   (ca. 1235–ca. 1280)
poet

Chiaro Davanzati was born in Florence, in the Italian province of Tuscany. Though the dates of his birth and death are not known for certain, he is recorded as having fought in the Battle of Montaperi in 1260 and maintaining a residence in the Santa Maria quarter of Florence with his wife and five sons. His surviving work includes 64 *canzoni,* or lyric poems, and about 100 sonnets on everything from philosophy and religion to politics and love.

His early poetry shows Davanzati borrowing largely from the lyric traditions of the Provençal TROUBADOURS and the vernacular tradition of Sicily. The next phase of his poetry shows him participating, along with his contemporaries Guittone d'Arezzo and Guido Guinizelli, in the development of a poetic style that came to be known as the *dolce stil nuovo* (the "new sweet style"), used by later poets Guido Cavalcanti, Cino da Pistoia, and, most famously, DANTE ALIGHIERI. Davanzati's later and more mature poetry shows, in the words of one biographer, "conservative imagery, graceful phrasing, and new themes and sentiments inspired by personal experiences and ardent patriotism." As a whole, the body of his poetry shows the broad range of Davanzati's interests, his personal commitment to his Florentine homeland, his ability to skillfully use the standard poetic imagery and devices, and his willingness to explore themes personally important to him, particularly political and ideological issues.

Translator Kenneth McKenzie says the Davanzati "is at his best in poems of a semi-popular style, when he casts loose from the conventionality and the metrical intricacy of the Sicilians, and appears as a poet of the Florentine people." Davanzati's poetry received little attention after his death, and for centuries he was discussed only as a forerunner to Dante. However, current scholarly opinion now recognizes him as an important and accomplished poet in his own right.

An English Version of a Work by Davanzati

Goldin, Frederick, ed. *German and Italian Lyrics of the Middles Ages.* Garden City, N.Y.: Doubleday, 1973.

A Work about Davanzati

"Davanzati, Chiaro." In *Cassell Dictionary of Italian Literature.* Edited by Peter Bondanella and Julia Conaway, 127–128. London: Cassell, 1996.

David of Sassoun (ca. 10th–12th centuries)
epic poem

A medieval EPIC poem, *David of Sassoun* is the most widely cherished literary work of the Armenian people.

Armenians have lived in the eastern regions of present-day Turkey and adjacent areas since the second millennium B.C. Though exposed to many diverse cultural influences, the common people preserved their own language even while the aristocracy adopted Greek during the Hellenistic and Byzantine eras.

After the country adopted Christianity around A.D. 400, an alphabet was developed and a literature emerged using a standard literary tongue that survived up to the 19th century. ORAL LITERATURE, however, continued to flourish in the spoken dialects of the various regions. For most of its history, the *David* cycle existed solely in oral form, the possession of often poorly educated bards and storytellers from every region of historic Armenia who, as early as the fifth century, performed at pagan festivals.

The cycle, whose stories may partly be based on incidents in ninth- and 10th-century Armenia, probably reached its highest development during the 11th century. Armenians were then reeling from the onslaughts of the Seljuk Turks, and the glorious victories of the epic's heroes may have consoled and inspired them. It probably reached its final form in the 12th century.

In the second half of the 19th century, a nationalistic cultural revival began to champion the popular dialects, both in West Armenia (under Turkey) and East Armenia (under Russia). In 1874 an Armenian bishop recorded and published the first *David* tale, causing a literary sensation. Over the next few decades, scholars combed the mountains of Armenia looking for storytellers who could add episodes and complete the cycle, publishing some 50 different versions. From 1936 to 1951, a major project was conducted in Soviet Armenia that published 2,500 pages of variants. In 1939 a standard version was issued in a unified dialect, though under Soviet aegis the Christian religious aspect was downplayed.

The work is divided into four sections, each dealing with a different hero, or pair of heroes, fighting to defend the common folk of the Sassoun region. Scholars detect echoes from many different episodes in the country's history, from prebiblical days to the struggles against the Arab Muslim invaders in the early Middle Ages. However, the details are confused, with cities, countries, and kingdoms exchanging names and switching centuries. Thus, the work cannot be a reliable guide to historical events.

The chief inspiration for the character of David, who gives his name to the entire work, may well have been Hovnan of Khout. Hovnan was a peasant youth who led a successful rebellion of Christian Armenians against Arab overlords in the Sassoun region in A.D. 851.

The *David* cycle is written in a mixture of prose and poetry; the poetry, originally meant to be sung, has a fairly loose meter and rhyming pattern. Action predominates, described in compact, vivid prose with many metaphors taken from rural life.

Though the saga in explicitly Christian, it also alludes to pagan legendary and mythological themes and symbols, such as apparent references to soma, the intoxicating beverage of Indo-European deities. Scholars find echoes from Sumerian, Hittite, Indian, Persian, Greek, and biblical literature. On the other hand, many Armenian critics detect a particular Armenian national ethos, or value set, that brings all the elements together.

David and the other heroes all show a strong sense of justice and duty. They are egalitarian and have no use for wealth and power, they marry princesses but reject the accompanying crowns, and they are steadfast in defense of the oppressed.

David of Sassoun, in its various classic and popular versions, has remained an important cultural reference point for Armenians in the home country and in the diaspora. The character of David, often represented in paintings and sculpture, acts as the Armenian national hero.

English Versions of *David of Sassoun*

Shalian, Artin K. *David of Sassoun: The Armenian Folk Epic in Four Cycles.* Athens: Ohio University Press, 1964.

Tolegian, Aram. *David of Sassoun: Armenian Folk Epic.* New York: Bookman Associates, 1961.

Works about *David of Sassoun*

Surmelian, Leon. *Daredevils of Sassoun.* Denver, Colo.: Alan Swallow, 1964.

Dead Sea Scrolls (ca. 200 B.C.–A.D. 135)
religious texts

The Dead Sea Scrolls are a collection of ancient Jewish religious manuscripts, written mostly in Hebrew on leather (parchment) or papyrus. They were discovered in the 1940s and 1950s in caves at various spots along the Dead Sea and the Jordan River Valley. They include the earliest known texts of the Hebrew BIBLE as well as other documents that shed light on early Judaism and Christianity.

The scrolls rank among the most important literary and religious discoveries of the 20th century. The dramatic story of how they were found, the controversies surrounding their eventual release to the public, and their interpretation have only added to their renown.

In the winter of 1946–47, a group of Beduin shepherds were tending their flocks near the ancient ruin of Qumran near the northern end of the Dead Sea, in what was then the British Mandate of Palestine. High up the cliffs they chanced on the narrow opening of a cave. One of them managed to pass inside, and he retrieved some moldy ancient scrolls wrapped in cloth.

After some months, the scrolls were brought to the attention of antique dealers and scholars. Further explorations in the region eventually yielded five major manuscript sites, including well over one dozen separate caves. In all, more than 15,000 fragments were retrieved, which scholars have assembled into some 800 discrete books, some with multiple copies.

Most of the manuscripts came into the possession of a scholarly committee, which began analyzing the material and publishing major documents. The slow pace of publishing and the restricted access to the fragments led to charges of a conspiracy to withhold documents that might overturn traditional views of early Christianity or Rabbinic Judaism. However, when all the fragments were released in the 1990s by the Israel Antiquities Authority, which had inherited control during the Six-Day War in 1967, no new surprises were uncovered.

After the original discoveries were made in the caves near the Qumran ruins, archeologists spent several years poring over the site on the theory that the manuscripts found nearby were written or owned by the original residents of the ruins. Most scholars believe that the ruins, and thus the manuscripts, belonged to the Essenes, an ascetic, messianic sect of the Jews mentioned by Josephus and other historians of the time. Many of the manuscripts seem to reflect the beliefs and practices of a tightly knit monastery or religious community. These beliefs generally conform to what was previously known about the Essenes.

Other scholars theorized that the Qumrun manuscripts, whatever their date and origin, constituted a "library" that was taken in its entirety from the

Temple and placed in the caves for safekeeping during the first-century revolt against the Romans. Still another theory emerged in which the caves' residents were said to be Sudducees, another Jewish faction.

Archeologists were eventually able to determine dates for most of the manuscripts. Accurate radiocarbon testing confirmed earlier guesses based on analysis of the various Hebrew, Aramaic, and Greek scripts used in the scrolls. Artifacts like pottery and coins associated with some of the finds also helped in pinpointing their period of origin—or at least the time they were deposited in the caves.

The manuscripts were written from as early as the third century B.C. up to the early second century A.D., during the time of the Jewish rebellion led by Bar Kochba against the Romans. Most of the material dates to the first century B.C.

In terms of Christian history, this is the era that precedes and frames the lifetime of Jesus. For Jews, the same period saw the rise and fall of the last independent Jewish dynasties, the Roman conquest, and the destruction of the Temple in Jerusalem. It was also the time when Rabbinic Judaism arose (so called because rabbis took the place of the temple priests in leading the people).

The documents that comprise the Dead Sea Scrolls fall into three major categories: texts from the Hebrew Bible; sectarian texts probably relating to the Qumran community; and other material, also for the most part of a religious nature.

Some 25 percent of the documents are biblical. Apart from the Book of Esther, every single book of the Hebrew Bible is represented, from a single fragment in the case of *Ezra-Nehemiah* and *Chronicles* to a nearly complete book of Isaiah (also represented by 20 partial copies). Thirty-seven partial copies of *Psalms* were found at Qumran, as were over 80 copies of the Books of Moses—including one scroll with both *Genesis* and *Exodus.*

These Bible manuscripts are about 1,000 years older than any previously known texts. In addition to the standard books found in Jewish Bibles, several of the apocryphal books found in some Christian Bibles were also found. Taken together, the findings shed dramatic light on the process by which the Bible was standardized.

When scholars compared the various fragments of biblical books from the Dead Sea hoards with the earliest previously known Hebrew, Greek, and Samaritan Bible manuscripts, several patterns appeared. Perhaps most importantly, scholars found that the later the fragment was in date, the closer it resembled the standard Hebrew text. Fragments from the Bar Kochba era (ca. A.D. 135) are virtually identical to Bibles in print today. This gives dramatic confirmation to extra-biblical evidence in later Jewish works such as the TALMUD, which seems to point to a similar date for the "canonization" or standardization of the Bible.

The earlier scrolls and fragments show hundreds of differences from the standard Bibles of today, but most of these are minor variations that do not affect the meaning of particular verses, let alone the message of the books. These variations include differences in spelling, the addition or deletion of a word or short phrase, and obvious copying errors.

Some texts showed more significant differences, such as the addition of several previously unknown psalms and the occasional insertion of explanatory verses. Scholars have noticed three different "textual families," that is, groupings of texts with similar variations. Some have made a case that these families are those that gave birth to the Septuagint (the Greek translation produced in Egypt in the third century B.C.); the Hebrew text in use today; and the Samaritan Bible, still used by the tiny community of Samaritans in Israel. The nonbiblical texts cover a large variety of genres, including hymns, commentaries on biblical books, so-called pseudepigraphic works (books supposedly written by prominent biblical characters), wisdom literature, and legal documents.

Many of these texts, including several large scrolls, have been labeled "sectarian," as they refer to the beliefs and practices of the Qumran sect (perhaps the Essenes). Some of the major sectarian texts are (in the names scholars have given them)

The Rule of the Community (Manual of Discipline), *The War of the Sons of Light against the Sons of Darkness,* and a commentary on the prophet Habakkuk. The Temple scroll, which is largely devoted to a plan for the construction of an ideal Holy Temple, may be connected to the sect as well.

The Community Rule, which was found in one fairly long scroll as well as fragments of about 10 other copies, is considered to be one of the oldest documents of the sect, composed around 100 B.C. Designed to be used by the Guardians or Masters of the community, it contains instructions concerning religious ceremonies and the holiday calendar, rules for entering the community, and guidance in disciplinary and penal matters.

The War scroll, found in seven copies, prophesizes a 40-year struggle between the sons of light and the sons of darkness, possibly including the entire Gentile world. It goes into great detail about battle plans, weapons, tactics, prayers, and personnel. In the end, God's intervention will ensure the prearranged victory of the just. Scholars have found correspondences between this scroll, composed in the early or mid-first century B.C., and certain concepts and language found in the New Testament.

The Habakkuk commentary gives some details on the origins of the sect, perhaps as early as the early second century B.C., during the struggles between Jewish traditionalists and those who favored assimilation into Hellenistic culture. It describes the conflict between the Teacher of Righteousness (perhaps the founder of the sect and probably a temple priest of Jerusalem) and the corrupt Wicked Priest (apparently a ruler of Israel who persecuted the members of the sect).

The Copper scroll, so called because it is embossed on copper foil, has also aroused great curiosity and analysis. It describes 64 hiding places for a huge quantity of silver, gold, and ritual objects. Some scholars believe the scroll refers to the treasure of the Temple in Jerusalem, either somehow rescued from the destruction of A.D. 70, or collected in the years thereafter in anticipation of its ultimate reconstruction.

All of the scrolls and fragments are now in the public domain and housed in the archaeology wing of the Israel Museum in Jerusalem, providing sufficient material to keep scholars and historians busy for years to come.

English Versions of the Dead Sea Scrolls

The Complete Dead Sea Scrolls in English. Translated by Geza Vermes. New York: Penguin, 1998.

The Dead Sea Scrolls Bible: The Oldest Known Bible Translated for the First time into English. Edited by Martin Abegg, Jr., Peter Flint, and Eugene Ulrich. San Francisco: HarperSanFrancisco, 1999.

Dead Sea Scrolls Reader: Exegetical Texts. Edited by Donald W. Parry and Emanuel Tov. Herndon, Va.: Brill Academic Publishers, 2004.

Works about the Dead Sea Scrolls

Alon, Hagit, et al. *The Mystery of the Dead Sea Scrolls.* Philadelphia, Pa.: Jewish Publication Society, 2004.

Palumbo, Arthur E., Jr. *The Dead Sea Scrolls and the Personages of Early Christianity.* New York: Algora Publishing, 2004.

Schiffman, Lawrence H. *Reclaiming the Dead Sea Scrolls: The History of Judaism, the Background of Christianity, the Lost Library of Qumran.* Philadelphia: Jewish Publication Society, 1994.

Thiede, Carsten Peter. *The Dead Sea Scrolls and the Jewish Origins of Christianity.* New York: Palgrave, 2000.

VanderKam, James C. and Peter Flinit. *The Meaning of the Dead Sea Scrolls: Their Significance for Understanding the Bible, Judaism, and Christianity.* San Francisco: HarperSanFrancisco, 2002.

Yadin, Yigael. *The Temple Scroll.* New York: Random House, 1985.

Demosthenes (384–322 B.C.) *orator*

Demosthenes was born in Athens to a wealthy sword maker who died in 377 B.C. When he reached his majority and discovered that his guardians had misused their power and brought his estate to near bankruptcy, Demosthenes made his first public speech in a lawsuit against his guardians and won some damages. This was surprising, since he suffered from a severe speech impediment; stammering made his words hardly distinguishable, and he was often the object of ridicule.

Demosthenes, however, overcame this hardship. To improve his speech, he would go to the beach and shout over the roar of the waves or talk with his mouth full of pebbles. To avoid distractions, he built himself a place underground and remained there for months, training himself to speak properly. He even went so far as to shave half his head so that he would not be tempted to make a public appearance before he was ready.

All Demosthenes' efforts paid off. At age 25, he entered public life as an influential orator, speechwriter, and politician. He wrote speeches for clients in law courts, but those he wrote for the general public concerning important political and social issues are among his best works. He became not only a leading speaker in Athens' assembly, but also a spokesman for the military and for Athens' need to be prepared for war. So effective was he as an orator and political leader that he was eventually forced into exile to escape prosecution for treason.

Demosthenes' death was as illustrious as his life. Tracked down at a temple where he was hiding, he asked for permission to write a letter. The guards granted him this right, not knowing that he had poison hidden in his pen, and after finishing his last letter, he bit his pen and died.

About 60 of Demosthenes' orations survive today. Most of them, such as *Against Polycles* and *Against Apatourius,* denounce political figures, while others, such as *Against Aristocrates,* criticize a particular social class. His *Erotic Essay* reflects on the nature of physical attractiveness and the often destructive effect it has on people.

Demosthenes' best-known works are the eloquent speeches in which he bids Athenians to unite against King Philip of Macedon, who was then conquering Greece. These speeches became known as *Philippics* (351, 344, and 341 B.C.), the work for which he is most widely famed.

Critical Analysis

One of Demosthenes' best orations was *On the Crown,* which he wrote to defend Ctesiphon, another orator, against Aeschines' claim that Ctesiphon had broken the law by suggesting that Demosthenes be given a golden crown in honor of his speeches for Athenian freedom. As a result of this speech, Aeschines, Demosthenes' opponent in the assembly, was forced into exile.

Demosthenes wrote *On the Crown* using short, concise sentences and avoiding excessive literary figures that might have confused or distracted his listeners. He makes his thoughts clear by using repetition and explanation. The logically sound structure of the speech is combined with highly emotional appeals, as when Demosthenes refers to Aeschines as a "bombastic phrase-monger."

In Ancient Greece, an oration was not only a piece of literature but also a performance. Thus, to make his argument more visual, Demosthenes presents different documents as evidence and invites witnesses who support his point. He denounces Aeschines by alluding to his mother's promiscuous behavior. A brilliant politician and spokesman, Demosthenes characterizes Aeschines as an incompetent, disrespectful fool, while portraying himself as noble and wise: "I saw a man enslaving all mankind, and I stood in his way."

It is this image of Demosthenes that remains: a hero who dared to stand up against the overwhelming political powers and who appealed to his people with passionate, patriotic speeches. In *Demosthenes: Statesman and Orator,* Ian Worthington says that Demosthenes is "regarded as the best of the Greek orators whose works have survived today." For contemporary readers, Demosthenes' speeches are an invaluable source of knowledge about Ancient Greek society and culture.

English Versions of Works by Demosthenes
On the Crown. Edited by Harvey Yunis. Cambridge, U.K.: Cambridge University Press, 2001.
On the False Embassy (Oration 19). Edited by Douglas M. MacDowell. Oxford: Oxford University Press, 2000.

Works about Demosthenes

Gibson, Graig. *Interpreting a Classic: Demosthenes and His Ancient Commentators*. Berkeley: University of California Press, 2002.

Johnstone, Christopher Lyle, ed. *Theory, Text, Context: Issues in Greek Rhetoric and Oratory*. Albany: State University of New York Press, 1996.

Worthington, Ian, ed. *Demosthenes: Statesman and Orator*. London; New York: Routledge, 2000.

deus ex machina   *term*

Deus ex machina, a Latin term that means "god from the machine," refers to a theatrical device used in ancient Greek drama, most conspicuously in the fifth century B.C. by the tragedian EURIPIDES. At the end of a play, when the character's difficulties seem beyond resolution, a deity such as Apollo or Athena (the "god") soars onto the stage in a basket maneuvered by a mechanical contraption (the "machine"), untangles the plot, and extricates the protagonist.

In contemporary usage, the term refers to any extraordinary mechanism or intervention used to resolve a situation in a theatrical or literary work. Even in Euripides' time, the agent was not always a *deus*, or god. For example, his *Electra* tells the tale of the ill-fated and murderous house of Aetreus and of the final deadly acts that will bring the familial curse to an end. While the great general Agamemnon is fighting in the Trojan War, his daughter Electra and son Orestes, with some justification, slay their adulterous mother and her lover. Immediately, they are stricken and incapacitated by what they have done, at which point Zeus's sons Castor and Polydeuces (the deus ex machina) appear overhead to mete out the appropriate punishment: Electra is exiled, and Orestes is pursued by vengeful spirits.

In another of Euripides' plays, *Medea*, the protagonist is princess of Colchis and a sorceress who has tricked her father, murdered her brother, and fled her homeland, all to help her beloved Jason procure the mythic Golden Fleece. The self-serving Jason, however, has taken a Corinthian princess as his bride. Medea punishes him by slaying their two young sons. As Jason swears vengeance, Medea appears above the house in a dragon-drawn chariot, poised to travel to Athens and seek refuge with the old king Aegeus. For some critics of deus ex machina, this is an unsatisfactory resolution to the plot, because Medea does not solve the princess's problem; rather, she complicates it.

A more satisfactory use of deus ex machina is in Euripides' *Alcestis*. In this play, Admetus, king of Thessaly, is fated to die young. The god Apollo intervenes on his behalf by persuading Death to take a substitute. Death agrees, on the condition the substitution is voluntary. Admentus assumes his elderly parents will die in his stead, but it seems they are enjoying their twilight years and refuse. Alcestis, Admetus's wife, however, volunteers to die in his place. The legendary hero Heracles, godlike but not a deity, travels to the underworld, successfully wrestles Death, and, as the deus ex machina, returns the queen of Thessaly to life.

The use of external or improbable means to solve a dramatic problem is generally considered a clumsy plot device and suggests the dramatist was unable to resolve the story in a more acceptable dramaturgical fashion. In the fourth century B.C., the philosopher ARISTOTLE gave his opinion of the use of such a device in his *Poetics,* an instruction manual of sorts for aspiring tragedians:

> In portraying character, too, as in constructing the events, the poet should always look for what is either necessary or probable, so as to have a given agent speak or *act* either necessarily or probably, and [hence] to have one event occur after another either necessarily or probably. It is evident, then, that the resolutions of the plots, too, should come about from the plot itself and not by the use of *deus ex machina,* as in the *Medea.* . . .

Some contemporary Euripedean scholars have argued that he deliberately used the device to make a dramatic statement. These scholars suggest that Euripides used supernatural or superhuman forces to make an ironic comment on the events and to restore a sense of myth and the supernatural to his stories after the tragic meaning of the human drama was already conveyed. Regardless of the impact of the earliest uses of deus ex machina, the device has evolved throughout time to become the means by which the resolution is achieved in most stories in world literature.

Works Featuring Examples of Deus Ex Machina

Euripides. *Euripides I.* Translated by Richmond Lattimore, et al. Edited by David Grene and Richmond Lattimore. Chicago: University of Chicago Press, 1955.

Euripides. *Euripides V.* Translated by Emily Townsend Vermeule, et al. Edited by David Grene and Richmond Lattimore. Chicago: University of Chicago Press, 1959.

A Work about Deus Ex Machina

Porter, John R. *Studies in Euripides' Orestes.* Leiden, Netherlands: Brill Academic Publishers, 1994.

Diodorus (Diodorus Siculus) (ca. 90–21 B.C.) *historian*

Although the city-states of ancient Greece had lost their political independence by the first century B.C., their culture remained intellectually vibrant, producing many great writers and thinkers; in particular, Greek historical writing continued to flourish. One of the Greek historians who lived and worked during the time of Roman domination was Diodorus.

Diodorus was originally from Agyrium, a Greek city on the island of Sicily. He lived during the time of Julius CAESAR, AUGUSTUS, Mark Antony, and Cleopatra, and traveled extensively throughout his life in Asia, Egypt, Europe, and other countries, living part of the time in Rome. He is known today for the massive history he composed, titled *Bibliotheca Historica* (Historical Library). This work was nothing less than a massive effort to record the universal history of the part of the world known to

Greeks and Romans. In *Bibliotheca Historica,* Diodorus discusses the ancient civilizations of Egypt, the Middle East, and the Mediterranean.

It took Diodorus approximately 30 years to compile *Bibliotheca Historica.* He divided it into 40 volumes, beginning with the mythical origins of various civilizations and continuing until his own time. Many of these volumes have vanished, and only fragments exist of others. Volumes one through five and 11 through 20 have survived completely intact.

Compared to other classical historians, such as HERODOTUS and THUCYDIDES, Diodorus is not particularly skilled as a historian, showing minimal understanding of historical cause and effect and making little effort to substantiate his claims. Nevertheless, his work is important for the information it provides on the people, culture, and events of ancient civilization, including Alexander the Great, Ptolemy, Eumenes, Macedonius, Antigonus, the Gallic Wars, India, Iran, and details of the first few years of the Roman Empire. *Bibliotheca Historica* also provides information on the now-lost written works of Hecataeus of Abdera, Ctesias, and Megasthenes, and draws on other histories (such as those written by Ephorus, Philistus, Hieronymus of Cardia, Timaeus, Philinus, and Posidonius), thus giving historians a means by which they can compare and confirm historical information. The *Bibliotheca Historica* is also important for the vast amount of information Diodorus provides on Sicily, information that would otherwise be lost.

English Versions of Works by Diodorus

Antiquities of Egypt: A Translation, with Notes, of Book I of the Library of History of Diodorus Siculus. Translated by Edwin W. Murphy. Somerset, N.J.: Transaction Publishers, 1990.

Diodorus Siculus: The Reign of Philip. Translated by E. I. McQueen. London: Bristol Classical Press, 1995.

Works about Diodorus

Sacks, Kenneth S. *Diodorus Siculus and the First Century.* Princeton, N.J.: Princeton University Press, 1990.

Stylianou, P. J. *Historical Commentary on Diodorus Siculus: Book 15.* Oxford: Oxford University Press, 1999.

Dionysius of Halicarnassus (ca. first century B.C.) *historian*

Dionysius was a Greek from the city of Halicarnassus who traveled to Rome in the late first century B.C., when civil war was transforming the Republic into the Roman Empire. He worked as a teacher for some time but soon turned to writing history.

Unlike other classical historians who wrote during the reign of the Roman Emperors, among them PLUTARCH or LUCAN, Dionysius does not focus on simply telling a good story or extolling the virtues of the noble man. His writing engages social history, and he was particularly concerned with the question of the origin of Rome and its connections with Greece. He did not think highly of historians who chose to write about useless subjects, and he criticized those who were careless in how they obtained their information. For Dionysius, writing history was a serious business.

In his best-known work, *The Roman Antiquities,* Dionysius analyzes the various claims made by previous historians concerning the rise of Rome. He provides historical details of Rome to 264 B.C. and of the Etruscans, who inhabited Italy before the rise of Rome. This information is invaluable to modern historians, as the works of many writers whom Dionysius mentions have disappeared, and their contents are known only through him.

Dionysius believed that the founders of Rome were, in fact, Greeks. By popularizing this theory, he attempted to spread the idea that the Greeks and Romans were one people. Similarly, VIRGIL's *Aeniad* portrays Trojans as the founders of Rome. Dionysius wanted to represent the Roman Empire not as a conquering force but as a universal Greco-Roman civilization.

In addition to his history, Dionysius also wrote *The Arrangement of Words, Commentaries on the Attic Orators,* and *On Imitation.* These works about rhetoric and composition were not as popular as his historical writing at the time, but they provide an important insight into Roman culture and thought. Three literary letters that survive are also much studied as examples of Dionysius's critical thought.

Dionysius pioneered techniques still used by modern historians. Extremely careful in the use of his sources, he believed in the study of cause and effect, and he believed a strong knowledge of history was important to society at large.

English Versions of Works by Dionysius of Halicarnassus

Dionysius of Halicarnassus: Critical Essays. Translated by Stephen Usher. Cambridge, Mass.: Harvard University Press, 1976.
On Thucydides. Translated by Kendrick Pritchett. Berkeley: University of California Press, 1975.
The Roman Antiquities. Translated by Earnest Cary. Cambridge, Mass.: Harvard University Press, 1974.

Works about Dionysius of Halicarnassus

Bonner, Stanley. *The Literary Treatises of Dionysius of Halicarnassus: A Study in the Development of Critical Method.* Amsterdam: Adolf M. Hakkert, 1969.
Gabba, Emilio. *Dionysius and the History of Archaic Rome.* Berkeley: University of California Press, 1991.
Roberts, W. Rhys. *Dionysius of Halicarnassus: The Three Literary Letters.* New York: Garland Publishers, 1988.

Donzella, Compiuta (La Compiuta Donzella) (13th century) *poet*

Nothing is known about Compiuta Donzella except that she lived and wrote in Florence, Italy, in the early 13th century. This was the time of the TROUBADOURS, who were spreading a new type of lyric poetry first developed in southern France. Donzella most likely considered herself a *trobaritz,* one of the female troubadours, and her poetry shows a familiarity with the themes and poetic devices used by the troubadours in their Provençal lyrics.

Donzella is sometimes referred to as "La Compiuta Donzella," which may have been a pen name because it effectively means, in Italian, "an educated lady" or "a lady of perfection." This was not an unheard-of practice, and other female *trobairitz* wrote under assumed names. For a time some scholars doubted that La Compiuta was an actual person, since nothing about her true identity was known. However, the fact that three sonnets attributed to her survive in a manuscript of early Italian poetry suggests that she did indeed possess a poetic skill, and two contemporary references during her own time indicate that La Compiuta was known to her larger literate society. Two sonnets of Maestro Torrigiano, also of Florence, referring to "a lady skilled in poetry" and a lady who "tries to rhyme," are thought to be speaking of Donzella. Also, a passage in a letter written by the Tuscan poet Guittone d'Arezzo expresses great admiration for Donzella and her work.

Donzella's surviving poems show her using the motifs and images common to troubadour poetry with an individual freshness and sadness. One of her sonnets opens with the declaration "I wish to leave the world and serve but God" and goes on to poignantly document the disillusionment of an idealist who, in the words of editor Rinaldina Russell, feels "contempt for a corrupt and vicious world." In another poem, a love sonnet in the Provençal and Sicilian traditions, the female poet speaks with independence and self-determination, adopting the narrative stance frequently adopted by male poets to address her beloved, another poet.

In a third sonnet, set in the "season when the world is leaves and flowers," the poet contrasts the images of the joyous rebirth of spring with her private despair over a marriage being forced upon her by her father. The beauty of the season accentuates her sadness over the fact that she has no choice over her future. Taken together, Donzella's three poems explore the only two life paths available to a woman in 13th-century Italy—to marry or lead a life of holy seclusion. "These motifs," Russell says, "are a sad commentary on the destiny of this talented and soon-forgotten poet and on the options open to women in medieval society."

Partly because of the lack of information about her life, and partly because so few of her poems survive, very little scholarship exists on La Compiuta Donzella. Yet she is considered the first known woman writing in Italian and, as such, begins a long tradition of literate Italian women producing works of art and poetry. Despite her awareness of and discomfort with the limited roles available to women in medieval culture, Donzella managed to make her voice heard. She and the other *trobaritz* mark the origin of feminist literature in the vernacular as known to Western Europe.

An English Version of a Work by Compiuta Donzella

"In the season when the world puts out leaves and flowers." In *An Anthology of Ancient and Medieval Woman's Song*. Edited by Anne L. Klinck. New York: Palgrave Macmillan, 2004. 113.

A Work about Compiuta Donzella

Cassell Dictionary of Italian Literature. Edited by Peter Bondanella and Julia Conaway. London: Cassell, 1996: 140.

Edda (ca. 800–ca. 1250) *Icelandic literature collections*

The term *Edda* refers to two key collections of medieval Icelandic literature, frequently distinguished by age as well as genre. The *Elder Edda,* also called *Poetic Edda,* is a collection of poems composed by a series of anonymous poets between 800 and 1100 and written down in Iceland between 1150 and 1250. The surviving manuscript, which dates to 1270, contains 33 lays, or poems, describing figures and events from Norse mythology (*see* MYTHOLOGY, NORSE). Though some of the material is not Scandinavian, these poems, which were originally written in Old Icelandic, vividly portray the heroic and frequently violent world of the pre-Christian Scandinavian cultures.

The *Younger* or *Prose Edda* (ca. 1220) is a guide to early Scandinavian poetry and mythology. SNORRI STURLUSON composed this *Edda* in an effort to preserve the art of Icelandic poetry. Together, the three books—"The Tricking of Gylfi," "The Language of Poetry," and the "List of Verse Forms"—provide a systematic review of the poetic rules and forms in addition to a comprehensive discussion of Norse beliefs on the creation and end of the world as well as the doings of various Norse gods. Part of his discussion contains advice on kennings, a poetic device that uses a compound descriptor to convey the qualities of a person or thing. The kenning often serves as a striking metaphor, for instance calling the sea the "whale-road," a person's speech a "word-hoard," and chest a "heart-locker."

The *Poetic Edda* shares material with the Icelandic *Volsunga Saga* and the German *Nibelungenlied,* while tales of Norse gods and heroes contained within the *Prose Edda* have inspired artists for centuries. German composer Richard Wagner (1813–83) based his *Ring of the Nibelung* on the *Poetic Edda,* and writer J. R. R. Tolkien (1892–1973) drew widely from the Norse myths for *The Hobbit* and *The Lord of the Rings.*

English Versions of the *Edda*

The Poetic Edda, 2d ed. Translated by Lee Hollander. Austin: University of Texas Press, 1986.

The Poetic Edda. Translated by Carolyne Larrington. Oxford: Oxford University Press, 1999.

Sturluson, Snorri. *Edda.* Translated by Anthony Faulkes. Rutland, Vt.: Charles E. Tuttle, 2002.

———. *The Prose Edda: Tales from Norse Mythology.* Translated by Jean L. Young. Berkeley: University of California Press, 2002.

Works about the *Edda*

Acker, Paul and Carolyne Larrington. *The Poetic Edda: Essays on Old Norse Mythology.* New York: Garland Publishing, 2001.

Wawn, Andrew. *Northern Antiquity: The Post-medieval Reception of Edda and Saga.* London: Hisarlik Press, 1994.

El Cid

See CID, EL.

Ennius, Quintus (239–169 B.C.) *poet, playwright*

Considered the first of the great Latin poets, Quintus Ennius is often referred to as the father of Roman poetry. His writings were the first examples of EPIC and tragic poetry to be written in the Latin language, and his influence touched almost every Latin writer who came after him.

Ennius was born in the town of Rudiae, southern Italy, in a region where Greek and Latin culture came together. His education provided a healthy mixture of Greek and Roman influences. While serving in the Roman army during the Second Punic War, his poetry was discovered by the Roman politician Cato the Elder, who brought Ennius to live in Rome. After settling down in the capital, Ennius pursued his literary ambitions by writing poetry and plays, both tragic and comic. Although he supplemented his income by working as a teacher and translator, and despite his numerous connections with noble Romans, he lived in poverty.

Unfortunately, only fragments of Ennius's works survive. It is known that he wrote at least 20 plays, many in honor of mythological heroes such as Ajax and Achilles. He also wrote a poem in honor of Scipio Africanus, the great Roman hero of the Second Punic War. He is most remembered, however, for the *Annals,* a history of Rome in the form of an epic poem. It covers the entire history of Rome from its legendary foundation by Romulus to the defeat of Hannibal, but only 550 lines of the epic survive today. Its popularity during Ennius's time may have been due as much to its patriotic vision of Rome's destiny as to Ennius's metrical use of language, specifically the hexameter, and other poetic devices and forms that he borrowed from Greek literature.

Ennius set the standard of Latin literature for many years. His work combines Greek and Latin influences, which has greatly affected Latin literature throughout its existence. The work of many of the great Roman writers of later centuries, particularly VIRGIL and LUCRETIUS, would be profoundly shaped by Ennius's earlier writings.

English Versions of Works by Quintus Ennius

Annals of Quintus Ennius. Edited by Otto Skutch. Oxford: Oxford University Press, 1985.

The Tragedies of Ennius: The Fragments. Edited by H. D. Jocelyn. London: Cambridge University Press, 1967.

A Work about Quintus Ennius

Conte, Gian Biagio. "Ennius" in *Latin Literature: A History.* Translated by Joseph B. Solodow. Baltimore, Md.: Johns Hopkins University Press, 1999, 75–84.

epic *term*

An epic is a lengthy narrative poem recounting in lofty language the feats of a heroic personage whose achievements either contribute to the development of a race or nation or reflect the ideals of a culture. Typically, the narrative announces the moment in the story at which the epic begins and then proceeds chronologically to the tale's completion. The epic hero is characteristically courageous, chivalrous, and proud. He is also accomplished on the battlefield, a seeker of glory who fears disgrace more than death and who may be more than a little pessimistic about the fate of mankind. Other characteristic elements of an epic include a central mission or journey upon which the hero embarks; encounters with mythic beasts, sorcerers, or deities that may be either threatening or auspicious;

promises of immortality; and a descent into the underworld.

Epic poetry has its origins in the oral tradition of storytelling. In ancient times, minstrels would travel to the courts of noblemen and entertain their patrons by singing of great heroes and their exploits. Some of the poem was memorized and some was improvised, and the songsters often re-used fixed descriptions or expressions for recurring subjects, such as sunrises and sunsets, meals, and the equipping of a hero with weapons. Metrical patterns and specific rhythms were also employed to help bards remember the words.

According to classics scholar W. F. Jackson Knight, specific types of literature arise from different social conditions, and oral poetry pertaining to action and adventure tends to be generated in a heroic age. This, according to Knight, is a time when an emerging culture is influenced by a more sophisticated and advanced neighboring culture and spawns an audacious, individualistic upper class that thrives on warfare and glory. The deeds of the heroes of this time are retold and in later generations develop into an epic tradition. Ancient Babylonia, Greece, Germany, Britain, and other countries have all produced epic literature.

Epics may be divided into two types. Folk epics are those that accumulated over time from works of various unknown poets, while classical epics are the product of a single known author. By far the best-known folk epics are the *Iliad* and the *Odyssey* (both eighth century B.C.), attributed to the Greek poet HOMER. Both poems begin with the traditional invocation of the muse, along with a statement of the purpose of the work, and feature numerous references to supernatural phenomena and deities. True to the oral tradition, Homer used numerous stock phrases (such as "swift-footed Achilles," "resourceful Odysseus," "the wine-dark sea, and "rosy-fingered dawn") to create his epic adventures. The *Iliad* tells how the great Greek warrior Achilles, insulted by his army's leader during the Trojan War, withdraws from the battlefield to sulk in his tent with disastrous consequences for the Greeks. The *Odyssey* follows the hero Odysseus's adventure-filled and mishap-laden efforts to return home to Ithaca after the war with Troy.

Other well-known folk epics include GIL-GAMESH (ca. 2500–1300 B.C.), the first great epic ever written, which relates the exploits of a semi-divine Babylonian king; the MAHABHARATA (ca. 400 B.C.–ca. 400 A.D.), an ancient Indian poem centering around royal brothers who battled for the throne; BEOWULF (A.D. 900s), an Old English tale of a dragon-slaying warrior; KALEVALA, the 2,000-year-old Finnish national epic; *El Cid* (ca. 1207; see CID, EL), concerning a Castilian warrior; and the medieval romances SONG OF ROLAND (ca. 1130–70), about a paladin in Charlemagne's court, and NIBELUNGENLIED (12th century), based on German folk legend.

Among the important classical epics are VIRGIL's *Aeneid* (19 B.C.), whose protagonist is a Trojan hero; DANTE's *Divine Comedy* (1321), which takes the reader through hell, purgatory, and heaven; *The Faerie Queene* (1590–96) by Edmund Spenser, an allegory of moral virtues; and *Paradise Lost* (1667), John Milton's account of man's expulsion from the Garden of Eden.

See also EPIC OF SON-JARA.

English Versions of Epic Works

Gilgamesh: A Verse Narrative. Translated by Herbert Mason. Boston: Houghton Mifflin, 2003.

Homer. *The Anger of Achilles: Homer's Iliad.* Translated by Robert Graves. Garden City, N.Y.: Doubleday & Company, 1959.

———. *The Odyssey.* Translated by Robert Fagles. Introduction and notes by Bernard Knox. New York: Penguin, 1996.

The Ramayana: A Modern Retelling of the Great Indian Epic. Translated by Ramesh Menon. New York: North Point Press, 2004.

Virgil. *The Aenied.* Translated by David West. London: Penguin Books, Ltd., 1990.

Works about Epic Literature

Miller, Dean A. *Epic Hero.* Baltimore, Md.: Johns Hopkins University Press, 2002.

Yamamoto, Kumiko. *Oral Background of Persian Epics: Storytelling and Poetry.* Leiden, Netherlands: Brill Academic Publishers, 2003.

Epic of Son-Jara   (13th century)   *epic poem*

The *Epic of Son-Jara* records the deeds and exploits of Son-Jara, otherwise known as SUNDIATA, a 13th-century king and the legendary founder of Mali, a West African kingdom. The original *Epic of Son-Jara* was composed in the Mande language as an oral tale passed down by generations of griots to their descendants. It is a story that is not only recited orally in social functions but also performed in accompaniment with music and dance. The griots (*jeli* in Manding) are keepers of oral traditions and can be compared to the minstrel knights of medieval Europe as they sing of the heroic deeds of the kings of the past.

The EPIC opens with a praise venerating the bravery, glory, and powers of Son-Jara, followed by a narration of the casting of Satan out of paradise and the genealogies of various religious figures such as Adam, Noah, and Konde. Konde is the family name of the Buffalo-Woman, Sogolon Konde, who would later give birth to Son-Jara. The story of Son-Jara begins midway through the long poem.

The poem relates Son-Jara's struggle in his childhood to overcome his handicap (at his birth he is crippled by a curse), his kindness and generosity to his people, as well as his filial piety to his mother, Sogolon. Unfortunately the wicked Sassouma, jealous of both mother and son, forces them into exile. The travels strengthen Son-Jara's character and give him the opportunities to learn new ideas and skills. With the help of his faithful sisters, half brother, and friends, Son-Jara successfully defeats the evil sorcerer, Sumamuru, and returns to Mali in triumph.

The *Epic of Son-Jara* as narrated by Fa-Digi Sisoko offers valuable information on the function of the bard, or griot, in traditional Mali society. Sisoko, it is said, attended a reroofing ceremony in Kaaba, West Africa, which improved his status and made him able to recite and thus preserve the epic

of the hero king Son-Jara. Kaaba was and is still considered the sacred center of the world in Mande traditions. The importance of the griot as a social recorder and observer is also represented in the character of Kouyate, Son-Jara's own griot within the story. In addition to being an adviser and spokesperson, the *griot* functioned as a historian, recording the important deeds and events in a king's life and singing him hymns of praise as well as of chastisement when necessary. As John William Johnson observes in his translation of *Son-Jara,* the interaction between music and words are essential to the performance of the tale.

Predestination and the supernatural constitute two major themes in the poem. The importance of destiny is represented in the prophecy of Son-Jara's birth and his future greatness. The prophecy is revealed first by the two hunters who brought Sogolon Kunde to Fara Mangan, king of the Manden and the father of Son-Jara. It is challenged briefly when Son-Jara is found to be crippled, but he eventually overcomes his handicap and displays his extraordinary strength by wielding a giant iron staff. Perhaps the importance of predestination is best represented in the inevitable battle between Son-Jara and Sumamuru. Son-Jara must defeat the sorcerer-king to fulfill his destiny, and his victory over the latter is not perceived as a victory of good over evil but as a completion of his predestined task.

The theme of the supernatural surfaces throughout the story. Son-Jara's prowess is derived from his maternal and paternal inheritances. He inherits occult power from his mother, Sogolon, the wraith of the Buffalo-Woman; and he derives grace and knowledge from his father, the descendant of Muslim migrants tracing their ancestry back to Bilal, the second convert of MUHAMMAD. Due to his lineage, Son-Jara possesses the ability to wield occult powers without succumbing to evil. This attests to his great strength, both physically and psychologically.

The *Epic of Son-Jara,* besides being a literary masterpiece and a representation of the richness of West African oral tradition, also contains important information about Mande culture. As Johnson observes in the introduction to his translations, the *Epic of Son-Jara* is "indeed filled with descriptions and catalogues of cultural information useful to those wishing to understand the remarkable society from which this famous epic has emerged."

See also SUNDIATA, AN EPIC OF OLD MALI.

An English Version of the *Epic of Son-Jara*
Sisoko, Fa-Digi. *The Epic of Son-Jara: A West African Tradition*. Translated by John William Johnson. Bloomington: Indiana University Press, 1992.

A Work about the *Epic of Son-Jara*
Austen, Ralph A., ed. *In Search of Sunjata: The Mande Oral Epic as History, Literature, and Performance*. Indianapolis: Indiana University Press, 1999.

Epictetus (55–135) *philosopher*
Epictetus was born a Greek slave in the Roman Empire and suffered from a permanent physical disability. These circumstances might have influenced him to turn to the philosophy of Stoicism, which promoted stern acceptance of all the external life facts without complaint or regret. At age 33, Epictetus finally gained his freedom but was expelled from Rome by Emperor Domitian. He settled down as a teacher of his own school of philosophy in Nicopolis, Greece.

Epictetus's teachings exist in two works compiled by Arrian, one of his students and a Greek historian and philosopher. One, the *Encheiridion (Handbook)*, exists in its entirety; of the other, *Discourses of Epictetus*, only four of eight books survive.

In *Discourses*, Epictetus explores the development of self-discipline and moral stamina as a means of accepting one's fate. "The good or ill of a man lies within his own will," he states. He also believed that in spite of hardships, people could live happy lives by accepting everything that comes their way as temporary and passing: "Make the best use of what is in your power, and take the rest as it happens."

Epictetus's teachings of morality, humanity, and freedom greatly influenced Stoicism and affected a great number of later writers, such as George Chapman, John Dryden, and Matthew Arnold.

English Versions of Works by Epictetus
The Art of Living: The Classic Manual on Virtue, Happiness, and Effectiveness. Translated by Sharon Lebell. New York: HarperCollins, 2004.
Discourses. Book I. Translated by Robert F. Dobbin. Oxford: Oxford University Press, 1998.
Enchiridion. Translated by George Long. Buffalo, N.Y.: Prometheus Books, 1991.
Virtue and Happiness: The Manual of Epictetus. Calligraphy by Claude Mediavilla. New York: Random House, 2003.

Works about Epictetus
Lillegard, Norman. *On Epictetus*. Florence, Ky.: Wadsworth Publishers, 2001.
Long, A. A. *Epictetus: A Stoic and Socratic Guide to Life*. Oxford: Oxford University Press, 2002.

Epicurus (341–270 B.C.) *philosopher*
Born on the island of Samos (in the Aegean Sea) to father Neocles and mother Chaerestrate, Epicurus was raised on a commune and later trained as a boy-soldier for the Athenian military. In approximately 306 B.C., he found his way to the city of Athens, where he established the center of his philosophical school in the garden of his home. The school attracted a devoted group of followers who separated themselves from the influences of city life and doggedly practiced the tenets of Epicureanism, the school of thought named for its founder. Epicureanism bases itself on the beliefs that man's existence is characterized by mortality; that the universe came about accidentally rather than as a result of divine design; and, perhaps most famously, that the pursuit of intellectual pleasure marks a fulfilled life.

Because its teachings flew in the face of more typical ascetic philosophies, some looked down on the Epicurean way. The Stoics, for instance, subscribing to a system of thought developed by Zeno around 308 B.C., believed that humans should seek to free themselves from passion and calmly endure all events as the decree of a divine will. Stoics regarded Epicureans as little more than flagrant hedonists, and critics purposely misunderstood Epicurus's teachings as instructions to blindly pursue one's every whim.

Still, Epicurus remains one of the most studied of the ancient thinkers, and scholarly investigations document that he produced more work than any other philosopher of his day—in total, 300 manuscripts covering topics from physics to love. Only a handful of these documents remain, all of which are included in *Lives of Eminent Philosophers, Book X* (translated by R. D. Hicks, Harvard University Press, 1925). We have gained a more comprehensive understanding of Epicurean philosophy, however, through the famed Latin poem by Lucretius, *De rerum natura* (On the Nature of Things).

Epicurus prioritized moral philosophy above all other categories of the discipline, as it concerns itself with how humans may become and remain happy. Pleasure, the main element of mortal happiness, comes about not when it is obsessively and inexhaustibly pursued, but when one's present desires are adequately satisfied and when these pleasures counterbalance the pains that inevitably accompany them. Philosophical study best cultivates the healthy quest for pleasure, since philosophy encourages the intellectual contemplation of corporeal pleasure rather than the actual acts of satisfying desires, which, Epicureanism argues, is less important than metaphysical rumination.

Famous works by Epicurus include *Letter to Herodotus,* a treatise on natural philosophy; *Letter to Pythocles,* which reflects on astronomy and meteorology; and *Letter to Menoeceus,* the definitive work of Epicurean moral philosophy. In this work, Epicurus makes clear his belief that the individual, and not a pantheon of ancient deities, retains the power to determine the course of his or her life. With the directness of a true metaphysician, Epicurus encapsulates his school of thought in *Menoeceus* 128: "We say that pleasure is the beginning and end of living happily."

English Versions of Works by Epicurus

The Epicurus Reader: Selected Writings and Testimonia. Edited by Brad Inwood and Lloyd P. Gerson. Introduction by D. S. Hutchinson. Indianapolis, Ind.: Hackett Publishing, 1997.
Fragments. Buffalo, N.Y.: Prometheus Books, 1992.

Works about Epicurus

De Witt, N. W. *Epicurus and His Philosophy.* Minneapolis: University of Minnesota Press, 1954.
Jones, Howard. *The Epicurean Tradition.* New York: Routledge, 1989.

Eschenbach, Wolfram von
See WOLFRAM VON ESCHENBACH.

Euclid (fl. ca. 300 B.C.) *mathematician*

Euclid lived in the time of the Egyptian king Ptolemy I, who had been a general in the army of Alexander the Great. Alexander's conquests had taken him to Egypt, where he founded the city of Alexandria on the Nile Delta in 332 B.C. The metropolis flourished, accumulating half a million residents and becoming the world's seat of scientific and literary scholarship. Among its chief attractions was the Alexandrian Library, which boasted more than 500,000 Greek manuscripts and translations.

Euclid, who probably received his mathematical education in Athens from followers of PLATO, was among the scholars drawn to Alexandria's offerings, and he established a school of mathematics there. It is said that one of his pupils asked Euclid what advantage he would gain by learning geometry. Euclid instructed his slave to give the boy a threepence, "since he must make gain out of what he learns."

The world's most famous geometer did not discover or invent the laws of geometry, as his theorems and proofs came from the existing body of Greek knowledge. Rather, his genius lay in organizing and presenting them in a logical fashion. *Stoicheia,* or *Elements,* totaling 13 books, is Euclid's masterpiece. The first six books cover plane geometry (straight lines, intersection of lines, angles), and the last three cover solid geometry (pyramids, cones, cylinders, spheres). The middle books address such subjects as ratios, proportions, magnitudes, and prime numbers.

Euclid begins *Elements* with 25 definitions of points, lines, plane surfaces, circles, parallels, and other terms. This is followed by a list of five postulates, which assume that it is possible, for instance, to draw a line from one point to another; and five axioms, such as "Things which are equal to the same things are also equal to one another" and "The whole is greater than the part." From these fundamentals, the first proposition—"On a given finite straight line to construct an equilateral triangle"—is demonstrated. From these elements plus the proven first proposition, the second proposition may be demonstrated, and so on. Each new proposition can be traced to the previously proven propositions on which it is based, all the way back to Euclid's initial descriptions of assumptions and self-evident truths. There are a total of 465 propositions. Ptolemy once wondered whether there was a shorter way to reach these invaluable conclusions, to which Euclid replied, "There is no royal road to geometry."

In addition to *Elements,* Euclid published several other less-famous works. *Fallacies,* no longer extant, provides methods for detecting illogical conclusions; *Data* proves that if certain magnitudes in a geometric figure are given, other magnitudes may be deduced; *Figures* shows how to divide figures proportionally; *Surface-loci* concerns curved surfaces; *Conics* studies cones; *Optics* addresses visual perspective; *Elements of Music* is based on Phythagorean theory; and in his pioneering work *Phenomena,* Euclid applies spheric geometry to astronomy.

Through the centuries, Euclid's *Elements* has appeared in more than 2,000 different versions. According to William Dunham, author of *Journey through Genius* (1991), "This work had a profound impact on Western thought as it was studied, analyzed, and edited for century upon century, down

to modern times. It has been said that of all books from Western civilization, only the Bible has received more intense scrutiny than Euclid's *Elements.*" Great minds from Archimedes and CICERO to Isaac Newton, Napoleon, and Lincoln have studied this classic work, and it remains the definitive geometry text in many classrooms.

English Versions of Works by Euclid

Euclid: The Thirteen Books of the Elements. Translated by Sir Thomas L. Heath. New York: Dover Publications, 1908.

Euclid's Phenomenon: A Translation and Study of a Hellenistic Treatise in Spherical Astronomy. Translated by Robert S. Thomas. Edited by J. L. Berggren. New York: Garland, 1996.

Works about Euclid

Artmann, Benno. *Euclid: The Creation of Mathematics.* New York: Springer-Verlag, 1999.

Mlodinow, Leonard. *Euclid's Window: The Story of Geometry from Parallel Lines to Hyperspace.* New York: Simon & Schuster, 2002.

Euripides (ca. 484–406 B.C.) *playwright*

Euripides was born on the Greek island of Salamis near Athens into a reasonably prosperous family. He made his home there, most likely on an estate owned by his father, and it is said he penned many of his dramas in a seaside cave. He was married twice, both times unhappily, and had three sons. A scholar and an intellectual, Euripides counted among his friends some of the leading philosophers of the day, including SOCRATES, an admirer of his plays; and the Sophist Protagoras, who debuted his agnostic work "Of the Gods" at Euripides' home.

Euripides saw roughly 88 of his plays produced, but he was honored at the Greek drama festivals only four times. Visionary and avant-garde, Euripides' plays reflected his unorthodox views, which were not shared by the general public during his lifetime. He was soundly ridiculed, and the comic playwright ARISTOPHANES parodied his plays in *The Thesmophoriazousai* (411 B.C.), which includes a group of women conspiring to punish Euripides for his depiction of deranged female characters.

Around 408 B.C., Euripides, an embittered, dispirited old man, went into self-imposed exile at the court of Archelaus of Macedon, where he wrote his masterpiece *The Bacchae*. There he died. His son Euripides the Younger produced the dramatist's final plays posthumously in Athens, where they won the prizes that had proven so elusive when their author was alive. It is said that the tragedian SOPHOCLES clad his own actors in mourning upon learning of his great rival's death.

Euripides was an iconoclast from the outset. He did not treat with the traditional reverence the legends that were a playwright's source material. Instead, he manipulated and reinterpreted them and introduced within that context the conflict between fate and free will. The "bad boy of Athenian drama," as Euripidean scholar Daniel Mendelsohn calls him, Euripides "questioned the established Olympian pantheon," slyly rearranging "traditional mythic material in bitter fables" and deconstructing tragic conventions. He also attacked traditional Greek customs and ideas, such as the treatment of women as inferior, the shaming of illegitimate children, the practice of slavery, and the glory of war.

Euripides' greatest contribution to dramatic art is his penetrating character studies, psychological analyses that investigate how human beings behave when they are subjected to sudden ill fortune. He creates pathos without descending to the maudlin or sentimental. The philosopher ARISTOTLE called Euripides the most tragic of the tragedians.

Improbably enough, Euripides' oldest surviving work, *Alcestis* (438 B.C.), is a comic drama. In this play, as in *Electra* (413 B.C.) and *Medea* (431 B.C.), Euripides uses DEUS EX MACHINA, a literary device in which the gods appear or an unexpected event occurs to resolve the conflict.

Other tragedies by Euripides include *Children of Heracles* (ca. 429 B.C.), which follows Heracles' disinherited family, who are persecuted by the king of Argos; *Hippolytus* (428 B.C.), in which a vengeful god causes a queen to fall in love with her stepson; *Hecuba* (ca. 424 B.C.), in which the Queen of Troy is driven mad by the brutality and injustice of the Trojan War and exacts violent revenge; and *Suppliant Women* (422 B.C.), which dramatizes the pleas of the mothers of fallen soldiers to bury their sons' bodies.

Euripides' later plays include *The Trojan Women* (415 B.C.), another compelling indictment of war. According to writer Erich Segal, "The ruthless tyrant Alexander of Pharae was so ashamed to be crying at the sorrows of Hecuba that he had to leave the theater before *The Trojan Women* was over."

Critical Analysis

The Bacchae (also *The Bacchants*, 408–406 B.C.) features a well-constructed plot in which the title characters are the priestesses and female worshipers of Bacchus, also known as Dionysis. Dionysis is the offspring of Zeus and of Semele, the deceased daughter of Cadmus, the Phoenician prince who founded Thebes.

Dionysis is a young and new god. When the play opens, he has returned to Thebes from his travels in the Orient. Slander against Semele is rife in the land of Dionysis' birth; the Thebans say that Zeus is not the father of Dionysis, that Cadmus perpetrated that rumor to save his daughter's good name, and that Dionysis is therefore not of divine birth.

To teach the city a lesson and assert his mystical powers, Dionysis has bewitched the women of Thebes, and the city "shrills and echoes to [their] cries":

> I bound the fawn-skin to the women's flesh
> and armed their hands with shafts of ivy. . . .
> I have stung them with a frenzy, hounded them
> from home up to the mountains where they
> wander, crazed of mind and compelled to wear
> my orgies' livery. . . .

Dionysis, disguised, appears in the city, where he is ill-treated by the young king Pentheus. Pentheus refuses to recognize Dionysis as a god, failing to realize that the stranger he repeatedly attempts to shackle and imprison, whose "girlish curls" he has forcibly shorn, is indeed the deity.

After repeated confrontations, Dionysis finally hypnotizes Pentheus into donning the outlandish attire of the Bacchae, complete with a blond wig, and a possessed Pentheus flees to the mountains to join the revelers. There, as a messenger later recounts in garish detail, Pentheus's own mother, Agave, "foaming at the mouth and her crazed eyes rolling with frenzy," leads a pack of madwomen who rip him limb from limb. In a ghoulish climax, Agave picks up her dead son's disembodied head and impales it on her staff. As she is released from the Dionysian spell and recognizes her trophy, Agave sees "the greatest grief there is," and the wretched woman is banished from Thebes.

The play demonstrates that the irrational, amoral, ferocious, chaotic forces of nature, as symbolized by Dionysis, can wreak hideous destruction if they are denied. Pentheus is a callow youth and vulnerable to the dangers of his own lack of self-knowledge. He rejects the god instead of embracing the primitive part of himself. According to translator William Arrowsmith, when Pentheus becomes a parody of Dionysis, "we see in his costume and madness not merely his complete humiliation but the total loss of identity the change implies."

Arrowsmith pronounces *The Bacchae* "a masterpiece: a play which, for dramatic turbulence and comprehensiveness and the sheer power of its poetry, is unmatched by any except the very greatest among ancient and modern tragedies."

Euripides' plays are frequently produced. His contemporary attitudes, social criticism, psychological insights, and especially his humanity make his work timeless.

English Versions of Works by Euripides

Euripides. Translated by Anne Marie Albertazzi. Edited by Harold Bloom. Langhorne, Pa.: Chelsea House Publishers, 2002.

Euripides I. Translated by Richmond Lattimore et al. Edited by David Grene and Richmond Lattimore. Chicago: University of Chicago Press, 1955.

Euripides' Alcestis. Notes by H. M. Roisman and C. A. Luschnig. Norman: University of Oklahoma Press, 2003.

Medea and Other Plays. Translated by John Davie. Introduction by Richard Rutherford. New York: Penguin Classics, 2003.

Works about Euripides

Conacher, D. J. *Euripidean Drama: Myth, Theme, and Structure.* Toronto: University of Toronto Press, 1967.

Mendelsohn, Daniel. *Gender and the City in Euripides' Political Plays.* Oxford: Oxford University Press, 2003.

Zacharia, Katerina. *Converging Truths: Euripides' Ion and the Athenian Quest for Self-Definition.* Leiden, Netherlands: Brill Academic Publishers, 2003.

Fan Chengda (Fan Ch'eng-t'a)
(1126–1193) *poet, travel writer*

Fan Chengda is one of the great poets of the southern Song (Sung) dynasty in China. He lived during a period of great political transition following the Qin (Ch'in) dynasty's conquest of the northern portion of the Song dynasty. He passed the important *jinshi* (*chin shih*) civil service examination for placement in the imperial bureaucracy in 1154. His friend and fellow poet, YANG WANLI, also passed the examination that year, and the two maintained a literary correspondence throughout their lives.

Fan Chengda's temperament and literary ability helped him to advance to high government positions during his career. In 1170 he became an ambassador to the Qin court in Beijing (Peking). This appointment served as the basis for one of his many travel writings, *Lanpei lu* (Lan-p'ei lu; Register of grasping the carriage reins). His travel writings provide a glimpse of the day-to-day life of a government official of the era and detail the local folklore, social and economic conditions, and natural wonders of the region. They also show Fan Chengda's familiarity with the works of earlier writers such as LI BAI and SU SHI.

Fan Chengda, like Yang Wanli and another friend and contemporary Lu Yu, achieved his greatest fame as a poet. His poetry combines Confucian, Buddhist, and Taoist elements while reflecting on nature and social concerns. Fan Chengda's poems consist of seven-character verses brimming with content. Some sing the praises of honest civil servants, others describe northern landscapes while infused with politics, such as the poem entitled "The Streets":

> *Nearby runs Heavenly Street*
> *Where elderly dwellers still await his*
>   *majesty*
> *They hold back tears and question his*
>   *envoy*
> *Shall we one day see his triumphal return?*

Fan Chengda's series of 60 poems, *Impromptu Verses on the Four Seasons of the Countryside*, is widely available in English translation.

English Versions of Works by Fan Chengda

Four Seasons of Field and Garden: Sixty Impromptu Poems. Translated by Lois Baker. Pueblo, Colo.: Passeggiata Press, 1997.

The Golden Year of Fan Chengda. Translated by Gerald Bullett. Cambridge, U.K.: Cambridge University Press, 1946.

Stone Lake: The Poetry of Fan Chengda. Translated and edited by J. D. Schmidt. Cambridge, U.K.: Cambridge University Press, 1992.

Farazdaq, al- (nickname of Tammām ibn Ghalib Abū Firās) (ca. 640–728) *poet*

Tammām ibn Ghālib Abū Firās, or al-Farazdaq ("lump of dough"), was one of the most prominent and widely popular of the "court poets" of the Ummayad, or early Muslim period. He was known for his dissolute life as well as his brilliantly insulting *hija* (lampooning).

Born and raised among the Tamim tribal confederacy in eastern Arabia, Farazdaq spent most of his career in the city of Basra in southern Iraq. At one point, he was forced to flee to Medina after choosing a too-powerful target for one of his *hija,* but he was expelled from Medina as well after a particularly indiscrete adulterous escapade.

Farazdaq made his living by writing fawning panegyrics (superlative praises) for the Ummayad caliphs and viceroys and by winning the patronage of other wealthy men who paid dearly to keep clear of his vicious pen. He was also an enthusiastic participant in Basra's intellectual and social life. According to some traditions, he was a supporter of ʿALĪ IBN ABĪ TALĪB, the murdered caliph, and was jailed for a while at the age of 70 for supporting ʿAli's grandson Zayn.

Farazdaq's personal life was stormy, which is not surprising in light of the venom and bragging found in his poetry. He had six or seven wives at various times, but none brought him happiness. The decades-long drama of his marriage with his cousin al-Nawar bint Aʿyun and then his longing for her and regrets after their divorce provided the subject of many of the poems in his *Divan.* "The repentance of Farazdaq" became a popular expression, fed by such lines as "She was my Paradise from which I was exiled, / like Adam when he rebelled against his Lord."

The poet is quite frank in describing his immoral personal life. Departing from the Arabic tradition of *ghazal* lyrics, which often depict passionate, unrequited love, Farazdaq's poems do not idealize his lovers nor show infatuation for them.

Farazdaq was an energetic, prolific writer whose poems display a rough style and diction as well as an awkward syntax. Some critics decry these characteristics as poetic incompetence, a clumsy attempt to exploit the rapid changes that were emerging in spoken Arabic. Others speculate that the poet was simply trying to update the literary language, in keeping with the brash and cosmopolitan urban life of the new Islamic Empire. Indeed, he was among the first generation of Arab poets to work in the cities and towns of Iraq and Syria, rather than the desert of the Bedouin.

Farazdaq's enduring fame, however, derives from a 40-year *naqa'id* (literary feud) that he pursued with rival poet Jarir ibn ʿAtiyya. The poems that resulted comprise the *Naqaith of Jarir and al-Farazdaq.* Although Arabic poetry was only just beginning to be written down in this era, the streams of rhymed, metered insults and obscenities that poured forth from the combatants were repeated by thousands of supporters of the two poets all across the Ummayad realm. The feud was originally based on tribal and political disputes, but it eventually became a debate over literary style. Arab literary circles have continued to debate the relative merits of the two camps ever since.

Farazdaq played a key role in developing Arabic literature from its spare desert origins to a vehicle more suitable for an urban-based empire. His sometimes-profane spirit won a wide mass audience for poetry in the new Islamic civilization.

An English Version of a Work by al-Farazdaq
The Naqaith of Jarir and al-Farazdaq. Translated by Arthur Wormhoudt. Oskaloosa, Iowa: William Penn College, 1974.

A Work about al-Farazdaq
Irwin, Robert. *Night & Horses & the Desert.* Woodstock, N.Y.: Overlook Press, 2000, 45–47, 56, 67.

Farīd od-Dīn

See 'ATTAR, FARĪD OD-DĪN.

Firdawsī (Abū ol-Qāsem Mansūr Firdousi) (ca. 935–1020 or 1026) *poet*

Firdawsī is considered the national poet of Persia. As author of the great epic the SHAHNAMEH (Book of Kings), he has been an enduring source of pride and entertainment to Iranians for more than 1,000 years.

Firdawsī was born in Tus, near present-day Mashhad, in the Khorasan region of Iran, and was apparently a modest landowner. To earn money for his daughter's dowry, he decided to write an epic poem devoted to Persian history. He planned to present it to the local governor, Abū Mansūr, a descendant of the old Sassanian royal dynasty and a generous patron of the arts.

Several of Firdawsī's immediate literary predecessors had been engaged in an attempt to free Persian literary language of the many Arabic words that had entered the language in the centuries following the Arab conquest in the seventh century. At the same time, a tradition of prose epics had emerged, celebrating the ancient glories of the Persian Empire. Firdawsī based his *Shahnameh* on one such prose epic. Like its predecessor, his poem was written in pure Pahlavi, a Middle Persian dialect. This has kept the work readable to the present day.

Firdawsī admitted that he built the poem's 60,000 couplets around an original core of 1,000 lines written by an earlier poet. This may have been a ruse to protect the poet from charges of pagan heresy, since the poem extols Zoroastrianism, the official religion of Persia before Islam.

The *Shahnameh* begins with the creation of the universe and ends with the defeat of Yazdigard, the last Sassanian king. The mass of material in the 50 intervening episodes is less a systematic history than a collection of legendary tales, historical exposition, lyrical interludes, and love stories. The heroes, all men, are larger than life and live and rule for hundreds of years. The chief hero is the fierce Rustam: "On the day of battle that worthy hero with sword, dagger, mace and lasso / Cut, tore, broke and bound, the heads, breasts, legs and hands of his foes." Rustam's many battles were won astride his horse Rakhsh. The horse's eyesight was so keen he could see an ant crawling on a piece of black felt two miles away on a dark night. The pair are often depicted in Persian miniatures.

Despite the storybook tone of the poem, Firdawsī includes many interesting details about ordinary life and material culture, especially in the Sassanian period, information which might otherwise have been lost to history.

More than 30 years after he began, Firdawsī completed the epic in 1010. By this time, a Turkish sultan, Mahmud of Ghazna, ruled Khurasan. Mahmud accepted the work but paid a paltry sum of 20,000 dirhams. He may have believed the charges that Firdawsī was a Shi'ite heretic, and he may have been unsympathetic to Persian national feeling. In a rage, Firdawsī gave the money away to a bath attendant and a beer seller. He then penned a 1,000-line satirical attack on Mahmud, which is still read with enjoyment today as a model of the genre. He then had to flee until the sultan's anger subsided. Some years later the sultan repented, but the 60,000-dirham prize came too late; the 90-year-old poet had died shortly before.

Firdawsī is revered by Iranians as one of the heroes of Persian culture. He is also recognized by Muslims in general as one of the greatest figures in Islamic cultural history, even though he never hesitated to honor pre-Islamic national and religious traditions.

Anthologies Containing English Translations of Works by Firdawsī

Hasan, Hadi. *A Golden Treasury of Persian Poetry.* Delhi, India: Ministry of Information and Broadcasting, 1986.

Arberry, A. J. *Persian Poetry: An Anthology of Verse Translations.* New York: E.P. Dutton, 1954.

Works about Firdawsī

Arberry, A. J. "II. From the Beginnings to Firdawsi" in *Classical Persian Literature*. London: Taylor & Francis, 1994, 42–52.

Thackston, Wheeler M. *A Millennium of Classical Persian Poetry*. Bethesda, Md.: Iranbooks, 1994.

Francis of Assisi, Saint (Francesco di Pietro di Bernardone) (ca. 1181–1226)
religious writer, poet

Francesco di Pietro di Bernardone was born in Assisi, Italy, to Pietro di Bernardone, a wealthy cloth merchant, and Madonna Pica di Bernardone. At the grammar school in Assisi, Francis learned only enough Latin to read the Psalter. The lively young man's imagination was aroused more by *chansons de geste* like the SONG OF ROLAND and the works of the TROUBADOURS.

Francis hoped to find glory as a knight, but in his first battle, with the neighboring town of Perugia, he was captured and imprisoned. Released after a year, he fell ill and almost died. When he recovered, he began to question his previous life and started caring for the lepers he had previously shunned. Finally he gave up all his possessions and began to serve God. In 1209, Francis and a few companions obtained Pope Innocent III's permission for their way of life, and they became known as the Order of the Friars Minor ("Lesser Brothers"), or the Franciscan Order. Inspired by hearing Francis preach, Clare of Assisi, the daughter of a count, left her home, took religious vows, and founded the Order of the Poor Clares, the sister order to the Franciscans.

Francis loved all nature and even preached to the birds, but most of all he pleaded for peace among the feuding factions in the Italian cities. He particularly stressed that greed for riches was the root cause of war. In 1219, he visited Egypt during the Fifth Crusade (*see* CRUSADES) in hopes of making peace between Christians and Muslims. Ill on his return, he devoted his last years to prayer. In 1224, while he was meditating on Mt. Alverna in Tuscany, the stigmata, or the marks of the passion of Christ, reportedly appeared on his body.

Francis believed that actions were more important than words. In his *Admonitions* to the friars, he said: "The saints have accomplished great things and we want only to receive glory and honor by recounting them." This may be why he left only a few short writings, most of which were dictated to scribes. His Latin works include the two rules for his order, *Admonitions,* some letters and prayers, his *Testament,* and a poem for Clare (later Saint Clare) and her sisters.

All of Francis's works are marked by poetic imagery, deep knowledge of the Bible and the courteous language of CHIVALRY. His most famous work, the *Canticle of the Sun,* is one of the earliest lyric poems in the Italian language. Francis wrote it in 1225, when he was dying and almost blind, yet it is the most joyous of his works. Written in his native Umbrian dialect, it is based on an irregular rhythm and has much assonance (the use of words with similar vowel sounds but different consonants) and rhyme. In *Canticle of the Sun,* Francis declares that humanity is not worthy of the goodness and power of God, who is to be praised instead through all His creation:

> *especially my Lord Brother Sun,*
> *who is the day and through whom You give us*
>   *light.*

Francis also calls for praise through Sister Moon, Brother Fire, Sister Water, and "Our sister, Mother Earth." He later added a stanza praising those who pardon others, and this was sung at his request to the quarreling bishop and mayor of Assisi, who immediately reconciled. A stanza written when he learned he was about to die adds "Sister Death" to the things that praise God. The principle of the song is mediation: God's praise extends from Himself and His own glory throughout creation, and is returned to Him by humanity through all created things.

Francis was so widely loved that only two years after his death at Portiuncula, Italy, he was canonized as a Catholic saint. His life and works were widely taught, and a collection of popular legends began to grow up about him, written down as the "Little Flowers of St. Francis of Assisi" in the early 14th century. By stressing the brotherhood of all men and women and all things created under God, Francis offered a corrective to the excesses of medieval asceticism and instead returned to the theme of the love of creation found in the Hebrew BIBLE. Partly because of his winsome biography, and partly because his teachings are primarily moral rather than doctrinal, which makes them easier to understand and identify with, Francis is one of the best-remembered saints in the Catholic calendar.

An English Version of Works by Saint Francis of Assisi

Armstrong, Regis J., O.F.M. Cap.; A. Wayne Hellman, O.F.M. Conv.; and William J. Short, O.F.M. *Francis of Assisi: Early Documents. Vol. 1: The Saint.* New York: New City Press, 1999.

Works about Saint Francis of Assisi

Chesterton, G. K. *St. Francis of Assisi; The Everlasting Man; St. Thomas Aquinas.* San Francisco: Ignatius Press, 1986.

Fortini, Arnaldo. *Francis of Assisi.* New York: Crossroad, 1992.

Fujiwara no Teika (Fujiwara Sadaie)
(1162–1241) *poet*

Fujiwara no Teika was born into a family of Japanese noblemen and poets. He was a direct descendant of Fujiwara Michinaga, who ruled Japan from 995 to 1028. However, his family line descended through a succession of younger sons, so his position in the Japanese court, while respectable, was not powerful. His father, Shunzei, was a great poet and literary critic who compiled the seventh imperial literary anthology, the *Senzaishu,* in 1183.

Fujiwara held minor court positions throughout his life. His opportunities for advancement through the imperial ranks were often stymied by

political intrigues or, in one case, by his own temperament, as evidenced when he struck a court official with a candlestick after being provoked. Still, Fujiwara's literary skill and his father's favorable reputation allowed him to achieve great fame as a poet and critic. He wrote and taught TANKA, and he was an accomplished essayist. For these reasons, he was asked to compile the eighth imperial anthology, the *Shinkokinshu,* by the ex-emperor Go-Toba in 1201. Fujiwara included many of his own poems in the collection.

Later in his life, Fujiwara began to teach young writers about poetry. His *Maigetsusho,* or *Monthly Notes,* was a detailed series of essays about poetic style and sensibility. He also collected shorter anthologies of representative poems that he used to teach young poets by example. He advised poets to look forward in their work and not to "become enamored of the archaic style." As a champion of poetry and as a master poet, Fujiwara continues to influence Japanese literature.

English Versions of Works by Fujiwara no Teika

Fujiwara Teika's Superior Poems of Our Time. Translated by Robert H. Brower and Earl Miner. Stanford, Calif.: Stanford University Press, 1967.

The Tale of Matsura: Fujiwara Teika's Experiment in Fiction. Translated by Wayne P. Lammers. Ann Arbor, Mich.: Center for Japanese Studies, 1992.

Fulgentius, Saint (Fulgentius of Ruspe, Fabius Claudius Gordianus Fulgentius)
(468–533) *theologian*

After the collapse of the western half of the Roman Empire in the fifth century, Western Europe entered a period of cultural decline and political disunity. The Christian Church, however, remained intellectually active, producing a large number of important theologians. One of these was Saint Fulgentius.

Fulgentius was born in the city of Telepte, North Africa, and received an excellent education in the Greek and Latin classics; it is believed he memorized all of HOMER's works. After beginning a political career, he abruptly took monastic vows and became a monk. Although he traveled throughout the Mediterranean, he lived in voluntary poverty for the rest of his life.

The early centuries of the Christian Church were a time of tremendous theological controversy and debate, as proponents of rival interpretations of Christianity struggled with one another for supremacy. Fulgentius was deeply involved in these intellectual quarrels, writing numerous theological treatises to promote his views of scripture. He believed fervently in the ideas of St. AUGUSTINE and accepted the absolute damnation of all nonbelievers, as can be seen in the three books that make up his *Ad Monimum.* He also struggled mightily against the Arian sect of Christianity, writing numerous sermons against them, including *Contra Arianos liber unus* (A Work Against Arians), which still exists today. By the time of his death, these struggles were not yet over, but they would end in triumph for the forces Fulgentius supported.

His best-known work, still extant, is "De Fide" ("Of Life"), about the matter of "true" faith. His "Liber ad Victorem" and "Liber ad Scarilam de Incarnatione" concern the religious view at the time of incarnation and the Holy Trinity. These, along with his other existing works, make Fulgentius one of the leading theologians of his day.

An English Version of Works by Saint Fulgentius
Fulgentius: Selected Works. Translated by Robert B. Eno. Washington, D.C.: Catholic University of America Press, 1997.

A Work about Saint Fulgentius
Ferguson, Thomas S. *Visita Nos: Reception, Rhetoric, and Prayer in a North African Monastery,* Vol. 203. New York: Peter Lang Publishing, 1999.

Galen (129–ca. 199) *physician, philosopher, treatise writer*

When Greece was absorbed into the Roman Empire, the Greeks' political freedom came to an end. But Roman domination did not prevent them from continuing to achieve great heights in culture and science. Indeed, some of the greatest Greek thinkers and writers produced their work after Greece had become part of the empire. One of the most important of these men was the brilliant physician and philosopher Galen.

The son of wealthy parents, Galen was born in the influential Greek city of Pergamon, in what is today Turkey. His family's status gave him the ability to study medicine in various Greek cities and undertake a serious study of physiology and anatomy. He dissected corpses to better understand the human body and became a highly skilled physician. He eventually won the favor of the Roman government and became the court physician to both Emperor Marcus AURELIUS and Emperor Commodus. In addition to his standard duties, he prepared a potion for Marcus Aurelius as a protection against assassination by poison. For unknown reasons, he left Rome for a time but eventually returned and resumed his place.

Fortunately for scholars, about 500 of Galen's works have survived. Many of them are in the original Greek or Latin, while others are translations made by later Arabic scholars. Galen wrote extensively on a multitude of medical topics. In his treatise *On the Uses of the Parts of the Body of Man,* he pays particular attention to questions regarding the circulation of the blood (describing how blood flows through arteries) and the functions of organs (describing the functions of the kidney and bladder). He also discusses the methods and treatments doctors should use with their patients.

Medicine was not very advanced in ancient times and Galen's writings were, in many cases, breakthroughs of medical knowledge. However, his writings still reflect the lack of scientific knowledge at the time. For instance, he believed in the then-traditional concept of the "four humors" as the basis of his medical theories, which has long since been proven false. Nevertheless, when viewed in the context of his time, Galen's work was astonishing, and he is considered one of the two greatest medical thinkers of the ancient world, the other being HIPPOCRATES.

In addition to his vast contributions to medicine, Galen was also a philosopher of considerable importance. He accepted many of Aristotle's ideas and expounded greatly on the need for direct observation as a basis for scientific knowledge. Galen also wrote on the subjects of history, linguistics, and philology, and social commentaries occasionally found their way into his writings.

In terms of his influence on later writers and thinkers, Galen must be ranked among the most important of classical figures. His emphasis on direct observation and experiment as the foundation of medical knowledge was critically important to the physicians who came after him, and his writings on medicine formed the basis of Western medical science for a millennium after his death.

An English Version of a Work by Galen

Galen on Food and Diet. Translated by Mark Grant. New York: Routledge, 2000.

Works about Galen

Bendick, Jeanne. *Galen and the Gateway to Medicine.* Bathgate, N.Dak.: Bethlehem Books, 2002.

Sarton, George. *Galen of Pergamon.* Lawrence: University of Kansas Press, 1954.

Gao Ming (Kao Ming) (1305–ca. 1370)
playwright

Though only one play by Gao Ming remains in existence, his work, *The Lute,* ranks among the greatest of China's literary creations. Gao Ming's early life was spent under Mongol rule. His father died when Gao was very young, and the playwright was raised by his mother. At an early age, he showed the deep respect for family tradition that would become a hallmark of his dramatic work.

Because the *jinshi* (*chin-shih*) examination, a civil service test, was not given during the Mongol regime, Gao Ming was not able to pursue a career in the government immediately after finishing his schooling. The *jinshi* was not reinstated until 1342, when Gao was almost 40 years old. He passed the exam in 1344 and received his first government post later that year as a judicial officer in Chuzhou (Ch'u-chou), where he became respected for his literary talents and his integrity. A transfer to a naval post in 1348 began a swift decline in his political ambitions.

Gao Ming retired from government service in the 1350s and moved to the town of Lishe (Li-she), where he began to develop his writing skills in earnest. He wrote *The Lute* during this period, as well as many poems (*shi,* or *shih*) and songs (*ci,* or *tz'u*). Though he achieved some fame during his lifetime for his poetry, only one *ci* and 50 *shi* remain in existence. As a result, *The Lute* is the source of Gao Ming's present fame.

The Lute tells the story of an ambitious young student, Cai Bojie (Ts'ai Po-chieh), who has spent his youth studying for the *jinshi* examination. However, when it is time to take the exam, Cai is reluctant to leave his poverty-stricken, ailing parents and his young wife, Wuniang (Wu-niang). After his parents and wife insist that he go to the capital to take the test, Cai reluctantly leaves and passes the test with the highest marks in the country. He marries the daughter of a government minister and lives in his father-in-law's mansion. Meanwhile, a famine ravages his hometown, and his parents soon die from malnutrition. Wuniang journeys to the capital in search of Cai, singing and playing the lute on her travels. When she reaches the imperial city, she is reunited with Cai, and the two, along with Cai's second wife, return to his hometown and observe the traditional three-year mourning period for Cai's parents. The play ends with Cai and his wives receiving a commendation from the emperor for their displays of virtue during their period of mourning.

The play has been recognized for its strong moralistic themes, and it is regarded as one of the Ming dynasty's greatest plays. Technically, *The Lute* also stands out for its complex songs and Gao Ming's use of colloquial and poetic dialogue. The play has become part of the standard repertoire of the Chinese theater and was adapted into a Broadway musical, *Lute Song,* in 1946.

An English Version of a Work by Gao Ming

The Lute: Kao Ming's P'i-p'a chi. Translated by Jean Mulligan. New York: Columbia University Press, 1980.

Geoffrey of Monmouth (ca. 1100–1155)
nonfiction writer, historian

In some of his writings, Geoffrey of Monmouth refers to himself as *Gaufridus Monemutensis,* which suggests he was born in Monmouthshire. Probably of Breton origin, he was raised in Wales. From 1129 to 1151, he lived in Oxford and was thought to have been a canon of the secular college of St. George. During his time there, he wrote his two well-known literary works, *Historia Regum Britanniae* (History of the Kings of Britain, 1136) and *Life of Merlin* (1148), both in Latin. His *Prophecies of Merlin,* first written as a separate piece, was later incorporated into the *History.*

In 1151, Geoffrey became bishop-elect of St. Asaph, in northern Wales. He was ordained priest at Westminster in 1152 and consecrated the same year at Lambeth by Archbishop Theobald. According to the Welsh Chronicles, he died in 1155.

Geoffrey's *History of the Kings of Britain* has held an important place in English literature since its completion. It is alternately a mere genealogy of royal primogeniture, a terse chronicle, a detailed sequence of dynastic lore, and a stirring narrative of an event or anecdote. Though the form and content of the *History* vary, the work as a whole is an epic tale spanning nearly 2,000 years. It begins with the fall of Troy in 1240 B.C. and tells the story of Brutus, great-grandson of the Trojan Aeneas, who was the first king of Britain and reigned for 23 years in the 12th century B.C. The epic ends with the death of the last British King Cadwallader in A.D. 689, after which the country was abandoned to the Saxons.

Geoffrey's remarkably vivid prose grips the reader and is as exciting today as it was in the 12th century. His purpose for writing the *History* was to highlight the story of the Breton and Welsh peoples, who were driven from the mainland by the Saxons, and to describe the dominions and ambitions of the Norman kings.

Some of Geoffrey's writings are rooted in facts he culled from various existing and authentic sources, including BEDE's *Ecclesiastical History of the English People,* the *British History* by Nennius, and *Concerning the Ruin of Britain* by Gildas. However, what material he couldn't find he simply made up.

To this day, Geoffrey is remembered for the romantic and heroic stories of valor, CHIVALRY, and mystery in his *History.* These stories occupy an important place in English literature through Geoffrey's well-paced, well-crafted, emotionally skillful handling of characters, places, and events. Readers of all ages continue to delve into his tales of King Arthur, Camelot, Avalon, the Knights of the Round-Table, Queen Guinevere, Lancelot, Mordred, and Merlin the Magician.

English Versions of Works by Geoffrey of Monmouth

The Historia Regum Brittanie of Geoffrey of Monmouth: Gesta Regum Britannie, Vol. 5. Edited by Neil Wright. Rochester, N.Y.: Boydell & Brewer, 1985.

The History of the Kings of Britain. Translated by Lewis Thorpe. New York: Penguin Classics, 1977.

Works about Geoffrey of Monmouth

Cooper, Helen. *Romance in Time: Transforming Motifs from Geoffrey of Monmouth to the Death of Shakespeare.* Oxford: Oxford University Press, 2004.

Curley, Michael J. *Geoffrey of Monmouth.* New York: Macmillan Library References, 1994.

Parry, John J. and Robert A. Caldwell. "Geoffrey of Monmouth." In *Arthurian Literature in the Middle Ages: A Collaborative History,* edited by Roger S. Loomis. Oxford: Oxford University Press, 1985.

Gilgamesh (ca. 2500–1300 B.C.) *epic*

In the second half of the third millennium B.C. (ca. 2500–2000), stories and poems about the half-legendary god-king Gilgamesh came to be widely told in Sumer. Within a few hundred years, these stories were compiled and edited into a long Babylonian poem, known today as the *Epic of Gilgamesh.* It can be considered the oldest surviving literary masterpiece in the world.

The Sumerian civilization is the oldest known to history. It emerged in the southern Tigris-Euphrates valley of Iraq (Mesopotamia) sometime in the fourth millennium B.C. Large city-states appeared by the third millennium, boasting massive civic and religious structures, elaborate irrigation systems, long-distance trade, a written language, and all the other attributes of a sophisticated culture. Hereditary kings, who attained semidivine status in the eyes of later generations, ruled the major cities.

One such king was Gilgamesh of Uruk (Erech of the Bible). According to inscriptions, he ruled sometime between 2700 and 2500 B.C., building up the walls of the city and dedicating a temple in Nippur. A body of oral legends soon grew up about his superhuman achievements; these tales began to be recorded on clay tablets soon after, written in cuneiform script in the Sumerian language.

By around 2000 B.C., Sumerian ceased to be a widely spoken language. However, the Babylonians, the neighboring people who eventually conquered all of Mesopotamia, accepted most elements of Sumerian civilization, including the literary and religious heritage. Babylonian scholars and scribes adapted their own language, Akkadian, to the Sumerian cuneiform script. They also kept Sumerian alive as a literary language, much the way Latin was kept alive in Europe long after the fall of Rome. Fortunately, they also preserved many old Sumerian texts by rendering them into Akkadian.

Though archeologists have found and deciphered several Sumerian-language Gilgamesh tablets, they have found many more such poems and stories in other, later languages at digs across the ancient Near East. The most famous and widely copied version of the Gilgamesh story was written in Akkadian, a Semitic language. That version was probably first composed in the Old Babylonian period (ca. 2000–1600 B.C.). It went through various permutations and adaptations in subsequent centuries, both in Akkadian and in Hittite and Hurrian translations.

Eventually, toward the end of the Middle Babylonian period (ca. 1600–1000 B.C.), the work seems to have settled into its final form. This revised edition, which included a new introduction and an additional section tacked on to the end, is generally known today as the "standard version." Ancient catalogues referred to it as the Gilgamesh "series" because it was written across several tablets. It was also known by its first line, "He who has seen everything."

A catalog from the library of Assyrian king Ashurbanipal attributes the standard version to a scholar/priest named Sin-Leqi-Unninni. His exact role in writing, editing, or transmitting the epic is not known, but scholars tend to agree that the work as we know it bears the stamp of a single writer.

Many ancient copies of the standard version have been uncovered in recent years, including a later Assyrian translation and a rendition in Elamite that may have been intended for performance as a religious ritual. The latter discovery has led some scholars to speculate that at least parts of the epic may have been performed at religious festivals in Babylonia too. The standard late Babylonian edition is the basis of all modern translations.

Critical Analysis

It should be noted that a complete text of *Gilgamesh* has not yet been found. Scholars have labored to piece together the existing fragments like a jigsaw puzzle and to fill in the remaining gaps with inspired literary guesswork. They know that the full text ran to 12 numbered tablets, with six columns of text on each.

Enough survives to make the work engaging even today. As it opens, the reader is drawn into the tale through a tour of the majestic walls of Uruk, built by the mighty Gilgamesh. Hidden in the walls is a copper box containing the tablets that tell the tale of "he who has seen everything . . . but then was brought to peace."

Though a great king, son of gods, supremely strong and beautiful, Gilgamesh oppresses the young men and women of Uruk. The gods decide to create a rival, Enkidu, who is depicted as an innocent child of nature, at home with the animals. Enkidu is soon seduced by a prostitute; he then makes his way to Uruk and challenges Gilgamesh. The king wins the hand-to-hand combat, but the two become fast friends despite the vast difference in status and personality. (Professions of friendship and love are a recurrent theme in the rest of the poem.)

Gilgamesh proposes a joint quest to visit the Cedar Forest and slay its demon protector Humbaba, thus gaining a kind of immortality through eternal fame. After a long journey, they succeed in slaying the demon, and Enkidu also fells the tallest cedar to use as a door in the famous temple at Nippur.

Feminist critics claim that the next episode, about the goddess of love, Ishtar, may signal a change in gender relationships in Babylon. After Gilgamesh rejects Ishtar's proposal of marriage, Ishtar has the gods send down the destructive Bull of Heaven. The hero slays the beast, reducing Ishtar and her priestesses to impotent grief.

The gods decide to kill Enkidu in punishment for the slayings of Humbaba and the Bull. When Enkidu asks for revenge against those who had seduced him away from his original state of innocence, the sun god Shamash lectures him on the simple civilized pleasures of food, wine, clothing, and friendship he has known, and assures him he will be properly mourned.

Gilgamesh cannot be consoled after the death of his friend. Consumed with despair about his own mortality, he decides to seek out Utnapishtim, the only human who ever achieved eternal life.

On the way, surviving a series of dangerous adventures, Gilgamesh is lectured on the futility of his quest. He is admonished to

"Make every day a delight,
Night and day play and dance . . .
Look proudly on the little one holding
    your hand,
Let your mate be always blissful in
    your loins,
This, then, is the work of mankind."

Ignoring this advice, the hero eventually succeeds in crossing over the Waters of Death. Utnapishtim recounts how he himself survived the great flood, which had been designed by the gods to exterminate all of mankind. He was granted immortality; perhaps if Gilgamesh can remain awake for seven nights, he, too, will receive the gift. But Gilgamesh drops off to sleep the moment he sits down. When a serpent then makes off with a youth-restoring herb that Utnapishtim has given him, Gilgamesh accepts that he must return to Uruk and reconcile himself to mortality.

Accompanied by the ferryman Urshanabi, Gilgamesh returns to Uruk. He invites Urshanabi to ascend and traverse the walls, in language that recapitulates the opening device; thus, the poem comes full circle.

As it has come down to us, *Gilgamesh* is an amalgam of many different elements. The basic Sumerian hero tales were enriched with motifs taken from royal hymns and temple hymns, independent creation myths, sacred marriage rituals, curse texts, and stories about deliverance from unjust rulers. The flood story seems to have been taken, albeit in modified form, from the Old Babylonian tale of *Atrahasis*. The style of the writing does not depart from tradition; there are many parallelisms and repetitive chant-like phrases, and a great deal of hyperbole.

Modern critics note that all these elements were gracefully unified to focus on a number of themes, centered on the problem of mortality. As more fragments are discovered, and more translations are made into modern languages, one conclusion becomes hard to evade. This ancient work, dating back almost to the dawn of literacy, shows a level of psychological and philosophical awareness that can speak to contemporary readers.

Gilgamesh the king became one of the most popular heroes of ancient times, at least amongst the scholarly elite. His bearded face and muscular body were depicted on cylinder seals, monuments, and other works of art. He was the model of the courageous but tragic figure whose search for fame, glory, and eternal life was doomed to ultimate failure.

Echoes of *Gilgamesh* have been discerned by some scholars in Greek mythology and in HOMER. Possible references to the king show up in the DEAD SEA SCROLLS and in a Syrian Christian manuscript from the seventh century A.D. Parallels with the Hebrew BIBLE have been widely debated, for example concerning concepts of life after death. The biblical story of Noah and the flood almost certainly drew on *Gilgamesh* or related Babylonian material.

When the civilization of Mesopotamia died by the end of the first millennium B.C., a moving and thought-provoking narrative that had entertained listeners and readers for some 2,500 years faded into oblivion. Thanks to the accumulated work of archeologists, historians, scholars, and poets, and the epic has been reborn.

English Versions of *Gilgamesh* (Including Notes and Analysis)

Gilgamesh: Translated from the Sin-Leqi-Unninni Version. Translated by John Gardner and John Maier. New York: Knopf, 1984.

Gilgamesh: A New Rendering in English Verse. Translated by David Ferry. New York: Farrar, Straus and Giroux, 1992.

The Epic of Gilgamesh. Translated and edited by Benjamin Foster. New York: W. W. Norton, 2001.

The Epic of Gilgamesh. Translated by Maureen Gallery Kovacs. Stanford, Calif.: Stanford University Press, 1989.

Works about *Gilgamesh*

Maier, John, ed. *Gilgamesh: A Reader.* Wauconda, Ill.: Bolchazy-Carducci, 1997.

Tigay, Jeffrey H. *The Evolution of the Gilgamesh Epic.* Philadelphia: University of Pennsylvania Press, 1982.

Gottfried von Strassburg (ca. 1180– ca. 1225) *poet, novelist*

Little is known about the life and personality of Gottfried von Strassburg because there are no records of his birth, activities, or death. All that remains are brief references to him in his own works and those of contemporary writers. It is not known exactly when Gottfried was born, but from his name it is to be assumed that he was active as a writer primarily in the city of Strassburg. In terms of a chronology, all that can be said is that he probably composed his masterpiece, *Tristan,* between 1210 and 1215. Though apparently not a nobleman, Gottfried nevertheless attained a high level of education in such fields as theology, mythology, and philosophy, and this education served as the foundation for his literary work.

Apart from individual poems in various anthologies of medieval German verse, Gottfried is known essentially only for one work—his Arthurian verse novel, *Tristan.* This book recounts the courtly adventures of the protagonist, culminating in his search for the HOLY GRAIL. At the center of the novel is the story of TRISTAN AND ISEULT (called Isolde in Gottfried's novel), who flee from the court of King Marke (Isolde's lover and Tristan's patron) to live together in forbidden love. It is this passage of the novel that has captured the imagination of artists over the centuries and given rise to any number of musical, literary, and artistic interpretations.

Left unfinished, presumably because of the author's early death, the general plots, as well as individual episodes of Gottfried's Tristan, are largely based on CHRÉTIEN DE TROYES's and WOLFRAM VON ESCHENBACH's Arthurian romances, as well as on the Middle English verse narrative of the same name. And yet Gottfried's *Tristan* departs from these sources to a great extent and is in many ways revolutionary for MIDDLE AGES literature and thought. For example, the lovers' insistence on personal happiness over the norms and expectations of society, and their disavowing of the knightly value system in the face of the intensity of their love set Gottfried's Tristan and Isolde apart from similar works. The couple's defiance of the aristocratic codes has in turn been read as a kind of criticism of courtly life and values in general This is an example of the great subtlety of Gottfried's writing, for although *Tristan* is a work primarily for and about the aristocracy, through the characters and their tragic fate Gottfried calls this aristocratic culture into question.

Other aspects of Gottfried's *Tristan* were also highly innovative and suggest an at-times surprisingly modern orientation on the part of the writer. The representation of love as the guiding life principle of the protagonists, more important than social norms and expectations, spoke against medieval ideas of societal harmony and individual submission. It would be this kind of vision of love, however, that would dominate in the Renaissance and modern eras, and in this sense Gottfried was far ahead of his time.

Gottfried von Strassburg was praised during his own time as a great artist and his *Tristan,* even in its unfinished state, was considered a masterpiece by audiences and peers. Later generations would also recognize the beauty and accomplishment of the work. In 1812 Jacob Grimm called Gottfried's *Tristan* "one of the most charming works of poetry ever written." More recently, the critic Rüdiger Krohn has said of Gottfried, "No author of the German Middle Ages was able to put into practice the ideal of medieval poetics with the same mastery (218)." It is Gottfried's version of the Tristan saga that has come to predominate in the European imagination through the 20th century and into the 21st, and in this way the mysterious author's legacy lives on through the present.

An English Version of a Work by Gottfried von Strassburg

Tristan. Translated by A. T. Hatto. New York: Penguin, 1960.

A Work about Gottfried von Strassburg

Batts, Michael S. *Gottfried von Strassburg.* New York: Twayne Publishers, 1971.

Greek and Roman mythology

See MYTHOLOGY, GREEK AND ROMAN.

Guillaume de Lorris (ca. 1215–ca. 1237)
poet

Guillaume de Lorris is the author of the first 4,000 lines of the French verse poem *Le Roman de la Rose* (ROMANCE OF THE ROSE, ca. 1225–40), one of the best-known love poems of the MIDDLE AGES. The remaining 18,000 lines were written by JEAN DE MEUN.

Nothing is known of De Lorris's life, but scholars speculate that he was most likely born in Lorris, a small town near Orleans, France. Based on his writing, he was probably an educated man, was familiar with OVID's *Art of Love,* and had an intimate knowledge of court society and courtly love poetry (*see* CHIVALRY AND COURTLY LOVE).

The *Romance of the Rose* is the story of a young man who tries to win the love of a young woman, personified as a rose. No one knows who the Rose is. She may have been De Lorris's beloved, his patroness, or a fictional character. In any case, the rose allegorically represents a beloved woman, while the garden in which the rose grows represents courtly life.

In the beginning of the poem, the poet suggests that the story is autobiographical and based on a dream that came true later in his life. It is, in essence, an ideal vision of the nature of love, and the poet prays:

> *That she for whom I write with favor look*
> *Upon my work, for she so worthy is*
> *Of love that well may she be called the Rose.*

De Lorris died before completing the poem, and despite the fact that Jean de Meun's section presents a more cynical view of love, *Romance of the Rose* remains one of the greatest achievements of courtly love poetry.

English Versions of a Work by Guillaume de Lorris

The Romance of the Rose by Guillaume de Lorris and Jean de Meun. Translated by Charles Dahlberg. Princeton, N.J.: Princeton University Press, 1995.

The Romance of the Rose. Translated by Harry W. Robbins. Edited by Charles W. Dunn. Syracuse, N.Y.: Syracuse University Press, 2002.

A Work about Guillaume de Lorris

Luria, Maxwell. *A Reader's Guide to the Roman de la Rose.* Hamden, Conn.: Archon Books, 1982.

Hadewijch (fl. mid-13th century) *poet, mystic, theologian*

Hadewijch lived in the duchy of Brabant, in what is now Belgium, around 1250. Her writings reveal that she was well educated and therefore probably a noble. She seems to have served as the leader of a group of Beguine women. Beguine communities, which first appeared in the late MIDDLE AGES, had less structure and fewer rules than traditional religious orders and consisted of individuals (usually women) who attempted to lead lives of poverty, prayer, and good deeds. Other members of Hadewijch's community eventually seem to have questioned her leadership, perhaps because of her unorthodox ideas about Christian love, and there is some speculation that they may have forced her to leave the community.

In the 1830s, German scholar F. J. Mone rediscovered Hadewijch's works, which had been preserved in 14th-century manuscripts. These works, which are written in Dutch, include 16 *Didactic Poems,* most of which are rhyming couplets; 45 *Poems in Stanzas;* 14 *Visions;* and 31 *Letters* to admirers and friends. They show that Hadewijch knew some Latin and French and that she had read many of the earlier Church fathers. She was aware of Ptolemy's theories on astronomy as well as contemporary ideas about music and rhetoric. Her writings also raise the possibility that she had read Pierre Abélard's poetry and listened to many TROUBADOURS' love songs.

Like her near-contemporary BEATRICE OF NAZARETH, Hadewijch concerns herself with the idea of Christian love. She writes in one letter that she has loved God since she was 10 years old: "In the end, I cannot believe that I have loved Him best, and yet I cannot believe that there is any living man who loves God as I love Him." In another writing, Hadewijch names individuals whom she sees as displaying a surpassing love for God. Her list includes the Virgin Mary, Mary Magdalen, Saint AUGUSTINE, HILDEGARD VON BINGEN, and Bernard of Clairvaux.

Bernard of Clairvaux had argued in the 12th century that individuals should strive above all to love God, because by doing so they could become one with God. Hadewijch, too, believes that through love an individual can become one with God. She perceives this union as both a burden and a joy: "We all want to be God along with God; but God knows that there are few of us who want to be man with Him in His humanity, to carry His

Cross with Him, to hang upon it with Him, to pay with Him the debt of human kind." It seems to some scholars that Hadewijch believed she was capable of such suffering. At the same time, she shows humility and an awareness of her own limitations in other works, as in her love poem "Drawing Close to Love:"

> I drew so close to Love
> That I began to understand
> How great the gain of those
> Who give themselves wholly to Love:
> And when I saw this for myself,
> What was lacking in me gave me pain.

Such expressions of belief and love were uncommon during her time, especially for laywomen of the Church, as was her style of writing. Unlike most medieval Christian writers, she rarely quoted the BIBLE. In addition, she wrote in a Brabantine dialect of Dutch, no Latin, and thus addressed a wider, less-learned audience. Rather than composing scholarly treatises that her audience would find incomprehensible, she communicated her thoughts in poetry, letters, and stories of visions. Even more remarkably, her descriptions of religious love contain passion and exaltation not often seen in religious writings of previous centuries. In one poem, love brings a "high, loud gift of low silence" and "completely rob[s] me of myself." Similarly, during one of her visions Hadewijch "remained in a passing away in my Beloved, so that I wholly melted away in him and nothing any longer remained to me of myself." When medieval writers employed such paradoxical, self-annihilating language, they usually had courtly love in mind (see CHIVALRY AND COURTLY LOVE), not religious love. Hadewijch was using the language and style of the troubadours.

Scholar J. Reynaert has recently argued that the "borrowing of a profane courtly model for communicating a religious 'content'" may not have originated with Hadewijch, and it did not make her unique. Nevertheless, it adds a layer of meaning and beauty to the mysticism that saturates her writing, as do her references to Love and the Soul as female:

> . . . The soul is the way that God goes when he proceeds from his depths to his liberty, that is into his ground, which is beyond the reach of all things but the soul's depths. And as long as God is not wholly her own possession, she will not be satisfied.
>
> ("The Deepest Essence of the Soul")

> In the beginning Love satisfied us,
> When Love first spoke to me of love—
> How I laughed at her in return!
> But then she made me like the hazel trees,
> Which blossom early in the season of
>   darkness,
> And bear fruit slowly.
>
> ("Love's Maturity")

English Versions of Works by Hadewijch

Hadewijch: The Complete Works. Translated and edited by Mother Columba Hart. New York: Paulist Press, 1980.

"Letters to a Young Beguine" and "Vision 7." In *Medieval Women's Visionary Literature*, edited by Elizabeth Petroff, 189–200. New York: Oxford University Press, 1986.

Works about Hadewijch

Reynaert, J. "Hadewijch: Mystic Poetry and Courtly Love." In *Medieval Dutch Literature in its European Context*, edited by Erik Kooper, 208–225. Cambridge: Cambridge University Press, 1994.

Milhaven, John Giles. *Hadewijch and Her Sisters: Other Ways of Loving and Knowing.* Albany: State University of New York Press, 1993.

Halevi, Judah (Yehuda ben Samuel Halevi) (before 1075–after 1141) *poet*

Judah Halevi is often considered the most exalted of all post-biblical Hebrew poets. His secular, religious, and national poetry have served as models for Jewish poets in various languages ever since.

Halevi was born in Toledo, the chief city of Christian Spain. He studied in Lucena and returned to Toledo to practice medicine. He later moved with his wife and daughter to Córdoba, then under Muslim rule. Overcome with longings for Zion, he left his family when he was in his 50s to go on a pilgrimage to the Holy Land. After visiting Cairo, Tyre, and Damascus, he disappeared; legend has it that he died a martyr at the gates of Jerusalem.

Halevi's secular poems, written mostly during his youth and early manhood, are linguistically rich and complex. They have a bright, harmonious, musical quality and a primarily optimistic tone. They vary in subject matter, from friendship, love, wine, and beauty to the vicissitudes of life.

For most of his life, however, Halevi focused his poetry on religious themes. Like most of his fellow Hebrew poets of the Andalusian school, he often expressed an intense longing for God. His God was a stern, distant ruler but also the ever-present source of love in nature and human affairs. In "Lord, Where Shall I Find You," he writes: "Lord, where shall I find You? Your place is lofty and secret. And where shall I not find you? The whole earth is full of Your glory."

It is Halevi's "national religious" poems that have endeared him to generations of pious and secular Jews. He lived in a more troubled era than the earlier poets of the Spanish Jewish Golden Age. His lifetime was marked by intermittent religious persecution in Spain from both Christian and Muslim rulers. In his poems, he frequently questions God's justice in allowing the Jewish people to suffer in exile. As the years pass, his sense of exile and longing for Zion grow stronger, as vividly recorded in his work. In perhaps his most famous poem, "My Heart Is in the East," he cries out: "My heart is in the East and I am at the edge of the West. / Then how can I taste what I eat, how can I enjoy it?"

Halevi's later poems chronicle his departure from Spain, his sea voyage, and his visit in Cairo on the way to the Land of Israel. Whether he ever reached Jerusalem, and what poetry he wrote there if he did, will probably never be known.

English Versions of Works by Judah Halevi

Book of Kuzari. Translated by Harwig Hirschfeld. Whitefish, Mont.: Kessinger, 2003.
In *Penguin Book of Hebrew Verse.* Edited by T. Carmi. New York: Viking, 1981.
In *Hebrew Poems from Spain.* Translated by David Goldstein. New York: Schocken, 1966.

A Work about Judah Halevi

Silman, Yochanan. *Philosopher and Prophet: Judah Halevi, the Kuzari, and the Evolution of His Thought.* Translated by Lenn J. Shramm. Albany: State University of New York Press, 1995.

Halle, Adam de la

See ADAM DE LA HALLE.

Hanged Poems (Mu'allaqāt, Seven Odes, Golden Odes) (sixth century)

Most Arabic poetry from the fifth and sixth centuries is attributed to anonymous authors. However, literary scholars generally agree that the *Hanged Poems* (also called the *Mu'allaqāt*, or "The hanging ones") were written by the following seven poets: IMRU' AL-QAYS, TARAFAH 'AMR IBN AL-'ABD, Zuhayr ibn Abi Sulma, LABID, Antara ibn Shaddad, 'AMR IBN KULTHUM, and al-Harith. They were displayed in the Ka'aba, the chief religious shrine in Arabia.

Little is known about the lives of most of these poets. They likely read their works aloud in a poetry competition during an annual meeting of the Arabic tribes. It is believed that the seven best of the *qasidas* (long poems or odes) chosen through these competitions were the ones hanged for display in the Ka'aba, hence their collective title as the "hanged ones." They address the topics of warfare, love, and famous cities of the region.

The oldest of the *Hanged Poems* was written by Imru' al-Qays, otherwise known as "the vagabond prince." He was of royal descent from the ancient kings of Yemen, and the stories about his life differ. In one telling, Imru' took vengeance on his father's murderer and then fled the region for fear of retaliation. In another story, Imru' became a wanderer because his father banished him for writing of love rather than spending more time warring. In both stories, Imru' eventually arrived in Constantinople and became a celebrated poet in the palace of the Roman emperor Justinian (530). He was later poisoned as punishment for falling in love with a Byzantine princess.

Imru' al-Qays is said to be the greatest of the *Mu'allaqāt* poets, the first to capture in a regular rhythm the chanting of the earlier desert singers. His poem speaks of the loss of love:

> There my companions halted their beasts awhile over me saying, "Don't perish of sorrow; restrain yourself decently!" Yet the true and only cure of my grief is tears outpoured: what is there left to lean on where the trace is obliterated?

Antarah, another of the poets, was a son of an Arab and his slave woman; he was raised as a slave in his father's house. He desperately loved Abla, a young woman of his tribe, but never had a relationship with her because his tribe did not consider Antarah, a slave, to be Abla's equal. His poem speaks of their unrequited love:

> I was enamored of her unawares, at a time when I was killing her people, desiring her in marriage; but by your father's life I swear, this was not the time for desiring.

The poet Zuhayr is regarded as the philosopher of the group of *Mu'allaqāt* poets, a man of rank and wealth from a family noted for their poetic skill and religious earnestness. He sought, through his poetry, to instill noble ideas in the people around him. In this poem, he encourages peace among the tribes:

> And war is not but what you have learnt it to be, and what you have experienced, and what is said concerning it, is not a story based on suppositions. When you stir it up, you will stir it up as an accursed thing, and it will become greedy when you excite its greed and it will rage fiercely.

Many of the Arabic tribal poets passed their works along orally. It was solely the public selection of these seven poems, which were said to have been written in gold on the walls of the Ka'aba, that allowed for their preservation for future generations.

English Versions of the *Hanged Poems*

Horne, Charles F. *Sacred Books and Early Literature of the East: Ancient Arabia, The Hanged Poems, The Koran.* Vol. 5. Whitefish, Mont.: Kessinger Publishing, 1997.

Jones, Alan. *Early Arabic Poetry, Vol. 2, Select Odes.* Reading, N.Y.: Garnet Publishing, 1996.

Works about the *Hanged Poems*

O'Grady, Desmond. *The Seven Arab Odes.* London: Agenda & Editions Charitable Trust, 1990.

Stetkevych, Suzanne Pinckney. *Mute Immortals Speak: Pre-Islamic Poetry and the Poetics of Ritual.* Ithaca, N.Y.: Cornell University Press, 1993.

Han Shan (fl. 750–800) *poet*

Little is known of Han Shan, not even his given name. While his poetry is well known and widely available, his life is shrouded in mystery. The poet was a Zen Buddhist recluse who lived in the Tientai (T'ien-t'ai) Mountains of Danxing (Tang-hsing), China, during the Tang dynasty (618–907); his name means, literally, "The Master of Cold Mountain." Han Shan lived on Cold Mountain with his friend, Shi De (Shih-te). Known for their lighthearted manner, the two men were immortalized in later pictures showing them laughing heartily.

Han Shan's poetry was introduced to China by a Tang government official, Lu Jiuyin (Lu Chiu-Yin), who met the poet while visiting the local Buddhist temple. Han Shan wrote more than 300 poems, which he inscribed onto trees, rocks, and walls. Lu Jiuyin took it upon himself to copy these poems, along with a few poems by Shi De, and collect them in a single volume, collectively known as Hanshan poetry.

Han Shan's poetry is deeply religious. He wrote mainly on Buddhist and Taoist themes, specifically enlightenment, in simple, colloquial language, using conventional Chinese rhyming schemes within the five-character, eight-line verse form. Although his poetry was not groundbreaking, the imagery and spirit of his poems in creating what scholar Burton Watson has called "a landscape of the mind" and his ability to express Buddhist ideals have given Han Shan a place among the finest of Chinese poets.

English Versions of Works by Han Shan

Cold Mountain: 100 Poems by the T'ang Poet Han-Shan. Translated by Burton Watson. New York: Columbia University Press, 1970.

The Poetry of Han-Shan. Translated by Robert Hendricks. Albany: State University of New York Press, 1990.

Han Yu (Han Yü) (768–824) *poet, prose writer*

Han Yu is one of the most important Neo-Confucian writers of the late Tang dynasty. The son of a minor government official, Han Yu was born in the Honan province of China. His father died when he was only two years old, and he was raised by his older brother, Han Hui, and sister-in-law. He spent his youth studying the Confucian classics in preparation for the *jinshi* (*chin-shih*) government examination, which he failed twice before passing in 792.

Han Yu showed a predilection for Confucian political critique early in his career. In 795 he wrote the government's ministers to seek employment and to remind them of their duty to surround themselves with talented writers and scholars, such as himself. His initial pleas did not work, and it was only after his marriage into a politically connected family in Loyang the following year that he obtained the first of many government posts.

Han Yu's first job was in Bianzhou (Pien-chou), an important military outpost, where he was in charge of supervising the provincial government examinations. Through this position, he developed a reputation as a man of letters, and a growing number of scholars and poets came to Bianzhou to become part of his circle. One such poet was Meng Jiao (Meng Chiao), with whom Han Yu developed a long literary relationship. In 806, the two wrote a series of "linked verses," poems in which the poets alternate sets of verses. Han Yu's assignment in Bianzhou ended in 799 with the death of the imperial governor Dong Jin (Jong Jin) and the subsequent mutiny of the soldiers under the new leadership.

Throughout his life, Han Yu used his connections with the imperial universities in Chang'an and Loyang to cultivate a group of Neo-Confucian scholars who would enter the imperial government after passing the examination. Despite his outspoken criticism of the bureaucracy and run-ins with many upper-level officials that led to several periods of exile, he was able to find allies within the administration who allowed him to return to the capital and positions of power.

Han Yu's strict Confucian adherence to proper bureaucratic procedures often gained him enemies, but his trustworthiness and moral code also allowed him to rise to great heights of power in his later years.

Critical Analysis

Throughout his career, Han Yu used his poetry and prose to elucidate political and social problems. He led what is known as the "ancient style" (*du-wen*) movement, which espoused clarity and simplicity in writing, and he combined his beliefs about how government should handle itself (sans heresy and decadence) with his beliefs about literary quality. In "An Enquiry into Slander," for example, he theorizes over the loss of morals in people of his day. He discusses how, in the past, men of high morals expected as much, if not more, from themselves as they did from others. "With the great men of the present day, however," he writes, "things are quite different. They make the most searching demands of others, but are sparing in what they ask of themselves. . . . How they can have any self-respect passes my understanding."

In another essay, "Against the God of the Wind," Han Yu uses satire to condemn the emperor's demand that taxes be paid during a hard year. "The sentence of Heaven will fall upon you; when it does there can be no repentance," he writes, adding, "even if you die, what man will mourn for you?"

Han Yu wrote a critique of the emperor's inept handling of the mutiny of 799 in his "Two Poems on the Bianzhou Rebellion." A later poem, "Craven," serves as a commentary on the social and political situation at his next posting in Zhengzhou (Cheng-chou) after the Yellow River flooded.

One famous critique, however, cost Han Yu his job and nearly his life. The incident involved a Buddhist relic purported to be the finger bone of the Buddha. In 819, the finger bone, normally kept in a Buddhist temple west of Chang'an, was put on display in the capital. According to tradition, the relic helped to ensure the health of the nation, and thousands of people flocked to the capital to pay their respects to this sacred piece of history. The relic also brought in a large amount of money for several government officials. Han Yu wrote "Memorial on the Bone of Buddha," in which he attacked those who catered to the emperor's use of the ritual to gain public favor. He addresses the emperor directly in the essay, saying, "Were he [the Buddha] still alive today, were he to come to court at the bidding of his country, your majesty would give him no greater reception than an interview in the Strangers' Hall, a ceremonial banquet, and the gift of a suit of clothes, after which you would have him sent under guard to the frontier to prevent him from misleading your people." Han Yu does not understand why the emperor insists on escorting the Buddha's bone into the building where it will be viewed by the masses. He says, "To my shame and indignation none of your ministers says

that this is wrong, none of your censors has exposed the error."

The emperor evidently read the essay as a ridicule of the ritual and a personal attack on himself rather than what it was—a call for government officials to demonstrate strong values and proper conduct. As a result, he commanded that Han Yu be executed for his insolence, but two ministers rallied support for Han Yu and were able to persuade the emperor to exile him instead to southern China. Han Yu immediately regretted his harsh testimonial and suffered the further pain of losing his 11-year-old daughter to illness on the journey south. The incident became famous in Chinese history and served as an indication of Han Yu's skill at using literature as social and political commentary.

An English Version of Works by Han Yu

Growing Old Alive: Poems. Translated by Kenneth O. Hanson. Port Townsend, Wash.: Copper Canyon Press, 1978.

Works about Han Yu

Hartman, Charles. *Han Yu and the T'ang Search for Unity.* Princeton, N.J.: Princeton University Press, 1986.
Owen, Stephen. *The Poetry of Meng Chiao and Han Yu.* New Haven, Conn.: Yale University Press, 1975.

Hartmann von Aue (ca. 1160–1200) *poet, novelist*

Like virtually all great writers of medieval Germany, little is known regarding Hartmann von Aue's life. From references made in his own works and in the writings of his contemporaries, it can be surmised that the writer was born to an aristocratic family and grew up near the southern German city of Freiburg. He likely received a clerical education and learned Latin and French before beginning his activities as a writer in royal and aristocratic courts.

Hartmann's first works were poetry and courtly religious tales, but his literary fame and importance rests on the strength of his longer verse narratives written between 1180 and 1200. His first novel, *Erec* (ca. 1187), was the first story about King Arthur's court written in the German language. He based *Erec* and his other Arthurian romance, *Iwein* (ca. 1193), on the work of the French writer CHRÉTIEN DE TROYES, but he often diverged from his source to impart his own unique vision of courtly life and morals.

Hartmann's most well-known and personal work is his *Poor Heinrich* (ca. 1200). Written in rhyming verse, the work tells the story of the hero's illness and ultimate physical and spiritual redemption. It is a kind of miracle tale with a strong Christian message. For his mercy and faith, Heinrich is ultimately healed by God and therefore serves as a model of Christian belief and self-sacrifice. Considered by many as Hartmann's masterpiece, *Poor Heinrich* established the writer as a key figure in medieval German literature, and the work has given rise to many modern interpretations and variations, from the Grimm Brothers' fairy-tale version to Longfellow's *Golden Legend.*

The scholar Volker Mertens has written of Hartmann von Aue, "In his poetic precision and sensibility . . . his mild irony and his feeling for social and existential problems . . . Hartmann emerges as a writer with modern subjectivity and vision." These qualities continue to make Hartmann's work both relevant and moving for present-day readers.

An English Version of Works by Hartmann von Aue

Arthurian Romances, Tales and Lyric Poetry: The Complete Works of Hartmann Von Aue. Translated by Frank Tobin, Kim Vivian, and Richard Lawson. University Park: Penn State University Press, 2001.

Works about Hartmann von Aue

Hasty, Will. *Adventures in Interpretation: The Works of Hartmann von Aue and Their Critical Reception.* Columbia, S.C.: Camden House, 1996.

Jackson, William H. *Chivalry in Twelfth-Century Germany: The Works of Hartmann Von Aue.* Rochester, N.Y.: Boydell & Brewer, 1995.

Mills, Mary Vandegrift. *Pilgrimage Motif in the Works of the Medieval German Author Hartmann Von Aue.* Lewiston, N.Y.: Edwin Mellen Press, 1996.

Heinrich von Veldeke (ca. 1140–ca. 1210)
poet

No official records have been found that give the exact birth and death dates of Heinrich von Veldeke, but it is known that he was a member of a family of minor nobility in Limburg, then a German province in what is now part of Belgium. He is best known for his medieval adaptation of VIRGIL's *Aeneid,* but he also wrote a narrative about the life and miracles of the fourth-century saint Bishop Servatius of Tongeren, as well as a series of love songs.

Heinrich began the *Eneit* around 1174 but did not finish it until 1190, during which time, as he relates in his epilogues, the manuscript was stolen. He supposedly loaned it to Margareta, the countess of Cleve and his patron. When she was married to Ludwig III of Thuringia, it was "stolen" by Count Heinrich (Ludwig's brother), who sent it home to Thuringia. Heinrich did not get the manuscript back until he journeyed to Thuringia nine years later. Count Palatine Hermann (another brother) finally returned it to him and asked that he finish the story. Thus the poet gained the patronage of the two counts.

Heinrich's *Eneit,* alternately called the *Eneas,* is based heavily on an anonymous French translation of the *Aeneid* called *Roman d'Eneas* (Book of Aeneas, ca. 1160). Heinrich had also read Virgil's epic in Latin, and the *Eneit* maintains Virgil's original narrative; Heinrich changed only those elements necessary in keeping with the Christian world of medieval CHIVALRY, adapting the epic to fit court fashions and customs of the 12th century and to emphasize activities, such as jousting, of the noble classes.

Perhaps the biggest difference between the two works involves details of the gods. In the *Eneit,*

Heinrich includes the pagan gods of Rome but gives them a much smaller role. As a whole, the characters in his adaptation have more responsibility over their choices, and the story is about both the struggle for self-fulfillment and the role of fate in our lives.

Love also plays a much more prominent role in Heinrich's version than it does in Virgil's. For example, Virgil uses the scene with Dido to explain the politics of Carthage and Rome, but Heinrich uses it to theorize on the meaning of love and obsession. As a result, the scene in the *Eneit* becomes much larger and more important to the poet's message. In addition, the relationship between Aeneas and Lavinia is established in a very minor scene in Virgil's *Aeneid,* but it carries more weight in terms of its relevance to the theme in the *Eneit,* revealing what love can be like when it is reciprocated. Heinrich's attention to the idea of love is a direct result of his having read OVID's works and his being aware of his audience—medieval nobles for whom courtly love was a way of life.

In terms of artistic achievement, the *Eneit* is no match for the *Aeneid;* however, it is important in that it was one of the first successful books to be written in vernacular German rather than in traditional Latin. This accomplishment made Heinrich one of the founders of German court EPIC poetry, and his influence on later German writers was profound. In the introduction to his translation of the *Eneit,* J. W. Thomas quotes the Middle High German poet GOTTFRIED VON STRASSBURG, who comments on Veldeke's influence:

> [I]t was he who made the first graft on the tree of German verse and that the shoot put forth the branches and the blossoms from which they took the art of fine composition. This craft has now spread so widely and become so varied that all who devise tales and songs can break off an ample supply of the twigs and blooms of words and music.

English Versions of a Work by Heinrich von Veldeke

Fisher, Rodney W. *Heinrich von Veldeke: Eneas: A Comparison with the "Roman d'Eneas" and a Translation into English.* Bern: Peter Lang, 1992.

Heinrich von Veldeke: Eneit. Translated by J. W. Thomas. New York: Garland Publishing, 1985.

Herodotus (ca. 480–425 B.C.) *historian*

Herodotus, whom the Roman statesman CICERO would later hail as the father of history, was born at the Greek colony of Halicarnassus in Asia Minor, now Bodrum on Turkey's Aegean coast. His mother and father, Lyxes and Dryo, were prominent in the community as well as wealthy and possibly aristocratic. Herodotus had at least one sibling, a brother named Theodoros.

Exposure to historical traditions was part of Herodotus's upbringing. The city of Halicarnassus maintained a listing of the priests who had served the temple of Isthmian Poseidon from the time of its founding 15 generations earlier. Furthermore, the EPIC poet Panyassis was a close relative, perhaps an uncle or a first cousin, who composed verse about the settlement of the Ionian cities in Asia Minor.

Herodotus's family relocated to the island of Samos to escape the tyrant Lygdamis, who put Panyassis to death. Herodotus returned to Halicarnassus years later to participate in Lygdamis's overthrow. When he was living for a time in Athens, Herodotus became an intimate of the tragedian SOPHOCLES. He finally made his home in Thurii, in southern Italy, when it was being colonized by the Greeks.

The first historian was an avid traveler, a zealous sightseer, and an intrepid explorer. His insatiable curiosity and hunger for knowledge led him to Egypt, Cyrene (now Tripoli), Babylon, Scythia in the Black Sea region, Ukraine, Thrace, North Africa, and India.

In the early years of the Peloponnesian War between Athens and Sparta, Herodotus published his life's work, *History*. In English, it is also sometimes called *The Histories, The Persian Wars,* or *History of the Persian Wars.* The work made Herodotus the first scholar to undertake research on the events of the past and impart them in a rational, rather than mythical, fashion.

Herodotus died in Thurii not long after publication of the *History*.

Critical Analysis

The *History* is contained in nine books, each named for one of the muses. Its subject matter is the legendary conflict between a motley band of Greek city-states and the mighty invading Persian Empire. Herodotus's intentions in producing this work, as he states in the very first lines, are to preserve the record of the events for posterity and to investigate why they occurred in the first place:

> These are the researches of Herodotus of Halicarnassus, which he publishes, in the hope of thereby preserving from decay the remembrance of what men have done, and of preventing the great and wonderful actions of the Greeks and the Barbarians from losing their due meed of glory; and withal to put on record what were their grounds of feud.
>
> (Book I)

Herodotus does not share his countrymen's disdain for foreigners. He did not use the word *barbarian* in a pejorative way; it was simply the Greek word for non-Greeks. His youth in a Greek city that was not in Greece and his travels to far-off, exotic lands had given him an outsider's perspective and an appreciation for other cultures that would inform his magnum opus. He presents a balanced treatment of the opposing sides and even reveals an admiration for the Persians, whom he finds valiant and heroic.

Herodotus represents the events in a vigorous and high-spirited prose style, casting the Persian Wars as a contest between tyranny and liberty; liberty emerges gloriously victorious. Freedom triumphs, he says, because the Greeks are free men defending their self-government, while the Persian soldiers are slaves risking their lives on behalf of a despot. But the Greeks are not inherently superior to the Persians; under tyranny, they behave similarly:

> And it is plain enough, not from this instance only, but from many everywhere that freedom is an excellent thing; since even the Athenians, who, while they continued under the rule of tyrants, were not a whit more valiant than any of their neighbors, no sooner shook off the yoke than they became decidedly first of all. These things show that, while undergoing oppression, they let themselves be beaten, since then they worked for a master; but so soon as they got their freedom, each man was eager to do the best he could for himself.

Although the Persian War is the ostensible reason for the tome's existence, Herodotus makes frequent digressions. Two-thirds of *Histories* is devoted to the oddities he witnessed, was told of, and otherwise learned about during his sojourns to far-off lands. The people, places, things, and incidents are recounted merely to set the stage for the central conflict. For example, Herodotus tells of one-eyed men, gold-digging ants, Babylonian temple treasures, Egyptian crocodile hunters, and men with the heads of dogs. He tallies the amount of money spent on radishes, onions, and garlic for the slaves who built the pyramids; describes what unattractive girls in Illyria do to get husbands and how people travel by boat over land when the Nile floods; reveals that Scythian royalty are buried in tombs containing sacrificed humans and horses, Libyan women are honored for having multiple lovers, Danube island dwellers become intoxicated by scents, and the king of Persia will drink only boiled water when he travels. More than the father of history, Herodotus was the father of ethnography, geography, archaeology, sociology—indeed, all the social sciences that are concerned with people, places, and customs.

In his translation of *The Persian Wars,* George Rawlinson writes:

Apart from all deficiencies of historical technique and all merits of intrinsic interest, charm of literary style, and more or less accidental preservation of important historical facts, one solid and important achievement stands out in the work of Herodotus. He has succeeded once and for all in expressing the conflict between the ideal of the free man defending his autonomy and basing his state on the rule of law, and the despot who bases his rule on force and whose subjects have the status of slaves.

English Versions of Works by Herodotus

Herodotus: The Wars of Greece and Persia. Translated by W. D. Lowe. Wauconda, Ill.: Bolchazy-Carducci Publishers, 1999.

The Histories. Translated by Aubrey De Selincourt. Introduction by John M. Marincola. New York: Penguin Classics, 2003.

The Histories. Translated by Robin A. Waterfield. Edited by Carolyn Dewald. Oxford: Oxford University Press, 1999.

Works about Herodotus

Mikalson, Jon D. *Herodotus and Religion in the Persian Wars.* Chapel Hill: University of North Carolina Press, 2003.

Selincourt, Aubrey de. *Phoenix: The World of Herodotus.* London: Phoenix Press, 2001.

Thomas, Rosalind. *Herodotus in Context: Ethnography, Science, and the Art of Persuasion.* New York: Cambridge University Press, 2002.

Hesiod (eighth century B.C.) *poet*

Hesiod's father was a seafaring merchant from Asia Minor who fell upon hard times and emigrated to Ascra, on the lower slopes of central Greece's Helicon mountain range, where he became a farmer. When the patriarch died, he left his farm to his sons, and Hesiod lived there most of his life.

According to legend, Hesiod visited a sacred grove in his later years and was slain by his hosts for seducing and impregnating their sister. His body was flung into the sea, but dolphins brought it ashore, where it was buried. The lyric poet Stesichorus is said to be the product of the illicit union.

Like his father, Hesiod was a poor farmer, for his primary occupation was poetry. He entered at least one poetry contest, at the funeral games of Amphidamas in Euboia, and won a prize. He may have been a contemporary of the epic poet HOMER, and the biographer PLUTARCH has him defeating Homer in a poetry competition.

Hesiod is often called the father of Greek didactic poetry. His *Works and Days* is an 800-line poem addressed to Perseus, his wastrel brother. It describes Ascra and the life of a farmer and also contains some elements of EPIC poetry (such as the use of hexameter verse, lofty language, and myths), which is perhaps why VIRGIL used the poem as a model for his *Georgics.*

In *Works and Days,* Hesiod observes the decline of the world since the glorious Golden Age, which was followed by the foolish Silver Age, the fierce Bronze Age, and the age of the Heroes. Now is the Age of Iron, which he characterizes as endless hard drudgery, hardship, and weariness; "And I wish that I were not any part of the fifth generation of men, but had died before it came, or been born afterward."

Works and Days is also scattered with tidbits of advice, such as "Get two strong, seasoned oxen and a mature, staid hired hand"; "Have one son to help with the chores"; and "When the cranes fly overhead, it's time for winter planting." Hesiod's descriptions and language have led translator Richard Lattimore to write: "Hesiod is the poet of the roadside grass and the many colored earth, and of men who live by the soil. . . . Echoes of ancient peasant wisdom and of the mysteries of the earth linger in his pages."

In another poem, *Theogony,* Hesiod describes in 1,000 lines the creation of the cosmos and the genealogy of the early gods. He begins by invoking the muses, who kept a sanctuary at Mt. Helicon. It was here, he says, when he was "shepherding his lambs," that the goddesses taught him his "splendid singing" (i.e., poetry). They handed him an olive staff, breathed a voice into him, and told him to sing "the race of the blessed gods everlasting."

Hesiod goes on to chronicle the origins of the earth, oceans, fate, death, and dreams in *Theogony.* He also personifies cheating Deception, loving Affection, malignant Old Age, and hateful Discord. He describes the origins of the more familiar deities as well: Zeus bedded Demeter, who bore him Persephone; he loved "Mnemosyne of the splendid tresses, from whom were born to him the Muses"; and from his head he produced gray-eyed Athena, leader of armies.

Hesiod did not name the gods, but he was the first to classify them. Greek scholar Edith Hamilton marvels that "a humble peasant, living on a lonely farm far from cities, was the first man in Greece to wonder how everything had happened, the world, the sky, the gods, mankind, and think out an explanation. . . ." It is this explanation that influenced later writers such as John Dryden, Edmund Spenser, and John Milton, and gave Hesiod a place in world literature.

English Versions of Works by Hesiod

Hesiod. Translated by Richmond Lattimore. Ann Arbor: University of Michigan Press, 1959.

Hesiod's Ascra. Translated by Anthony T. Edwards. Berkeley: University of California Press, 2004.

Hesiod: Theogony, Works and Days, Shield. Translated by Apostolos N. Athanassakis. Baltimore: Johns Hopkins University Press, 2004.

Works about Hesiod

Hamilton, Richard. *Architecture of Hesiodic Poetry.* Baltimore, Md.: Johns Hopkins University Press, 1976.

Lefkowitz, Mary R. *The Lives of the Greek Poets.* Baltimore: Johns Hopkins University Press, 1981.

Marsilio, Maria S. *Farming and Poetry in Hesiod's Works and Days.* Lanham, Md.: University Press of America, 2000.

Peabody, Berkeley. *Winged Word: A Study in the Technique of Ancient Greek Oral Composition as Seen Principally through Hesiod's Works and Days.* Albany: State University of New York Press, 1975.

Hildegard von Bingen (1098–1179)
religious writer, mystic, composer

Hildegard von Bingen was born of noble parents in Bockelheim, West Frankonia (now Germany). She was educated at the Benedictine cloister of Disibodenberg by the prioress, Jutta, whom she succeeded in 1136. Throughout her life she was subject to mystical visions, which she reported to her confessor at age 43. The archbishop of Mainz called a committee of theologians to convene to confirm the authenticity of her visions, after which a monk was appointed to help her record them in writing. The finished work, *Scivias,* which took over 10 years to complete, contains 26 of her prophetic and apocalyptic visions concerning the church, redemption, and the relationship between God and humans. The vivid images and poetic symbols of *Scivias* have been compared to those of William Blake and DANTE ALIGHIERI. One such image is her portrayal of "life's journey as a struggle to 'set up our tent.'" As Matthew Fox writes in his foreword to *Hildegard von Bingen's Mystical Visions,* "The tent, in Hildegard's view, comes folded up in us at the time of our birth as original blessings. But our life journey is that of setting up the tent."

In 1147 Hildegard founded a new convent at Rupertsberg, where she continued to record her visions. She also wrote prolifically on a variety of other subjects such as medicine, natural history, and the lives of saints. Her *Symphonia armonie celestium revelationum* (The Symphony of the Harmony of Celestial Revelations), which she finished in the early 1150s, is a collection of 77 of these lyric poems and chants, each with a musical setting. As she states in her letters, she regarded music as divine inspiration: "Sometimes when we hear a song we breathe deeply and sigh. This reminds the prophet that the soul arises from heavenly harmony." *The Symphony* has recently enjoyed renewed critical interest.

Before 1158, Hildegard completed another musical work, *Ordo,* a collection of 82 melodies that is important as one of the first morality plays, in which good is pitted against evil. In her lifetime,

Hildegard von Bingen overcame almost insurmountable obstacles as a medieval woman and was consulted by bishops, popes, and kings for her religious insight. Though she has not been formally canonized, she is listed as a saint in the Roman Martyrology.

English Versions of Works by Hildegard von Bingen

Hildegard von Bingen's Mystical Visions. Translated from *Scivias* by Bruce Hozeski. Introduction by Matthew Fox. Santa Fe, N.Mex.: Bear & Co., 1986.

Mystical Writings. Edited and introduced by Fiona Bowie and Oliver Davies with new translations by Robert Carver. New York: Crossroad, 1990.

A Work about Hildegard von Bingen

Flanagan, Sabina. *Hildegard of Bingen, 1098–1179: A Visionary Life.* London; New York: Routledge, 1998.

Hippocrates   (ca. 460 B.C.–ca. 377 B.C.)
physician, medical writer

During the fourth century B.C., the classical civilization of ancient Greece flourished. The Greeks, particularly the Athenians, achieved new heights in art, literature, and science that have remained a standard of human accomplishment up to the present day. Of the many great thinkers and philosophers who lived and worked during this time, one of the most important and influential was the physician Hippocrates, often considered the father of medicine.

Hippocrates was born on the island of Cos, in the Aegean Sea. Aside from his birthplace and the years in which he lived, very little is known about his life. It is known that the city-state of Cos contained a thriving medical school, which may be attributed to Hippocrates' presence. His teachings, however, are well known because they were collected into a series of books known as the *Hippocratic Corpus.*

Before Hippocrates, medicine in the ancient world was hardly more advanced than superstition. Illness and disease were thought to be caused by evil spirits or the disfavor of the gods. The remedies provided for patients were more like religious rituals than medical treatments.

Hippocrates changed this by transforming medicine into an empirical science, based on observation and experiment. He taught his students to search for natural explanations of medical symptoms, as opposed to attributing illnesses to supernatural phenomena. Rather than relying on rituals or prayers to heal the sick, Hippocrates favored the use of dietary changes and other such devices. Although his medical knowledge was primitive compared with that of the modern world, the fact that he recognized the empirical basis of medicine was a considerable achievement.

Hippocrates is also famous for the so-called "Hippocratic Oath." A modified version of the oath is still taken by many graduates of medical schools today. By taking the oath, doctors swear to assist any person who needs help, no matter whom they are or what they may have done, and they also pledge never to harm any patient under any circumstances.

The teachings of Hippocrates are collected in the *Hippocratic Corpus.* It consists of about 60 books, written on a variety of medical subjects. Most of them were likely written by Hippocrates' students rather than by Hippocrates himself. In addition to suggested treatments for a variety of ailments, the *Hippocratic Corpus* speculates on the causes of disease in general and can be considered a philosophical and scientific text or a collection of medical treatises.

Hippocrates' teachings greatly influenced the development of medicine and science. The Roman doctor GALEN, the second most important physician of ancient times, greatly respected Hippocrates. Indeed, Hippocrates' work dominated Western medical thinking until the Renaissance, 2,000 years later. Although the medical knowledge of the modern world far surpasses that known to Hippocrates, he is still greatly respected for his teaching of medicine as an empirical science.

English Versions of Works by Hippocrates

Hippocrates: Ancient Medicine, Airs, Waters, Places, Epidemics 1–2, Oath, Precepts, Nutriment, Volume 1. Loeb Classical Library. Translated by W. H. Jones. Cambridge, Mass.: Harvard University Press, 1992.

Hippocrates: Places in Man, General Nature of Glands, Fleshes, Use of Liquids, Ulcers, Fistulas, Haemorrhoids, Volume 8. Loeb Classical Library. Edited by Paul Potter. Oxford: Oxford University Press, 1994.

Works about Hippocrates

Craik, Elizabeth M. *Hippocrates: Places in Man.* Oxford: Oxford University Press, 1998.

Jouanna, Jacques. *Hippocrates.* Translated by M. B. Debevoise. Baltimore, Md.: Johns Hopkins University Press, 2001.

Temkin, Owsei. *Hippocrates in a World of Pagans and Christians.* Baltimore, Md.: Johns Hopkins University Press, 1995.

Hirtius, Aulus (ca. 90–43 B.C.) *historian, politician*

During the first century B.C., the Roman Republic was thrown into political and social chaos as rival generals and politicians fought one another for supremacy. Despite this anarchy, however, many Romans continued to make important intellectual and literary contributions. One of these men was Aulus Hirtius.

Hirtius was a military and political ally of Julius CAESAR who served as a general in numerous military campaigns, as well as an administrator in various political posts. Caesar apparently trusted him enough to nominate him to become a consul, which was the most important office in the Roman Republic. After Caesar's assassination, Hirtius became an ally of Mark Anthony but was persuaded by the orator CICERO to switch sides. During an attack on Anthony at the Battle of Mutina, in which Anthony was defeated, Hirtius was killed.

Hirtius's literary reputation comes from his important historical contributions to Caesar's *Commentaries.* It is thought that he authored the eighth book of Caesar's *Commentaries,* including *De Bello Gallico* (The Gallic Wars) and *Bellum Alexandrinum* (The Alexandrian War). It is for these contributions, as well as his written records of Caesar's African and Spanish campaigns, that Hirtius is remembered.

English Versions of Works by Aulus Hirtius

Caesar, Julius. *Caesar's Gallic War.* Translated by W. A. McDevite and W. S. Bohn. Harper's New Classical Library. New York: Harper & Brothers, 1869.

Gallic War: Seven Commentaries on the Gallic War with an Eighth Commentary by Aulus Hirtius. Translated by Carolyn Hammond. Oxford: Oxford University Press, 1998.

Holy Grail *religious object*

The Holy Grail has been variously identified as a cup, dish, or a life-giving stone, but each story about it has shown it to be mysterious and spiritual in nature. According to legend, the Grail has magical powers and can only be found by someone who fulfills the highest ideals of Christianity and CHIVALRY. Whatever it was or is, some scholars believe the Grail originated from the sacred cauldron of Celtic mythology (*see* MYTHOLOGY; CELTIC); others say that legend became combined with apocryphal Christian stories about Joseph of Arimathea, the rich man who buried Christ in his tomb, then took the Grail with him and supposedly ended up in Britain. The early 20th-century folklorist Jessie Weston sees the Grail and its mystic powers of restoring potency and youth as a vestige of pagan spring renewal ceremonies.

The great French poet CHRÉTIEN DE TROYES first mentions the Holy Grail in his last unfinished work, *Perceval* (1190). According to Chrétien, Perceval, a young, inexperienced knight of King Arthur's court, witnesses a solemn procession in which a beautiful maid carries a beautiful golden platter with a single Mass wafer. This item sustains the Fisher King, a wounded leader whose kingdom has become barren. Only a pure and chivalrous knight who can ask the right question about the procession can eventually heal the Fisher King and restore his kingdom to plenty.

Shortly after Chrétien de Troyes failed to finish *Perceval,* Robert de Boron wrote *Le Roman du Graal* (1200). His contribution to literature about the Grail identifies it as the vessel used by Christ at the Last Supper and by Joseph of Arimathea to catch Jesus' blood as He hung upon the cross. Significantly, this characterization of the Grail not only became the dominant one in legend and literature but also spiritualized the quest motif. This spiritual quest can be seen as well in *Le Haut Livre du Graal* or *Perlesvaus,* written around the same time as Boron's work by the monks of Glastonbury. Their text emphasized adventure and chivalry (through the characters of Lancelot, Gauvain, and Perceval) as a means by which the monks could attract wealthy nobles to support an abbey known for its Arthurian relics. This theme of spiritual quest and chivalric adventure was continued in a later collection of Arthurian stories, *La Queste del saint Graal* (1225), in which Galahad, the son of Arthur's greatest knight, Lancelot, becomes the only knight pure enough to find the Grail.

Chrétien's unfinished poem also influenced one of the greatest works of medieval literature, the *Parzival* (1200) of WOLFRAM VON ESCHENBACH. Wolfram's version is more serious and allegorical than Chrétien's, as it portrays Parzival's spiritual growth. In his poem, the Grail is a stone that fell from heaven during Lucifer's fall. As in Chrétien's version, Parzifal fails to ask the right question about the Grail that will lead to the Fisher King's healing, but Wolfram has Parzifal going through a long process of spiritual purification and successfully fulfilling his task.

Wolfram's version became the most influential in Germanic literature and inspired the 19th-century composer Richard Wagner's great opera *Parsifal.* Alfred, Lord Tennyson's *Idylls of the Kings* (1869) was also inspired by the legend of the Holy Grail, as were Sir Thomas Malory's *Le Morte D'Arthur* (ca. 1469), T. H. White's Arthurian novels *The Once and Future King* (1958) and *The Sword in the Stone* (1937), Charles Williams's novels *Taliessin through Logres* (1938) and *The Region of the Summer Stars* (1944), and T. S. Eliot's *The Waste Land* (1922).

The motif of the Holy Grail quest gave a serious moral and spiritual weight to the adventures of King Arthur's knights, which dominated the medieval and early Renaissance imagination. It exists to this day as a symbol of perfection, spirituality, and Christianity in literature, art, and music.

English Versions of Works about the Holy Grail

Chrétien de Troyes. *Arthurian Romances.* Translated by William W. Kibler and Carleton W. Carroll. New York: Penguin, 1991.

Wolfram von Eschenbach. *Parzival.* Translated by A. T. Hatto. New York: Penguin, 1980.

Works about the Holy Grail

Kennedy, Elspeth. *Lancelot and the Grail: A Study of the Prose "Lancelot."* Oxford: Clarendon, 1986.

Lacy, Norris J. and Geoffrey Ashe with Debra N. Mancoff. *The Arthurian Handbook.* New York: Garland, 1997.

Locke, Frederick W. *The Quest for the Holy Grail: A Literary Study of a Thirteenth-Century French Romance.* New York: AMS Press, 1967.

Maddox, Donald. *The Arthurian Romances of Chrétien de Troyes: Once and Future Fictions.* Cambridge, U.K.: Cambridge University Press, 1991.

Sacker, Hugh D. *An Introduction to Wolfram's "Parzival."* Cambridge, U.K.: Cambridge University Press, 1963.

Weston, Jessie L. *The Quest of the Holy Grail.* New York: Barnes & Noble, 1964.

Homer   (eighth century B.C.) *epic poet*

Homer is the name given to the man credited with composing the *Iliad* and the *Odyssey,* great Greek EPIC poems that are the earliest surviving examples of European literature. The *Iliad,* or "poem about Ilion (Troy)," recounts an episode during the Trojan War with Greece. The *Odyssey* follows one

Greek warrior, the shrewd and wily Odysseus, as he wends his way back home after the siege of Troy.

Almost nothing is known about Homer, including whether he truly existed, but the ancient Greeks in the centuries that followed the poems' composition considered him a distinct individual and depicted him in sculpture. Many scholars are convinced that the two epic poems were created by the same person, as they seem stamped with a single artistic sensibility, sharing such traits as individualized characters, humor (often derived from the all-too-human antics of the gods on Mount Olympus), and deeply moving scenes. They are written in hexameter verse and reveal a structural, stylistic, and dramatic harmony. The narratives are characterized by swift descriptions, straightforward storytelling, generous use of simile (but little if any metaphor), and such oft-repeated epithets as "swift-footed Achilles," "gray-eyed Athena," "resourceful Odysseus," "Hector, tamer of horses," and "Zeus the cloud-gatherer." Common themes include a reverence for lineage and the heroic code, destiny and fate, and the role therein of the gods, who guide arrows, bring false dreams, and directly and indirectly influence human lives.

These masterpieces influenced almost all Greek poetry that followed and much of Western literature. As H. C. Baldry, a scholar of Greek literature, wrote, "For epic [Homer's poems] were accepted as models which all must imitate but none could equal."

It is not known whether Homer was literate or composed the poems orally while others wrote them down. It is known that what has come to us of the *Iliad* is not entirely the original composition. The ancient Athenians altered the narrative to enhance their role in the Trojan War. Additionally, each of the poems was divided long after their creation into 24 convenient sections, or "books."

Of the two eminent Homeric epics, the *Odyssey* was probably composed first, although the events it relates take place at a later date than those in the *Iliad*. The first four books of the poem tell two important background stories, one concerning Mount Olympus and the other concerning the state of Odysseus's household in Ithaca. This is the first documented use of the narrative device in which the story is begun in the middle, and the beginning is recounted at a later stage of the tale. The Roman epic poet VIRGIL used this strategy in the *Aeneid*.

As the story opens, the war goddess Athena had been the Greeks' greatest divine ally, but after the Greeks sacked Troy they failed to pay proper tribute to the gods, so she gives them bitter homecomings. Odysseus, who had spent 10 years fighting the Trojan War, is doomed to spend another decade returning home from it. His son Telemachus, who had been an infant when Odysseus left, is now a fine young man.

Meanwhile, in Ithaca, Odysseus's wife Penelope, beautiful, wealthy, and presumably a widow, is fighting off an onslaught of suitors who have taken up residence in Odysseus's home, devouring his provisions and ordering his servants about. To discourage the parasitic petitioners, Penelope tells them she cannot select a husband from among them until she has finished weaving a shroud for Odysseus's father; and she delays the odious obligation by unraveling by night what she has woven during the day.

Odysseus ventures into many a familiar folktale. He escapes from the island of Calypso, a sea nymph who loves him and wants to give him immortality, and is washed up on the shores of Scheria, home of the mythic Phaeacians, whose king is a grandson of the sea god Poseidon. Here, Odysseus tells of his adventures since he left Troy: He and his crew had traveled to the land of the Lotus-eaters, where men forgot their pasts; blinded the Cyclops, a one-eyed monster; encountered the sorceress Circe, who turns men into swine; traveled to the underworld; averted being tempted by the Sirens' singing by placing wax into their ears; and tried, not altogether successfully, to avoid being eaten by the sea serpent Scylla.

The Phaeacians return Odysseus to Ithaca, where he summarily slaughters his wife's wooers in a gruesome bloodbath. Penelope, no less cunning and resourceful than her husband, tests him to make sure he is who he claims to be. When Odysseus reminds her that he built one of their bedposts out of a growing olive tree, Penelope welcomes her husband home.

Critical Analysis

The *Iliad*, sometimes titled "The Wrath of Achilles," takes place over a few action-packed days during the 10-year conflict between Troy and Greece. Paris, the son of Priam, king of Troy, has absconded with the beauteous Helen, wife of Menelaus, king of Sparta. In retaliation, the Greeks, led by Agamemnon, Menelaus's brother, have waged war on the Trojans. At the opening of the poem, a priest of the sun god Apollo visits the Greeks' camp to request the return of his daughter, who has been kidnapped to serve as Agamemnon's concubine. To appease Apollo, Agamemnon agrees, but he insists that one of his colleagues give up his own mistress to replace the girl he is relinquishing. Achilles, the Greeks' greatest warrior, objects, so Agamemnon punishes him by seizing Achilles' mistress to take the place of the priest's daughter.

An enraged Achilles retreats from the battlefield and withdraws his men. He prays to his mother, Thetis, a sea nymph, to persuade Zeus to give the Greeks ill fortune in battle so Agamemnon will be humiliated and his fellow soldiers will realize how essential Achilles is to their victory.

A series of savage battles follows. The Trojans, led by Hector, son of Priam and brother of Paris, and assisted by Zeus, trounce the Greeks in the next day's battle. Alarmed, Agamemnon sends an envoy to Achilles, still sulking in his tent, offering many gifts and honors if Achilles will return to the battlefield. The warrior rejects the attempt at reconciliation, but when his dearest friend, the kindhearted Patroclus, is slain by Hector, he leaps to his feet and lets forth his famous war cry:

> There he stood, and shouted, and from her
>   place Pallas Athene
> gave cry, and drove an endless terror upon
>   the Trojans.

> As loud as comes the voice that is screamed
>   out by a trumpet
> by murderous attackers who beleaguer a
>   city,
> so then high and clear went up the voice of
>   Aiakides.
> But the Trojans, when they heard the
>   brazen voice of Aiakides,
> the heart was shaken in all, and the very
>   floating-maned horses
> turned their chariots about, since their
>   hearts saw the coming afflictions . . .
> Three times across the ditch brilliant
>   Achilleus gave his great cry,
> and three times the Trojans and their
>   renowned companions were routed.
>   (XVIII, 217–224)

With reinforcement from Achilles, the Greeks massacre the Trojans. Achilles slays Hector and drags his body by the heels behind his chariot around the walls of Troy and back to the army base. Patroclus's body is buried amid much ceremony, and Achilles is persuaded by Priam to permit Hector to have a suitable burial as well.

Critic David Denby describes the vividness of the poetry:

> The brute vitality of the air, the magnificence of ships, wind, and fires; the raging battles, the plains charged with terrified horses, the beasts unstrung and falling; the warriors flung facedown in the dust; the ravaged longing for home and family and meadows and the rituals of peace, leading at last to an instant of reconciliations, when even two men who are bitter enemies fall into rapt admiration of each other's nobility and beauty—it is a war poem, and . . . it has an excruciating vividness, an obsessive observation of horror that causes almost disbelief.

According to scholar Howard W. Clarke, Homer's epics have "retained a primacy . . . as the first and probably the finest example of its genre, the beginning of the Western literary tradition, and the ideal introduction to literature. . . ."

English Versions of Works by Homer

The Iliad of Homer. Translated by Richmond Latti-
    more. Chicago: University of Chicago Press, 1951.
The Odyssey. Translated by Robert Fagles. Introduc-
    tion and notes by Bernard Knox. New York: Pen-
    guin, 1996.
The Poetry of Homer. Translated by S. E. Bassett.
    Edited by Bruce Heiden. Lanham, Md.: Rowman
    & Littlefield, 2003.

Works about Homer

Clayton, Barbara. *A Penelopean Poetics: Reweaving the
    Feminine in Homer's Odyssey.* Lanham, Md.: Row-
    man & Littlefield, 2004.
Knight, W. F. Jackson. *Many Minded Homer.* New
    York: Barnes & Noble, 1968.
Powell, Barry. *Homer.* Oxford, U.K.: Blackwell, 2003.

Horace (Quintus Horatius Flaccus) (65– 8 B.C.) *poet*

Horace was born at Venusia in southern Italy. His first memories were of a nurse, so his mother must have died when he was young. His father, Flaccus, was a freed slave who farmed a small plot of land and may have elevated himself to the position of district tax collector. Flaccus made a modest living, but he was able to save his money and accompany his talented and vivacious young son to Rome for a better education than could be had in their isolated village. In Rome, Horace received scholarly instruc-tion and moral training. Flaccus remained in the city, walking the boy to and from his classes. After he became a poet, Horace wrote movingly about his father's devotion and sacrifice on his behalf.

When he was about 19, Horace traveled to Athens to complete his education with the study of philosophy and Greek poetry. Some two years later, in 44 B.C., Julius CAESAR was slain. Brutus, one of his assassins, arrived in Athens, filled with patri-otic zeal for the tradition of aristocratic republi-canism, to recruit officers for his army. He was an imposing presence, the very embodiment of the republican ideal, and his fervor was infectious, leading Horace, among many others, to join Bru-tus's forces.

It was an inauspicious career move that came to an end, along with dreams of a republican revival, at the battle of Philippi in 42 B.C. Horace returned to Rome and meager prospects. His father had died; what little Horace might have inherited had been confiscated by Octavian, Caesar's adopted son and heir (later Emperor AUGUSTUS), and his old friends had fallen out of political favor.

A failed revolutionary, Horace took a menial job as a magistrate's clerk. Undefeated in spirit, however, he began spending his leisure time com-posing verse and hoping to secure the support of a benefactor. He became intimate friends with the fledgling Roman poet VIRGIL, and his fortunes soon brightened. Virgil recommended Horace to Mae-cenas, the trusted counselor of Augustus and, like the emperor, a generous patron of literature. (This era would become known as the Golden Age of Roman literature.) Around 33 B.C., Maecenas made Horace a gift of the Sabine Farm, some 25 miles northeast of Rome, complete with tenants and servants, so he might devote all of his time and energy to writing poetry. Horace's subsequent fame reflected well on Maecenas for having "dis-covered" the brilliant lyricist.

Horace's friendship with the powerful political adviser, his talent, and his considerable social skills (he loved parties and flirtations and was a shrewd observer with a good sense of humor) provided him entry into the upper crust of Roman society, and his eminent friends found their way into his poetry. Although the poet had opposed the future emperor at Philippi, he developed a sincere patri-otic devotion to the new regime, its leader, and peace. These sentiments, too, he expressed in his writings.

Upon the unexpected death of his dear friend Virgil in 19 B.C., Horace became the official poet of the Augustans. As such, he was chosen to commem-orate and immortalize imperial affairs in verse. These compositions became his celebrated *Odes* and ensured his enduring fame. He died shortly before his 58th birthday and a few weeks after the passing of his benefactor and friend Maecenas.

Horace's first published works, written between 41 and 30 B.C., were called *Satires,* but they do not contain the caustic invective we associate with satire today. Rather, they poke gentle fun at human foibles (avarice, the yearning for wealth and status, hypocrisy), cults of philosophy, various fashions of the day, or whatever strikes the poet's fancy (a journey from Rome to Brundisium with Maecenas; Flaccus's devotion to his son). While the tone is affectionate and good-natured and the style chatty, the poems signify Horace's distinguished intellect, sharp wit, and sophistication. He frequently identifies by name exactly whom he is caricaturing, and Horace himself is no less than others a target of his own barbs.

The *Epodes* were published around 29 B.C. They serve as a transition between the *Satires* and the *Odes,* with the controversial character of the former and the lyric form of the latter. Their subject matter ranges from a tribute to friendship, to the joys of country living (his farm at Sabine was a constant source of pleasure to Horace), to the ill effects on one's social life of eating garlic.

The *Odes* were first published in 23 B.C., followed by two books of *Epistles,* or letters, in roughly 20 and 14 B.C. The *Epistles* are addressed to Horace's friends, including Maecenas and Augustus, and feature agile, entertaining, and erudite ruminations on contemporary life and art.

Critical Analysis

The brilliant and lyrical *Odes* "at once raised Horace to the front rank of Roman poets," writes translator C. E. Bennett, and their popularity has proved enduring. By the time he wrote these poems, Horace was a more recognized artist than he was when he composed his previous works. He was self-sufficient and established, professionally, socially, and financially. These factors are reflected in a more confident and authentic poetic voice.

Because Horace was interested in artistic experimentation, each of the first nine poems exhibits a different meter and a range of subject matter: a dedication to Maecenas; a tribute to Augustus; Virgil's voyage to Greece; the arrival of springtime; an entreaty to a flirt; and an exhortation to enjoy the indoor pleasures of wine, women, and song while winter rages outdoors. Other subjects in these works include the gods, pastoral life, jealousy, vanity, and the poet's immortality. The *Odes* are by turns patriotic and sentimental, formal and light-hearted, dotted with laughter and lamentations, entertaining, and profoundly philosophical.

The *Odes* are presented in four books. The best-known and most beloved poems are I:XI, to which C. E. Bennett gave the title "Enjoy the Passing Hour!"; and the dignified, majestic first six poems of the third book, known as the Roman Odes, particularly IV:VII, "Spring's Return," on the constant beat of the passage of time; and *Carmen Saeculare,* a hymn that was officially commissioned by Augustus to be sung at the ceremonies of the Secular Games that celebrated the peace and prosperity of the age.

Horace's poem "Carpe Diem" is also well-known because it introduces the enduring concept of CARPE DIEM, or "seize the day," a concept Horace also uses in Ode I:XI: "Life Is Brief," the poet counsels. "Even while we speak, envious Time has sped. Reap the harvest of to-day, putting as little trust as may be in the morrow!" Carpe diem later became a pet motif among 17th-century English lyric poets.

"Spring's Return" is rich in mythological, theological, and natural imagery:

> *The snow has fled; already the grass is returning to the fields and the foliage to the trees. Earth is going through her changes. . . . The Grace, with the Nymphs and her twin sisters, ventures unrobed to lead her bands. . . . The cold gives way before the zephyrs; spring is trampled underfoot by summer, destined likewise to pass away so soon as fruitful autumn has poured forth its harvest; and lifeless winter soon returns again.*

In his translation of Horace's works, C. E. Bennett calls Horace "unexcelled among Roman poets."

English Versions of Works by Horace

Odes and Epodes. Translated by C. E. Bennett. Cambridge, Mass.: Harvard University Press; London: William Heinemann Ltd., 1964.

The Odes and Epodes. Translated by Niall Rudd. Cambridge, Mass.: Harvard University Press, 2004.

The Satires, Epistles, and Art of Poetry. IndyPublish.com, 2004.

Works about Horace

Anderson, William Scovil, ed. *Why Horace? A Collection of Interpretations.* Wauconda, Ill.: Bolchazy-Carducci Publishers, 2001.

Coolidge, Olivia. *Lives of Famous Romans.* Boston: Houghton Mifflin Company, 1965.

Feeney, Denis and Tony Woodman, eds. *Traditions and Contexts in the Poetry of Horace.* New York: Cambridge University Press, 2002.

Mendell, Clarence W. *Latin Poetry: The New Poets & The Augustans.* New Haven, Conn.; London: Yale University Press, 1965.

Watson, Lindsay C. *Commentary on Horace's Epodes.* Oxford: Oxford University Press, 2003.

Hsieh Ling-yün

See XIE LINGYUN.

hubris   term

Hubris is a literary term meaning "overweening pride." It was originally used to describe a theatrical or literary device employed in classical tragic drama but is more often used now to describe people who exhibit too much pride, to their own and others' detriment.

The word was introduced by the Greek philosopher and scholar ARISTOTLE in his work of literary criticism, the *Poetics,* of which only fragments remain. Aristotle defined the term *hamartia* as a tragic flaw or error in judgment that leads to a hero's inevitable downfall. Hubris is a type of *hamartia:* excessive insolence, overconfidence or arrogance that causes a great (or, at least, honorable) man to disregard the warnings of the gods, ignore the established moral order, or violate the heroic code. Examples of hubris can be seen in the writings of the EPIC poet HOMER, the *Histories* of HERODOTUS, and the tragedies of SOPHOCLES and EURIPIDES.

Homer's masterpiece, the *Iliad,* recounts events that take place over a few days' period toward the end of the war between Troy and Greece. Achilles, Greeks' greatest warrior, has received a young woman, Briseis, as a sort of war trophy. The commander in chief of the Greeks, Agamemnon, has been compelled to appease the gods by surrendering his own mistress and so seizes Briseis to take her place. Achilles wages a monumental tantrum, withdraws from combat, and prays to his mother, who has influence with the gods, to cause the Greeks to be defeated in the next battles. Agamemnon tries to make amends, but Achilles continues to pout. As a result of his hubris, Achilles' comrades are massacred, including his best friend, whose death rouses Achilles to revenge. In brutally executing his friend's killer, however, Achilles precipitates his own demise; for it has been preordained that his death would soon follow that of the man he has slain. Achilles' hubris hastens his own death.

Herodotus, considered the world's first historian, wrote an exhaustive account of the great wars between the Persian Empire and Greece. Persia was a colossal force, while Greece was just a fledgling group of city-states, poorly organized and barely united. But the Greeks prevailed, Herodotus suggests, because of Persia's hubris. The invading empire's arrogance lay in the belief that it was appropriate for the mighty to enslave and tyrannize the weak and in its attempts to achieve victory in battle by dominating and defying nature (diverting a river's natural flow, for example). These actions brought divine retribution, and so the Persian Empire was defeated. The tragedian AESCHYLUS dramatizes a corresponding point of view in *The Persians* (472 B.C.).

In *Oedipus Rex,* SOPHOCLES tells of the Theban king and queen Laius and Jocasta, who learn from a prophesy that their son will murder his father and marry his mother. When Jocasta bears a son, the couple casts him out to be exposed to the elements, but unbeknownst to them, he survives. Later, when Laius is traveling on a sacred mission, he is killed on the road by bandits. Oedipus then arrives in Thebes and saves the city from the monstrous Sphinx with his cleverness. As a reward, he is pronounced king and marries the widow Jocasta. But a terrible plague descends on Thebes, and when a prophet presages blindness and ruin for Oedipus, the king dismisses him. Oedipus's exceeding confidence in his own cunning and omniscience has tragic consequences. When they discover the truth—Oedipus was, of course, Laius's murderer and he has indeed married his mother—Jocasta commits suicide and Oedipus blinds himself with her brooches and condemns himself to exile. Laius and Jocasta, too, have been punished for their own arrogant conviction that they could defy an oracle from the gods.

The Bacchae, Euripides' master work, has as its main characters Dionysis, a novice god who represents primal forces, and Pentheus, who is the young ruler of Thebes. With the reckless self-assurance of youth, Pentheus refuses to recognize Dionysis as a god and treats him with bald-faced contempt. Pentheus's hubris leads him to reject both religion and nature. As a consequence, he is killed by his own mother, who has been hypnotized by Dionysis.

Greek myths, as documented by OVID, HESIOD, and others, also feature examples of hubris. Among the most memorable is the tale of Prometheus, who steals fire from the gods to give it to humans. He is punished by being shackled to a cliff and ultimately cast into the underworld.

Works Exemplifying Hubris

Euripides. *Euripides V.* Translated by Emily Townsend, et al. Edited by David Grene and Richmond Lattimore. Chicago: University of Chicago Press, 1959.

Herodotus. *The Histories.* Translated by Robin A. Waterfield. Edited by Carolyn Dewald. Oxford: Oxford University Press, 1999.

Hesiod. *Hesiod.* Translated by Richmond Lattimore. Ann Arbor: University of Michigan Press, 1959.

Homer. *The Anger of Achilles: Homer's Iliad.* Translated by Robert Graves. Garden City, N.Y.: Doubleday & Company, 1959.

Ovid. *Metamorphoses.* Translated by A. D. Melville. Oxford: Oxford University Press, 1998.

Sophocles. *Sophocles I.* Translated by David Grene. Chicago: University of Chicago Press, 1991.

Works about Hubris

Gowan, Donald E. *When Man Becomes God: Humanism and Hubris in the Old Testament.* San José, Calif.: Pickwick Publications, 1975.

Mann, Mary Anneeta. *Construction of Tragedy: Hubris.* Bloomington, Ind.: AuthorHouse, 2004.

Ibn Gabirol, Solomon ben Yehuda
(Abu Ayyub Sulaiman Ibn Yahya Ibn Jabirul, Avicebron) (ca. 1021–1058) *poet, philosopher*

Solomon Ibn Gabirol, one of the giants of Hebrew poetry, was born in Malaga, Spain, around 1021. His deeply personal poems are the source of most of what is known of his life, though two critiques from those days also survive. One Arab poet called him a brilliant if shy student of philosophy, while the Hebrew literary historian Moshe Ibn Ezra wrote of his "angry spirit" and "his demon within."

The poet was raised in Saragossa and educated in literary Arabic, biblical Hebrew, and Greek philosophy. Frail, short, and ugly by his own description, he was beset in his teens by the painful ailments that would embitter his life. In T. Carmi's translation (*The Penguin Book of Hebrew Verse*), Ibn Gabirol writes: "Sickness burned my innards with a fever like fire, till I thought my bones would melt."

Ibn Gabirol suffered one reversal after another, beginning with his father's death, followed by the death of his court patron Yequtiel Ibn Hasan. Still, by age 19, Ibn Gabirol had made his name as an accomplished poet.

After his mother died, Ibn Gabirol moved to Granada and attached himself to its vizier (minister of state), Samuel HaNagid, himself a great Hebrew poet who influenced the young Solomon. His ambition stymied by court intrigues and the jealousy of lesser men, whom he skewered in verse, Gabirol departed for Valencia, where he died while still in his 30s. Over 400 of his poems survive, covering the full range of secular, religious, and philosophical Hebrew forms. He also wrote a major work of philosophy, *Fons Vitae* (The Well of Life), an ethical treatise, *On the Improvement of the Moral Qualities;* and some 20 other books that have apparently been lost.

Ibn Gabirol was one of the founders of the "Andalusian school." Nourished in the aristocratic courts of the region, these poets derived their secular subject matter and their "quantitative" meters from Arabic models while continuing to embellish the rhyming traditions of the earlier Jewish religious poets (*paytanim*). They helped revive biblical Hebrew as a literary medium, building on the linguistic studies of such scholars as the 10th-century Babylonian rabbi Sa'adia Gaon.

Ibn Gabirol's nature and love poems can be intensely lyrical, as evidenced in his poem "The Garden":

Its beads of dew hardened still,
he sends his word to melt them;

they trickle down the grapevine's stem
and its wine seeps into my blood.

These secular verses, written for a sophisticated public or for wealthy patrons, are considered less innovative than Ibn Gabirol's religious poetry. His most famous work, *Keter Malkhut* (A Crown for the King) is still read on Yom Kippur in Sephardic congregations. It combines exalted visions of the creation according to Ptolemaic cosmology with a humble plea for divine mercy, totally out of keeping with the poet's otherwise arrogant persona. "Adon Olam" (Master of the Universe), perhaps the most popular hymn in the Jewish liturgy, is usually attributed to Ibn Gabirol as well.

The poet's religious works attest an ecstatic love of God as his only consolation. In the poem "In Praise of God," he professes:

I sigh for You with a thirsting heart; I am
like
the pauper begging at my doorstep. . . .

Other poems, such as "Pitiful Captive," show a yearning for Jewish national redemption that may have influenced the later poet Judah Halevi.

Ibn Gabirol is considered one of the transmitters of Neoplatonism to the Christian scholastics of the high MIDDLE AGES. They knew only the Latin translation of his *Fons Vitae* (The Well of Life), and thought the author to be a Muslim or Christian. The 19th-century discovery of Hebrew excerpts rendered from the Arabic original helped identify Ibn Gabirol as the true author.

In the *Fons,* Ibn Gabirol connects the earthly and heavenly realms, composed alike of matter impressed with form. By a spiritual effort, we can exploit this similarity to achieve divine wisdom and bliss. His treatise *On the Improvement of the Moral Qualities* was the first systematic Hebrew work of ethical philosophy. He claims a close correlation between moral impulses and physical senses, which can be trained to promote right conduct.

From his day to the present, Ibn Gabirol has kept his place in the Jewish literary canon. His original mix of secular and religious achievement influenced Hebrew poets for 400 years in Muslim and Christian Spain and continued to bear fruit in other lands even after the decline and destruction of the fabled Spanish Jewish community.

English Versions of Works by Solomon Ibn Gabirol

The Fountain of Life: Fons Vitae by Solomon Ibn Gabirol (Avicebron). Translated by Harry E. Wedeck. New York: Philosophical Library, 1962.

Keter Malkhut: A Crown for the King by Solomon Ibn Gabirol. Translated by David R. Slavitt. New York: Oxford University Press, 1998.

Selected Poems of Solomon Ibn Gabirol. Translated by Peter Cole. Princeton, N.J.: Princeton University Press, 2001.

Works about Solomon Ibn Gabirol

Halkin, Abraham S. "Judeo-Arabic Literature." In *The Jews: Their Religion and Culture.* Edited by Louis Finkelstein. New York: Schocken, 1971.

Loewe, Raphael. *Ibn Gabirol.* London: Weidenfeld & Nicholson, 1989.

Ibn Sīnā

See AVICENNA.

Imam 'Alī

See 'ALĪ IBN ABĪ TALĪB.

Imru' al-Qays   (Amru al-Qays, Ibn Hujr)
(d. ca. 550) *poet*

Imru' al-Qays is considered the most important of the pre-Islamic Arab poets—those who lived and wrote in the era before MUHAMMAD. He is traditionally credited with formalizing the rules of Arab poetry, and his work has influenced Arab poets throughout the centuries.

Imru' lived in the mid-sixth century. His father was king of the Kinda tribe of central Arabia, which was in turn part of the Qays clan, which boasted the finest Arabic poetry of that era. Imru's pleasure-loving youthful years ended abruptly when his father was killed as a result of feuds with rival clans. The rest of his life was a fruitless quest to regain power and avenge his father's death. In his *Mu'allaqāt* ode, he writes: "Many a desolate wadi have I crossed wherein a wolf howled . . . and when it howled I replied: 'We are both destitute.'" After finding refuge with the Jewish chief Samuel of Taima, Imru' won the support of the Byzantine emperor Justinian, but when he seduced the emperor's daughter, Justinian had him poisoned.

In Imru's era, poetry was still transmitted orally. Imru's works were collected into a *diwan*, or anthology, but scholars doubt the authenticity of many of them. The poet is mostly known for a long, complex poem (untitled) that was included in the *Mu'allaqāt* (The Seven Odes), also called the Hanged Poems) an anthology of major pre-Islamic poems first collected 200 years after the poet's death.

Imru's *Mu'allaqāt* poem has 82 lines. It is constructed along fairly conventional lines, but its imagery and descriptive power have made it one of the most popular poems in the Arabic repertoire. It begins with an unusually erotic, self-congratulatory account of former lovers, recalled in sadness at a deserted campsite: "Stop, both of you. Let us weep for the memory of a beloved and an abode in the lee of the sands." This is followed by the obligatory animal section, which praises the poet's horse and describes an antelope hunt, and, finally, by a powerful rendering of a thunderstorm.

Muhammad considered Imru' the greatest of the Arab poets. Subsequent generations of Arab critics have confirmed that judgment.

See also HANGED POEMS.

English Versions of Works by Imru' al-Qays
Arberry, A. J., trans. *The Seven Odes: The First Chapter in Arabic Literature.* 61–66. New York: Macmillan, 1957.

Lichtenstadter, Ilse. *Introduction to Classical Arabic Literature.* New York: Twayne, 1974.

A Work about Imru' al-Qays
Huart, Clement. *A History of Arabic Literature.* Beirut: Khayats, 1966.

Isaeus (fourth century B.C.) *lawyer, orator, speechwriter*

During the Golden Age of ancient Greece, which was dominated by the powerful city-state of Athens, questions concerning legal issues became extremely important. With commerce expanding and wealth increasing, a profession of lawyers developed whose requirement it was to deal with questions concerning property and personal estates. One such lawyer was Isaeus, of whose life virtually nothing is known. It is believed that he was born in the Greek town of Calcis, he was a student of ISOCRATES, and he subsequently passed on his knowledge of rhetoric to the Athenian orator DEMOSTHENES.

Only a very small portion of Isaeus's works has survived: 11 speeches involving inheritance cases and a fragment of a speech protesting a man's exclusion from citizenship. Isaeus wrote most of his speeches for other people, yet he is counted among the ten ATTIC ORATORS (a group of public speakers and speechwriters). His writing and speaking style, as revealed in his extant texts, were direct and to the point but rather dry and academic, characteristic of the Attic style. He was also not above making personal attacks against his opponents, a common practice among lawyers in ancient Greece.

Despite the limited information on his life and the small amount of surviving material, Isaeus's works provide important historical information on the legal, social, and economic conditions of Greece during his lifetime.

An English Version of a Work by Isaeus
Isaaus. Translated by Edward Seymour Forster. New York: G.P. Putnam's Sons, 1927.

A Work about Isaeus
Robinson, Charles Alexander. *The Tropes and Figures of Isaeus: A Study of His Rhetorical Art.* Princeton, N.J.: C.S. Robinson & Co., 1901.

Isocrates (436–338 B.C.) *orator, teacher, speechwriter*

In the fourth century B.C., the city-states of ancient Greece were caught up in political turmoil and constant warfare. At the same time, the Greeks were making astonishing advances in literature, art, and science. During this turbulent time, many great thinkers and writers lived and worked, among them Isocrates.

Isocrates was an Athenian, born into a well-to-do family that lost most of its property during the Peloponnesian War. After receiving a good education, he turned to speechwriting and teaching to make a living. He developed strong opinions about politics and education, and established a school in Athens that soon rivaled the famous Academy of PLATO.

Isocrates believed that an effective education, particularly in the art of speaking, was extremely important for the people who would become leaders of the Greek city-states. Students such as ISAEUS, Timotheus, and Hyperides came from all over Greece to study at Isocrates' school, and many of them went on to outstanding political careers. The concept of a well-rounded, humanistic education, which became a crucial part of Western civilization, was largely his creation.

Isocrates also believed that the disunity plaguing Greece was its chief weakness. He believed Greeks to be superior to all other people and called on them to unite in a great crusade against their mutual enemy, the Persian Empire. In particular, he believed that a single strong leader was needed to bring the Greeks together, and toward the end of his life, he came to feel this man was Philip II, king of Macedonia and father of Alexander the Great.

All but 21 of Isocrates' speeches have been lost. In a speech titled *Panegyricus,* he states his belief that being Greek is more about believing in Greek culture and adopting a Greek mind-set than about simply being born Greek. In many other speeches, he repeatedly states his belief that the Greeks must stop fighting amongst themselves and unite against the Persians. In his most famous speech, *Philip,* he calls on King Philip II to unite all city-states under his leadership.

Isocrates was a fierce opponent of the Athenian statesman DEMOSTHENES, who was strongly against Philip. By the time Isocrates died, Philip was close to consolidating his control over Greece, just as Isocrates had hoped.

An English Version of a Work by Isocrates

Isocrates I. Translated by David Mirhady & Yun Lee Too. Austin: University of Texas Press, 2000.

Works about Isocrates

Poulakos, Takis and David J. Depew. *Isocrates and Civic Education.* Austin: University of Texas Press, 2004.

Yun Lee Too. *Rhetoric of Identity in Isocrates: Text, Power, Pedagogy.* New York: Cambridge University Press, 1995.

Izumi Shikibu (ca. 970–1030) *poet, diarist*

Izumi Shikibu lived during the highest point of the Heian era and is considered by many to be one of the greatest Japanese female poets. Little is known of her early life, but historical and literary texts indicate that at age 18 she married a provincial official (the lord of Izumi Province) and had a daughter named Koshikibu. Despite her marriage, she began a passionate affair with the Empress Masako's stepson, Prince Tametaka, when she joined the court. Disowned by her family, she was separated from her husband, and then her lover died, leaving her heartbroken.

Three years later, Izumi became the mistress of her dead lover's brother, Prince Atsumichi, and moved into the royal compound. When Atsumichi died, Izumi went into a period of mourning, during which she wrote more than 240 poems about her loss.

Izumi eventually returned to court and became a lady-in-waiting to Empress Akiko, along with MURASAKI SHIKIBU, author of *The Tale of Genji.* At age 36, she married again and accompanied her husband, Fujiwara no Yasumasa, to his post in the provinces. She never returned to court.

Although Izumi is best known for her poetry, there is also a diary associated with her called the *Izumi Shikibu Nikki* (*Izumi Shikibu Diary,* also referred to as *The Tale of Izumi Shikibu*). This diary is written in a mixture of poetry and prose, a common form for diaries written during the Heian era, and mostly describes the events surrounding Izumi's relationship with Prince Atsumichi. There is some question as to whether Izumi actually wrote the diary, as the entries are not dated, and while the narration is intensely personal, it is written in the third person.

Little doubt exists about the authorship of her poetry, however, for it was well known even in her own time, and 67 of her poems appeared in the *Goshuishu,* the Imperial anthology compiled in 1086. Her poetry often uses highly stylized language, but it is also deeply emotional and at times intensely erotic. Much of her work also reflects a strong religious consciousness and her interest in exploring the fleetingness of love and life:

> The fleeting world
> of white dew,
> fox fires, dreams—
> all last long,
> compared with love.

Izumi's poetry, written mostly in the TANKA form, shows both a great passion for life and a great sense of melancholy. She is regarded as one of the few female tanka poets of the first century worthy of note.

English Versions of Works by Izumi Shikibu

The Ink Dark Moon: Love Poems by Ono No Komachi and Izumi Shikibu, Women of the Ancient Court of Japan. Translated by Jane Hirshfield and Mariko Aratani. New York: Vintage Books, 1990.

The Izumi Shikibu Diary: A Romance of the Heian Court. Translated by Edwin A. Cranston. Cambridge, Mass.: Harvard University Press, 1969.

A Work about Izumi Shikibu

Keene, Donald. "The Izumi Shikibu Diary" in *Travelers of a Hundred Ages: The Japanese as Revealed Through 1,000 Years of Diaries.* New York: Columbia University Press, 1999, 36–39.

Jacopone da Todi (Jacopo dei Benedetti) (ca. 1230–1306) *poet, prose writer*

Jacopone da Todi, along with DANTE, was the greatest religious poet of his time. Born into an aristocratic family in Todi, Italy, he studied law and became a notary. He lived a worldly and sensual life until he married Vanna di Bernardino di Guidone around 1267. Only a year later, his young wife died in an accident. Jacopone, shocked out of his complacent life, spent the next 10 years dressed in rags and living as a wandering penitent, influenced by the spirituality of FRANCIS OF ASSISI.

In 1278, Jacopone became a friar at the Franciscan convent of San Fortunato in Todi. Though the friars there lived according to the relaxed interpretation of the Francisan rule, Jacopone sympathized with the Spirituals, those who wanted to emulate the complete poverty of St. Francis.

In 1294, the unexpected election of Pier da Morrone, a poor hermit, as Pope Celestine V, excited the Spirituals. They sought his protection against the Conventuals, the friars who favored a more relaxed rule. Many Spirituals saw Celestine as a savior who would end the greed and corruption of the clergy. But Jacopone was more skeptical, writing in one of his poems:

> Now we'll see what comes
> Of all those meditations in your hermit's
>   cell.
> Disappoint those who have placed their
>   hopes in you
> And they will rain curses on your head.
> (Lauda 54)

As Jacopone feared, Celestine proved weak and soon abdicated. His successor, Boniface VIII, withdrew the protection that Celestine had accorded the Spirituals. In 1297, the Spirituals defied the pope but were defeated, and Jacopone was thrown into prison, where he continued to write poems. He was freed in 1303 and died three years later.

During his life, Jacopone wrote approximately 100 poems, called the *Laude* because many were written in the style of the popular religious songs (*laude*) sung by wandering groups of flagellants in imitation of St. Francis. The poems are difficult to interpret, however, since scholars do not agree on the order in which the poems were written, or which of the many poems attributed to Jacopone are really his.

Jacopone's poems describe his spiritual experiences and political and religious struggles. Some poems satirize businessmen who grasp after material things and, metaphorically, the friar whose learning does him no good now that he is dead. Other poems describe Jacopone's imprisonment and denounce Boniface VIII.

Two other prose works have been attributed to Jacopone: *Il Tratatto,* a Latin treatise interpreting his more philosophical poems; and the *Detti,* or sayings written down by his admirers.

Jacopone's religious poems celebrate the Nativity, Franciscan poverty, and above all his intoxication with God and the steps by which he passed from grief for his sins to mystical contemplation. Many of his works use the techniques and imagery of the Provençal TROUBADOURS and the Italian poets who imitated them; yet, rather than describing love for a woman as the troubadours did, Jacopone focuses on loving God.

"Amor de caritate" (Lauda 90), like the Provençal *tenson,* is a dialogue in verse. Evelyn Underhill, a student of mysticism, calls it "a masterpiece of dramatic construction." Jacopone begins by exulting in the contemplation of Christ:

My heart melts, like wax near fire.
Christ puts his mark on me, and stripped of
myself (O wondrous exchange) I put on Christ.
Robed in this precious garment,
Crying out its love,
The soul drowns in ecstasy!

But Christ answers him with

O you who love me, put order into your love,
For without order, there is no virtue!

Jacopone replies:

If it was temperance you wanted,
Why did you lead me to this fiery furnace?

The language of ecstatic love and the images of the furnace and the heart melted like wax are typical of the 13th-century Tuscan and Sicilian poets.

Another of Jacopone's most famous *laude,* "Lady of Heaven," is a dramatic dialogue between

the Virgin Mary, her son Jesus, and the bystanders at the Crucifixion, and it influenced the development of medieval Italian drama. A popular Latin hymn of the MIDDLE AGES with a similar theme, the *Stabat Mater,* has been erroneously attributed to Jacopone.

Jacopone's religious lyrics were popular throughout the Middle Ages, but modern critics outside of Italy have neglected his work. Some consider him coarse, unbalanced, and often incomprehensible, but Jacopone's works have recently attracted new interest. George Peck writes that "Rarely has a poet revealed the marrow of his inner life with more precision and more passion."

An English Version of a Work by Jacopone da Todi

Jacopone da Todi: The Lauds. Translated by Serge and Elizabeth Hughes. New York: Paulist Press, 1982.

Works about Jacopone da Todi

Peck, George T. *The Fool of God: Jacopone da Todi.* Tuscaloosa: University of Alabama Press, 1980.
Underhill, Evelyn. *Jacopone da Todi: A Spiritual Biography.* New York: Books for Libraries Press, 1972.

Jāhiz, al- ('Abu 'Uthmān 'Amr ibn Bahr ibn Mahbūb al-Jāhiz) (ca. 776–868)
essayist

Al-Jāhiz (meaning "goggle-eyed") was a very prolific prose writer who authored nearly 200 books of essays covering a very broad range of topics from science to politics. He is considered the foremost Arab intellectual of his era.

Al-Jāhiz was born in Basra, reportedly the grandson of a black porter. He lived most of his life there. Basra was then at the peak of its economic and cultural glory under the new Abbasid Caliphate, as Arab civilization began to assimilate the cultural contributions of all the great peoples that had been assembled together in the realm of Islam.

Al-Jāhiz was known for his cosmopolitan knowledge; his clear, accessible prose; the logic of his argumentation; and most of all for his talent to entertain. There was no topic in the sciences, literature, religion, or philosophy that escaped the attention of his pen. He treated all subjects with the same combination of seriousness and humor. His humor, however, led some critics to accuse him of triviality, and indeed it is not always clear whether or not al-Jāhiz is being sarcastic; for example, he wrote one book condemning wine and another defending it.

Al-Jāhiz was a master of rhetorical argument, often specializing in *munazara,* or parallels, a contemporary genre in which different people, animals, objects, or concepts argue their respective virtues. Not surprisingly, he wrote a popular book on rhetoric, titled *Kitab al-Bayan wa al-tabayyun* (The Book of Excellence and Rhetoric). Among the many topics he illuminated were the conduct of kings, the customs of misers, the virtues of the Turks, cripples, bureaucrats, mispronunciation, singers, Christianity, and jokes. One widely read work was a collection of sayings attributed to Ali, MUHAMMAD's son-in-law.

Like many Basrans, al-Jāhiz was a Mu'tazilite, one whose relatively rationalist Islamic philosophy held that the current caliph could supplement the laws of the KORAN with new rulings. He is considered one of the first great practitioners of *adab,* or the cultivation of worldly knowledge. However, al-Jāhiz was also a consistent defender of Arab and Islamic culture against the claims of Greeks, Indians, and Persians. He participated in the great literary debate against the Shu'ubites, who sang the virtues of the non-Arab Muslim cultures, especially that of Persia.

Al-Jāhiz gained his greatest renown with his seven-volume *Kitab al-Hayawan* (Book of Animals). In addition to animals, it addressed many other topics in endless digressions, including religion, climate, crime, and the nature of matter. His underlying purpose may have been to demonstrate that Arabic scientific and practical knowledge had become equal or even superior to its pagan predecessors in Greece and Persia.

Al-Jāhiz's life was a celebration of the culture of books. As he wrote in the *Book of Animals:* "[A book] will amuse you with anecdotes, inform you on all manner of astonishing marvels, entertain you with jokes or move you with homilies, just as you please. . . . there is no pleasanter neighbor, no more fair-minded friend, no more amenable companion."

In the final irony, al-Jāhiz's love of books proved his undoing. From time to time, he would have himself locked into a bookstore at night to read through the stock. On one such occasion, when he was 92, a pile of books collapsed and crushed him to death.

An English Version of Works by al-Jāhiz
Nine Essays of al-Jāhiz. Translated by William M. Hutchins. New York: P. Lang, 1989.

Works about al-Jāhiz
Pellat, Charles. *The Life and Works of Jāhiz.* Translated by D. M. Hawke. Berkeley: University of California Press, 1969.
Huart, Clement. *A History of Arabic Literature.* Beirut: Khayats, 1966.
Nicholson, R. A. *A Literary History of the Arabs.* Cambridge, U.K.: Cambridge University Press, 1966.

Jataka (fifth century) *sacred texts*
The Jataka tales constitute part of the canon of sacred Buddhist literature. The main body of Jataka literature is a collection of 547 stories of Buddha's previous births in prose and verse, written in Pali. Originally the Jatakas were oral tales that came from the Varanasi region of north central India and consisted of both animal and human tales as well as parables for instruction. These were then absorbed into the Buddhist literary canon, and the stories later became an important part of the Southeast Asian canon of Buddhist literature after its indigenous kingdoms adapted Indian cultural and religious philosophy.

The Jatakas contain stories that relate the self-sacrificing spirit of the Buddha in his previous lives. Several major themes and types are represented in the stories. These consisted of pre-

Buddhist animal fables, heroic adventure tales, tales of renunciation, and tales exemplifying total charity and generosity. The themes of sacrifice and continuous rebirth reveal the similarity between Buddhist and Hindu beliefs regarding reincarnation. They also represent Buddhist and Hindu aims to escape the cycle of rebirth by attaining enlightenment or release from this world.

Though the stories originated as oral fables, Buddhists believe that the Buddha told these stories as lessons to his followers. In the Theravada Buddhist areas of Burma and Thailand, the most popular Jataka is the story of Prince Vessantara, who is known for his charitable nature; this a virtue that most Buddhists wish their kings would emulate. Vessantara leaves the comforts and luxuries of his palace to wander all over his kingdom. In his travels, he gives away many of his possessions, including his wife and children when he has nothing else to give away. The last 10 Jatakas, including the story of Vessantara, are frequently depicted in murals, temple reliefs, and paintings in Burma and Thailand.

English Versions of the Jataka

Jataka Tales: Animal Stories. Retold by Ellen C. Babbit. New York: Appleton-Century-Crofts, 1940.

Jataka Tales, Birth Stories of the Buddha. Retold by Ethel Beswick. London: J. Murray, 1956.

A Work about the Jataka

Cummings, Mary. *The Lives of the Buddha in the Art and Literature of Asia*. Ann Arbor: University of Michigan, Center for South and Southeast Asian Studies, 1992.

Jaufré Rudel (Jaufré Rudel II, lord of Blaye [Gironde]) (early 12th century)
troubadour, poet

Jaufré Rudel was born into a noble French family in the first half of the 12th century. He inherited the lordship of Blaye, a territory in southwest France, from his father Girard after 1126 and be-

came known as a TROUBADOUR. He joined the Second Crusade (*see* CRUSADES) in 1147, arriving in Palestine in 1148, where he seems to have died.

According to legend, Jaufré fell in love with the Countess of Tripoli, a woman he had never met, and supposedly wrote several songs about her, including the following lines from "When the Days Are Long in May":

> But I'll find no love or joy
> without the joy of my love far away,
> for I know none gentler, better,
> north or south, near or far away;
> so high is her true and fine worth
> that upon Saracen earth
> I'd be called captive for her.

As the legend continues, Jaufré also became a crusader in order to travel to Tripoli, where the countess was alleged to be, but unfortunately fell ill on the way. After his arrival in Tripoli, the countess visited his sickbed. Jaufré thanked God for allowing him to see his love and then died.

Six of Jaufré's poems remain in existence, along with the melodies meant to accompany four of them. As most troubadour songs do, Jaufré's concern courtly love (*see* CHIVALRY AND COURTLY LOVE) and are written in Provençal, which he calls "a plain old Romance tongue." As scholar Frede Jensen notes, "troubadours of southern France were the first European poets to write in the vernacular" rather than in Latin.

Jaufré's songs are comprised of lines of seven or eight syllables. Between six and eight lines make up each stanza, and each poem contains five to eight stanzas. "When the days are long in May," which is regarded as his best song, repeats the same rhyme scheme (ababccd) for seven stanzas, then concludes with a final three lines whose rhyme scheme is ccd.

While Jaufré lingers on the feelings he has for his "distant love," he remains vague about whom the "distant love" is. Some critics have theorized that his poems were really about a love for the Virgin Mary or for Jerusalem. Others have pointed out that Jaufré occasionally speaks of his beloved in words that could only apply to a living woman. Either interpretation could be correct.

Perhaps partly because of their ambiguity, the poems reach beyond the time and place of their composition to speak to readers of every century. During World War II, French exiles and prisoners of war read and reread Jaufré's poems. In addition, his works and legendary life have inspired numerous writers, including the author of the French MEDIEVAL ROMANCE *Guillame de Dôle;* Petrarch, who mentions Jaufré in his "Triumph of Love"; the 19th-century poet Robert Browning, who wrote a poem entitled "Rudel to the Lady of Tripoli"; and the 20th-century poet Ezra Pound, who refers to Jaufré in his *Cantos.*

Jaufré's poems remain appealing less because of their beauty than because they describe a universal feeling: the longing for love. As scholar James Wilhelm writes, Jaufré acknowledges his "earthbound condition" yet "constantly keeps striving for higher ideals. These ecstatic flights, more clearly pronounced in him than in any other troubadour, show him as a forerunner of DANTE."

See also MIDDLE AGES.

English Versions of Works by Jaufré Rudel

The Poetry of Cercamon and Jaufré Rudel. Edited and translated by George Wolf and Roy Rosenstein. New York: Garland, 1983.

Songs of Jaufré Rudel, Vol. 41. Translated by Rupert T. Pickens. Toronto: Pontifical Institute of Mediaeval Studies, 1978.

Works about Jaufré Rudel

Rosenstein, Roy. "A Medieval Troubadour Mobilized in the French Resistance," *Journal of the History of Ideas* 59, no. 3 (1998), 499–520.

Wilhelm, James J. *Seven Troubadours: The Creators of Modern Verse.* University Park: Penn State University Press, 1970.

Jean de Meun   (Jean de Meung, Jean Chopinel, Jean Clopinel of Meung-sur-Loire)   (ca. 1240–ca. 1305)   *poet, translator*
Jean de Meun, best known as the author of the final 18,000 lines of the ROMANCE OF THE ROSE, was born in the French town of Meun-sur-Loire. Very little is known about his life. Since he was known to contemporaries as Master Jean de Meun, scholars believe that he received a Master of Arts degree at the University of Paris and that he likely taught there. He was living near the university at the time of his death. His work contains satires of the Franciscan and Dominican orders of friars, who were under attack at the university at the time. He had also studied Alan of Lille and other philosophical poets of Chartres who exalted Nature.

Jean's works show that he was an expert in Latin with an encyclopedic knowledge of many subjects. He describes himself in the *Romance of the Rose* as "joyous of heart, agile and sound of limb." He also describes himself as a lifelong servant of love. His style is lively and filled with satirical wit, and he popularizes abstract philosophical ideas through the pungent dialogue of his characters.

The variety of works attributed to Jean reflect the interests that led him to complete the *Romance of the Rose.* Among these works is his translation of the Latin work *de re Militaria* by Vegetius, which he called *The Art of Chivalry* (1284). He also translated *The Consolation of Philosophy* by BOETHIUS and the letters of the famous lovers ABÉLARD AND HÉLOÏSE. Two other works, the *Testament of Jean de Meun* and the *Codicil of Jean de Meun,* have also been attributed to him. The dedications of his works show that he had many friends in high places, including Jean de Brienne, count of Eu, and King Philip the Fair of France (1285–1315).

De Meun said that he read GUILLAUME DE LORRIS's *Romance of the Rose* and liked it so much that he decided to finish it. But he had things in mind that went beyond Guillaume's work. While Guillaume wrote somewhat uncritically from within the courtly tradition (*see* CHIVALRY AND COURTLY LOVE), De Meun, writing as a next-generation poet, had a more critical, satirical view of courtly love and its conventions. He brings in satire of women and relations between the sexes, and sets forth arguments that passionate love has no importance in comparison with procreation. His digressions are encyclopedic in length and cover a wide range of topics to interest his medieval listeners.

De Meun's contribution to the *Romance of the Rose* was a popular one; all of the medieval manuscripts except one include his continuation of the text. The work has both survived and become controversial because of him.

An English Version of a Work by Jean de Meun

The Romance of the Rose by Guillaume de Lorris and Jean de Meun. Translated by Charles Dahlberg. Princeton, N.J.: Princeton University Press, 1995.

Works about Jean de Meun

Hill, Jillian M. L. *Medieval Debate on Jean de Meung's Roman de la Rose: Morality Versus Art.* Lewiston, N.Y.: Edwin Mellen Press, 1992.

Kay, Sarah. *The Romance of the Rose.* London: Grant & Cutler, 1995.

Jerome, Saint (Sophronius Eusebius Hieronymus) (ca. 340–420) *translator, prose writer*

Saint Jerome was born in Strido, where Croatia is now, into a family that highly valued education. Although they were Christian, Jerome's parents sent their young son to a prominent pagan school in Rome, where he studied classical literature and became fluent in Latin and Greek.

Concerned that secular studies had corrupted his love of God, Jerome left Rome and spent many years traveling. He befriended monks and other young Christian scholars who had renounced material concerns to dedicate themselves to their faith. This spiritual quest led him to the Syrian desert, where he lived as a hermit for several years.

Taunted and tempted by memories of Roman decadence, Jerome gained mastery over his desires with acts of penance, contemplation, and the discipline of learning Hebrew. He then journeyed to Turkey and became engaged in the theological debates of the day. Sharp-tongued and hot-tempered, Jerome strongly criticized the clergy's worldly pursuits, earning himself many foes. While addressing these controversies at a council in Rome, Jerome found favor with Pope Damasus, who made him his private secretary. At Damasus's behest, Jerome translated the New Testament into contemporary Latin. He also translated the Old Testament from Hebrew to Latin. For centuries, Jerome's Vulgate ("of the common people") was the only version of the Bible sanctioned by the Catholic Church.

When his champion Damasus died, Jerome left Rome and established a monastery at Bethlehem. There, he reportedly extracted a thorn from the paw of a lion, who remained his loyal companion.

While the Vulgate was his crowning triumph, Jerome was also a prolific writer of letters, commentaries, biographies, and translations of historical works. In the MIDDLE AGES, Jerome was designated "Doctor of the Church" for his outstanding piety, contributions to Christianity, and learnedness.

Jerome is the patron saint of translators. "One need only utter the name of Jerome and the most humble of us immediately feels taller, and reminded of the duties and the honor of his calling," wrote 20th-century translator Valery Larbaud.

An English Version of Works by Saint Jerome

Select Letters of St. Jerome. Translated by Frederick Adam Wright. Cambridge, Mass.: Harvard University Press, 1999.

Works about Saint Jerome

Hodges, Margaret. *St. Jerome and the Lion.* London: Orchard Books, 1991.

Larbaud, Valery, *An Homage to Jerome: Patron Saint of Translators.* Translated by Jean-Paul De Chezet. Marlboro, Vt.: Marlboro Press, 1984.

Josephus, Flavius (Joseph ben Mattathias) (ca. 37–ca. 101) historian

Flavius Josephus was born in Jerusalem during Roman rule. His father was a Jewish priest, and his mother was a member of Jewish royalty. He was well-educated, studying both Greek and Hebrew literature, and it is said that at one point he spent three years with a hermit in the desert.

In his early 20s, Josephus traveled to Rome to negotiate the release of several Jewish priests held hostage by Emperor Nero. When he returned home after completing his mission, his nation was beginning a revolution against the Romans (ca. 66). Josephus immediately became a commander of the revolutionary forces in Galilee (present-day Israel).

In one battle, Josephus successfully defended the fortress in Jotapata for almost two months. He eventually surrendered and was taken prisoner by the Roman general Vespasian, who planned on sending him and other prisoners to Emperor Nero, who most likely would have had them executed. Josephus avoided this fate by presenting himself as a prophet and professing Vespasian's rise to imperial power. After this successful move, Josephus served the Romans by assisting them in understanding and negotiating with the Jewish nation. The Jewish revolutionaries considered Josephus a traitor and refused to follow his advice to surrender. Thus he became a witness to the destruction of Galilee, Judea, and the Holy Temple. When Vespasian released him, Josephus joined Vespasian's family name, Flavius, with his own, and eventually followed Vespasian's son Titus to Jerusalem (70).

Josephus's experience as Vespasian's captive resulted in his first work, *Jewish War,* which was published in seven books in 78, when its author was serving at the Flavian court in Rome. The work did not merely state the facts of the war but proclaimed the emperor's military might, flattered his wisdom, and warned other nations against opposing his power. A significant part of the *Jewish War* is devoted to poorly masked adulation of its author's qualities as a warrior and a writer. Josephus first wrote the book in his native language of Aramaic but then translated it into Greek, which was the most widely used language of the Roman Empire.

Josephus's later work *Jewish Antiquities* was published in 93 or 94 in 20 books. In this written work, entirely in Greek, Josephus explains the history of the Jews to the general non-Jewish audience of the time and explains the title of his work by emphasizing the age of the Jewish culture and the Bible. Almost half of the work consists of Josephus's rephrasing of the Hebrew BIBLE, for which he used the works of earlier historians as his sources. *Jewish Antiquities* was zealously read by the early Christians, and numerous translations in later centuries revived interest in the work. One of the best English translations was done by William Whiston (1667–1752) in 1737.

Two shorter works by Josephus include *Autobiography* (or *Life*), in which the historian attempts to justify his position at the beginning of the Jewish uprising; and *Against Apion,* in which he refutes Apion's charges against the Jews in the first century. This, like Josephus's other works, provide significant details on the Roman-Jewish conflict of the ancient world, as well as information about written texts that no longer survive.

English Versions of Works by Flavius Josephus

Life of Josephus: Translation and Commentary. Translated by Steve Mason. Boston: Brill, 2003.

The Jewish War. Translated by H. St. J. Thackeray. Cambridge, Mass.: Harvard University Press, 1997.

Works about Flavius Josephus

Colautti, Federico M. *Passover in the Works of Josephus.* Boston: Brill, 2002.

Feldman, Louis H. *Studies in Josephus' Rewritten Bible.* Boston: Brill, 1998.

Juan Chi

See RUAN JI.

Juvenal (Decimus Junius Juvenalis)

(ca. 50–ca. 127) *poet*

Throughout history, writers have sought to use sarcastic comedy as a means to express their concerns about the society in which they live. Such authors as Voltaire and Jonathan Swift achieved their fame through satire, while also articulating important observations about life. Among the ancient Romans, no one made better use of satire than Juvenal.

Juvenal was born in the town of Aquinum, Italy, at a time when the Roman Empire was at its height. This age was known as the *Pax Romana*, or "Roman Peace." The empire controlled the entire Western world, ruling millions of people and outwardly appearing to be a model of tranquillity and stability. All was not perfect, however, and Juvenal's writings articulated this fact quite well.

Little is known about Juvenal's life. He came from a wealthy family and served both in the army and as a public official. It is not known if he ever married or had children, but records indicate that MARTIAL was one of his friends. His knowledge of the workings of rhetoric schools have led some to speculate that he might have been a teacher, but there is no proof.

Juvenal's writings got him into trouble with the authorities, a fate suffered by many other socially conscious writers both before and after him. The Emperor Domitian sent him into exile for having criticized Domitian's favorite comedian, but Juvenal was apparently held in high regard by another emperor, the cultured Hadrian.

Juvenal wrote his most important work between 110 and 130, during which time he published his 16 major satires, composing them in dactylic hexameters. His themes vary, but every satire revolves around Juvenal's conviction that Roman society was rapidly decaying and losing its sense of purpose. He writes about the corruption of the aristocracy, moral degeneration and sexual depravity among all classes, congestion in Roman cities, and numerous other social ills. He also displays strong anti-Semitism as he approaches all of his subjects with derisive sarcasm and intense bitterness.

Juvenal did not expend all his energy on serious social commentary. Some of his works also lampoon less crucial problems. In his *Satire I*, for example, he begins by making fun of banal and long-winded poets:

> Must I always be stuck in the audience at
>   these poetry-readings, never
> Up on the platform myself, taking it out on
>   Cordus
> For the times he's bored me to death with
>   ranting speeches
> From that Theseid of his?
> . . . When you find
> Hordes of poets on each street-corner, it's
>   misplaced kindness
> To refrain from writing. The paper will still
>   be wasted.

By cloaking these feelings with wit and humor, Juvenal both infuriates and amuses his readers. Furthermore, his meticulous and precise style gives his works a sense of poetic perfection, which was emulated by many poets who came after him.

One of Juvenal's most famous phrases became a part of the lexicon of historians who studied Rome. Juvenal claimed the Roman people were interested only in "bread and games." In other words, as long as Roman citizens had enough to eat and were entertained, they did not care about the critical issues facing their society, such as reforming the government, managing the economy, or protecting the borders from barbarian enemies. The "bread and games" observation thus became an analogy for everything that caused the collapse of the Roman Empire.

Juvenal's works are important for several reasons. From a purely literary standpoint, his poetic style and satirical technique served as models for many later writers. He also provides information that has been extremely useful to historians as they attempt to piece together a picture of Roman culture during the *Pax Romana*. Finally, the social ills Juvenal lampooned were hardly unique to his own time and culture, and his bitter criticisms, aside from his anti-Semitism, can be seen as a warning to our current societies, just as they were to his own.

English Versions of Works by Juvenal

Juvenal in English. Edited by Martin M. Winkler. New York: Penguin Books, 2001.

The Sixteen Satires. Translated by Peter Green. New York: Penguin, 1999.

Works about Juvenal

Colton, Robert E. *Juvenal's Use of Martial's Epigrams: A Study of Literary Influence.* Amsterdam: Benjamins, John Publishing, 1991.

Wehrle, William T. *Satiric Voice: Program, Form, and Meaning in Persius and Juvenal.* Hildesheim, Germany: Georg Olms Publishing, 1992.

Kagero Diary
See MOTHER OF FUJIWARA MICHITSUNA.

Kalevala (400 B.C.–A.D. 1849) *Finnish national epic*

In the early 19th century, Finnish folklore was assembled into a massive EPIC called the *Kalevala* (Land of Heroes). Compilers from the universities of Turku and Helsinki traveled throughout Finland collecting these stories, called runes, which had been transmitted orally for centuries, a task deemed necessary before Finland's oral traditions were lost to modernization. Fifty runes consisting of almost 23,000 lines of poetry had been collected by 1849, and Elias Lönnrot, the Finnish philologist who discovered the *Kalevala*, worked to organize them into a cohesive whole. (An earlier collection was published by Zacharius Topelius in 1822.)

The *Kalevala* (pronounced *Kah* leh *vah* luh) contains the songs and stories of the ancient Finnish people and includes the beginnings of Christianity in Finland. It has been compared to other national mythologies, specifically Vedic mythology from India. For example, in both traditions the myths surrounding the origin of the world—stating that it was hatched from an egg—are very similar.

The ancient Finnish people were animists, which means they worshipped nature and believed that everything around them had an inner spirit. Seers and shamans, key figures in Finnish mythology, undertook visionary journeys, using the reindeer as their animal spirit companion. Many of the songs in the *Kalevala* come from shamanistic ceremonies, and it was believed that some of these songs, or chants, had healing powers. Other chants were said to take shamans, in spirit, to the origins of the world.

The three main characters of the *Kalevala* are Väinämöinen, Lemminkäinen, and Ilmarinen, all sons of *Kalevala*. Väinämöinen is the primal first shaman. He is the master word-weaver and musician in the tales, offering counsel to his people. Lemminkäinen is a young romantic adventurer whose exploits are recounted in many of the runes. Ilmarinen is the primeval smithy, the master architect of the stellar dome and forger of the Sampo. The Sampo is a central object in the *Kalevala*, described as a spinning wheel and seen as a magic mill that grinds out food, money, or gold. The Sampo can also be seen as a cosmological image of the spinning World Axis centered upon the Pole

Star. In Finland the Pole Star can be seen almost straight ahead in the night sky.

The epic was originally written in the trochaic tetrameter, which means each verse had four meters written in the pattern of one accented (long) syllable followed by one unaccented (short) syllable. The following lines from Eino Friberg's 1988 translation are a good example of the style and philosophical subject matter of the runes: "Knowledge cannot stay concealed, / Hidden in some secret burrow; / Words of wisdom never vanish, / Though the wise men pass away."

The *Kalevala*'s words of wisdom remain vital to the Finish people because it contains their traditions, such as the Finnish wedding ceremony, as well as magical incantations and ancient spells. It also gives a specific spiritual outlook connected to the traditional emphasis on nature. Most importantly, the *Kalevala* provides the Finnish people with a connection to their past and a sense of national pride. Pekka Ervast describes the impact of this epic in his work *The Keys to the Kalevala*: "From the rune stories of the *Kalevala* arose a lively picture of the Finnish people's past, their religion, traditions, struggles, ideals, and heroes." Similarly, as Jaakko Ahohas states in *A History of Finnish Literature*, the *Kalevala* "supported [the Finns'] belief in the creative powers of the Finnish nation and in this way contributed to the development of Finnish literature. . . ."

An English Version of the *Kalevala*
The Kalevala: Epic of the Finnish People. Translated by Eino Friberg. Helsinki: Otava Publishing, 1988.

Works about the *Kalevala*
Bosley, Keith. *The Kalevala: An Epic after the Oral Tradition.* New York: Oxford University Press, 1989.
Ervast, Pekka. *The Keys to the Kalevala.* Nevada City, Calif.: Blue Dolphin Publishing, 1999.

Kalidasa (fifth century) *playwright, poet*
Much of Kalidasa's life is surrounded by legend. One of the most common stories about Kalidasa, whose name means "servant of Kali," is that he was born a fool and begged the goddess Kali for wisdom so that he could marry a cunning princess. In reality, he is said to be the son of Pandit Sadasiva Nyayavagisa ("pandit" means "scholar") of Paundra, India, and most scholars associate Kalidasa's life with the reigns of Chandragupta II and Skandagupta in the fifth century.

Many consider Kalidasa, who was called one of the nine gems for his expertise in poetry and drama, the greatest Sanskrit writer of all time. Most of his plays have happy endings, and most of his works are about love. He uses five different kinds of meter based on various patterns of long and short syllables, as well as frequent alliteration and assonance to express the sounds of nature.

Sanskrit poetry is a form of music, and Kalidasa's poems have the lilting rhythm and sensual tone of many love songs. For example, in *Ritusamhara* (The Seasons), a famous poem of 144 stanzas, Kalidasa relates nature to emotion:

> *Their cliffs are cloud-kissed by the midst of lotus white, . . .*
> *They're spread with thick masses of dancing peacock flocks;*
> *They make the heart yearn, do these earth-supporting rocks!*

Another of Kalidasa's poems is "Megha Duuta" ("The Cloud Messenger"), an elegy divided into two parts: The first 63 stanzas are called "Purva-megha" ("The Former Cloud"), and the final 52 stanzas are called "Uttara-megha" ("The Latter Cloud"). The poem tells of Yaksha, a young man, and his sorrow at being separated from his wife. In "The Former Cloud," Yaksha describes the cloud's journey, and in "The Latter Cloud," Kalidasa tells us what Yaksha's message is and describes his wife. The poem is written in the Mandakranta ("slow-stepping") meter to create a sense of the cloud's movement (as the wind blows it on its way) and sound (as rain pours forth from it). In the following lines, Yaksha addresses the cloud, praising it for its beauty:

While favouring breezes waft thee gently
forth,
And while upon thy left the plover sings
His proud, sweet song, the cranes who know
thy worth
Will meet thee in the sky on joyful wings
And for delights anticipated join their rings.
(ll. 41–45)

Such beauty and lyricism did not escape Kalidasa's plays, most of which are based on stories told in the MAHABHARATA. His themes, however, are love and courtship, and the plays were very popular in the royal court. In his most famous play, *The Recognition of Sakuntala,* Kalidasa tells the story of Sakuntala and King Duhsanta. After Sakuntala is cursed, the king loses his memory of her, and Sakuntala must find a ring that he gave her to restore his memory. In another story, *Malavikagnimitra* (Malavika and Agnimitra), Kalidasa describes how King Agnimitra falls in love with the picture of an exiled servant girl named Malavika. In *Vikramorvashe* (Urvashi Conquered by Valor), he tells how King Pururavas falls in love with a celestial nymph named Urvashi.

Kalidasa's works were highly praised during his time, and they continue to be popular today. For many centuries after he wrote "The Cloud Messenger," so many poets imitated his style that their Sanskrit poems were collectively called "Duuta poems." He was admired by the German poet Goethe and imitated by Schiller (in his play *Maria Stuart,* 1800). Later playwrights have written stories about the legends surrounding Kalidasa's life. For example, Shri Mathura Datt Pandey's play *Kalidasakavyasambhavam* (1979), tells the origins of "The Cloud Messenger," a poem about which scholar Arthur Berriedale Keith comments in *A History of Sanskrit Literature:*

It is difficult to praise too highly either the brilliance of the description of the cloud's progress or the pathos of the picture of the wife sorrowful and alone. Indian criticism has ranked it highest among Kalidasa's poems for brevity of

expression, richness of content, and power to elicit sentiment, and the praise is not undeserved.

Similar praise abounds for Kalidasa's *Sakuntala,* as critics continue to praise his language for its clarity, his imagery for its power, and his verse for its perfection.

English Versions of Works by Kalidasa

Kalidasa: Shakuntala and Other Writings. Translated by Arthur W. Ryder. New York: Dutton, 1959.
Malavikagnimitram of Kalidasa. Translated by M. R. Kale. Delhi: Motilal Banarsidass, 1985.
The Recognition of Sakuntala: A Play in Seven Acts. Translated by W. J. Johnson. Oxford: Oxford University Press, 2001.
The Seasons: Kalidasa's Ritusamhara. Translated by John T. Roberts. Tempe: Center for Asian Studies, Arizona State University, 1990.

Works about Kalidasa

Singh, A. D., ed. *Kalidasa: A Critical Study.* Columbia, Mo.: South Asia Books, 1977.
Thapar, Romila. *Sakuntala: Texts, Readings, Histories.* London: Anthem Press, 2002.
Tilakasiri, J. *Kalidasa's Imagery and the Theory of Poetics.* New Delhi, India: Navrang Publishers, 1988.

Kama Sutra (Kamasutra, Kama–sutra) (fourth century) *scriptural manual*

The *Kama Sutra* is an Indian text, written in Sanskrit, which provides a prescriptive set of instructions elevating the pursuit of pleasure to an art. Hindus of the fourth century, when the *Kama Sutra* was composed, believed that a properly fulfilling life required balanced attention to three areas: religious piety or duty (dharma), material provisions or success (*artha*), and sensual pleasure (*kama*). Complementing other Hindu texts that provided instruction in the first two areas, the *Kama Sutra,* or "pleasure treatise," advised readers on how to maximize their enjoyment of the sensual pleasures of life, in everything from home furnishing to interpersonal relationships.

The original author of the *Kama Sutra* was Vatsyayana Mallanga, about whom nothing is known outside of what the text reveals. He appears to have been a Brahman, a member of the priest caste, who resided in the city of Pataliputra in southern India during the Gupta era when Indian arts, culture, and literature were flourishing. In his text, Vatsyayana claims he compiled the *Kama Sutra* for two main reasons: first to ensure the survival of works on the subject, and second to cater to the needs of circles of educated and refined connoisseurs who would appreciate good poetry. He also claims that he wrote the work "in chastity and highest meditation," which may mean that ancient Hindus cultivated the pursuit of pleasure as sincerely as they practiced religious devotion. The number of serious passages in the text suggests that, unlike OVID's *Art of Love* (ca. 1 B.C.), Vatsyayana expected readers to put weight on his advice and regard the pursuit of love and pleasure as an important aspect of human life.

Being born into the priestly caste, Vatsyayana would have received a brahminical education, which included knowledge of the teachings of the Vedas and the grammatical structure of the Sanskrit language. He cites earlier sages and works who have treated the topic of love, but Vatsyayana's is the first work to offer a comprehensive guide to living the sensual life. Though a precise date of composition cannot be safely ascribed to the *Kama Sutra,* the classical poet Subandhu, who lived in the court of the Gupta monarch Chandragupta II during the fourth century, mentions the *Kama Sutra* in his own work.

The first extant commentary on the *Kama Sutra* was written in the 12th century by the Indian scholar Yasodhara, which began a tradition of translation and interpretation continuing up to the present time. Narsingha Shastra wrote a commentary called the *Sutra Vritti* in the 18th century. The work of contemporary Hindi scholar Devadatta Shastri puts the *Kama Sutra* in the context of a continuing Indian literary tradition and also presents a new assessment and interpretation of the concept of *kama.*

Critical Analysis

Complementing the *Artha Shastra* and the *Dharma Shastra,* to which it makes frequent reference, the *Kama Sutra,* in the words of translator Alain Daniélou, offers "a picture of the art of living for the civilized and refined citizen, competing in the sphere of love, eroticism, and the pleasures of life." The text of the *Kama Sutra* is divided into seven books, which together address all aspects of a man's adult life.

The target audience of the work includes both the *rasikas* (connoisseurs) within the Gupta ruler's court and the city dwellers, or *nagaraka,* a class of men who possess both the wealth and leisure to cultivate artistic pursuits. As Book 1 makes clear, one must possess all the conveniences and facilities of a *nagaraka* to properly enjoy sensual pursuits. The author recommends establishing a pleasant home within the confines of a city and equipping its spacious rooms with comfortable beds, garden access, and plenty of fresh flowers. Vatsyayana's ideal city may be his native Pataliputra, but he refers to other cities in India, including Gandhara and Bactria. In these details, as well as in the rules of etiquette discussed throughout the text, the *Kama Sutra* offers a useful source of information on the culture of Indian cities during the first century.

Book 2, which contains a discussion of recommended sexual techniques, is undoubtedly the most-translated and the reason the *Kama Sutra* is frequently, but erroneously, thought to be exclusively and explicitly a sex manual. Books 3 through 7 go on to advise young men on how to approach virgins, how to marry and establish their own households, and how to conduct extramarital affairs and seduce other men's wives. Book 6 discusses the patronage of courtesans, and Book 7 addresses the aging man's anxieties about how to preserve his attractiveness and his libido.

Throughout, the *Kama Sutra*'s advice reveals the standards and habits of conduct for men and women of various classes. Some of the advice seems surprisingly progressive; for example, the text makes reference to same-sex relationships and acknowledges the existence of variant groups later marginalized in many societies. In fact, according to Vatsyayana, male homosexual prostitutes are people to know in Indian society; they symbolize good luck and should be invited to weddings to bestow good fortune on the newlyweds. Courtesans, too, are considered essential members of an urban society. The courtesans were themselves art lovers, or *rasikas,* who perfected techniques of music and dance. A number of these courtesans fulfilled religious roles as temple dancers.

The *Kama Sutra,* though directed at men, acknowledges that women can be equal participants in erotic activities and equally capable of sexual pleasure. For example, Books 3 and 4 contain information instructing women on how to attract men and how to be good wives. It tells a wife how to keep her husband happy, and how to deal with his infidelity, recommending that she scold him both when they are alone and in company. At the same time, the *Kama Sutra* contains instructions that some readers may find objectionable. If a young girl is too resistant to advances, for instance, the text recommends getting her drunk and then taking advantage of her. Also, while it presumes that a good wife is faithful, the attention devoted to discussing extramarital affairs suggests that many wives were not.

Overall, the main purpose of the *Kama Sutra* is to explain how supreme enjoyment of the divine can be achieved through the successful blending of eroticism and mysticism. It therefore serves as both a popular manual on erotic practices and as a sacred text. In later periods of Indian history, the pursuit of pleasure was relegated to a lesser status in the context of Hindu life. However, sections of the *Kama Sutra* continued to be used as a text in Indian schools, though with much of the erotic material excised. Certain later commentaries inserted concepts such as suttee, the requirement that a widow cast herself on her dead husband's funeral pyre, into a text originally free of these ideas.

The great popularity of the *Kama Sutra* in the Western world rested for a long time on its misin-

terpretation as a pornographic text. Victorian adventurer Sir Richard Burton obtained and published an English translation of the *Kama Sutra* in 1883. Burton's version focused on the erotic material, largely ignoring the spiritual seriousness of the advice, which reflected the tendencies of Burton's own society to limit the agency of and deny the capacity for sexual pleasure to women. More recent translations, such as the one undertaken by Professor Wendy Doniger, attempt to do justice to the original work. In Doniger's words, the *Kama Sutra* reflects a time "when the erotic was associated with all that was bright, shining and beautiful in the ordinary world." For this reason, its appeal is universal; as Daniélou observes, "the *Kama Sutra* retains a surprising topicality. It is a breviary of love valid for all times and places."

English Versions of the *Kama Sutra*

The Complete Kama Sutra: The First Unabridged Modern Translation of the Classic Indian Text by Vatsyayana. Translated by Alain Daniélou. South Paris, Maine: Park Street Press, 1994.

Kamasutra. Translated by Wendy Doniger and Sudhir Kakar. Oxford: Oxford University Press, 2003.

Works about the *Kama Sutra*

Doniger, Wendy and Sudhir Kakar, trans. *Kamasutra: The Acclaimed New Translation.* Philadelphia: Running Press, 2003.

Verma, Vinod. *The Kamasutra for Women: The Modern Woman's Way to Sensual Fulfillment and Health.* Tokyo: Kodansha International, 1997.

Kamo no Chomei (ca. 1155–1216) *poet, essayist*

Kamo no Chomei was born into a family of Shinto priests in Kyoto, Japan, during the late Heian period (794–1192). In the 1170s and 1180s, political power shifted from the court at Kyoto to the newly established shogunate (military government) in Kamakura. During Kamo's youth, inept and inefficient governance in the capital resulted in the mismanagement of various natural disasters that struck Kyoto. Kamo lived through a huge fire, a tornado, an earthquake, and lingering famine and pestilence that the government could not seem to eradicate. The famine of 1181 killed more than 42,300 people in just two months, and Kamo was an astute and horrified observer of these disasters and their effects. As he remarks in his essay *Hojoki,* "I have seen not a few strange happenings."

As a poet, Kamo showed talent at a young age and eventually was named to the Imperial Poetry Bureau by the retired emperor. The bureau was made up of Japan's leading poets, and Kamo quickly found his place among them. Eventually, however, disgusted with life in the city and exhausted by the overwhelming disasters, he moved into the wooded mountains, where he set up a new life in a small, isolated hut. There, at age 60, he produced his masterpiece, an essay account of the events of his youth and his subsequent retreat to isolation. In poetic detail, he describes his solitary life, writing that "the hut in which I shall spend the last remaining years of my dew-like existence, is like the shelter that some hunter might build for a night's lodging in the hills, or like the cocoon some old silkworm might spin." The work, called *Hojoki* (*An Account of My Hut*), is recognized as a masterpiece of the Japanese essay tradition and is one of the earliest examples of literature as conscience.

In *Hojoki,* Kamo describes the horrific sights and smells of famine in detail, tells of the other disasters he lived through, and then extols the virtues of solitude and isolation. He finds the serenity of his life favorable to the turbulence of city life, preferring his quiet days of chores and walks to the human misery he encountered in the past. At the end of the work, however, he questions his own sanity, wondering whether he has not grown too attached to detachment in the world he has cultivated.

Kamo also wrote the *Heike Monogatari,* a story of the rise and fall of the Heike clan of Japan, which was the most dramatic such political epic in the history of the empire. In the story, the chaos brought on by the Heike clan's decline is the background to Kamo no Chomei's fraught life. His sentiment is genuine as he describes the clan's tragic end; defeated by the Minomoto clan, the leaders of the Heike throw themselves into the sea to drown.

By confronting the horrors of his past while cultivating a contented yet reclusive life, Kamo no Chomei addresses the universal human concerns of suffering, moral reflection, and recovery.

English Versions of Works by Kamo no Chomei
Hojoki: Visions of a Torn World. Translated by Yasuhiko Morigushi and David Jenkins. Berkeley, Calif.: Stone Bridge Press, 1996.

The Ten-Foot-Square Hut and Tales of the Heike. Translated by A. L. Sadler. Westport, Conn.: Greenwood Press, 1970.

A Work about Kamo no Chomei
Pandey, Rajyashree. *Writing and Renunciation in Medieval Japan: The Works of the Poet-Priest Kamo no Chomei.* Ann Arbor: University of Michigan Center for Japanese Studies, 1997.

Kebra Nagast Chronicles (The Book of the Glory of the Kings of Ethiopia)
(13th century) *chronicle*

The *Kebra Nagast Chronicles* contain the history of the origins of the line of Ethiopian kings who claimed descent from Solomon. The text is widely perceived to be the authority on the history of the conversion of the Ethiopians from their indigenous, animistic worship to Christianity.

The book opens with the origins of the Christian religion, beginning with the decision of the Trinity to make Adam. It asserts that the Trinity lived in Zion, the Tabernacle of the Law of God. The foremost purpose of the *Chronicles* is to legitimize the authority of the Solomon line of the Ethiopian kings. They were credited with the bringing of Christianity to the eastern kingdom of Ethiopia, or Axum, as it was known in those days. The text suggests that Christ descended from Solomon. The main theme deals with the legendary relationship between Queen Makeda of Sheba and King Solomon of Jerusalem.

The *Chronicles* describes Makeda as a beautiful, intelligent, and wealthy queen who lives in the southern regions of the African continent. She desires to meet King Solomon after hearing about his power and wisdom. Makeda leaves her kingdom and travels to Jerusalem, where she is won over by the king's wisdom and his staunch faith. She decides that her descendants will abandon their worship of the sun and adopt Christianity as their new religion. After frequent visits with the king, Makeda eventually sends a message informing Solomon of her impending return to her country. The king invites her to a banquet and requests that the queen spent the night on his couch. Makeda agrees on the condition that the king promises not to take her by force. In return, she grants Solomon's request not to take anything that is in his house. The richness of the meats of the banquet unfortunately made the queen extremely thirsty, and when she seizes a vessel of water to drink, the king surprises her by accusing her of breaking her promise. Unable to suppress her thirst, Makeda agrees to sleep with Solomon, and from their union springs a line of Ethiopian kings.

The *Kebra Nagast Chronicles* became known to the Western world through European excursions into Africa during the 16th century. Many sources indicate that P. N. Godinho (a traveler, historiographer, or writer) was probably the first European to publish accounts of King Solomon and his son, Menyelek, in the first quarter of the 16th century. In the following century, Baltazar Teilez (1595–1675), author of the *Historia General de Etiopia Alta* (1660), incorporated stories from the *Chronicles* into his text. Later authors, including Alfonson Mendez and Jerónimo Lobo (1595–1678), used information from the *Kebra Nagast* in their histories. The most complete and possibly least-known of the translations is the *History of the Kings of Ethiopia* by Enrique Cornelio Agrippa, published in 1528. Manuel Almeida (1580–1646), a Jesuit priest who went to Ethiopia as a missionary, learned about the *Kebra Nagast* and translated the chronicles in his *History of Ethiopia*.

The original text remained unknown until explorer James Bruce's travels to Ethiopia near the close of the 18th century. Bruce (1730–94), who went to Ethiopia in search of the Nile, received several valuable Ethiopian manuscripts from King Takia Haymanot of Gondar. Among these was a copy of the *Kebra Nagast*. The third volume of Bruce's *Travels in Search of the Sources of the Nile* (1790) contained a detailed description of the contents of the original text. The documents obtained during Bruce's expeditions now reside in the Bodleian Library at Oxford University.

The various versions of the *Kebra Nagast* and generations of copying and recopying by scribes have made the task of dating and ascertaining the identity of the compilers exceedingly difficult. Scholars such as Almeida and E. A. Wallis Budge were nonetheless fully aware of the value of this text. As Budge writes in his preface to his translation, "This work has been held in peculiar honour in Abyssinia for several centuries, and throughout that country it has been, and still is, venerated by the people as containing the final proof of their descent from the Hebrew Patriarchs, and of the kinship of their kings of the Solomonic line with Christ, the son of God."

An English Version of the *Kebra Nagast Chronicles*
Budge, E. A. Wallis. *The Queen of Sheba and Her Only Son Menyelek (I).* London: Oxford University Press, 1932.

A Work about the *Kebra Nagast Chronicles*
Brooks, Miguel F. *A Brief History of the* Kebra Nagast. Lawrenceville, N.J.: Red Sea Press, 1996.

Khansā', al- (Tumadir bint 'Amr ibn al-Hārith ibn ash-Sharīd al-Khansā')
(575–ca. 645) *poet*
Al-Khansā', whose name means "the snub-nose" or gazelle, is the foremost exponent of the Arabic *ritha*,

or funeral elegy. She is also considered perhaps the greatest female Arabic poet of the classical period (ancient and medieval).

Few biographical details are known about al-Khansā' apart from her six children and unhappy marriage. She was born a pagan but converted to Islam, traveling to Medina with tribesmen to meet MUHAMMAD. Her brothers Sakhr and Mu'awiya were killed in different tribal battles early in her life. Lamenting these losses and demanding revenge from her Banu Sulaym tribesmen became her chief poetic themes, as can be seen in the poem "The Dust Is Blown Over His Beauties."

The *ritha* was a particularly important genre in pre-Islamic Arabic poetry, which generally celebrated military prowess and courage. Most of these dirges were written by women, and Al-Khansā' was the first to render these themes in exalted literary meters and rhymes.

Contemporary and later poets celebrated Al-Khansā''s passion and intensity. She would recite her poetry as if in a trance, adding great emotional impact:

> To the pool that all men shun in awe
> you have gone, my brother, free of blame,
> as the panther goes to his fight, his last,
> bare fangs and claws his only defense.
>   (from "For Her Brother")

Al-Khansā' reputedly won a competition in the annual gathering of poets at the 'Ukaz market, and so impressed was Muhammad with her recitation that he made her repeat several lines over and over. As a result of the quality of her work, Muhammad's appreciation, and her own passion for poetry, al-Khansā' became a much-imitated model for later generations of Arabic women poets.

An English Version of Works by al-Khansā'

Selections from the Diwan of al Khansa'. Translated by Arthur Wormhoudt. Oskaloosa, Iowa: William Penn College, 1977.

Works about al-Khansā'

Irwin, Robert. *Night and Horses and the Desert.* Woodstock, N.Y.: Overlook Press, 2000, 25–27, 239.

Nicholson, R. A. *A Literary History of the Arabs.* Cambridge: Cambridge University Press, 1966, 126–127.

Ki no Tsurayuki (ca. 872–946) *poet, travel writer, literary theorist*

Ki no Tsurayuki was born to a prominent family in Japan. Little is known of his personal life, but Tsurayuki served as a government official and librarian of the Imperial Records Office in the early 10th century. Between 902 and 905, he was asked by the Imperial Court to compile a collection of Japanese poetry, the *Kokinshu,* or *Collection of Old and New Japanese Poems.* He was also given the task of writing the Japanese preface to the collection, in which he provided an explanation of how to criticize poetry. Believing that the artistic value of poetry lay in its effect on the emotions, he wrote: "It is poetry which, without effort, moves heaven and earth, stirs the feelings of the invisible gods and spirits, smooths the relations of men and women, and calms the hearts of fierce warriors."

Tsurayuki was himself a first-rate poet. His collection *Tsurayuki Shu* appeared first with 700 poems, and in a second version containing 900 poems. Translator William Porter says his poetry is distinguished by "artless simplicity and quiet humor." In addition, he wrote a travel book, *Tosa nikki,* or *The Tosa Diary,* (935), in which he relates the details of a journey that he took from Tosa to Kyoto in 934. *The Tosa Diary* ranks among the Japanese classics, and is valued as a model for composition in native Japanese style. The *Diary* introduced a significant development into Japanese literature because Tsurayuki wrote this work, as he had the preface to *Kokinshu,* in the phonetic *kana* syllabary, rather than in Chinese characters. The use of phonetic characters was considered "women's language," as opposed to the ideographic characters that constituted the "men's language;"

therefore, in the *Diary,* Tsurayuki writes from the point of view of a woman character and refers to himself in the third person. Altogether, Tsurayuki's brilliant prose and poetry rank him among the greatest of Japanese writers of the early Heian period (794–1185).

English Versions of Works by Ki no Tsurayuki

Kokinshu: A Collection of Poems Ancient and Modern. Translated by Laurel Rasplica Rodd and Mary Catherine Henkenius. Edited by Mary Catherine Henkenius. Boston: Cheng & Tsui, 1999.
The Tosa Diary. Translated by William N. Porter. Rutland, Vt.: Charles E. Tuttle, 1981.

A Work about Ki no Tsurayuki

Schalow, Paul Gordon and Janet A. Walker, eds. *The Woman's Hand: Gender and Theory in Japanese Women's Writing.* Stanford, Calif.: Stanford University Press, 1996, 5, 41–71, 78.

Kojiki (712) *historical and literary compilation*

The *Kojiki*—literally Record of Ancient Things—was compiled by Ō no Yasumaro. At the behest of Japan's Emperor Temmu, Yasumaro put together a history of Japan's emperors, ceremonies, mythology, magical practices, and legends. The subject matter of the *Kojiki,* already considered ancient history by the eighth century, became the official sourcebook of Japanese culture and customs for future generations. The process of compiling the records took many years, and Temmu died before the *Kojiki* was completed. Empress Gemmei, his niece and daughter-in-law, urged Yasumaro to complete the collection, and he presented the finished books to her in 712.

The *Kojiki* also contains 111 songs that are among the oldest recorded in the Japanese language, many of them describing scenes of hunting, fishing, farming, and other humble activities. Several texts and songs in the *Kojiki* recount the adventures of the legend of Jimmu,

an invading god/emperor, the gods who came before him, and the Mikados who came after him. All of this also appears in the *Nihon shoki,* although that work reflects a heavy Chinese influence. The first English translation of the *Kojiki* was undertaken by B. H. Chamberlain and published in 1882.

The *Kojiki* is the oldest extant book in the Japanese language, and because of its references to the origins of the imperial and leading families of Japan, it serves not only as a source for the beginnings of Japan as a nation but also, as translator Donald Philippi observes, as "a compilation of myths, historical and pseudo-historical narratives and legends, songs, anecdotes, folk etymologies, and genealogies." The *Kojiki,* written before the influence of the Chinese, and the *Nihon shoki,* which was completed in 720, serve as sacred texts in the Shinto religion.

English Versions of the *Kojiki*

Kojiki. Translated by Donald L. Philippi. New York: Columbia University Press, 1982.
Kojiki: Records of Ancient Matters. Translated by Basil Hall Chamberlain. Rutland, Vt.: Charles E. Tuttle, 1982.

Works about the *Kojiki*

Brownlee, John S. *Political Thought in Japanese Historical Writing from Kojiki 712 to Tokushi Yoron 1712.* Waterloo, Ontario, Canada: Wilfrid Laurier University Press, 1991.
Norinaga, Motoori. *Kojiki-Den.* Translated by Ann Wehmeyer. Ithaca, N.Y.: Cornell University Press, 1997.

Komachi, Ono no
See ONO NO KOMACHI.

Kong Qiu (K'ung Ch'iu)
See CONFUCIUS.

Koran (Qur'an) (ca. 610–632) *sacred scripture of Islam*

Muslims believe that the Koran (or Qur'an, Arabic for "recitation") is the word of God as revealed to MUHAMMAD in a process that began in the year 610, during the month of Ramadan, when the angel Gabriel called out to him and commanded him to "recite in the name of the Lord." For more than 20 years, until his death in 622, Muhammad continued to receive further revelations when in a trance-like state, and he would then convey the words to his followers. Each revelation eventually became part of a *surah,* or chapter, in the Koran.

After the prophet's death, different versions and arrangements of the *surahs* began to spread across the expanding Muslim realm. To counteract this trend, Muhammad's secretary, Zayd Ibn Thabit, collected all the written fragments he could find and recorded the recollections of those "reciters" who had memorized parts of Muhammad's visions.

Together with other scholars, Zayd produced an authoritative text sometime during the reign of the Caliph 'Uthman (ruled 644–56). This text is the basis of all subsequent editions of the Koran and is recognized by all Muslims, regardless of doctrinal differences.

Muslims often refer to the Koran as the "Arabic Koran (Recitation)." It is considered impossible to translate and impious even to try. Thus, non-Arab Muslims use the Arabic original for prayer, recitation, and study. When Muslims render the text into other languages, it is considered a paraphrase or interpretation.

The written Koran has always been intended for reading aloud, following carefully preserved traditions of pronunciation and emphasis. In this way, difficult Arabic passages can be made accessible. Translators of the Koran will generally add additional wording to preserve the meaning.

Printed editions of the Koran appeared in Europe from the Renaissance on, first in Arabic and then in European languages. Eventually, critical editions were published in Europe in which the text was often rearranged and "corrected" in light of modern linguistic and historical research. Scholarly but strictly orthodox Arabic versions also appeared in the 20th century.

Critical Analysis

Muslims consider the classical Arabic of the Koran to be the very standard of purity, grammar, and diction. Nearly all the vocabulary is of Arabic origin, although some words appear to scholars to be derived from Greek, Aramaic, and Hebrew.

There are also several different styles of writing in the Koran. Many of the short, earlier verses are written in the clipped rhymed prose of the *kahins,* or pagan priests. Other verses in the *khatib* style have the flavor of sermons, while still others follow the style of stories or dramatic poetry. Finally, many of the legal rulings follow the format of treaties or agreements.

Most of the verses appear to be spoken by God. Many of those spoken by Muhammad begin with the command, "Say," often when the prophet is being instructed to answer questioners or doubters.

English-language prose versions of the Koran run to about 400 pages. The content is divided into 114 chapters. Some chapters correspond to individual revelations, while others are composites that Muhammad himself assembled from shorter revelations.

In the standard text, the chapters are presented roughly in size order, rather than following a chronology or thematic plan. The longer chapters appear near the beginning, even though many of them date from the last years of the prophet's life. For example, following a brief introductory chapter invoking God's guidance, Chapter 2 has 286 verses, while the final 10 chapters range from three to seven verses each.

The verses themselves (*ayat* in Arabic) vary greatly in length. Many of them, especially in the shorter chapters, consist of one brief line, while the longer verses run the length of a full paragraph.

The title of each chapter is taken from its text but does not necessarily describe the chapter as a whole. Beneath the title is an indication of whether the *surah* was revealed at Mecca or Medina, followed by the number of verses the chapter contains. All but one chapter continues with the standard invocation, "In the name of Allah (God), the Compassionate, the Merciful." Finally comes the text itself, except for 29 chapters that precede the text with some stand-alone letters whose mystical significance is not known.

In terms of content, the main theme of the Koran is that the world was created and is ruled by a single all-powerful and merciful God, who demands both faith and righteousness. Failure to obey will result in punishment on the Day of Judgment, when evildoers will be sent to hell and the righteous to heaven.

The Koran says that God, to instruct human beings in proper faith and conduct, sent a series of prophets at different times and to different peoples, all with the same essential teaching. The last prophet was Muhammad, who was sent to the Arabs in particular and to the entire world.

Among the Old Testament characters found in the Koran are Adam and Eve; Cain and Abel; Abraham, Isaac, Ishmael, and Jacob; Joseph and his brothers; Moses and Aaron; David and Solomon; Job; and Jonah. The most important of these figures are Moses, who freed the Israelites from Egypt and led them to the Promised Land, and Abraham. The Koran praises Abraham as the first man to abandon idol-worship. It also credits him with building the sacred Ka'bah shrine in Mecca, which Muhammad later designated as the holiest site in Islam. Interestingly, the Koran considers Ishmael, the ancestor of the Arabs, to be Abraham's heir, while the Hebrew BIBLE attributes that role to Isaac, the ancestor of the Jews.

The Koran also contains many references to Jesus, who is revered as a prophet and miracle worker, and Mary, but the Koran rejects the Christian concept of the Trinity and denies that Jesus was crucified.

Many of the later chapters of the Koran (which appear earlier in the standard text) deal with laws and society. These chapters have been carefully studied by generations of Muslim legal scholars and form the basis of much Islamic law. Among the topics treated are the laws of prayer, purification, fasting, and pilgrimage; almsgiving and respect for the poor; theft, violence, and revenge; the distribution of spoils when fighting nonbelievers; usury, debts, and inheritance; food and drink; marriage; and the role of women.

Muslims consider the Koran to be the miraculous, infallible, primary source for all basic legal and religious doctrines. The Koran we know is said to be a reflection of a divine, uncreated Koran that has always existed. Because of the crucial importance of every word in the text, many schools of interpretation (*tafsir*) have arisen over the centuries, using a variety of approaches. The earliest interpreters actually created the science of Arabic linguistics to fix the exact meaning of the text. They pored over every word and studied other contemporary and earlier Arabic writings for clues to meaning, even studying pagan poetry.

Scholars collected and commented on the vast body of *hadith,* the traditions about the life and sayings of Muhammad not found in the Koran, hoping to clarify the meaning of disputed passages. Each of the many theological camps within medieval Islam produced its own interpretation, and mystics from the Sufi tradition wrote allegories as an aid to understanding the Koran.

In the 19th century, European scholars began to approach the Koran with the linguistic and historical tools developed in the critical study of the Hebrew and Christian Bibles. They challenged the authenticity of some of the *surahs* (chapters) and published editions that rearranged the material in a more chronological fashion.

In recent decades, some academic specialists have gone further. They claim that parts of the Koran were written perhaps a century later than the date of Muhammad's death. They also speculate that the Koran was largely composed in Syria and Palestine. Other secular scholars dispute these conclusions.

To date, very few Muslim scholars have shown an interest in such speculation, for the historical validity and divine origin of the entire book remains a matter of faith for nearly all Muslims. Researchers and critics have compared the Koran to both the Hebrew Bible (noting differences between the two texts) and the Hebrew *midrash,* folktales and sermons that were recorded in the centuries after the Bible was completed (noting similarities). Regardless of ongoing scholarship and debate, one fact remains true: The Koran has had a profound influence on all subsequent Arabic literature and continues to influence contemporary religion, culture, and literature.

English Versions of the Koran

The Essential Koran: The Heart of Islam. Translated by Thomas Cleary. Edison, N.J.: Castle, 1998.

The Glorious Koran. Translated by Muhammad Marmaduke Pickthall. Elmhurst, N.Y.: Tahrike Tarsile Qu'ran, 2000.

The Koran. Translated by J. M. Rodwell. London: J. M. Dent, 1994.

Works about the Koran

Ali, Abdullah Yusuf. *The Meaning of the Holy Qur'an.* Beltsville, Md.: Amana Publications, 2004.

Barazangi, Nimat Hafez. *Woman's Identity and the Qur'an.* Gainesville: University Press of Florida, 2004.

Schwartz-Barcott, Timothy P. *War, Terror & Peace in the Qur'an and in Islam.* Carlisle, Pa.: Army War College Foundation Press, 2004.

Sells, Michael. *Approaching the Koran: The Early Revelations.* Ashland, Ore.: White Cloud Press, 1999.

Kulthum, 'Amr ibn

See 'AMR IBN KULTHUM.

K'ung Fu-tzu (Kongfuzi)

See CONFUCIUS.

L

Labid (Diwan Labid ibn Rabi'a al-'Amiri)
(ca. 560–661) *poet*
Labid, the son of a celebrated philanthropist, Rabi'a, was born into a prominent family in the 'Amir tribe in central Arabia. As a teenager, he made his name at the court of the Lakhmid king, a famous patron of poetry. He was said to have converted to Islam while visiting Medina and after hearing Muhammad recite verses from the KORAN. His own poems display a deep religious feeling, but there is speculation among scholars that he abandoned poetry after his conversion.

Labid's brother Arbad was killed by lightning, inspiring a very famous elegy, "The Deserted Camp," in which Labid philosophically laments the futility of human existence and the difficulties of old age: "Man is but a little flame. A little while after it has risen into the air, it turns to ashes."

One of Labid's longer poems was later included in the *Mu'allaqāt* (The Seven Odes), an anthology of major pre-Islamic poems collected in the late eighth century. While Labid's odes follow the traditional format, he is noted for his vivid animal descriptions and intense celebration of his tribe's noble qualities and traditional customs and laws. He calls his tribesmen "generous, assisting liberality, gentlemanly, winning and plundering precious prize, sprung of a stock whose fathers laid down a code for them." Labid was among the prominent pagan poets who converted to Islam, and his poems celebrate the Bedouin values that served as models for later Muslim poets.

See also HANGED POEMS; TARAFAH 'AMR IBN AL-'ABD.

An English Version of a Work by Labid
Arberry, A. J. *The Seven Odes: The First Chapter in Arabic Literature.* New York: Macmillan, 1957.

Works about Labid
Allen, Roger. *An Introduction to Arabic Literature.* Cambridge, U.K.: Cambridge University Press, 2000.
Huart, Clement. *A History of Arabic Literature.* Beirut: Khayats, 1966.

Laozi (Lao Tzu, Master Lao, Li Erh) (sixth century B.C.) *philosopher, essayist*
Laozi was born in the Quren (Ch'ü-Jen) hamlet of Li village in the state of Chu. There is no information on his life and exploits, as there exists no comprehensive or even brief description of Laozi's life other than that found in Sima Qian's (Ssu-ma Chien's) works and a few other isolated statements in historical documents of the Chu and Zhou (Chou) states.

There are, however, legends and traditions associated with Laozi. According to one legend, he lived in the state of Zhou for a long time as the keeper of the imperial archives. Disappointed with the decline, constant chaos, and disorder of the state, he saddled a water buffalo and set off for the West.

Sima Qian's brief biography of this old sage contains two interesting facts. The first pertains to a meeting between Laozi and CONFUCIUS during which Confucius asks Laozi to instruct him in the performing of ancestral rites, then chastises and rejects him for his ignorance. This episode of the meeting between the two philosophers set the basis for a philosophical rivalry that was perpetuated by their followers. The second fact relates Laozi's westward journey through a mountain pass. According to Sima Qian, the keeper of the pass pleaded with the old man to write a book. Laozi did, and the book became known as the *Daodejing (Tao Te Ching)*, Laozi's definitive work. Based on the *Daodejing*, most scholars consider Laozi to be the founder of Daoism (Taoism), an important school of thought in China and Chinese-influenced areas.

One of the basic concepts of Laozi's teachings is *wuwei*, which means "no excessive action." This has often been misinterpreted to mean passivity, but Laozi emphasized nonaction as the most effective form of action because he believed that if people are immersed in activity, they will become one with the act, rather than becoming bored or restless and looking for something else to do or forcing acceptance. The emphasis of nonaction is on softness, endurance, and adaptability. As Laozi explains in the *Daodejing*:

> Less and less do you need to force things,
> until finally you arrive at non-action.
> When nothing is done,
> nothing is left undone.

In spite of Laozi's teachings of *wuwei*, he was at times dissatisfied with his wandering lifestyle:

> I alone am inert, showing no sign of desires,
> like an infant that has not yet smiled.

> Wearied, indeed, I seem to be without a
> home.
> The multitude all possess more than
> enough,
> I alone seem to have lost all . . .
> Common folks are indeed brilliant;
> I alone seem to be in the dark.

The *Daodejing*'s importance has not diminished with time. It has had a deep influence on Chinese culture, thought, and literature throughout history, and it is one of the most widely read books in both China and the world. In English alone, there exist well over 30 translations. Not only does the *Daodejing* embody and reflect the variety of teachings and ideology that emerged during the chaotic period of the Warring States (402–221 B.C.), it also exemplifies the literary creativity of what is often perceived as the Golden Age of Chinese philosophical thought.

Critical Analysis

The key idea in Laozi's text is the *Dao* (referred to as both "the way" and "the One"):

> The way that can be spoken of
> Is not the constant way.
> . . . .
> The valley in virtue of the One is full;
> The myriad creatures in virtue of the One
> are alive;
> Lords and princes in virtue of the One be-
> come leaders
> in the empire.
> It is the One that makes these what they
> are.

Laozi saw the *Dao* as the essence, or foundation, for the creation and preservation of the universe. The idea of the *Dao* as the creator of the universe deviates from the traditional Chinese concept of Heaven, or *Tien*, as the entity that created the universe.

The central idea of the *Daodejing* is simple: Human beings should model their lives on the *Dao*. Whether people are rulers of nations or peasants working in fields, they must first and foremost survive. According to Laozi, it is submissiveness that enables people to live life most efficiently. The *de* element of Laozi's philosophy, which refers to "virtue," constitutes the manner in which a person must live according to the *Dao.*

There are, however, some contradictions within the *Daodejing.* For example, Laozi believed people became enlightened when they learned to accept life as it is. Yet he states at one point in the text, "The reason I have great trouble is that I have a body. When I no longer have a body, what trouble have I?" This idea of transcending the limits of corporeal form hints at the influence of Hindu-Buddhist ideology and repudiates to some extent the Daoist belief in nonaction.

In another part of the *Daodejing,* Laozi comments on the balance of opposition:

> Thus Something and Nothing produce each
> other;
> The difficult and the easy complement each
> other;
> The long and the short off-set each other;
> The high and the low incline towards each
> other;
> Note and sound harmonize each other;
> Before and after follow each other.

As explained in the passage, what is high is determined by its opposite, which is low. If either one is removed, the other cannot exist in isolation. Therefore, perhaps Laozi's comment on transcending life balances the realities of life with dreams, for what person does not dream beyond their real abilities?

This balance is most clearly revealed in the *Daodejing*'s themes: the mundane and worldly concerns of human life and mysticism. Laozi clearly presents these themes in two distinct types of passages. The first concerns cosmogony and the origins of the universe. A common metaphor that he uses in these passages is the womb. Just as living beings emerge from a mother's womb, so is the universe born from the womb of what Laozi refers to as the "mysterious female":

> The spirit of the valley never dies.
> This is called the mysterious female.
> The gateway of the mysterious female
> Is called the root of heaven and earth. . . .

The second type of passage details the actions and practices of the individual. Laozi uses the image of a newly born baby to represent a being that is submissive, weak, and helpless. The baby's frailty and innocence has the power to cause adults to care for it. Ironically, this frailty symbolizes strength, and this, Laozi suggests, is the ideal form of human virtue.

Laozi's descriptions of balance—nonaction as effective action, having all and nothing, everything in view of the One, submissiveness and force, acceptance versus transcendence, reality versus dream, and the worldly versus the mystical—are what have made the *Daodejing* a work for all ages and all time. As Stephen Mitchell states in the introduction to his translation of the text, "Like an Iroquois woodsman, [Laozi] left no traces. All he left us is his book: the classic manual on the art of living, written in a style of gemlike lucidity, radiant with humor and grace and large-heartedness and deep wisdom: one of the wonders of the world."

English Versions of the *Daodejing*

Lao Tzu Tao Te Ching. Translated with an introduction by D. C. Lau. Middlesex, U.K.: Penguin Books, 1963.

Tao Te Ching. Translated with foreword and notes by Stephen Mitchell. London: Macmillan, 1988.

Works about Laozi

Fung-Yu Lan. *A History of Chinese Philosophy,* Translated by Derk Bodde. Princeton, N.J.: Princeton University Press, 1952, 171–172, 186–190.

Legge, James. *The Texts of Taoism. Sacred Books of the East,* Vol. 40. New York: Dover, 1962, Chapters 3 and 4.

Wing-Tsit Chan. *A Sourcebook in Chinese Philosophy.* Princeton, N.J.: Princeton University Press, 1969.

Latini, Brunetto (Brunetto Buonaccorso Latini) (ca. 1212–ca. 1294) *translator, nonfiction writer, poet*

Brunetto Latini was a native of Florence, Italy, a married man, and the father of three children. He belonged to a powerful family and enjoyed a long and distinguished public career that began in 1254. In 1260, as Manfred of Sicily threatened to invade Florence, Latini headed a diplomatic mission to seek help from Alfonso X of Spain. Unfortunately, Manfred's army conquered Florence before Latini returned home, and for the next seven years, he lived in exile in France. After Manfred died in 1266, Latini returned to his native city, where he soon resumed his political career.

In addition to his political activities, Latini worked as a teacher, training his students by having them copy translations of Pier delle VIGNE's letters. The most famous of his students was DANTE ALIGHIERI, who placed Latini (for reasons now unknown) among the Sodomites in Canto 15 of his *Inferno.*

Latini's literary works include Italian translations of works by CICERO; the *Favolello,* a letter containing poetry about friendship; and *Tesoretto* (Little Treasure), an allegory written in rhyming couplets. Scholar Julia Bolton Holloway believes Latini composed *Tesoretto* for Spain's King Alfonso. Partially modeled on the ROMANCE OF THE ROSE, the poem includes scenes in which Latini meets Nature, escapes the garden of Love with OVID's help, and talks to Ptolemy. It may be the first Italian poem intended to educate more than to entertain.

Latini's most popular and enduring work, composed while he was in exile (1260–66), was *The Book of the Treasure.* Europeans of the MIDDLE AGES placed little value on originality; they viewed authors who referred to (or even copied) well-known works as more knowledgeable and authoritative.

Thus, many medieval books are essentially compilations of earlier writings. Latini's *Book of the Treasure* is just such a compilation. Holloway posits that Latini intended it to teach Charles of Anjou the proper way to govern. Other scholars speculate that the book targeted less-prominent readers who wished to advance in the world. Latini most likely intended the work to be used by learned men as a reference source, for he begins with an appeal to the wise:

> This book is called the *Treasure,* for just as the lord who wishes to amass things of great value . . . puts into his treasure the most precious jewels he can gather together according to his intention, in a similar manner the body of this book is compiled out of wisdom, like the one which is extracted from all branches of philosophy in a brief summary.

Latini divides the *Treasure* into three parts. In the first part, he discusses "the nature of all things celestial and terrestrial." It includes a history of the world, much of which comes from the BIBLE; information on astronomy and the elements; and a BESTIARY. In the second part, he discusses ethics, "what things one should do and not do," drawing heavily on ARISTOTLE's writings. Finally, in the third section, he discusses rhetoric and city government—or, as he says, "knowing and demonstrating why one should do some things and not others." In this section he mentions Cicero's ideas about rhetoric and describes his personal experiences as a government official.

Chapter headings of the *Treasure* include "The paths of day and night, and heat, and cold"; "How one should choose land for cultivation"; "The cetacean called whale"; "The three manners of good"; "The five parts of rhetoric"; and "Which man should be elected to be lord and governor of the city".

Adding to the *Treasure*'s authority, Latini mentions and uses information from the works of Aristotle; Cicero; PLATO; SOCRATES; SALLUST; LUCAN;

Palladius; SENECA; VIRGIL; JUVENAL; MARTIAL; HORACE; AUGUSTINE, SAINT; JEROME, SAINT; BOETHIUS, and AMBROSE, SAINT.

Translators Paul Barrette and Spurgeon Baldwin note that the *Treasure* appeared "in the very twilight of the life of such compendia," meaning it was one of the last of its breed. Nevertheless, it enjoyed great popularity for being the first compendium to be written in a vernacular language (French) rather than in Latin and for its extravagance of information based on the classics. In their translation of the work, Barrette and Spurgeon write, "Another key to [its] special popularity seems to be associated with Brunetto's skillfully organized plan . . . but the most compelling reason would have to be the venerable and unassailable authority of Brunetto's sources."

English Versions of Works by Brunetto Latini

Il Tesoretto (The Little Treasure). Translated and edited by Julia Bolton Holloway. New York: Garland, 1981.

The Book of the Treasure (Li Livres dou Tresor). Translated by Paul Barrette and Spurgeon Baldwin. New York: Garland, 1993.

Works about Brunetto Latini

Holloway, Julia Bolton. *Brunetto Latini: An Analytic Bibliography.* London: Grant and Cutler, 1986.

———. *Twice-Told Tales: Brunetto Latino and Dante Alighieri.* New York: Peter Lang, 1993.

Li Bai (Li Bo, Li Po, Li Pai, Li T'ai Po)
(701–762) *poet*

Li Bai was born in Sujab, near Lake Balkash in then-Chinese Central Asia. When he turned five years old, he was brought back to Jiangyu (Chiangyu) County in Sichuan (Szechuan), where he spent most of his boyhood and youth until he turned 18. Li Bai wrote poetry for a living, and his greatest supporters were members of the official class. He traveled extensively during his lifetime, and his easygoing personality enabled him to make many friends wherever he went. For a brief time, Li Bai enjoyed the favor of Emperor Xuanzhong (Hsüan-tsung) and lived in the palace until his involvement in political intrigue resulted in his banishment to the southwest. He later died of sickness at Tangtu, in modern Anhui, when he was 61.

Of Li Bai's 20,000 poems, only 1,600 survive. The main themes of his poetry are beautiful women and friendship. Some of his most moving poems deal with the sadness that results from the separation of friends. His poems also reflect the influence of the Chinese philosophy of Daoism (Taoism). An example of a poem containing Daoist imagery is "Dialogue in the Mountains," in which Li Bai describes his love of nature:

> You ask why I dwell in the green hills
> Smiling, I reply not, heart in peace.

This otherworldliness in his poetry has gained Li Bai the title of "Poetic Immortal." His disregard for convention reveals itself in the free style and lack of rules in the structure of his poetry.

Li Bai's masterpieces are his *Yueh Fu*, songs, which exemplify his romantic style and celebrate his carefree spirit and his love for both wine and lovely women. His fellow poet Du Fu (Tu Fu) praised him, saying that his name would survive for 10,000 years. Translator Rewi Alley agrees, saying Li Bai "had a magic touch which took men high above the mundane affairs of life."

English Versions of Works by Li Bai

Li Pai: 200 Selected Poems. Translated by Rewi Alley. Hong Kong: Joint Publishing Co., 1980.

Selected Poems of Li Bo. Translated by David Hinton. New York: New Directions Publishing, 1996.

Works about Li Bai

Hu, Patricia Pin-ching. "Tang's Golden Age." In: *Random Talks on Classical Chinese Poetry.* Hong Kong: Joint Sun Publishing Co., 1990.

Varsano, Paul M. *Tracking the Vanished Mortal: The Poetry of Li Bo and its Criticism.* Honolulu: University of Hawaii Press, 2003.

Li He (Li Ho) (791–817) poet

Li He was born in Henan (Honan) province in central China, the son of a minor bureaucrat who was descended from a cadet branch of the ruling Tang dynasty. One story holds that he composed his first verse at age seven in honor of a visit by the famous poet HAN YU. By the time of his father's death in 805, he had acquired a considerable literary reputation. Five years later, at age 21, he arrived at the imperial capital at Chang'an to take the Confucian examinations for a prestigious career in the imperial civil service.

Li He promised to excel in the arduous literary examinations, and some historians believe the newcomer's obvious brilliance excited the envy of higher-placed yet mediocre poets. Incredibly, officials barred him from the exams because of an arcane technicality known as a "character taboo": a Chinese written character in his father's name had the same sound as a character in the title of the exam. Heartbroken and embittered, Li He accepted a menial post in the Chinese bureaucracy, but he resigned only two years later. In dire poverty, he turned to his friend Han Yu for aid in finding another position, but five years of disappointment and struggle had taken their toll. He died in Changgu (Ch'ang-ku) at age 26, supposedly summoned from this world by a heavenly messenger on a red dragon.

Literature remembers Li He as a "demon-gifted" poet who composed his later verses in a unique fashion. Each morning, he would ride through the countryside on horseback, followed by a servant boy carrying an embroidered black bag on his shoulder. As inspiration struck, he would jot down single lines at random on small strips of paper, drop the strips into the bag, and assemble a finished poem from the strips in the evening.

In contrast to the formal, concrete, and traditional styles favored by most poets of the later Tang period, Li He's dark and sensual work is characterized by its beautiful imagery, unique word choice, jarring metaphors, and, not infrequently, pessimism tinged with compassion, the last undoubtedly stemming from the poet's melancholy life. In the words of translator David Hodges, "This poet is very much an aesthete, drawn to curious artifacts, ancient legends, beautiful women (courtesans and dancing girls), picturesque ruins and strange rites."

"Haunting" is the adjective modern scholars most often use to characterize Li He's verses. One of the most famous of these is "Song of the Jade-hunter," about an elderly jade-cutter in rural China, one of the men who daily risked their lives in conditions of great privation to procure the prized stone:

> Like the blood that wells from the cuckoo's
>   maw
> Are the old man's tears

Another of Li He's verses noteworthy for its imagery and metaphors is "Cold is the North," describing a river in winter:

> The Yellow Stream—all ice, so fish and
>   dragon died.
> Tree barks, three foot—a script of frost-
>   cracked runes.

A common Chinese aphorism, comparing Li He with two of his better-known and more conventional contemporaries, holds that Du Fu's (Tu Fü's) genius was that of a Confucian sage, Li Bai's of a Daoist (Taoist) immortal, and Li He's of a ghost or demon. To quote Hodges, Li He was "a poet so striking and so different that readers are still not sure what to think of him." Although he is not as famous today as several other poets of the Later Tang period, many scholars believe that the untimely and tragic death of the "Chinese Keats" deprived his nation of one of its greatest poets-to-be.

English Versions of Works by Li He

Five Tang Poets. Translated by David Young. Oberlin, Ohio: Oberlin College Press, 1990.

Goddesses, Ghosts, and Demons: The Collected Poems of Li He. Translated by J. G. Frodsham. San Francisco: North Point Press, 1983.

Poems of the Late Tang. Translated by A. C. Graham. New York: Penguin, 1977.

Works about Li He

Fusheng Wu. *The Poetics of Decadence: Chinese Poetry of the Southern Dynasties and Late Tang Periods.* Albany: State University of New York Press, 1998, 77–116.

Kuo-ch'ing Tu. *Li Ho.* Boston: Twayne, 1979.

Li Po (Li Bo)

See LI BAI.

Li Qingzhao (Li Ch'ing-chao) (1083–ca. 1141) *poet, nonfiction writer*

Li Qingzhao, who is considered China's greatest female poet, was born in Shandong (Shantung) Province to Li Gefei (Li Ko-fei), a famous prose writer; her mother was also a poet. Being born into such a family allowed Li Qingzhao to cultivate her natural talents as a writer at a time when women were not often permitted to be educated.

At the age of 18, Li Qingzhao married Zhao Mingzheng (Chao Ming-cheng), a student at the Imperial Academy who later served in the imperial administration. During this time, Li Qingzhao was able to write poetry, acquire a vast collection of books, and, with her husband, collect antiques such as bronze vases, goblets, pots, and stone inscriptions. She also wrote a book on antiquities with her husband called *Critical-Analytical Studies of Metal and Stone Inscriptions.*

Li Qingzhao and her husband loved each other very much, and their poems to each other, vivid and sensuous, reflect their delight in the married state. In "Plum Blossoms" the poetess speaks of their love as a flower and compares the reunion with her lover to the coming of spring, saying:

> I come, my jade body fresh from the
> bath . . .
> Even Heaven shares our joy.

In 1126, Zhao Mingzheng was appointed the Magistrate of Zizhuan (Tzu-chuan) in Shandong. As first lady of the province, Li Qingzhao retained her vigorous love for both poetry and the beauty of nature. Relatives told stories of how she would climb the city walls, even in the middle of a snowstorm, to gain poetic inspiration from the view of the mountains in the distance. Then tragedy struck in 1127, when the city was invaded by the Jin (Chin), a tribe of barbarians from the north, who burned Li Qingzhao's home, including her 10 rooms of books. When her beloved husband fell ill and died, her poetry acquired a tone of terrible sadness. In "Remorse," the narrator wanders in a dark room, looking at the rain, and says in her grief:

> Every fiber of my soft heart
> Turns to a thousand strands of sorrow.

Even after she remarried, Qingzhao wrote poetry to her first husband that expressed her loss and her longing, as in "Boat of Stars," where she writes:

> . . . since you've gone
> even the wine has lost its flavor.

Several of her poems lament the passing of time, as in "The Washing Stream," with its tone of wistful sadness:

> The pear blossoms fade and die
> and I can't keep them from falling.

Poetry of Li Qingzhao's time was largely set to music, and the manuscripts of her poems contain directions for the tune to which each poem is to be performed. The work of her mature years lack the patriotic fire of some earlier poems, but they still reflect her continued sense of the beautiful and the artistic. Often her later poems contain a haunting sense of exile and loneliness, as in these lines from an untitled lyric:

This year I am at the corner
Of the sea and the edge of Heaven.
I am old and lonely.

Li Qingzhao was the only Chinese woman author to write in both the *shi* (*shih*) and *ci* (*tz'u*) forms of poetry, and she used a wide variety of styles and imagery. She had a great feeling for nature and lived a life filled with love and loss. Translator Sam Hamill calls her a "stylistic innovator" whose writing is "remarkable for its emotional integrity, poetry at once beautifully erotic, coyly charming, while retaining an inner tensile strength of self-assurance." Altogether she wrote six volumes of poetry, and the 50 poems which remain in existence today are enough to justify her title as the "Empress of Song."

English Versions of Works by Li Qingzhao

Li Ch'ing-chao: Complete Poems. Translated by Kenneth Rexroth and Ling Chung. New York: New Directions, 1979.

The Lotus Lovers: Poems and Songs. Translated by Sam Hamill. St. Paul, Minn.: Coffee House Press, 1985.

Plum Blossom: Poems of Li Ching-chao. Translated by James Cryer. Chapel Hill, N.C.: Carolina Wren Press, 1984.

Works about Li Qingzhao

Ho, Lucy Chao. *A Study of Li Ch'ing-chao, her life and works.* South Orange, N.J.: Seton Hall University Press, 1965.

Pin-Ching, Hu. *Li Ch'ing-chao.* New York: Twayne, 1966.

Pollard, D. E., ed. *Translation and Creation: Readings of Western Literature in Early Modern China.* Amsterdam: Benjamins, 1988, 105–126.

Li Shangyin (Li Shang-yin) (ca. 813–858)
poet

Li Shangyin was born in Zhengzhou (Cheng-chou) in southeastern China. He grew up in various cities throughout the region because his father was a government official who was often transferred to different towns. After his father's death in 821, Li Shangyin and his mother moved back to Zhengzhou, where he was taught the Confucian classics by a scholarly uncle. Consequently he became a literary prodigy.

Despite Li Shangyin's obvious talents, in 833 he failed the government-administered literary examination, a test that identified qualified candidates for government positions. In 835, he failed the test once more, but finally passed it two years later. After his successful examination, Li obtained a position on the staff of a military leader, Wang Maoyuan. Soon after, he married one of Wang's daughters, and though he held a succession of minor government posts, he never rose to a high rank. One reason for this might have been his reputation for writing political poems, some of which may have ruffled the feathers of his superiors.

Li Shangyin's poetry also gained him the notice of the famous poet BAI JUYI. Legend has it that Bai Juyi wished to return as Li Shangyin's son after his death. Upon Bai Juyi's death in 846, Li wrote the older poet's epitaph, an indication of the high regard he had for his colleague.

Li Shangyin died relatively young, at age 45. In the years before his death, he began to study Buddhism and made many donations to temples in his area. His devoutness in his later years runs counter to his reputation, gained through his romantic poetry, as a man who had many secret love affairs. It is not known for certain, however, whether this reputation was justified. Li Shangyin's poetry ran the gamut from political commentary, as in his long poem "Written While Traveling through the Western Suburbs," to romance, exemplified in his series of poems dedicated to a young girl he calls "Willow Branch," who fell in love with him during one of his official assignments. Whether writing of political intrigues or love affairs, Li Shangyin remains one of the great poets of the Tang dynasty.

English Versions of Works by Li Shangyin

Five T'ang Poets: Field Translation Series. Translated by David Young. Oberlin, Ohio: Oberlin College Press, 1990.

The Poetry of Li Shang-Yin, Ninth-Century Baroque Chinese Poet. Translated by James J. Y. Liu. Chicago: The University of Chicago Press, 1969.

Livy (Titus Livius) (59 B.C.–A.D. 17) *historian*

Livy was born in the Northern Italian city of Padua and spent most of his life in Rome. His family did not belong to the influential circles of the Roman Empire, yet Livy early attracted the attention of AUGUSTUS and was invited to supervise the literary activities of the young Claudius, who later became the Roman emperor. Augustus appreciated Livy's independent and sincere mind, and he expressed his respect by giving Livy the nickname "Pompeian."

At a young age, Livy started his work entitled *The History of Rome from Its Foundation,* a history of the Romans from ancient times to his day. Initially, he published his writing in units of five books, the length of which was determined by the size of the ancient papyrus roll. With time, however, his work became more complex; Livy abandoned the symmetrical pattern and wrote 142 books. Books 11–20 and 46–142 have been lost; they are known mostly from surviving summaries. Letters from Livy to statesman PLINY THE YOUNGER reflect the historian's doubts about his work and his fears that the scope of the undertaking was too huge. However, the work turned out to be so fascinating that he continued writing. As a result, he became famous and was deeply respected throughout the Roman Empire.

What attracted contemporary readers to Livy's work was the way he explained history. Unlike his predecessors, who were entangled in political battles that affected what they wrote, Livy saw history in more personal, moral terms. This tendency to step away from the politics and concentrate on moral values was characteristic of Augustus's rule. Through legislation and propaganda, Augustus tried to strengthen moral ideals. Such prominent figures as HORACE and VIRGIL wrote poetry stressing the same message—that moral qualities make the Roman Empire great and allow Rome and its citizens to retain their power. Ironically, the Italian historian Niccolò Machiavelli (1429–1527), who was known for his deceit in diplomatic negotiations, wrote an in-depth analysis of Livy's *History,* titled *Discourses on Livy* (1551), in which he espouses the ideals of an autocratic government made effective only by conflict, rather than stability—a far cry from the morality Livy discusses.

In addition to his contributions to the moral ideals of the Roman Empire at the time, Livy also affected the use of Latin as the language of writing. The earliest Romans wrote in Greek, which was considered the language of culture. Therefore, Latin had formed no appropriate style for the recording of history. Livy filled this void. In his *History,* he developed a varied and flexible style that the ancient critic QUINTILIAN described as "milky richness."

By contemporary standards, Livy can hardly be considered a serious scholar. His history is more personal than "formal," and some of the information he includes in *History* can hardly be considered faultlessly accurate. In addition, he borrows greatly from Virgil's *Aeneid,* giving his work almost a fictional aspect. His *History,* however, tells much about the moral values and attitudes of the Romans: who they were and what they thought of themselves and the rest of the world in the first century. The *History* became a classic in Livy's own lifetime and exercised a profound influence on the style and philosophy of historical writing down to the 18th century.

English Versions of a Work by Livy

The Early History of Rome. Translated by Aubrey De Selincourt. Introduction by R. M. Ogilvie. New York: Penguin Classics, 2000.

Rome and the Mediterranean. Books XXXI–XLV of 'The History of Rome from its Foundation.' Translated by Henry Bettenson. Introduction by A. H. McDonald. Hammondsworth, U.K.: Penguin, 1976.

Works about Livy

Briscoe, John. *A Commentary on Livy.* Oxford, U.K.: Clarendon Press, 1981.

Chaplin, Jane D. *Livy's Exemplary History.* Oxford: Oxford University Press, 2000.

Feldherr, Andrew. *Spectacle and Society in Livy's History.* Berkeley: University of California Press, 1998.

Machiavelli, Niccolò. *Discourses on Livy.* Oxford's World Classics Series. Translated by Julia Conaway Bondanella and Peter Bondanella. Oxford: Oxford University Press, 2003.

Longinus (ca. A.D. first century) *rhetorician, literary critic*

Very little is known about the Greek writer called Longinus. His writings describe early travels with his parents, which he said enlarged his mind and diversified his experience. He studied humanities and philosophy and was well acquainted with the genius and spirit of Greek literature. Eventually he established residence in Athens, a seat of learning in the world of ancient Greece. One tradition identifies him with the third-century Cassius Longinus, described in PORPHYRY's *Life of Plotinus (see* PLOTINUS) who was hired by Queen Zenobia to educate her children. When she was defeated by Emperor Aurelian, she and Longinus fled but were captured, and Longinus was executed. For centuries this commonly held but possibly inaccurate belief cast a heroic glow on the man otherwise established as an important literary critic. The majority of scholars place him in the first century, but most modern researchers recognize that it is now next to impossible to identify the real man. If he indeed lived in the first century, Longinus would have been contemporary with DIONYSIUS OF HALICARNASSUS, another critic of the Augustan age.

The early biographer Eunapius described Longinus as "a living library and a walking university." The scope of his learning reveals itself in his one known work, *On the Sublime.* Also known as "the Golden Treatise," this work ranks only slightly less important than the *Poetics* of ARISTOTLE in the field of literary criticism and the history of aesthetics. *On the Sublime* is also one of the earliest "how to write" manuals. Longinus defines the sublime as "an image reflected from the inward greatness of the soul."

This quality, also translated as "height," distinguishes the greatest writing and explains the impact that the most profound poetry has upon readers.

Longinus begins the treatise with an address to his friend Terentianus declaring his threefold purpose: to outline a method, to be useful to those who use the art of public speaking, and to provide a moral answer to the question: "How can we develop our natural capacities to some degree of greatness?" His scheme for recognizing and cultivating the sublime involves a combination of nature and craft. The artist must possess the ability to perceive or entertain important thoughts ("high thinking"); the ability to experience profound emotion ("high feeling"); and the command of imagery, diction, and composition that would enable the best expression of these combined thoughts and emotions. The sublime was not simply the result of natural genius, but aptitude disciplined with knowledge. Longinus wrote that "greatness, when left to itself with no help from knowledge, is rather precarious—unsupported and unballasted . . . as greatness often needs the spur, so too it needs the rein." Good fortune, he concludes, must be tempered with good judgment.

To support his points, Longinus draws examples of both successes and failures from the long tradition of Greek literature, including HOMER, HESIOD, PLATO, XENOPHON, DEMOSTHENES, and EURIPIDES. The treatise ends with a lament that materialism, moral decline, and greed are responsible for the decline in the quality of literature. This sentiment, it must be observed, was already a literary commonplace by the first century, also expressed by but not original to Plato. For Longinus the sublime was a moral as well as a stylistic ideal, and integrity was a prerequisite for great writing. Only "the man of dignity and integrity who does his duty in human society and understands his station as a citizen of the cosmos" was capable of high thought and feeling. Longinus shares this ideal with other Latin rhetoricians, including CICERO, SENECA, and QUINTILIAN.

Editor D. A. Russell observes that the work of Longinus had "an immense influence on critical thinking" and "retains a power of immediate attraction." Alexander Pope and Jonathan Swift, in their works of literary criticism, stressed the importance of reading Longinus's work. The standard translation of *On the Sublime* was published by Nicolas Boileau in 1674, and subsequent readers regarded Longinus as a critic and hero in the tradition of SOCRATES and Cato. Philosophical thought focused once more on the sublime in the 18th century and the beginning of the Romantic movement in English literature. Even to the modern eye the book has a certain appeal, perhaps because, as Russell says, Longinus simply "loves literature and wants to communicate his love to others."

English Versions of Works by Longinus

On Great Writing (On the Sublime). Translated by G. M. A. Grube. Indianapolis, Ind.: Hackett Publishing Company, 1991.
Poetics: Longinus on the Sublime, Demetrius on Style. Edited by Stephen Halliwell, et. al. Cambridge, Mass.: Harvard University Press, 1996.

Works about Longinus

Arieti, James A. and John M. Crossett. *On the Sublime: Longinus*. New York: E. Mellen Press, 1985.
Russell, D. A. *Longinus on the Sublime*. Oxford, U.K.: Clarendon Press, 1964.

Longus (third century) *poet*

Nothing at all is known about Longus but that he composed the first pastoral romance, titled *Daphnis and Chloë*. The Latin style of Longus's name may suggest he was a native of Italy, but it is also possible that Longus was a *nom de plume*, or pen name. Some scholars suggest that he was born on the Aegean island of Lesbos, also home to the poet SAPPHO. The story is set there, and the author describes the setting as though he were familiar with it.

Daphnis and Chloë is a prose poem in Greek that tells the story of the love of Daphnis, a goatherd, for Chloë, a shepherdess. It combines two traditions that emerged around 300 B.C.: the development of the novel, and the pastoral tradition, which concerns the doings of simple folk in an idyllic country setting. Critics often classify *Daphnis and Chloë* as a romance or a love story of the type also written by XENOPHON and Heliodorus. The Greek novel, as developed by such writers as LUCIAN and PETRONIUS, typically featured themes of love, separation, and mutual fidelity, and the lively plots contained kidnappings, pirates, near escapes, wolves, feasts, people falling in love, trials, weddings, and grand reunions. Longus's story incorporates all of these elements. In addition, he enlivened a genre that had come to rely on formulaic plots, stock characters, and mundane sentiment by adding irony and sophisticated humor. The story shows that Longus was familiar with the EPICS of HOMER and VIRGIL; the dramas of EURIPIDES, ARISTOPHANES, MENANDER; and even the history of THUCYDIDES. He frequently references the pantheon of Greek gods, some of whom function as characters. Though Longus likely lived at the same time as the influential Christian teachers and thinkers Origen and Clement of Alexandria, his work adheres closely to the ancient pagan tradition. Scholar William McCulloh calls *Daphnis and Chloë* "the last great creation in pagan Greek literature."

True to pastoral convention, Daphnis and Chloë lead an idealized country life, tending their animals in the peaceful countryside. As infants, both were abandoned in the woods, taken in by animals, and finally discovered and raised by humble families. This plot device was not so far-fetched then as it seems now; it was a Greek practice to expose unwanted children on the hillside, leaving a token that could identify the infant if necessary. The young Daphnis and Chloë meet while pasturing their animals, and as it is springtime, they naturally fall in love. Enforced separations test their innocent passion in the form of accidents, rival suitors, abductions, and deceit, but throughout they remain true and devoted to each other. Their fidelity convinces the gods to intercede and arrange matters so that Daphnis and Chloë may be together. Ultimately their birth tokens reveal that both of them are the offspring of rich and upper-class parents, so the last impediments to their marriage are removed.

Longus's *Daphnis and Chloë* has had a pervasive influence on art, music, and literature. Early manuscripts survived into the 16th century, but with missing passages. Jacques Amyot published the first print translation in French in 1559, and Angell Daye brought out an English version in 1587. In 1809 excitement stirred the world of Longus scholars when a French soldier in Italy discovered an earlier manuscript containing the missing portions, and the first complete Greek text was released in 1810. The pastoral setting used by Longus inspired later writers in the English tradition, particularly the *Arcadia* of Philip Sidney. The novels of Samual Richardson and Henry Fielding also borrow from the pastoral ideal.

Throughout the ages the critical reception of the work has varied widely; Goethe called *Daphnis and Chloë* a masterpiece, and Elizabeth Barrett Browning referred to it as "an obscene text." But the story is no more obscene than any of the Greek romances of its kind, and more restrained than some. The author proposed to write of love as a means of both comforting and instructing his readers. In his Prologue he hopes his story will be "something to heal the sick and comfort the afflicted, to refresh the memory of those who have been in love and educate those who have not. For no one has ever escaped Love altogether, and no one ever will." Aided by the straightforward language, which retains its beauty even in translation, the story of Daphnis and Chloë continues to appeal to modern readers by its focus on that most universal and ageless of themes, the triumph of love.

An English Version of a Work by Longus

Longus: Daphnis and Chloe. Translated by Paul Turner. New York: Penguin Books, 1989.

Works about Longus

MacQueen, Bruce D. *Myth, Rhetoric, and Fiction: A Reading of Longus's Daphnis and Chloe.* Lincoln: University of Nebraska Press, 1991.

McCulloh, William E. *Longus.* New York: Twayne Publishers, 1970.

Lorris, Guillaume de
See GUILLAUME DE LORRIS.

Lucan (Marcus Annaeus Lucanis)
(39–65) *poet*

Lucan was one of the most influential writers of the *Pax Romana,* or Roman Peace. A nephew of the writer and philosopher SENECA, Lucan was born in Córdoba, Spain, and educated in Athens, where he became interested in the philosophy of Stoicism. He later moved to Rome to serve in the government of Emperor Nero. When accused of plotting against Nero, he committed suicide in A.D. 65.

During his brief life, Lucan produced many poems and became a very popular writer. He was greatly influenced by earlier Roman writers, especially LIVY and VIRGIL, and much of his poetry was written in praise of the Emperor Nero.

Lucan's most famous and only extant work is the *Pharsalia,* also called the *Civil War,* which poetically describes the civil war between CAESAR and Pompey. The 10 books of the *Pharsalia* begin with Caesar's crossing of the Rubicon and end with his exploits in Egypt. More dramatic than historical, the work is about 8,000 lines long and was left unfinished at Lucan's death. He possibly planned more books narrating the events leading to Caesar's assassination in 46 B.C.

A primary theme of the *Pharsalia* is the idea that a republican form of government is better than a monarchy. The poem portrays Caesar as an ambitious villain who seeks only personal power. The hero of the poem is the republican figure Cato, who is portrayed as fighting for Rome's freedom. Other themes of the work are horror at the idea of family members fighting against one another, dismay at the failure of the Roman Republic to live up to its potential, and despair at the collapse of cosmic order.

Though notably inaccurate in its historical details, the *Pharsalia*'s dramatic appeal led readers of the MIDDLE AGES and Renaissance to place Lucan in the ranks of the classic writers he so admired, including Virgil, HOMER, and OVID.

An English Version of a Work by Lucan
Lucan: Civil War. Translated by Susan H. Braud. Oxford: Oxford University Press, 1992.

A Work about Lucan
Ahl, F. *Lucan: An Introduction.* Ithaca, N.Y.: Cornell University Press, 1976.

Lucian (ca. 115–ca. 180) *poet, satirist*
Long after the Greek city-states had lost their independence to the might of the Roman Empire, Greek cultural and literary life continued unabated. The stability provided by Roman military and political power, along with the respect many Romans held for Greek culture, allowed Greek writers and thinkers the freedom to explore new subjects and themes. One of the men who took advantage of this was the poet Lucian.

Lucian was born in the city of Samosata in Syria, then part of the Roman Empire. He was not of a distinguished family and worked as a stonemason. Wanting more out of life, he educated himself in the areas of rhetoric and philosophy, and soon began working as a lawyer and lecturer. He also developed great interest and knowledge in the important philosophical and political issues of his time. He apparently traveled across the Roman Empire, serving as a public speaker, and finally settled in Athens.

Lucian was a satirist, always seeking to use humor to express his feelings on various subjects. He was particularly adept in his development of satiric dialogue. Like future satirists, such as Voltaire and Jonathan Swift, Lucian's writings ridicule superstitious and false philosophy. For example, in *True History* he parodies the facts of the world as expressed by early historians and poets. This fantastical tale of journeys to the moon and within a monster's belly influenced the French satirists François Rabelais' *Pantagruel* and Cyrano de Bergerac's *Voyages to the Sun and Moon* as well as Swift's *Gulliver's Travels*.

Among the best known of Lucian's works are the *Dialogues of the Gods*. In these short pieces, Lucian uses conversations among the Olympian gods to demonstrate human folly and gullibility, with the gods themselves playing the part of the humans Lucian was trying to deride.

One of the main targets of Lucian's ridicule was organized religion. He believed that religion was merely a tool used by many to take advantage of gullible people, and he had nothing but contempt for people possessed of false religious convictions. He did not target any particular faith; rather, he criticized the use of religion as a tool to control the masses and lampooned society's inability to pursue enlightenment rather than temporal wealth and luxury. In essence, Lucian was a writer who sought to amuse his audience with his wit while also expressing his skepticism and derision. His skill made him one of the greatest writers of the Silver Age of Greek literature.

English Versions of Works by Lucian
Lucian: A Selection. Edited by M. D. MacLeod. Wiltshire, U.K.: Aris & Phillips, 1991.
Selected Satires of Lucian. Translated by Lionel Casson. New York: W. W. Norton & Co., 1968.
True History. Translated by Paul Turner. Bloomington: University of Indiana Press, 1958.

Works about Lucian
Allinson, Francis G. *Lucian, satirist and artist.* New York: Cooper Square Pub., 1963.
Anderson, Graham. *Studies in Lucian's Comic Fiction.* Leiden, Netherlands: E. J. Brill, 1976.
Baldwin, Barry. *Studies in Lucian.* Toronto: Hakkert, 1973.
McIntyre, Ann. *Culture and Society in Lucian.* Cambridge, Mass.: Harvard University Press, 1986.

Lucius Apuleis
See APULEIUS.

Lucretius (Titus Lucretius Carus) (ca. 99– ca. 55 B.C.) *poet*

Biographical information about Lucretius is scant, untrustworthy, and inconsistent. The translator and essayist St. JEROME wrote in the fourth century that a love potion drove Lucretius mad, that he composed his poetry in moments of clarity between bouts of insanity, that his works were improved on by CICERO, and that he committed suicide. Jerome's reportage should be approached with some skepticism, however: As a doctor of the Christian Church and the translator of the Old Testament from Hebrew to Latin and the New Testament into modern Latin, Jerome may have been motivated to discredit a man who rebelled against conventional religion.

It is known that Lucretius lived during the years that saw the demise of the great Roman republic at the hands of Julius CAESAR, accompanied by rampant decadence, corruption, and conspiracy. It is also known that he died when he was in his 40s, at the height of his poetic powers.

Further details of Lucretius's life can be assumed from fashions of the day or from details in his writings. He was very well educated and well read, with a fluency in both Greek and Latin. He may have been well traveled, too; it is suggested he had journeyed throughout Italy and to Greece, Sicily, and other parts of the eastern Mediterranean and southwest Asia. Although it is not known whether Lucretius was of noble birth, he was almost certainly integrated into aristocratic society, as was the tendency for writers of note during that era. Lucretius was familiar with the pageantry, hustle, and glamour of city living, as well as its well-designed public spaces and architectural constructions. He also knew and loved the recreational and sensuous pleasures the countryside had to offer.

Critical Analysis

Scholar Olivia Coolidge states that *De Rerum Natura*, Lucretius's only known work, is "one of the world's great poems, magnificent in its courage, and glorious in its feeling for nature." Translated as "On the Nature of Things," or sometimes as "The Way Things Are," the poem is based on the beliefs of the Greek philosopher EPICURUS and his followers. The Epicureans believed that the world's matter is made up of atoms, that all knowledge is derived from the senses, which "we trust, first, last, and always" (*De Rerum Natura*, I.423), and that pleasure is the supreme good.

Lucretius's work, which he left unfinished, is written in hexameter verse in six segments, or books. As was the custom among the poets of his day, Lucretius begins by invoking a goddess. This is curious, however, given Lucretius's (and the Epicureans') hostility toward religious tradition. Indeed, we soon find him asserting, "religion has prompted vile and vicious acts" (I.83), giving as an example the commander in chief of the Greek army who, according to legend, sacrificed his daughter on the altar of the goddess Diana on the eve of the Trojan War. (This tale is dramatized in EURIPIDES' tragedy *Iphigenia at Aulis*.)

Most of Book I of *De Rerum Natura* concerns the theories of atoms, which Lucretius precedes with an entreaty to his readers to keep an open mind:

> Now turn attentive ears and thoughtful
> mind,
> by trouble undistraught, to truth and
> reason;
> my gifts displayed for you in loyal love
> you must not scorn before you grasp their
> meaning.
> For I shall tell you of the highest law
> of heaven and god, and show you basic
> substance,
> whence nature creates all things and gives
> them growth,
> and whither again dissolves them at their
> death.
> "Matter," I call it, and "creative bodies,"
> and "seeds of things" . . . for with them
> everything
> begins.
>
> (I.50–61)

Being is created out of matter, Lucretius states, as a consequence of natural law, not by miracles or divine intervention. The atoms that constitute everything cannot be destroyed, only changed. Although objects seem solid to us, they are actually made up of widely dispersed, always moving atoms. Differences in atomic density account for differences in weight. Wherever atoms are absent, there is void; these are the only two forms of matter.

Book II explains that not only is pleasure, or mind-body harmony, the only true criterion of the good, but also that nature wants it for us: "[N]ature demands no favor but that pain / be sundered from the flesh, that in the mind be a sense of joy, unmixed with care and fear!" (II.17–19) Wealth, status, and power cannot benefit the soul unless they eliminate the fear of death, and they do not; only human reason can do that. Book II also discusses at greater length the ways in which atoms travel and mutate and how different shapes produce different physical sensations when we perceive them through our senses.

The fear of death is the source of almost all human ills, according to Book III, which undertakes to dispel this fear. The soul is corporeal, made of atoms like any limb or organ. The idea that the immortal (soul) and mortal (physical body) can coexist is nonsense. When the soul's vessel, the human body, dies, the soul ceases to exist. If the soul dies, it cannot possibly suffer; so fear of death is foolish. There is no afterlife, according to Lucretius, and "Hell is right here [on earth], the work of foolish men!" (III.1023) Therefore, superstitions are a waste of time and prayers are a waste of breath.

In Book IV, Lucretius explores the mechanics of the senses and thought vis-à-vis atomic theory. For instance, we are able to see because the images release atoms that strike our eyes; sounds and speech are matter and also cause hearing via physical impact. Sounds must be matter, Lucretius argues, because it is well known that "he who speaks at length loses some weight"! (IV.541) Contrary to popular belief, echoes are not caused by supernat-

ural beings, but rather occur when sound-matter strikes a surface and is thrown back to the speaker. The atoms that cause odors are languid—they do not travel as far as sound and sight—and large, as they do not readily penetrate walls. Lucretius goes on to say that mistakes in sense perception occur because the mind has reached an erroneous conclusion, not because the organs of sense perception are faulty.

Lucretius discusses astronomical and cosmological matters in Book V. Earth came about due to the forces inherent in natural law and had nothing to do with the activities of any deities or divine beings. The celestial bodies, the sea, and the land are not made of godlike stuff, eternal and fixed; rather, the earth as we know it is a combination of atoms and void. In other words, matter cannot exist indefinitely and will one day perish.

Lucretius then provides an anthropological account of the increasing refinement of the human race, concluding:

> Navigation, agriculture, cities, laws
> war, travel, clothing, and all such things else,
> money, and life's delights, from top to bottom,
> poetry, painting, the cunning sculptor's art,
> the search, the trial and error of nimble minds
> have taught us, inching forward, step by step.
> Thus, step by step, time lays each fact before us,
> and reason lifts it to the coasts of light;
> for men saw one thing clarify another
> till civilization reached its highest peak.
> (VI.1448–1457)

Book VI acts as a summary of sorts in which Lucretius recounts some of his previous insights. His lyricism in this book is characteristic of the work as a whole.

In the introduction to *Lucretius* (Basic Books, 1965), Donald R. Dudley states that Lucretius "is, pre-eminently, the poet of the intelligible world, of the processes which govern it, and of the intellect by which these processes are revealed." And, according to translator Frank O. Copley, "Lucretius saw into the hearts of individual men as they faced the immediacies of their lives. But his sympathy and understanding not of man, but of *this* man and *that* man, not of mankind, but of people, was hardly surpassed in antiquity, and perhaps has never been equaled."

English Versions of a Work by Lucretius

De Rerum Natura: The Poem on Nature. Translated by C. H. Sisson. London: Routledge, 2003.
On the Nature of Things. Translated by W. E. Leonard. Mineola, N.Y.: Dover Publications, 2004.

Works about Lucretius

Campbell, Gordon. *Lucretius on Creation and Evolution: A Commentary on de Rerum Natura 5.772–1104.* Oxford: Oxford University Press, 2003.
Kennedy, Duncan F. *Rethinking Reality: Lucretius and the Textualization of Nature.* Ann Arbor: University of Michigan Press, 2002.

Lute, The

See GAO MING.

Lysias (459–380 B.C.) *orator, speechwriter*

Lysias was a *metic:* a resident of Athens, but not a full Athenian citizen. His family was associated with the democratic movement in Athens, and his life was deeply affected by large-scale political changes in the country. During the revolution of 404–403 B.C., for example, the Thirty Tyrants of Athens killed Lysias's brother and confiscated the shield factory that belonged to his family. Lysias left Athens, returning only when the Thirty Tyrants had been overthrown (403 B.C.).

His brother's murder became the motivating force for Lysias's development as an orator. He is partially known for his writing a defense speech for SOCRATES, when the philosopher was taken to court. Socrates rejected the speech because he wanted to defend himself, but the simple yet eloquent oration by Lysias became famous.

Indeed, it is Lysias's simplicity, as well as his clarity of thought and purity of language that make his works profound. As an ATTIC ORATOR, he composed speeches covering a wide range of public and private issues, including citizenship, misuse of public funds, the removal of a sacred olive stump, adultery, and slander. One of his best-known speeches is *On the Murder of Eratosthenes.* Written in Lysias's usual direct style, the speech paints a portrait of a simple-minded, naive peasant who murders Eratosthenes because he could not have acted otherwise when he caught his wife with a lover.

Against Eratosthenes is considered the best of Lysias's 30 orations, and its success in his lifetime resulted in Lysias becoming one of the best and most highly paid Athenian speechwriters and lawyers. His works are important for the details they provide of ancient Athenian thought and culture.

English Versions of Works by Lysias

Lysias. The Oratory of Classical Greece Series. Translated by S. C. Todd. Austin: University of Texas Press, 1999.
Lysias orations I, III. Commentary by Ruth Scodel. Bryn Mawr, Pa.: Thomas Library, Bryn Mawr College, 1986.
Selected Speeches. Edited by C. Carey et al. Cambridge, U.K.: Cambridge University Press, 1990.

A Work about Lysias

Dover, Kenneth James. *Lysias and the Corpus Lysiacum, Vol. 39.* Berkeley: University of California Press, 1968.

M

Ma'arrī Abū al-'Alā', al- (Ahmad ibn 'Abd Allāh al-Ma 'arri) (973–1058) *poet, philosopher*

Al-Ma'arrī, a Syrian poet, is considered one of the key figures in the history of Arabic literature. Blind from childhood, ascetic, and skeptical, he was unwilling to participate in the Arabic poetic traditions of flattery or boasting panegyrics (praises to a patron). He toiled in seclusion for years to produce a body of technically innovative poetry, original narrative prose, and criticism that won him fame and honor both in his lifetime and beyond.

Born in Ma'arra (hence his name), al-Ma'arrī lost his sight to smallpox at age four but compensated for the loss with his phenomenal memory for books. He was educated in his home town and in nearby Aleppo. Thus began a lifelong investigation of Arabic poetics, grammar, and philology that informed many of his poems.

Al-Ma'arrī's prose and poetry reflect the pessimism and misanthropy for which he became famous. Contemptuous of all the heroic, romantic, and nostalgic themes of traditional Arabic poetry, he cultivated a tone that at times approaches despair. Ironically, despite his constant refrain that "My clothing is my shroud, my grave is my home; my life is my fate, and for me death is resurrection"

(*The Constraint of What is Not Compulsory*), he lived to a ripe old age in comfort and prosperity.

Although al-Ma'arrī's philosophic writings were obscure, perhaps to defend against charges of heresy, he appears to have disbelieved in an afterlife, favored cremation of the dead, and opposed sex as sinful, even for the purpose of having children. Critics attacked his book of moral and religious admonitions, *Paragraphs and Periods,* a tour de force of rhymed prose, as a parody of and al-Ma'arrī's attempt to imitate the style of the KORAN.

After early successes as a poet and scholar, the writer spent an unsuccessful 18 months during his 30s trying to make his fortune in Baghdad. Unable to assimilate himself into the court life of the Abbasid capital, he retired in 1010 to his hometown, where he remained the rest of his life, supporting himself by teaching poetry.

Though many of al-Ma'arrī's works cited by biographers have not survived, a good deal of poetry, belles lettres, prose, and criticism remains. His most famous prose work is "The Epistle of Forgiveness" (ca. 1033), which takes the form of a letter to his friend Ibn al-Qarih and recounts the tale of al-Qarih's death and his subsequent journeys to Paradise (where he converses with famed poet AL-KHANSĀ') and hell (where he converses with

TARAFAH 'AMR IBN AL-'ABD and other poets). The conversations within the text cover a wide range of topics, including heresy and atheism.

Another unusual work is "Letters of a Horse and Mule" in which a horse, a mule, and other animals discuss philology as well as taxation, warfare, and other topics.

Al-Ma'arrī collected three volumes of his own poems in his lifetime. The first of them, *The Spark from the Fire-stick,* includes a series of his earliest poems. The second collection, *On Coats of Mail,* contains poems about armor. The third collection is his most celebrated, *The Constraint of What Is Not Compulsory,* which includes more than 1,500 poems. Most of these are written in a rhyme scheme far more elaborate than required by the rules of Arabic verse and are replete with plays on words so complex that the poet had to write a commentary on his own work. Al-Ma'arrī's pessimism and cynicism reach full expression in this volume, with lines such as: "If only a child died at its hour of birth and never suckled from its mother in confinement. / Even before it can utter a word, it tells her: Grief and trouble is all you will get from me." Despite the outlook on life portrayed in his works, al-Ma'arrī is remembered not only for the volume of work he produced but also for his imagery and elaborate style.

English Versions of Works by Abū al-'Alā' al-Ma'arrī

Arberry, A. J., ed. *Arabic Poetry: A Primer for Students.* Cambridge, U.K.: Cambridge University Press, 1965.

Lichtenstadter, Ilse, ed. *Introduction to Classical Arabic Literature.* New York: Twayne, 1974.

A Work about Abū al-'Alā' al-Ma'arrī

Irwin, Robert, ed. *Night and Horses and the Desert.* Woodstock, N.Y.: Overlook Press, 2000, 31, 58, 203, 263, 315, 354.

Mahabharata   (ca. 400 B.C.–ca. 400 A.D.)

The *Mahabharata* is one of India's two great literary EPICS; the other is the *RAMAYANA* (*see* VALMIKI, MAHARSHI). It consists of a series of verses originally composed for oral recitation; most of the verses are couplets containing 32 syllables. As a whole, the *Mahabharata* contains no fewer than 73,000 verses, and some editions contain as many as 100,000, making it eight times longer than HOMER's *Iliad* and *Odyssey* combined.

The *Mahabharata* may be based on actual events from the eighth or ninth century B.C. It seems to have come into existence around the fourth century B.C., the same time as the *Ramayana*. Numerous copyists and reciters added to it and modified it over time until it reached its current form, around or before A.D. 400. It now contains 18 major books, each divided into a number of chapters. The text also breaks down into 100 minor books.

The *Mahabharata* has exercised an extraordinary influence over Indian literature and culture. KALIDASA's plays drew inspiration from it, as did the works of many other writers. Painters and sculptors depicted scenes from it, and a cult grew around its heroine, Draupadi. In the MIDDLE AGES, knowledge of the *Mahabharata* spread as far as Java and Bali. More recently, Indian comic books have retold the epic story.

As scholar Bruce Sullivan has noted, the *Mahabharata* represents the "desire to conserve and preserve for everyone the wisdom enunciated by a dharma-knowing sage." (Dharma involves the way things should be and the way one should behave.) Thus, the epic holds a significant place in the history of Indian thought. Editor and translator J. A. B. van Buitenen points out that the *Mahabharata*

> contains a large number of philosophical chapters that are among the oldest documents for more or less systematic "Hindu" thought. Likewise, the history of Indian law cannot be properly understood without the epic, where the law is the single greatest concern.

The *Mahabharata's* importance is demonstrated by the fact that the BHAGAVAD GITA, which has become a key text in Hinduism, is only a small part of the great epic. In the end, however, the highest praise for the *Mahabharata* comes from the epic itself:

> Once one has heard this story so worthy of being heard[,] no other story will please him: it will sound harsh as the crow sounds to one after hearing the cuckoo sing. . . . No story is found on earth that does not rest on this epic. . . . Whatever is found here may be found somewhere else, but what is not found here is found nowhere!

Critical Analysis

The *Mahabharata's* plot is complex. In essence, it tells of a bitter and bloody conflict between two sets of cousins, the Pandava brothers and the Dharatarastra brothers. Both wish to rule Kuruksetra, a kingdom in northern India.

The trouble begins when King Vicitravirya dies without heirs. His half brother Krsna Dvaipayana, also called Krsna Vyasa, fathers sons on the king's two widows and a maidservant. The first son, Dhartarastra, is blind. As a result, the second son, Pandu, becomes king. After Pandu has ruled for some time, however, he finds it necessary to retire to the forest. Dhartarastra now rules the kingdom.

Pandu has five sons, while Dhartarastra has 100. The eldest Pandava, Yudhisthira, was born before any of his Dharatarastra cousins and therefore claims the throne. Unfortunately, one of the Dharatarastras, Duryodhana, wants to become king himself. He tries to kill Yudhisthira and the other Pandavas.

After two assassination attempts have failed, and the Pandavas have acquired allies, Duryodhana agrees to divide the kingdom with his cousins. The Pandavas travel to their part of the kingdom and found a new capital city. Seeing them prosper, Duryodhana's jealousy gets the better of him again. He challenges Yudhisthira to a dice game during a ritual intended to consecrate the latter as king. The game is rigged; Yudhisthira loses his brothers' freedom, his own freedom, and the Pandavas' common wife, Draupadi. He also loses a rematch. The Pandavas agree to spend 12 years in exile and live in disguise for a 13th year.

When the 13 years have passed, the Pandavas and their allies return to the capital to claim the throne for Yudhisthira. Duryodhana refuses to yield. A war ensues that lasts for 18 days and takes in the entire world. Duryodhana and most of the Dharatarastras perish, as do the Pandavas' relatives, allies, and unborn children. The five Pandavas, however, survive, and Yudhisthira takes the throne. Years later, his descendant hears this story, the *Mahabharata*, recited by a disciple of Krsna Vyasa.

Krsna Vyasa, the grandfather of the Pandavas and Dharatarastras, is an important figure in Hindu tradition. According to legend, he composed not only the PURANA but also the *Mahabharata*, which he dictated to the god Ganesh. He appears in the *Mahabharata* as a wise and powerful man. Ironically, as Sullivan points out, he is also partly responsible for the bloody war between his grandchildren. He deliberately made his son Dharatarastra blind and thus complicated the line of succession; he supervised the ritual during which Yudhisthira lost everything in a dice game; and he failed in his attempts to pacify his grandchildren and prevent the war.

Yet it seems the war was unavoidable. Indeed, the inevitability of fate is a theme of the *Mahabharata*. Dharatarastra says, "My old age, the destruction of all my relatives, and the death of my friends and allies happened because of fate." Time, says the *Mahabharata*, is merciless and inescapable:

> [Time] brought the Pandava and [Dharatarastra] armies together in that place and there destroyed them. . . . Time ripens the creatures. Time rots them. . . . Whatever beings there were in the past will be in the future, whatever are busy now, they are all the creatures of Time—know it, and do not lose your sense.

In keeping with its theme of time, the *Mahabharata* depicts the war between the Dharatarastras and Pandavas as the end of one stage of history and the beginning of another. Characters are described as incarnations of either gods or demons, battling each other in human form. Van Buitenen argues that this mythical imagery is a late addition to the epic and cheapens its story. Sullivan, in contrast, believes that "the conflict between the gods and demons" is a central theme of the epic, just as the conflict between gods and giants is a central theme in Norse mythology (*see* MYTHOLOGY, NORSE).

English Versions of the *Mahabharata*

Carrière, Jean-Claude. *The Mahabharata: A Play Based Upon the Indian Classic Epic.* Translated by Peter Brook. New York: Harper & Row, 1987.

The Mahabharata. 3 vols. Translated and edited by J. A. B. van Buitenen. Chicago: University of Chicago Press, 1973–78.

The Mahabharata. Translated and edited by William Buck. Berkeley: University of California Press, 2000.

Works about the *Mahabharata*

Chaitanya, Krishna. *The Mahabharata: A Literary Study.* New Delhi: Clarion Books; Flushing, N.Y.: Asia Book Corp. of America, 1985.

González Reimann, Luis. *The Mahabharata and the Yugas: India's Great Epic Poem and the Hindu System of World Ages.* New York: Peter Lang, 2002.

Matilal, Bimal Krishna. *Moral Dilemmas in the Mahabharata.* Shimla: Indian Institute of Advanced Study, 1989.

Sullivan, Bruce M. *Krsna Dvaipayana Vyasa and the Mahabharata: A New Interpretation.* New York: E.J. Brill, 1990.

Maimonides, Moses (Moses ben Maimon, Rabbi Moses ben Maimon, RaMBaM) (1135–1204) *philosopher, physician, nonfiction writer*

Moses Maimonides, known in Hebrew literature by the acronym RaMBaM, was born in Córdoba, Spain, to Rabbi Maimon ben Joseph, a judge of the rabbinical court, and a mother (name unknown) who died at his birth. He became a Talmudic scholar and philosopher, studying and writing books as he wandered throughout Andalusia.

In 1160, Maimonides and his family fled Spain to evade the Muslim Almohades, who were invading Spain and persecuting Jewish communities. They traveled to several different countries, going first to Morocco, where they still had to hide their Jewish origins. After an abortive attempt to move to Israel, they settled in Egypt, first in Alexandria and then in Fustat, close to Cairo, where Maimonides started studying medicine. He was eventually able to gain a position as chief physician at the court of Saladin. He also became a respected citizen and served as the leader of the Cairo Jewish community.

Many fantastical myths and legends have grown up around Maimonides over the years, which is ironic since the philosopher himself was very skeptical of all superstition, magic, and myth. He was, philosophically speaking, a religious rationalist. He did not take seriously the ideas, common in his day, of witchcraft, astrology, mysticism and speaking in tongues. Nonetheless, the stories surrounding him include accounts of his miraculous birth and death, tales of mysterious circumstances surrounding his travels and burial, and tales of his raising people from the dead.

Despite his obligations as chief physician and leader of the Cairo Jewish community, Maimonides continued with his scholarship and produced a large body of written work on the TALMUD, Jewish law, medicine, and philosophy. He was the first person ever to codify Jewish law systematically, the product of which is the *Mishnah Torah* (1180). In one section of this work, Maimonides defines repentance: "Repentance involves forsaking sins and removing such thoughts from one's way of thinking and resolving firmly never to do it again. . . ." Another of his works, *The Guide to the Perplexed*, is regarded as one of the great philosophical works on Judaism. Maimonides based his interpretation of Jewish law on ARISTOTLE's philosophy, and his work influenced such later writers as Benedict Spinoza and Saint Thomas Aquinas.

In his time, Maimonides was a hero throughout the Jewish world. Upon his death, Egyptian Jews mourned for three days. The credo of Judaism that he formulated, expressed in 13 articles of faith, was reworked into the *Yigdal* prayer, which is included in most Jewish prayer books. Today Maimonides is regarded as one of the foremost Jewish philosophers of all time, and his work is still widely read and respected.

English Versions of Works by Maimonides

Codex Maimuni: Moses Maimonides' Code of Law: The Illuminated Pages of the Kaufmann Mishneh Torah. Budapest: Corniva, 1984.

The Guide to the Perplexed, Vols. One and Two. Translated by Shlomo Pines. Chicago: University of Chicago Press, 1974.

Rambam, Readings in the Philosophy of Moses Maimonides. Translated by Lenn E. Goodman. Los Angeles: Gee Tee Bee, 1985.

Works about Maimonides

Davidson, Herbert A. *Moses Maimonides: The Man and His Works.* Oxford: Oxford University Press, 2004.

Robinson, Ira and Lawrence Kaplan. *The Thought of Moses Maimonides: Philosophical and Legal Studies.* (Studies in the History of Philosophy, Vol. 17). Lewiston, N.Y.: Edwin Mellen Press, 1991.

Rosner, Fred and Samuel S. Kottek, editors. *Moses Maimonides: Physician, Scientist, and Philosopher.* Northvale, N.J.: Jason Aronson, 1993.

Twersky, Isadore. *Introduction to the Code of Maimonides (Mishneh Torah).* New Haven, Conn.: Yale University Press, 1982.

Manco Capac, myth of

See MYTH OF MANCO CAPAC.

Marcus Aurelius Antoninus (Marcus Aelius Aurelius Antoninus) (121–180)
philosopher, Roman emperor

Marcus Antoninus Aurelius was born in Rome. When he was young, he lost his father, and from his earliest years enjoyed the friendship and patronage of Emperor Hadrian, who provided him with special educational privileges. Thus, at age eight Aurelius became a member of the Salian priesthood. He was adopted by Hadrian's successor, Antoninus Pius (his uncle by marriage), whose daughter he later married.

Aurelius is known as one of the greatest emperors in Roman history (reigned 161–180). In times of plague and famine, he sold many of his own possessions to help the poor. This and other similar acts made him one of the "Five Good Emperors" (an ironic title, given that he also persecuted the Christians as a threat to Roman rule). As a military and civic leader, he won several important wars and successfully dealt with serious internal disasters. His personal life, however, was not as successful. His wife was unfaithful, and his heir (an adopted nephew whom some scholars believe was responsible for Aurelius's death) was disappointing. In addition, Aurelius was plagued by self-doubts regarding his adequacy as an emperor, for although he was a sound military leader, he was troubled by the nature of war. These doubts and contemplations were perhaps what led him to write *Meditations* (first published in 1555). Originally written in Greek, the work exists in 12 volumes. It is Aurelius's interpretation of and "meditations" on Stoic philosophy, specifically those elements of it that extolled reason, virtue, freedom, and morality.

In light of the personal conflicts and military matters that Aurelius dealt with, it is not surprising that he turned to Stoicism to find the moral stamina to deal with adversity. Some critics have gone so far as to suggest that Aurelius's commitment to Stoicism interfered with his ability to be an effective emperor. His successful campaigns against the Parthians (166) and the Germans (167) as well as his commitment to the welfare of his people suggest otherwise. Aurelius died from the plague on March 17 in what is now Vienna.

Aurelius's *Meditations* provide an in-depth look at the man, the emperor, and the philosopher. One of the central ideas of *Meditations,* and Stoicism, is unity. Stoics believed that all "parts" were part of a "whole," that all things—even thoughts and emotions—were entwined and could not be logically viewed as separate. In *Meditations,* Aurelius writes:

> All things are implicated with one another, and the bond is holy; and there is hardly anything unconnected with any other things. . . . For there is one universe made up of all things, and one god who pervades all things, and one substance, and one law, and one reason.
>
> (7.9)

According to this theory, Aurelius reasons that people, as a natural part of the universe, must abide by "natural" laws:

> We are made for cooperation, like feet, like hands, like eyelids, like the rows of the upper and lower teeth. To act against one another then is contrary to nature.
>
> (2.1)

To Aurelius, harmony is a natural state of being. He believed that happiness can be achieved by anyone, and that external circumstances should not prevent one from finding harmony. This is somewhat characteristic of the Roman ideal of success—to work toward a goal without allowing the possibility of failure to alter action. In *Meditations,* he says:

> [I]f you work at that which is before you, following right reason seriously, vigorously, calmly without allowing anything else to distract you, but keeping your divine part pure . . . you will be happy.
>
> (4.7)

Meditations is not only an invaluable sample of early introspective writing, illuminating the development of Aurelius's thoughts and ideas; it is also an extensive explanation of Stoic philosophy. The work influenced such later writers as Petrarch, Michel de Montaigne, George Chapman, Matthew Arnold, and others.

English Versions of Works by Marcus Aurelius Antoninus

Marcus Aurelius. Loeb Classical Library. Edited by G. P. Goold. Translated by C. G. Haines. Cambridge, Mass.: Harvard University Press, 1988.
The Meditations. Everyman's Library. Translated by A. S. L. Farquharson. Introduction by D. A. Rees. New York: Alfred A. Knopf, 2003.
Thoughts of the Emperor Marcus Aurelius Antoninus. Translated by George Long. Watchung, N.J.: Albert Saifer, 1995.

Works about Marcus Aurelius Antoninus

Birley, Anthony. *Marcus Aurelius: A Biography.* New York: Barnes and Noble, 1999.
Farquharson, A. S. L. *Marcus Aurelius, His Life and His World.* Oxford, U.K.: Greenwood Publishing, 1975.
Rutherford, R. B. *The Meditations of Marcus Aurelius: A Study.* Oxford: Oxford University Press, 1989.

Marcus Fabius Quintilianus

See QUINTILIAN.

Marie de France (ca. 1150–ca. 1200) *poet, translator*

All that is known of Marie de France, one of the first women writers in French literature, comes from her texts. At the end of one her tales, she writes, "My name is Marie and I come from France." Most of her work was written between 1175 and 1190.

Marie wrote *lais,* short narrative poems, and translated some of AESOP's fables and a saint's life of Saint Patrick. In her work, she demonstrates familiarity with classical literature and contemporary

Latin and Anglo-Norman literature. Most scholars believe that she either lived or spent time in the courts of Henry II and Richard I of England; the English and French kings were related, and the two courts strongly influenced each other. Marie wrote her poetry in Anglo-Norman French, which was a widely used and easily understood dialect.

Marie's poetry has survived because of its sophisticated narrative voice and condensed structure. "Chevrefoil" ("Honeysuckle"), her most famous *lai*, focuses on an episode from TRISTAN AND ISEULT, the most famous love story of the MIDDLE AGES. In this poem, Tristan has been banished from court, but he sends Queen Iseult a secret message carved on a hazel branch. It compares their love to the honeysuckle that entwines the hazel tree; neither of them can live without the other. Marie's use of a specific object integral to the plot as a metaphor for the story's theme occurs in several of her other *lais*, and it shows the elegant economy and sophistication of her style.

English Versions of Works by Marie de France

The Lais of Marie de France. Translated by Glyn S. Burgess. New York: Penguin, 1999.

The Lais of Marie de France. Translated by Robert Hanning and Joan Ferrante. Durham, N.C.: Labyrinth Press, 1982.

A Work about Marie de France

Mickel, Emanuel J., Jr. *Marie de France.* New York: Twayne, 1974.

Martial (Marcus Valerius Martialis)
(ca. 40–ca. 104) *poet*

Marcus Valerius Martialis, later called Martial, was born at Bilbilis, a town in northeast Spain, to parents named Fronto and Flacilla. Then a province of the Roman Empire, Spain was also the birthplace of the first-century writers SENECA, LUCAN, and QUINTILIAN. In 64, during the reign of Nero, Martial went to Rome. He received a thorough education in grammar and rhetoric, which was standard for the time, but declined to pursue a profession. Because he wanted to write poetry, he sought the favor of wealthy patrons who would compensate him for his work in return for flattery. He never married but still enjoyed the social benefits reserved for those who had parented three children. Emperor Titus made him a tribune, which raised him to the equestrian class.

Though he spent most of his working life in one of the multilevel flats that housed the bulk of the common population of Rome, Martial also had a small country estate, where he took up residence in 94. Four years later, he returned to his birthplace, aided by his friend PLINY THE YOUNGER. His patroness there, a generous lady named Marcella, made life so agreeable that Martial wrote to his friend JUVENAL expressing his delight with country life. Though he missed the city, he never returned to Rome.

Martial scorned the artificial style of EPIC writers like Statius and instead adopted the straightforward, personable style he admired in the poet Gaius Valerius CATULLUS, which his audience appreciated. His earliest surviving work is *The Book of Spectacles,* written to celebrate the opening of the Colosseum in 80. He wrote *The Xenia* in 83 and *The Apophoreta* in 85 to celebrate the Roman feast of the Saturnalia. *Xenia* was a word used to describe the leftovers of the feast as gifts, and *apophoreta* referred to traditional gifts. These early epigrams were so popular that Martial thereafter began to write whole books of them, collected in the 12 books of *Epigrams* that appeared between 85 and 102.

The epigram emerged originally in Greece as a verse form used in inscriptions on monuments or artworks, or to accompany gifts. Concise out of necessity, the poem could be simply descriptive or commemorate a person or event. After CALLIMACHUS, other poets employed the form for a wide variety of subjects, but it remained extremely simple and stylistically pure. After Martial, the epigram was irrevocably linked with satire. In the words of scholar Peter Howell, Martial brought this short but powerful form to "a pitch of technical perfection never afterwards rivalled."

Later generations found the *Epigrams* somewhat obscene, but Martial's frankness is familiar to the modern eye. The satire in most of the poems is comparatively gentle, since a man of his position could scarcely afford to alienate the wealthy and influential. It required shrewdness and ingenuity to live the life of a perpetual hanger-on; therefore, when Martial pokes fun at his fellows, it seems in good spirit, as can be seen in James Michie's translation of the third poem of Book I:

> . . . Nobody sneers as loud
> As a Roman: old or young, even newly-
>   born,
> He turns his nose up like a rhino horn.

As a whole, the *Epigrams* offer a vivid picture of life in Rome near the end of the first century. The poems reveal practices of city life as well as common attitudes, for instance in the complaint that appears in the ninth poem of Book V:

> I was unwell. You hurried round,
>   surrounded
> By ninety students, Doctor. Ninety chill,
> North-wind-chapped hands then pawed
>   and probed and pounded.
> I was unwell: now I'm extremely ill.

In all the 12 books of the *Epigrams,* the voice of the poet mocks the foolishness and vanity of human nature but never seems to hold himself apart or superior. As Howell says of Martial, "mankind is his concern. It is his acute perception of human nature, and boundless interest in the life around him, that makes him so permanently interesting." Martial's influence spread through the late Roman poets to the medieval writers, and Renaissance and Baroque authors revived the epigram as a way of making a concise and cutting statement. Eighteenth-century poets and writers in the European tradition, with their relish for caricature, considered Martial the master, and even poets of the 19th century, such as Lord Byron, found that even

if one did not appreciate Martial, it was still necessary to read him.

English Versions of Works by Martial

Martial: The Epigrams. Translated by James Michie. New York: Penguin Books, 1973.
Martial: Select Epigrams. Translated by Lindsay Watson, et al. New York: Cambridge University Press, 2003.

Works about Martial

Boyle, A. J. and J. P. Sullivan, eds. *Martial in English.* New York: Penguin Books, 1996.
Hull, K. W. D., ed. *Martial and His Times.* London: Bell, 1967.

medieval romance
See ROMANCE, MEDIEVAL.

Menander (ca. 342–292 B.C.) *playwright*

At the height of Greek cultural importance, the city-state of Athens was the home of many distinguished literary figures. Before the rule of Alexander the Great, Athens had been dominant in both a political and a cultural sense. Later, in the Hellenistic Age, Athens was no longer an important political or military power, but it remained a center of Greek culture. One of the most distinguished literary figures that Athens produced during this time was the playwright Menander.

The nephew of another playwright, Menander came from a wealthy and respected family. He began writing early in his life, producing plays as early as his mid-20s, and continued writing throughout his life. One of his teachers was the philosopher and writer THEOPHRASTUS, who had been a student of ARISTOTLE. Menander was highly regarded by his fellow Athenians and included the philosopher EPICURUS among his friends. He regularly participated in the drama contests of which the Athenians were so fond, winning eight prizes over the course of his life. Despite invitations from King Ptolemy I of Egypt to come to Alexandria, then in the process of eclipsing Athens as the center of Greek culture, Menander loved his home too much to move away from it. He was around 50 when he drowned while swimming in Piraeus harbor.

It is thought that Menander wrote more than 100 plays over the course of his life, most of them comedies. Scholars have recovered some fragments of Menander's works, but the only complete surviving play is titled *Dyskolos* (The Misanthrope, or The Bad-Tempered Man). The main plot deals with a man who intensely dislikes everyone else, particularly the man his daughter wishes to marry. Later on, his daughter's fiancé saves his life, forcing him to allow the wedding.

This play, like so many others Menander wrote, is one reason scholars view the playwright as being the greatest representative of a form of Greek drama called the New Comedy (as opposed to the Old Comedy of a century earlier, adhered to by such playwrights as ARISTOPHANES). Unlike the works of Old Comedy dramatists, Menander's works do not dwell on pressing social or political issues. Rather, they are concerned with commonplace situations to which any human being, of any time period, can easily relate. Similarly, they feature ordinary men and women instead of characters from Greek mythology.

Other Menander plays that have partially survived include *The Arbitrators, The Woman of Samos, The Ogre,* and *The Man from Sicyon.* As with *Dyskolos,* these works seem to share many of the same themes and styles. One common theme is that of a young man trying to win the love of a young woman but facing unexpected and often absurd obstacles in his quest for love. Also common are stories of separated twins causing confusion and of parents having difficulty dealing with ridiculously disobedient children. These themes allowed Menander to create wonderful and successful comedy and also became a means through which he expressed important truths about human nature and personal relationships.

Although not as well known as many other Greek playwrights, Menander had a great influence on the development of dramatic comedy. His plots, though familiar today, were unique during

his own time, and his literary style and wit were such that later writers, such as PLAUTUS and TERENCE, adapted and imitated his works.

English Versions of Works by Menander

The Bad-Tempered Man (Dyskolos). Translated by Stanley Ireland. Wiltshire, U.K.: Aris & Phillips Ltd., 1995.

Four Plays of Menander: The Hero, Epitrepontes, Periceiromene, Samia. Edited by Edward Capps. Berlin: Melissa Media, 1981.

Menander: The Grouch, Desperately Seeking Justice, Closely Cropped Locks, the Girl from Samos, the Shield. Edited by Palmer Bovie, et al. Philadelphia: University of Pennsylvania Press, 1998.

Menander: The Plays and Fragments. Translated by Maurice Balme. Oxford: Oxford University Press, 2002.

Works about Menander

Heath, Malcolm. *Menander: A Rhetor in Context.* Oxford: Oxford University Press, 2004.

Walton, J. Michael and Peter D. Arnott. *Menander and the Making of Comedy.* Westport, Conn.: Greenwood Press, 1996.

Zagagi, Netta. *The Comedy of Menander: Convention, Variation, and Originality.* Bloomington: Indiana University Press, 1995.

Meun, Jean de

See JEAN DE MEUN.

Middle Ages (ca. 450–ca. 1450) *era*

The Middle Ages is a label traditionally used to describe a 1,000-year period in western Europe spanning the Early Middle Ages (450–900), the High Middle Ages (900–1200), and the Late Middle Ages (1200–1450).

Historians traditionally describe medieval society as being made up of three classes or estates: the class that fights, the class that prays, and the class that tills the land. This model distinguishes among the clerics, or those who belong to the

Church; the kings and nobles, who own the land; and the peasants, who comprise the bulk of the population.

Medieval European society was governed by feudalism, a system of mutual oaths and loyalties that bound the peasants who lived on the land (and provided the means of survival for all classes by producing food, clothing, and other necessities) to the nobles and knights who owned the land. Knighthood, attained after a long and arduous apprenticeship as a squire, came to be synonymous with the French concept of *chevalerie,* or CHIVALRY, which was basically a military code governing conduct both on and off the battlefield. While originally a martial concept requiring loyalty, bravery, physical strength, and battle prowess, in the 12th century the concept of chivalry became identified with the practice of courtly love. The concept of courtly love, originated and spread by the French TROUBADOURS, came to be an important part of the social and literary culture of the Middle Ages.

Historians estimate that 80 percent of the people living on feudal estates were peasants. About half were freemen, who could leave when they chose, and the other half were serfs, legally bound to the land. While Early Middle Ages systems of production were essentially agrarian or based on farming, the increasing settlement of cities and the development of commercial exchange led, in the Late Middle Ages, to a thriving city culture characterized by a growing middle class and the antecedents of modern industry. Where those bound to the land were at the mercy of their overlord, and often caught up against their will in the disputes of the upper class, the growing cities were self-governing, and their residents answered only to the king. This led to the eventual decline of feudalism and the rise of parliamentary structures.

The church of the Middle Ages was the Roman Catholic Church, which governed the lives of those of all estates. Christianity, the official religion of the Roman Empire in its last years, retained its center of power at Rome in the form of the pope, who sent missionaries to the "barbarians" until, by the High Middle Ages, all the lands of western Europe were Christian. The Church used Latin as its official language, though the native or vernacular languages continued to be spoken among the laypeople or those not under religious vows. Monastic orders or cloisters formed where the truly devoted could dedicate their lives to contemplation. Some monasteries (for men) and convents or nunneries (for women) developed into powerful centers of culture and learning.

The Church also inspired art, including music and painting, but was primarily responsible for education. Priests and those in religious orders were the most highly educated members of society. Lay literacy evolved and spread slowly. The BIBLE, translated by Saint JEROME, was in Latin. Philosophical works, such as those composed by AUGUSTINE, BOETHIUS, and FRANCIS OF ASSISI, were written in Latin. Histories, such as BEDE's *Ecclesiastical History of the English People,* or pseudo-histories, such as GEOFFREY OF MONMOUTH's *History of the Kings of Britain,* were composed in Latin. Members of religious orders communicated to each other in Latin, as did ABÉLARD AND HÉLOÏSE in their letters, and clerics recording individual experiences, like Julian of Norwich and HILDEGARD VON BINGEN, did so in Latin. The Christian Church and the classics of ancient Rome, the poetry of authors like VIRGIL and OVID, were the primary authorities for medieval literature.

Despite the romantic light cast by chivalry and courtly love, the Middle Ages were a time of almost continual warfare and disease, beginning with the fall of Rome in 476. After the Germanic Franks and Anglo-Saxons settled France and England in the fifth and sixth centuries, in the eighth through 10th century the Vikings harried European shores. In 800, Pope Leo III crowned Charlemagne emperor of the Holy Roman Empire. In 1066, at the Battle of Hastings, King Harold of England was defeated by Duke William of Normandy, thus introducing French culture into England. In 1076, Pope Gregory VII excommunicated Henry IV, the German emperor. In 1095, the CRUSADES launched a planned counterattack against Islam as articulated by MUHAMMAD. In 1215, the barons of England wrote the *Magna Carta,* and in 1295, Edward I of England formed a model parliament. Between 1338 and 1471, France and England were constantly at war.

While attacks of the plague occurred frequently, the Black Death, which first reached Italy from the Middle East in 1347, proved the worst medical disaster of the Middle Ages, reducing the population of Europe by a third. Still, as trade routes opened and western Europe came in contact with the civilizations and technologies of the East through the travels of explorers like Marco POLO, information concerning new civilizations, technologies, and products revitalized medieval culture.

In 1453, the Ottoman Turks conquered Constantinople, bringing an end to the Byzantine Empire, the last center of Roman civilization. Those witnessing the rebirth of learning that characterized the European Renaissance viewed the thousand-year period after the fall of Rome as a lapse, a "Dark Age." DANTE ALIGHIERI, on the cusp of the new humanism movement born in Italy in the 13th century, not only coined the term *Middle Ages* but also proved that great literature could be written in the vernacular.

Critical Analysis

Early medieval literature is largely EPIC in nature. The BARDIC POETRY of Celtic-speaking peoples, the OLD ENGLISH POETRY of the Anglo-Saxons, the Scandinavian EDDA, and the Germanic SAGAS largely focus on great events. Many of the heroes they describe, such as King Arthur, Finn, BEOWULF, or the actors in the NIBELUNGENLIED, are historical figures cloaked in the glamour of fantastical myth.

Along with the invention of Western romantic love, the French are credited with the invention of MEDIEVAL ROMANCE in the form of the *chansons de geste,* or songs of adventure. The SONG OF ROLAND, the Arthurian romances of CHRÉTIEN DE TROYES, the legends of TRISTAN AND ISEULT and the HOLY GRAIL, the ROMANCE OF THE ROSE, and the Spanish *El CID*—all capture the essential qualities of romantic literature. Women like MARIE DE FRANCE and Christine de Pisan proved that literature was not entirely a

male domain. The French historiographers Geoffroi de VILLEHARDOUIN and Jean Froissart gave their chronicles a romantic cast. However, Dante's *New Life* and *Divine Comedy* became the models for literature that all later authors aspired to use.

Some of the most important information about daily life in the Middle Ages comes from literature like Giovanni Boccaccio's *The Decameron* (1352), Geoffrey Chaucer's *The Canterbury Tales* (1390s), and François Villon's *Ballade,* or *The Testament* (1461). As do Fabliaux and the ROMAN DE RENART of French literature, these works provide vivid portraits of a cross section of the traditional medieval estates, as well as satiric glimpses of courtly culture.

Other works of literature demonstrate the prevailing ethos of the Middle Ages. Tales like *Sir Gawain and the Green Knight* explore the demands of the courtly code, while poems like William Langland's *Piers Plowman* examine the philosophical foundations of medieval society. In addition, theatrical works like the MYSTERY, morality, and miracle plays used allegorical characters and biblical stories to dramatize current issues and events.

The discovery of the printing press ultimately revolutionized medieval literature. Thanks to Johannes Gutenberg's invention of movable type in 1458, not only did the Bible become available to a broader audience, but publishers could circulate works of secular literature as well, as William Caxton did with Thomas Malory's *Le Morte D'Arthur* (1485). This, along with the growth of Italian humanism and the decline of feudalism, paved the way for the Renaissance in Europe.

Works about the Middle Ages

Cantor, Norman F. *The Civilization of the Middle Ages.* New York: Harper Perennial, 1994.

Gies, Frances and Joseph. *Daily Life in Medieval Times.* New York: Black Dog & Leventhal, 1999.

Hay, Jeff, ed. *The Middle Ages,* Vol 3. San Diego, Calif.: Greenhaven Press, 2002.

Steinberg, Theodore L. *Reading the Middle Ages: An Introduction to Medieval Literature.* New York: McFarland & Company, 2003.

Tuchman, Barbara W. *A Distant Mirror: The Calamitous 14th Century.* New York: Ballantine Books, 1987.

Mohammed
See MUHAMMAD.

Mother of Fujiwara Michitsuna
(Fujiwara Michitsuna no haha)
(936–995) *diarist*

The Mother of Fujiwara Michitsuna, a high court official, lived during the middle of the Heian period, a time when Japanese literary traditions were at its peak. She was a member of the middle-ranking aristocracy and was 19 when she married Fujiwara no Kaneie, from a distant but more powerful branch of the family. The main source of information on her life is her influential work, the *Kagero Diary,* which details not only her thoughts but also the crises and events that occurred during her life. It is believed that she began writing her diary around 971 as a way to preserve her life experiences for posterity. The *Kagero Diary* stands as one of the earliest and best examples of women's autobiography and it greatly encouraged the realistic mode of writing adopted during the height of Japanese literary development.

Several themes are represented in Fujiwara Michitsuna's mother's writing. The foremost is the theme of romance. Her portrayal of herself in the diary reflects the Japanese ideal of a romantic heroine whose expectation of romance in her marriage falls sadly short of her ideal. In the initial exchange of love letters between her would-be husband and herself, she saw him as "a tall tree among oak trees." This image dissipated after their marriage, when her husband began to neglect her. Her diary records her despair:

> Just as I thought would happen, I have ended up going to bed and waking up alone. So far as the world at large is concerned, there is nothing unsuitable about us as a couple; it's just that his heart is not as I would have it; it is not only me who is being neglected, I hear he has stopped visiting the place he has been familiar with for years.

Language also plays an important part in Fujiwara's mother's work. The themes of self-creation and self-consciousness develop throughout the text. On one level, Fujiwara's mother's decision to record her personal experiences and let them be made known to the world suggests a certain degree of self-awareness and self-recognition. On another level, the theme of self-consciousness is effectively reflected in her use of the first-person point of view. Her voyage in writing poetry, interspersed throughout the diary, can be seen metaphorically as a voyage of self-discovery in which she realizes her independence and identity.

A unique blend of Buddhism and Shintoism entwines throughout the *Kagero Diary.* The Buddhist premise that life is suffering pervades the work. The author's awareness of the transitory nature of human life enables her to cope with various difficult events in her life, including separations from her husband and sister and the deaths of those close to her. At the same time, this level of awareness allows her to maintain a certain distance and detachment from the suffering caused by those events. The diary suggests the author found no contradiction in visiting both Buddhist and Shinto shrines.

The *Kagero Diary* is divided into three parts. The first part covers the first 14 years of the author's married life and conveys an ambivalent mood of wistful reminiscing and lamentation as she relives the romantic high points of her marriage. The second part of the diary spans the three years of discontentment and unhappiness following her discovery that her husband has taken another lover. In this part, the author slowly takes on a more philosophical view of her life, using her mastery of prose to regain a symbolic control over her life.

The final section of the book, covering another three years of the author's life, lacks the emotional fervor that marks the first two parts. Gradually she transcends the emotional intensity of her problems to examine events from a more detached point of view.

On the whole, the *Kagero Diary* remains an important document about the interior life of a woman, transcribed by her own hand and recorded in her own voice. It provides valuable information about the life of women in the Heian dynasty, but aside from that, it remains a touching account of one woman's struggles to come to terms with her own circumstances and make peace with herself.

An English Version of the *Kagero Diary*

The Kagero Diary: A Woman's Autobiographical Text from Tenth-Century Japan. Translated by Sonja Arntzen. Ann Arbor, Mich.: Center for Japanese Studies, 1997.

Works about the Mother of Fujiwara Michitsuna

Arntzen, Sonja. "Translating Difference: A New Translation for the Kagero Diary." *Japan Foundation Newsletter* 21, no. 3 (December 1993): 16–19.

McCullough, William and Helen C. McCullough, trans. *A Tale of Flowering Fortunes: Annals of Japanese Aristocratic Life in the Heian Period [Eiga monogatari].* 2 vols. Stanford, Calif.: Stanford University Press, 1980.

Sarra, Edith. *Fictions of Femininity: Literary Inventions of Gender in Japanese Court Women's Memoirs.* Stanford, Calif.: Stanford University Press, 1996.

Mu'allaqāt

See 'AMR IBN KULTHUM; *HANGED POEMS*; IMRU' AL-QAYS; LABID; TARAFAH 'AMR IBN AL-'ABD.

Muhammad (Mohammed, Muhammad ibn 'Abd Allāh ibn 'Abd al-Muttalib ibn Hāshim, Abu al-Qāsim) (ca. 570–632)
prophet

Muhammad (also known as Mohammed) was the founder of Islam, the first leader of the Muslim community, and the author or transmitter of the KORAN, the sacred scripture of the Muslim religion. Nearly everything that is known about Muhammad, whom his followers called "the Prophet," comes from Muslim tradition. The main sources are the Koran, Islam's holiest book; and the *hadith,* oral stories about Muhammad that were written in early Muslim times.

Muhammad was born in Mecca, a trading city in the Hijaz region of the Arabian Peninsula and the site of a pagan shrine, the Ka'bah. His family was prominent, but he became an orphan at an early age with no inheritance. He was raised by his uncle Abu Talib, a prominent merchant and head of the noble Hashem clan, part of the Quraysh tribe that dominated Mecca.

Around 595, Muhammad married Khadija, who remained his sole wife until her death in 619. Celebrated in the Koran, she bore four daughters; all of their husbands eventually played prominent roles in the early Muslim community. Khadija's wealth gave Muhammad both trading capital and the independence to pursue his religious ideas and political ambitions.

Muhammad was said to have frequented a cave near Mecca to think in solitude. There, one day in 610, he had a frightening vision of an angelic being, whom he believed to be God, who told him, "You are the messenger of God." This was followed by many further revelations, often delivered while the prophet was in a trance. Because Muhammad could not read or write, he related the revelations to his followers, at first a small band. According to some traditions, he had many of the verses recorded by scribes. The stories were eventually collected and edited into the Koran about 20 years after the prophet's death.

Research has revealed that Muhammad supplemented the actual revelations with his own comments and explanations. In this way, he eventually learned, and conveyed to his followers, all the basic precepts of what became Islam. He also laid the groundwork for the legal and social practices that later became the basis of Muslim law. Many Muslims insist that every word of the Koran is divine and immutable; thus, Muhammad became one of the most influential figures in the Islamic world, and the Koran one of the most influential works of world literature.

Muhammad began preaching publicly around 613. He attracted supporters among the younger members of the chief merchant families and also among the poor, who were attracted by his criticism of the wealthy for not helping the "weak." His supporters came to be called Muslims, or those who had submitted to God.

Muhammad's fame soon extended beyond Mecca, but he still faced opposition from the powerful leaders of the city. After negotiating with tribal leaders and Muslims in Medina, a city to the north, the prophet and about 70 supporters left Mecca for Medina. This event, known as the *hijra* (hegira), took place in the year 622, which thus became year one of the Muslim calendar.

At Medina, Muhammad gradually reduced intertribal warfare and sent his followers off on raids against Meccan caravans. In the 620s, he had a falling-out with the Jewish clans, who were prominent in both agriculture and trade in Medina. Refusing to recognize his claims to being God's prophet, they were all eventually expelled or killed. Previously, Muslims had prayed toward Jerusalem; thereafter, they prayed toward Mecca and its Ka'bah shrine. Following Muhammad's victory in 624 in a battle with a Meccan force at Badr, most Arabs of Medina rallied to his cause. By 629, further military losses to Muhammad's supporters convinced the Meccans to accept his rule. Many soon became Muslims as well, as did many pagan tribes.

Among Muhammad's last campaigns was a large raid near Syria in 630, in which the Muslims confronted several Christian Arab tribes. This completed the break of Islam with the previous monotheistic religions.

Muhammad died in 632. Although his failure to appoint a successor led to future conflicts among the faithful, he left Arabia united for the first time in history. The new, highly motivated confederation of Arabic tribes soon launched a series of campaigns that succeeded in spreading Arab rule, and the Muslim religion, to a large part of the civilized world.

An English Version of a Work by Muhammad

The Koran. Translated by J. M. Rodwell. London: J. M. Dent, 1994.

Works about Muhammad

Armstrong, Karen. *Muhammad: A Biography of the Prophet.* San Francisco: HarperSanFrancisco, 1992.

Forward, Martin. *Muhammad: A Short Biography.* Oxford: One World, 1997.

Lings, Martin. *Muhammad: His Life Based on the Earliest Sources.* New York: Inner Traditions International, 1983.

Rodinson, Maxime. *Muhammad.* New York: The New Press, 1980.

mummers' plays (ca. 1200s–present) *term*
The term *mummers* describes a set of actors reenacting a type of folk drama that has been performed for centuries in the British Isles, beginning perhaps as early as the 13th century and continuing today. The term has been variously traced to words in German, Danish, and French that indicate the use of disguise. Mummers' plays are short, seasonal performances that address the theme of death and resurrection and frequently involve foolery and nonsense language. The actors' dis-

guises include anything from blacking the face to assuming a mask or dressing a man as a woman.

The existing texts of mummers' plays reveal that the most common plots are those of the hero-combat (involving folk heroes like St. George or Robin Hood, or a doctor and a fool), the sword dance, the plough play (so called because it makes reference to an offstage plough), and a wooing (also offstage). The plays are very short, involve only a handful of characters, and are staged with minimal props. In the past, these plays were often performed in a small area in the middle of the street, usually at Christmas, Easter, and other festival days. Many mummers' plays, however, show a remarkable absence of Christian influence or doctrine. Instead, generic characters such as Father Christmas and Beezlebub appear.

Like morality, miracle, and MYSTERY plays, mummers' plays were originally aimed at a broad public. The setting is historically generic; Oliver Cromwell might be on the stage with Saladin, Napoleon chatting with Charlemagne. The themes of death and resurrection and their seasonal characteristics suggest the mummers' plays capture a folk memory of ancient pagan rituals associated with planting and harvesting, an agricultural death and renewal. Controversy among scholars concerning the pagan roots of mummers' plays is ongoing.

Texts of existing mummers' plays, while they follow the same broad outlines, show many local variations; in fact, each of the hundreds of extant texts is unique. Efforts to document the plays began in the 17th century, but the mummers have been performing for centuries and continue to this day, a testament to the power of theatrical tradition.

Published Editions of Mummers' Plays

Helm, Alex. *Eight Mummers' Plays*. London: Ginn, 1971.

Miller, Katherine. *St. George: A Christmas Mummer's Play*. New York: Houghton Mifflin, 1967.

Stevens-Cox, James. *Mumming and the Mummers' Plays of St. George*. Beddington, Surrey, U.K.: Toucan Press, 1970.

Works about Mummers' Plays

Brody, Alan. *The English Mummers and Their Plays: Traces of Ancient Mystery*. Philadelphia: University of Pennsylvania Press, 1970.

Helm, Alex. *The English Mummers' Play*. Cambridge, U.K.: D. S. Brewer, 1981.

Murasaki Shikibu (ca. 978–ca. 1016)
novelist, diarist, poet

The true name of the writer known as Murasaki Shikibu is not known. Murasaki is the name of a central character in her novel *The Tale of Genji*, and Shikibu is the name of a position held by the writer's father. Upper-class women in the Japan of Murasaki's time lived secluded lives, their charm intensified by the mystery that surrounded them, and that mystery surrounds the writer still.

It is known that Murasaki was born into a minor branch of the Fujiwara family, the clan that held most of the power in Japan of the Heian period (794–1185); her father was a provincial governor. Murasaki had a brother and was able to eavesdrop on the lessons in Chinese that, as a young nobleman, he was obliged to master. In her diary she records her father's reaction when he realized that she was quicker than her brother at understanding difficult passages: "'Just my luck!' he would say. 'What a pity she was not born a man!'" The diary goes on to relate how she gave up reading Chinese because she was criticized for using a skill that was considered inappropriate for women.

In 998 Murasaki was married to Fujiwara no Nobutaka, an older man who already had more than one wife. Her daughter, Katako, was born in 999, and her husband died two years later. It was as a widow that she began to write her great novel. In 1005 or 1006, she entered the service of the emperor's powerful right-hand man, Fujiwara Michinaga (966–1027), as a companion to his daughter, who was to become the Empress Shoshi (988–1074). Shoshi loved learning, and she and Murasaki took to secretly reading Chinese classics together. Murasaki says in her diary, "we carefully chose a time when other women would not be present." Although they had to be discreet about their study of Chinese, composing poetry in Japanese—especially improvising a poem in response to the immediate situation—was a highly valued skill in the ritualized world of the court, and Murasaki excelled at it. Some of her poems are preserved in her diary. There are also 795 poems included within the text of *The Tale of Genji*.

Murasaki kept her diary for about two years during her time at court. It records intricate details of court life—its etiquette, its ceremonies, and the complex rivalries among the women. It also reveals Murasaki's struggles with loneliness and with the sense of helplessness that accompanied being a woman without a male protector in a male-dominated world, as well as her efforts to attain the sense of detachment from worldly passions that is the Buddhist ideal. Of her own personality, she says:

> Pretty and coy, shrinking from sight, unsociable, fond of old tales, conceited, so wrapped up in poetry that other people hardly exist, spitefully looking down on the whole world— such is the unpleasant opinion that people have of me. Yet when they come to know me they say that I am strangely gentle, quite unlike what they had been led to believe. I know that people look down on me like some old outcast, but I have become accustomed to all this, and tell myself, "My nature is as it is."

Empress Shoshi was widowed in 1011 and moved to a mansion outside the court; it is likely that Murasaki moved with her. There are suggestions in Murasaki's writings that she may have retired to a Buddhist convent.

Critical Analysis

The Tale of Genji centers on the character of the fictitious Prince Genji, "the shining prince," a man of devastating charm who loves and is loved by many women. But its action, divided into 54 books or chapters, covers four generations and nearly 100 years, and there are more than 400 characters.

In the very first sentences, aspects of Murasaki's approach can be discerned. The book begins:

> In a certain reign there was a lady not of the first rank whom the emperor loved more than any of the others. The grand ladies with high ambitions thought her a presumptuous upstart, and lesser ladies were still more resentful. Everything she did offended someone. Probably aware of what was happening, she fell seriously ill and came to spend more time at home than at court. The emperor's pity and affection quite passed bounds. No longer caring what his ladies and courtiers might say, he behaved as if intent upon stirring gossip.

The lady whose predicament is so sympathetically described here is a minor character in that she dies on the fourth page, after having given birth to Genji. Her influence is felt throughout, however, because her early death is clearly central to the personality development of Genji, who spends his life seeking someone to take the place of his beautiful mother. The passage introduces themes that run throughout the book: the obsession with rank and its collision with human affection, and the damaging resentments that inevitably arise among women when they are confined and must jostle for the attention of men who are free to come and go as they please.

There are aspects of the supernatural in the plot involving one of Genji's rejected lovers, the Lady of Rokujo. Consumed by jealousy and resentment, she becomes a malicious spirit who is capable of taking hostile possession of the bodies of Genji's more valued lovers, even after her own physical death; the deaths of two characters are attributed to her malevolent influence. Lady Rokujo's pain is presented so vividly that her supernatural power gains psychological conviction.

The story of Genji's career as a government official—successful in spite of setbacks caused by repercussions from his amorous affairs—and of his loves occupies the first 41 chapters. Genji is presented as artistically talented, sensitive, and capable of love, yet somehow blind to his own responsibility for the pain suffered by the women he loves or has loved. The remainder of the book focuses on Kaoru, the son of Genji's second principal wife, Princess Nyosan, who learns as an adult that he is not in fact Genji's son. Kaoru's friendship with his cousin, Prince Niou, dissolves in an amorous rivalry that has tragic consequences for all involved. The action of this section takes place in a small town, away from the luxury and glamour of the court, and the tone is much darker.

The Tale of Genji is not only widely recognized as the finest of all Japanese novels; it is the first work of prose fiction anywhere in the world to present rounded characters with psychological depth.

English Versions of Works by Murasaki Shikibu

The Diary of Lady Murasaki. Translated and with an introduction by Richard Bowring. New York: Penguin, 1996.
Murasaki Shikibu, Her Diary and Poetic Memoirs. Translated by Richard Bowring. Princeton, N.J.: Princeton University Press, 1982.
The Tale of Genji. Translated by Edward G. Seidensticker. New York: Alfred A. Knopf, 1978.

Works about Murasaki Shikibu

Bowring, Richard. *Murasaki Shikibu: The Tale of Genji.* New York: Cambridge University Press, 1988.
Field, Norma. *The Splendor of Longing in "The Tale of Genji."* Princeton, N.J.: Princeton University Press, 1987.
Keene, Donald. *"The Tale of Gengi"* in *Seeds in the Heart: Japanese Literature from Earliest Times to the Late Sixteenth Century.* 477–514. New York: Henry Holt & Co., 1993.
Knapp, Bettina L. *Images of Japanese Women: A Westerner's View.* Troy, N.Y.: Whitston Publishing, 1992.
Morris, Ivan I. "Murasaki Shikibu" in *The World of the Shining Prince: Court Life in Ancient Japan.* 251–264. New York: Kodansha International, 1994.
Shirane, Haruo. *The Bridge of Dreams: A Poetics of "The Tale of Genji."* Stanford, Calif.: Stanford University Press, 1987.

Mutanabbī, al- (nickname of Abū at-Tayyib Ahmad ibn Husayn al-Mutanabbī) (ca. 915–965) *poet*

Al-Mutanabbī (meaning "the would-be prophet") was born in the city of Kufa to a Yemenite father. Most of his poems were flattering panegyrics, distinguished by their complex style and imagery and written for a succession of powerful patrons. The poems were extremely popular in al-Mutanabbī's time.

The poet was educated in a Shi'ite Muslim school and may have had some Greek education as well. As a young man in the 930s, he passed several years among the Bedauin in Syria, promoting a revolutionary new religion. The miracles he claimed to perform led to his nickname, al-Mutanabbī, which remained with him all his life. Freed in 937 after a four-year jail term for banditry, he decided to confine his career to poetry and began a lifelong struggle to find patrons who would support him. His greatest success was a nine-year stay at the court of the Hamdanid ruler Sayf al-Dawla in Aleppo, starting around 948. His panegyrics to Sayf were noted for their vivid battle scenes as well as for his tendency to address the ruler as a beloved, as he does in the poem "To Sayf al-Dawla on His Recovery from an Illness."

Like other poets at the court, al-Mutanabbī would accompany Sayf al-Dawla on many of his *jihad* (holy war) campaigns against the Christian Byzantine empire and record their events in verse. One poem, "A Congratulatory Ode on the Occasion of the Feast of Sacrifices," proclaims:

> Every man has a habit to which he dedicates his time, and the habit of Sayf al-Dawla is thrusting at the enemy
>
> . . .
>
> Many an arrogant man, who knew not God for a moment, has seen his sword in his hand and promptly professed the faith.

After falling from Sayf's grace, al-Mutanabbī traveled to Cairo, where he managed to antagonize the famous regent Kafur by brutally satirizing the former slave in poems that destroyed the ruler's historical reputation. He was more successful in Persia, until he was ambushed by relatives of one of his satirical victims. Reminded of his celebrated lines: "I am known to night and horses and the desert, to sword and lance, to parchment and pen," the poet unsheathed his sword and was promptly killed.

Al-Mutanabbī's fame spread to Andalusia in Spain and to Persia, where he is said to have influenced the new school of Persian poetry, especially its greatest master, RUMI. In Arabic literary criticism he is considered a champion of ethnic Arabs in the Muslim world, and he remains a favorite among modern Arabic nationalists.

English Versions of Works by al-Mutanabbī

The Diwan of Abu Tayyib Ahmad ibn al Husain al Mutannabi. Translated by Arthur Wormholdt. Oskaloosa, Iowa: William Penn College, 1995.
Poems of al-Mutanabbi. Translated by A. J. Arberry. Cambridge, U.K.: Cambridge University Press, 1967.

A Work about al-Mutanabbī

Hamori, Andras. *The Composition of Mutanabbī's Panegyrics to Sayf al-Dawla.* New York: E. J. Brill, 1992.

mystery plays   (13th–16th centuries)   *drama*

Mystery plays were a type of drama that flourished in the later MIDDLE AGES in England. Cycles of plays drew together a series of shorter scripts dramatizing stories from the Christian Bible, spanning the Creation to the Last Judgment. Cycles are frequently referred to by the name of the town in which they are recorded as having been staged. Full cycles survive from four towns: York (48 plays); Wakefield (32 plays, also called the Townley cycle); Chester (24 plays); and N-Town (42 plays, formerly referred to as the Coventry Cycle). Single plays in English survive from at least four other towns, and one cycle exists written in the Cornish language. A great number of English towns of all sizes, including Canterbury and London, document the staging of mystery plays as early as the mid-1200s, though the manuscripts for these plays may be lost. Records suggest that the cycles began evolving in the 13th century, though existing manuscripts are of later dates.

Plays were staged within a particular town in connection with a celebrated event, perhaps a feast day, which is the case of the plays associated with Corpus Christi. Performances took place outdoors, sometimes on a pageant wagon that was pulled through the town. The term *mystery* refers to the guild or craft organizations that sponsored the events (the term comes from the secret rites or mysteries of their trades, which the guilds protected fiercely). The actors, in most cases, belonged to the guild. Productions were often elaborate; the Chester cycle took three days to perform. Often the guilds selected episodes that could best illustrate the nature of their craft; for instance, the shipwrights of York commonly presented the story of Noah and the Flood.

The authors of mystery plays were most likely clerics. As the plays evolved, several different hands made revisions and changes to the existing scripts. Certain playwrights showed more skill than others, and some made greater contributions, as is the case with the "York Realist" and the "Wakefield Master."

Naturally, certain stories of the Bible lent themselves well to dramatization, blending high tragedy with low comedy. Favorite scenes from the Old Testament included the rebellion of Lucifer, the creation and fall, the story of Cain and Abel, Abraham and Isaac, and the exodus from Egypt. The central images of the cycles are the life, death, and resurrection of Christ. Characteristics shared among the plays of different towns point to the development of popular stereotypes, such as the depiction of Noah's wife as a scold who had to be forced to board the ark, and the portrayal of Joseph as a somewhat feeble and gullible old man. The dialogue and action of the plays show biblical characters speaking and behaving exactly like contemporary English citizens, which suggests the plays gave voice not only to the religious tradition but also to contemporary social concerns. For the audience, the battle between good and evil was not an abstract concept but a real issue that had bearing on their individual lives as they daily faced death, disease, poverty, and political unrest.

The mystery plays, like the miracle plays, evolved from the Latin tradition of religious drama. The morality plays, which developed slightly later, had a different subject and purpose. Performances of mystery plays provided a way to join the community in entertainment and in worship. In the 16th century, opposition to mystery plays based on religious controversy and concerns for public order led to their suppression. Plays surviving from the Elizabethan and Jacobean periods were written and produced for court patrons, no longer a common audience. These plays had their roots in the lively and complex tradition of the mystery, miracle, and morality plays. Modern companies have revived the mystery plays, and productions of the indigenous cycles take place with regular frequency in Chester and York.

English Versions of Mystery Plays

Beadle, Richard and Pamela M. King, eds. *York Mystery Plays: A Selection in Modern Spelling.* Oxford: Oxford University Press, 1999.

Happe, Peter, ed. *English Mystery Plays: A Selection.* New York: Viking Press, 1979.

Rose, Martial, ed. *The Wakefield Mystery Plays.* New York: W.W. Norton & Co., 1969.

Works about Mystery Plays

Davidson, Charles. *Studies in the English Mystery Play.* Brooklyn, N.Y.: M.S.G. Haskell House, 1969.

Diller, Hans-Jürgen. *The Middle English Mystery Play: A Study in Dramatic Speech and Form.* Cambridge, U.K.: Cambridge University Press, 1992.

Prosser, Eleanor. *Drama and Religion in the English Mystery Plays: A Re-Evaluation.* Palo Alto, Calif.: Stanford University Press, 1961.

myth of Manco Capac (ca. 1200– ca. 1544) *fiction*

Manco Capac is the legendary founder of the Incan empire that flourished in the Andean mountains of South America and had its capital in what is now Cuzco in modern-day Peru. Existing versions of legends, which first were recorded in the 1200s, differ slightly in the details of Manco Capac's parentage. In some accounts, he is the son of Mama Huaco, one of the Ayar siblings who, with her four brothers and three sisters, came forth from a cave called Pacauitambo in search of fertile lands to settle and farm. Mama Huaco possessed two golden shafts that she threw north, and where one shaft sank into the ground, Manco Capac led a group of people there to settle.

In other versions, Manco Capac was a son of the sun, the Life-Giver and the chief deity in the pantheon of Incan divinities, who sent Manco forth to bring the gifts of civilization and culture into the world. Along with his sister-wife, Mama Ocllo, Manco Capac set forth from their dwelling in Lake Titicaca and headed north in search of a place to settle. Where Manco Capac's golden divining rod sank into the earth indicated that they had reached a favorable place, and so the city of Cuzco was founded. Manco Capac taught the settlers there the art of agriculture, and Mama Ocllo taught them how to weave and spin, laying the foundations for Incan civilization and history.

In truth, Andean civilizations had existed for centuries, and the Inca were no more than one of several tribes flourishing in the region around 1200. The Inca, however, showed a talent for conquest, and as they began to expand, they brought neighboring tribes under their rule. At the peak of expansion, achieved in the mid-15th century, the Inca governed what they called Tahuantinsuyu, the "Land of the Four Quarters," with its center at Cuzco, which they regarded as the center of the earth. Calling themselves by a Quechua word meaning "People of the Sun," the Inca treated their ruler or emperor (also called the Inca) as the human embodiment of the sun on earth. Incan government, represented by a well-organized system of administration, penetrated every level of society in a way meant to represent the breadth of the sun's rays. In this way, even as the Incan system of worship evolved to regard the figure of Viracocha as the ultimate creator, Manco Capac was referred to as the Son of the Sun and acknowledged as a divine figure. In their practice of sun worship, the Inca were said to decorate lavishly with gold, which is one reason the Spanish were eager to appropriate their wealth.

During the reign of the Inca, Quechua was not a written language, and history was communicated in the form of verse narratives, paintings, and a method of accounting involving knotted strands of multicolored rope called *quipu*. The verse narratives recording oral history might be revised by the royal poet-historian to avoid offending the current ruler, and therefore the accounts of Inca history recorded by Spanish chroniclers are often confusing and sometimes contradictory. The conquistador Francisco Pizarro and his band of less than 200 men found the Incan Empire in a state of civil war in 1532 and quickly exerted control. After imprisoning, holding for ransom, and then executing the reigning king, Pizarro made another Manco ruler of the Inca in 1534. He was largely acknowledged to be a puppet ruler and did not survive past 1544.

In this way, Manco Capac can be called the first and last ruler of the Incan Empire. The Spanish chroniclers, writing largely between 1533 and 1608, capture his story in conflicting versions. In *Commentary on the Inca* (1609), Garcilaso de la Vega (El Inca) gives the account of the origin in Lake Titicaca and the aid of the golden divining rod. Pedro Sarmiento de Gamboa in *History of the Incas* (1572) records Manco Capac, Mama Huaco, Sinchi Roca, and Mango Sapaca as the four founders of Cuzco, while other chroniclers such as Cristóbal de Molina, in *Myths and Rites of the Inca* (1575), give slightly differing accounts. The myth of Manco Capac most likely preserves the memory of an early migration of the Inca in search of lands favorable for farming, and its later ornamen-tation is as elaborate and fantastic as Incan civilization itself.

English Versions of the Myth of Manco Capac

Ferguson, Diana. *Tales of the Plumed Serpent: Aztec, Inca and Mayan Myths*. London: Collins & Brown, 2000, 107–112, 148.

Urton, Gary. "Origin Myths of the Inca State" in *Inca Myths: Legendary Past*. Austin: University of Texas Press, 1999.

Works about the Myth of Manco Capac

Bierhorst, John, ed. and trans. *Black Rainbow: Legends of the Incas and Myths of Ancient Peru.* New York: Farrar, Straus and Giroux, 1976.

Canseco, María Rostworowski de Deiz. *History of the Inca Realm*. Translated by Harry B. Iceland. Cambridge, U.K.: Cambridge University Press, 1999, 8–15.

Hemming, John. *The Conquest of the Incas.* Fort Washington, Pa.: Harvest Books, 2003, 52, 97, 132, 298.

mythology, Celtic

Celtic mythology refers to a series of myths and legends from the British Isles and northwestern Europe. These myths represent part of the oral tradition of Ireland, England, and Wales. Prior to and throughout the MIDDLE AGES, the myths were retold by bards, most notably Taliesin, the chief bard of Britain and a Celtic shaman who lived during the late sixth century. The tales were later written down by monks and have since influenced literature around the world.

Many of the richest myths originated in Ireland and Wales. The ancient Celtic myths are divided into four cycles of stories: the Mythological Cycle, the Ulster Cycle, the Fenian (or Ossianic) Cycle, and the Cycle of Kings (or the Historic Cycle). These stories concerned heroic events in Celtic history, the underworld, great warriors, and magical events. The Celts also had a strong connection with nature, and many tales featured animal transformations. In some tales, natural elements, such as trees or streams, had human characteristics.

The Mythological Cycle provides the best information available about pagan Ireland. These stories center on the Tuatha Dé Danann (or People of Dana) who make up the Celtic pantheon. The Tuatha Dé Danann arrived in Ireland from northern Greece, where they developed their skills in magic and druidism, so it was told, to such an extent that they became known as gods. Their arrival in Ireland is recorded in the *Lebor Gabala* (The Book of Invasions), which gives a complete account of the pantheon of early Celtic gods. According to this book, the Tuatha Dé Danann were involved in several major battles against other early Irish people, the Fir Bolg, who had also emigrated from Greece, and the Fomorians, a race of brutal giants. The Tuatha Dé Danann defeated the Fir Bolg at the First Battle of Moytura and forced them to flee to islands off the coast of Ireland. Later, the Tuatha Dé Danann conquered the Fomorians at the Second Battle of Moytura, where Lugh the Long Arm led the Tuatha Dé Danann to victory against the giant King Balor.

The arrival of the Milesians from Spain marked the beginning of Gaelic rule in Ireland. Emer, Donn, and Eremon were the sons of Mil of Spain, and they came to Ireland to establish a new kingdom. According to legend, they fought fiercely with the Tuatha Dé Danann and were able to overcome the gods' powers. The two groups agreed to a truce that allowed the Tuatha Dé Danann to rule over all the territory in the Irish underworld and the Milesians to rule over all the territory aboveground. The Tuatha Dé Danann then lived in *sídh* (or fairy mounds) belowground and were only able to return to the surface of the earth on Samain (or Halloween). Other famous stories from the Mythological Cycle concerning the Tuatha Dé Danann include those about the Children of Lir, the Children of Tuirenn, and the Wooing of Étáin.

The Ulster Cycle concerns the heroic feats of the greatest of the Knights of the Red Branch, Cu Chulainn, who lived during the first century B.C. This was during the time of Conchobar Mac Nessa's and Medb's reigns. Mac Nessa was the King of Ulster, whose castle was called Red Branch, and Medb was the Queen of Connacht. Cu Chulainn was thought to be the son, or reincarnation, of Lugh the Long Arm, one of the Tuatha Dé Danann leaders. The most famous tale in the Ulster Cycle is the *Tain Bo Cuailnge,* or *The Cattle Raid of Cooley.* The story tells of Queen Medb's desire to steal the Black Bull of Cooley from Ulster. Medb amasses a large army to go to Ulster to steal the bull, which is renowned for its fertility. Because of a curse on Ulster, all the soldiers except Cu Chulainn are rendered unable to fight when the Connacht army approaches. Cu Chulainn single-handedly holds off the army's advance and defeats the Connacht troops. Despite Cu Chulainn's heroics, the Black Bull is stolen and taken to Connacht, where he is placed in battle with that town's White Bull of Ailill. The Black Bull defeats the White Bull, after which the two kingdoms end their fighting.

Another Ulster Cycle tale, *Bricriu's Feast,* concerns a feast held by a wealthy Celt named Bricriu. In the story, three heroes of Ulster, including Cu Chulainn, compete for a prize of wine, a boar, a cow, and wheat cakes. A giant named Bachlach must find out who is the bravest of the warriors by means of a wager that allows a hero to cut off Bachlach's head one night if the hero promises to allow Bachlach to cut off the hero's head the next. The first hero cuts off Bachlach's head, which the giant then finds and places back on his shoulders. However, the first hero fails to return the next night to complete his part of the wager. Only Cu Chulainn returns the second night to keep his covenant. Bachlach is so impressed by Cu Chulainn's honor that he pronounces him the bravest of the Ulster warriors and awards him the prize Bricriu had promised. This story served as a model for the later medieval tale *Sir Gawain and the Green Knight.*

The Fenian (or Ossianic) Cycle consists of tales about Finn Mac Cumhail and the Fenians, who lived in County Kildare in eastern Ireland around the third century. Many of the tales of the Fenian Cycle are recorded in *The Book of the Dun Cow* (ca. 1100). Unlike the myths of the other cycles, these stories do not focus on tribes but on families of heroic hunters. These tales concern the quarrel between the family of Cumhaill and the family of Morna. The greatest rivalry was between Finn Mac Cumhaill and Goll Mac Morna, who had brutally killed Finn's father in battle.

One tale in this cycle is that of Diarmuid and Grainne, one of the greatest Irish love stories. It recalls the legend of the maiden Grainne, who is to be married against her will to the much-older Finn Mac Cumhaill. But Grainne is a strong-willed woman who wants to marry only someone she loves. She meets Diarmuid during a great feast and asks him to take her away and be her husband. Their flight leads the Fenians to hunt all over Ireland for the couple. The story ends tragically with Diarmuid's death at the hands of Finn, who regretfully decides not to administer a healing potion to his mortally wounded foe. The Fenian Cycle remains a popular series of myths in Irish folklore and the public imagination. James Joyce's final work, *Finnegan's Wake,* contains many references to the events of the cycle.

The Cycle of Kings stories are a mixture of myth and historical events. These stories include the tales of King Arthur and his Round Table, which were first written down by GEOFFREY OF MONMOUTH. The French medieval court poet CHRÉTIEN DE TROYES also preserved many of the chivalric tales first told by bards throughout the British Isles and northern France.

In addition to the four cycles, Welsh tales form an important part of Celtic mythology. *The Mabinogian* is a collection of 11 tales from Wales. The title roughly translates to stories concerning the conception, birth, and life of a particular hero. The most famous of these tales are "The Four Branches of the Mabinogian," stories of magic and chivalry, which comprise "Pwyll, Lord of Dyfed"; "Branwen, Daughter of Llyr"; "Manwydan, Son of Llyr"; and "Math, Son of Mathonwy." Other Welsh tales were collected in the Middle Ages in the *White Book of Rhydderch* and *Red Book of Hergest.*

Celtic mythology continues to inspire writers and readers today. The Irish poet W. B. Yeats was heavily influenced by Celtic literature. Many elements of Celtic myth can also be seen in works such as Morgan Llywelyn's *The Red Branch,* Edward Rutherford's *The Princes of Ireland,* and J. R. R. Tolkien's *Lord of the Rings* trilogy. In her book *Gods and Heroes of the Celts,* Marie-Louise Sjoestedt says, "Some people, such as the Romans, think of their myths historically, the Irish think of their history mythologically." Perhaps it is this portrayal of history as myth that has made and continues to make Celtic mythology so compelling.

See also BARDIC POETRY; ORAL LITERATURE/TRADITION.

Works of Celtic Mythology

Early Irish Myths and Sagas. Translated with notes and introduction by Jeffrey Gantz. New York: Penguin, 1982.

Ellis, Peter Berresford. *The Chronicles of the Celts: New Tellings of Their Myths and Legends.* New York: Carroll & Graf Publishers, 1999.

Glassie, Henry. *Irish Folk History: Texts from the North.* Philadelphia: University of Pennsylvania Press, 1982.

Greeley, Andrew M. *Emerald Magica.* New York: Tor Books, 2004.

Green, Miranda Jane. *Celtic Myths.* London: The Trustees of the British Museum, 1993.

Rutherford, Ward. *Celtic Mythology.* New York: Sterling, 1990.

Works about Celtic Mythology

Bernard, Catherine. *Celtic Mythology.* Berkeley Heights, N.J.: Enslow Publishers, 2003.

Matthews, Caitlin. *The Celtic Tradition.* Shaftesbury, Dorset, U.K.: Element, 1995.

Matthews, John. *Taliesin: Shamanism and the Bardic Mysteries in Britain and Ireland.* Rochester, Vt.: Inner Traditions International, 2002.

Monaghan, Patricia. *The Red-Haired Girl from the Bog: Celtic Spirituality and the Goddess in Ireland.* Novato, Calif.: New World Library, 2003.

mythology, Greek and Roman

Mythology comes from a Greek word that means simply "stories," but the term is now used to refer to ancient tales, especially those from Greece and Rome, that attempt to account for such mysteries as the origins of the world and the vagaries of human behavior within the context of the religious beliefs of the time. If the story was satisfying enough, no one required proof of its veracity. In true storytelling fashion, the oft-told tales, the characters that populated them, and the events they related grew more incredible with time.

Nearly every region of the ancient world has its own body of mythology. The stories evolved and expanded as different cultures mixed—due to military invasions, for instance, or commercial trade—and became aware of one another's traditional narratives. "Goddess-worshipping native cultures were conquered by foreign patriarchies; Asian cosmology was imported along with metals and spices; monsters from abroad crossed paths with local champions," writes Michael Macrone, author of *By Jove! Brush Up Your Mythology.* "The result was a common pantheon of capricious, anthropomorphic gods who camped on [their dwelling place] Mount Olympus and pursued their separate interests on earth."

Initially, the births, exploits, and scandalous carryings-on of the divine Olympians were committed to memory. In the eighth century B.C., the Greeks HOMER and HESIOD compiled these stories and gave them narrative structure in their poems the *Iliad,* the *Odyssey,* and *Theogony.* These works recount, respectively, an episode during the Trojan War that involves gods behaving badly; the adventures of a Greek warrior returning home from the Trojan War who is waylaid by a succession of mythical creatures; and the origins of the universe and the genealogy of the deities. Each of the Greek gods exhibited a distinct personality and displayed passions and weaknesses that humans readily recognized. They also possessed the supernatural powers they needed to satisfy their desires, punish their adversaries, and wreak havoc.

The Roman pantheon, on the other hand, was originally occupied by incorporeal agents who instigated events but were not exactly "beings" and did not mingle with one another. Eventually, through interactions with Greece, the Romans adopted the Greek stock of deities, renaming them appropriately; for instance, "Zeus" became "Jupiter." The Romans also incorporated tales and legends that arrived from Egypt and Asia into their own mythologies. The Roman poets VIRGIL and OVID elaborated on these myths to render their own works, the *Aeneid* and the *Metamorphoses,* respectively, more powerful artistically and politically.

According to Greek and Roman myth, the first gods on earth were the Titans, including Atlas, Prometheus, and the leader Cronus (Latin name: Saturn), who fathered the first six Olympian gods. Cronus was told that one of his children would dethrone him, so he swallowed his offspring at birth. But when his sister-queen, Rhea, delivered Zeus (Jupiter), she hid him and gave Cronus a rock to swallow in his place. Accordingly, Zeus later overthrew his father, became ruling power among the deities, and punished the conquered Titans. Atlas was compelled to bear the cruel weight of the sky and the earth upon his shoulders. His brother, Prometheus, who gave men fire, was shackled to rocks in Tartarus, the depths of the underworld.

Twelve gods followed the Titans. Besides Zeus, there were Hera (Juno in Latin), his long-suffering wife and protector of marriage; Poseidon (Neptune), god of the sea; Hades (Pluto), god of the underworld; and Athena (Minerva), the goddess of war and of wisdom, who sprang from Zeus's head fully formed and outfitted for battle. Apollo is the god of poetry and healing. His twin sister, Artemis (Diana), is a patroness of the forest and goddess of the moon. Aphrodite (Venus) is the goddess of love and beauty and, as such, causes more than her share of discord. Hermes (Mercury) is a messenger god. Ares (Mars), the war god, was more revered by the Romans than the Greeks. Hephaestus (Vulcan), god of the forge, is a patron of craftsmen; and Hestia (Vesta) is the virgin goddess of the hearth.

One of the best-known myths features Demeter (Ceres), the daughter of Cronus and Rhea. The goddess of grain, wheat, and the harvest, she is one of the oldest divinities. Demeter had a daughter, Persephone, sired by Zeus. When the girl lived on earth, it was always springtime. But Hades stole Persephone away to be queen of the underworld. The bereft Demeter searched for her beloved daughter, during which time the earth and its flora began to wither. Without the fond attentions of its patroness, the world was thrust into a permanent state of winter. Zeus at last dispatched Hermes to liberate Persephone. Before she left the land of the dead, she was tricked into eating a pomegranate seed. Demeter knew this would kill her, so she and Hades struck a deal in which Persephone would spend part of the year with the dead and the other part with the living. When Persephone is with Hades and Demeter is forlorn, the crops die, darkness descends, and cold comes. When Persephone is on earth, springtime returns. This myth accounts for the seasons of the year.

The myth of Epimetheus explains how evil was introduced into the world. The foolish Epimetheus ("afterthought") was the brother of the cunning Prometheus ("forethought"). They were charged with the tasks of creating animals and man, respectively. Epimetheus gave the animals formidable qualities such as strength and speed, leaving none left over for humans. Prometheus retaliated by making man in the image of the gods and stealing fire from Mount Olympus for use by the creatures. An angry Zeus sent Pandora, the first woman, to Epimetheus, armed with a box that they were told must forever remain shut. Overwhelmed by curiosity, however, Pandora lifted the lid and unleashed misery and affliction to plague mankind forevermore. But the vessel also contained hope, which helps humans endure inevitable suffering.

Contemporary language reflects the enduring influence of these and other classical myths. "Such ancient Greek and Roman tales have enlivened English speech for centuries," according to author Michael Macrone. "In fact, you probably invoke at least one god a day." Chaos, a disorganized mass, was the first power in the universe, according to Hesiod's *Theogony;* "aphrodisiac" is derived from the name of the love goddess Aphrodite; "cereal" comes from Ceres; Flora and Faunus were gods of nature; and the Amazons were bellicose superwomen living along the Black Sea.

The works influenced by classical mythology are endless. In DANTE ALIGHIERI's *Divine Comedy,* the narrator takes Virgil as his guide and names Homer and Ovid among the great writers. Other works include William Shakespeare's *Venus and Adonis,* Christopher Marlowe's *Doctor Faustus,* and Edmund Spenser's *Faerie Queen.* Even John Milton's *Paradise Lost* uses mythological imagery, despite its Christian subject matter.

European poets and dramatists who relied on myth include Pierre Corneille, Jean Racine, Gotthold Lessing, Friedrich Schiller, Johann Wolfgang von Goethe, as well as England's Romantic poets. In the 20th century, the playwright Eugene O'Neill used myth as the basis for *Desire Under the Elms.*

Artists from Rubens in the baroque period to Matisse during the 20th century have used mythological subjects, and operas from George Frideric Handel, Wolfgang Amadeus Mozart, Ludwig von Beethoven, Richard Wagner, and Benjamin Britten all exhibit the influence of the classics. The George Bernard Shaw play *Pygmalion* and the musical *My Fair Lady* by Frederick Loewe and Alan Jay Lerner, to name just a couple of contemporary theatrical examples, are derived from the myth of a king who sculpted a statue so beautiful he fell in love with it.

"Every age has reinvented old myths in line with its new sensibilities turning them into romances or satires, demonic histories or heavenly allegories," writes Michael Macrone. Psychoanalyst Sigmund Freud used the story of Oedipus, dramatized by SOPHOCLES, to identify psychological phases and disorders and also saw a relationship between myths and dreams. Carl Jung demonstrated that myths feature archetypal characters that serve as models of behavior and project the "collective unconscious" of a society or community. And finally, the sociologist Claude Lévi-Strauss considered myths a form of communication within a culture.

English Versions of Works of Greek and Roman Mythology

Great Classical Myths. Edited by F. R. B Godolphin. New York: Random House, 1964.

Hesiod. *Hesiod.* Translated by Richmond Lattimore. Ann Arbor: University of Michigan Press, 1959.

Ovid. *Metamorphoses.* (Oxford World's Classics). Translated by A. D. Melville. Oxford: Oxford University Press.

Virgil. *The Aeneid.* Translated by David West. New York: Penguin Books, 1990.

Works about Greek and Roman Mythology

Buxton, Richard. *The Complete World of Greek Mythology.* London: Thames & Hudson, 2004.

Campbell, Joseph. *The Power of Myth.* New York: Anchor Books, 1988.

Edinger, Edward F. and Deborah A. Wesley, eds. *Eternal Drama: The Inner Meaning of Greek Mythology.* Boston: Shambhala Publications, 2001.

James, Vanessa. *The Genealogy of Greek Mythology: An Illustrated Family Tree of Greek Mythology from the First Gods to the Founders of Rome.* New York: Gotham Books, 2003.

Macrone, Michael. *By Jove! Brush Up Your Mythology.* New York: HarperCollins, 1992.

Wilson, Donna F. *Ransom, Revenge, and Heroic Identity in the Iliad.* New York: Cambridge University Press, 2002.

mythology, Norse

Norse mythology consists of stories that pre-Christian Scandinavians told about supernatural beings, superhuman heroes, and the world around them. Norse myths share stories and themes with Germanic and with Celtic MYTHOLOGY. They have provided inspiration for countless writers, including William Shakespeare, who took *Hamlet*'s plot from myth; and J. R. R. Tolkien, who drew heavily on Celtic and Norse mythological ideas and language for his *Lord of the Rings* trilogy.

Norse myths began as ORAL LITERATURE. Few were written down before Iceland's conversion to Christianity in A.D. 1000. Sources for these myths include rune-covered objects, rock carvings, and articles found in graves. In addition, some Scandinavian places have names derived from myth. The scholar, E. O. G. Turville-Petre notes that these place-names "show how eminent were some of the gods and goddesses, such as Ull (Ullinn) [and] Hörn . . . who, for us, are only shadowy figures." Descriptions written by foreign observers, including TACITUS, have also provided information.

Written sources native to Scandinavia have preserved myths in greater detail. Although these sources exhibit a Christian influence, some of the stories they contain are clearly centuries older than the manuscripts in which they appear. They include a history written by Saxo Grammaticus (born ca. 1150), SAGAS, and poetry. Scaldic poetry, which usually focuses on contemporary events, is full of kennings, riddling descriptions that often involve mythology. For instance, a poet might mention "the blood of Ymir," alluding to the story that Ymir's blood created the sea. Finally, the *Poetic EDDA* and SNORRI STURLUSON's *Prose Edda* are Norse mythology's greatest literary monuments.

According to Norse myth, an ash tree, Yggdrasill, forms and surrounds the entire cosmos. The *Poetic Edda* describes the early cosmos in the following words:

> *Nothing was there when time began,*
> *neither sands nor seas nor cooling waves.*
> *Earth was not yet, nor the high heavens,*
> *but a gaping emptiness nowhere green.*

Eventually, drops from melting icicles formed a frost giant, Ymir, the progenitor of all giants. Other water drops became a cow, who licked ice until it formed a man, Buri. Buri's grandchildren were the gods Odin, Vili, and Ve. They killed Ymir and built the Earth from his body. In a scene with parallels in

Oceanic MYTHOLOGY, they then created man and woman from "two feeble trees, Ash and Embla."

Norse gods include Odin, god of poetry and battle, who gave up an eye in exchange for wisdom; Thor, who uses his dwarf-forged hammer to kill giants and protect the world; Freyja, a fertility goddess who weeps golden tears; Baldr the Beautiful, who is destined to be killed by a sprig of mistletoe; and Loki. Like the Hopi's Coyote (*see* COYOTE TALES) and Oceanic mythology's Maui, Loki is a trickster. Unlike Coyote and Maui, he has an evil side and brings about Baldr's death. His children include Hel, goddess of death; the wolf Fenrir; and the serpent that surrounds Midgard ("middle earth," humanity's home).

Loki and his children will fight against the gods in the final battle between gods and giants. In preparation for this battle, known as Ragnarok, Odin sends winged female beings called valkyries to battlefields. They bring fallen warriors to Odin's palace, Valhalla, where the warriors drink, eat, and await the coming of Ragnarok.

Norse myths also celebrate human heroes. In the words of translator Patricia Terry, such heroes receive praise for their "courage, strength, and loyalty," while "ordinary men are praised for prudence." The *Lay of Volund* describes how Swedish royals capture Volund, a Finnish prince, while he is waiting for his valkyrie wife to return from war. Volund eventually takes a horrible revenge. Other poems tell of the warrior Helgi and the valkyrie Sigrun. Most famous of all is Sigurd, whose story is a Norse version of the German *NIBELUNGENLIED* and is also related to the English *BEOWULF*.

Norse heroes struggle to reconcile their duties to kinsmen, spouses, lords, lovers, and friends. Sigrun, for instance, laments when she learns that Helgi has won her as his bride by killing most of her family.

Although female goddesses receive less attention than their male counterparts, Norse mythology is full of women like Sigrun, strong yet suffering. "For the most part women and warriors are praised for identical qualities," notes Terry. "The poets seem to have been particularly inter-ested in the heroines, perhaps because they may be . . . both convincing victims and daughters of Odin."

See also KALEVALA.

English Versions of Norse Mythology

The Norse Myths. Retold by Kevin Crossley-Holland. New York: Pantheon, 1980.

Poems of the Elder Edda. Translated by Patricia Terry. Introduction by Charles W. Dunn. Philadelphia: University of Pennsylvania Press, 1990.

The Sagas of the Icelanders: A Selection. Preface by Jane Smiley. Introduction by Robert Kellogg. New York: Viking, 2000.

Sturluson, Snorri. *The Prose Edda: Tales from Norse Mythology.* Translated by Jean Young. Berkeley: University of California Press, 1992.

Works about Norse Mythology

Davidson, H. R. Ellis. *Gods and Myths of Northern Europe.* Baltimore: Penguin, 1964.

Lindow, John. *Norse Mythology: A Guide to the Gods, Heroes, Rituals, and Beliefs.* Oxford: Oxford University Press, 2002.

Orchard, Andy. *Cassell's Dictionary of Norse Myth & Legend.* London: Cassell, 2003.

Turville-Petre, E. O. G. *Myth and Religion of the North: The Religion of Ancient Scandinavia.* New York: Holt, Rinehart and Winston, 1964.

mythology, Oceanic

Oceania encompasses a large number of Pacific islands, including Polynesia, Micronesia, Melanesia, Australia, and New Zealand, and sometimes the Malay Archipelago. Its inhabitants have developed a vast number of myths. Some appear to be from only one or two islands, while others exist in dozens of versions across much of Oceania.

Oceania's myths took on written form beginning with the visits of European missionaries and explorers in the 18th and 19th centuries. Before that, they had existed for centuries as ORAL LITERATURE. They held and continue to hold fundamental roles in Oceanic cultures. They explain how the world in general, and humanity in particular, came to be; describe the lives and activities of gods and human (or superhuman) heroes; and, finally, serve to display individual composers' artistry and entertain listeners.

Polynesian islanders have developed two types of creation myths. In one, the world gradually grows out of darkness into its present state. The Hawaiian *Kumulipo* is one myth of this type. Another is the Maori creation chant *Te Po*, which in James Irwin's translation begins:

> *The recital of the great dark*
> *The great unknown*
> *The deep unknown . . .*
> *The unknown that is being revealed.*

From the darkness come forth Father Sky, Ranginui, and Mother Earth, Papatuanuku. They have children, who are trapped between the two parents. Finally, the children, led by Tane, push their mother and father apart, thus separating sky from earth. Their parents grieve over this forced separation and produce rain and mists.

On other islands, the primeval father Rangi appears as Atea Rangi or Atea. Mother Papa occasionally appears under a name related to coral and coral growth. The Mangaian islanders tell how the world is contained inside a coconut shell named Avaiki, whose first inhabitant Vari (mud) pulled Father Sky from her side.

In the second kind of creation myth, a preexisting, all-powerful creator brings forth the world. Inhabitants of Samoa, Tonga, and the Ellice Islands tell how Tangaloa created everything from the "Illimitable Void."

Micronesian myths place less emphasis on world creation than do Polynesian myths, but the Micronesians do have origin myths. In some stories, just as in Norse mythology (*see* MYTHOLOGY, NORSE), a primeval being's body parts make up the world. In the Marshall Island myths, islands appear when the god Lowa says, "mmmm." In other Oceanic myths, Ancient Spider creates the world, and the eel Riiki separates earth and sky.

Many Australian myths postulate a primeval Dreamtime during which spirit beings walk on the earth. Australian myths also emphasize the separation of earth and sky, which was accomplished by eucalyptus trees, mountains, or even a magpie using a stick. In contrast, Melanesian myths, while they can involve raising the sky, tend to emphasize the creation and release of the sea.

Ancient Oceanic peoples had many gods about which they told stories. Australian myths have the powerful Rainbow Snake as well as Bat, Eaglehawk, and Sun. Easter Island myths include the creator god Makemake, and Hawaiian myths have Pele, the volcano goddess. Gods widespread throughout Polynesian myths include Tane (Kane in Hawaii), god of forests and animals; Tangaroa, the ocean god; Rongo (also known as Ono or Lono), the god of sound and cultivated food; and Tu, god of war, whom the Hawaiians called "Ku-of-the-deep-forest," "Ku-the-snatcher-of-lands," and "Ku-with-the-maggot-dropping-mouth." Also popular is the goddess Hina-of-the-moon.

Some myths explain humanity's origins. Various Australian aboriginal tribes tell of a goddess who emerged from the sea to create life; Bunjil, who made men from clay, while Bat made women from water; and the Numbakulla brothers, who cut humans out of unformed, sightless beings. According to other Oceanic myths, a god makes men out of maggots, sand, or wood; humans grow out of trees or develop from stones, blood clots, maggots in a dead wallaby. The Maori believed that Tane not only made a woman from red earth but also brought humanity baskets of knowledge.

Oceanic myths also tell of heroes. In their equivalent of VIRGIL's *Aeneid*, the inhabitants of Ma'uke (one of the Cook Islands) explain how 'Uke, son of the god Tangaroa, left the mythical homeland Avaiki to settle on their island. The Maoris' Hutu and the Marquesan Kena resemble Greek mythology's (*see* MYTHOLOGY, GREEK) Orpheus in that they visit the underworld to retrieve a dead loved one. In the Bismarck Archipelago, the brothers To Kabinana and To Karvuvu create women, release the sea, and fish up land. The incompetent To Karvuvu also creates sharks and brings about death. The Polynesian hero Tawhaki, who seeks to avenge his father's death, also has a less-competent brother. Their adventures are part of a lengthy myth cycle that includes the story of Tawhaki's grandson Rata. Meanwhile, the Melanesians tell of Qat and his 11 brothers.

The most popular and widely known hero of Oceanic mythology is Maui. Like the Hopi's Coyote (*see* COYOTE TALES), Maui is almost always a trickster, but he also accomplishes great deeds. He fishes up land, steals fire, kills monsters, and snares the sun so that days will be longer. According to the Maori, humans die because Maui's attempt to gain immortality was unsuccessful.

The myths of Oceania reflect innumerable elements in the lives of peoples surrounded by sky and water. As with all myths, there is an element of historical truth concerning the social, cultural, economic, and political developments of a time long past.

English Versions of Oceanic Mythology

Anderson, Johannes C. *Myths and Legends of the Polynesians.* Rutland, Vt.: Charles E. Tuttle, 1969.

Luomala, Katherine. *Voices on the Wind: Polynesian Myths and Chants.* Honolulu: Bishop Museum Press, 1955.

Works about Oceanic Mythology

Luomala, Katharine. "Survey of Research on Polynesian Prose and Poetry (in Oceania and Australia)," *Journal of American Folklore,* 74, no. 294 (Oct.–Dec. 1961): 421–439.

Poignant, Roslyn. *Oceanic Mythology: The Myths of Polynesia, Micronesia, Melanesia, Australia.* London: Paul Hamlyn, 1967.

Swain, Tony and Garry Trompf. *The Religions of Oceania.* Library of Religious Beliefs and Practices. London: Routledge, 1995.

Nahuatl poetry, ancient (Aztec poetry)

Nahuatl has for centuries been an indigenous language of the peoples of Mexico. Prior to the arrival of Spanish explorers, it was the language spoken by inhabitants of the México-Tenochtitlán region, who called themselves Mexicas or Tenochcas, but whom the Spanish referred to as Aztecs. It is likely that Nahuatl was also the language of the Toltecs, who predated Aztec civilization and whose culture was absorbed into the Aztecs' in many ways. Nahuatl was a spoken as well as a written language. Priests, rulers, and their counselors preserved their knowledge and written history in a form of ORAL LITERATURE aided by pictoglyphic accounts recorded in paintings and books they called *cuicamatl*, or "papers of songs." The recitation of Nahuatl verse was, in fact, a reading of pictures, to which the language of the poetry often makes reference.

Some of the Nahuatl poetry records history, from the beginnings of Toltec civilization in the first century A.D. to the Spanish conquest in 1521. The poetry was meant to be sung, and some records involve musical notation or directions on intonation. The meter of the poetry is varied and complex, and poems frequently pair images and lines to convey a single idea. For instance, the words *xochitl* (flower) and *cuicatl* (song) are frequently used together, and a "flower-song" might represent art, poetry, or the idea of symbolism itself.

Genres of poems range from songs celebrating war, rulers, women, and ancient wisdom to songs about nature, including the seasons and certain favorite images such as doves, fish, flowers, birds, and eagles. A number of the surviving songs are anonymous, while others are attributed to rulers and sages referred to as *cuicahuicque*, "composers of songs." Many poems glorify Aztec conquests in war and explain their religion, a system of sacrifice built on the premise that it was human responsibility to ensure the continuation of sun, moon, earth, and stars in what they counted the fifth incarnation of the universe. Other poems celebrate love and friendship. Many of the poems addressed to nature contain a theme of lament on the transitional nature of life.

The most famous of the ancient Nahuatl poets, and the most-praised in his own time, is Nezahualcoyotl (1402–72), ruler of Tezcoco, an architect, legislator, and sage as well as a poet. His poetry shows a profound depth of thought and an artful blend of two distinct traditions—that of the ancient Chichimecs of the north and that of the Toltecs, who attribute their arts, crafts, philosophy, and wisdom to the divine figure and culture hero Quetzacoatl. His poetry also reflects the somber meditation that all on earth must pass away, as in these lines translated by Miguel León-Portille in *Fifteen Poets of the Aztec World*. Observing that nothing lasts forever, the poet says sadly:

> Though it be jade it falls apart,
> though it be gold it wears away,
> though it be quetzal plumage it is torn
>   asunder.

Mortality, Nezahualcoyotl writes, means eventual loss and departure: "Like a painting / we will be erased." But if there is an afterlife, he speculates, then nothing ever really disappears.

While untold numbers of artifacts, manuscripts, and other records of Aztec culture were systematically destroyed by the Spanish, some early missionaries took an interest in the native language and literature. Many of them attempted to preserve customs, histories, and poems by transcribing them in either Nahuatl or Spanish. Most of the existing works of ancient Nahuatl poetry survive in three collections: the "Romances of New Spain," collected and recorded by Juan Bautista Pomar as part of his history *Geographical Relation of Tezcoco* (1582); the anonymous *Cantares Mexicanos* (Mexican Songs) compiled between 1565 and 1597; and the songs recorded by Bernardino de Sahagún in the Florentine Codex (1560). In addition to these, native speakers like Alva Ixtlilxóchitl adopted the Spanish alphabet for their own language and made a similar effort to preserve their heritage before it was entirely lost. These collections show very little influence of European thought or religion, preserving the native beauty and spirit of Nahuatl poetry.

English Versions of Ancient Nahuatl Poetry

Cantares Mexicanos: Songs of the Aztecs. Edited by John Bierhorst. Palo Alto, Calif.: Stanford University Press, 1985.
Poems of the Aztec Peoples. Translated by Edward Kissam and Michael Schmidt. Ypsilanti, Mich.: Bilingual Press, 1983.
A Scattering of Jades: Stories, Poems, and Prayers of the Aztecs. Translated by Thelma D. Sullivan. Edited by Timothy J. Knab. Tucson: University of Arizona Press, 2003.

Works about Ancient Nahuatl Poetry

León-Portilla, Miguel. *Aztec Thought and Culture: A Study of the Ancient Nahuatl Mind.* Translated by Jack Emory Davis. Norman: University of Oklahoma Press, 1990.
———, ed. *Fifteen Poets of the Aztec World.* Norman: University of Oklahoma Press, 1992.
———. *Pre-Columbian Literatures of Mexico.* Translated by Grace Lobanov. Norman: University of Oklahoma Press, 1986.

Native American literature

See CHINOOK MYTHS AND TALES; COYOTE TALES; CREATION MYTHS; NAHUATL POETRY, ANCIENT; NAVAJO NIGHTWAY CEREMONY SONGS; OJIBWAY MYTHS AND LEGENDS; OKLAHOMA CHEROKEE FOLKTALES; *TELAPNAAWE* NARRATIVES; *TUUWUTSI* NARRATIVES; *WAIKAN* NARRATIVES; WHITE MOUNTAIN APACHE MYTHS AND TALES; *WORAK* NARRATIVES; YAQUI DEER SONGS; ZUNI NARRATIVE POETRY.

Navajo Nightway Ceremony songs

Music plays a major role in the traditional ceremonies of the Navajo people. Their songs, such as "Song from the Mountain Chant" and "Song of the Earth," are deeply bound to ceremonies performed for a variety of reasons, such as to evoke cures for the ill or to celebrate and honor the gifts bestowed by nature.

The Nightway Ceremony is a nine-day Navajo healing ceremony undertaken to relieve stricken people and in a larger sense to reharmonize and reorder the natural world. The songs that comprise the ceremony number into the 400s. The ceremony is carefully constructed as a means of rebalancing relationships with the Navajo universe and between people, especially along lines of gender, authority, and age. In general, the goal of the activity is to reestablish beauty and remove ugliness from the universe.

Well-trained medicine men, prepared by decades of study in arcane details of the Navajo healing arts, run the ceremonies. Many, including current public-health officials of the Navajo, contend that the Nightway Ceremony is effective in healing the sick and ordering social relations among the participants.

Navajo history has it that the Holy People gave the Nightway to the Navajo after the earth was rid of monsters. At that time, Holy People became invisible and began to live in caves, mountaintops, and sacred sites from where they could watch over mortals below. This change in the status of the Navajo Holy People can be set shortly after the year 1000, a date fairly late in the Navajo cosmic history.

Songs are probably the most significant element of the Nightway Ceremony. A varied litany of songs and chants, accompanied by instruments such as the gourd rattle and the basket drum, are meant to instruct, evoke, and exalt. There are unfortunately few systematic records of the songs, partly because Western ears have not been sensitive to the differences among the various chants, and partly because the medicine men have been reluctant to have their ceremonies taped. Therefore the songs have had to be re-created outside the actual Nightway, a method that often creates a slightly artificial reproduction. Nonetheless, full records of the various song sets used in the ceremonies have been enumerated, bearing such names as *Songs of the Highest Mountains, Songs of the Navajo Canyon, Songs of the Sand Painting, Songs of the Killer Enemies,* and *Songs of the Fringed Mouth Gods.*

English Versions of Navajo Nightway Ceremony Songs

Levy, Jerrold E. *In the Beginning: The Navajo Genesis.* 18, 41–42, 126–128. Berkeley: University of California Press, 1998.

Wiget, Andrew. *Handbook of Native American Literature.* 59–60, 112, 348. New York: Garland Publishing, 1996.

A Work about the Navajo Nightway Ceremony Songs

Faris, James. *The Nightway: A History and a Documentation of a Navajo Ceremonial.* Albuquerque: University of New Mexico Press, 1990.

Nezāmī (Nizāmī, Elyās Yūsof Nezami Ganjavī, Nizāmī Ganjavī, Abu Muhammad Ilyas ibn Yūsuf ibn Zaki Mu'ayyad) (ca. 1141–ca. 1203) *poet*

Nezāmī was born in Ganja, the capital of Arran, an area of Transcaucasian Azerbaijan. His father was from Qom in Iran and might have been a civil servant, while his mother is believed to have been the daughter of a Kurdish chieftain. Nezāmī was orphaned early, brought up by his uncle, and married three times. In Nezāmī 's day, Ganja was a center of literary activity, and poets there enjoyed the patronage of provincial governors, receiving upkeep and distribution of their poetry. Persian poets of that time, Nezāmī in particular, were well versed in many subjects such as languages, mathematics, astrology, astronomy, Muslim law, philosophy, and history.

Nezāmī was a classical Persian poet who wrote on the themes of women, love, and science. His style of poetry is lyrical and sensuous, made especially alive by intense imagery and complicated symbolism. He is best known for five long lyrical works: *Khamse,* or *The Five Treasures* (1173, also known as *The Quintuplet*), a collection of five long poems in which he expresses his views on a number of cultural and aesthetic issues; *Khosrow and Shīrīn* (1181), a collection of lyric poems about the pure love shared by the title characters; *Layli and Majnun* (1188), a romance about the extremes of passion and forbidden love; *Haft Paykar,* or *Seven Beauties* (1197), a romance told by the character Bahram V Gur, modeled after the ruler who led the Sassanian Empire from 421 to 439; and *Iskandar-Nama* (1201), a poem about Alexander the Great.

The themes in Nezāmī 's writing involve problems of self-knowledge, the problem of identity, and the difficulty of the protagonist's interpretation of his role as a lover. Nezāmī stresses the romantic atmosphere, exploiting the pathos of his stories. He expresses his ideas of love from the standpoint of a society that tried to strictly control the effects of love and marriage. For example, in the nearly 4,000 stanzas of his most famous poem, *Layli and Majnun,* Nezāmī vividly portrays both love's destructive force and one lover's willingness to become victim to love's excesses. He thus creates a love story and an allegory.

The two main characters of *Layli and Majnun* are cousins who fall madly in love, Majnun to the point of obsession. When Majnun makes a public display of his sentiment, he damages Layli's honor and incurs her father's disfavor. Layli's father forbids the marriage, and Majnun responds with a public display of grief, ripping his clothes and crying Layli's name. Majnun's father takes him to Mecca in an attempt to heal him, but Majnun's madness is simply confirmed when he proclaims, "A love as steadfast as this, let it increase a hundred fold."

Majnun becomes alienated from society, starts wandering naked in the desert, and finally, in a last show of madness, rejects Layli, who has been faithfully waiting for him. She does not match the image of her that Majnun had been carrying in his head and heart, so he cannot love the real Layli. She dies of grief as a result of his rejection.

Layli and Majnun and Nezāmī's other works reflect his intellectual background. He used literature as a means through which he could challenge current societal conventions, and he beautifully depicts his ethical viewpoints of love, science, and women in poems that reveal his prodigious creative talent.

English Versions of Works by Nezāmī

The Haft Paykar: A Medieval Persian Romance. Translated by Julie S. Meisami. Oxford: Oxford University Press, 1995.

Lailāi and Majnuän: A Poem from the Original Persian of Nizami. Translated by James Atkinson. New Delhi: Asian Publication Services, 2001.

Layla and Majnun. Translated by Colin Turner. London: Blake Publishing, 1997.

Story of the Seven Princesses. Translated by G. Hill. Edited by R. Gelpke. Mystic, Conn.: Verry, Lawrence, Inc., 1976.

Works about Nezāmī

Binyon, Laurence. *The Poems of Nizami, Described by Laurence Binyon.* London: The Studio Limited, 1928.

Meisami, Julie S. *Medieval Persian Court Poetry.* Princeton, N.J.: Princeton University Press, 1987.

Talattof, Kamran, K. Allin Luther, and Jerome W. Clinton, eds. *The Poetry of Nizami Ganjavi: Knowledge, Love, and Rhetoric.* New York: Palgrave Macmillan, 2001.

Nibelungenlied (12th century) *epic poem*

The *Nibelungenlied* (Song of the Kings of Burgundy) is a verse narrative written in 12th-century Germany by an author whose identity remains unknown. The *Nibelungenlied* inherits from both the EPIC or heroic poetry of the Germanic peoples (of which BEOWULF is a classic example) and the tradition of ORAL LITERATURE in Scandinavian cultures. It builds on the stories of Norse mythology (*see* MYTHOLOGY, NORSE), stories collected in the EDDA, and other SAGAS. Most English translations of the *Nibelungenlied* are based on what is commonly referred to as the B text, compiled ca. 1205 by a cleric serving the bishop of Passau.

The text of the *Nibelungenlied* exists in 34 manuscripts compiled and circulated in southern Germany between the 13th and 16th centuries. Together the manuscripts present various versions of the basic story, with fairly subtle differences. Presenters giving an oral performance of the poem would have added their own interpretations of specific events or characters, thus giving the text an evolution of sorts through the ages.

As editor Francis Gentry observes in *German Epic Poetry,* "Few works have exercised such a hold on later generations as this epic narrative of the deeds of bold warriors and lovely ladies, of high-spirited festivals and solemn ceremonies, of great battles, and, foremost, of revenge." Part of the *Ni-*

belungenlied's appeal is that it blends the heroic themes of loyalty, murder, and vengeance with a courtly setting drawn from MEDIEVAL ROMANCES. Its main characters are kings and queens, its warriors follow the code of CHIVALRY, and interspersed with the moments of mass violence are poetic descriptions of courtly ceremonies and behaviors.

Divided into two main parts, this long poem (there are 2,379 stanzas) organizes its episodes into chapters or "adventures." When pronounced aloud, the four-line stanzas, separated by a *caesura* or line break, create a rhythmic, thunderous quality suitable to the unfolding events. Most of the action centers on the courts of Worms in southwestern Germany and Xanten in present-day Holland.

The hero Siegfried is depicted as a knightly prototype, daring and chivalrous but also demanding. To win the heart of Kriemhild, Siegfried offers his services to the court of Burgundy and is eventually granted her hand in marriage by King Gunther. Ten years after this marriage, Kriemhild argues with Queen Brünhild, Gunther's wife, over which man is the better champion. In the resulting struggle, Brünhild has Hagan murder Siegfried, and Kriemhild is left friendless and defeated. Kriemhild seeks revenge in the second part of the work, killing Hagan and King Gunther before losing her own life at a banquet hosted by Attila the Hun, where fighting ensues between the Huns and the Burgundians.

Part of the artistry of the *Nibelungenlied* is due to the personalities of its characters, who are portrayed as dimensional figures neither purely heroic nor purely villainous; all have strengths and weaknesses, and all possess tendencies toward good and evil. Siegfried is initially described as a man possessing skill at arms and physical beauty, whose accomplishments have won him wide renown, but through the course of the narrative he displays arrogance, ruthlessness, and callousness along with a sort of carefree ignorance. Hagen, Gunther's chief counselor, is a complex figure whose desire for power leads him from the most exemplary loyalty to the most profound betrayal. Far from being passive heroines, the women of the *Nibelungenlied*

are forceful, determined, and fully responsible for their actions, including their failures.

The *Nibelungenlied* is a tragic epic, and its theme is perhaps best personified by the character of Kriemhild, the Burgundian queen who opens and closes the tale and whose career demonstrates that joy is ever blended with sorrow. Introduced as "a royal child in Burgundy— / In all the world none lovelier than she," she is murdered by Hildebrand in the closing stanzas, proving that "ever pleasure turns to pain when all is done."

The *Nibelungenlied* has held an enduring fascination for readers, inspiring plays, poems, novels, music, and Richard Wagner's opera, *Ring of the Nibelung*. The discovery of the C text in 1755 at a castle in Austria revived interest in the epic and led to new editions, translations, and imitations. As Germany became a unified nation in the 19th century, the *Nibelungenlied* was cited as proof of the common mythology, literature, and history of German peoples. Today the text can still be appreciated for its dramatic quality, as well as its poetic beauty and sophistication.

English Versions of the *Nibelungenlied*
Nibelungenlied. Translated by A. T. Hatto. New York: Penguin, 1965.
The *Nibelungenlied*. Translated by D. G. Mowatt. London: Dover Publications, 2001.
Song of the Nibelungs: A Verse Translation. Translated by Frank G. Ryder. Detroit: Wayne State University Press, 1982.

Works about the *Nibelungenlied*
Andersson, Theodore M. *A Preface to the Niebelungenlied*. Stanford, Calif.: Stanford University Press, 1987.
Haymes, Edward. *The Nibelungenlied: History and Interpretation*. Urbana: University of Illinois Press, 1986.

Njal's Saga (ca. 1280) *prose narrative*
Written by an unknown author, *Njal's Saga* is widely considered among the finest of all classical Icelandic

SAGAS. The original manuscript for *Njal's Saga* has been lost; the earliest extant vellum manuscript is from ca. 1300. In its time the saga enjoyed great popularity, which is perhaps why many of its manuscripts have survived.

Broadly based on historical events that took place some 300 years earlier, *Njal's Saga* tells the story of ordinary people in medieval Iceland became caught in a complex web of revenge and murder. Honor and familial obligation play a large part in the events that unfold, as any insult, whether real or imagined, must be revenged.

In straightforward, economical prose, the story centers on Njal Thorgeirsson, an influential lawyer and sage who becomes embroiled in a 50-year feud that ultimately leads to his doom. Njal and his family are drawn irrevocably into conflict through his friendship with Gunnarr, who is portrayed as a brave and honest man. The beginning of the conflict is Gunnarr's marriage to Hallgerd (a match that meets with Njal's disapproval). Hallgerd, who is portrayed as very beautiful yet morally corrupt, then sets in motion a bitter set of feuds, beginning with her rivalry with Njal's wife, Bergthora. The following passage shows their initial exchange of insults (characteristic of most family sagas):

> Hallgerd seized hold of her hand and said, "There's not much to choose between you and Njal; you have turtle-back nails on every finger, and Njal is beardless." "That is true", said Bergthora . . . "But your husband Thorvald wasn't beardless, yet that didn't stop you from having him killed."

A killing match ensues, and seven men die before the feud is stopped. Meanwhile, however, Gunnarr's mortal enemy, Mord, succeeds in bringing about Gunnarr's downfall, and the violence continues. Eventually Njal and his family are burned to death in their own home as a result of Mord's further machinations.

As a form of literary art, *Njal's Saga* ranks among the best of Icelandic sagas. Its characters are highly developed and represent a broad range of human characteristics—all of which play a role in the development of a complex story riddled with conflict. It is the saga's human elements that make it appealing even to modern readers and that have given it a place in world literature.

An English Version of *Njal's Saga*
Njal's Saga. Translated by Robert Cook. New York: Penguin Classics, 2002.

Works about *Njal's Saga*
Byock, Jesse L. *Medieval Iceland: Society, Sagas, and Power.* Berkeley: University of California Press, 1988.
Helgason, Jon Karl. *Rewriting of Njabl's Saga: Translation, Ideology, and Icelandic Sagas.* Clevedon, U.K.: Multilingual Matters, 1999.

Norse mythology
See MYTHOLOGY, NORSE.

Nukada, Princess (Nukata Okimi)
(fl. seventh century) *poet*

Princess Nukada, also known as Nukata Okimi, is considered Japan's first lyric poet. Like other members of the Japanese cultural elite at this time, she may have been of Korean origin. She was first the consort of Emperor Kobun, to whom she bore Prince Katsuragi; after the emperor's death, she married Emperor Temmu, to whom she bore Princess Toichi. She also had a relationship with Emperor Tenchi; in one poem she describes herself as waiting for him, using an image of nature to express her restlessness and longing:

> *Swaying the bamboo blinds of my house,*
> *The autumn wind blew.*

Emperor Tenchi, a great patron of the arts, encouraged Nukada's compositions. Princess Nukada's favored medium of poetic expression was the TANKA, a traditional poetic form consisting of five lines and 31 syllables. Her tanka were known for their graceful symmetry and forceful rhythms. The Princess's poetry focused as frequently on political issues as on her personal life. Indeed, her position at court demanded that her life be political. But she is at her best in evoking metaphors of nature to portray a state of mind, as in one poem where she compares picking flowers in spring to flowers in autumn, and concludes simply: *Akiyama ware wa* — "But the autumn hills are for me."

Several of Princess Nukada's poems were collected in the *Manyoshu, The Ten Thousand Leaves* (called by some *The Ten Thousand Ages*), a collection of Japanese literature compiled by the poet OTOMO YAKAMOCHI. This collection, like the folk poems of the *KOJIKI* (compiled in 712), provides a valuable record of life in Japan during the Heian era.

English Versions of Works by Princess Nukada

The Penguin Book of Women Poets. Edited by Carol Cosman. 72–73. New York: Viking Press, 1986.

The Ten Thousand Leaves. Translated by Ian Hideo Levy. Princeton, N.J.: Princeton University Press, 1981.

A Work about Princess Nukada

Singer, Kurt. "Asuka and Nara Periods (A.D. 592–794)" in *The Life of Ancient Japan*. New York: Routledge, 2002.

Oceanic Mythology
See MYTHOLOGY, OCEANIC.

Ojibway myths and legends

The Ojibway Indians, also known as the Chippewa or the Anishinaubaek (pronounced nish-NAH-bek, meaning "the good people") people, inhabited the Great Lakes region of North America in the late 17th century. For most of the year, the Ojibway spent their time farming and hunting for food and pelts for the fur trade. However, because the winters in the Great Lakes region are so bitterly cold and snowy, the Ojibway people spent these months gathered around fires indoors. It was around their fires that the Ojibway oral tradition developed. In fact, their myths were told only during the winter months.

One of the central characters in many Ojibway myths is Wenebajo, also known as Manabozho. Wenebajo was a mythical figure, not quite human and not quite animal. He was alternately portrayed as a trickster (a common character in Native American mythology), a kind of superhero, and the creator of the Ojibway people. He fought many monsters and protected humans against danger and disease.

Other Ojibway myths and legends include "A Gust of Wind," which tells the story of how the first males were born; "The Foolish Girls," which tells the story of how two girls learn not to be foolish; "The Father of Indian Corn," which tells the story of a boy named Wunz who asks the Chief of Sky Spirits to help him find a way to feed his people; "How Dog Came to the Indians," a tale about a giant who gives his pet dog to a pair of men so they can find their way home; and stories of supernatural spirits called the Manitous.

The Ojibway myths and creation stories were among the first such Native American tales to be collected by white American settlers. Henry Rowe Schoolcraft from Michigan published two books of Ojibway tales in the early 19th century. These books also served as source material for the poet Henry Wadsworth Longfellow's epic poem *The Song of Hiawatha*.

See also ORAL LITERATURE/TRADITION.

Works of Ojibway Myths

Broker, Ignatia. *Nightflying Woman: An Ojibway Narrative*. St. Paul: Minnesota Historical Society, 1983.

Johnston, Basil H. *Tale of the Anishinaubaek*. Toronto: Royal Ontario Museum, 1993.

————. *The Manitous: The Supernatural World of the Ojibway.* New York: HarperCollins, 1996.

Schoolcraft, Henry Rowe. *The Myth of Hiawatha, and Other Oral Legends, Mythologic and Allegoric, of the North American Indians.* Philadelphia: J.B. Lippincott, 1856.

Oklahoma Cherokee folktales

The Cherokee nation originally inhabited the Appalachian region of the United States, but a relocation effort begun by the U.S. government in 1838 removed huge numbers of Cherokee to Oklahoma via a route called the "Trail of Tears." Currently, the Cherokee Nation of Oklahoma comprises a little over half the total Cherokee living in the United States. The folktales of the Oklahoma Cherokee preserve the beliefs, customs, and spiritual resiliency of a culture that has managed to survive enormous obstacles while maintaining its native dignity and strength.

The tales of the Oklahoma Cherokee are inherited, in many ways, from older myths of shared ancestry with the Eastern Band Cherokee. One example is the story of Selu, the corn goddess, and her husband Kana'ti. These two, who were among the first humans on earth, established the division of labor that would subsequently be practiced in the Cherokee tribe. Kana'ti (whose name means "hunter" in Cherokee) established that men would be responsible for bringing home animals to provide meat, while Selu (whose name means "corn") was able to produce corn by shaking it out of her body and established that women would take care of planting, harvesting, and food preparation.

Other folktales describe the origin of natural phenomenon. For instance, "How the Deer Got His Horns" explains how Deer competed in a race with Rabbit in which a pair of antlers was the prize. As James Mooney tells the story in *Myths of the Cherokee,* the judges discovered that Rabbit had cheated by gnawing a shortcut through the bushes. Therefore:

> They agreed that such a trickster had no right to enter the race at all, so they gave the horns to the Deer, who was admitted to be the best runner, and he has worn them ever since. They told the Rabbit that as he was so fond of cutting down bushes he might do that for a living hereafter, and so he does to this day.

Some of the Oklahoma Cherokee folktales are what Mooney calls "wonder tales," stories of magic and enchantment that might include spirits, giants, personified elements like Thunder, or similar supernatural events. Other folktales serve as records of historical traditions, preserving accounts of trade, interaction with other tribes, wars, and the first contacts with Europeans. Some tales provide a simple moral lesson.

Though they may simply appear to be entertaining stories, these Cherokee folktales act as valuable cultural records, preserving and communicating Cherokee ways of life and modes of thought. Aside from offering information about diet, economics, social structures, and tribal etiquette, the folktales preserve sacred religious teachings and offer myths that explain how the Cherokee understood and interpreted the world. Many of the folktales incorporate the foundational Cherokee understanding of the nature of the world as a union of the Upper World, and Lower World, and the earth world (called in the creation tales the "Ball of Mud"), which must be kept in a state of balance.

Moreover, despite their age and the fact that they have survived a centuries-long oral tradition (*see* ORAL LITERATURE/TRADITION), these tales offer a perspective on the world that can benefit present-day readers. In Marilou Awiakta's *Selu: Seeking the Corn-Mother's Wisdom,* Wilma Mankiller, the principal chief of the Cherokee Nation of Oklahoma, reminds readers that these old folktales teach lessons that still have currency in contemporary life. She writes:

> We human beings are sometimes so oriented toward scientific explanations for everything that we seldom are able to suspend that analytical state of mind. . . . We have never really understood that we are one small part of a very

large family that includes the plant world, the animal world and our other living relations.

In addition to being entertaining stories that audiences of all ages and backgrounds can enjoy and appreciate, the folktales of the Oklahoma Cherokee remind readers of the subtle balance that must be maintained in all things as well as the connection to the larger world for which each individual is responsible.

English Versions of Oklahoma Cherokee Folktales

Cherokee Folk Tales & Myths. Translated by Agnes Cowen. Park Hill, Okla.: Cross-Cultural Education Center, 1984.

Kilpatrick, Jack F. and Anna G. *Friends of Thunder: Folktales of the Oklahoma Cherokees.* Norman: University of Oklahoma Press, 1995.

Living Stories of the Cherokee. Edited by Barbara R. Duncan and Davey Arch. Raleigh: University of North Carolina Press, 1998.

Mooney, James. *Cherokee Animal Tales.* Edited by George F. Scheer. New York: Holiday House, 1968.

Works about Oklahoma Cherokee Folktales

Mooney, James. *History, Myths, and Sacred Formulas of the Cherokees.* Asheville, N.C.: Bright Mountain Books, 1992.

———. *Myths of the Cherokee.* New York: Dover Publications, 1995.

Old English poetry (ca. 650–ca. 1050)

Old English was the vernacular language spoken by the Angles, Saxons, Jutes, Frisians, and other Germanic tribes that began to migrate to Britain in the fifth and sixth centuries. British resistance to the Germanic invaders gave rise to the legends of Arthur, who would reach great fame in the MIDDLE AGES. The Germanic tribes brought with them a non-Christian religion, deriving from Norse MYTHOLOGY and accounted for in the early SAGAS. New efforts to convert the Angles and Saxons began in 597 with the missions of Augustine. The Church taught and wrote in Latin, as did the ruling class. Yet the Anglo-Saxon culture, which flourished from the first settlements until the time of the Norman Conquest in 1066, included a vernacular poetry of a range, depth, and complexity quite unrivaled by any other medieval European literature. The Old English poetry that survives shows a blending of the newer Christian beliefs with the ancient heroic code adhered to by the Germanic tribes, who were historically governed by a warrior elite and bound by ties of kinship and loyalty.

The greater part of Old English poetry is contained in four surviving manuscripts. The BEOWULF manuscript contains, among other fragments, the famed EPIC poem of that name. *Beowulf* is the best example of Germanic heroic poetry and the crown jewel of the Old English poetic corpus. The Junius manuscript contains various poems retelling stories from the Christian Bible, including an intriguing dialogue, *Christ* and *Satan.* The Exeter Book contains the largest number of poems, which range from religious verses and allegorical poems to charms, riddles, and gnomic verses which offer priceless insights into Anglo-Saxon folk wisdom. The Vercelli Book, discovered in Italy, includes the innovative poem thought to be the most beautiful of Anglo-Saxon religious verse, *The Dream of the Rood.*

Due to the near-constant warfare of the Anglo-Saxon period, first between neighboring tribes and then against Danish invaders or Vikings who raided the coast, the poems in the manuscripts are often damaged and in many cases reduced to fragments. Almost all the poems are anonymous. Old English poetry was an ORAL LITERATURE, developed and maintained by *scops,* or poet-singers, who functioned like the bards of the celtic BARDIC POETRY. The *scops* served as the living memory of the tribe, recording their history, genealogy, and social codes, all in rhymed verse. Evidence exists to suggest that women served as *scops,* though they too remain unnamed. The only Anglo-Saxon poet who personally signed his works was the cleric Cynewulf, writing in the late eighth century, who added his autograph so that readers might pray for him.

Critical Analysis

Most Old English poetry employed a poetic line with a four-beat meter, consisting of two half-lines of two stresses each. The half-lines were typically linked by alliteration, the use of similar-sounding consonants, which gave the words an aural music complemented by the accompaniment of a stringed instrument, probably a harp. A distinct feature of Anglo-Saxon verse is the use of the kenning, a compound descriptor that employs a striking image or metaphor to convey the qualities of the thing it describes. Old English vocabulary included a striking range of words to describe a single thing (dozens of different words existed, for example, as synonyms for "warrior," "battle," and "sword," suggesting that these items were featured often in the poetry), and the use of varied adjectives or kennings along with the strict alliterative meter required no small skill of the poet. A brief poem by CAEDMON encapsulates all of these features in its opening lines on the creation:

> Now must we praise heaven-kingdom's
>   Guardian,
> the might of the Measurer and his mind-
>   thoughts,
> the Glory-Father's work, since he . . . made
>   the beginning.

Caedmon's achievement is remarkable because he was supposedly an illiterate shepherd who, some time between 658 and 680, spontaneously began devising poetry after an angel visited him one night in a dream. "Caedmon's Hymn," commonly accepted as the oldest Anglo-Saxon poem on record, is preserved in BEDE's *Ecclesiastical History of the English People.*

Anglo-Saxon poetry after Caedmon can be discussed according to type. Excepting *Beowulf,* the best example of heroic poetry is the *Battle of Maldon,* composed to record the defeat of the famed warrior and Essex ealdorman Byrhtnoth in a battle against Danish invaders which took place at Maldon in 991. *Maldon* aptly and lyrically expresses the basic tenets of the warrior code: to fight bravely no matter the odds, never abandon kin to the enemy, and avenge fallen chiefs or fellow warriors. Byrhtnoth dies gloriously, due to a fatal move in which he allowed the Danish armies to compensate for a territorial disadvantage. The dramatic tension of the poem lies precisely in this tragic defeat, and the vividness with which the clash of battle is evoked marks the anonymous poet's skill:

> Thus the brave men stood firm in battle,
> each sought eagerly to be first in
> with his spear, winning the life and
>   weapons
> of a doomed warrior; the dead sank to the
>   earth.

A similar example of heroic poetry is preserved in the ANGLO-SAXON CHRONICLE entry for 937, describing the Battle of Brunanburh. The Anglo-Saxon corpus also preserves a unique set of heroic poems about women: *Judith, Juliana,* and *Elene,* who are collectively referred to as the "fighting saints." Though they are about Christian warriors, these poems preserve traces of the sacred role of women in early Germanic society as advice-givers, equal rulers, and weavers of peace.

A second well-represented type of Old English poetry is the elegy. Much of the Anglo-Saxon corpus touches on themes of separation and grief, but the so-called elegies deal specifically and lyrically with loss: loss of a spouse, loss of a beloved chief, loss of hearth and family. *The Seafarer* evokes the exile of a warrior who has left his home and is in search of another lord who will take him on as a retainer. The poet uses the natural imagery of his current surroundings, the icy seas and the freezing winds, to contrast the warm companionship of the mead-hall:

> The cry of the gannet was all my gladness,
> the call of the curlew, not the laughter of
>   men,
> the mewing gull, not the sweetness of mead.

The poet in *The Wanderer* sings a similar lament as he searches for a new lord. This poem contains a classic expression of the *ubi sunt* motif, which mournfully asks, "Where?" The warrior laments:

> Where has the horse gone? Where the man?
> Where the giver of gold?
> Where is the feasting-place? And where the
> pleasures of the hall?

Two other elegies portray sadness from a woman's point of view. The wife in *The Wife's Lament* mourns her separation from her husband, and the female narrator of *Wulf and Eadwacer* sorrows that she was forcefully separated from her lover.

The religious poetry of the Anglo-Saxons is distinctly compelling in the way it blends Christian beliefs with the heroic inheritance of their Germanic forebears. For instance, the *Genesis* poem offers, in part B, a unique account of the biblical book. Dealing with a culture in which women were valued as counselors and it was reasonable for a man to listen to the advice of his wife, the *Genesis B* poet complicates the ancient story and distributes the guilt equally.

The Anglo-Saxons were also hugely fond of riddles, which survive in the Exeter Book, though without solutions. The accompanying charms, remedies, and bits of gnomic wisdom preserved in verse offer a glimpse into a day-to-day life in which ancient pagan beliefs and Christian doctrine existed side by side.

The latest example of Anglo-Saxon poetry is probably Layamon's *Brut,* which is a translation of Wace's French version of GEOFFREY OF MONMOUTH's *History of the Kings of Britain.* After the Battle of Hastings in 1066, the introduction of French language and culture turned the Anglo-Saxon world into the Anglo-Norman world, and the language evolved into Middle English. Some examples of Middle English poetry attempt to preserve the older alliterative verse forms; *Sir Gawain and the Green Knight, Pearl*, and William Langland's *Piers Plowman* are examples. The English Renaissance witnessed a fantastic rediscovery of and renewed appreciation for the poetry that had formed so essential a part of the native culture and literature.

English Versions of Old English Poetry

The Anglo-Saxon World: An Anthology. Translated by Kevin Crossley-Holland. London: Oxford University Press, 1999.

Beowulf. Translated by Seamus Heaney. New York: W. W. Norton & Company, 2000.

Works about Old English Poetry

Klinck, Anne L. *The Old English Elegies.* Buffalo, N.Y.: McGill–Queen's University Press, 1992.

Lambdin, Laura Cooper and Robert Thomas. *Companion to Old and Middle English Literature.* Westport, Conn.: Greenwood Press, 2002.

O'Keefe, Katherine O'Brien, ed. *Old English Shorter Poems: Basic Readings.* New York: Garland Publishing, 1994.

Swanton, Michael. *English Poetry before Chaucer.* Exeter, U.K.: University of Exeter Press, 2002.

Omar Khayyám (Abū ol-fath 'Omar, Gheyās od-Dīn Abū ol-fath 'Omar ebn Ebrahīm ol-Khayyāmī) (ca. 1048–1131)
scientist, mathematician, poet

Omar Khayyám was born in Nishapur, Persia, in what is now Iran. Since the literal translation of his birth name, al-Khayyámi, means "tent-maker," it is possible to assume that his father made tents for a living. Although Omar received an education in philosophy, he was highly gifted in many areas. Before he turned 25, he wrote a book on music, a book on algebra, and his famous *Problems of Arithmetic.* In 1070, he moved to Samarkand in Uzbekistan, where he devoted himself to algebra and astronomy. A talented scientist and mathematician, he calculated the length of the year with precision; created the Jalali Calendar, which is more accurate than the Julian; created a geometric solution of cubic equations; and created accurate astronomical tables. He achieved all of these accomplishments while performing as a court astronomer for the king of Malekshah. During his 40s, he traveled to

Baghdad, Mecca, and other areas of the Middle East, returning to Nishapur to spend his remaining years teaching.

During Omar's lifetime, the political situation in Persia was unstable: rulers competed for power, and radical groups tried to establish a state based on orthodox Islam. At one point, Omar became the subject of the radicals' attacks because they felt that his questioning mind did not conform to conservative faith. He was targeted especially by the Sufis, whose practices he ridiculed.

In addition to conducting scientific and mathematical research, Omar also wrote poetry. Perhaps because he was too honest or logically-minded, though, he never developed his poetry in a mystical fashion, as did some of the Sufi poets such as Hafiz.

Omar Khayyám's most famous work is the *Rubáiyát,* a collection of about 1,000 poems, each written in an epigrammatic style and consisting of quatrains, four line groups. About 600 of the poems were translated by Edward Fitzgerald (1809–83) in 1859. The translation was well received and maintains the spirit of Omar's original reflections on humanity, nature, life, and mortality.

Critical Analysis

Scholars have taken two opposing views of Omar Khayyám's *Rubáiyát.* Some claim that the poet was highly influenced by Islamic mysticism and that his references to wine and lovers are allegorical expressions of the mystical wine and divine love. Others argue that Omar understood his mortality, had a pessimistic view of the spiritual nature of life, and celebrated only sensual, temporal pleasures. These scholars view references to wind and lovers in the *Rubáiyát* as literal. The truth of Omar's message perhaps lies between these two schools of thought. As a scientist, he had a trained mind and a natural inclination to view the world and himself through "clinical" eyes, but as a man, he also felt passion, love, hatred, sadness, and joy.

The *Rubáiyát* reveals the soul of a romantic disillusioned by hypocrisy and futility and, at the same time, aware of beauty and spirituality. In some quatrains of the *Rubáiyát,* the poet realizes

that his love for truth and sincerity will not win him the sympathy of the world, and he understands that all he possesses—his scientific talent, his intellect—are useful to society only as long as he conforms to those upon whom he is dependent for survival, or as long as society needs him. At times, the truth of the poet's situation reveals his bitterness:

> *The good and evil that are in man's heart,*
> *The joy and sorrow that are our fortune*
>   *and destiny,*
> *Do not impute them to the wheel of heaven*
>   *because, in the light of reason,*
> *The wheel is a thousand times more help-*
>   *less than you.*
>
> (Stanza 34)

Yet the disillusioned man can, at other times, find peace and comfort in simple pleasures:

> *I need a jug of wine and a book of poetry,*
> *Half a loaf for a bite to eat,*
> *Then you and I, seated in a deserted spot,*
> *Will have more wealth than a Sultan's*
>   *realm.*
>
> (Stanza 98)

Themes of merrymaking and enjoying wine, the company of good friends, and beautiful women constitute a significant part of the *Rubáiyát,* but the man Omar seemed to find it difficult to reconcile the critical and scientific with the sensual and spiritual. At times, this lack of reconciliation comes across in the poet's CARPE DIEM outlook on life:

> *Khayyám, if you are drunk on wine,*
>   *enjoy it,*
> *If you are with the tulip-cheeked, enjoy her:*
> *Since the world's business ends in nothing,*
> *Think that you are not and, while you are,*
>   *enjoy it.*
>
> (Stanza 140)

The momentary, transient nature of human life is another prevalent theme of the *Rubáiyát*. Realistically, Omar perceived mortality as inevitable, so much so, however, that it prevented him from finding peace in religion, faith, or spirituality:

> Oh what a long time we shall not be and
>   the world will endure,
> Neither name nor sign of us will exist;
> Before this we were not and there was no
>   deficiency,
> After this, when we are not it will be the
>   same as before.
>
> (Stanza 51)

It is perhaps this duality of humanity that Omar portrays with aching clarity that makes the *Rubáiyát* one of the most treasured works in world literature. It has been translated into most major languages, and Omar Khayyám's sharp wit, polished form, and depth of meaning remain highly relevant for readers of all epochs and cultures.

English Versions of a Work by Omar Khayyám

Rubáiyát of Omar Khayyám. Edited and translated by Peter W. Avery and John Heath-Stubbs. Harmondsworth, U.K.: Penguin Books, 1981.

Rubáiyát of Omar Khayyám: A Critical Edition. Translated by Edward Fitzgerald. Edited by Christopher Decker. Charlottesville: University Press of Virginia, 1997.

Works about Omar Khayyám

Alexander, Doris. *Creating Literature Out of Life: The Making of Four Masterpieces.* University Park: Penn State University Press, 1996.

Bjerregaard, C. H. *Sufi Interpretations of the Quatrains of Omar Khayyam and FitzGerald (1902).* Whitefish, Mont.: Kessinger Publishing, 2003.

Thompson, Eben Francis. *Wisdom of Omar Khayyam.* New York: Kensington Publishing, 2001.

Yogananda, Paramahansa. *Rubáiyát of Omar Khayyám Explained.* Nevada City, Calif.: Crystal Clarity Publishers, 1994.

Yogananda, Paramahansa. *Wine of the Mystic: The Rubáiyát of Omar Khayyám: A Spiritual Interpretation, from Edward Fitzgerald's Translation of the Rubáiyát.* Los Angeles: Self-Realization Fellowship Publishers, 1996.

Ono no Komachi (fl. ca. 850) *poet, playwright*

Many fantastic legends have grown up about the life of Ono no Komachi, since few facts are known. She lived in the early period of Heian Japan (794–1185) and was a lady-in-waiting in the imperial court around 850. She was said to be the daughter of Yoshisada, the lord of Dewa. A later poem supposedly written by "Komachi's grandchild" suggests she had at least one child.

The legends held that Ono no Komachi was adored at court for her poetic skill and was considered the most beautiful Japanese woman who had ever lived. She had many passionate affairs but spent the last years of her life in solitude and abject poverty. Tales were told about her skull, which survived in a field where it complained in verse about the grasses growing up around it.

Several Noh plays written in the mid- to late-Heian period perpetuate the figure of Ono as being a beautiful and manipulative courtesan who ends up abandoned and rejected. The legends may draw partially on the themes within the surviving TANKA poems attributed to her. Eighteen of her poems were collected in the *Kokinshu* anthology (905) compiled by KI NO TSURAYUKI. Fujiwara no Kinto named her the sole woman among the ranks of the *Rokkasen*, the Six Poetic Geniuses. The collection of poems ostensibly written by Ono no Komachi, the *Komachishu*, was compiled between 1004 and 1110. Of the 100 poems it contains, only about 45 are thought to actually be Ono's, while the rest are poems written by others, some addressed to her.

Ono no Komachi was one of the first female Japanese poets to write about her love and longing with great passion. Many of her poems speak eloquently of unrequited love, and one much-anthologized poem compares a man's heart to a blossom "whose colors, unseen / yet change." Other poems show the influence of Buddhism, and contain thoughtful meditations on the nature of reality, observing that one cannot know if love is real or a dream

> *when both reality and dreams*
> *exist without truly existing.*

Stylistically, Ono's poems are clever and graceful, often making use of the *kakekotoba*, or pivot-word, which contains two different meanings that simultaneously reflect the imagery and subject matter of a poem. In one poem she uses the word *tsuki*, which means both "way" and "moon." In this poem, she is waiting for a man who does not come, and the moonless night, leaving her without a way to see her lover, symbolically represents her fears about the future of their relationship.

Desolation is a frequent topic of Ono's poetry, and one she describes with painful grace. In the earlier poems her grief is frequently due to neglect or abandonment by lovers. In one poem she pictures herself in "a sad floating boat," and says,

> *there is not a single day*
> *that I am not drenched by the waves.*

Other poems show a growing sense of isolation and a feeling of disconnectedness. In one haunting poem, Ono compares her body to "floating sad grasses / severed from their roots," and says, "if there were waters that beckoned / I should go, I think." Her later poems express grief over the loss of beauty and a melancholy view of old age:

> —*how sad this is!*
> —*to think that my body*
> *has become useless.*

Some critics tend to describe Ono's poetry as "weak," since so much of it deals with love, loss, and longing. Yet, as scholar and translator Terry Kawashima observes, "tropes of fleetingness and sadness over the changing state of things are common in *waka* poetry," the tradition within which Ono was writing. In addition, several of her dream poems show, as Kawashima puts it, "a strong-willed woman who goes against custom, even if only in a dream." Later Japanese writers, such as IZUMI SHIKIBU, were inspired by Ono's passionate imagery and insight into human emotion. Her biography continues to be the subject of plays and studies, and her lyric poetry intrigues and fascinates lovers of poetry around the world.

English Versions of Works by Ono no Komachi

The Ink Dark Moon: Love Poems by Ono No Komachi and Izumi Shikibu, Women of the Ancient Court of Japan. Translated by Jane Hirshfield and Mariko Aratani. New York: Vintage Books, 1990.

Japan's Poetess of Love Dream and Longing, Ono no Komachi: 117 poems. Translated by Howard S. Levy. Yokohama, Japan: Warm-Soft Village Press, 1984.

Ono No Komachi: Poems, Stories, and Noh Plays. Translated by Roy E. Teele. Edited by James J. Wilhelm. London: Taylor & Francis, 1993.

A Work about Ono no Komachi

Kawashima, Terry. "Part II: Komachi" in *Writing Margins: The Textual Construction of Gender in Heian and Kamakura Japan.* Cambridge, Mass.: Harvard University Press, 2001.

Ō no Yasumoro

See KOJIKI.

O'othham Hoho'ok A'agitha Papago and Pima Indian folklore

The *O'othham Hoho'ok A'agitha* are a collection of legends and myths of the Papago and Pima Indians, collectively known as the O'othham, who are native to southern Arizona and northern Mexico. The Hohokam (which means "finished ones" in Pima) settled in the American southwest from Mexico between 750 and 900; around 1400, they disappeared either through migration or warfare.

The Pima and Papagos peoples, who lived in the former Hohokam territory, retained their ORAL LITERATURE and communicated the stories for centuries, using them as educational tools that taught traditional values and customs. For the Pima and Papago, these tales were their history, not fiction.

Because of their remoteness from Spanish and Mexican power, the Pima and Papago did not fall under European rule and were not introduced to Christianity until 1694. The native man-god described in the Hohokam chronicles, who was murdered and then departed from the world, bears some parallels to but is not patterned after the Christian Jesus. The tale of creation describes how God created the world so he might live on it. Called the Earth-Doctor, he makes the world out of shavings of his own skin, and then creates the sun, moon, stars, and the first humans. Together, the sun, moon, earth, and sky then make Siuuhu the Drinker and the Coyote.

Other stories tell of the origin of wine and of irrigation. In them, wind, clouds, rains, and seeds are gathered from the corners of the universe and used to plant and water the fields. The ritual involving saguaros, or cactus wine, is used to invite rain. A later story tells of the death and resurrection of Siuuhu.

Thanks to careful collaborations between scholars and native speakers in the last century, the O'othham tales have been preserved and are an important source of information about the elements of Native American mythologies prior to their discovery by Europeans.

An English Version of the *O'othham Hoho'ok A'agitha*

O'otham Hoho'ok A'agitha: Legends and Lore of the Papago and Pima Indians. Translated by Dean and Lucille Saxton. Tucson: University of Arizona Press, 1973.

Works about the *O'otham Hoho'ok A'agitha*

Bahr, Donald, et. al, eds. *The Short Swift Time of Gods on Earth: The Hohokam Chronicles.* Berkeley: University of California Press, 1994.

Underhill, Ruth M. *Papago Indian Religion.* New York: Columbia University Press, 1946.

Zepeda, Ofelia, ed. *When it Rains: Papago and Pima Poetry.* Tucson: University of Arizona Press, 1982.

oral literature/tradition

The literature of every culture from every corner of the world shares one thing in common: It originates in the spoken word. Long before and after a culture develops written systems of communication, the oral exchange of stories forms an essential part of a people's emotional and spiritual life. In daily life, stories serve as a means of connection and a way of establishing a shared humanity. Every society uses stories to retain and transmit its shared history, accumulated wisdom, cultural values, and beliefs.

Oral literature, as scholars define it, can include any fictive utterance, from folklore and mythology to jokes and nursery rhymes. Scholarly discussions of oral tradition often focus on oral poetry in the form of historical narratives or wisdom tales. As a culture evolves, it commemorates its history and ancestors in narratives that are passed on in the form of a heroic story or EPIC. The Sumerian GILGAMESH, the long poems of HOMER, and compositions like the Finnish KALEVALA or the Persian SHAHNAMEH all originated as oral poems relating events that a culture considered part of its history. The Mande EPIC OF SON-JARA or the Incan MYTH OF MANCO CAPAC, though they belong to different continents, both retell foundation myths of how a civilization came to be. In many cultures, the earliest written literature preserves stories that had already been told for centuries. In fact most of the sacred literature of the world, including the Hebrew BIBLE, is thought to have its roots in oral tradition.

Narratives of mythology develop as humans attempt to explain their own existence and understand the world around them. Creation stories like the Native American CREATION MYTHS or the Hawaiian *Kumulipo* describe how a culture accounts for the order of the world and its creatures. From the beginning, these and other stories communicated through oral exchange offered a way to instruct listeners and celebrate shared beliefs. Cultures develop an oral tradition as a way to remember and ritually convey stories for the benefit of succeeding generations.

Oral traditions may be communicated in the form of prose, but most cultures develop a poetic tradition to remember and relate their stories. Historians of oral tradition have learned that rhythm and rhyme function as mnemonic devices to enhance the memories of performers as well as audiences. In oral poetry, meter serves as a way to structure the poem and to organize information. Once the meter is established, the poet draws on certain ready-made compositional devices. This is seen in oral traditions of all ages and cultures, from the Vedas or PURANA of India to the BARDIC POETRY of the Celts. Longer tales require more compositional devices, such as typical details, formulaic lines or diction, and recurrent situations. The WHITE MOUNTAIN APACHE MYTHS AND TALES, for example, end each line or phrase with "they say" to emphasize the fact that the tale has been handed down by others.

Oral literature is meant to be performed. In performance, poetry differs little from song, and most oral performances involve musical or visual accompaniment. Interaction with the audience opens and sustains the performance, making the story or poem uniquely different each time it is recited.

Despite the advantages of print culture in preserving and disseminating knowledge, it would be false to say that cultures no longer have or depend on oral traditions. Folklore exists today in the form of urban legends; elders tell us about their history and experience, friends share stories about their day. Human experience is defined by, understood through, and shared in story, and the oral tradition of a culture preserves its origins, its foundations, and its essential character in a way that written literature can perpetuate but never duplicate.

English Versions of Works of Oral Literature

Courlander, Harold. *A Treasury of Afro-American Folklore.* New York: Marlowe & Company, 2002.

Haa Shuka, Our Ancestor: Tlingit Oral Narratives. Edited by Nora Dauenhauer. Seattle: University of Washington Press, 1987.

Pham, Loc Dinh. *A Glimpse of Vietnamese Oral Literature: Mythology, Tales, Folklore.* Philadelphia: Xlibris, 2002.

Stories that Make the World: Oral Literature of the Indian Peoples of the Inland Northwest. Edited by Lawrence Aripa, Tom Yellowtail, and Rodney Frey. Norman: University of Oklahoma Press, 1999.

Works about Oral Literature/Tradition

Fontes, Manuel de Costa. *Folklore and Literature: Studies in the Portuguese, Brazilian, Sephardic, and Hispanic Oral Traditions.* New York: State University of New York Press, 2000.

Okpewo, Isidore. *African Oral Literature: Backgrounds, Character, and Continuity.* Indianapolis: Indiana University Press, 1992.

Ramirez, Susan Berry Brill de. *Contemporary American Indian Literatures and the Oral Tradition.* Tucson: University of Arizona Press, 1999.

Warner, Keith Q. *Kaiso! The Trinidad Calypso: A Study of Calypso as Oral Literature.* Pueblo, Colo.: Passeggiata Press, 1999.

Yamamoto, Kumiko. *The Oral Background of Persian Epics: Storytelling and Poetry.* Boston: Brill Academic Publishers, 2003.

Ostromir Gospel (ca. 1057) *liturgical text*

Composed between 1056 and 1057 by a cleric known as Deacon Gregor, the *Ostromir Gospel* is the oldest extant Russian manuscript and thus the first text of Russian literature. Almost nothing is known about Deacon Gregor's life. From the text itself it is clear that he possessed exceptional learning and artistic skill. Though he belonged to no specific religious order, as a clergyman and scribe he would have obtained the education and skills necessary for the work. It is believed Deacon Gregor was active in Novgorod, but he must have been born or spent considerable time in Kiev, as traces of his native Russian dialect show in the language of his work.

The *Ostromir Gospel* was commissioned by Ostromir, the *posadnik,* or city governor, for the Cathedral of St. Sophia in Novgorod. It follows the model of the Aprokos Gospel used in Greek manuscripts in that it is divided into two sections. The first and largest section contains the gospel texts, drawn from the Acts and Epistles of the Apostles in the New Testament of the Christian Bible. Since the gospel readings began at Easter and were normally concluded by Pentecost, the *Ostromir Gospel* recommends Scripture to read for the remaining Saturday and Sunday services of the year. The second section provides a calendar of readings and notes which saints are to be commemorated on which days. The text is richly decorated throughout, with elaborate lettering and miniature portraits of the apostles that show the influence of the Old Byzantine style.

The *Ostromir Gospel* is invaluable to linguists because it is written in Old Church Slavonic, a medieval language in which very few manuscripts survive. Christianity reached Slavic-speaking lands between 865 and 883 through the missionary efforts of Cyril and Methodius, and it continued to spread as rulers converted and their subjects followed suit. Under the reign of Jaroslav of Kiev, called "the Wise" (1019–54), a considerable number of churches and monasteries were built. The services at these churches, such as masses and other celebrations, were conducted in the native language rather than the Greek used earlier in the Orthodox Church. Thus the spread of Slavonic rites fostered the need for Slavonic books. As a substantial body of Christian literature already existed in eastern Bulgaria, the *Ostromir Gospel* and its companion works are thought to be translated from manuscripts obtained from Balkan lands through either plunder from war or peaceful trading contacts. Throughout the medieval period, Church Slavonic was used by the Russian Orthodox Church for both ecclesiastical and literary purposes, much the same way that Latin was used by the Roman Catholic Church. The vernacular Slavic dialects were used for everyday purposes.

Four other manuscripts in Old Church Slavonic contain material from the Gospels, and three other manuscripts contain parts of prayerbooks, hymns, and saints' lives. Until the secularization of Russian society that took place under Soviet influence, the Orthodox Church was not simply the official religion but the most prominent cultural institution. For this reason, the *Ostromir Gospel,* preserved in the National Library of Russia, remains one of the cultural treasures of the Russian people. The history of Russian literature begins with this document. A key artifact in the evolution of the Russian language, it is a valuable resource that speaks to the development of Christian religion and culture in Eastern Europe, as well as a beautifully crafted piece of art.

Works about the *Ostromir Gospel*

Goldblatt, Harvey and Riccardo Picchio. "Old Russian Literature." In *A Handbook of Russian Literature,* edited by Victor Terras, 316–322. New Haven, Conn.: Yale University Press, 1985.

Moser, Charles, ed. *The Cambridge History of Russian Literature.* 2, 4. Cambridge, U.K.: Cambridge University Press, 1992.

Otomo Yakamochi (Otomo no Yakamochi) (718–785) *poet*

The detailed information on Otomo Yakamochi's life comes from his poetic journal and his contributions to the poetry anthology *Man'yōshū* (The collection for ten thousand leaves [pages], compiled from 686 to 784). Otomo grew up in Dazaifu, a city home to some of the most important Japanese poets of the time. His father Tabito's high place in government and the tutoring of his aunt, Otomo Sakanoue, prepared Otomo for a life as an imperial official and a poet in his own right.

In 741 Otomo was made an attendant to the emperor, and from 745 until his death he was promoted continuously. In 777 he was made *Daisi* ("Great teacher") and became a chief imperial counselor. Late in life he was implicated in a murder trial but was pardoned.

Otomo lived at a time when Japanese culture was greatly influenced by the Tang Chinese, and his poetry reflects his efforts to reconcile tensions between the older Japanese form of society, governed by a warrior elite, and the modern forms of political administration. As a young courtier he experimented with the fashionable court styles, writing occasional poetry to be recited at official occasions or banquets and love poetry addressed to a series of women.

In his mid-20s and 30s, Otomo produced most of his mature verse and began editing the *Man'yōshū*. This work, in its final form, spans 20 volumes and contains 4496 *uta* (song poems), from elegies to poems on love, the seasons, travel, and royal events. In 746, Otomo became the governor of Etchū, where he wrote the majority of his poems. His varied and original verses cover a wide range of subjects, blending artful observations of nature with a poignant undertone of melancholy and yearning, as expressed in this poem, number 3967 in the *Man'yōshū*:

> If I could show you but a glimpse
> Of the cherries blooming
> In the mountain gorges.

Translator Paula Doe notes that Otomo was "in large part responsible for the preservation of the ancient poetic tradition" and adds that "he laid the foundation for Japanese poetry for centuries to come."

An English Version of Works by Otomo Yakamochi

Written on Water: Five Hundred Poems from the Man'yōshū. Translated by Takashi Kojima. Rutland, Vt.: Charles E. Tuttle, 1995.

A Work about Otomo Yakamochi

Doe, Paula. *A Warbler's Song in the Dusk: The Life and Work of Otomo Yakamochi (718–785)*. Berkeley: University of California Press, 1982.

Ouyang Xiu (Ou-yang Hsiu) (1007–1072)
poet, historian

Ouyang Xiu was born in Mianyong (Mien-yang), in the Sichuan (Szechuan) province of China. After his father died, he and his mother moved to Hubei (Hupeih) to live with his uncle. Legend has it that Ouyang lived in such poverty that he learned to write with a stick in the sand. At age 23, he became a judge in Loyang, and during his three years there, he spent much time developing his literary talents.

During his life, Ouyang Xiu held a number of government positions and wrote many essays, poems, and songs. Although his public-service career was plagued by a series of exiles, he remained dedicated to his literary pursuits. In his mid-20s, he composed *New History of the Five Dynasties,* a documentation of China's political history during the 10th century. In his 30s, he served as governor of Chuzhou (Ch'u-chou), where he built the "Old Drunkard's Pavilion," about which he wrote a famous essay. In his 40s, he hosted legendary parties for literary friends in which his famous *ci* (*tz'u*) (songs) were performed, and he began work on the *New History of the Tang Dynasty* (completed in 1060). He retired from public service in 1071.

Many of Ouyang's works continued the classical style of writing initiated by HAN YU, and he became one of the leading literary figures of the Sung dynasty. His essays focus on Confucian philosophy, history, and politics, but he is best remembered for the poetry and songs in which he uses images of nature to explore the human spirit. In his poem "Autumn," for example, he compares images of the dying landscape to the decay of the human soul:

> . . . The trees will fall
> In their due season. Sorrow cannot keep
> The plants from fading. Stay! there yet is
>   man—
> Man, the divinest of all things, whose heart
> Hath known the shipwreck of a thousand
>   hopes,
> . . . whose soul

Strange cares have lined and interlined,
   until
Beneath the burden of life his inmost self
Bows down. And swifter still he seeks decay
When groping for the unattainable
Or grieving over continents unknown.

As translator L. Cranmer-Byng says in *A Lute of Jade,* "Autumn," like many of Ouyang Xiu's poems, is worthy of praise: "With its daring imagery, grave magnificence of language and solemn thought, it is nothing less than Elizabethan, and only the masters of that age could have done it justice in the rendering."

An English Version of a Work by Ouyang Xiu

A Lute of Jade. Translated by L. Cranmer-Byng. Indy-Publish.com, 2003.

A Work about Ouyang Xiu

Egan, Ronald C. *The Literary Works of Ou-yang Hsiu (1007–72).* Cambridge, U.K.: Cambridge University Press, 1984.

Ovid (Publius Ovidius Naso) (43 B.C.– ca. A.D. 18) *poet*

Ovid was born into a well-to-do and socially prominent family living in Sulmo (modern Sulmona), some 90 miles east of Rome. His father, a member of the wealthy Equestrian class, provided him and his older brother with the Roman education in rhetoric and law, as well as a grand tour of Greece and Asia Minor.

The young Ovid was a gifted student of rhetoric (the art of using language effectively and persuasively), and he habitually added lyrical touches to his academic exercises and assignments. However, he had no taste for the law and no skill in politics. His father tried repeatedly to dissuade him from his chosen path, admonishing him that even HOMER died broke. Ovid reportedly penned a promise to stop writing poetry—in dactylic hexameter.

Ovid's work was an immediate success among fashionable society, as it reflected their disillusionment with the breakdown of the classical republican ideals of Rome at the time. Many scholars have contrasted the positive light of Ovid's work to the "darker" works of his older counterparts, the Augustans, for his work resembles neither that of the patriotic satirist HORACE nor that of the melancholy and moralistic VIRGIL. His inventive, refined, and metrically brilliant poetry seems effortlessly composed and depicts a cosmopolitan, secular sensibility that derived from both his inherent skill and the peace and prosperity of AUGUSTUS's reign. His spirited, graceful elegies and epistles reveal the soul of a true romantic.

Ovid was prolific as well as popular; more than 35,000 lines of his verses survive. His first published poems were a collection of playful and lighthearted love poems, *Amores* (Loves), first published 20–16 B.C. in five books and later, in 2 B.C., reduced to three.

Around the same time as the *Amores,* Ovid composed the *Heroides* (Heroines), a collection of imaginary love letters between 15 mythological women and their lovers or husbands. In these letters he takes minor characters appearing in other works and gives them psychological depth and complexity by using the first person to reveal the personalities of these famous and doomed women. The characters typically seen as pure evil, such as Medea, Ovid humanizes by explaining their motives or casting them in a light of pitiful ignorance, as he does with Helen of Troy. Those women customarily seen as noble and guiltless, like the abandoned Dido or the bereft Hero, Ovid complicates by revealing their sinister thoughts and occasional selfishness. Altogether, the *Heroides* so captured the imagination of readers that subsequent authors added six more letters to Ovid's collection.

Ovid also wrote a tragedy called *Medea* (no longer extant), most likely to take advantage of the boom in theater construction during 13–11 B.C. *Ars amatoria* (*The Art of Love*) appeared in 1 B.C., offering, in three books of mock didactic verse, a satirical instructional manual on the art of seduction. This was followed shortly by *Remedia Amoris* (Remedies for Love), an even more mocking sequel.

Between A.D. 1 and 8, Ovid worked on *Metamorphoses* concurrently with *Fasti* (*Religious Holidays*), a calendar of Roman feast days that he never completed. The six books of *Fasti* cover the first six months of the Roman year and are now a valuable source of information about Roman religious practice. In addition, they include lively episodes of Greek MYTHOLOGY, Roman history, and astronomical observations.

Augustus's banishment of Ovid around A.D. 8 is generally attributed to an "unknown indiscretion," but it was probably brought about by a number of factors: The eroticism and immorality of Ovid's works were not in keeping with the emperor's efforts at moral reform; the poet may have witnessed scandalous behavior in the imperial family; and he was decidedly unpatriotic and indifferent to religion and politics. Although the emperor supported the arts, he sent Ovid to live the rest of his days at the furthest edge of the Roman Empire, far from the center of literary arts and cultural entertainments upon which the poet thrived. During his exile, Ovid wrote the *Tristia* (*Songs of Sorrow*) and *Epistulae ex Ponto* (*Letters from the Black Sea*). In these works, he unsuccessfully asks to be pardoned and allowed to return to Rome.

Critical Analysis

The work that secured Ovid's fame to future generations and his acknowledged place among the master artists of world literature is the 15-book *Metamorphoses*. In this project, Ovid underwent a change of his own, turning from elegy and its meter to EPIC and the nobler and more appropriate hexameter. He declares his purpose in the first four lines of the poem:

> My intention is to tell of bodies changed
> To different forms; the gods, who made the
>   changes,

> Will help me—or I hope so—with a poem
> That runs from the world's beginning to
>   our own days.

The theme of *Metamorphoses* is the transforming power of love, and the brief, fanciful tales that make up the work relate numerous metamorphoses: men turn into birds, boys become trees, a magic spell makes a woman a spider, and an ivory statue comes to life. For a work of such disparate elements, the narrative's continuity is striking.

The poem begins with the creation of the world and ostensibly covers the course of history up to the deification of Julius CAESAR. Ovid concludes the work with a suggestion that Augustus will be similarly venerated:

> Later than our own era, when Augustus
> Shall leave the world he rules, ascend to
>   Heaven,
> And there, beyond our presence, hear our
>   prayers!

If this was an attempt to curry favor, it did not succeed in recalling the poet from exile.

Many of the stories in *Metamorphoses* are implicit or explicit statements about power dynamics, examining (and subtly criticizing) power imbalances between gods and humans, rulers and subjects, women and men. The stories are by turns gay and tragic; Ovid turns his pen to charming subjects such as courtship with the same ease he uses to describe horrifying violence, like the battle of the Centaurs or the rape of Philomela. Love and betrayal are constant themes throughout the books, and doomed lovers scatter Ovid's landscape as thickly as trees. In the first four books, infidelities of the gods intertwine with the story of Cadmus and the founding of Thebes. Books 5 through 8 describe the adventures of the ancient heroes Perseus, Jason, and Theseus. Book 9 introduces Hercules, and Book 10 narrates a series of famous love affairs: Orpheus, Ganymede, Pygmalion, and Venus and Adonis.

After the story of Midas in Book 11, the focus turns in Book 12 to the fall of Troy, and, in 13 and 14, the voyage of Aeneas, the hero of Virgil's epic. Book 14 then progresses to the legendary early history of Rome, reaching at last the event which in Ovid's time marked the end of the Roman Republic: the ascent of Caesar. Altogether, Ovid's vivid and elaborate tapestry of narratives contains within it, in the form of story, all the changes that brought forth the world he knew.

In his introduction to *Metamorphoses,* translator Rolfe Humphries writes, "The enormous influence of *The Metamorphoses* on pre-nineteenth century Europe cannot be disputed: it is all but omnipresent, in prose as well as in poetry, in painting as well as sculpture." He adds that the work "was, more than any other work, the medium by which classical mythology was known and understood." According to translator Horace Gregory, *Metamorphoses* is continually being rediscovered: "Something of its original importance is beginning to be understood. Its collection of myths . . . has taken on fresh color and richness . . . and contemporary anthropologists are finding new meaning in Ovid's 'fables' and miracles."

Throughout the European MIDDLE AGES, Ovid and Virgil were considered the unparalleled exemplars of the Latin tradition. Ovid's treatment of love influenced the development of courtly love (*see* CHIVALRY AND COURTLY LOVE) and gave a language of passion to such famous lovers as ABÉLARD AND HÉLOÏSE. Stories from *Metamorphoses* reappeared in the poetry of DANTE, Petrarch, Chaucer, and Gower, and influenced the Renaissance playwrights and poets Christopher Marlowe, Edmund Spenser, and William Shakespeare.

English Versions of Works by Ovid

The Art of Love. Translated by James Michie. Introduction by David Malouf. London: Random House, 2002.

Fasti. Edited by A. J. Boyle and R. D. Woodard. New York: Penguin Classics, 2000.

Metamorphoses. Translated by Rolfe Humphries. Bloomington: Indiana University Press, 1955.

The Metamorphoses. Translated by Horace Gregory. New York: The Viking Press, 1958.

Ovid: Selected Poems. London: Phoenix House, 2004.

Ovid: Selections from Ars Amatoria, Remedia Amoris. Edited by Graves Haydon Thompson. Wauconda, Ill.: Bolchazy-Carducci, 1999.

Works about Ovid

Holzberg, Niklas. *Ovid: The Poet and His Work.* Translations by G. M. Goshgarian. Ithaca, N.Y.: Cornell University Press, 2002.

Lindheim, Sara H., ed. *Mail and Female: Epistolary Narrative and Desire in Ovid's Heroides.* Madison: University of Wisconsin Press, 2003.

Spentzou, Efrossini. *Readers and Writers in Ovid's Heroides: Transgressions of Genre and Gender.* Oxford: Oxford University Press, 2003.

Tissol, Garth. *The Face of Nature: Wit, Narrative, and Cosmic Origins in Ovid's Metamorphoses.* Princeton, N.J.: Princeton University Press, 1996.

Panchatantra (ca. second century B.C.)
collection of stories

The *Panchatantra* belongs to the rich tradition of ORAL LITERATURE in India. It is a collection of tales populated mainly with animal characters acting as heroes and villains and executed with a moralistic content and a clearly instructional tone. The Preamble to the *Panchatantra* offers the information that the tales were composed (or perhaps compiled) by the 80-year-old sage Visnu Sarma as part of his efforts to both entertain and educate the three sons of King Amara-sakti.

The *Panchatantra* is a complex group of tales, interwoven into a series of frame stories, which operate on several allegorical levels. The characters are given names suggestive of the qualities they represent, and their animal personas transparently reveal the human personalities beneath. Throughout the *Panchatantra*, the natural world functions as a metaphor for the human world; it is, in effect, a treatise on moral philosophy disguised as a set of fabulous narratives.

Dating the *Panchatantra* is difficult. Scholars have suggested dates as early as the second century B.C., though no records of a manuscript exist prior to A.D. 570. Analogues exist in other cultures, such as the fables of AESOP and PHAEDRUS, and certain tales of the *Panchatantra* parallel stories from the JATAKA and *Tipitaka*. This is hardly surprising, since oral literature passes through many hands, possibly being reworked and embellished each time, which also makes ascertaining authorship difficult. The existence of Visnu Sarma has been questioned, since no evidence for him occurs outside the *Panchatantra* itself. He was possibly the *kavi*, or court poet, for the king of "the southern lands" mentioned in the same stanza. He may also be a fictional character created as part of a literary device of the narrative.

Nevertheless, an authorial hand of no little genius is evidently at work. The content and tone of the stories suggest that the author knew the ways of royal courtiers and was a sharp-witted observer of the behavior and morals of all levels of Indian society. His overall purpose is to edify, for the Preamble states that the work is a *nitisastra*, a set of instructions on wise conduct, set forth for the purpose of "awakening young minds." The dramatic and elegant style of his prose and verse convey a deep understanding of philosophical issues and also of human nature. Visnu Sarma's ability to interweave humor and wit into his narratives also gives his tales a satiric edge that supports the often poignant tone.

Critical Analysis

The *Panchatantra* is written in both prose and verse forms, a characteristic of the genre of Sanskrit literature referred to as *champu.* Dialogue and narrative are offered in prose, while verse is employed to articulate concepts, provide moral instruction, and describe emotional behavior and sentiment. Verse usually appears in the beginning and end of the text to emphasize the moral of the tale, while the prose form is used primarily to recount the story's developments.

The *Panchatantra* is structured as a series of tales within tales, with the Preamble functioning as the highest level or frame. The five books that follow each offer another frame story, within which more stories are nested. This nesting technique appears in other Sanskrit literature, notably in the Indian EPIC the MAHABHARATA and to some extent in Vedic literature. Within the *Panchatantra*, Book 1, "The Estrangement of Friends," contains the most subsidiary tales. Each successive book addresses a different theme: Book 2 examines the "Winning of Friends," Book 3 speaks "Of Crows and Owls," Book 4 discusses "Loss of Gains," and Book 5 provides examples of "Rash Deeds."

The philosophical structure that runs through the narrative structure carries out the author's intention to provide a *nitisastra.* In Hindu belief, the path to living wisely and well required the equal and balanced pursuit of three aims: *dharma,* described as duty, compliance with the law, or right conduct; *artha,* wealth or material possessions, since money was considered a requirement for gracious living; and *kama,* which includes love and sensual fulfillment. These concepts are dealt with separately in other Sanskrit texts, including the *Dharmasastra,* the *Arthasastra,* and the KAMA SUTRA, but the *Panchatantra* incorporates instructions on all three areas into a single context.

Books 2 and 5, for example, speak to the concept of *artha,* or the acquisition of material resources, when the characters describe the evils of poverty. A verse from Book 5 vividly captures the correlation between wealth and acquisition of knowledge, suggesting one can only successfully meditate and acquire wisdom if one has a full stomach:

> Wit, kindliness and modesty,
> Sweetness of speech and youthful beauty,
> Liveliness too and vitality;
> Freedom from sorrow, and joviality;
> Uprightness, knowledge of sacred texts;
> The wisdom of the Preceptor of the
>   Immortals;
> Purity as well of mind and body;
> Respect too for rules of right conduct:
> All these fine attributes arise in people,
> Once their belly-pot is full.

Part of dharma means fulfilling the duties required of one's station in life, which Cloud Hue, the King of Crows, encounters in Book 3 when he must defend his kingdom and subjects from a cruel enemy. Dharma dictates the behavior of all beings, including the snake in Book 1, who informs the priest that he bites not to hurt anyone, but only does so in self-defense.

The third element of *kama* is reflected in the theme of friendship that pervades all five books. This verse from Book 2 meditates on how to achieve happiness:

> Those who enjoy happy times,
> Friends with dear friends,
> Lovers with their beloved,
> Joyful with the joyous. . . .

True friendship, where beings are connected like flesh and claw, is illustrated in Book 2's story of Goldy, a mole; Lightwing, a crow; and Slowcoach, a tortoise. Goldy and Lightwing, as his friends, successfully extricate Slowcoach from his neurotic obsession and restore him to serenity and happiness.

The consequence of a balanced approach to dharma, *artha,* and *kama* is a harmonious order within society, which the *Panchatantra,* in the Preamble, sets out to illuminate. Prominent signposts in various parts of the narrative constantly remind the reader that these stories are parables about human society and human virtues, vices, and frailty. A good example is "The Singing Donkey" of Book V, a pretentious soul who claims to know everything about music except how to sing.

In the *Panchatantra,* the natural world and the human world mirror each other. Two main devices achieve this effect. The narrative uses analogy to portray similarities in social and political hierarchy and organization between the two worlds. For example, the king of the human world parallels the characteristics of the animal king of the forest. The second literary device, the use of allegory, anthropomorphizes or projects human characteristics onto the animal characters in the stories. Just like the three princes in the Preamble who desire to learn moral conduct, most of the good characters in the stories strive to attain the highest level of education. Animal characters such as Lively the bull and Goldy the mole represent the perfect model citizens with their judicious blend of good learning and sound practical sense.

As Franklin Edgerton observes in the *Panchatantra Reconstructed:* "No other work of Hindu literature has played so important a part in the literature of the world. . . . Indeed, the statement has been made that no book except the BIBLE has enjoyed such an extensive circulation in the world as a whole." The influence of the *Panchatantra* in both its structural format and its dual purposes of entertainment and enlightenment can be traced in works as diverse as the THOUSAND AND ONE NIGHTS, Giovanni Bocaccio's *Decameron,* Geoffrey Chaucer's *Canterbury Tales,* and Jean de La Fontaine's *Fables.* Its canny characters and lively plots surface in the fairy tales of the Grimm Brothers and the Br'er Rabbit stories of the American south. The sheer number of translations of the *Panchatantra* provide proof of its popularity. No other work of Indian literature, and perhaps no other work of world literature, has had such an ageless and universal appeal.

English Versions of the *Panchatantra*

The Panchatantra. Translated by Chandra Rajan. London: Penguin Books, 1993.
The Panchatantra: The Book of India's Folk Wisdom. Translated by Patrick Olivelle. Oxford: Oxford University Press, 1997.

Works about the *Panchatantra*

Amore, R. C. and L. D. Shinn. *Lustful Maidens and Ascetic Kings: Buddhist and Hindu Stories of Life.* New York: Oxford University Press, 1981.
Edgerton, Franklin. *The Panchatantra Reconstructed, I: Text and Critical Apparatus.* American Oriental Series 2. New Haven, Conn.: American Oriental Society, 1924.

Pausanias (115–180) *historian, travel writer*

Born in Greece, next to Mount Sipylos, Pausanias was a Greek traveler who lived during the height of Rome's rule in Greece. His writing—the only source of information about his life—reveals that he lived a long life, witnessed many important historical events, and traveled extensively throughout Greece and the Greco-Roman world. His major work is *Hellados Periegesis* (Description of Greece), which exists in 10 books; the first was completed after 143, the last before ca. 176.

As a whole, *Description of Greece* serves as a type of guidebook for the places Pausanias visited. As he reached each city, he first recorded the location's history. He then visited sacred sites or monuments within or near the city, describing them and other important religious, artistic, and architectural achievements. He also reflects on the customs, peculiarities, and daily lives of the local population of each region, including descriptions of folklore, local legends, and ceremonial rituals. Based on surviving structures and artworks, as well as archaeological evidence, Pausanias's descriptions are remarkably accurate.

Description of Greece provides modern readers with a unique opportunity to journey through ancient Greece with an educated and curious companion, one whose knowledge of history and culture also provides a wealth of information that continues to aid in research of the ancient world.

English Versions of a Work by Pausanias

Pausanias' Guide to Ancient Greece. Translated by Christian Habicht. Berkeley: University of California Press, 1985.

Pausanias's Description of Greece. Translated with a commentary by J. G. Frazer. New York: Biblo and Tannen, 1965.

A Work about Pausanias

Alcock, Susan E., John F. Cherry, and Jajs Elsner, eds. *Pausanias: Travel and Memory in Roman Greece.* Edited by Lysiacum. Oxford: Oxford University Press, 2001.

Petronius (Gaius Petronius) (27–66) poet

Petronius lived during the time of the Roman Empire and served as Emperor Nero's adviser in matters of luxury and extravagance. His sophistication in sensual pleasure even earned him the title *arbiter elegantiae;* TACITUS in his *Annals* refers to Petronius as a sensualist "who made luxury a fine art." Petronius managed to combine his official duties with a chaotic lifestyle, sleeping during the day and living during the night, but his life ended tragically when he was betrayed by a rival and dismissed by Nero. As a result, he committed suicide, which Tacitus described as the ultimate act of refined self-control.

For contemporary readers, Petronius is famous for his *Satyricon,* a brilliant satire of excesses in Nero's Rome. Although only fragments of this work survive, enough of the text remains to provide evidence of Petronius's satirical talent and in-depth knowledge of Roman society at the height of the empire's prosperity. He demonstrates a thorough knowledge of the language and sociology not only of the Roman elite but also of the lower classes.

The *Satyricon* also is the best existing evidence of the prominence of homosexuality in the Roman Empire, which Petronius describes in a vivid, lively manner. The main character of the work is Encolpius, a student whose name, according to some translators, means "crotch." Encolpius offends the god Priapus, and as a result he is forced to undergo a sequence of painful but generally comic misadventures, mostly of a sexual nature. The world of the *Satyricon* resembles a sexual carnival, where gender and orientation are easily interchangeable. This work unambiguously articulates a very specific philosophy, which was, according to the author, widespread among the Roman Empire's elite. According to this philosophy, the only real sin consists in denying one's sexual appetites. To do so is considered blatant hypocrisy and is punished, generally through comic ridicule. This view on morality is explicitly expressed in the paired tales of the Widow of Ephesus and of the Boy of Pergamon.

Written in A.D. 61 and first printed in 1664, the *Satyricon* has since become a prototype for a number of novels about homosexuality. The first English translation was published in Paris in 1902 and attributed to Sebastian Melmoth, a well-known pseudonym of Oscar Wilde. Contemporary works using the legacy of the *Satyricon* include John Rechy's *City of Night* (1963), Daniel Curzon's *The Misadventures of Tim McPick* (1975), and Luis Zapata's *Adonis Garcia* (1979). In these novels, as in the *Satyricon,* travel is portrayed as a license or venue for sexual experimentation and indulgence. The film version of Petronius's masterpiece was produced by Federico Fellini in 1968. Though the film succeeds in capturing *Satyricon's* grotesquerie and powerful homoeroticism, it loses most of Petronius's humor.

Petronius is remembered as much for the content of his *Satyricon* as for his elegant prose and verse, including even the colloquialisms and common language of some of its characters. The *Satyricon* is the earliest example of the picaresque novel in European literature.

An English Version of a Work by Petronius

The Satyricon. Translated by P. G. Walsh. New York: Oxford University Press, 1996.

Works about Petronius

Conte, Gian Biagio. *The Hidden Author: An Interpretation of Petronius' Satyricon.* Translated by Elaine Fantham. Berkeley: University of California Press, 1996.

Courtney, Edward. *A Companion to Petronius.* New York: Oxford University Press, 2001.

Phaedrus (first century) *poet*

Most of what is known about Phaedrus has been deduced or inferred from his work *Fabulae Aesopiae,* a collection of writings commonly referred to as the *Fables.* He was originally a slave of the first Roman emperor, AUGUSTUS, but was later freed. He claimed to have been born in Thrace, in the region of the Pierian Mount on the southeast coast of Macedonia. This reference has been questioned, since the legendary AESOP was thought by some to be from Thrace. (Elsewhere Phaedrus says that Aesop came from Phyrgia.) Likewise, the Mount of Pieria was the mythical birthplace of the Muses, so attributing his birth to the Muses' domain may have been Phaedrus's attempt to legitimize his claims to literary fame and inspiration. One remark in the *Fables* that scholars often take seriously is his hint that he was at some point persecuted by Sejanus, the ambitious general under Emperor Tiberius whom Tiberius executed for treason in 31. Other references in the *Fables* suggest that Phaedrus lived through the stormy rule of Caligula and into the time of Claudius.

Critical Analysis

The first portions of Phaedrus's five books of *Fables* borrow from Aesop, the slave who lived in the sixth century B.C. The Greek tales attributed to Aesop were originally written in prose. Phaedrus, in the beginning of the first century A.D., and Babrius, who lived in the second half of the century, were the first to put these fables into verse. As

prose they functioned as collections of myth, providing stories that could be used to reinforce a rhetorical point or lesson. As verse, however, the fables could be considered literature, and Phaedrus seems to be consciously maneuvering for a place in the literary tradition, despite his background as a slave. (HORACE was himself the son of a freedman, and it was not unknown for slaves to be educated.)

For his source on Aesop, Phaedrus used the manuscript of Demetrius of Phaelerum, compiled around 300 B.C. The first two books he published feature a series of brief tales, their animal characters familiar to readers of Aesop. The author's point of view is frequently dark and cynical as he looks upon a world where injustice exists and the whims of the mighty prevail, sometimes not for the good of all. The fables ridicule vanity, conceit, and arrogance and consider ignorance the cardinal sin. Though a pessimistic mood seems to pervade the stories as the author repeatedly showcases objectionable behavior, the fables clearly intend to educate readers on the simple morals required to live in the world. "Be unkind to no man," Phaedrus declares in the fable of "The Fox and the Stork," for, he goes on to explain, "mean behavior is liable to rebound." In a society where those in power cannot always be counted on to behave with respect and mercy, the best option, Phaedrus seems to say, is to remain humble, keep quiet, and simply try to blend in.

As the books progress, the author moves away from predominantly beast fables to material of his own making. Though he cannily continues to attribute his work to Aesop and often uses Athens as a setting for his fables, Phaedrus clearly depicts the daily life and political situations of first-century Rome. Some disguise and circumspection were no doubt necessary to avoid angering certain civic authorities. In the preface to Book 3, Phaedrus claims: "My purpose is not to pillory any person, / But to illustrate life and the ways of the world." His frequently biting and often unflattering portraits of those in power, however, obviously led some authority figures to identify themselves with the wolves, lions, and other predators of Phaedrus's fables and to take issue with him, as Sejanus apparently did. For the common person, the best defense is sometimes silence, as Phaedrus suggests in the epilogue to Book 3 in which he refers to the maxim he learned as a youth: "For a man of humble birth / It is not proper to protest in public." Phaedrus speculates that the first fables were invented because the first slaves, "exposed to incessant hazards, / Unable openly to express what [they] wanted," found they could safely express their personal opinions by masking them in the form of fictional fables. In writing his books, Phaedrus wrote that he had merely taken that route and "enlarged it to a highway," so to speak, by adding to the themes bequeathed him by Aesop.

Certain stories in Book 3 show how Phaedrus expands on his material and brings in morals from his own experience. In "On Believing and Not Believing," the author recommends that readers "find out the truth, before faulty thinking / Leads to a stupid and tragic outcome." He offers what he says is a story from his own experience, in which a man, on the treacherous advice of his secretary, ends up killing his son and then himself, leaving his innocent wife to be accused of double murder. The terrible story turns into an episode praising the justice and wisdom of Augustus, who sorts out the messy details of the case, and Phaedrus returns to his moral with the announcement "[T]rust no one you don't know." Then, in a tag at the end, he ironically adds that he told this story at length because "a few friends have informed me / That they find my fables somewhat too short." Using the premise of a fable to explain a tragedy of which he knows, Phaedrus manages to praise his patron and also insert his own somewhat discouraging but perhaps hard-learned advice. He also uses Book 3 to talk back to his critics—for instance, in the fable of "The Cock and the Pearl," which tells the story of a rooster finding a pearl as he digs for food. Although he recognizes the value of the pearl, he declares that it is no use to him in his hunger. This fable is directed, Phaedrus concludes, at "people who fail to appreciate my work."

The five books of *Fables* were apparently composed over the course of Phaedrus's life. In the last fable of Book 5, "The Old Dog and the Hunter," he depicts himself as the old dog scolded by his master because he can no longer perform the same services he could in his youth. "It's strength, not spirit, that's deserted me," the dog says in his defense and implores his master to "give me credit for what I was." Some later collections contain appendices of additional fables attributed to Phaedrus, such as the 15th-century translation of Nicholas Perotti, but these are often thought to be later, anonymous additions.

The later Roman fabulists Avianus and Pilpay borrowed from Phaedrus, and he was read frequently in the MIDDLE AGES. The genre of the beast fable influenced medieval poems like the *ROMAN DE RENART* and authors such as DANTE. The French writers MARIE DE FRANCE and Jean de La Fontaine are known for their collections of fables. Christopher Smart composed a rhyming translation of Phaedrus in 1765 as a text meant for instruction of young readers. Phaedrus's work was often a teaching text in English schools during the 18th century, when he was classified as one of the great classical authors along with Horace, VIRGIL, and OVID. He is much less familiar to modern readers, who tend to confuse Phaedrus the fabulist with Phaedrus the Greek philosopher of the fifth century B.C.

Despite the dark view of the animal world in the *Fables*, scholar Anne Becher notes that Phaedrus is important because he "speaks for the oppressed and is concerned about the abuse of power and the exploitation of the poor and weak." He can be legitimately remembered as the first proletarian poet and satirist. In choosing the fable as his genre, Phaedrus chose to transmit and contribute to source material that was already ancient by the time of Aesop but continued to be relevant across cultures. Certain subjects and themes of the original Greek fables have analogues in the Arabic "Fables of Bidpai," translated by Symeon Seth in 1080, and in the fables of the Indian *PANCHATANTRA* and the Buddhist JATAKA.

English Versions of Works by Phaedrus

The Fables of Phaedrus. Translated by P. F. Widdows. Austin: University of Texas Press, 1992.

The Poetical Works of Christopher Smart: A Poetical Translation of the Fables of Phaedrus, Vol 6. Edited by Karina Williamson. Oxford: Clarendon Press, 1996.

Works about Phaedrus

Henderson, John. *Telling Tales on Caesar: Roman Stories from Phaedrus.* New York: Oxford University Press, 2001.

Perry, Ben Edwin. *Babrius and Phaedrus.* Cambridge, Mass.: Harvard University Press, 1965.

Pindar (ca. 522–ca. 438 B.C.) *lyric poet*

The man considered the greatest of the Greek lyric poets was a native of Cynoscephalae, a town just outside of Thebes in the region of Boeotia. Pindar was born into an aristocratic family at a time when the noble class in Greece was waning; his parents were Daïphantus and Cleodicê. He considered himself Theban and took pride in the land of his birth and the aristocratic ideal. His uncle Scopelînus taught Pindar how to play the flute, an instrument that was a vital element in the worship of Apollo, the god of poetry, music, and the sun.

Pindar studied lyrical composition in Athens, where he may have met the tragedian AESCHYLUS. When he returned to Thebes, he embarked upon his career, counting among his patrons a number of prominent Greek families and political leaders who commissioned him to write odes. His earliest works flouted literary tradition by failing to make use of myths. The noted Boeotian poetess Corinna reportedly called attention to this deficiency. Pindar's next offering teemed with mythological references, whereupon Corinna is said to have admonished him, "One must sow with the hand and not with the whole sack."

Of Pindar's 17 existing works, only the odes composed to celebrate a victory at one of the Panhellenic festivals (the precursor to the modern-day Olympic Games) survive in substantially complete form. These are the Olympian, Pythian, Nemean, and Isthmian Odes, and collectively they are known as the Epinician (or Victory) Odes. These choral poems solemnly compare the victor of the athletic contest to the legendary and mythic figures from the glorious days of yore. The competition itself becomes a device for providing metaphors and similes for achievement and valor. The odes laud the champion's family, ancestors, and homeland, and recount legends originating in his place of birth.

The longest of all of Pindar's odes is *Pythian IV,* which was commissioned by an aristocrat by the name of Dâmophilus, who had been banished to Thebes from the kingdom of Battus IV of Cyrene, in modern Libya. The king's son, Arcesilas, prevailed in the chariot races in the Pythian games of 462 B.C., and Dâmophilus sought to appease Battus with an extravagant lyric tribute penned by Pindar and performed in the palace at Cyrene:

> Thou must stand, my Muse! to-day in the
>   presence of . . .
> the king of Cyrene with its noble steeds, that
>   so,
> beside Arcesilas, while he celebrateth his
>   triumph,
> thou mayest swell the gale of song. . . .

To suggest the idea of reconciliation between Dâmophilus and the king of Cyrene, Pindar quotes HOMER: "A good messenger bringeth highest honor to every business." The song praises Dâmophilus's "righteous heart" and his exemplary life; the exile wants nothing more than to play his harp once again by Apollo's fountain at Cyrene. An attempt to flatter the king is made when the poet compares him with the sovereign among gods: Even Zeus forgave the Titans.

Characteristic features and themes of Pindar's works include the use of myth, heroic legends, reverence for deities, the repetition of important words, and a recurring format: prelude, beginning, transition, midpoint (during which the ancient myth is narrated), transition, and conclusion. His framework, now called a Pindaric ode, includes three parts: a strophe (the part of an ancient Greek choral ode sung by the chorus when moving from right to left); an antistrophe (the part of the choral ode in which the chorus sings its answer to the strophe while moving from left to right); and the epode (the part of the choral ode that follows, as a rule, the strophe and antistrophe). This framework was admired by the Roman HORACE and the English John Dryden, Alexander Pope, and Thomas Gray.

The architectural perfection of Pindar's odes and his bold use of metaphors led PAUSANIAS, a Greek traveler and geographer of the second century, to comment:

> . . . [B]ees flew to him, and placed honey on his lips. Such was the beginning of his career of song. When his fame was spread abroad from one end of Greece to the other, the Pythian priestess . . . bade the Delphians give to Pindar an equal share of all the first-fruits they offered to Apollo.

English Versions of Works by Pindar

The Odes of Pindar. Translated by Sir John Sandys. Cambridge, Mass.: Harvard University Press, 1957.

Pindar: Olympian Odes, Pythian Odes. Edited and translated by William H. Race. Cambridge, Mass.: Harvard University Press, 1997.

Pindar's Victory Songs. Translated by Frank J. Nisetich. Baltimore, Md.: Johns Hopkins University Press, 1980.

Works about Pindar

Hamilton, John T. *Soliciting Darkness: Pindar, Obscurity, and the Classical Tradition.* Cambridge, Mass.: Harvard University Press, 2004.

MacKie, Hillary Susan. *Graceful Errors: Pindar and the Performance of Praise.* Ann Arbor: University of Michigan Press, 2003.

Segal, Charles. *Pindar's Mythmaking: The Fourth Pythian Ode.* Princeton, N.J.: Princeton University Press, 1986.

Plato   (ca. 428–ca. 348 B.C.)   *philosopher*

Plato's family was aristocratic and claimed great distinction. His paternal ancestry reportedly goes back to the old Athenian kings, and his mother counted among her forbears Solon, an influential statesman who is considered the father of Athenian democracy.

The future philosopher was born during the age of Pericles, a political leader and champion of Athenian democracy. Under Pericles, the world's first great democratic system flourished, and potentially contentious subjects like religion, philosophy, morality, and affairs of state were discussed freely. Early on, Plato aspired to the legislative and social pursuits in which a young man of his class was expected to engage.

Plato may have become acquainted with SOCRATES in his childhood, for the great philosopher was friendly with some members of the youngster's extended family. What is certain is that during his late teens and early 20s, Plato was among Socrates' ardent pupils, and his experiences during this time would become the subject matter of Plato's future writings.

Athens was defeated by Sparta in the Peloponnesian War in the early 400s B.C., and Plato was repelled by the tyranny and injustice that followed. After Socrates' conviction for impiety and execution in 399 B.C., Plato became embittered and left his homeland. The works he wrote soon after are, like nearly all of his writings, written in dialogue and feature Socrates as the consummate seeker of truth.

The so-called Socratic Method employed in Plato's dialogues has the great thinker and teacher feigning ignorance of critical ethical and social issues, such as the nature of justice, whether virtue can be taught, and the best form of government. Although Socrates resembles the historical personage, he is primarily a vehicle by which Plato expresses his own intellectual interests and processes. As such, Socrates asks a group of listeners a series of pointed questions. After listening to their answers, Socrates demonstrates their illogical thinking and erroneous conclusions. As the conversations persist, the players begin to contradict themselves, and they become hesitant. By the end of these discourses, the value of independent thinking and the unrelenting pursuit of truth have been brought to light.

In other discourses, the dialogues often end inconclusively since, according to Plato, the purpose of reason—a faculty that only humans possess—is to strive toward definition with disciplined thinking and to illuminate the natural world, not to limit its possibilities. This philosophy can be seen in some of the works Plato produced during his years of self-imposed exile and travel: *Lysis,* which asks, "What is friendship?"; *Euthyphro* ("What is piety?"); *Charmides* ("What is temperance?"); and *Theatetus* ("What is knowledge?").

In the 380s B.C., Plato returned to Athens to establish the school that would become known as the Academy, which emphasized pure research and discourse on the topics of mathematics, astronomical disciplines, government, natural sciences, and rhetoric. Plato spent two decades of his life as an educator and director of the Academy. It was most likely during this time that he produced the bulk of his 29 treatises. Among these were *The Symposium,* which takes place at a banquet whose guests, including Plato's friend ARISTOPHANES, attempt to define love; *The Republic,* Plato's magnum opus; and *Phaedo,* purportedly an account of the exchange between Socrates and his followers and friends on the eve of his execution. (In reality, due to illness, Plato was not among Socrates' visitors.) During the exchange, Socrates explains that the philosopher should not fear death, as he does not, because only without the burden of corporeal form can the eternal soul come to know the pure truth and splendor that mortal beings seek during their existence on earth.

In the late 360s B.C., Plato twice visited Dionysius II, the "tyrant of Syracuse," to put to the test his theories regarding the education of philosopher-kings as described in *The Republic,* and to persuade the ruler to implement a platonic government. Plato's ambitions were not realized, and he returned to the Academy, where he remained until his death.

Critical Analysis

Contained in 10 books, *The Republic* is Plato's longest finished work; Professor Allan Bloom's seminal translation runs 300 pages long. Appearing initially to be an inquiry into the nature of justice, the discourse soon turns toward an attempt to define and describe a "just man" and a "just city." Ultimately, the soul of the just man is shown to be a microcosm of the operations of a just state.

Early in the dialog, Socrates and his interlocutors deduce how a city comes about:

> [It] comes into being because each of us isn't self-sufficient but is in need of much. . . . So, then, when one man takes on another for one need and another for another need, and, since many things are needed, many men gather in one settlement as partners and helpers, to this common settlement we give the name city, don't we?
>
> (II.369b–c)

In essence, Plato is saying that no one can provide entirely for himself; a city needs farmers, house builders, weavers, shoemakers, carpenters, herdsmen, merchants, and laborers. But life would be bleak without luxuries such as olives, furniture, perfumes, embroidery, and ivory. Therefore many more people are needed, including poets, servants, beauticians, and chefs.

The dramatis personae agree with Socrates that "each of us is naturally not quite like anyone else, but rather differs in his nature; different men are apt for the accomplishment of different jobs" (II.370a–b). They also agree that it is appropriate for one person to practice one art rather than many arts.

The philosophical discussion of *The Republic* then leads the characters to deduce that the existence of valuables in the city will lead to crime, which in turn creates a need for military forces. The "origin of war," says Socrates, lies "in those things whose presence in cities most of all produces evils both private and public" (II.373e). The characters' final conclusion regarding the formation of a just city is that there should be three classes: the merchants or money-makers, the armed forces or auxiliary, and the ruling class.

The discussion then turns to the question of who should rule. Ultimately, they determine that thinkers should become the rulers-philosopher-kings because they themselves are governed by reason and harmony. Furthermore, precisely because the true philosopher has no worldly ambitions—in fact, he "despises political offices" (VII.521b)—he cannot be corrupted or made to impose his rule on a reluctant populace. "Unless," Socrates asserts, "philosophers rule as kings or those now called kings and chiefs genuinely and adequately philosophize, and political power and philosophy coincide in the same place . . . there is no rest from ills for the cities . . . nor I think for human kind, nor will the regime we have now described in speech ever come forth from nature, insofar as possible, and see the light of the sun" (V.473c–d).

Plato employs sunshine as a symbol of enlightenment in another important part of *The Republic,* when Socrates presents the famous "Allegory of the Cave" (Book VII). The benighted, Socrates says, are shackled in cavernous hollows of ignorance and believe the shadows cast on the cave walls represent reality, when they are, in fact, merely illusions. The light of day represents a cosmos of perfect being, where the universal ideals—the Forms—exist. Here, there are ideals not only for concrete items, like "chair," but also abstractions like "circle" and "good."

Most individuals do not "see the light," nor do they realize that there is an alternative to their shadowy netherworld or that what they perceive as reality is a mere approximation of the ideal (or Platonic) Form. These representations merely refer to the Form; they do not duplicate it.

The Republic, wrote critic David Denby, is

the single most widely read work of philosophy in the West, and for immediately obvious reasons. Plato, an entrancing writer, had perfected the form of a dialogue, with its gracefully sinuous plait of questions and answers, its antici-

pation of the readers' objections, its courtesies that are really a form of sly mockery.

Within a framework of spirited debate, Plato addresses the most profound questions of human existence that remain relevant to this day. His influence on Western thought over thousands of years is immeasurable and cannot be overstated. As the English philosopher Alfred North Whitehead says, "all philosophy is a set of footnotes to Plato."

English Versions of Works by Plato

The Complete Works of Plato. Edited by John M. Cooper and D. S. Hutchinson. Indianapolis, Ind.: Hackett Publishing, 1997.
Phaedo. Translated by G. M. A. Grube. Indianapolis: Hackett Publishing Company, Inc., 1976.
The Republic of Plato. Translated by Allan Bloom. New York: HarperCollins, 1991.

Works about Plato

Brann, Eva. *The Music of the Republic: Essays on Socrates' Conversations and Plato's Writings.* Philadelphia: Dry, Paul Books, 2004.
Dickinson, G. Lowes. *Plato and His Dialogues.* La Vergne, Tenn.: University Press of the Pacific/ Ingram Book Group, 2003.
Heidegger, Martin. *Essence of Truth: On Plato's Parable of the Cave and the Theaetetus.* Translated by Ted Sadler. London: Continuum International Publishing, 2002.
Johansen, Thomas. *Plato's Natural Philosophy: A Study of the Timaeus-Critias.* Cambridge, Mass.: Cambridge University Press, 2004.
Kunkel, John H. *Winged Soul: Plato's Autobiography.* Philadelphia: Xlibris, 2003.
Michelini, Ann N., ed. *Plato as Author: The Rhetoric of Philosophy.* Leiden, Netherlands: Brill Aca-demic Publishers, 2003.

Plautus, Titus Maccius (254–184 B.C.)
playwright

From the beginning of his life in the tiny mountain village of Sarsina, Titus Maccius Plautus was called just Plautus, which means "flatfoot." Because he was not a Roman citizen, Plautus was not entitled to a full name. Driven by his love for theater and adventure, as a boy he left his native village by joining a traveling theatrical troupe. He later tried various other jobs, at one point becoming a soldier for the Roman Empire.

During his military service, Plautus was introduced to the concept of Greek theater, specifically Greek New Comedy and the plays of MENANDER. After leaving the service, he supported himself by working around the Roman stages as a carpenter or mechanic; opening his own business, which failed; and becoming a miller, cruising the streets with his hand-mill.

Fascinated by the theater, Plautus soon tried his own hand at writing. He wrote his earliest plays, *Addictus* and *Saturio,* while working as a miller, and it was not long before his work made him the Roman Empire's best-known playwright. He won instant popularity partly because his plays appealed to the tastes of the uneducated public, which cared only for the entertainment and not for the contemplation of serious political issues. Knowing that he had to keep his audience interested—an audience that was accustomed to bear baiting and gladiator fighting—Plautus purposely engaged the common public's appreciation for the vulgar and ignored the manners and language of the aristocracy. His works are therefore a valuable documentation of the live, vivacious, conversational vernacular Latin of the third and second centuries B.C.

Despite the crudity of words and idiomatic expressions that populate Plautus's plays, his plots, characters, and settings reveal the markings of great literature. He generously employs puns, alliterations, and plays on words, most of which cannot be effectively reproduced in translation. On the other hand, translations of his rich metaphors (some taken from military operations), descriptions of business transactions, and portrayals of the trades of artisans reveal the clarity of a well-rounded literary and social thinker.

Plautus composed approximately 130 pieces, 21 of which survive to this day. The play considered his

masterpiece is *Captives.* The German playwright and critic Gotthold Lessing once described it as "the best constructed drama in existence." Other significant works include *Menaechmi* (The Twin Brothers), his first comedy to be translated into English; and *Miles Gloriosus* (The Braggart Soldier), another comedy in which Plautus created the archetype of a swaggering soldier, which, in turn, became very popular in Renaissance literature.

Due to his outstanding achievements, Plautus was eventually granted citizenship and given permission to assume a full name. Among the names he chose for himself was Maccius, which means "clown," revealing his penchant for humor.

What is perhaps most remarkable about Plautus's works is that they represent a clear exception to the didactic and moral characteristics of most Roman literature of his time. Between the uniqueness of his comedy and the clarity of the elements of his drama, it is no wonder that Plautus's plays influenced a number of later writers. Molière and Dryden imitated his *Amphitryo.* From *Aulularia,* Molière borrowed the subject for his own *Miser,* and Shakespeare's *The Comedy of Errors* is adapted from Plautus's *Menaechmi.* Today his plays are studied by students and critics alike and performed on stages across the globe, attesting to a timeless appreciation for Plautus's work, and especially his comedies.

English Versions of Works by Plautus

Four Comedies. Translated by Erich Segal. New York: Oxford University Press, 1996.

Plautus: Amphitruo. Edited by David M. Christenson. Cambridge, U.K.: Cambridge University Press, 2000.

Works about Plautus

Moore, Timothy J. *The Theater of Plautus: Playing to the Audience.* Austin: University of Texas Press, 1998.

Riehle, Wolfgang. *Shakespeare, Plautus and the Humanist Tradition.* Rochester, N.Y.: Boydell & Brewer, 1991.

Segal, Erich. *Roman Laughter: The Comedy of Plautus.* Oxford: Oxford University Press, 1987.

Pliny the Elder (Gaius Plinius Secundus)
(23–79) *historian, nonfiction writer*
Gaius Plinius Secundus, known in English as Pliny the Elder, was born in Como, Italy, to parents of the equestrian class, which meant wealth and position in the world of ancient Rome. As a youth he studied rhetoric, the art of speaking in public, and also traveled. At age 23 he joined the military and was made tribune, a common entry point for sons of the equestrian or senatorial classes. He worked his way up to a cavalry unit and was stationed in present-day Germany.

During his years of service on the Rhine, Pliny wrote a short treatise, now lost, on spear-throwing from horseback, based on his observations of the Germanic tribes. He followed this work with a biography of his teacher and military commander, Publius Pomponius Secundus. After a brief visit to Rome in 52, he returned to Germany and began his 20-volume *History of the Germanic Wars.* This work, also lost, had an immense impact on his fellow historians; TACITUS and Suetonius quote Pliny a great deal.

Returning again to Rome in 59, Pliny withdrew from the military to practice law and turn his attention to writing. His next works were not considered particularly original or inspiring. *The Scholar,* for example, was a training manual for orators and rhetoricians, and its advice would be surpassed in both substance and style by QUINTILIAN. The eight-volume *Problems in Grammar* was perhaps the only subject Pliny could find to write about that would not incur the wrath of the capricious Emperor Nero. His *Continuation of the History of Aufidius Bassas* updated events at Rome from the late 40s to his own time. None of these works, unfortunately, have survived to the present time.

In 69, after a succession of emperors, Pliny returned to favor under Vespasian, with whom he was previously acquainted. He served as procurator in a series of provinces and was then made prefect of the Roman navy stationed at Misenum, in the Bay of Naples. He was killed while attempting to evacuate people from Pompeii when Vesuvius erupted on August 24, 79. His nephew, PLINY THE YOUNGER, wrote in one of his letters:

> The fortunate man, in my opinion, is he to whom the gods have granted the power either to do something which is worth recording or to write what is worth reading, and most fortunate of all is he who can do both. Such a man was my uncle.

By the time of his death, Pliny had published 75 books and left behind 160 volumes of unpublished work. His crowning literary achievement, the only one that survives, was the encyclopedic *Historia naturalis,* or *Natural History,* consisting of 37 books, published in 77. In these volumes, Pliny deals with the entirety of creation, from cosmology to anthropology, geography to biology, as well as horticulture and agriculture, medicine, magic, and the properties of metal and stone. In fact the work covers all things natural and in addition contains frequent accounts of human inventions and institutions. The work reflects Pliny's systematic mind, his immense curiosity, and his tireless working habits. The younger Pliny said of him: "He had a keen attention, incredible devotion to study, and a remarkable capacity for dispensing with sleep." It was said that he even dictated notes to his secretary while in the bath.

The *Natural History* freely mixes fact with fiction, since the author, though a Stoic like most educated men of his day, possessed a great love of the curious. The *Natural History* was frequently read and relied on during the MIDDLE AGES, when some of its more peculiar notations were taken as literal fact—for instance, when Pliny describes certain peoples of the East as having ears that they can tie around their heads or heads set directly upon shoulders, with no neck at all. To the modern reader the work may often appear simply quaint, as, for example, when Pliny speculates that people in Ethiopia grow tall due to their country's climate, because "the juice is called away into the upper portions of the body by the nature of heat." In other places he flatly contradicts current knowledge—for instance, when he declares that the earth is clearly the center of the universe.

The *Natural History* is still valuable as an anthropological document reflecting the world of the first century as Pliny knew it, and his process of direct observation remains a foundational method for conducting scientific research.

An English Version of a Work by Pliny the Elder
Natural History: A Selection. Translated by John F. Healy. New York: Penguin Books, 1991.

Works about Pliny the Elder
Beagon, Mary. *Roman Nature: The Thought of Pliny the Elder.* Oxford, U.K.: Clarendon Press, 1992.
Healy, John F. *Pliny the Elder on Science and Technology.* Oxford, U.K.: Oxford University Press, 2000.

Pliny the Younger (Gaius Plinius Caecilius Secundus) (ca. 61–ca. 112)
lawyer, orator, letter writer, poet
By the first century, after hundreds of years of bitter warfare, Rome had established uncontested dominance through the entire Mediterranean region. All independent powers had bowed to the might of the Roman legions, and no sovereign state remained to challenge Rome's supremacy. At the same time, after a series of civil wars, the republican form of government had been overthrown, and Rome had become an empire. Though the imperial government was autocratic, it brought political and social stability to the Mediterranean region for centuries. This period is now known as the *Pax Romana,* or "Roman Peace," the stability of which allowed literature and art to flourish. One of the best-known and most influential literary figures of this time was Pliny the Younger.

Born in the Roman city of Novum Comum, Pliny was the nephew and adopted son of the fa-

mous Roman writer, soldier, and statesman, PLINY THE ELDER. His uncle moved him to Rome to ensure that he received an excellent education and the opportunity to enter the legal profession, which Roman society considered very honorable.

In 79, Pliny the Younger witnessed the famous eruption of Mount Vesuvius and the destruction of the cities of Pompeii and Herculaneum, having gone there with his uncle, the commander of the fleet that was sent to help the citizens evacuate. Pliny the Elder was killed during the evacuation, and Pliny the Younger wrote an account of the entire event in a letter to the Roman historian TACITUS. The letter has been preserved and provides the best firsthand information concerning what happened at Mount Vesuvius.

Pliny eventually became a lawyer in Rome, arguing his first case when he was only 19. He made excellent connections with important people in Roman society and before long embarked on a prosperous career within the imperial administration. He served three different emperors—Domitian, Nerva, and Trajan—working in military, judicial, and administrative capacities, as well as sitting as a member of the Senate. He was clearly efficient as a civil servant, and his contributions were highly valued, as evidenced by the numerous letters that he exchanged with Emperor Trajan.

In the year 100, Trajan made Pliny a consul, the highest position in the Roman government besides emperor. To express his thanks, Pliny made a famous speech on the floor of the Senate to thank Trajan for the honor bestowed upon him, an oration that has become known as the *Panegyricus Trajani.* In this speech, Pliny praises Trajan's qualities and compares him favorably to other emperors. Although it was an unabashed eulogy of Trajan, the content of this speech provides historians with important information about the early events of Trajan's reign. As an orator, Pliny was greatly influenced by CICERO, an earlier Roman orator whom he greatly admired and tried to emulate.

In 114, not long after assuming a position in the Roman province of Bithynia, Pliny the Younger died. His public career had been uneventful, but he was universally respected for the sobriety of his private life and his compassion as a magistrate.

Critical Analysis

Pliny the Younger's fame rests on his correspondence. Despite the demands of his duties in the imperial government, he found time to devote himself to a life of literature and letters. Although much of what he wrote has been lost, including most of his poetry, 247 of his letters survive in a collection known simply as *Letters*. This work is accessible to modern readers and provides a priceless account of what life was like among the upper classes during the time of the *Pax Romana*.

During Pliny's time, letter writing was a crucially important skill. Not only personal matters but also affairs of state and government had to be communicated entirely by letter. This was particularly true of the Romans, who had the burdens of communicating across a vast empire and dealing with a variety of administrative and military matters.

In addition to official administrative matters, the subjects covered in Pliny's letter are numerous. He discusses everything from Roman literary life and his own intellectual interests to the weather conditions in the place from which he is writing. The letters also provide a fascinating glimpse into the personality of Pliny himself, revealing a man of both kindness and vanity.

Scholars have organized the *Letters* into 10 different books, although each was likely intended as an entirely independent piece. In addition to simple communications between friends, Pliny clearly intended his letters to be presented for publication, which he states in the first letter of the first book.

Two letters in particular have become famous. The first is the one addressed to Tacitus in which Pliny describes the eruption of Mount Vesuvius and the death of his uncle. The second letter, addressed to Emperor Trajan, was written when Pliny was governor of the province of Bithynia and concerns the persecution of the Christians.

This second letter is significant because it sheds considerable light on the Romans' general attitude toward Christians during the early days of Christianity. In it, Pliny writes to Trajan requesting guidance on how he should deal with Christians brought to him for trial, pointing out that he has never presided over such a trial before. He states that he executes those who admit to being Christians and refuse to recant, but he lets go those Christians who do recant their faith. He also states that he has received anonymous accusations against a number of people, charging them with being Christians, but most of these prove to be harmless. This letter to Trajan is interesting to historians for its firsthand account of the persecutions of Christians.

Other letters deal with mundane matters. In one letter to Tacitus, he describes his own surprise at killing three boars while on a hunt, even though his personal preference is to study rather than hunt. In another letter to his friend Sura, he describes ghost stories he has heard. Such letters offer a fascinating record of Roman life at the time, making them invaluable historical documents.

English Versions of Works by Pliny the Younger

Letters of the Younger Pliny. Translated by Betty Radice. New York: Penguin Classics, 1990.

The Letters of the Younger Pliny: First Series, Vol. 1. Available online. URL: IndyPublish.com. Accessed 2002.

Works about Pliny the Younger

Bell, Albert A., Jr. *All Roads Lead to Murder: A Case from the Notebooks of Pliny the Younger*. Boone, N.C.: High Country Publishers, 2002.

Gamberini, Federico. *Stylistic Theory and Practice in the Younger Pliny*. Hildesheim, Germany: Georg Olms Publishers, 1983.

Hoffer, Stanley E. *Anxieties of Pliny the Younger*. Oxford: Oxford University Press, 1999.

Plotinus (205–270) *philosopher*

All that is known of Plotinus comes from the *Life of Plotinus* composed by his student PORPHYRY, who published the biography as a preface to his collected treatises about 30 years after the philosopher's death. His arrangement of Plotinus's writing into six sets of nine tracts each, ordered by subject and named the *Enneads* (which means 'nines' in Greek), remains the sole means by which the ideas of Plotinus have survived.

Plotinus was born in Lycopolis in Upper Egypt, and at age 28 he began to study philosophy at Alexandria under Ammonius Saccas. Wishing to study Persian and Indian philosophy, he joined the military expedition of Emperor Gordian III to the East in 243. After Gordian was murdered in Mesopotamia, Plotinus fled to Antioch and, in 244, made his way to Rome, where he began to teach. Ten years later, at 50, he began to write.

Plotinus's pupils included doctors, politicians, literary men, and women. His method of teaching consisted of conversation; sessions would begin with a reading of a commentary on PLATO or ARISTOTLE and proceed to a debate of certain points of philosophy. Though he had no political aspirations of his own and believed philosophers should not be involved in reform of the state, Plotinus did ask permission from his friends, the Emperor Gallienus and Empress Salonina, to establish a city called Platonopolis. He envisioned a community founded entirely on the ideals of Plato. However, too many people opposed the plan for it to become feasible. In 269 an illness, probably leprosy, forced him to retire to the country estate of one of his pupils, where he died the next year.

The scholar Dominic O'Meara correctly notes that "many paths lead back to Plotinus." Plotinus and his successors, known as the Neoplatonists, continued their teachings during late antiquity in the great schools of philosophy in Syria, Athens, and Alexandria, which in their turn shaped the philosophical foundations underlying the Islamic, Byzantine, and Western worlds of the MIDDLE AGES, Renaissance, and Enlightenment.

Plotinus's main achievement was a systematized worldview in which he ordered and defined important metaphysical concepts. For him, philosophy was a religion, a way for the mind to ascend from the material to God. Building on the ideas of Plato, Aristotle, and the Stoics, he conceived of reality as a hierarchy of spiritual powers that all had their source in an infinite and transcendent entity he called the First Principle or the One. The One, he believed, contained and was the source for all being. The next state of being he called the *Nous*, a Greek word roughly meaning Divine Intellect. This was the force that ordered the world, a finite entity comprised of the sum of all living things.

The third state Plotinus called the Soul of the World, and he described it in two parts, the first consisting of intelligence and reason, and the second consisting of material being or nature. For Plotinus, evil and imperfection existed only in the state of matter, and the material could be transcended through contemplation. Contemplation, which turned away from the material or external and focused on the inner soul or true self, was the way an individual could unite with the Universal Soul and, from there, the *Nous*. The purpose of existence was to strive for moral and intellectual perfection, which would ultimately bring the soul closer to the First Principle or the One, the source of all life. Evil and suffering, though a necessary part of the plan, were caused by a selfish attachment to the body and could be conquered through moral goodness, discipline, and wisdom.

Plotinus revived and popularized the ideas of Plato and Aristotle in the Latin world and became the chief exponent of Neoplatonism. He influenced the Byzantine scholar Michael Psellus, and Arabic translations of the *Enneads*, particularly the "Theology of Aristotle," circulated in the medieval Islamic world. He also influenced Christian theologians, such as Gregory of Nyssa, AMBROSE, and AUGUSTINE, and the medieval philosophers BOETHIUS and Macrobius. Translator H. A. Armstrong calls him "metaphysician and mystic, a hard and honest thinker who enjoyed intense spiritual experience and could describe it in the language of a great poet." His ideas have contributed to philosophy, art, literature, and religious thought.

See also PLUTARCH.

An English Version of a Work by Plotinus

The Enneads. Translated by Stephen MacKenna. Edited by John Dillon. New York: Penguin Books, 1991.

Works about Plotinus

Hadot, Pierre. *Plotinus or the Simplicity of Vision.* Translated by Michael Chase. Chicago: University of Chicago Press, 1998.

Miles, Margaret Ruth. *Plotinus on Body and Beauty: Society, Philosophy, and Religion in Third-Century Rome.* Oxford, U.K.: Blackwell Publishers, 1999.

Plutarch (ca. 50–ca. 125) *biographer, essayist, philosopher*

Plutarch was born in the city of Chaeronea, in the ancient Greek district of Boeotia, where his family had long been established. He studied in Athens under Ammonius, traveled to Rome, and became equally at home in both cultures. He was extraordinarily erudite and particularly knowledgeable in the areas of literature, contemporary history, and PLATO's philosophy. Plutarch married, fathered five children, and spent much of his life in Chaeronea, where he involved himself in community activities and served in public office.

Plutarch's range of experience and scholarship allowed him to pursue a variety of careers: as Delphic priest, lecturer, archon, and influential leader in the literary and intellectual circles of the court of the Roman emperor Trajan. During Trajan's reign (98–117), Plutarch produced his masterpiece, *Parallel Lives.* This set of biographies of famous Greeks and Romans reflects the sensibilities of his age, putting Roman traditions and achievements on a level with Greece's glory-filled history. It was the belief at the time that studying the individual accomplishments and mistakes of histori-

cal persons was a character-building pursuit. Plutarch, a moralist and ethicist after the fashion of ARISTOTLE, wrote to improve the moral fiber of his audience.

Parallel Lives reveals Plutarch's pride in the heritage of Greek thought and classic ideals, his profound admiration for Roman civilization, and his attempt to reconcile the two. The treatise offers 23 pairs of biographies. The portrait of a Greek statesman or military leader is presented first, and the life story of his Roman counterpart follows for purposes of comparison. Plutarch creates both inner and spoken dialogue, stages dramatic scenes, and narrates anecdotes to depict his subjects as men of honor, principle, and integrity. His protagonists are at turns dutiful and self-important, outraged and triumphant, generous and petty, autocratic and heroic, and censured and rewarded.

One of the finest and most appropriate pairings within *Parallel Lives* is that of DEMOSTHENES, the Greek orator, and CICERO, the Roman orator. Demosthenes' oration shows "thoughtfulness, austerity, and grave earnestness" displayed by his morose countenance and anxious aspect. On the other hand, Cicero is "disposed to mirth and pleasantry," and his "love of mockery often [runs] him into scurrility; and in his love of laughing away serious arguments in judicial cases by jests and facetious remarks . . . he [pays] too little regard to what [is] decent."

Another of Plutarch's important works is the series of essays on moral philosophy called the *Moralia.* The topics of these more-than-70 essays range from education, religion, and literary criticism to psychology, politics, and matters of etiquette. Jacques Amyot's French translations of the *Lives* (1559) and *Moral Essays* (1572) made Plutarch available to such thinkers and artists as Rabelais, Montaigne, Racine, and Molière.

Translated into English by Philemon Holland in 1603, the *Lives* provided fertile ground for English playwrights, including Ben Jonson and William Shakespeare. Shakespeare, in particular, borrowed from Plutarch's writings and used the Greeks' analysis of human behavior to embellish the action and characters of his history plays, including *Julius CAESAR*. Later, John Dryden was inspired to write *Life of Plutarch* (1683), in which he analyzes the structure and style of *Parallel Lives*. The *Moral Essays* influenced English poets and thinkers like John Lyly, George Chapman, Jeremy Taylor, and John Milton.

Plutarch's reputation has varied over the ages, since his historical approach was somewhat unreliable and his facts often inaccurate. However, his purpose was edification and instruction, and his works reflect a vigorous mind. His *Lives* in particular provided models for biographers to follow. As a moralist, he addresses questions of enduring concern, and as literature his works provide an enduring fascination.

English Versions of Works by Plutarch

Essays. Edited by Ian Kidd. New York: Penguin Classics, 1993.

The Life of Alexander the Great. Translated by John Dryden. Introduction by Victor Davis Hanson. New York: Random House, 2004.

Plutarch: The Lives of the Noble Grecians and Romans. Translated by John Dryden. Edited by Arthur Hugh Clough. New York: Random House, 1992.

Works about Plutarch

Barrow, R. H. *Plutarch and His Times.* Bloomington: Indiana University Press, 1967.

Mossman, Judith, ed. *Plutarch and His Intellectual World.* London: Duckworth, 1997.

Pelling, Christopher B. *Plutarch and History.* Cardiff: The Classical Press of Wales, 2002.

Po Chü-i

See BAI JUYI.

poetry

See BARDIC POETRY; NAHUATL POETRY, ANCIENT; OLD ENGLISH POETRY; *PURANA*; TANKA; TROUBADOURS; ZUNI NARRATIVE POETRY; *and titles of specific works.*

Polo, Marco (1254–1324) *traveler, writer*

Marco Polo's account of his experiences in Asia shaped the western European vision of the East. He was born to a merchant family in Venice, and his uncle and father owned a trading house in Soldaia, a Crimean port on the Black Sea.

According to Polo, during their travels to the East, his father and uncle had met the Great Khan and promised to return to his court with Christian missionaries. After returning to Venice in 1271, the pair reunited with the 17-year-old Marco and then, with him, headed back to China. They traveled from Acre through Jerusalem, overland through Armenia and Persia (now Iran) to Central Asia, across the Pamir mountains, along the Takla Makan Desert in Western China, through the Gobi Desert and finally reached the summer court of Kubla Khan in Shangdu, which was about 200 miles north of modern Beijing. They arrived in 1275 and stayed there for the next 17 years.

During this period, Polo claims that Kubla Khan was so impressed with his intelligence and diligence that he appointed him to diplomatic missions that took him to southern China and northern Burma (now Myanmar). Polo also claims that he was governor of Yangzhou, a large commercial city, but this has not been confirmed by scholars.

The Polo family finally had an opportunity to return home when they were appointed to escort a Mongol princess en route to Persia to get married. This time they went by sea, setting off from the southern Chinese port city of Quanzhou in 1292 and traveling to Sumatra, Ceylon (now Sri Lanka), southern India, and through the Persian Gulf. After leaving the princess in Persia, the Polos traveled on land through Turkey, where they sailed from Constantinople (now Istanbul) to Venice in 1295.

After being captured in a sea battle in 1296, Marco Polo was imprisoned in Genoa. There he met a Pisan romance writer named Rustichello, who collaborated with him on his only book, *Il milione* (called variously *The Description of the World; The Book of Marvels; The Book of Marco Polo;* and, most commonly, *The Travels of Marco Polo*).

Polo was released from prison in 1298 and returned to Venice in 1299, where he married and ran several businesses. He became famous in Venice for telling stories of his travels, despite the fact that some people questioned the validity of his tales. When he lay dying on January 8, his friends and relatives begged him to recant his stories, but he insisted that he had not told half of what he had seen. Marco Polo was buried in the church of San Lorenzo in Venice.

Critical Analysis

The Travels of Marco Polo poses several interesting questions for readers and critics. One is the issue of classification: Is the book a travelogue, a merchant's handbook, an autobiography, or even a fantasy? As a person, Marco Polo does not come alive on the page; the reader cannot define his likes, dislikes, or reactions to his experiences, so his work is generally not considered an autobiography.

Unlike earlier travelogues, Polo does not emphasize the dangers or strangeness of what he encounters. Instead, with minimal comment, he catalogues the religions, appearances, and customs of the people he encounters and focuses more on the general and objective in his descriptions of cities and regions. His emphasis on the varieties of goods and spices found in the various ports throughout his travels have led some scholars to conclude that the book is no more than a guide for the medieval Venetian merchants who dominated trade with the East. However, as John Lerner points out in *Marco Polo and the Discovery of the World,* existing merchant guidebooks do not include the interest in the Mongol Empire's government and court, as well as the spectacular buildings and statues that Polo describes.

Finally, since the 17th century, when enduring contact with China was established by Jesuit missionaries, many readers, critics, and scholars have questioned whether Polo went to China at all. Several scholars, most notably Leonardo Olschki, have pointed out how Polo does not mention any of the same Chinese phenomena that other travelers of the time mention in their books: no Great Wall, no tea, no chopsticks or footbinding. Polo's supporters argue that Polo seems to have spent his years in China as part of the Mongol emperor's court and that his knowledge of customs is based on what he observed there, rather than on native Chinese practices. If, as Lerner theorizes, Marco Polo spent his time in the East as a minor civil servant of the Mongol Empire, then he would have had little contact or interest in native Chinese customs. On the other hand, he is knowledgeable and enthusiastic about the Great Khan's court, describing in detail the protocol for holidays and banquets. For example, the servers who bring the Khan food and drink "are all obliged to cover their noses and mouths with handsome veils or cloths of worked silk, in order that his victuals or his wine may not be affected by their breath."

Some may say that Marco Polo was a precursor of things to come, for behind Christopher Columbus's voyage and his unexpected discovery of the New World lay the marvelous East. While Polo does describe some implausible events, such as the use of eagles in gathering diamonds, his work relies little on stories of mythical beasts and human monsters, as did earlier travelogues and even imitation travelogues, such as the travels of Sir John Mandeville. Polo recorded the flora, fauna, and especially riches of the places he visited and thus helped shape the Far East's image as a fabulous place of bizarre customs and unimaginable wealth. His book also inspired 14th-century cartographers to change their maps and record the geography and cities he had visited. The spices and riches he describes only heightened the curiosity and longing of Europeans to trade with the East.

The Travels of Marco Polo has been translated into many languages from its original Italian. Columbus owned a copy of the work, which has been preserved. The first English translation, by John Frampton, appeared in 1579, followed by a more accurate English version by W. Marsden in the early 19th century and another English version with notes by Sir Henry Yule in 1871. Polo is remembered for his grand tales of adventure as well as the information his work provides on the Mongol culture and customs of the 13th century.

English Versions of a Work by Marco Polo

Travels. New York: Konemann Publishers, 2000.

The Travels of Marco Polo. Edited by Manuel Komroff. New York: Liveright Publishing, 2003.

The Travels of Marco Polo: The Complete Yule-Cordier Edition, Vol. 1. Edited by Henry Yule and Henri Cordier. Mineola, N.Y.: Dover Publications, 1993.

Works about Marco Polo

Feeney, Kathy. *Marco Polo: Explorer of China.* Berkeley Heights, N.J.: Enslow Publishers, 2004.

Larner, John. *Marco Polo and the Discovery of the World.* New Haven, Conn.: Yale University Press, 2001.

Olschki, Leonardo. *Marco Polo's Asia: An Introduction to His "Description of the World" called "Il milione."* Translated by John A. Scott. Berkeley: University of California Press, 1960.

Wood, Frances. *Did Marco Polo Go to China?* London: Secker & Warburg, 1995.

Porphyry (Porphyrius, Malchus) (ca. 232–ca. 303) *philosopher, biographer, editor*

By the third century, Greek philosophy was beginning to lose the creativity and vitality that had nourished it for so long. The rise of Christianity and the country's long subjugation by Rome had eroded Greek intellectual activity. Among the last of the great philosophers was Porphyry, who was a great exponent of the philosophy known as *Neoplatonism.*

Little is known about Porphyry's life. He was from the city of Tyre, on the Mediterranean coast of what is now Lebanon. During his life, the social order of the Roman Empire was beginning to collapse, and barbarian invasions were penetrating the imperial frontiers. In the midst of all this, the Christian Church was growing rapidly, altering both society and intellectual and philosophical thought.

Porphyry came into contact with many of the great intellectuals and philosophers of his day, and was a disciple of PLOTINUS, who largely developed Neoplatonism. It is unknown precisely when the two philosophers met, but they remained companions until 268. Porphyry not only edited Plotinus's works, creating his *Enneads* (ca. 301), but also wrote a biography of his teacher. Another of Porphyry's teachers was the philosopher LONGINUS, and he was also acquainted with the great Christian thinker, Origen.

Based on these influences and his own studies, Porphyry authored many philosophical works, most of which have been lost. Perhaps his most famous work is *Against the Christians* (ca. 270), in which he attempts to show that the ideas of pagan Greek philosophers, such as PLATO and ARISTOTLE, were superior to the new ideas of the Christian Church. Porphyry also wrote *Life of Pythagoras,* a biography of the great philosopher and mathematician; and numerous commentaries on Aristotle's works, including *Eisagoge* (an introduction to Aristotle's *Categories*), which would greatly influence medieval philosophy.

Porphyry was not nearly as important to the development of Neoplatonism as was his teacher, Plotinus, but his contributions were nevertheless significant. Further, it was because of Porphyry that much of the philosophical thinking of Plotinus, PYTHAGORAS, and Aristotle has been preserved.

English Versions of Works by Porphyry

Porphyry's Against the Christians. Translated by Joseph Hauffmann. Buffalo, N.Y.: Prometheus Books, 1994.

Porphyry's Launching-Points to the Realm of the Mind: An Introduction to the Neoplatonic Philosophy of Plotinus. Translated by Kenneth Sylvan Guthrie. Grand Rapids, Mich.: Phanes Press, 1989.

A Work about Porphyry

Smith, Andrew. *Porphyry's Place in the Neoplatonic Tradition: A Study in Postplotinian Neoplatonism.* New York: Kluwer Academic Press, 1975.

Proclus (ca. 410–485) *philosopher*

By the fifth century, Greek philosophy was in decline. The rise of Christianity and the steady collapse of political institutions contributed to this deterioration, and Greece was no longer producing thinkers such as PLATO and ARISTOTLE. The last major movement within pagan Greek philosophy, which took place during this time, was known as Neoplatonism, which had been expounded by the philosophers PLOTINUS and PORPHYRY. Among those who promoted Neoplatonism was Proclus, who was born in Constantinople (now Istanbul) sometime in the early fifth century. Little is known of his life. He lived and worked in the city of Athens, which remained an intellectual center despite the fact that its political and economic importance had long since faded.

Proclus, who became head of the Platonic Academy in Athens, was the author of several works concerning Neoplatonism, including *On Platonic Theology, Elements of Platonic Theology,* and *Commentary on the Timaeus.* In these works, he describes the most important aspect of Neoplatonism as the separation of the body and the mind, through which Proclus and most Neoplatonists believed that people could transcend physical limitations to reach a mystical union with the "One." Christian thinkers later adopted this and other aspects of Neoplatonic philosophy in developing their theology. One such person was the theologian Dionysius the Areopagite (ca. 500), whose *The Celestial Hierarchy* and *The Divine Names* (treatises of mystical and speculative theology) greatly affected the intellectual development of medieval Europe.

Proclus was not as influential as other Greek philosophers. His major achievement was to develop and extend the Neoplatonic theories articulated by Porphyry. Through his work on spreading the philosophy of Neoplatonism through the Greek-speaking world, Proclus contributed to the development of Christian theology.

English Versions of Works by Proclus

Fragments that Remain of the Lost Writings of Proclus. Translated by Thomas Taylor. Whitefish, Mont.: Kessinger Publishing, 2003.

Proclus of Constantinople and the Cult of the Virgin in the Late Antiquity: Homilies 1–5, Texts and Translations. Translated by Nicholas Constas. Leiden, Netherlands: Brill Academic Publishers, 2003.

Works about Proclus

Bos, Egbert P. and P. A. Meijer, eds. *On Proclus and His Influence in Medieval Philosophy.* Leiden, Netherlands: Brill Academic Publishers, 1991.

Edwards, Mark J., trans. *Neoplatonic Saints: The Lives of Plotinus and Proclus by Their Students.* Liverpool, U.K.: Liverpool University Press, 2001.

Siorvanes, Lucas. *Proclus: Neo-Platonic Philosophy and Science.* New Haven, Conn.: Yale University Press, 1996.

Propertius, Sextus (ca. 50–ca. 15 B.C.) *poet*

Sextus Propertius was born in Italy near Assisi, later home to Saint FRANCIS OF ASSISI. His parents belonged to the wealthy equestrian class, and although his family lost properties in the confiscations of 41 B.C., Propertius never needed to pursue a profession to earn his living, nor did he require a patron, as did his contemporaries VIRGIL and HORACE. He established an enduring friendship with the wealthy statesman Maecenas, who was patron to several other artists and who accepted Propertius into his literary circle. Though the precise dates in which his books appeared are not known, one of his elegies is addressed to a woman who died in 16 B.C. OVID, writing the *Remedy for Love* in A.D. 2, implies that Propertius was dead by this time.

Propertius is known for four books of *Elegies,* a total of 92 poems. The fame of these books earned him a place alongside CATULLUS and Ovid in the tradition of classical love poetry. QUINTILIAN considered him second only to Tibullus as an elegiac poet. The elegiac meter had become the accepted form for poetry as early as Mimnermus (ca. 630 B.C.). Though it was also used for martial verse, dirges, and lamentations, it was most widely used for love poems.

Traditionally, the love poets professed enslavement to one woman, an attachment that the 12th-century TROUBADOURS of southern France would imitate and that DANTE would continue in his poems addressed to Beatrice and Petrarch in his sonnets to Laura. Catullus addressed his mistress as Lesbia, Cornelius Gallus wrote to Cytheris, and Tibullus professed devotion to Delia. Propertius's love was a Roman lady whom he named Cynthia.

The first book is completely dominated by Propertius's experience of falling in love with Cynthia; as he declares in the very first poem: "No girl but Cynthia ever caught my eye / or stormed by my heart or felled my passionate pride." These initial poems portray love as an external force that has thoroughly overcome the poet, and, in keeping with tradition, he grows ill with unrequited love. Passionate descriptions of Cynthia's worth and beauty alternate with declarations of despair over her coldness and neglect. The second book also addresses Cynthia. Propertius opens this book by declaring that even if he were gifted enough to write of gods, heroes, and epic battles, he would still write of Cynthia because, he says,

> To die for love is glory; glory also
> to love one only; I would have that joy.

His Cynthia is more constant than Helen, more enchanting than Circe, more beautiful than any of the goddesses.

By his third book, Propertius has widened the scope of his art. The poet's voice here seems more often disenchanted with love and concerned for the things that do last. Mournfully he remarks in the second poem of the third book, "from remembered genius, fame shall flower. / It is only wit that death does not devour."

The fourth book contains only the rare reference to Cynthia, and the poet turns his attention to the legendary past of Rome, occasional poems, letters, and an elegy. More than any of the others, this book demonstrates Propertius's professed identification with the aesthetics of the Alexandrian poet CALLIMACHUS. The fourth book shows the true breadth of Propertius's talent, and together the *Elegies* chart the maturation of a poet, his struggle to learn from his experiences, and his quest to discover and define his own personality.

Translator Constance Carrier calls Propertius a "daring, difficult, experimental writer." Scholar Margaret Hubbard concludes that Propertius has no characteristic or distinguishable style, but rather draws on a variety of influences and is highly inventive, especially in his use of imagery and metaphor. Though not as often read in later centuries as the EPIC poets, whose ranks he declined to join, Propertius is nonetheless remembered in the *Roman Elegies* (1788) by Goethe and in *Homage to Sextus Propertius* (1917) by Ezra Pound.

English Versions of Works by Sextus Propertius

Propertius: Elegies. Edited by G. P. Goold. Cambridge, Mass.: Harvard University Press, 1990.
Propertius: Elegies. Translated by R. I. V. Hodge and R. A. Buttimore. London: Bristol Classical Press, 2002.

Works about Sextus Propertius

Benediktson, D. Thomas. *Propertius: Modernist Poet of Antiquity.* Carbondale: Southern Illinois University Press, 1989.
Carrier, Constance. *The Poems of Propertius.* Bloomington: Indiana University Press, 1963.
Hubbard, Margaret. *Propertius.* London: Bristol Classical Press, 2001.

purana (first–15th centuries) *Hindu scriptural genre*

The Sanskrit word *purana* means "ancient" and refers to a genre of sacred Hindu scripture describing the mythological history of India. There are 18 *mahapurana*, or major *puranas*, and 18 *upapurana*, or minor *puranas*. Each *purana* celebrates a different aspect of the Hindu trinity, or Trimurti: Brahama, Vishnu, or Shiva. Devotees of Sakti, the Divine Mother, sometimes include the *Devi Bhagavata* as a major *purana*.

According to tradition, all the *purana* were composed by the sage Vyasa, to whom is attributed the epic of Indian literature, the MAHABHARATA. The *puranas* were compiled and recited over centuries, perhaps from as early as the first century to as late as 1400. Each *purana* is essentially a long poem composed in two-line stanzas called *slokas*. In content, they use short stories and dialogue between gurus and students to explain concepts contained in the Vedas, the oldest and most sacred Hindu scriptures. Strictly speaking, a *purana* should address five subjects: the first stage of the creation of the universe (*sarga*), the second stage of creation (*pratisarga*, or *visarga*), genealogies of kings and gods (*vamsa*), the reigns of the Manus (*manvantaras*), and the histories of the solar and lunar dynasties.

In practice, each *purana* is structurally unique and the content varies widely, covering a breathtaking scope of theology and philosophy. None are brief, though the lengths also vary. The *Vishnu Purana*, sometimes thought to be the oldest of the *puranas*, is called the *Puranatna*, or Gem of the Puranas, as it most conforms to the specified subjects. It contains 23,000 verses or *slokas*. The *Bhagavata Purana*, sometimes called the *Srimad Bhagavatam*, contains perhaps the most widely translated and the most-quoted writings on Hindu spirituality. Also dedicated to Vishnu, this *purana* most likely took shape between the first half of the sixth century and the second half of the eighth. It contains 18,000 verses.

Like the BHAGAVAD GITA, the *purana* are concerned with devotion to God but, due to their narrative style and poetic beauty, are accessible to laypeople. Together they form a substantial contribution to the development of Hindu thought.

An English Version of the *Purana*

Bhagavata Purana. Translated by G. V. Tagare. Columbia, Mo.: South Asia Books, 1989.

Works about the *Purana*

Brown, Cheever MacKenzie. *The Triumph of the Goddess*. New York: State University of New York Press, 1990.
Winternitz, Maurice. *History of Indian Literature: Introduction, Veda, Epics, Puranas and Tantras*. Columbia, Mo.: South Asia Books, 1981.

Q

Qu Elegies (Ch'u Elegies, Chu Ci, Ch'u Tz'u, Songs of Ch'u, Elegies of Ch'u, Songs of the South) (fourth century B.C.)
collection of verses

The *Qu Elegies* is a great collection of Chinese poems second only to the renowned BOOK OF SONGS. This collection of verses records the legends, myths, religious philosophy, and social commentaries of the tumultuous Warring States period (403–221 B.C.). when imperial power broke down and rival feudal states fought among one another almost constantly.

The most important of these songs was attributed to QU YUAN, who is generally regarded as the father of Chinese poetry. He composed the *Lisao* (translated in English variously as The *Lament, Encountering Sorrow,* or *A Song on the Sorrows of Departure*), which in 375 lines relates the poetic account of a man's spiritual journey from birth to death. The poem's somber mood and melancholy reflect the poet's disillusionment and the rejection he felt after his master, the emperor, betrayed him.

Several major themes are represented in the collection of songs, the foremost being the theme of quest. A number of the elegies are religious texts that relate the story of a shaman who embarks on a spiritual journey to the supernatural realm. For instance, in *Nine Songs* (*Jiuge [Chiu-ko]*), the protagonist is a religious figure who goes in search of gods and goddesses who may or may not show themselves. A similar theme is explored in another song, *The Far-off Journey* (*Yuanyu*), in which the main character encounters and interacts with many deities along his circular pilgrimage, which culminates in his achieving his goal in the center of the cosmos.

Lisao also contains strong imagery of the poet's quest for virtue or for a virtuous person to guide him on his path. His quest proves fruitless, ending in his eventual decision to seek solace in death by drowning himself in the river. This image combines the poet's quest with another significant theme of the poem: Nature's reflection of the human condition, especially the subjection of humans to the forces of fate, or predestination. As the writer Richard Strassberg points out in his introduction to *Inscribed Landscapes*, Qu Yuan "in the end, was unable to view Nature as a mirror of personal virtue, a scene of transformation, or a soothing refuge. The environments he visited prove to be merely extensions of his anguished sorrow and feelings of misunderstanding."

The literary styles of the elegies continue to explore the relevance of nature. The general feature of the elegies or "parallel prose" (*bianwen* or *pianwen*) is the pervasive use of couplets of four or six char-acters that maintain metrical symmetry. The key rhetorical device used is the prevalent imagery of polarities or binary opposites, such as the moun-tain and water (or landscape) (*shansui*) imagery, heaven and earth, and yin and yang (the dual, or opposing nature of things). An example of this is the asymmetry of beauty and pestilence repre-sented in the reference to flowers and weeds in the *Lisao.* The poet, Qu Yuan, laments, "I grieve that fragrant flowers grow amidst patches of weeds."

Another important poem in the *Qu Elegies* is the *Tian Wen* (Tien Wen) or *Heavenly Questions.* This poem is comprised of rhymed riddles and questions regarding the creation of the universe and China's early history. Most of the questions re-main unanswered except for a few, which allude to answers derived from earlier oral traditions. Al-though *Tian Wen* may appear to be a rather bewil-dering work, it contains important information on the myths and early beliefs of Chinese society in the Warring States and earlier periods.

The *Qu Elegies*'s expansion of the more restric-tive four-syllabic verse form of the *Book of Songs* greatly influenced the development of later forms of writing in China. It is deemed to have had con-siderable impact, for example, on the prose form of *fu* poetry and the five-syllabic verse form of the *shih* poetry of the Han dynasty (206 B.C.–A.D. 220). In addition to the *Book of Songs,* the *Qu Elegies* serves as one of the best collections of vernacular literature in China and has served as a model of poetry and inspiration for many authors writing both inside and outside of the Chinese tradition.

An English Version of the *Qu Elegies*

Ch'u Tz'u, The Songs of the South: An Ancient Chinese Anthology. Translated by David Hawkes. Taipei: Tun Huang Publications, 1968.

Works about the *Qu Elegies*

Strassburg, Richard E., trans. *Inscribed Landscapes: Travel Writing from Imperial China.* Berkeley: Uni-versity of California Press, 1994, 24, 199.

Wang, C. H. *From Ritual to Allegory: Seven Essays in Early Chinese Poetry.* Hong Kong: Chinese Univer-sity Press, 1988.

Waters, Geoffrey. *Three Elegies of Ch'u: An Introduction to the Traditional Interpretation of the Ch'u Tz'u.* Madison: University of Wisconsin Press, 1985.

Quintilian (Marcus Fabius Quintilianus)
(ca. 40–ca. 96) *rhetorician, nonfiction writer*

Quintilian was born in Calagurris in Spain, a Roman province that was then a center of culture and the birthplace to other notables, including the elder and younger SENECA and the poet MARTIAL. By the year 57, Quintilian had traveled to Rome to study rhetoric under Domitius Afer. Following Afer's death, he returned to Spain to teach and practice law, but in 68 he came once more to Rome in the company of Galba, who briefly became em-peror in 69. In 71–72 he received a subsidy from the emperor Vespasian, who supported education in hopes of forming an educated citizenry. During this time, from 68 to 88, he taught oratory in Rome and became head of the first public school there in 88. He retired two years later.

In 89 Quintilian published *On the Causes of Corrupted Eloquence,* a work now lost. He began writing his major work, *On the Education of the Orator,* around 92 and published it in 94 or 95. In this work, Quintilian synthesizes a lifetime of ex-perience in speaking and writing and blends it into a work that is at once a treatise on education, a manual of rhetoric, a recommended reading list, and a handbook of moral duties. For Quintilian, excellence in oration could not be separated from excellence of mind. Thus, his teaching emphasized the development of moral principles as well as artistic skill. In his own words, oratory is "the good man speaking well." (At this time girls could re-ceive a basic education in grammar, but only young men were allowed to study rhetoric, or the uses of language and literature.)

Through its 12 books, *On the Education of the Orator* charts a progression through the steps of education. Quintilian's recommended teaching techniques include imitation, memorization, translation, recitation, the study of history, and literary criticism, among others. The first two books provide the foundation of the work by defining rhetoric and outlining the purposes and uses of education. For Quintilian, education was a lifelong pursuit that required turning every life experience to instructional advantage. The product of his educational system was a student schooled in both eloquence and ethical conduct, equipped to act justly in public affairs.

Most innovative, and most appealing to the modern reader, is the attention Quintilian pays to the development of the small child. From the moment of birth, he maintains, care should be taken to expose the child only to constructive influences and moral teachers, even in the appointment of the child's nurse. Education can begin with music, such as the lullabies sung to babies, since music helps develop taste and a sense of aesthetic distinction. He recommends giving exercises such as puzzles and problems of geometry to small children to stimulate their minds and hone their intellect. As the child develops, the relationship between student and teachers should be based on love. Quintilian urges the pupil to love his tutors as much as his studies, and he likewise instructs tutors to hold their pupils in true affection. He further states that if a student proves unequal to certain tasks, the teacher should direct him toward exercises in which he would have a chance of success. Most importantly, the subjects of education should be varied so as to create a well-rounded individual who can excel in both physical and mental tasks, for oration in particular required mastery of every skill. "Eloquence is like a harp," Quintilian wrote, "not perfect unless with all its strings stretched, it be in unison from the highest to the lowest note."

Quintilian's impact on the history of education has been profound. Remarks by his contemporaries JUVENAL and PLINY THE YOUNGER reveal the esteem in which he was held in his own time. The *Dialogue on Orators* by TACITUS borrows from Quintilian, and so do JEROME's instructions on the education of Christian girls. Quintilian's ideas enjoyed great attention during the period of late antiquity, and he was often quoted in the works of French scholars during the 12th century. The humanist movement looked again to Quintilian, with scholars such as Petrarch, Erasmus, Martin Luther, and Philip Melanchthon enlarging on his program. In England, Ben Jonson and Alexander Pope both read and praised Quintilian, and his techniques remained part of the English system of education well into the 19th century. Even in the 20th century, Quintilian is still recognized as a landmark figure in the history of education.

English Versions of Works by Quintilian
Quintilian: The Orator's Education, Books 3–5. Edited by Jeffrey Henderson and D. A. Russell. Cambridge, Mass.: Harvard University Press, 2002.
Quintilian on the Teaching of Speaking and Writing. Edited by James J. Murphy. Carbondale: Southern Illinois University Press, 1987.

Works about Quintilian
Kennedy, George. *Quintilian.* New York: Twayne Publishers, 1969.
Tellegen-Couperus, Olga, ed. *Quintilian & The Law: The Art of Persuasion in Law & Politics.* Leuven, Belgium: Leuven University Press, 2003.

Qur'an
See KORAN.

Qu Yuan (Ch'ü Yüan) (332–296 B.C.) *poet*
Qu Yuan was born in Zhikui (Chih-K'uei), Hubei (Hupeh) province, China, during the chaotic period of the Warring States (403–221 B.C.), when the authority of the Zhou (Chou) dynasty was decentralized among seven rival feudal states. Qu was a descendant of the royal family of Qu and later became the Left Counselor of King Huai of Qu. He belonged to the anti-Qin (Ch'in) party in the court,

which unfortunately went against his favor. Qu Yuan was sent into exile twice by two different Qu kings because he advised them not to continue diplomatic relations with the court of the rival state of Qin. For many years, he roamed from place and place before finally drowning himself after learning that the Qu dynasty had fallen to the Qin armies.

During his exile, Qu Yuan vented his grievances through his poems, such as the *Lisao,* the most famous of his works. The longest of Qu Yuan's lyrical poems, the *Lisao* reveals his devotion to and love of his country and his unyielding desire and determination to persuade his erring kings to avoid committing the gravest mistake by cultivating friendly relations with the treacherous Qin state. *Lisao* is divided into three sections. The first describes the ancestors, biographical details, and poet's desire to serve his king. A female character, probably the poet's sister, dominates the second section, in which she tries to persuade the poet of his foolhardiness. The final section contains a vivid description of Qu Yuan's imaginary pursuit of hope and truth. The poem ends on a despondent note as the poet laments:

> *Alas! All is over.*
> *My fellow countrymen know me not*
> *Why should I pine for my native land?*
> *Since there is none to govern well with me.*
> *I shall join Beng Xian's abode.*

It is this keenness of expression which makes the *Lisao* a valuable document in the tradition of important Chinese literature, both as a poetic biography and as a model of poetic style and sentiment.

English Versions of Works by Qu Yuan

Li Sao, A Poem on Relieving Sorrows. Translated by Jerah Johnson. Miami: Olivant Press, 1959.
Tian Wen: A Chinese Book of Origins. Translated by Stephen Field. New York: New Directions, 1986.

A Work about Qu Yuan

Hu, Patricia Pin-ching. "Poet of Man's Ingratitude." In *Random Talks on Classical Chinese Poetry.* Hong Kong: Join Sun Publishing Co., 1990.

R

Ramayana

See VALMIKI, MAHARISHI.

Rig-Veda (ca. 1500–600 B.C.) *sacred text, poem*

The oldest of the Vedas, the four books that make up the Hindu scriptures, is the Rig-Veda. Along with the Sama-Veda, the Yajur-Veda, and the Atharva-Veda, the Rig-Veda sets out the creation stories, the religious rituals, and the early prayers of the Hindu religion.

The Vedas were created as part of the Brahmanical tradition of the ancient Aryans, nomadic people who settled in the Indus River valley between 3000 B.C. and 2000 B.C. Their religion was based on the use of fire during sacrifices and the consumption of an intoxicating drink called soma, made from a plant that may be related to the mushroom known as "fly-agaric." The Aryan Brahmanical tradition also placed a heavy emphasis on social order and served as a precursor to the later Hindu caste system.

The Rig-Veda contains 1,028 hymns, the earliest of which were probably composed around 1500 B.C. The hymns, or *mantras,* were recited by priests and preserved through an oral tradition (*see* ORAL LITERATURE/TRADITION) for hundreds of years. After 1000 B.C., the Rig-Veda was written down in Sanskrit, making it the oldest work in the Indian tradition and one of the oldest works of any kind in the Indo-European language system. The Sanskrit word *veda* means "knowledge." Thus, the Rig-Veda concerns knowledge through hymns to the gods.

The central figures of the Rig-Veda are Indra, the god of thunder and battle; Agni, the god of fire; Varuna, the god of truth and order; and soma, the powerful intoxicating plant. Two other gods, Vishnu and Shiva, although of lesser importance in the Rig-Veda, later became two of the three most important gods in the Hindu religion.

More than 200 of the Rig-Veda's verses are devoted to Indra. He was the most popular god in the Indo-Aryan pantheon and a devoted user of the plant soma. His heroic exploits helped to create the Indo-Aryan civilization. One of the most famous sets of hymns tells of his destruction of the serpent Vrtra, who had encompassed all the universe's elements, including Water, the Sun, the Moon, the heavens, and the earth, within his coils. By destroying Vrtra, Indra released the elements that allowed life to flourish.

The importance of Agni in the Rig-Veda lies in his connection with fire and sacrifice. The early Indo-Aryan religion was a fire cult, and as the god of fire, Agni was worthy of many hymns of praise. Agni served as a messenger between people and gods. Through the use of fire sacrifice, the Indo-Aryans were able to communicate with the gods and ensure their health and protection.

Soma was an essential part of the Indo-Aryan religion. The plant is mentioned nearly 1,000 times in the Rig-Veda, and the entire ninth book is devoted to hymns praising it. The plant's juice produced an effect on its users that allowed them to achieve superhuman tasks. Indra's use of soma, for example, allowed him to defeat Vrtra and other monsters throughout the text. Soma was also praised in the works of the Zoroastrian religion in Iran around the same time that the Rig-Veda was written.

Varuna played the god of order and Truth (or Rta), an extremely important role in the Indo-Aryan religion. Varuna's presence regulated the universe and kept all things from falling into chaos. He has often been portrayed as a moon god, though his role is more accurately described as god of the heavens, as well as of Truth. Though he held a position of great importance in the early religion, he was later eclipsed by Vishnu and Shiva in the Hindu pantheon.

The Rig-Veda's dual role as a sacred scripture of the early Indo-Aryan fire cults and of the Hindu religion have given it a place of the utmost importance in the history of religion and literature.

English Versions of the Rig-Veda

The Rig-Veda: An Anthology. Selected, Translated and Annotated by Wendy Doniger O'Flaherty. New York: Penguin, 1981.

The Hymns of the Rig Veda, 3d ed., complete in two volumes. Translated by Ralph T. H. Griffith. Benares, India: E. J. Lazarus and Co., 1920–26.

Works about the Rig-Veda

Gonda, Jan. *Vedic Literature (Samhita and Brahmanas)*. Wiesbaden: Harassowitz, 1975.

Hillebrandt, Alfred. *Vedic Mythology.* Translated by Sreeramula Rajeswara Sarma. Delhi: Motilal Banarsidass Publishers, 1980.

romance, medieval (12th–14th centuries)
literary genre

In 12th-century France, the term *romanz* referred to a work written in the vernacular literature rather than in Latin, which was the language used by scholars, lawmakers, the religious, and the ruling class. First used to indicate a poem that related historical facts, the term *romance* soon came to designate a new literary genre. This genre did not come about spontaneously; rather, it found its beginnings in ancient Greek, Arabic, and Celtic literatures. For example, medieval society was familiar with the triumph of love in CALLIMACHUS's works as well as Celtic stories, such as the romance of TRISTAN AND ISEULT. Medieval romances were also influenced by Arabic songs, brought into contact with Western culture through the CRUSADES, and by the political history of the province of Aquitaine in present-day France. William of Poitou, Duke of Aquitaine, who fought in the First Crusade, was also the earliest recorded TROUBADOUR. His granddaughter, Eleanor of Aquitaine, became Queen of France and then Queen of England, carrying to both courts a new tradition of love poetry that evolved into a code of CHIVALRY and COURTLY LOVE.

From 1150 until the end of the 14th century, the romance was the most popular secular genre in the literature of England and France. Scholars later tried to organize the immense proliferation and colorful variety of texts by organizing them into three main areas: the Matter of Britain, which involves the adventures of King Arthur and his knights; the Matter of Charlemagne, which includes the stories of Roland; and the Matter of Rome, which includes tales about Alexander the Great and the fall of Troy. Arthur, Alexander, and Roland all take their place among the favorite heroes of medieval romances. Even those narratives that are not related to these cycles share certain characteristics with the most famous and influential of the romance tales.

The first romance distinguishable as such may be the *SONG OF ROLAND*, which was composed in the latter half of the 11th century. Some scholars maintain that the *Song of Roland* is still an example of the older heroic poetry similar to the Anglo-Saxon BEOWULF or the EPICS of ancient Greece and Rome. In addition, the *Romance of Thebes, The Romance of Aeneas,* and *The Romance of Troy,* written between 1150 and 1165, all deal with the matter of Rome, retelling the epic stories in romance form. During these same years, Béroul wrote his *Tristan* and CHRÉTIEN DE TROYES his *Arthurian Romances,* which forever shaped the way these characters were known and continue to be perceived. Later writers also added to the treasury of stories, among them MARIE DE FRANCE and Robert de Boron, whose verse romances develop the story of the HOLY GRAIL and add to the Arthurian romances. Around 1225, GUILLAUME DE LORRIS began an elaborate allegorical poem called The ROMANCE OF THE ROSE, which was continued later by JEAN DE MEUN and which left an enduring stamp on the romance genre and the way love was poetically treated in the Western world.

From its roots in France, the romance tradition spread to Italy, England, Germany, the Netherlands, Portugal, Greece, and Spain. Two of the most popular Spanish romances, *The Book of Apollonius* and *The Book of Alexander,* composed between 1220 and 1240, return to the Matter of Rome. In England the most popular romances dealt with the legends of King Arthur, such as *Sir Gawain and the Green Knight* or Sir Thomas Malory's *The Death of Arthur.* In Germany, the romances of WOLFRAM VON ESCHENBACH and GOTTFRIED VON STRASSBURG also contributed to the Matter of Britain, and the most celebrated authors of Italian romances—Boiardo, Ariosto, and Torquato Tasso—all used characters from the Roland tradition.

Critical Analysis

As a genre, the medieval romance is distinct from the chronicle, which purported to relate a true history. The romance is also quite different from epics or the earlier heroic poetry. David Staines, who translated the Arthurian romances of Chrétien de Troyes, puts it thus: "Traditionally, the epic and the chronicle depict a nation; their characters are the embodiment of a national destiny; their ultimate concern is the nation itself. By contrast, the romance depicts the individual." Scholar Foster Guyer also observes that the romance introduced several innovations into the literature: "important feminine roles, a love element in narrative form, a refined style, and an entirely new kind of plot."

All romances share certain motifs, which scholar John Stevens identifies as the following: the hero's sense of a vocation or quest; the presentation of the heroine as distant, beautiful, and desirable; the essential isolation of the hero and his experience; and the feeling of involvement in a mystery. Romances also frequently feature magic elements or supernatural experiences.

Medieval romances were popular because they focused their attention not on national character but on human character. As Terence McCarthy says, "Romance takes us close to its heroes; we share their thoughts and see into their hearts." The romance genre also explored in a new way the treatment of women in the medieval world. Scholar Rosamund Allen observes that in literature prior to romances, "Women were notoriously excluded from positions of authority in medieval society." For this reason, women in literature frequently appeared "in the archetypal roles of mother, sister, daughter, wife and queen-consort"; in short, female characters were defined by their relationship to men. On the surface, medieval romances seemed to elevate women by putting them in positions of power and worshipping them for their grace and beauty. Upon closer investigation, however, feminist scholars observe that by making them the focus of the male quest, trapping them in towers or prisons, and valuing them for beauty or wealth rather than for personality or achievements, medieval romances simply continued to treat women as powerless objects in stories dominated by men.

Almost as soon as it was established, the romantic tradition began to investigate and even parody itself. Romances frequently use humor to describe situations in which the hero finds himself, and even moments that the author intended to be serious and tragic may appear funny to modern eyes in their extravagant detail and sensational excess. Certain authors of the later MIDDLE AGES questioned the romance with particular skill. In his *Troilus and Criseyde,* Geoffrey Chaucer examines the clash between the epic and romance genres that inevitably happens when an ancient tale is recast in romance form. Ariosto draws away from the romantic tradition in his *Orlando Furioso,* offering a comic treatment of the repetitive and formulaic nature of romance episodes and devices. And *Don Quixote* (1605), by Miguel de Cervantes, is frequently seen as the last great parody and the final break with romance as a leading medieval literary genre.

Still, romantic conventions persisted in literature. In the English tradition, many of William Shakespeare's plays stage a return to romance, but with remarkably more complex psychological detail. The Renaissance figures Sir Philip Sidney and Edmund Spenser revived elements of the medieval romance in *Arcadia* and *The Faerie Queene,* respectively, but in these works the once-viable characteristics of the romance appear archaic and even quaint. In its farthest reaches, however, the medieval romance is considered the precursor to the modern novel. Even the contemporary definition of *romance* inherits some qualities of its older counterparts. In modern terms, a romance is inevitably a love story and typically involves the quest of a hero or heroine whose experiences and emotions are the main focus of the tale; thus, this most popular genre of secular medieval literature permanently affected the way literature is received in the modern world.

English Versions of Medieval Romances

Béroul. *The Romance of Tristan.* Translated by Alan S. Fedrick. New York: Viking Press, 1978.

Boron, Robert de. *Merlin and the Grail.* Translated by Nigel Bryant. Cambridge: D.S. Brewer, 2001.

Chrétien de Troyes. *Arthurian Romances.* Translated by D. D. R. Owen. Rutland, Vt.: Charles E. Tuttle, 1997.

Guillaume de Lorris and Jean de Meun. *The Romance of the Rose.* Translated by Charles Dahlberg. Princeton, N.J.: Princeton University Press, 1995.

Marie de France. *The Lais of Marie de France.* Translated by Glyn Burgess. New York: Penguin, 1999.

The Song of Roland. Translated by Glyn Burgess. New York: Penguin, 1990.

Works about Medieval Romance

Barron, W. R. J. *English Medieval Romance.* New York: Longman, 1987.

Krueger, Roberta L., ed. *The Cambridge Companion to Medieval Romance.* Cambridge, U.K.: Cambridge University Press, 2000.

Mills, Maldwyn, Jennifer Fellows and Carol M. Meale. *Romance in Medieval England.* Cambridge, U.K.: D. S. Brewer, 1991.

Romance of the Rose (ca. 1225–1277)
allegorical poem

The *Roman de la Rose* (Romance of the Rose) is one of the most famous and influential courtly love poems of the MIDDLE AGES. Written by two French authors, GUILLAUME DE LORRIS and JEAN DE MEUN, *Romance of the Rose* is an allegory in which emotions and abstract ideas such as Reason and Nature are personified by the story's characters.

The story tells how a young man in courtly society (represented in the literal story by a garden) seeks to win a young woman's love (represented by a rose). The man's attempt to seduce the woman is aided by her friendliness (or Fair Welcome), and by her passion (Venus), and repulsed at other moments by her haughtiness (as represented by the character of *Dangier*).

According to author C. S. Lewis, *Romance of the Rose* is "a love story of considerable subtlety and truth" in which the poets create the psychology of their characters by constructing an imaginary world in which the lovers' passions move and impress themselves vividly on the reader's mind.

Guillaume de Lorris, about whom almost nothing is known, composed the first 4,000 lines of the poem. After his death, the work's popularity led more than one writer to try to complete it. A first, very short anonymous conclusion was probably written shortly after the original, but much more famous is the long continuation and conclusion by Jean de Meun.

Guillaume's major inspiration was the ideology and poetry of CHIVALRY and courtly love in which the lady plays the dominant role, kindly granting her favors or not, and the lover strives to please her in all things and be worthy of her. This type of love was an innovation and in direct contrast with the current idea of marriage in which the husband was expected to have complete control and domination over his wife. Guillaume and Jean de Meun also recognized that the love they were portraying contradicted the medieval ascetic tradition that condemned passion for its ability to destroy a person's reason; hence the appearance of Reason, whose character argues in vain against love.

Jean de Meun's sources included the works of Alan of Lille, a 12th-century poet of the school of Chartres, who wrote philosophical poetry about nature and creation. His other sources included Greek and Roman mythology (*see* MYTHOLOGY, GREEK AND ROMAN) and the allegorical traditions found in the BIBLE and in the works of ancient poets.

Critical Analysis

Romance of the Rose begins with the narrator dreaming of entering the beautiful Garden of Delight by permission of the gatekeeper Idleness. As he explores the garden, he looks into a well, where he sees two crystal stones and, reflected in them, a Rose growing a little way off. The God of Love shoots him with his arrows, and he falls in love and tries to reach the Rose. But he must first surrender to the God of Love, whom he takes as his lord, saying:

> This heart is yours; it is no longer mine;
> For good or ill it does as you command.

With the help of the lady's initial friendliness (Fair Welcome), the Lover tries to win the Rose's love. He grows too bold and is soon rebuffed by her *Dangier*. At this point, Reason, a beautiful woman, urges him to give up his quest.

> Nothing but foolishness is this disease

> called Love; 'twere better if it were folly
> named.

The Lover rebuffs Reason and perseveres. Another character, Friend, who is already experienced in the ways of love, advises him on how to placate Dangier. The Lover again makes headway and soon asks if he can kiss the Rose. Fair Welcome at first demurs:

> . . . So help me God, dear friend,
> If Chastity did not so frown on me,
> I'd not deny you; but I am afraid
> Of her and would not act against her will.

At Venus's (desire's) arrival, however, Fair Welcome capitulates, and the lover kisses the Rose. Malebouche (Evil Mouths or gossip) spreads the news, and Jealousy builds a fortress around the Rose and imprisons Fair Welcome in its tower. The lover laments his defeat. It is at this point that Guillaume de Lorris's story ends and Jean de Meun's begins.

Sarah Kay describes Jean's conclusion, which is more than four times longer than Guillaume's beginning, as "less an expansion than an explosion of the original *Rose.*" Around the framework of the simple story of the Lover and the Rose, Jean weaves vast discourses on dozens of subjects, including free will and predestination, the planets, and hypocritical religions. He displays a more critical and cynical attitude toward idealized courtly love and includes a number of satirical passages on women and relations between the sexes. One of the most famous characters, *Vekke,* the old woman who guards Fair Welcome, speaks at length about how women should take many lovers, cheat on them, and get expensive presents from them.

Jean de Meun's conclusion tells how the Lover argues again with Reason, who explains that those who engage in love for pleasure alone, without the desire to procreate, are wrong. The God of Love agrees to help the Lover, calling on his forces to storm the castle where the Rose is kept prisoner. They are defeated and finally call on Venus.

While this is happening, Jean introduces Nature's character, whose beauty the narrator cannot describe:

> *For God, whose beauty is quite measureless,*
> *When He this loveliness to Nature gave*
> *Within her fixed a fountain, full and free*
> *From which all beauty flows.*

As she is working in her forge to repair the ravages of death by the birth of new human beings, Nature hears of the Lover's quest. She goes to her confessor Genius (the god of reproduction) and complains of the disobedience of humans who refuse to procreate as God ordains. Genius goes to Love's forces, excommunicates those who refuse Nature's laws, and absolves those who are about to fight. Above all, he exhorts them to live so as to be worthy of the Park of the Lamb of God, for the beauty of the Garden of Delight is only an illusory image of the beauty of heaven. During the storming of the castle, Venus throws her torch and destroys the Rose's prison; at last the Lover enjoys and apparently impregnates his love.

Countless other authors have quoted *Romance of the Rose* and imitated its symbolism and imagery. It has been translated twice into Italian (*Il Fiore* and *Il Detto d'Amore*), numerous times in Middle English (a version often attributed to Geoffrey Chaucer) and Modern English, and in many other languages. Chaucer used the poem as one of his sources when creating the different moods of the heroine Criseyde in his long narrative poem *Troilus and Criseyde* (early 1380s). John Gower also used the poem as a source for his *Confessio Amantis* (The Lover's Confession, 1390s), in which he, too, portrays Genius as a confessor, this time for the lover. Later medieval authors, including Jean de Montreuil and Christine de Pisan, debated the morality of the poem and its treatment of women.

Modern critics disagree about Jean de Meun's ultimate intentions, questioning whether he approved of Guillaume de Lorris's original poem, whether he intended his cynical views to overshadow his religious views, and whether Nature or Genius represent his true beliefs. Perhaps the answers to such questions lie somewhere in between. According to scholar Maxwell Luria, Jean de Meun's subject can be summed up as "Love itself, man's multifarious and conflicting and sometimes treacherous attraction toward the whole spectrum of created goods and their uncreated Maker." Within this subject there is room for both delight in and cynical realism about human love, as well as yearning for the divine. Scholar R. Allen Shoaf takes a broader look at the poem, viewing it as a form of criticism. In his essay "Rose Oser Sero Eros: Recent Studies of the *Romance of the Rose*," Shoaf writes that *Romance of the Rose* succeeds as a criticism of love "largely because Jean de Meun saw and expressed the inescapable mutual contamination of the languages of love, philosophy, and theology. . . ." Wherever future debates and scholarly criticism of the poem might lead, there seems to be no question that the *Romance of the Rose* will continue to be regarded as a masterpiece of medieval French literature.

English Versions of *Romance of the Rose*

The Romance of the Rose. Translated by Frances Horgan. Oxford: Oxford University Press, 1999.

The Romance of the Rose by Guillaume de Lorris and Jean de Meun. Translated by Charles Dahlberg. Princeton, N.J.: Princeton University Press, 1995.

Works about *Romance of the Rose*

Brownlee, Kevin, and Sylvia Huot, eds. *Rethinking the Romance of the Rose: Text, Image, Reception.* Philadelphia: University of Pennsylvania Press, 1992.

Heller-Roazen, Daniel. *Fortune's Faces: The Roman de la Rose and the Poetics of Contingency.* Edited by Stephen G. Nichols and Gerald Prince. Baltimore: Johns Hopkins University Press, 2003.

Huot, Sylvia Jean. *Romance of the Rose and Its Medieval Readers: Interpretation, Reception, Manuscript Transmission.* Cambridge, Mass.: Cambridge University Press, 1993.

Kelly, Douglas. *Internal Difference and Meanings in the Roman de la Rose.* Madison: University of Wisconsin Press, 1995.

Roman de Renart (ca. 1175–1250) *satirical fable*

The *Roman de Renart* (Romance of Reynard) is a series of French tales composed over a span of several years. Altogether the poem covers tens of thousands of lines and has 27 branches, or episodes. The earliest recorded branches emerged in 1170, and additions continued until 1250. About 20 different poets had a hand in writing the stories, and although the names of Pierre de Saint-Cloud, Richard of Lison, and a priest of Croix-en-Brie are linked with certain early branches, most of the writers remain anonymous.

The French tale is stylistically the most sophisticated rendition of the hugely popular tradition of Reynard the Fox, which appears elsewhere in Dutch, German, and English literature. The character of the trickster fox hails back to the fables of AESOP, but fragments of medieval Latin poems contain some source material, including *Ysengrinus*, written at Ghent in 1148. As with many stories from folklore, the precise origins of the Reynard characters are obscure. The names are arguably Germanic; Reynard probably derives from Raginhard, which means "strong in counsel." The German *Reinhart* manuscript, dated to 1180, and the Flemish variations of the stories likely draw on now-lost French originals that first circulated in the region of Alsace-Lorraine. The 13th-century English poem *Of the Fox and of the Wolf* and the Italian *Rainardo* also used the Reynard material. The *trouvères* (TROUBADOURS) of northern France developed these popular folktales into a work that is at once a fabulous epic BESTIARY and a political allegory, cultural commentary and verse romance, fireside story and literary parody.

Critical Analysis

Though a folk hero and an epic figure, Reynard is a trickster: This is the definitive aspect of his personality. As a fox, he uses trickery to get food, avenge himself, and defend himself against his enemies. Other characters in the story are Noble the Lion, Chanticleer the Rooster, Bruin the Bear, and Isengrin the Wolf. Together these figures represent the main branches of feudal society: royalty, the nobility, the clergy, and the peasantry, respectively. The laws and morals that govern them strongly resonate with the ruling ideology of 12th-century France.

The story of Reynard begins, as do many MEDIEVAL ROMANCES, with the king—in this case, Noble the Lion—organizing a feast and calling all the animals to attend. The animals comply, and all of them have one complaint or another against Reynard. Curtois the Hound complains that Reynard has stolen food from him; Chanticleer the Rooster claims that Reynard has killed a hen. Corbant the Raven says that Reynard murdered his wife by pretending to be dead; when his wife approached to lay her ear to the fox's mouth, Reynard snapped her up and ate her so quickly that only a few feathers remained. The king decides that Reynard must come forward to answer the charges.

No one has managed heretofore to convict Reynard of a crime. He is a master of deception, and with a seemingly reasonable explanation he always manages to befuddle his accusers. For instance, Reynard claims that Corbant the Raven's wife died from eating too many worms. And when danger threatens, Reynard resorts to tricks; for instance, when Bruin is sent to bring him to court, Reynard bribes him with honey and traps the bear in a tree.

In time Reynard is at last brought to court and put on trial for his crimes. Despite his smooth talking, he is condemned to the gallows and only narrowly escapes death. Thereafter Reynard is sent on a pilgrimage as penance, and more adventures ensue, during which it becomes clear that he has not repented at all. When the fox is brought once more to trial, Isengrin determines to get revenge, still humiliated from a famous episode wherein Reynard pretended to teach the wolf how to fish with his tail and then took him to a frigid lake, where Isengrin became trapped when his tail froze in the ice. This battle between Reynard and Isengrin crowns the collection.

Scholars have long debated the literary qualities of *Renart*. Some claim that because he is a fox, all of Reynard's activities can be explained by his motive to survive. Other critics read the animals more imaginatively as the human types they were intended to represent in later versions of the stories. Roger Bellon says of Reynard that his "character is fully rounded, with a psychological richness which is the product of his trickery." Though a fox, he possesses the human capacities of reason and intelligence. He also has the capacity for human affection and piety, as in this touching passage in William Caxton's version when Reynard takes leave of his wife:

> Reynard said to his wife, "Dame Ermelin, I betake you my children that you see well to them and specially to Reynkin, my youngest son. He belikes me so well, I hope he shall follow my steps. And there is Rossel, a passing fair thief. I love him as well as any may love his children. If God give me grace that I may escape, I shall when I come again thank you with fair words."
> Thus took Reynard leave of his wife.

Originally the Reynard tales were intended for purposes of entertainment, not instruction. In the earlier tales, the doings of Reynard and his counterparts had a largely comic relevance and helped create a new genre of literature: the beast fable, which blended the conventional fable with the epic. Translator Joseph Jacobs observes, "One of the chief points of interest in the study of the Reynard is this mixture of literature and folklore which thus gave rise to a new form of literature." This genre proved to have important and innovative uses in attacking and exposing the follies of certain social, political, and religious aspects of medieval society.

As the stories of Reynard's trickery grew, the beast fables turned into cutting satire. *Renart* contains many layers of tension, not the least being that because Renart's character is a trickster, he is not the typical romance hero. As an animal, he is motivated by survival instincts, but as a being who can speak and reason, he also has the ability to deceive. He is treated as a comic character, yet his stories are often used to make a moral point. It is not always easy to sympathize with Reynard's victims; sometimes they deserve what they get. Later, Reynard became an emblem of hypocrisy among monkish orders. Certain stories show him donning a monk's garb to outwit his foes or attending confession, being absolved of his sins, and promptly going forth to engage in more immoral behavior. After 1250, no new branches of the *Renart* cycle appeared, but poets such as Philippe de Novare and RUTEBEUF adopted the character of Reynard for moralizing purposes.

Another key characteristic of the Reynard stories, which may account for their popularity, is the fact that they are one of the few medieval genres developed for the enjoyment of the nonaristocratic classes. Like the fabliaux or the poetry of François Villon, the beast fables addressed life in the lower classes and examined the struggles of those who were, by the rules of feudalism, the hardest working and least powerful. In a world ruled by wealth and military might, cunning was often the only recourse against a tyrant, which may explain the enormous amount of sympathy and interest that audiences felt for the crafty fox. For some readers, Reynard symbolizes the resistance of the little man against more powerful foes and echoes other stories like David and Goliath or Jack and the Beanstalk.

Like many other French romances, *Renart* circulated beyond France into England, Germany, and the Low Countries (modern Belgium, Luxembourg, and the Netherlands), where several analogues or similar stories appear. An episode borrowed from the Reynard tradition appears in The Nun's Priest's Tale in *The Canterbury Tales* of Geoffrey Chaucer, where the protagonist of the story is Chanticleer the rooster and Russell is the name of the wily fox. William Caxton's *History of Reynard the Fox,* based on a Dutch version, appeared in 1481. Goethe reworked the material into *Reinecke Fuchs* in 1794, and the English poet John Masefield's hunting poem *Reynard the Fox* appeared in 1921, attesting to the continuing folkloric memory and comic appeal of this immortal and charismatic trickster.

See also SONG OF ROLAND.

English Versions of *Roman de Renart*

Caxton, William, trans. *The History of Reynard the Fox.* Edited by N. F. Blake. Rochester, N.Y.: Boydell and Brewer, 1970.

The Romance of Reynard the Fox. Translated by D. D. R. Owen. Oxford: Oxford University Press, 1994.

Renard the Fox. Translated by Patricìa Terry. Boston: Northeastern University Press, 1983.

Works about *Roman de Renart*

Lodge, Anthony and Kenneth Varty. *Earliest Branches of the Roman de Renart.* New Alyth, Scotland: Lochee Publications, 1989.

Varty, Kenneth, ed. *Reynard the Fox.* New York: Berghahn Books, 2000.

Ruan Ji (Juan Chi) (210–263) *poet*

Ruan Ji was born into a traditional Confucianist family of government officials in Wei-shih, China. His father, Ruan Yu, was a minor poet and government official under Cao Cao (Tsa'o Tsa'o), a Wei warlord. Ruan Ji entered government service in 239 and served the Wei dynasty until its overthrow by Sima (Ssu-ma) I in 249. The coup d'etat against the Wei dynasty was a turning point in Ruan Ji's life. Although his father and grandfather had served the Wei dynasty, Ruan Ji accepted nonpolitical posts under the new dynasty. One scholar describes Ji's efforts as a form of "passive resistance in which he could 'serve without serving.'"

Ruan Ji's poetry was a groundbreaking extension of his passive resistance. Some of his poems are an expression of his deeply personal thoughts and reflect his familiarity with Taoist philosophy. In this poem, for example, he describes an immortal "tortured" by his isolation and his apparent search for the meaning of life:

> Long ago there was an immortal man
> who lived on the slope of Shooting
>   Mountain . . .
> He could be heard, but not seen,

> sighing sorrows and full emotion
> self-tortured he had no companion
> grief and heartbreak piled upon him
> "Study the familiar to penetrate the
>   sublime"
> But time is short and what's to be done?

Other poems are filled with biting political satire and commentary and allusions to government figures and events, many of which were so obscure they could not be identified.

Ruan Ji served as a model for later poets who lived during similar years of political chaos, and he remains justly famous for his work.

A Work about Ruan Ji

Holzman, Donald. *Poetry and Politics: The Life and Works of Juan Chi,* A.D. *210–263.* Cambridge: Cambridge University Press, 1976.

Rudel, Jaufré

See JAUFRÉ RUDEL.

Rumi, Jalaloddin (Jalāl ad-Dīn ar Rūmī) (1207–1283) *poet*

Jalaloddin Rumi was born in Balkh, Afghanistan, to a family of learned theologians; his father was known as the "Sultan of Scientists." Escaping a Mongol invasion, Rumi and his family fled Afghanistan, made a pilgrimage to Mecca, and finally settled in Konya, Anatolia (Asia Minor). At age 24, Rumi, already a distinguished scholar, followed in his father's footsteps as a teacher and preacher of religious sciences at the college in Konya.

Rumi lived a wealthy, respectful life. The most distinguished philosophers of the time visited to discuss ideas with him, and his lectures in mosques drew enormous crowds. He became the sultan's consultant on law, and his opinion was considered the highest authority. However, he was dissatisfied and sought ways in which to learn more and impart his knowledge to others. Then, at age 37, he met a wandering dervish (a Muslim religious order) named Shamsuddin of Tabriz.

Shamsuddin saw that Rumi's creative potential was stifled by the weight of his scholarly knowledge and the burden of authority. Consequently, Rumi spent 90 days in a private retreat with Shamsuddin, from which both men emerged spiritually transformed.

As a result of Shamsuddin's instruction, Rumi gave up everything he had in life and devoted himself exclusively to a prolific outpouring of poetry. He later named his collection the *Diwan-i Shams-i Tabriz-i* (The Works of Shams of Tabriz) in honor of Shamsuddin. The *Diwan* consists of about 40,000 verses, arranged according to rhythm, and was written over a period of 30 years.

Rumi wrote thousands of poems glorifying life and love for God, and he became the spiritual founder of the Mawlawi Sufi order, a leading mystical brotherhood of Islam that practiced "ecstatic whirling" as a form of glorifying life and God. When he died, his grave became a place of pilgrimage for people all over the world. The day of Rumi's death was named "Night of Union," and it is celebrated to this day in honor of his life and works.

Critical Analysis

Among the great variety of themes in Rumi's poetry, love in all its forms is manifest. The poet explores the immortal theme of love as passion in such poems as "Love Is the Master," "After Being in Love, the Next Responsibility," and "The Interest without the Capital." He sees passionate love as a selfless experience that enriches one's life:

> The lover's food is the love of the bread;
> no bread need be at hand:
> no one who is sincere in his love is a slave to
>   existence.
>   (*Mathnawi* 3, 3020–3024)

Almost all of Rumi's love poems are ambiguous; they can be interpreted as addressing both the earthly love that exists between two people and the higher love that exists between humans and God:

> A house of love with no limits,
> a presence more beautiful than venus or the
>   moon,
> a beauty whose image fills the mirror of the
>   heart.
>   (*The Divani Shamsi Tabriz*, XV)

Other of Rumi's poems, called his "Spiritual couplets," give vivid depictions of the mystical experiences of ecstatic worship. These experiences are based on expressing love for God and life through a combination of poetry, music, and dance:

> This is love: to fly to heaven, every moment
> to rend a hundred veils;
> At first instance, to break away from
> breath—first step, to renounce feet . . .
>   (*Mystical Poems of Rumi*)

Beyond Rumi's mystical poems of passionate worship is his major work, the *Mathnawi* (Poem on Hidden Meaning). Compared to Rumi's mystical poems, the *Mathnawi* is relatively sober and reasoned. It comprises six books of poetry in a didactic style intended to convey instruction, information, pleasure, and entertainment. The poems take the form of engaging anecdotes or tales, with numerous digressions. Rumi tells each story to illustrate and discuss a moral, similar to what is done in AESOP's fables, and within this anecdotal structure, he illustrates the idea that it is important to distinguish between *form* (the external appearance of things) and *meaning* (internal, invisible reality):

> Form is a Shadow,
> Meaning is the Sun.
>   (*Mathnawi*, 6, 4747)

Rumi used various sources to derive the material for these tales, including the KORAN and miscellaneous folktales. In spite of the striking variety of his sources and forms, the *Mathnawi* is a unified work, planned around a central theme and aimed at proving different points, such as those found in Sufi's interpretations of Islamic wisdom.

In the *Mathnawi*, Rumi expresses pity for people who live as he used to—blind to the fact that the surrounding world is just a blanket covering reality. He describes the tangible things in life as dreams or prisons:

> *Meaning of the wind makes it rush*
> *about like a mill wheel—an internal*
> *prisoner of a stream.*
>
> (*Mathnawi*, 1, 3333)

For the poet, reality is love, and materialism and tangibility only fog its shining essence. He urges people to shake off the stifling cover of everyday life and to discover the real world:

> *Let go of your worries*
> *and be completely clear-hearted,*
> *like the face of a mirror*
> *that contains no images.*
>
> (*The Divani Shamsi Tabriz*, XIII)

Rumi's poetry has influenced not only Islamic literature and civilization but also world literature, philosophy, and culture. Some elements of Hegel's philosophical teachings were inspired by Rumi, whose works have been translated into most world languages. The importance of Jalaloddin Rumi, "Teacher with Glowing Heart," as he is often called, cannot be overrated.

English Versions of Works by Jalaloddin Rumi

The Book of Love: Poems of Ecstasy and Longing. Translated by Coleman Barks. New York: Harper-Collins, 2003.

Mathnawi. Translated by E. H. Whinfield. London: Watkins Publishing, 2002.

The Soul of Rumi: A New Collection of Ecstatic Poems. Translated by Coleman Barks. San Francisco: HarperSanFrancisco, 2001.

Works about Jalaloddin Rumi

Friedlander, Shems. *Rumi and the Whirling Dervishes.* New York: Parabola Books, 2003.

Johnson, Will. *Rumi: Gazing at the Beloved: The Radical Practice of Beholding the Divine.* Rochester, Vt.: Inner Traditions International, 2003.

Lewis, Franklin D. *Rumi—Past and Present, East and West: The Life, Teachings and Poetry of Jalal al-Din Rumi.* Oxford, U.K.: Oneworld Publications, 2004.

Rutebeuf (fl. 1245–1285) *poet, playwright, hagiographer*

Very little is known of Rutebeuf's life, except that he lived in Paris, introduced a sense of individualism into medieval French poetry, and produced his works between 1248 and 1272. He apparently died before 1285.

Rutebeuf wrote in a variety of genres: hagiography (biography of saints' lives), drama, and of course, poetry. Rutebeuf mastered the various intricate forms of medieval French poetry, proving to be a virtuoso in rhyme. His poems range from moral polemics to crusade propaganda to political satire and to personal complaints of his poverty and misfortune.

Some of Rutebeuf's personal problems may have stemmed from his involvement in religious and political events of the time. Starting in 1252, the masters of the University of Paris quarreled with the Mendicant friars over authority in parish duties and teaching positions in the theology faculty. Although Pope Alexander IV ruled in favor of the friars in 1255, the secular masters of the university refused to recognize the ruling and continued to stage protests and resist the Mendicants' attempts to take control of parish duties and the theology faculty. The university masters hired Rutebeuf to write poems that explained and popularized their viewpoints while satirizing and attacking the friars' positions.

Rutebeuf also attacked the clergy in a morality play, *Le Miracle de Théophile* (The miracle of Théophile). Théophile is a cleric who makes a deal with the devil to regain his wealth and power, which he then uses to insult his bishop and other priests. After seven years, Théophile repents to save his soul, and the Virgin Mary fights the devil and reclaims the priest's soul for heaven. Théophile publicly repents and summarizes his sin:

> The devil, who assaults good men,
> Made my soul commit a sin
> For which I should die;
> But Our Lady, who directs her own,
> Turned me from the path of wrong
> Where I had strayed
> And lost my way.

Rutebeuf used another genre, the fabliau (a short, comic tale), to attack the self-interest and hypocrisy of both church and state in *Renart le Bestourné* (Renart the Hypocrite). This poem uses the characters from the ROMAN DE RENART to portray a society ruined by corruption and lies.

While poverty and bad luck were a common poetic trope of medieval poets, Rutebeuf gave it a personal stamp that prefigures the poetry of François Villon. Many scholars see these complaints as Rutebeuf's greatest contribution to medieval French poetry. As the literary historian David Coward says, it "goes beyond a literary persona and expresses not collective values but a distinctive individual consciousness."

An English Version of Works by Rutebeuf
Medieval French Plays. Translated by Richard Axton and John Stevens. New York: Barnes & Noble, 1971.

Works about Rutebeuf
Coward, David. "Lyric Poetry to Rutebeuf" in *A History of French Literature: From Chanson de Geste to Cinema.* Oxford, U.K.: Blackwell, 2002.
Ham, Edward Billings. *Rutebeuf and Louis IX.* Chapel Hill: University of North Carolina Press, 1962.
Regalado, Nancy Freeman. *Poetic Patterns in Rutebeuf: A Study in Noncourtly Poetic Modes of the Thirteenth Century.* New Haven, Conn.: Yale University Press, 1970.

Saadī (Sadī, Mosharref od-Dīn ibn Mosleh od-Dīn Sa'dī) (ca. 1210–ca. 1290)
poet, writer

Mosharref od-Dīn ibn Mosleh od-Dīn Sa'dī, known simply as Saadī, was born in Shiraz, Persia (present-day Iran). He received traditional Islamic education at the renowned Nezamiyeh College in Baghdad. The unsettled conditions following the Mongol invasion caused Saadī to leave his native land and wander for years through the lands of Syria, Iraq, Egypt, India, and Central Asia. After 30 years of wandering, he returned to Shiraz as an old man. His tomb in Shiraz is a revered shrine.

Saadī was a great master of love poetry and prose, rich with similes and metaphors: "She came forth as morn succeeding a dark night, or as the waters of life issuing from the gloom." Another distinguishing feature of his writing is its symbolism; for example, when he uses love to represent a spiritual quest for fulfillment or knowledge: "The thirst of my heart cannot be slaked with a drop of water, nor if I should drink rivers would it be lessened."

In his works, Saadī demonstrates a subtle understanding of human emotions and a great practical wisdom. Many of his quotations have become aphorisms because of their humor and precise phrasing, such as this one from an autobiographical sketch in which an old man tells the tired author, who has traveled hard and stopped his journey at the foot of the mountain: "It is better to walk and rest, than to run and be oppressed."

Saadī's main works are the *Bustan* (The place of sweet scents, 1257) and the *Golestan* (The rose garden, 1258). The *Bustan,* a book of moral anecdotes in verse, is divided into several parts according to various aspects of human thought and behavior, as evidenced by the chapter titles: "On Justice, Wisdom, and Common Sense"; "On Love, Infatuation, and Insanity"; and "On Being Satisfied by the Little," to name a few.

The *Golestan* is a combination of prose and poetry. It contains tales, personal anecdotes, humorous reflections, and moral advice. These works reveal Saadī's preference for the freedom of dervishes, who choose their one way in life, over the fate of those who depend on others for their survival or happiness.

Saadī's subtle humor and wisdom garnered him the title "The Genius of Shiraz," for he is and continues to be one of the greatest masters of love poetry and philosophical aphorism.

English Versions of Works by Saadī
The Bostan of Saadi: (The Orchard). Translated by Barlas M. Aqil-Hossain. London: Octagon Press, 1998.

Morals Pointed and Tales Adorned: The Bustan of Saadi. Translated by G. M. Wickens. Toronto: University of Toronto Press, 1974.

Works about Saadī

Anonymous. "Sa'di-e-Shirazi." Available online. URL: http://shirazcity.org/shiraz/Shiraz%20Information/Famous%20People/Sa'di%20e.htm. Downloaded on April 8, 2004.

Bashiri, Iraj. "A Brief Note on the Life of Shaykh Muslih al-Din Sa'di Shirazi." Available online. URL: http://www.angelfire.com/rnb/bashiri/Poets/Sadi.html. Downloaded April 8, 2004.

Shah, Idries. *The Sufis.* New York: Anchor Books, 1971, 111–116.

saga (12th–14th centuries) *literary genre*

The saga, as a literary term, generally refers to a cycle of stories composed and written in the medieval Norse, Icelandic, and Germanic worlds. Though other cultures use the form of the saga in their literature (for instance, Celtic cultures retell family sagas in works of BARDIC POETRY), the Norse and Icelandic sagas are important for what they reveal about the history and mythology (*see* MYTHOLOGY, NORSE) of the Scandinavian cultures sharing a Germanic origin. Largely written in the 13th century, the stories in the sagas were composed and communicated for centuries as a type of ORAL LITERATURE and were recorded only when Christian missionary efforts brought a new type of literacy, and a new literary history, to Scandinavia. While works such as SNORRI STURLUSON's *Prose EDDA* reflect knowledge of the BIBLE as well as the myths of HOMER and VIRGIL, the sagas reveal native customs, beliefs, and social mores associated with Icelandic, Norse, and Germanic cultures.

Most of the sagas are assumed to have taken their final shape by the beginning of the 12th century, when efforts to record them began. Depending on where they were transcribed, most of the existing manuscripts were written in Old Icelandic and Old Norse. The scribes recording them would most likely have been educated through the Church and would therefore have been Christian. The histories and tales recorded in the sagas, however, date almost entirely to a pre-Christian era when northern Europe was ruled by the Scandinavian tribes collectively known as the Vikings. Vikings are traditionally depicted as adventurers, merchants, and warriors with a strong appreciation for challenge who also celebrated achievement in battle. They migrated widely, and their explorations were broader still, reaching the eastern coast of North America sometime in the 10th century. Viking tales preserve a strong heroic code most aptly shown through fierceness in battle. In the sagas, human figures battle with or against divine creatures, and legends that abound in supernatural elements just as accurately represent the cultural values and religious beliefs of the pre-Christian Icelandic, Norse, and German peoples.

Many of the sagas, in addition to gods, kings, queens, and mighty warriors, feature a *Valkyrie* figure. These were the divine women who served mead in *Valhalla,* the hall where spirits of those killed in battle feasted and fought after their mortal deaths. They were also the choosers of the slain, and they decided who would die on the field of battle.

Although the Icelandic NJAL'S SAGA and Norse *Egil's Saga* are frequently read and referenced, the most famous saga has to be the *Volsunga Saga,* or *Song of the Volsungs* (ca. 1270), the Icelandic version of the NIBELUNGENLIED (ca. 1205). The Norweigian version, *Saga of Thidrek of Bern* (ca. 1250), replaces the hero with Thidrek (Dietrich to the Germans), but the outlines of the story remain the same. Sigurd, among his many other adventures, slays a dragon, finds the hoard of Nibelung gold, and rescues the warrior maiden Brynhild. He is later forced, through a magic drink, to marry Gudrun, and Brynhild plots revenge. In addition to a portrayal of the Germanic warrior code, the *Volsung* cycle contains echoes of CHIVALRY/COURTLY LOVE that reflect the influence of outside cultures and beliefs during the reign of King Haakon IV.

Other sagas composed in the 13th century include the *Eyrbyggia Saga,* which tells of the feud between the Snorri family and Thorolf Twist-foot.

Viga Glum's Saga, whose eponymous hero was a king who ruled Iceland around 940, portrays the social manners and legislative practices of 10th-century Iceland as well as the religious ideas of the time. The *Laxdaela Saga* (ca. 1245), thought by many to have been composed by a woman, tells the story of Aud the Deep-minded and her descendants. Weland the smith, who has semimagical powers, appears frequently in the Germanic sagas, as well as in the poem BEOWULF and certain OLD ENGLISH POETRY, indicating the shared Germanic origins of the peoples of northern Europe.

The color, vitality, violence, and poetry of the sagas continue to inspire retellings, perhaps most famously in the operas of Richard Wagner and *The Lord of the Rings* trilogy by J. R. R. Tolkien.

English Versions of Sagas

Egil's Saga. Translated by Hermann Palsson and Paul Edwards. New York: Penguin Classics, 1977.

The Saga of the Volsungs. Translated by Jesse L. Byock. New York: Penguin Classics, 2002.

The Sagas of the Icelanders. Edited by Robert Kellogg. New York: Penguin 2001.

Sagas of Warrior-Poets. Translated by Diana Whaley. New York: Penguin Classics, 2002.

Seven Viking Romances. Translated by Hermann Palsson and Paul Edwards. New York: Penguin Classics, 1985.

Works about the Sagas

Byock, Jesse L. *Feud in the Icelandic Saga.* Berkeley: University of California Press, 1993.

Jones, Gwyn. *A History of the Vikings.* Oxford: Oxford University Press, 2001.

Roberts, David and Jon Krakauer. *Iceland: Land of the Sagas.* New York: Villard, 1998.

Saints

See AMBROSE, SAINT; AUGUSTINE, SAINT; FRANCIS OF ASSISI, SAINT; FULGERTIUS, SAINT; JEROME, SAINT.

Sallust (Gaius Sallustius Crispus) (86–35 B.C.) *historian*

Sallust was a Roman historian and political propagandist who lived and worked during a time of great unrest in the Roman world. The old order of the Roman Republic was breaking down, and new demagogic leaders, particularly Julius CAESAR, were coming to power.

Sallust was born in the town of Amiternum. Throughout much of his life, he played an important role in the political events in Rome. As a member of the Senate, he supported Caesar's ambitions and also served as the commander of one of Caesar's legions. For his loyalty, Caesar rewarded Sallust by making him governor of Numidia, a province in North Africa. As a governor, Sallust was more interested in making money for himself than in benefiting the people for whom he was ostensibly responsible. After Caesar's assassination in 44 B.C., Sallust fell out of favor and retired to his estate. No longer directly involved in politics, he turned his thoughts to intellectual pursuits and labored on his scholarly projects until his death.

One of Sallust's most important works is his *History of the Roman Republic,* which was written in five volumes, of which only fragments remain. Despite its title, the work does not cover the history of Rome, only the political unrest which Sallust either participated in or witnessed.

Sallust's best-known work is a monograph titled *The Conspiracy of Catiline,* about the famous events of 63 B.C. The conspiracy was an attempted coup by Catiline, a disaffected Roman politician who had failed to achieve high office through constitutional means. He sought to raise a rebellion against Rome, burn the city, and seize power in the resulting chaos. In his monograph, Sallust details the course of events during Catiline's bid for power and how the plot was defeated.

The style of *Catiline* is largely based on the writings of THUCYDIDES, and it is also clear that much of Sallust's political philosophy comes from PLATO.

The historian emphasizes drama over accuracy and seems to be more interested in telling a good story than in telling a truthful one. Therefore, although his writings are the best source of information on the Catilinian conspiracy, many of its details are questionable.

Furthermore, as Sallust had been deeply involved in politics himself, his own personal feelings clearly interfered with his presentation of historical facts. As he had been allied with Caesar, his depiction of Caesar's opponents is highly negative, aside from the famous statesman Cato, whom Sallust seems to have respected. Sallust's style betrays a feeling of resentment toward those with views different from his own, and much of the material in his monograph seems to be simple moralizing rather than historical reconstruction.

Sallust's other important work, less famous than *Catiline,* is another monograph called *War against Jugurtha,* also known as *History of the Jugurthine War.* Jugurtha was a North African king against whom Rome fought a bitter and difficult war from 111 to 105 B.C., and it is through Sallust's writings that modern historians have a good understanding of this war's events. Nevertheless, as with the *Catiline,* the account and details are biased.

Sallust's writings are important for their historical and literary significance. Despite their inaccuracies, his works provide much valuable information on the Roman world during a highly confusing period. Sallust's literary style, based largely on earlier Greek writers such as Thucydides, greatly influenced later authors. The Roman historian TACITUS, in particular, clearly took much of his stylistic inspiration from Sallust.

English Versions of Works by Sallust

Histories. Edited by Patrick McGushin. Oxford: Oxford University Press, 1992.
The Jugurthine War and the Conspiracy of Catiline. Translated by S. A. Hanford. New York: Penguin Classics, 1978.

Works about Sallust

Syme, Ronald. *Sallust.* Berkeley: University of California Press, 2002.
Wilkins, Ann Thomas. *Villain or Hero: Sallust's Portrayal of Catiline.* New York: Peter Lang Publishers, 1994.

Sappho of Lesbos (fl. ca. 610–ca. 580 B.C.)
lyric poet

Sappho was born on the prosperous Aegean island of Lesbos, a seat of intellectual and cultural activity, and spent most of her life in Mytilene, its largest city. Her father, Skamandronymos, and her mother, Kleïs, were of the aristocracy and also had a son, Charaxos. Sappho married Kerkylas of Andros, a prosperous businessman with whom she had a daughter named Kleïs, after Sappho's mother. Near the end of her life, it is believed she may have been exiled to Sicily.

On Lesbos, the poet established a school to instruct the daughters of well-to-do families in the arts of poetry and music. Sappho, with her pupils—who had little contact with men until they were betrothed—formed a cult devoted to Aphrodite, the goddess of beauty and love. Based on the scant evidence found in her poetry, it appears Sappho taught her young students, not inappropriately, to luxuriate in their loveliness and to look forward to matrimony. In "Song of the Wedding Bed," for example, she espouses the emotional and carnal pleasures of marriage:

> Bride, warm with rose-
> colored love, brightest
> ornament of the Paphian,
> come to the bedroom now,
> enter the bed and play
> tenderly with your man.
> May the Evening Star
> lead you eagerly
> to that instant when you

will gaze in wonder
before the silver throne
of Hera, queen of marriage.

Sappho's poems were originally collected in nine books, of which only a few fragments and one complete poem ("Prayer to Aphrodite") still exist. The last of her nine books comprised "Epithalamia," lyric nuptial odes sung at different phases of wedding ceremonies. She wrote in the Lesbian-Aeolian dialect, and her themes were primarily of personal relationships (often with other women) and love.

It is tempting to believe the much-perpetrated legend that the passionate poetess ended her life by flinging herself from a cliff into the sea because her love for a beautiful youth, Phaon, was unrequited. However, this tale probably arose from a misinterpretation or mistranslation of some ancient work, for the facts of Sappho's death simply are not known.

Critical Analysis

Sappho's poetry arose from oral tradition, in which poems were sung or recited, often to the accompaniment of music (*see* ORAL LITERATURE/TRADITION). Unlike her predecessors, however, Sappho experimented with rhythm, meter, and monody, a technique characterized by a single line of melody. She invented, or at least perfected, the so-called Sapphic strophe, a complex, rigorous, and challenging four-line verse later adapted by Roman poets.

Sappho dedicated many of her poems to her pupils, of whom she clearly had favorites. Her devotion to them and her anguish when they left the school, withdrew their love from her, or transferred their affections to others, is obvious. In "To Atthis," she addresses this torment:

Love—bittersweet, irrepressible—
loosens my limbs and I tremble.

Yet, Atthis, you despise my being.
To chase Andromeda, you leave me.

And in "To Anaktoria," she expresses her sorrow at a loved one's departure:

Some say cavalry and others claim
infantry or a fleet of long oars
is the supreme sight on the black earth.
I say it is

the one you love. And easily proved.
Didn't Helen—who far surpassed all
mortals in beauty—desert the best
of men, her king,
and sail off to Troy and forget
her daughter and dear kinsmen? Merely
the Kyprian's gaze made her bend and led
her from her path;

these things remind me now
of Anaktoria who is far,
and I
for one

would rather see her warm supple step
and the sparkle of her face—than watch all
    the
dazzling chariots and armored
    hoplites of Lydia.

In "Prayer to Aphrodite," we see Sappho's dedication to and the manner of her dependence on the goddess:

On your dazzling throne, Aphrodite
sly eternal daughter of Zeus,
I beg you: do not crush me with grief,
but come to me now . . . and free me
from fearful agony.

In other lines from the poem, we see an external outpouring of Sappho's thoughts and beliefs concerning her loves, losses, and evidence of Aphrodite's aid. ". . . Come to me now," Sappho begs, "as once / you heard my far cry, and yielded." Aphrodite replies, "What does your mad heart desire? / Whom shall I make love you, Sappho, / who is turning her back on you?" And upon agreeing to make Sappho's loved one love her in return,

Aphrodite warns, "She will love you, though unwillingly."

Sappho has been censured throughout history for her erotic expressions of affection for her pupils, but it is entirely possible that what is translated as "I" was originally written to denote "we." This means poems that appear to express the exquisite longing of a single individual were actually written to be performed in public by choruses made up of Sappho's young students. In addition, modern readers must take into account that the affection Sappho reveals in her poetry may have been the norm in her time and culture.

In other poems, such as "Kleïs," we see not only Sappho's simplicity of style and skillful use of words, but also her love for her daughter:

> I have a small daughter who is beautiful
> like a gold flower. I would not trade
> my darling Kleïs for all Lydia or even
> for lovely Lesbos.

Critic Daniel Mendelsohn writes, "With a directness seemingly unmediated by vast stretches of time, Sappho seems to speak to us quite clearly today . . ." Centuries after Sappho flourished, Plato wrote, "Some say nine Muses—but count again. / Behold the tenth: Sappho of Lesbos." What comes to us of Sappho's simple yet evocative and provocative verse—by turns witty, graceful, and fraught with passion—has a radiant vitality that still resonates with modern audiences.

English Versions of Works by Sappho of Lesbos

If Not, Winter: Fragments of Sappho. Translated by Anne Carson. New York: Alfred A. Knopf, 2003.

Sappho's Lyre: Archaic Lyric and Women Poets of Ancient Greece. Translated by Diane Rayor. Berkeley: University of California Press, 1991.

Works about Sappho of Lesbos

Mendelsohn, Daniel. "In Search of Sappho." *The New York Review of Books* L, no. 13 (August 14, 2003): 26–29.

Reynolds, Margaret. *The Sappho History.* New York: St. Martin's Press, 2003.

Sei Shōnagon (ca. 965–unknown)
memoirist, poet

Sei Shōnagon was born to a father named Motosuke, a member of the Kiyo-wara family, who worked as an imperial official and was also a scholar and poet. Some historians believe that Sei Shōnagon was briefly married to a government official named Tachibana no Norimitsu, with whom she had a son. It is known for certain that she served as a lady-in-waiting to Empress Sadako until Sadako's death in 1000. After her service with the empress ends, nothing more about Sei's life is known, including the date of her death. Tradition has it that she died lonely and in poverty, but this may be the invention of those who disapproved of her worldly ways.

Her name may be a title obscuring her given name: *Shōnagon* means "minor counselor," and *Sei* refers to her father's family. However, her contemporary and fellow court writer MURASAKI SHIKIBU, who wrote *The Tale of Genji*, mentions Sei Shōnagon in the context of "those Chinese writings of hers that she so presumptuously scatters about the place . . . full of imperfections." Murasaki calls her a "gifted woman, to be sure," but utterly frivolous. This scorn perhaps reflects a competitive spirit prevalent at a court where Sei's intelligence, wit, sensitivity to beauty, observation of detail, and occasional intolerance and callousness were perceived as a threat.

What is known about Sei Shōnagon's life survives in the *Makura no Soshi*, or *Pillow Book*, which she began writing in 994 and continued for more than 10 years. The *Pillow Book* is a miscellany of lists, vignettes, descriptions, thoughts, and poems. None of the 300 selections in the book are longer than a few pages, and they are arranged in no obvious order. During the Heian period in Japan, both upper-class men and women were educated and literate, and many frequently recorded thoughts and informal notes that they kept in their sleeping quarters, possibly in the drawers of their wooden pillows. Sei's book makes reference to the works of at least a dozen other authors, only one of whose manuscripts survives.

Sei is remembered as a snob for the occasional derision she shows to those of the lower classes; she is equally critical of people with poor grooming habits or unattractive appearances. Nonetheless, the minute detail, rhythmic language, and frank tone of her work provide a varied and engaging look at court life in imperial Japan.

Sei's *Pillow Book* established a tradition of *zuihitsu*, or "random notes," which continues to the present day and represents some of the most valuable works of Japanese literature. Despite Murasaki Shikibu's criticism Sei's language is pure Heian Japanese, with very few Chinese words or inflections. Historians appreciate the wealth of information her work provides about life in Japan over 1,000 years ago.

In her writing, Sei Shōnagon's approach to life is primarily aesthetic. Her frequent use of the words *okashi* (charming) or *medetashi* (splendid) not only serve as descriptive terms but also create a repetitive, incantatory writing style that can prove difficult to translate into modern English. Sei evaluates things by the feelings they provoke and thoughtfully analyzes the qualities of both ugliness and beauty. Among her many lists are those things that give a feeling of heat (such as a very fat, hairy person or a coppersmith at work) and a list of unpleasant things (including people who show off their children, mosquitoes who appear just when one is about to sleep, and having a story interrupted by someone who has just entered the room).

Other sections of the *Pillow Book* recount events at court or offer vignettes of Sei's life and observations, showing her keen awareness of the transient nature of life. Although not sexually explicit, the *Pillow Book* also speaks candidly of Sei's—and others's—love affairs.

The original manuscript of the *Pillow Book* disappeared, and the earliest manuscript that survives was compiled 500 years after the period during which Sei Shōnagon wrote. The work was popular enough to be recopied many times, but copyists frequently made changes that have led to several different existing versions, many with the sections arranged in varying order. The *Pillow Book* was issued as a printed book in the 17th century and has become a revered classic in Japan.

English Versions of a Work by Sei Shōnagon
The Pillow Book of Sei Shōnagon. Translated by Ivan Morris. New York: Columbia University Press, 1991.
The Pillow Book of Sei Shōnagon. Translated by Arthur Waley. New York: HarperCollins, 1979.

A Work about Sei Shōnagon
Blensdorf, Jan. *My Name is Sei Shōnagon.* New York: Overlook Press, 2003.

Seneca (Lucius Annaeus Seneca, "Seneca the Younger") (ca. 4 B.C.–A.D. 65)
philosopher, orator, essayist, dramatist, nonfiction writer

Of Spanish descent, Seneca was born in Cordova into a distinguished family of some means. As a young boy, he went to Rome to pursue an education. His father, Seneca the Elder, was of the wealthy equestrian class and spent a great deal of time in Rome. A renowned orator, Seneca the Elder counted among his intimates the outstanding rhetoricians of the time. In his declining years, at the urging of his three sons, he penned his memoirs, basing them on recollections of his eminent colleagues. He was also an exacting disciplinarian who planned his sons' education to prepare them for prominent political positions in Rome.

Seneca's mother, Helvia, was a woman of exceptional intelligence with a profound interest in philosophy. She might have pursued formal study if her husband, 30 years her senior, had not opposed it. However, she played an influential role in her son Seneca's career.

Seneca was frail and perpetually dogged by ailments, but he overcame his frailty and compensated for his physical limitations by exercising his mind. A self-disciplined and enthusiastic pupil, he received instruction in language, literature, and rhetoric, for which he proved to have a natural flair. His teachers of philosophy included Attalus the Stoic and representatives from the Cynic sect and the Pythagorean school.

Having spent his early adulthood visiting Egypt, Seneca returned to Rome in the year 31 to launch his political career. His aunt, into whose care he had been entrusted in Rome, was married to the governor of Egypt and used her influence to get Seneca elected to the quaestorship (a financial administrative position); later, he became a magistrate of public works. As a lawyer, Seneca's trenchant oratory and pithy observations secured his reputation and earned him a private fortune. Regrettably, these orations, and all his works prior to 41, have been lost.

The emperor Caligula was jealous of Seneca's fame and talent and would have condemned him to death if a courtesan had not persuaded Caligula that Seneca was in poor health and soon to die. Ironically, this brush with mortality prompted Seneca to abandon his profession in favor of writing and philosophical study. During Claudius's reign, though, the milieu of political intrigue nearly undid him once again when the emperor's third wife, Messalina, unjustly charged Seneca with illicit goings-on in the company of the princess. An execution was ordered, but his sentence was later commuted to banishment, and Seneca spent eight years in Corsica.

In *Ad Helviam Matrem de Consolatione* (Consolation to Helvia), Seneca uses his rhetorical eloquence to entreat his mother not to lament his fate, making the Stoic argument that the mind is boundless, infinite, beyond time and place, and incapable of being "exiled." He goes on to explain that while he may be banished physically, he still possesses the knowledge of nature's beauty and his own goodness.

Ad Polybium was also written and published during this period. Addressed to one of the em-peror's freedmen, it is written in a spirit very different from the philosophy with which Seneca consoled his mother. The exile describes his abject misery and heaps extravagant praise upon the attendant in an effort to have his expulsion retracted. Though these appeals were fruitless, Seneca was eventually recalled from Corsica in 49 by Agrippina, Emperor Claudius's fourth wife, to tutor her son, Nero, in rhetoric and etiquette.

Five years later, Agrippina poisoned Claudius, and Nero acceded to the throne. For the next five years, under the tutelage of Seneca and Burrus, the young emperor's prefect, Nero administered the public affairs in Rome with integrity and benevolence. Seneca recognized Nero's brutal nature, however, and wished to instill in him a sense of mercy and forbearance. Agrippina, on the other hand, scorned moral instruction and, as a result, Seneca retired from public life.

During his retirement, Seneca wrote a multitude of works, but his writing ended when, in the year 65, he was accused of complicity in a conspiracy to assassinate Nero, who subsequently ordered him to commit suicide, an order he obeyed with stoic courage.

Critical Analysis

Although Seneca dabbled in diverse schools of philosophical thought, he was particularly influenced by Stoicism, the creed of the Roman aristocrat, which found its way into even his courtroom discourse. Stoicism held that nature is governed by divine reason, and since humans should strive to coexist in concert with nature, living a life illuminated by reason is the ultimate virtue. Those who conduct themselves in this way have no fear of ill fortune, nor should they be tempted by good fortune, for they are masters of their inner domain. Seneca also believed that when he encountered vice in others, it was his obligation to attempt reform. These tenets must have provided no small comfort to him when he was expelled to Corsica, particularly his self-assurance of his own virtue.

Seneca's *Epistulae morales,* a collection of 124 moral essays, largely reflect and promote Stoic ethics, morals, and social outlook, with numerous asides providing an insider's glimpse into Roman political life in the mid-first century. They include *De Providentia* (On Fortune), which explores why bad things happen to good people; and *De Ira* (On Anger), which conveys Seneca's aversion to anger and the blood lust and unbridled violence that it engenders. He argues that greatness exists only in tranquillity; that people of character may choose not to act impulsively; and that by cherishing others, people can set aside real and imagined abuses.

De Clementia (On Mercy), another moral essay, was intended as instruction for Nero. Mercy, Seneca says, means refraining from retaliation or punishment when one has the power to inflict it. In one particularly persuasive passage, he reminds Nero of an incident in which the emperor demonstrated leniency. Burrus was about to execute two outlaws and produced paper on which Nero was to seal their fate, but the emperor cried out, "Would that I had not learned to write." Seneca praises Nero lavishly for his response:

> What an utterance! All nations should have heard it. . . . What an utterance! It should have been spoken before a gathering of all mankind, that unto it princes and kings might pledge allegiance. What an utterance! Worthy of the universal innocence of mankind. . . .

Seneca also suggests that if Nero continues to behave in such a manner, his greatness will be assured:

> That kindness of your heart will be recounted, will be diffused . . . throughout the whole body of the empire, and all things will be molded into your likeness. . . . There will be citizens, there will be allies worthy of this goodness, and uprightness will return to the whole world. . . .
> (*De Clementia*, Book II)

Throughout the centuries, Seneca has inspired thinkers and artists—Romantics, transcendentalists, absurdists, existentialists, and more—who

have been attracted by the Stoic belief in self-reliance, the notion that God is present in both the natural and the rational, the refusal to become embroiled in a civilization gone mad while maintaining a sense of responsibility to society and humankind, and the fascination with the questions of death and suicide. As Anna Lydia Motto writes in her work *Seneca:*

> Among the outstanding personalities of imperial Rome there is no one who can more readily arouse our interest and admiration than Lucius Annaeus Seneca. Tutor, guardian, minister, victim of Nero, author of tragedies, scientific treatises, philosophical essays, and moral epistles, he was a man to honor—and to serve—any age. . . .

From Seneca's *Epistulae morales* and other surviving works, it can be deduced that his philosophical and literary training served him well. His *Naturales quaestiones* (Natural Questions) is a seven-book scientific discourse on the natural universe, most notably cosmology. *Apocolocyntosis divi Claudii* (The Pumpkinification of the Divine Claudius) is a satire, and his 10 tragedies—including *Phaedra, Agamemnon, Oedipus, Medea, Thyestes,* and *Hercules Enraged*—are adaptations of Greek myths and legends (*see* MYTHOLOGY, GREEK AND ROMAN). These works, as scholar Kenneth J. Atchity points out, reflect "the hope and despair of a progressively decadent empire" and reveal Seneca's knowledge of "the darkest recesses of the human heart." Perhaps this is why Seneca holds a significant place in the body of world literature, for despite the passage of time, the heart of the matters upon which he expounded remain timeless.

English Versions of Works by Seneca

Hercules. Translated by Ranjit Bolt. New York: Theatre Communications Group, 1997.

Moral and Political Essays. Translated by John M. Cooper. Cambridge, U.K.: Cambridge University Press, 1995.

Oedipus of Lucius Annaeus Seneca. Translated by Michael Elliot Rutenberg. Wauconda, Ill.: Bolchazy-Carducci, 2001.

Seneca: Tragedies: Hercules, Trojan Women, Phoenician Women, Medea, Phaedra, Vol. 1. Edited by John G. Fitch. Cambridge, Mass.: Harvard University Press, 2002.

Works about Seneca

Henderson, John. *Morals and Villas in Seneca's Letters: Places to Dwell.* Cambridge, U.K.: Cambridge University Press, 2004.

Mayer, Roland. *Seneca: Phaedra.* London: Gerald Duckworth & Co., 2003.

Motto, Anna Lydia. *Seneca.* New York: Twayne Publishers, 1973.

Pratt, Norman T. *Seneca's Drama.* Chapel Hill: University of North Carolina Press, 2001.

Veyne, Paul. *Seneca: The Life of a Stoic.* Translated by David Sullivan. London: Taylor & Francis, 2002.

Sextus Empiricus   (ca. 150–ca. 225)
philosopher

Sextus Empiricus was a Greek physician most likely connected with one of the great schools in Athens, Alexandria, or Rome. The ideas set forth in his *Outlines of Pyrrhonism* form the basis of our understanding of the philosophy of skepticism as founded by Pyrrho (ca. 360–270 B.C.). The philosophies of SOCRATES, PLATO, and ARISTOTLE, though not strictly Pyrrhonian in practice, also rest on the exercise of doubt and inquiry to advance knowledge and discover truth. For Sextus, the practice of skepticism required setting one judgment against another, or contrasting one appearance with another, to successively undermine the validity of any form of knowledge and finally reach a suspension of judgment. Only in this manner could one avoid dogmatism. The ultimate goal of skeptical inquiry was to achieve *ataraxia*, a state of unperturbedness equated with peaceful living and tranquility. Two other contemporary philosophies, those of the Stoics and of EPICURUS, sought the same end but through slightly different means.

In total, 11 books by Sextus survive, in which he applies his trademark skeptical methodology to the fields of logic, physics, natural philosophy, and ethics. *Against the Physicists* (sometimes translated as *Against the Mathematicians*) and *Against the Logicians* (also known as *Against the Dogmatists,* or *Against the Professors*) have been translated and studied by generations of scholars. The rediscovery of Sextus's works in Europe in the 16th century influenced other skeptics such as Michel de Montaigne and René Descartes.

English Versions of Works by Sextus Empiricus

Against the Ethicists. Translated by Richard Bett. Oxford, U.K.: Oxford University Press, 2000.

Against the Grammarians. Translated by David L. Blank. Oxford: Oxford University Press, 1998.

Outlines of Pyrrhonism: Sextus Empiricus. Translated by R. G. Bury. Amherst, N.Y.: Prometheus Books, 1990.

Works about Sextus Empiricus

Bailey, Alan. *Sextus Empiricus and Pyrrhonian Skepticism.* Oxford, U.K.: Clarendon Press, 2002.

Floridi, Luciano. *Sextus Empiricus: The Transmission and Recovery of Pyrrhonism.* Oxford: Oxford University Press, 2002.

Hallie, Philip P., ed. *Sextus Empiricus: Selections from the Major Writings on Scepticism, Man, & God.* Indianapolis, Ind.: Hackett Publishing, 1985.

Shahnameh   *(Shah-nama, Shahname, The Epic of Kings, The Book of Kings)*
(10th century) *Persian epic*

The *Shahnameh*, an EPIC poem, is not only a masterpiece of Persian literature but also an important work for Persian national identity. It was written in the 10th century, after three centuries of Arab yoke, when Persian nationalism was slowly reviving.

The *Shahnameh*, was created by Abū ol-Qāsem Mansūr, later known as FIRDAWSĪ, a highly educated Persian intellectual who lived in the late 10th and early 11th centuries. In the text of the *Shahnameh*, Firdawsī repeatedly emphasizes that his role as author is minor, that all he did was versify the myths and narratives of the ORAL LITERATURE/TRADITION of his people. Yet his accomplishment is profound. The *Shahnameh* contains approximately 50,000 couplets that contain multiple stories and a host of heroes.

The first two-thirds of the *Shahnameh* include ancient myths, legends, and historical figures, such as Alexander the Great, dating back to the sixth century B.C. The last third of the poem contains fictionalized stories about historical people, kingdoms, and events, including the Parthian and Sassanian dynasties, ending around the middle of the A.D. seventh century.

The *Shahnameh's* themes are as varied as its stories. They include fate, immortality, filicide, and God's preference for Persia (modern-day Iran) above other nations. Indeed, the poem ends when, in 652, Persia's ruler, Shah Yazdegerd III, is killed. The theme that holds all of the stories together concerns the Persian belief in the role of kings; as long as the kings survive, so does Persia.

Many of the characters in the *Shahnameh* are ancient Persian heroes—generals and commanders who defended the country against its enemies. In vivid and eloquent verse, Firdawzi tells of a multitude of battles and other challenges to Persian sovereignty. His central character is Rostam, called Jahan-Pahlavan ("Champion of the World"), the guardian of the divine right of kingship in Persia and a symbol of the king's sovereignty.

Perhaps the most compelling story in the *Shahnameh* is "The Story of Sohrab and Rostam," in which Rostam kills his son Sohrab for assaulting the ruling *shah* (king). The story is fast-paced, with battles, romance, and inherent conflicts. In addition, the tragic scene in which Rostam realizes the wrongness of what he has done is one of the most poignant scenes ever written in verse. When Rostam removes Sohrab's armor and discovers the man he has mortally wounded is his son, he says:

"Oh, brave and noble youth, and praised
     among
All men, whom I have slain with my own
     hand!"
He wept a bloody stream and tore his hair;
His brow was dark with dust, tears filled his
     eyes.
Sohrab then said, "But this is even worse.
You must not fill your eyes with tears. For
     now
It does not good to slay yourself with grief.
What's happened here is what was meant
     to be."
     ("The Death of Sohrab," ll. 71–78)

Thus, Sohrab's death underscores the poem's theme of God-chosen rulers. By attacking the shah, Sohrab goes against the "natural order" of the world; in turn, Rostam goes against the same when he kills his own son. Yet none can deny that the king Sohrab attacked continues to live for a reason: It is God's will.

Yet another important aspect of the *Shahnameh* is its language. In the 10th century, when the epic was written, the dominant language of literature and culture was Arabic. Persian was deeply affected by this dominance, and more and more Arabic words were entering the Persian language. In his epic, Firdawzi made a conscious effort to avoid words of Arabic origin, using Middle and Modern Persian instead.

The only complete English translation of the *Shahnameh* was published in 1925 by Arthur George and Edmond Warner, while Reuben Levy wrote a prose translation of select verses in 1967, titled *The Epic of the Kings*. The *Shahnameh*, written in rich, expressive language, is considered to be a great masterpiece of world literature and the embodiment of the Persian national spirit.

English Versions of the *Shahnameh*

The Epic of the Kings; Shah-nama, the National Epic of Persia. Translated by Reuben Levy. Chicago: University of Chicago Press, 1967.

Robinson, B. W. *Persian Book of Kings: An Epitome of the Shahnama of Firdawsi.* London: Taylor & Francis, 2002.

The Tragedy of Sohrab and Rostam from the Persian National Epic, the Shahname of Abol-Qasem Ferdowsi. Translated by Jerome W. Clinton. Seattle: University of Washington Press, 1996.

Works about the *Shahnameh*

Davidson, Olga M. *Poet and Hero in the Persian Book of Kings.* Ithaca, N.Y.: Cornell University Press, 1994.

Davis, Dick. *Epic and Sedition: The Case of Firdawzi's Shahname.* Fayetteville: University of Arkansas Press, 1992.

Hillenbrand, Robert. *Shahnama: The Visual Language of the Persian Book of Kings.* Aldershot, Hampshire, U.K.: Ashgate Publishing, 2003.

Shikishi, Princess (d. 1201) *poet*

Princess Shikishi was a 12th-century Japanese poet who wrote in the TANKA form. Like many women in the imperial court, little is known about her life. She was the third daughter of Go-Shirakawa, who became Japan's 77th emperor in 1155. Early in her life she was selected to become a high priestess of the Kamo Shrines, but illness required her resignation. Sometime during the 1190s, she became a Buddhist nun and acquired the Buddhist name Shonyoho.

Shikishi was well known for her poetry, much of which centers on her isolation. Fifteen of the 21 imperial anthologies include 155 of her poems, and 399 poems altogether have been recovered. The majority of her work appears in 100-poem sequences called *hyakushu-uta,* which translator Hiroaki Sato described as a "mosaic describing the changing of the seasons, love, and other matters."

In *Go-Kuden,* a treatise on poetics, Emperor Go-Toba (1180–1239) calls Shikishi one of the most outstanding poets of their time. Her seasonal poems show great sensitivity and creativity in addressing traditional tanka themes, such as the arrival of spring and the scattering of cherry blossoms:

> Though warblers
> have not called,
> in the sound of cascades
> pouring down rocks
> spring is heard.

Her poems about love, on the other hand, focus more on the psychological impact of love than on the meditation of natural images:

> My sleeves' hue
> Is enough to make folk ask—
> I care not!
> The depth of my love—
> If only you would believe in it . . .

Shikishi's poetry is important in that it provides a rare glimpse of a woman's perspective in 12th-century Japan and because it reflects a spiritual dimension that offers several layers of meaning. In addition, Shikishi shows a clear understanding of the Buddhist way of life, full of compassion and detachment from earthly pursuits. Its role in her poetry rivals the animistic themes and passionate passages.

An English Version of Works by Princess Shikishi

String of Beads: Complete Poems of Princess Shikishi. Translated and edited by Hiroaki Sato. Honolulu: University of Hawaii Press, 1993.

Snorri Sturluson (1179–1241) *poet, historian*

A descendant of the poet and hero of *Egils Saga,* Egill Skallagrimsson, Snorri Sturluson was born in Iceland and brought up at Oddi in the home of Jon Loptsson, the most powerful chieftain of his time, from whom he gained a deep appreciation of Icelandic tradition. In 1199 Snorri married an heiress and began to acquire land and power, settling in Reykjaholt, where he wrote most of his works, between 1223 and 1235. He also served as "lawspeaker," or president, of the Icelandic commonwealth for many years. In 1218, he traveled to Norway as a guest of King Haakon IV. As a result of this visit, he became entangled in various political intrigues that ultimately led to his assassination.

Snorri wrote prolifically on a wide range of topics. He is best known for two works, both vast in their scope. The first is the *Prose Edda* (also known as *Younger Edda*), a handbook of poetics that recounts the various legends of Norse mythology (*see* MYTHOLOGY, NORSE) and catalogs the variety of poetic meters used in Icelandic verse. He also wrote the *Heimskringla* (ca. 1220–35), a history of Norwegian kings beginning with their legendary descent from Odin, the Norse warrior-god up to 1177.

Much of the information detailed in Snorri's histories was gathered from ORAL LITERATURE/TRADITION transmitted from the times of the actual events. His genius lay in his ability to utilize his firsthand knowledge of 13th-century politics to illuminate the past. As Magnus Magnusson and Hermann Palsson state in their introduction to Snorri Sturluson's *King Harald's Saga*, "It is primarily the vastness of the conception of *Heimskringla,* the sweep and range of its scope, that marks it out from all the many other Icelandic saga-histories. . . . No one, before or after, attempted anything on such a grand scale."

English Versions of Works by Snorri Sturluson

Heimskringla: History of the Kings of Norway. Translated by Lee M. Hollander. Austin: University of Texas Press, 1991.

King Harald's Saga: Harald Hardradi of Norway. Translated by Magnus Magnusson and Hermann Palsson. New York: Penguin, 1966.

Prose Edda: Tales from Norse Mythology. Translated by Jean I. Young. Berkeley: University of California Press, 2002.

Works about Snorri Sturluson

Bagge, Sverre. *Society and Politics in Snorri Sturluson's Heimskringla.* Berkeley: University of California Press, 1991.

Byock, Jesse L. *Medieval Iceland: Society, Sagas, and Power.* Berkeley: University of California Press, 1988, 32, 53, 54, 71, 73, 74, 78, 89, 99, 133.

Ciklamini, Marlene. *Snorri Sturluson.* Farmington Hills, Mich.: The Gale Group, 1978.

Socrates (ca. 469–399 B.C.) *philosopher, teacher*

Socrates was born in an Athenian township, the child of Sophroniscus, who may have been a sculptor or stoneworker, and Phaenarete, a midwife. The family must have had some financial resources but were certainly not wealthy, for Socrates would later serve with the hoplites, heavily armed foot soldiers who defended the Greek city-states. (According to regulations, citizens who could afford the equipment—helmet, shield, armor, weapons—but could not afford horses served as hoplites.) Socrates distinguished himself numerous times during the course of the Peloponnesian War between Athens and Sparta (431–404 B.C.), a monumental conflict that ultimately stripped Athens of its empire.

The arts, sciences, culture, and civilization of ancient Greece were at their zenith in Socrates' time. The Greek city-states had defeated the mighty Persian Empire in two wars, heroic conflicts that were immortalized as history by HERODOTUS and as drama by AESCHYLUS. SOPHOCLES, EURIPIDES, THUCYDIDES and ARISTOPHANES also flourished during the fifth century B.C.

Socrates was a product of his time, a philosopher who sought to understand the inner self and human behavior, rather than to explain the phenomena of the outside world. Originally, he studied cosmological and natural philosophical theories, but he found them confusing and contradictory. Moreover, he was disappointed that they did not address the issues of selfhood and human morality that had begun to preoccupy him.

There is an often-told—and probably true—tale accounting for Socrates' transformation into a wry and sardonic interrogator. According to the story, Chaerephon, a friend and follower, asked the Oracle at Delphi whether any living man was wiser than Socrates. "No" was the answer. Pondering this, Socrates realized how little he really knew and concluded that he must have been proclaimed wisest only because he appreciated how ignorant he was. His mission, then, would be to procure the assistance of other wise men in his quest for that which is invariably and eternally true, particularly regarding the virtues of individuals and societies.

From this is derived the image that most people today have of Socrates (probably an accurate one): a barefoot, robed, bearded individual wandering and pondering throughout the city of Athens. He has also been described as being subject to fits of abstraction, and Aristophanes has depicted him as strutting like a duck and habitually rolling his eyes, until he arrives at some suitably public arena. Here, he buttonholes an ostensibly wise man—a teacher or a politician, for example—and grills him before an audience in a painstaking truth-seeking exercise that ultimately shows the supposed authority to be uninformed at best, foolish at worst, and always a less-than-rigorous thinker.

This process was the so-called Socratic method, exemplified by the philosopher PLATO, Socrates' most illustrious pupil, in many of his dialogues. Critic David Denby describes the Socratic method like this:

> Socrates the great teacher seems to flatter his students and friends, praising them extravagantly. Oh, yes, they're so wise, so clever, and his own powers are so feeble, so terribly feeble! But he'd just like to ask them some small question: What do they mean by such-and-such a word, such-and-such an idea? And then *wham!* he catches them in some contradiction or confusion, and they're knocked sprawling.

According to Plato, Socrates himself referred to the process as "midwifery," believing the answers already existed in the minds of his students and needed merely to be "birthed" by a skilled specialist. It can be assumed that Socrates' principal goal was elucidation and not humiliation, but that did not detract from the entertainment value of his methods.

Socrates' marriage to Xanthippe is another detail of the great philosopher's life with which most modern readers are familiar. History paints her as a scold, a nag, and a shrew. Another viewpoint depicts her as a devoted and long-suffering woman whose husband did not provide adequately for his family. (Socrates and Xanthippe had at least one son, possibly two or more.) As the scholar I. F. Stone suggests, "Xanthippe had a lifetime of trying to make ends meet and feed the children while [Socrates] went around enjoying himself in philosophical discourse. Socrates' constant boast that unlike the Sophists he never took a fee from his pupils was a luxury for which his poor wife paid the bill."

After Sparta's victory in the Peloponnesian War, Athens was ruled briefly by a brutal right-wing oligarchy known as the Thirty Tyrants. When democracy was restored, Socrates was brought to trial on two charges: "not worshipping the gods whom the State worships, but introducing new and unfamiliar religious practices" and "corrupting the young." Some critics have suggested that Socrates was really indicted because he had been the teacher of two of the rebels and because he remained in Athens during the terrorist dictatorship without protesting the activities of the regime. In any event, he was found guilty and sentenced to death. Plato's *Phaedo* claims to recount the last day of Socrates' life, which ended when he drank hemlock, a poison. (In fact, Plato was absent from that occasion due to travel or illness.)

Critical Analysis

What is known of Socrates' teachings and beliefs has been construed from his biographers and defenders, namely XENOPHON, ARISTOTLE, Aristophanes, and especially Plato.

Xenophon, a historian, former pupil, and disciple, defended Socrates against his indictment by portraying him as a popular teacher of morality and ethics, while Aristotle praised Socrates' use of "inductive arguments" and "universal definitions." Xenophon's works about Socrates include his *Memorabilia* and *Symposium*. In *Clouds*, Aristophanes depicts a deceitful farmer who enrolls his son in a school of philosophy known as the Thinkery, hoping he will become crafty enough to figure out how to erase his debts. Socrates is depicted as "traversing the air and contemplating the sun." Plato, in his Dialogues, attributed some beliefs to Socrates that were not his, like the theory of Forms that is so characteristic of Platonism.

Socrates was, first and foremost, concerned with ethics and human excellence, and he looked for generalities or universal definitions through specifics. He classified values as either intrinsic or instrumental, i.e., serving as a means or agent to another end. Knowledge, integrity, and valor have intrinsic value since they are esteemed for themselves, whereas physical beauty, wealth, and power have only instrumental value as they are appreciated only because of what further use they can be, and may be ill-used as well. Only that which has intrinsic value can give an individual excellence and make him happy. Socrates believed that virtue was synonymous with wisdom and that happiness lies in virtue. Therefore, wickedness could only be a consequence of ignorance, for why would someone knowingly choose to be unhappy? In Plato's *Apology*, the character of Socrates describes himself like this:

> "And so I go about the world obedient to the god, and search and make inquiry into the wisdom of anyone, whether citizen or stranger, who appears to be wise, and if he is not wise, then in vindication of the oracle I show him that he is not wise; and my own action quite absorbs me, and I have not time to give either to any matter of public interest or to any concern of my own."

In the Prelude to *The Trial of Socrates* (which begins, "No other trial, except that of Jesus, has left so vivid an impression on the imagination of Western man as that of Socrates"), I. F. Stone discusses the mutual debt of Plato and Socrates:

> It is to Plato's literary genius that Socrates owes his preeminent position as a secular saint of Western civilization. And it is Socrates who keeps Plato on the best-seller lists. Plato is the only philosopher who turned metaphysics into drama. Without the enigmatic and engaging Socrates as the principal character of his dialogs, Plato would not be the one philosopher who continues to charm a wide audience in every generation.

Yet it is Socrates who has influenced the whole of Western thought. His teachings on ethics and the way he lived his life—according to his beliefs—have been followed by philosophers ever since. Socrates' impact on modern thought continues to the present day in the way we define such concepts as ethics, morals, ignorance, and wisdom.

Works about Socrates

Bowen, Richard and Iassen Ghiuselev. *Socrates: Greek Philosopher*. Broomall, Pa.: Mason Crest Publishers, 2002.

Brann, Eva. *The Music of the Republic: Essays on Socrates' Conversations and Plato's Writings*. Philadelphia: Paul Dry Books, 2004.

Kreeft, Peter. *Philosophy 101 by Socrates: An Introduction to Philosophy*. Ft. Collins, Colo.: Ignatius Press, 2002.

Plato. *Apology*. Edited by James J. Helm. Wauconda, Ill.: Bolchazy-Carducci, 1997.

Plato. *Phaedo*. Translated by G. M. A. Grube. Indianapolis: Hackett Publishing, 1976.

Stone, I. F. *The Trial of Socrates*. New York: Doubleday, 1989.

Xenophon. *Conversations of Socrates*. Translated by Hugh Trednnick. New York: Penguin Classics, 1990.

Song of Igor, The (1185–1196) *epic poem*

Composed between 1185 and 1196 in southern Russia, *The Song of Igor* is a heroic EPIC recounting the defeat of Prince Igor's forces from the city of Novgorod-Seversk by a Polish army. Apparently composed by a well-educated nobleman whose name is no longer known, it is said to be the most artistically complete work of old Russian epic literature.

Like most traditional epics, *The Song of Igor* was intended to be performed and accompanied by music, and was only later set down in writing. The book is divided into five sections. In the introduction, the author addresses his audience as brothers and explains that, unlike other epics, he has striven not only to create beautiful music but also to recount historical events. He then begins his narration of Igor's adventures. Despite the bad omen of a solar eclipse, Igor, his brother Vsevolod, and their sons prepare themselves for battle against a nomadic Polish force, a battle they will ultimately lose.

To contrast this defeat, which is caused by Igor and his brother's egoistical quest for personal glory, the second chapter recounts the victorious battle of the righteous Grand Duke Svyatoslav in the old Russian capital of Kiev. This is followed by a complaint spoken by Igor's young wife for her absent husband, who has been imprisoned by the Polish enemy. The poem closes with a retelling of Igor's daring escape from prison and return to his wife.

Though the heroic epic enjoyed a golden age in the old Russian capital of Kiev in the 12th century, *The Song of Igor* stands apart for its poetic sophistication and dramatic force. Characters' moral and political predicaments are vividly described, and the action itself is presented with much energy and pathos. These elements allow favorable comparison of the work to other medieval European epics, from the Old English BEOWULF, to the Middle High German NIBELUNGENLIED to the Old French SONG OF ROLAND.

The manuscript of *The Song of Igor,* together with other old Russian texts, was discovered in a monastery library in the late 18th century by Count Mussin-Puschkin, the Procurator-General of the Holy Synod in St. Petersburg. Copies of the manuscript were published in 1800, and it found a large audience due to the newfound interest in Russia and Europe, in medieval nationalistic epics, and in the high literary quality of the work. The original manuscript was later lost in a fire, but thanks to the 1800 republication, the work has been preserved in its entirety.

An English Version of *The Song of Igor*

The Song of Igor's Campaign, An Epic of the Twelfth Century. Translated by Vladimir Nabokov. New York: Ardis, 1989.

A Work about *The Song of Igor*

Mann, Robert. *Lances Sing: A Study of the Igor Tale.* Columbus, Ohio: Slavica, 1990.

Song of Roland (Chanson de Roland) (ca. 1030–1070) *epic poem*

The best-known French EPIC poem of the MIDDLE AGES, the *Song of Roland*, is an exciting story of war and treachery, heroic knights and Christian faith—all set in a medieval world in which loyalties and chivalry collide. One scholar, Bernard Cerquilini, has said, "The reason we are medievalists is to study the *Song of Roland.*"

The poem is based on an actual event. In 778, Charlemagne, the king of the Franks, who had been campaigning in Spain, was returning to France through the Pyrenees Mountains when his rearguard was ambushed by Basques at a pass called Roncevaux and killed to the last man. The dead included Roland, Lord of the Breton Marches. The story of this attack was recorded earlier by the Frankish noble Einhard (*Life of Charlemagne,* ca. 829–836). Almost 200 years later, the story of this battle became the focus of an Anglo-Norman French poem called the *Chanson de Roland* (Song of Roland). The poem is now housed in a manuscript in the Bodleian Library in Oxford, England, and its last line reads: "Ci faut la geste ke

Turoldus declinet," which means, "Here ends the tale that Turoldus used for his poem."

The true source or sources for the poem, however, are not known. The *Song of Roland* makes mention several times of an *ancienne geste* or *geste Francor,* a tale of heroic deeds written by the baron Saint-Gilles, who was supposedly present at the battle of Roncevaux. But this source, which may have been in Latin and was certainly much later than the battle, has not survived.

The poem may have originally been the work of a *jongleur* or minstrel, who sang it to entertain noble audiences. Many later manuscripts of the *Song of Roland* are based on the Bodleian manuscript, though they all differ in many ways from the original.

The date of the French poem indicates that it was influenced by the Christians' struggle against the Muslims in the first CRUSADE (1095–99). The author turned the original story (where Charlemagne actually fought in alliance with a Muslim prince in Spain) into a fight between the forces of Islam and Christendom.

Critical Analysis

The *Song of Roland* consists of some 4,000, 10-syllable lines, divided into *laisses,* or strophes of varying numbers of lines. The poetic technique is that of assonance, or similar vowel sounds at the ends of lines, and occasional rhymes. There is some repetition and sometimes different versions of the same lines within the poem, perhaps because it was copied incorrectly or because more than one source manuscript was used.

The story begins by telling us that Charlemagne has been fighting the Saracens in Spain for seven years. The Saracen king of Saragossa, Marsile, admits that his army cannot defeat the Christians. After he decides to pretend to convert to Christianity and become Charles' vassal to get the Christians to leave the country, he sends messengers to Charlemagne's camp.

Roland, the emperor's nephew and a favorite and most valiant knight, opposes the plan, warning that the Saracens have been treacherous in the past, killing the envoys Basan and Basile. Ganelon, Roland's stepfather, thinks they should accept the offer. When another knight, Naimon, argues persuasively that it is best to show mercy to an enemy who cannot win, the army finally agrees.

Charles decides to send a messenger to Marsile with the news, but when Roland volunteers, Charles refuses to let him go. Roland then suggests that Ganelon should go, and everyone agrees, but Ganelon is angered because he perceives Roland's suggestion as an insult to his honor, perhaps for not having volunteering himself. Roland does not take Ganelon's anger seriously and laughs, unwittingly inciting Ganelon's desire for revenge. As a result, when Ganelon meets with Marsile, they plot together to destroy Charlemagne's rearguard.

Ganelon returns to the Christian army with hostages that Marsile sends as a false pledge of good faith. As the army is about to cross the Pyrenees, Ganelon convinces Charlemagne that Roland should be left in command of the rearguard. Roland, though he does not know the whole of Ganelon's treachery, realizes his suggestion is malicious. He denounces Ganelon but accepts the task, swearing that Charlemagne will cross safely over the mountains.

When the main part of the army is over the pass, the Saracens attack the rearguard as Ganelon had planned. Oliver, Roland's friend, sees them coming and asks Roland to blow his horn to summon Charles and the rest of the army back to help them fight the Saracens. Roland refuses because he feels it is his duty to fight the battle for his lord; anything less, he believes, would be shameful. Roland and Oliver quarrel over this, but Roland will not be moved.

The battle is bloody. Beside Roland and Oliver is Archbishop Turpin, a priest, who does not hesitate to kill Saracens with his own hands. Roland soon realizes, despite some initial success, that the rearguard has no chance of winning the battle. When he finally blows his horn to alert Charlemagne to the ambush, the veins in his temple burst. Oliver too has been mortally wounded, and as they both lay dying, they make up their quarrel.

Only when he is the last man alive does Roland lie down under a tree and take his final breath:

> *He proffered his right glove to God;*
> *Saint Gabriel took it from his hand.*
> *Roland laid his head down over his arm;*
> *With his hands joined, he went to his end.*
> (ll. 2389–92)

The Archangel Gabriel and St. Michael are sent from God to bring Roland's soul to heaven.

When he hears the horn, Charlemagne realizes Ganelon's treachery and has him put in chains. He finds the bodies of Roland and the other heroes, then pursues the Saracens and defeats them. In the meantime, the emir Baligant has roused an enormous force of Saracens from the eastern kingdoms, and they arrive in Spain to help Marsile. Charlemagne defeats and kills the emir in single combat.

On their return to Aix-la-Chapelle, Ganelon is put on trial. He defends himself by saying he had the right to avenge his honor, which Roland had impugned. His ally, Pinabel, concurs with this view and says that anyone who wants to convict Ganelon must fight him. The court is ready to acquit Ganelon when Thierry, one of the smallest and slenderest of the knights, agrees to fight Pinabel. Because God is with Thierry, he defeats Pinabel, and Ganelon is executed. Only then does the Archangel Gabriel return to call Charlemagne back to war.

Some critics, including Pierre Le Gentil, see the *Song of Roland* as a tragedy, believing that Roland's pride and anger against Ganelon lead to an unnecessary loss of life at Roncevaux. The poem contains details that skillfully foreshadow the tragedy, as when Ganelon drops the glove that Charlemagne holds out to him as he accepts his mission. Other critics, however, including Robert Cook, believe that Roland is not proud but acts in perfect accord with the rules of CHIVALRY: "He is at Roncevaux to represent Charles, and his first duty is not to himself. . . . Roland has already committed himself to fight if attacked, and if he calls for help instead he will be breaking his word."

The characters in *Song of Roland* are portrayed as larger than life. Roland is the fiercest knight, Oliver the wisest. Charlemagne is portrayed as a venerable old man with a white beard, though in reality he was only 36 at the time of the Saracen battle. He is a religious leader as well as a warrior for whom God works miracles, making the sun stand still while he fights the Saracens.

The author seems to have known very little about the actual beliefs of Muslims. He represents them as "pagans," worshipping not only MUHAMMAD but also Apollo as idols. Nevertheless, the poet celebrates the bravery of individual Muslims. Of Baligant he says, "Oh God, if he were a Christian, / what a noble baron!" (l. 3164). For Christians, on the other hand, fighting with a pure heart against God's enemies means martyrdom and an assurance of reaching heaven. The poem's ultimate message appears to be that individual destinies and quarrels have no place when the ultimate fate of Christendom is at stake. The times called for heroism from every man.

The *Song of Roland* had an immense influence on the development of medieval epics. Later poets from many lands developed the legend of Roland and Charlemagne's other warriors into a whole series of epics, including Matteo Maria Boiardo's *Orlando Innamorato* (1487) and Lodovico Ariosto's *Orlando Furioso* (1516).

An English Version of the *Song of Roland*
The Song of Roland. Translated by Glyn Burgess. New York: Penguin Books, 1990.

Works about the *Song of Roland*
Cook, Robert Francis. *The Sense of the Song of Roland.* Ithaca, N.Y.: Cornell University Press, 1987.
Le Gentil, Pierre. *The Chanson de Roland.* Translated by Frances F. Beer. Cambridge, Mass.: Harvard University Press, 1969.

Sophocles (ca. 496 B.C.–ca. 405 B.C.)
playwright

Sophocles, son of the wealthy Sophilus of Colonus, was born near Athens. He was good-looking and a talented dancer and musician who led public victory hymns as a teenager. His lyre instructor was Lamprus, who was a widely celebrated master of traditional Greek music. Sophocles' true love, however, was the theater, and after a few appearances as an actor in his own youthful productions, he devoted himself entirely to the writing of Greek tragedies.

Sophocles was widely admired and his work was a popular success. His first of 24 competitive dramatic victories came in 468 B.C., when he bested the venerable AESCHYLUS in a theatrical contest. He penned nearly 125 dramas—of which a mere seven survive—and supplanted Aeschylus as the poet of Athens.

Sophocles was also active in public life, serving as treasurer of the Athenian Empire (443–442 B.C.) and as general (441–440 B.C.). During the unsuccessful revolt of Samos around 412 B.C., he was appointed to a board of commissioners in the aftermath of the doomed Sicilian expedition. He was also a lay priest in the cult of Asclepius, a deity of healing, and was associated with other well-known men of letters, including the historian HERODOTUS; Archelaus, a natural scientist and teacher of SOCRATES; and the many-talented and prolific Ion of Chios.

Upon the death of his fellow tragedian EURIPIDES in 406 B.C., Sophocles expressed his respect and grief by clothing actors in mourning dress during a rehearsal for a drama competition. He himself died not long after, and his play *Oedipus at Colonus* was produced posthumously by his grandson. Yale professor Eric A. Havelock writes that Sophocles "was remembered and celebrated as an example of the fortunate life, genial, accomplished, and serene."

Sophoclean tragedy is tense, startling, and disquieting. The cast of characters tends to be comparatively small, and the individuals' personal natures are boiled down to the essentials, so the significance of each action is intensified. Action in Sophocles' plays is always indicative of character. Causality is a prominent theme, with separate factors often combining to produce to an inevitable result. Sophocles' tragic vision is that life exists only at the price of suffering.

Ajax was produced around 442 B.C. and is thought to be Sophocles' earliest extant play. Its title character is a Trojan warrior whose bitterness over losing the armor of the legendary Achilles to a rival drives him mad, and he slaughters a flock of sheep, believing they are his Greek foes. When Ajax regains his reason, shame drives him to take his own life. His compatriots are persuaded to give him an honorable burial in a typically Sophoclean scene that sees an outcast reconciled with God and society.

The Women of Trachis (ca. 420s B.C.) is one of the few Greek tragedies that features Heracles (Hercules in Latin). Although a stunningly popular mythological figure, Heracles was rarely a theatrical subject. The play takes place during the last of Heracles' famed 12 labors. His wife is duped into giving him a poisoned garment that so scalds his skin he chooses to be burned alive on a pyre.

In *Electra* (ca. 415 B.C.), the playwright tells of the familial curse on the House of Atreus that Aeschylus so thoroughly dramatized. The title character in *Philoctetes* (ca. 409 B.C.) is a Greek hero who has angered the gods by accidentally stumbling onto one of their sacred sites. He suffers divine retribution but is mysteriously rescued from his punishment. Critics, including ARISTOTLE, have censured the play's use of the artificial device of DEUS EX MACHINA to bring the play to a conclusion.

Oedipus the King (ca. 427 B.C.) dramatizes the deeply tragic yet fascinating story of the King of Thebes and how he unwittingly brought pestilence to his realm and ruin to his family and himself. In *Oedipus at Colonus,* the erstwhile sovereign—aged, exiled, blinded, and broken—is sent by the gods to his death, but not before finding redemption. Produced at roughly the same time as *Ajax, Antigone* follows one of the daughters of the late king, whose only crime is wishing to see her slain brothers buried properly, and who pays for it with her life.

These three productions are collectively known as the "Theban Plays."

Critical Analysis

As *Oedipus the King* opens, a group of suppliants stands before the royal palace beseeching their ruler to save Thebes from a deadly blight that has ravaged the city: plants are not bearing fruit, livestock are sick, and women are barren.

A priest reminds Oedipus that he rescued the city once before, directly upon his arrival in Thebes, when he freed the people from the tyranny of the cruel Sphinx by solving the beast's riddle. (The riddle asks what walks on four legs in the morning, two in midday, and three at night, and the answer is "Man": as a crawling infant, as an adult, and as an elderly person with a cane.)

Oedipus's brother-in-law, who has just paid tribute at the temple of Apollo, reports that, according to the god, the land has been defiled by the presence of the slayer of King Laius, who was killed by robbers while in an embassy. Shortly thereafter, Oedipus muses how, having restored order in Thebes, he had won the hand of Laius's widowed queen, Jocasta.

The murderer must be located and either exiled or executed, according to the report; only then will Thebes be purified and fruitfulness restored. Oedipus promises that anyone who comes forth with knowledge of the homicide will not be harmed, but all Thebans are forbidden to shelter the guilty man. As for the killer himself, Oedipus proclaims:

> Upon the murderer I invoke this curse—
> whether he is one man and all unknown,
> or one of many—may he wear out his life
> in misery to miserable doom! If with my
> knowledge he lives at my hearth
> I pray that I myself may feel my curse.
>
> (ll. 246–251)

Little by little, the awful saga unfolds. Jocasta reveals that, years ago, an oracle had warned Laius that he would die at the hands of their son; so when a son was born, they left him abandoned on a hillside. Oedipus, with growing dread, recalls that, although he was reared by the king and queen of Corinth and considered them his parents, he was once accused by a drunken dinner guest of being illegitimate. Furthermore, an invocation of Apollo foretold his doom: to murder his father and lie with his mother. With horror, monstrous realization dawns: Oedipus was the abandoned son. He had encountered Laius that fateful day and murdered him in a fit of pique, then married his wife—Oedipus's mother. A tortured Jocasta hangs herself, while Oedipus puts out his own eyes with her brooches and banishes himself:

> I do not know with what eyes I could look
> upon my father when I die and go
> under the earth, nor yet my wretched
>   mother—
> those two to whom I have done things
>   deserving
> worse punishment than hanging. . . .
> And my city,
> its towers and sacred places of the Gods,
> of these I robbed my miserable self
> when I commanded all to drive him out,
> the criminal since proved by God impure
> and of the race of Laius.
>
> (ll. 1372–1383)

Sophoclean audiences would have been familiar with the tale of Oedipus, so the tragedian's task was to make the narrative interesting in a new way. He did this by introducing irony into every possible situation to create intense dramatic tension. Oedipus, the famed solver of riddles, is stumped by the circumstances of his own birth, marriage, and kingship. He is symbolically blinded by pride and arrogance when he is literally a seeing man, and after he "sees" the truth, he blinds himself physically. He accuses a blind prophet, a "seer" who grasps that Oedipus killed his father and married his mother, of lying in an effort to seize the throne.

However, like Sophocles' other protagonists, Oedipus is shown ultimately to be a man of some honor, as he refuses to take his own life, but rather accepts the fate that he himself meted out and the gods ordained.

"A full study of the influence of Sophocles on modern literature has yet to be written," according to Harvard professor Ruth Scodel. "The task would be immense, touching on the histories of scholarship, reading and education. . . . While works which use explicitly Sophoclean themes are not hard to find, often those where Sophocles has been used less obviously have used him more profoundly. . . . At once satisfying, disturbing, and frightening, the Sophoclean world seems inexhaustible."

English Versions of Works by Sophocles

The Oedipus Plays of Sophocles: Oedipus the King, Oedipus at Kolonos, and Antigone. Translated by Robert Bagg. Introduction by Mary Bagg. Boston: University of Massachusetts Press, 2004.

Sophocles I. Translated by David Grene. Chicago: University of Chicago Press, 1991.

Theban Plays. Translated by Peter Meineck and Paul Woodruff. Oxford, U.K.: Oxford University Press, 2004.

Works about Sophocles

Beer, Josh. *Sophocles and the Tragedy of Athenian Democracy.* Oxford, U.K.: Greenwood Publishing, 2004.

Budelmann, Felix. *Language of Sophocles: Communality, Communication and Involvement.* Cambridge, U.K.: Cambridge University Press, 2000.

Scodel, Ruth. *Sophocles.* Boston: Twayne Publishers, 1984.

Strabo (ca. 63 B.C.–ca. A.D. 24) *geographer, historian*

With the rise of the Roman Empire, the political influence of the Greeks diminished. However, Greece remained a center of intellectual and literary activity throughout the era of the Roman Empire. One of the important Greek writers of this time period was Strabo, the first great geographer in history.

As with so many other figures in ancient times, little is known of Strabo's life. He was born in the Greek city of Amasia, in today's northern Turkey. He received an excellent education and was deeply influenced by Stoical philosophy. While he traveled extensively throughout the ancient world, it is believed that he probably lived in Rome. Despite the fact that Strabo was a Greek, he was of the opinion that the Roman Empire was a positive influence on the world. The order and stability it provided allowed people like him to pursue intellectual and literary activities, without being interrupted by war or politics. This attitude is clearly expressed in his writings.

Strabo was the author of 47 books known as the *Historical Sketches* (compiled in 20 B.C.), a history of Rome of which only fragments remain. His greatest work, most of which is extant, is *The Geography,* or *Geographical Sketches.* This work, written in 17 volumes, was a general survey and summary of the geographic world familiar to the Greeks and Romans: Europe, India, Syria, and Asia, among other countries. Strabo describes the various mountains, rivers, and regions that had been explored up to that time. He also discusses important cities, the cultural tradition of various tribes and nations, and the art and architecture of many of the places he visited. *The Geography* is invaluable not only for its historical information, but also for what it reveals about the extent of geographic knowledge possessed by the ancient Greeks and Romans.

English Versions of Works by Strabo

The Geography of Strabo. Translated by Horace Leonard Jones. Cambridge, Mass.: Harvard University Press, 1967.

Isaeus. Loeb Classical Library. Translated by Edward Seymour Forster. Cambridge, Mass.: Harvard University Press, 1992.

Works about Strabo

Dueck, Daniela. *Strabo of Amasia: A Greek Man of Letters in Augustan Rome.* London: Routledge, 2000.

Syme, Ronald. *Anatolica: Studies in Strabo.* Edited by Anthony R. Birley. Oxford: Oxford University Press, 1995.

Strassburg, Gottfried von

See GOTTFRIED VON STRASSBURG.

Sturluson, Snorri

See SNORRI STURLUSON.

Sundiata, an Epic of Old Mali (13th century) *epic poem*

Sundiata, an Epic of Old Mali relates the story of Sundiata (also called Son-Jara), the 13th-century hero-king of Mali, a kingdom in West Africa. The *Sundiata* is a conceptual prose rendition of the original EPIC poem (*see* EPIC OF SON-JARA), written in the Mande language. D. T. Niane, the compiler, adopted this approach to make the story of Sundiata more accessible to non-Mande speakers. Niane's translation retains the general chronology of events as well as the main themes and ideas contained in the original.

The book begins with the prophecy of the future king's birth and the meeting and marriage between Sogolon Kunde (the Buffalo-woman) and the then-king of Mali. Their union produces the future king, Sundiata, who must go through a series of tests and trials, including exile, before he returns triumphantly as the hero after defeating the evil king Soumaroa Kante.

The epic addresses several important themes, including destiny, bravery, and friendship. The importance of prophecy is emphasized in Sundiata's transformation from a cripple into a powerful and remarkable king. The irreversibility of destiny is clearly shown in the eventual reclaiming of the Mali kingship by Sundiata, despite the many attempts made by his enemies, among them the wicked Sassouma, to foil his destiny.

Bravery constitutes another important theme of the book. The young and crippled Sundiata shows great courage and fortitude in his determination to overcome his handicap and protect his family from harm. He goes to battle with Soumaroa Kante, the sorcerer king, even when he has not discovered the secrets of the latter's prowess.

Another major theme is friendship, represented in the loving and sacrificial relationship between Sundiata and his half brother Manding Bory. Because of their close friendship, both characters are able to survive their trials and tribulations and remain undaunted as they resist their enemies. Sundiata willingly goes into exile to ensure that Manding Bory remains unharmed.

This tale, originally told by griots, or the West African keepers of oral traditions, gives invaluable information about not only the rich oral traditions of West African society, but also about its history and heroic past.

See also ORAL LITERATURE/TRADITION.

English Versions of *Sundiata, an Epic of Old Mali*

The Epic of Son-Jara: A West African Tradition. Translated by John William Johnson. Text by Fa-Digi Sisoko. Bloomington: Indiana University Press, 1992.

Niane, D. T., Comp. *Sundiata: An Epic of Old Mali.* Translated by G. D. Pickett. London: Longman, 1969.

Sunzi (Sun Tzu, Sun–tzu) (late sixth century B.C.) *military strategist, essayist*

Sunzi was a native of the Qi (Ch'i) state who worked as a military adviser of the kingdom of Wu ruler, He Lu. Not much is known about Sunzi's early life, as there are few existing works containing only scant biographical information; however, an anecdote of how he came to the Wu king's attention is contained in the work of Sima Qian (Ssu-Ma Ch'ien), the grand chronicler of pre-Han China. As the story goes, Sunzi was asked to demonstrate how he could put his theories of military organization into practice. Sunzi convinced the Wu king of his ability when he was able to transform a cohort of the king's concubines into an organized and disciplined drill unit. Scholars have estimated that this incident probably occurred not long after He Lu came to the throne.

According to Sima Qian and the *Shiji (Shi-chi),* Sunzi most probably died before his patron's death in 496 B.C. The last time Sunzi was mentioned was in connection with his role in assisting He Lu in his defeat of the Qu (Ch'ü) state in 512 B.C. Sunzi's greatest legacy is his composition on military strategies, titled *Ping-fa* (The Art of War). In his translation and commentary on Sunzi's work, Lionel Giles praises the author's genius: "They [Sunzi's words] reflect the mind not only of a born strategist, gifted with a rare faculty of generalisation, but also of a practical soldier closely acquainted with the military conditions of his time."

The Art of War represents the work of an experienced warrior. This has led to speculation that Sunzi began to write this work close to the end of his career when He Lu's military adviser. The work contains 13 chapters, each one examining a particular military topic or strategy. *The Art of War* is not merely a collection of sound and effective military plans and strategies; it is also a historical text that describes the events and personalities of Sunzi's lifetime. In two passages, for example, Sunzi refers to the size of the armies of the Wu kingdom and its adversaries, the Yueh.

Sunzi's work attained recognition and status from not only his contemporaries but also later generations of famous generals and warriors. Military leaders, including Han Xin (Han Hsin) and

Yue Fei (Yueh Fei), learned much from *The Art of War* and acknowledged their debt to it. Even purely literary men such as SU SHI's father, Su Xun, paid compliments to the great strategist.

The scholar Zheng Hou (Cheng Hou) also praised Sunzi in this extract contained in *Impartial Judgements in the Garden of Literature*:

> Sun Tzu's 13 chapters are not only the staple and base of all military men's training, but also compel the most careful attention of scholars and men of letters. His sayings are terse yet elegant, simple yet profound, perspicuous and eminently practical. Such works as the *Lun Yu,* the *I Ching* and the great Commentary, as well as the writings of Mencius, Hsun Kuang and Yang Chu, all fall below the level of Sun Tzu.

Sunzi's work continues to influence present-day society, in both military and commercial matters. Modern writers have tried to adapt Sunzi's ingenious cunning to the new competitive age of commerce and international business. Examples include Mark McNeilly's work *Sun Tzu and the Art of Business: Six Strategic Principles for Managers* and Check Teck Foo and Peter Grinyer's book *Organizing Strategy: Sun Tzu's Business Warcraft.*

An English Version of a Work by Sunzi

The Art of War. Translated by Lionel Giles. Singapore: Graham Brash, 1988.

Works about Sunzi

Foo, Check Teck and Peter Grinyer. *Organizing Strategy: Sun Tzu's Business Warcraft.* Boston and Singapore: B-H. Asia, 1994.

McNeilly, Mark. *Sun Tzu and the Art of Business: Six Strategic Principles for Managers.* Washington, D.C.: National Defense University Press, 1997.

———. *Sun Tzu and the Art of Modern Warfare.* Oxford and New York: Oxford University Press, 2001.

Zi Chang Tang. *Principles of Conflict: Recompilation and New English Translation with Annotation on Sunzi's Art of War.* San Rafael, Calif.: T. C. Press, 1969.

Su Shi (Su Shih, Su Tung-po) (1037–1101)
poet

Su Shi was born in Meishan in the Sichuan (Szechwan) Province of China. He was educated at home by his Buddhist parents and then later at a private school by a Taoist priest. In 1056, he went to the capital, Kaifeng, with his older brother to take the civil service examination. Both brothers passed with distinction. In 1060, after observing the customary three-year mourning period following his mother's death, Su Shi returned to the capital with his father and brother, and all were assigned government posts.

During his first years in the government, Su Shi became an outspoken critic of the reform program, the "New Laws," of the ruling party in Kaifeng. In 1079, he fell out of favor with the leader of the ruling party, Wan Anshi (Wang An-shih), and was tried for slander. The "New Laws" party used Su Shi's own poems as evidence against him, and the poet was banished to Huangzhou (Huangchou), an insignificant town on the banks of the Yangtze River. Su Shi was able to return to the capital the following year, after the "New Laws" party lost power. He was banished a second time, however, when the party returned to favor in 1094. He remained in southern China for the rest of his life and never returned to the capital. Because of Su Shi's political situation, most of his poems were banned during his lifetime, and it was not until after his death that his works were widely distributed and read.

Despite his political failings, Su Shi was one of the great poets of the Sung dynasty, and more than 2,400 of his poems have survived. His poetry was heavily influenced by the Buddhist and Taoist education he received in his youth. During his political career, he spent a great deal of time visiting Buddhist temples, and many of his poems reflect his ongoing association with the Zen Buddhist school of thought, as can be seen in these lines from "Water Music Prelude" (addressed to his younger brother):

> The moon should have no regrets.
> Why is she always at the full when men are
>   separated?
> Men have their woe and joy, parting and
>   meeting;
> The moon has her dimness and brightness,
>   waxing and waning.
> Never from of old has been lasting
>   perfection.
> I only wish that you and I may be ever well
>   and hale,
> That both of us may watch the fair moon,
>   even a thousand miles apart.

Su Shi experimented with all styles of poetry: five- or seven-character *shi* (*shih*) poems; *ci* (*tz'u*), or songs; and rhapsodic prose poems called *fu*. Most of his works deal with his personal life and his deep Taoist connection to nature. Perhaps the best example of Su Shi's ability to connect nature with emotion can be found in his poem "Tune: The Charms of Nien-nu," which he wrote 10 years after his wife passed away:

> Last night in a dream I returned home
> And at the chamber window
> Saw you at your toilet;
> We looked at each other in silence and
>   melted into tears.
> I cherish in my memory year by year the
>   place of heartbreaking,
> In the moonlit night
> The knoll of short pines.

Su Shi's brilliance is evident not only in the sheer volume of his poems, but also in his poignant expression of emotion. As translator Burton Watson remarks, "A great [poet] had to have such complete mastery of the [poetic] tradition that he could at the same time express his own thoughts freely and naturally, and could advance and enrich the tradition in some way, adding new depth and nuance. This [Su Shi] did."

English Versions of Works by Su Shi

Su Tung-p'o: Selections from a Sung Dynasty Poet. Translated by Burton Watson. New York: Columbia University Press, 1965.

The Prose-Poetry of Su Tung-p'o. Translated by Cyril Drummond Le Gros Clark. New York: Paragon, 1964.

A Work about Su Shi

Egan, Ronald C. *Word, Image, and Deed in the Life of Su Shi.* Cambridge, Mass.: Harvard University Press, 1994.

Tacitus, Cornelius (ca. 56–ca. 120)
historian, biographer, essayist

Tacitus was born into a wealthy family in Northern Italy. He received an education appropriate for a Roman from a good family, mastering public speaking skills, oratory, and debate. Throughout his life, he occupied prestigious high-ranking positions in the Roman Empire, beginning his career as a senator, then becoming a consul and, finally, a governor of Anatolia, one of the largest provinces of the empire. Most of what we know about Tacitus's life comes from his works and letters he exchanged with his good friend PLINY THE YOUNGER.

Though Tacitus was very successful politically, it is as a historian and moralist that he is best remembered. As a writer of history, he sought "to distinguish right from wrong, the useful from the dangerous" (*Annales* 4, 33). As a result, much of his writing is focused on denouncing the Roman emperors for their cruelty, attributing the decline of the Roman Empire to this and other imperial vices.

In the year 98, Tacitus wrote his first work, *Agricolae De Vita Iulii,* a biography of his father-in-law, after whom the book is named. In this work, Tacitus expresses his respect and admiration for Agricola as a highly virtuous man. Soon after, he wrote the treatise *Concerning the Origin and Location of the Germans,* commonly called *Germania* (Germany, ca. 98). Although the book contains a detailed description of the customs and geographic locations of Germanic tribes, it is not an objective ethnographic study since the essence of the work is political. It is colored with subtle irony toward some of the German tribes' primitive customs, descriptions that glorify the simple German way of life, and comparisons of these with the corruption and luxurious immorality of the Romans.

Around the year 81, Tacitus composed his *Dialogus de Oratoribus* (Dialogue on Orators), an essay on education, the art of oratory in Rome, and oratory's decline. It is written in the style of CICERO and, as was typical of the declamatory genre, is rich with rhetorical figures and metaphors, illustrating Tacitus's talent as an expressive speaker. He became one of the foremost prosecutors of his day, but after the year 100 he gradually devoted more time to writing until his death in Rome.

Critical Analysis

Tacitus is most famous for his *Annals* (ca. 115–117) and *Histories* (ca. 104–109). In these historical works, the traditional declamatory writing is replaced by a highly individual, polished style that makes use of rich vocabulary and diverse sentence structure and is reminiscent of LONGINUS. Both works contain bitter criticism of imperial power. Tacitus believed that the emperor had so much power that no one could occupy the throne without being corrupted by that power. Therefore, his history is a tale of a succession of corrupt despots, lust for power, and government scandal.

Histories presents a history of the Roman Empire from the year 69 until the death of Domitian in 96. The original work comprised 14 books, but only the first four books and part of the fifth have survived.

Tacitus's later work, *Annals,* of which 16 books are preserved, is a history of the emperors from Augustus to Nero (37–68). Throughout *Histories* and *Annals,* Tacitus makes good use of sarcasm. The surviving fragments describe the revolt by the northern tribes of Gaul, their defeat at the hands of the Roman army, and the establishment of the Pax Romana (Roman Peace) in the Gallic territories. While he describes some emperors, namely Augustus, with belittling innuendos, he describes others with severe criticism. Emperor Tiberius, for example, is portrayed as sinister and cruel, a man who purges his opponents from the Senate by having them tried for treason and executed. Claudius and Nero are painted in similarly dark colors. The account contains incisive character sketches, ironic passages, and eloquent moral conclusions about how the Roman character was declining due to the lack of character in its rulers. In *Annals,* Tacitus remains faithful to the spirit of passionate criticism of the emperors' cruelty and inhumanity. Thus, he describes the terror that Nero imposed on Christians who deviated from the traditional worship of Greco-Roman gods:

> Nero created a diversion and subjected to the most extra-ordinary tortures those hated for their abominations by the common people called Christians. Mockery of every sort was added to their deaths. . . . Covered with the skins of beasts, they were torn by dogs and perished, or were nailed to crosses, or were doomed to the flames. These served to illuminate the night when daylight failed"
>
> (*Annales* 15, 44)

Tacitus's works differ from the usual panegyric writing, which expresses admiration of the deeds of those in power regardless of their actions. By contrast, Tacitus provides a new perspective on the personalities and deeds of these great historical figures, allowing for a better understanding of the events and people who colored his world.

English Versions of Works by Cornelius Tacitus

Agricola and Germany. Translated by Anthony Birley. Oxford: Oxford University Press, 1999.

Annals and the Histories. Translated by Alfred J. Church and William J. Brodribb. New York: Random House, 2003.

Histories. Book I. Edited by Cynthia Damon et al. Cambridge, U.K.: Cambridge University Press, 2003.

Tacitus: Dialogus de Oratoribus. Edited by Roland Mayer et al. New York: Cambridge University Press, 2001.

Works about Cornelius Tacitus

Haynes, Holly. *The History of Make-Believe: Tacitus on Imperial Rome.* Berkeley: University of California Press, 2003.

Mellor. Ronald. *Tacitus.* London: Routledge, 1994.

O'Gorman, Ellen. *Irony and Misreading in the Annals of Tacitus.* New York: Cambridge University Press, 2000.

Tale of Genji, The

See MURASAKI SHIKIBU.

Talmud (ca. 200–ca. 550)

The Talmud is a collection of writings concerning Jewish religious and civil law. It contains scriptural interpretations of the Five Books of Moses (Genesis, Exodus, Leviticus, Deuteronomy, and Numbers) as well as complete guidelines according to the rabbinic authorities for human conduct in daily life. Known as the Oral Torah because it was handed down and built upon by teachers through the ages, the Talmud is studied together with the Written Torah (the Five Books of Moses, the Prophets, and the Scrolls) and forms the core of Jewish learning. The Talmud is considered the next most important text in the Jewish religion after the BIBLE itself.

The Talmud was born in the wake of the catastrophic destruction of the Second Temple in Jerusalem by the Romans in 586 B.C. The Temple had been the core of the Jewish people who were forced to leave Israel and became scattered throughout Babylon. In an effort to keep the Jewish people unified, exiled leaders who possessed the ancient Jewish teachings in the form of oral and written doctrine from the Temple established study houses. In these houses, which came to be known as synagogues, sacred learning was available to the Jewish masses. This development in Judaism, though spawned by dire necessity, was revolutionary. Until the destruction of the Temple, only the priests had been allowed to read the doctrines. The result of mass learning and prayer in the synagogues instilled in the exiles a love of Jewish scripture, creating the need for a new class of teachers.

The foremost of these teachers was a religious scholar named Ezra, who adapted the ancient doctrines to make them appropriate for a group of people living in exile. He then founded what was called the Great Assembly, a core group of teachers to whom he gave the amended doctrine. He saw this doctrine as a way of instructing people to live a moral and ethical life that would unify them with one another and with God, thus preserving the existence and integrity of the Jewish people. The members of the Great Assembly, in turn, gave this doctrine to the teachers in the synagogues.

The passage of time and the political and social changes that occurred demonstrated the need for the Torah to be a living document that could be adapted to the Jews' changing lives. Thus the teachers, or rabbis, developed the Talmudic method of scriptural interpretation, a systematic way of questioning scripture, finding answers through the use of intellect and reason, to understand what God wants for and from his people. The result of this method of religious study resulted in the development of an exhaustive code of conduct that applied to every aspect of human life, including marriage and bodily hygiene. The rabbis taught this code to the masses in the synagogues, both in Palestine and throughout Babylon. As the Talmud's founding teacher Ezra had held, the rabbis of generations following also believed that the devoted study of the Talmud and practice of its teachings would promote the individual's compassionate treatment of his fellow people and bring the Jews closer to God.

Critical Analysis

Two versions of the Talmud exist. The first is the Palestinian Talmud (also called the Jerusalem Talmud), which was written by Palestinian scholars from the third century to the early fifth century (ca. 408). The second is the Babylonian Talmud, which was written by scholars from the third century to the early sixth century (ca. 500).

There are numerous historical translations of and commentaries on the Talmud. The British rabbi Isidore Epstein was the first scholar to translate the Babylonian Talmud into English, a task that lasted from 1935 to 1952. The Palestinian Talmud was translated into Latin by the Italian historian Blasio Ugolino, who titled the work *Thesaurus Antiquitatum Sacrarum* (1744–69). Before this, Moses MAIMONIDES, a Spanish philosopher and physician, wrote *Mishnah Tora* (Repetition of the Torah, ca. 1180), and French and German rabbis wrote numerous commentaries on the Talmud from the 12th to 14th centuries.

The Talmud is composed of three main parts: the Mishnah, the Gemara, and the Midrash. The Mishnah, completed around 352, contains six sections called Orders, which are each broken down into chapters. The Orders deal with laws concerning agriculture, observance of the Sabbath and other Festivals and Holy Days, women, legal matters, rituals concerning daily life and dietary laws, and cleanliness of body and home. The following example from Dr. Abraham Cohen's English translation of the Talmud concerns medical treatment and gives an excellent example of the way in which Talmudic rabbis interpreted scripture to promote ethical treatment of human beings:

> If the patient says he wants something and the physician says he may not have it, the former is listened to. For what reason? "The heart knoweth its own bitterness."
>
> (Proverbs 14:10)

The Gemara, as it has been recorded, is actually a series of lively debates between scholars and students who disagreed on the interpretations found in the Mishnah. This form of scholarly debate provides the system of Jewish learning and continues to this day.

The third portion of the Talmud is the Midrash (derived from the Hebrew word *darash*, meaning "to reason or search out"), which was developed during the same period as the Mishnah. A Midrash can best be described as a story the rabbis invented to answer questions that arise from passages in the Bible that seem unclear. The story is then used as a tool for understanding God's will for mankind. For example, in Genesis 1:27, the Bible says: "So God created man in his own image, in the image of God created he him; male and female created he them." The story of God's creation of woman from Adam's rib does not occur until Chapter 2 in Genesis. The rabbis used midrash to explain this gap by creating the legendary story of Lilith, the first woman, who would not act as a helpmate to Adam. In the midrash, Lilith treats Adam as an enemy rather than as a husband; therefore, she is banished from the Garden of Eden to wander as a demon. The Rabbis used this story to show the importance of a man and woman's cooperation in life.

The Talmud has proven to be the unifying force its originators intended it to be, and history attests to this cohesive force. With the rise and passing of numerous cultures throughout the centuries, Judaism as a religion and culture has survived and continues to thrive.

English Versions of the Talmud

Talmud. Translated by H. Polano. Whitefish, Mont.: Kessinger, 2003.

The Jerusalem Talmud. Edited by Heinrich W. Guggenheimer. Berlin: Walter de Gruyter, 2000.

Wit and Wisdom of the Talmud: Proverbs, Sayings, and Parables for the Ages. Edited by George J. Lankevich. Garden City Park, N.Y.: Square One Publishers, 2001.

Works about the Talmud

Bokser, Ben Zion. *The Wisdom of the Talmud.* New York: Kensington, 2001.

Cohen, Norman J. *The Way into Torah.* Woodstock, Vt.: Jewish Lights Publishing, 2004.

Grishaver, Joel Lurie. *Talmud with Training Wheels: Courtyards and Classrooms.* Los Angeles: Torah Aura Productions, 2004.

Kolatch, Alfred J. *Masters of the Talmud: Their Lives and Views.* Middle Village, N.Y.: Jonathan David Publishers, 2001.

Rubenstein, Jeffrey L. *The Culture of the Babylonian Talmud.* Baltimore, Md.: Johns Hopkins University Press, 2003.

tanka   *Japanese poetic form*

A tanka poem comprises 31 syllables, ordered into five lines of five, seven, five, seven, and seven syllables, respectively. The form dominated Japanese poetry for more than 1,000 years. Today the haiku has in some ways replaced tanka in popularity, but the tanka form is still quite commonly used. Since it is somewhat longer than haiku, tanka has a more lyrical quality and is highly valued for its concise nature:

> *I shall pass away*
> *soon. To keep your memory*
> *in that other world*
> *I so long to see your face*
> *again, for just one last time.*
>
> (Izumi Shikibu)

Tanka poets rely on internal alliteration (the repetition of consonants), assonance (the repetition of vowels), an absence of rhyme, and the use of concrete images to express intense emotional experiences and moods and to describe everyday events.

An English Version of Works by Tanka Poets
The Ink Dark Moon: Love Poems by Ono No Komachi and Izumi Shikibu, Women of the Ancient Court of Japan. Translated by Jane Hirshfield and Mariko Aratani. New York: Vintage Books, 1990.

Tao Yuanming (T'ao Yüan-ming, Tao Qian [Tao Ch'ien]) (365–427) *poet*
Tao Yuanming was one of the first in the tradition of the Chinese recluse poets; HAN SHAN is another notable example. Tao spent the early part of his life as a government official after the collapse of the Han dynasty. This tumultuous period in Chinese history was marked by intermittent clan wars, weak rulers, and political instability. As a result, the life of many government officials at the time was fraught with danger. Tao's Confucian principles made him loathe to support or serve a government that was not equal to his ideals. These principles conflicted with the only avenue that was available to him for living a life of wealth and privilege. In "The Return," he says, "My instinct is all for freedom, and will not brook discipline or restraint. Hunger and cold may be sharp, but this going against myself really sickens me." Finally, at age 40, Tao's principles rose to the forefront, and he abruptly resigned his government post, retiring with his family to a farm in the Lu Mountains.

Tao Yuanming, whose name translates as "the recluse Tao," found true happiness after his retirement. He wrote many pastoral poems extolling the virtues of the simple life to be found on a farm. While he and his family lived in poverty, Tao found his life in the mountains to be much more rewarding than his former career: "My home remains unsoiled by worldly dust / Within bare rooms I have

my peace of mind." ("Returning to the Farm to Dwell," ll. 17–18).

Tao Yuanming's poems reflect his calmness and the joy he found in moments of idleness. He wrote often about honor, the ills of seeking money, and the pleasures of observing nature and sharing good wine with friends. His lyrics served as models for many great poets, such as WEI ZHUANG, LI BAI, and Tu Fu, who followed.

An English Version of Works by Tao Yuanming
The Selected Poems of T'ao Ch'ien. Translated by David Hinton. Port Townsend, Wash.: Copper Canyon Press, 1993.

A Work about Tao Yuanming
Hightower, James R. and Florence Chia-Ying Yeh. *Studies in Chinese Poetry.* Cambridge, Mass.: Harvard University Press, 1998.

Tarafah 'Amr ibn al-'Abd (543–ca. 569) *poet*
Tarafah 'Amr ibn al-'Abd is one of the most important poets of the pre-Islamic Arabic world and one of the seven celebrated authors of the *Mu'allaqāt,* (the Golden Odes; see HANGED POEMS). Born into the Bakr tribe in the Bahrain region of the Persian Gulf, Tarafah led a life that is a matter of colorful legend. Traditional accounts claim that in his youth he developed dissolute habits as well as a talent for satire, which led to his exile from the tribe. After gaining recognition for his *mu'allaqah,* or ode, he—along with his uncle and fellow poet Mutalammis—was favored by Amr ibn Hind, who became king of al-Hirah in 554.

It was said that Tarafah's sarcastic tongue soon caused trouble because of a verse in which he declared he would rather have a bleating sheep than Amr bin Hind around his tent. Lascivious advances to the king's sister, a reported beauty, earned Tarafah and his uncle a mission to return to Bahrain with a pair of sealed letters for the governor. Mutalammis opened his and discovered its contents contained a death warrant, which he quickly destroyed. Tarafah, determined to meet his fate, delivered his letter and was thereupon imprisoned and executed. His early and avoidable death (tradition held that he was still in his 20s) earned him the title "the murdered lad."

Though other fragments of his poetry survive in various collections, Tarafah is best known for his *qasidah* of about 100 lines. The *qasidah* was a popular form of poetry that generally contained two sections: a glimpse of the beloved and then an enforced exile involving a dangerous journey through the desert, where the poet's only companion was his camel. Tarafah's ode contains the traditional description of the beloved, which according to translator A. J. Arberry in *The Seven Odes* translates to a "young gazelle, dark-lipped, fruit-shaking." It also gives a quite detailed and extensive description of the camel.

Tarafah's ode incorporates themes that probably helped fuel the legends about his rebellious and libertine ways. Historian Reynold Nicholson, in *A Literary History of the Arabs,* calls Tarafah's *mu'allaqa* "a spirited portrait of himself." His ode shows his appreciation for and generosity with his *khamr,* or wine, in these reckless lines (translated by Philip Kennedy in *The Wine Song in Classical Arabic Poetry*): "Whenever you come to me in the morning, I give you a cup of wine that quenches your thirst; if you can do without it, then do without it and more!" Elsewhere Tarafah offers his philosophy on life, sagely saying, "A noble man satiates himself in life, for you will know / if we die tomorrow which of us is thirsty." Kennedy calls this "the clearest and most direct expression of CARPE DIEM [seize the day]," which seems to be the poet's personal motto.

Tarafah's ode also incorporates the classic element of *fakhr,* or self-glorification. He portrays himself as important and the center of attention, claiming, "I am not one that skulks fearfully among the hilltops . . . / if you look for me in the circle of the folk you'll find me there." The *qasidah* frequently ends with a celebration of pleasure and an image of repatriation into the tribe. The images in Tarafah's homecoming involve all three of his favorite things—wine, boon companions, and a beautiful woman—indicating, as Nicholson says, the poet's "insistence on sensual enjoyment as the sole business of life."

In the century following Tarafah's death, Arabic poetry changed in significant ways. The first movement of the *qasidah* evolved into the *ghazal,* a highly influential form of love poetry. In the 600s, the birth of the prophet MUHAMMAD brought profound changes to Arabic culture with the introduction of Islam, and the poetry changed in tone.

The *Mu'allaqāt* was compiled in the mid-eighth century by Hammād al-Rāwiyah, who selected seven poets as the exemplars of pre-Islamic poetry. IMRU' AL-QAYS, Zuhayr ibn Abi Sulma, LABID, Antara ibn Shaddad, 'AMR IBN KULTHUM (the very king supposedly responsible for Tarafah's death), and al-Harith join Tarafah in this esteemed group. *Mu'allaqāt* is traditionally interpreted to mean "the suspended ones," alluding to a practice where the prize-winning works of poetry contests would be written out in letters of gold and suspended, or hung, for viewing in a public place. Later compilers added to or changed the *Mu'allaqāt* as they wished, but Tarafah is customarily included. His appeal endures not only in his fantastic biography of a daring rebel killed in his prime, but also in the evidence of his poetic gifts and his personal resolution to live life to the fullest.

An English Version of a Work by Tarafah 'Amr ibn al-'Abd

"The Ode of Tarafah." In *The Seven Odes: The First Chapter in Arabic Literature.* Translated by A. J. Arberry. London: George Allen & Unwin, 1957.

Works about Tarafah 'Amr ibn al-'Abd

Kennedy, Philip F. *The Wine Song in Classical Arabic Poetry.* Oxford: Oxford University Press, 1997.
Nicholson, Reynold A. *A Literary History of the Arabs.* New York: Kegan Paul International, 1998.

telapnaawe narratives (*telapnanne narratives*) *Zuni tales*

For more than 2,000 years, the Zuni were pueblo dwellers in what is now New Mexico. Today, only about 12,000 Zuni still live in New Mexico, but their culture is rich with tradition, religion, art, music, and dance.

Religion, which is at the center of the Zuni culture, is told through stories and myths. Similar to the Winnebago WAIKAN and WORAK NARRATIVES, Zuni myths and folktales are divided into two types: creation stories known as *chimiky'ana'kowa* (meaning "the beginning"), based on true events; and *telapnaawe* (or telapnanne), entertaining, fictional stories. The creation stories are told only by priests during religious ceremonies. *Telapnaawe* narratives, on the other hand, are relayed by *telaapi,* or storytellers, who tell their tales only during the winter.

Zuni scholar Dennis Tedlock notes that the *telapnaawe* begin with a traditional exchange between storyteller and listener. The listener will ask the *telaapi* to "take up a tale," to which he will respond, "Now we take it up." The tales can last from 30 minutes to one hour or longer. The stories' subjects range from the trickster Coyote (*see* COYOTE TALES) to marriage, family, and hunting.

Some *telapnaawe* tales include "The Boy and the Deer," a story about a boy who is raised by deer; "The Hopis and the Famine," a story of a scorned husband who seeks revenge by causing a famine; and "The Girl Who Took Care of the Turkeys," a story about a girl who abandons the turkeys she cares for to go to a dance.

Frank Hamilton Cushing was the first white American to collect and translate Zuni myths. He lived with the Zuni in the late 19th century and published many books and articles on Zuni culture. In the 20th century, anthropologist Franz Boas and his student Ruth Benedict also studied Zuni culture and published numerous works on the subject. Scholar Dennis Tedlock translated many Zuni tales into English, maintaining the complexity and integrity of the Zuni originals.

English Versions of *Telapnaawe* Narratives

Benedict, Ruth. *Zuni Mythology*. New York: Columbia University Press, 1935.
Cushing, Frank Hamilton. *Zuni Folk Tales*. New York: G. P. Putnam's Sons, 1901.
Peynetsa, Andrew and Walter Sanchez. *Finding the Center: The Art of Zuni Storytelling*. Translated by Dennis Tedlock. Lincoln: University of Nebraska Press, 1999.

Works about *Telapnaawe* Narratives

Shell, Marc. *American Babel: Literatures of the United States from Abnaki to Zuni*. Cambridge, Mass.: Harvard University Press, 2002.
Tedlock, Barbara. *The Beautiful and the Dangerous: Encounters with the Zuni Indians*. Albuquerque: University of New Mexico Press, 2001.

Terence (Publius Terentius Afer) (ca. 185– 159 B.C.) *playwright*

Terence was born in Carthage to Libyan parents and brought to the Roman Empire as a slave. His family name, Afer, means "African," which probably reflects his origin. His owner was a Roman senator, Terentius Lucanus, who quickly recognized his slave's ability and not only emancipated Terence but also provided him with a classical Roman education. Terence became popular among the Roman aristocracy and was also highly respected by such distinguished thinkers as CICERO and HORACE. He died an early, tragic death; before he turned 30, he was lost at sea during his journey to Greece. It is said that Terence translated 108 of MENANDER's plays, all of which were lost in the same shipwreck.

Terence wrote his first play, *Andria* (The Maid from Andros), when he was only 19. The play is a romantic comedy about a long-lost daughter's return to her home, a story Terence adapted from one of Menander's plays.

Like PLAUTUS, Terence adapted Greek plays from the late phases of Attic comedy (farcical dramas that evolved from fertility rites mixed with song and rudimentary dialogue produced in the region known as Attica during the third and fourth centuries B.C.). However, he differed from his predecessor in his choice of style. While Plautus wrote for the Roman public, who were hungry for anything vulgar, Terence delighted in subtle irony and refined yet natural expression. In addition, Terence's plots far surpassed those of Plautus.

A perfectionist, Terence polished his works until they were flawless. He wrote only six plays, all of which survive to this day, and his skill progressed with each completed work. First staged in 160, *The Eunuch,* a tale of the love exploits of two brothers, was met with such success that it was performed twice a day. Other plays include *Adelphi* (The Brothers), in which Terence explores how the upbringing of two brothers (one strict, the other not) affects their behavior as adults; *Hecyra* (The Mother-in-Law), in which a man discovers that he is the one who raped his wife and got her pregnant; and *The Phormio,* which is based on one of APOL-LODORUS's plays and tells the story of how a sycophant helps two brothers convince their father to accept their lovers.

Terence's refined comedies remained popular throughout the MIDDLE AGES and the Renaissance. The medieval playwright Hroswitha of Gandersheim claims to have written her plays so that her nuns would spend less time reading Terence. His comedies also influenced the works of a number of later authors. Molière adapted Terence's *Phormio* in one of his earliest plays, *The Trickeries of Scapin* (1671), and Richard Steele adapted Terence's *Andria* in his play *The Conscious Lovers* (1722).

English Versions of Works by Terence

The First Comedy of Pub. Terentius, Called Andria. Translated by Joseph Webbe. London: Scolar Press, 1972.

Plautus and Terence: Five Comedies. Translated by Deena Berg and Douglass Parker. Indianapolis, Ind.: Hackett Publishing, 1999.

Terence: Eunuchus. Edited by John Barsby et al. New York: Cambridge University Press, 1999.

Terence: The Woman of Andros, The Self-Tormentor, The Eunuch, Vol. 1. Translated by John Barsby. Cambridge, Mass.: Harvard University Press, 2001.

Works about Terence

Leigh, Matthew. *Comedy and the Rise of Rome.* Oxford, U.K.: Oxford University Press, 2004.

Moore, Timothy J. "Terence and Roman New Comedy" in *Greek and Roman Comedy: Translations and Interpretations of Four Representative Plays.* Translated by George F. Franko, et. al. Edited by Shawn O'Bryhim. Austin: University of Texas Press, 2001.

Theophrastus (Tyrtamus) (ca. 372–ca. 287 B.C.) *philosopher, rhetorician, scientist, teacher, nonfiction writer*

The son of a fuller, or cloth handler, Theophrastus was born in Eresus on the island of Lesbos. Certain biographers suggest he studied at PLATO's Academy in Athens. By age 25 he had formed close ties with Plato's favorite student and successor ARISTOTLE, whom he accompanied to the court of Philip of Macedonia when Aristotle was hired to tutor the young prince Alexander. Upon their joint return to Athens in 334, Aristotle founded the Peripatetic school, where Theophrastus became his most gifted student. After Alexander's death, the Athenian democracy experienced civil disorder as various persons struggled for control of the city. Theophrastus spent a year in exile when a political decree banished all philosophers, but in 306, when the decree was revoked, he returned and took over as head of the Peripatetic. Under his leadership, the school enjoyed the peak of its influence and success, attracting more than 2,000 students. When Theophrastus died, Athenians accompanied his bier on foot as a mark of honor.

Originally named Tyrtamus, Theophrastus, which means "divine speaker," earned the name by which he is known through his impressive command of rhetoric. STRABO said that "Aristotle made all his students eloquent, but Theophrastus most eloquent." Like his mentor, Theophrastus's interests ranged from the natural sciences to logic, metaphysics, rhetoric, poetics, politics, and ethics. His ideas on philosophy and metaphysics built on the ideas of Plato and Aristotle, though during Theophrastus's tenure at the Peripatetic, Zeno was formulating Stoic philosophy and EPICURUS founded his own Epicurean school at the Garden.

Diogenes Laertius, who wrote an early biography of Theophrastus, called him "a very intelligent and industrious man . . . ever ready to do a kindness and a lover of words." Laertius attributed 224 works to Theophrastus, everything from 24 books on law to treatises on the winds, types of sweating, tiredness, plagues, fainting, and dizziness. The sheer diversity and breadth of topics shows the extraordinary breadth of his knowledge and the inquisitiveness of his mind. He wrote on abstractions such as flattery and piety and on practical activities such as sleep and dreams, music, and judicial speeches. He analyzed virtually every aspect of the natural world, from fruits and flavors to wine and olive oil. He meditated on emotions, virtue, and the nature of the soul and wrote manuals on kingship, the rearing of children, and the art of rhetoric. Other topics he studied included melancholy, derangement, slander, metals, fire, and old age, to name just a few.

What remains of Theophastus's work, aside from scattered fragments and quotations in texts of late antiquity and the MIDDLE AGES, are two treatises on botany and assorted essays on natural sciences, sense perception, and metaphysics. His most-remembered work is what was, perhaps to him, his most unimportant: the *Characters,* which became a paradigm for European literature and contributed to the development of the English essay.

Critical Analysis

The work *Characters* consists of a table of contents, a preface explaining the purpose of the collection, and 30 chapters, each devoted to a different aspect of personality. None of the listed traits are very pleasant or admirable. Each individual chapter is titled with the trait under attack and commences with a general definition, leading to a description of the characteristic actions of a person of this sort. Some sketches are followed by moralizing epilogues, which scholars suspect are later additions. The true worth of *Characters* lies in the detailed descriptions of each figure, which read like a series of lecture notes or scribbles in a personal sketchbook. The structure of these descriptions is uniformly peculiar and distinctive: Each begins with the formula "X is the sort who . . ." and commences with a series of modifiers listing the behaviors to which this sort of person is prone. The details are vivid and often hilarious. There are no virtues featured in these sketches; the characters are buffoons, braggarts, tricksters, and examples of all sorts of vice.

Theophrastus, along with his students, had a reputation for dressing finely and living well, which may explain why so many of the characters he writes about are parodies of stinginess. He was also known for his elegant manners and sophistication, so several of the bumbling characters lack social graces. The work is clearly not meant to instruct, either on the basis of ethical behavior or as an example of rhetorical style; alone of Theophrastus's compositions, *Characters* seems designed for sheer entertainment. What moral judgments that exist are thought to be the interpolations of later authors. Theophrastus takes the stance of the natural scientist—studying, classifying, and remarking on distinct traits, without attempting to moralize or rationalize upon them.

The details of the descriptions clearly anchor them in Athens in the last decades of the fourth century B.C., revealing the city's customs, institutions, practices, and prejudices. The sketches were likely composed over a decade or so, and most of the internal evidence, or references within the work, suggest dates between 325 and 315 B.C. The descriptions abound with fascinating information about everyday life in Athens, as can be seen in this description of the character Obsequiousness:

He gets frequent haircuts and keeps his teeth white, and discards cloaks that are still good, and anoints himself with perfumed oil. In the marketplace he goes frequently to the money-changers; among gymnasia he spends his time at those where the ephebes work out; in the theater, whenever there is a show, he sits next to the generals. He buys nothing for himself, but for foreigners he buys letters of commission for Byzantium, and Laconian dogs for Kyzikos, and Hymettos honey for Rhodes, and as he does so tells everybody in town about it.

Despite the specificity of the detail, however, Theophrastus's characters do not belong only to ancient Greece. When he summarizes the ungenerous person as "the sort who, if he wins the tragedy competition, dedicates to Dionysus a strip of wood with only his own name written on it," even readers unacquainted with this practice can guess readily enough what it means. Many of Theophrastus's characters are universal types.

In his approach to the work, Theophrastus uses a theory of personality predicated on the belief that traits may be isolated and separately studied. He inherited from Aristotle the idea that badness of character resulted from excess or extremes. Excellence of character—what we would call virtue—required moderating or balancing between the extremes. While Theophrastus's characters borrow from Aristotle's *Ethics,* at least in their examples of vice, he also incorporates elements of comedy and satire perfected by the dramatists, for example ARISTOPHANES. MENANDER's style of New Comedy owes much to the philosophy of character contained in Theophrastus. After Theophrastus, character writing was often imitated, most successfully by SENECA and PLUTARCH. The works of HORACE, MARTIAL, JUVENAL, and LUCIAN all demonstrate their knowledge of the *Characters.*

The several existing copies of the manuscript, in various stages of decay, owe their survival to the frequency with which the work was anthologized in manuals of rhetorical instruction. The character sketch was a rhetorical exercise recommended by CICERO and QUINTILIAN as a way of developing writing skill as well as providing an understanding of human nature. Medieval writers borrowed the technique of a gallery of personality portraits; the most notable examples are the Prologue to *The Canterbury Tales* by Geoffrey Chaucer, the catalog of the Seven Sins in *Piers Plowman* by William Langland, and *Ship of Fools* by Sebastian Brandt. The 1592 edition of *Characters* by Issac Casaubon inspired renewed attention to the character sketch.

Renaissance writers showed a keen interest in the literature and ideals of the ancient Greeks, among them François Rabelais, Miguel de Cervantes, Desiderius Erasmus, Michel de Montaigne, and Ben Jonson. Several writers of the 17th century attempted their own series of characters modeled after Theophrastus, most notably Jean de La Bruyère, who translated Theophrastus and then continued with his own updated character sketches. Though the technique of the literary "portrait" belonged to the 17th and 18th centuries, the art of describing characters through descriptions of manners and behaviors was adapted by 19th-century novelists from Charles Dickens to George Eliot. In many ways, therefore, the technique of characterization used in the modern-day novel can be dated all the way back to the height of ancient Greece and the work of Theophrastus.

English Versions of Works by Theophrastus

Theophrastus: Characters. Edited James Diggle et al. New York: Cambridge University Press, 2004.
Theophrastus: Enquiry Into Plants. Translated by Arthur F. Hort. Cambridge, Mass.: Harvard University Press, 1989.

Works about Theophrastus

Baltussen, Han. *Theophrastus Against the Presocratics and Plato.* Boston: Brill Academic Publishers, 2000.
Huby, Pamela and William W. Fortenbraugh. *Theophrastus of Eresus: Sources for his Life, Writings, Thought and Influence.* Boston: Brill Academic Publishers, 1999.

Van Ophuijsen, Johannes M. and Marlein Van Raalte, eds. *Theophrastus: Reappraising the Sources.* Somerset, N.J.: Transaction Publications, 1998.

Thomas Aquinas, Saint (ca. 1224–1274)
theologian, philosopher

Thomas Aquinas was born at the castle of Roccasecca, near Naples, Italy, to a noble family. He was sent away before he was five to be educated at the Benedictine monastery of Montecassino, where his father's brother was abbot. Later he studied at the University of Naples. In this culturally rich environment Thomas became familiar with the writings of the Muslim thinkers AVICENNA and AVERROËS, whose study of the Greek philosopher ARISTOTLE, the ideas of whom had been almost forgotten following the collapse of the Roman Empire, was beginning to attract the interest of Christian Europe. Thomas Aquinas was among those who studied Aristotle's theories.

In Naples, Aquinas also met members of the new Dominican order of mendicant friars, who led a more austere and self-denying life than that practiced by the older established monastic orders such as the Benedictines. Aquinas was still a teenager when he decided to join the Dominicans. His family opposed this decision and held him captive for more than a year, trying to force him to change his mind. Eventually they had to accept that their efforts were wasted, and he was allowed to take his vows in 1244.

The Dominicans sent young Thomas to Cologne to study with the scholar Albertus Magnus (later known as Saint Albert the Great, ca. 1200–80). Albertus Magnus had made an extensive study of Aristotle, and this shared interest contributed to the close relationship between master and pupil, which lasted for many years. Aquinas moved to Paris when Albertus Magnus took up a teaching position there in 1245. After completing his studies, he remained in Paris as a professor for another three years. He then spent 10 years in Italy, much of the time in attendance on the pope, but

returned to Paris for another three years before taking up a teaching position at the University of Naples. A mystical experience in 1273 that made all his work seem to him "like straw," as he told a friend, led to his ceasing to write, but he continued with his teaching and administrative work. When he was about 50 years old, he was on his way to Lyons on church business when he died, not far from his birthplace.

Critical Analysis

Thomas Aquinas wrote more than 60 works, all in Latin, the language of scholarship in his day. There are sermons, biblical commentaries, polemical tracts (he was often called on by Church leaders to respond to controversies and potential heresies), philosophical expositions, and theological works. His 13 commentaries on the works of Aristotle are still valued by students of philosophy for the help they give in understanding Aristotle's ideas, but as a Christian philosopher, Aquinas probably saw them more as a means to a clear understanding of the unity of God's creation.

The early medieval Catholic Church tended to dismiss classical philosophers like Aristotle, who had lived before the time of Christ, as pagan and therefore irrelevant or even harmful to Christianity. Aquinas demonstrated that Aristotle's ideas were in fact compatible with Christian teaching. Aristotle's confidence in the capacity of human reason to uncover the underlying order in the universe by studying the details of creation was pursued by Aquinas, who identified that underlying order with God. Aristotle's proof of the existence of a prime mover was developed by Aquinas as proof of the existence of God. His modification of Aristotle's approach was to argue that human reason could not discover everything, and God's revelation was needed to discover the fullness of truth.

Aquinas's greatest book, the *Summa Theologica*, which he began around 1265 and was still working on when he stopped writing in 1273, was conceived as an aid to students of theology and metaphysics. The original title, *Summa Totius The-*

ologiae, may be translated as "the summary of all theology," and the work is indeed ambitious. It has three parts, dealing with the nature of God, ethics, and Christ. In a logical progression of ideas, Aquinas takes a philosophical and theological approach to reconciling the concepts of reason and faith. He includes commentaries by such philosophers, theologians, and scholars as Avicenna, IBN GABIROL, Averroës, AUGUSTINE, and MAIMONIDES.

Aquinas was the most important Christian theologian of the European MIDDLE AGES, providing a new balance between theology and philosophy that held until the age of science began in the 17th century.

Aquinas was officially recognized as a saint by the Church in 1373, and his teachings (collectively known as "Thomism") have become identified with the doctrine of the Roman Catholic Church. His work is still studied by modern philosophers.

English Versions of Works by Saint Thomas Aquinas

Aquinas: Selected Philosophical Writings. Edited by Timothy McDermott. New York: Oxford University Press, 1998.

A Shorter Summa: The Essential Philosophical Passages of Saint Thomas Aquinas' Summa Theologica. Edited by Peter Kreeft. San Francisco: Ignatius Press, 1993.

St. Thomas Aquinas on Politics and Ethics: A New Translation, Backgrounds, Interpretations. Translated by Paul E. Sigmund. New York: Norton, 1988.

Works about Saint Thomas Aquinas

Flannery, Thomas L. *Acts Amid Precepts: The Aristotelian Logical Structure of Thomas Aquinas's Moral Theory.* Washington, D.C.: Catholic University of America Press, 2001.

McInerny, Ralph. *A First Glance at Thomas Aquinas: Handbook for Peeping Thomists.* Notre Dame, Ind.: University of Notre Dame Press, 1990.

Nichols, Aidan. *Discovering Aquinas: An Introduction to His Life, Work, and Influence.* Grand Rapids, Mich.: Eerdmans, 2003.

Thousand and One Nights, The *(Alf Layla wa-Layla, Arabian Nights)*
(9th–13th centuries) *Islamic story collection*

The Arabic *Alf Layla wa-Layla* (*The Thousand and One Nights*) is a vibrant and extensive collection of stories brought together in the Islamic world of the ninth–13th centuries. Also known as *The Arabian Nights,* the original tales have Indian, Persian, and Arabic antecedents and were likely told for centuries before being written down.

A cycle of tales with no single author and no single source, *The Thousand and One Nights* is enormously diverse and entertaining. Long regarded as a collection of fairy tales, like the folklore of the Grimm brothers or the fables of AESOP, the tales, as Robert Irwin observes in *The Arabian Nights: A Companion,* include "long heroic epics, wisdom literature, fables, cosmological fantasy, pornography, scatological jokes, mystical devotional tales, chronicles of low life, rhetorical debates and masses of poetry."

Though compilers can select among hundreds of original stories, the traditional opening remains the same. Long ago, Sultan Shahryar, bitterly disappointed by the infidelity of his wife, vowed never again to trust a woman. He proposed instead to marry a new wife each night and have her killed the next morning. After some time had passed, the beautiful and clever Scheherazade developed a plan to end the tyranny. She persuaded her father to marry her to the sultan, then begged the sultan to allow her sister, Dunyazad, to spend her last night on earth with her. Just before dawn, Dunyazad woke Scheherazade and asked her to tell a story. When dawn broke, the story was unfinished, and the sultan realized he must keep her alive in order to hear the end. By the next morning the tale was still unfinished, and once more the execution was delayed. This cycle continued for more than three years—for a total of 1,001 nights—during which time Scheherazade bore the sultan three healthy sons, and he fell deeply in love with her.

The Thousand and One Nights entered Western consciousness with the French translation by Antoine Galland (1646–1715) of a Syrian manuscript dating to the 14th or 15th century. His publication, preserved at the National Library in Paris, is now the oldest extant manuscript of the *Nights.* Edward Lane undertook an English translation in 1838–41, with large sections excised to suit the sensitivities of 19th-century Victorians. The 1885 translation by Sir Richard Burton, who traveled widely through the Middle East and India (and also introduced the English-speaking world to the KAMA SUTRA), is not entirely faithful to the Arabic versions, mixing in tales by Geoffrey Chaucer and François Rabelais. Since some of Galland's added stories have been translated into Arabic, it is now virtually impossible for any but the most devoted scholar to trace the complex web of influences. Readers can therefore simply relax into the magical world of *The Thousand and One Nights,* losing themselves among its colorful characters: brave travelers and lovely princesses; capricious rulers and trickster magicians; and the demons, witches, and clever genies who constantly test human ingenuity.

Critical Analysis

The narrative technique of using a frame story to link a series of smaller tales is a standard feature of ORAL LITERATURE and also appears in such written works as the PANCHATANTRA of India, OVID's *Metamorphoses,* Chaucer's *Canterbury Tales,* and Giovanni Boccaccio's *Decameron.* The multitude of stories in *The Thousand and One Nights* are linked by the irresistible figure of Scheherazade, who, in Burton's translation, is both educated and beautiful:

> . . . indeed it was said that she had collected a thousand books of histories relating to antique races and departed rulers. She had perused the works of the poets and knew them by heart; she had studied philosophy and the sciences, arts, and accomplishments; and she was pleasant and polite, wise and witty, well read and well bred.

In addition to the stories told by Scheherazade, the other characters begin to tell their own stories, and the narrative thread can become quite compli-

cated. Readers of *The Thousand and One Nights* find this interweaving of narratives one of its most appealing characteristics. Novelist A. S. Byatt, in the introduction to the Modern Library edition of Burton's translation, celebrates this structure and sees it as supporting a larger theme:

> A character in a story invokes a character who tells a story about a character who has a story to tell. . . . Everything proliferates. The *Nights* is a maze, a web, a network, a river with infinite tributaries, a series of boxes within boxes, a bottomless pool. It turns endlessly on itself, a story about storytelling. And yet we feel it has to do with our essential nature, and not just a need for idle entertainment.

For Scheherazade, storytelling is the way to extend her life. The themes of the individual stories continually echo the themes of the larger work: kings and powerful beings like genies constantly demand to hear stories; the weak or oppressed are constantly brought to judgment and must use their wits to protect their lives; wily sages and thieves pop out of corners to trick honest citizens out of their earned wealth; the stouthearted undertake fantastic voyages and return with remarkable tales. Magic elements abound in the stories, but human cleverness predominates.

An example of the nested narrative technique appears in the tale of "The Fisherman and the Genie," where the genie, waiting for the fisherman to return to fulfill a sentence of execution, is approached by an old man and a hind, and so begins the story "The Old Man and the Hind." The narrative thread always finds itself, however; the first story ends with the fisherman tricking the genie into going back into his bottle, and the sly fisherman quickly stoppers it up.

Although certain translators have tended to regard *The Thousand and One Nights* as no more than engaging tall tales, and to collect them as *The Arabian Nights' Entertainments*, these ostensibly diverting stories carry a prickly subtext. Certain tales seem uncannily modern, as in the tale of "The

Ebony Horse," where a sage creates a flying machine that an enterprising prince learns to operate. Moreover, close readers will observe that the *Nights* offers an intriguing series of lessons on public relations. The tales expose a broad view of all classes and levels of society, creating a stage where kings rub elbows with street thieves. Through frequent praises and invocations, Allah serves as a constant presence and a unifying force that binds the tales; Burton's translation illuminates this in its opening and closing addresses to MUHAMMAD. Characters of different races and religions populate the *Nights,* offering glimpses into the diverse world of the Middle East. The seemingly riotous tales of crosses and double-crosses include useful advice on how to operate within a society where it is accepted that women occupy subordinate positions, class differences are distinct and insurmountable, and rulers have the power to distribute justice, grant life, and demand death.

The Thousand and One Nights has had a profound impact on all the cultures it has reached. In their childhoods, the English poets Samuel Taylor Coleridge and William Wordsworth and the Victorian novelist Charles Dickens immersed themselves in tales of the Arabian nights; both Marcel Proust and Edgar Allan Poe saw themselves as Scheherazades of sorts. Twentieth-century novelists have composed modern versions of oriental fables—for example, Salman Rushdie in *Haroun and the Sea of Stories* and Naguib Mahfouz in *Arabian Nights and Days.* The *Nights* have sparked the imagination of filmmakers and musicians, and almost any child has heard at some point, and in some version, the tale of Aladdin and his enchanted lamp, the seven voyages of Sinbad the Sailor, and the tale of Ali Baba and the Forty Thieves. Many a child has perhaps wished for a lamp containing a wish-granting genie without realizing the true moral of Aladdin's story: that genies are tricky creatures and wishes are dangerous things.

Some maintain that *The Thousand and One Tales* is an achievement unparalleled by any work of literature in any other culture. Its sheer volume, diversity, and complexity are unrivaled. It sheds light on the culture of its creators, and it continues to spark the imagination of new generations with its promise of magic and its lesson that storytelling is the only sure way to achieve immortality.

English Versions of *The Thousand and One Nights*

The Arabian Nights. Translated by Husain Haddawy. New York: Everyman, 1990.

Arabian Nights: Tales from a Thousand and One Nights. Translated by Richard Burton. New York: The Modern Library, 2001.

The Book of Thousand Nights and One Night. 4 vols. Edited by E. P. Mathers and J. C. Mardrus. New York: Routledge, 1994.

Works about *The Thousand and One Nights*

Caracciolo, Peter L., ed. *The Arabian Night in English Literature: Studies in the Reception of Thousand and One Nights into British Culture.* New York: St. Martin's Press, 1988.

Hovannisian, Richard and Georges Sabagh. *The Thousand and One Nights in Arabic Literature and Society.* Cambridge, U.K.: Cambridge University Press, 1997.

Irwin, Robert. *The Arabian Nights: A Companion.* New York: Penguin Books, 1994.

Thucydides (ca. 460–ca. 400 B.C.) *historian*

Very little is known about the life of Thucydides, particularly his early years. He was born and raised in Athens as an aristocrat, "son of Olorus," as he described himself, and apparently relished his status.

Athens and Sparta were both military superpowers; the former ruled the seas and the latter boasted the world's greatest army. After the Greek city-states unexpectedly defeated the powerful Persian Empire in the early fifth century B.C., the alliance between Athens and Sparta disintegrated. The allies became adversaries, each struggling for dominance, leading to the Peloponnesian War.

Thucydides fought for Athens in the war, and by 424 B.C., he had been designated a general. Stationed in the Balkans in a region called Thrace, he failed to thwart the capture of the strategically positioned port city of Amphipolis. When he described the incident in his only known work, the *History of the Peloponnesian War,* Thucydides defended his good intentions, saying that even though he "sailed in haste with seven ships," the citizens surrendered before he could reach them. For this mistake, he was exiled from Athenian territory for 20 years, until the end of the war, when Sparta, with the aid of Persia, annihilated the mighty Athenian navy, cut off the food supply until the city surrendered, and installed an oligarchy at Athens.

From adversity arose opportunity. "Because of my exile," Thucydides wrote, "I was enabled to watch quietly the course of events." Like his older colleague HERODOTUS, Thucydides became an observer and investigator of both warring factions. He was permitted to return to Athens in 404 B.C., but he must have died within a few years of his return, for he never completed his *History of the Peloponnesian War.*

Critical Analysis

Whatever his feelings about his exile, Thucydides wrote *History* without rancor or prejudice. He gives equal attention to both parties, who perpetrated brutality and bloodshed in an acquisitive and ruthless grasp for power. His *History* is an important treatise on the nature and causes of war, its impact and consequences, and under what circumstances it will continue to disgrace and destroy civilization.

Unlike Herodotus, who often digresses during his history of the Persian War, Thucydides remains focused on recording military events and their implications. He divides *History of the Peloponnesian War* into three military phases. The first covers the conflict between Sparta and Athens, which lasted from 431 to 421 B.C. The second covers the Athenians' expedition into Sicily and its failure during the years 415 to 413 B.C. The third phase covers the new war between Sparta and Athens, which lasted from 413 to 404 B.C., although Thucydides's writing ends in 411 B.C.

The historian begins his opus by clarifying his methodology and assuring readers that his conclusions are reliable, based on the "clearest data." He acknowledges, however, that memories are imperfect, impressions fallible, and eyewitnesses biased. Unlike "the compositions of the chroniclers that are attractive at truth's expense" (presumably Herodotus), "[t]he absence of romance in my history will . . . be judged useful by those inquirers who desire an exact knowledge of the past as an aid to the interpretation of the future. . . . I have written my work . . . as a possession for all time."

Thucydides concludes in his introduction, "The real cause" of the Peloponnesian War was "the growth of the power of Athens, and the alarm which this inspired in" Spartan territory, which "made war inevitable." Important throughout the *History* is his ongoing comparisons of the two antagonists. Athens was a democracy that had only recently gained influence in Greece. Because its power was naval, its economy was a commercial one. Thucydides believed, incorrectly, that Pericles, a statesman and military commander of the time, perfected Athenian democracy; thus, he includes several of Pericles' speeches in Book II of his *History.*

In Sparta, government was controlled by a handful of powerful men, and the city-state was known for its long-standing power and military prowess. As its forces were land-based, so was its agrarian economy. If Athens was enterprise and innovation, Sparta was fortitude and discipline.

A turning point in the war occurred after the revolt of Mytilene, the chief city on the prosperous island of Lesbos, home of the lyric poet SAPPHO. All of Attica had been ravaged by the Spartans, and Athens had been blockaded. Teeming with refugees who had fled the countryside, the city succumbed to overcrowding, creating abysmal sanitary conditions and a plague that killed Pericles. During the Mytilene uprising, Athens was still reeling from the devastation, but its forces nevertheless laid siege to Mytilene, which finally succumbed when conditions there became intolerable.

The rulers of Athens were in no mood to be magnanimous in dealing with the insurrectionists;

the assembly voted to slaughter the men and sell the women and children. A warship was promptly dispatched, but the assembly soon regretted its decree. Wholesale extermination would eliminate potential friends as well as foes; it might trigger rebellion rather than suppress it; and Mytilene had military and monetary resources that could help Athens defeat Sparta. Even though Cleon, Pericles' successor, insisted that mercy was not in the empire's best interests, cooler heads prevailed, and the two cities eventually became allies.

Throughout the remainder of the *History*, Thucydides characterizes Athens as increasingly bloodthirsty and repressive, and less the idealistic, enlightened force depicted at the beginning. He emphasizes how the Athenians compromised their principles, gave way to revenge, attained a feverish level of ruthlessness, and justified murder for political gain despite their democratic ideals.

Just one example of this overriding desire for power appears in Thucydides' account of the conflict between Athens and Melos. Melos was a colony of Sparta that endeavored to remain neutral during the Peloponnesian War. Athens, affronted, tried to force an alliance with the small island city-state, to no avail. According to Thucydides, during a conference between councils for the two entities, the Athenian representative asserted that the "will to power" is a fundamental human drive and, essentially, that "might makes right":

[We] both alike know that into the discussion of human affairs the question of justice only enters where the pressure of necessity is equal, and that the powerful exact what they can, and the weak grant what they must. . . . For . . . of men we know, that by a law of their nature wherever they can rule they will. This law was not made by us, and we are not the first who have acted upon it; we did but inherit it, and shall bequeath it to all time, and we know that you and all mankind, if you were as strong as we are, would do as we do.

In 416 B.C., the Athenians inflicted on Melos and other Greek city-states what it had spared Mytilene: massacre, slavery, and occupation. As the war persisted, Thucydides portrayed Athenians as becoming weak in body and spirit, fractious and factious; he saw the ideal of Athenian democracy deteriorating as a result. According to Harvard professor John H. Finley, Jr., the end of the *History* expresses "a mood of fear, instability and division" among the Athenians. "As description, the account of the slow death . . . of Athens' strength and hope is Thucydides' masterpiece and one of the masterpieces of all historical writing."

Classics scholar H. C. Baldry writes:

Thucydides' proud claim to immortality has proved correct: his book is still absorbing reading. . . . His swift narrative . . . breathes the spirit of contemporary rationalism yet has an old-fashioned flavor; it is concise and austere, yet forceful and impassioned. [Thucydides is] deeply moved by Athens' folly . . . and its disastrous results; yet he austerely surveys the whole story as a clinical example of human behavior under the stresses of imperialism and war.

As such, the *History of the Peloponnesian War* influenced a host of Greek writers, politicians, and historians, including XENOPHON, Cassius Dio (ca. 164–ca. 229), Polybius (ca. 200–ca. 118 B.C.), Thomas Hobbes (1588–1679), and more recently author Lewis Lapham. More importantly, however, Thucydides' *History* has influenced the perception of war—its philosophy and politics—throughout the ages and up to the present day.

English Versions of Works by Thucydides

On Justice, Power, and Human Nature: Selections from History of the Peloponnesian War. Translated by Paul Woodruff. Indianapolis, Ind.: Hackett Publishing, 1998.

The Peloponnesian War: The Complete Hobbes Translation. Translated by Benjamin Jowett. Buffalo, N.Y.: Prometheus Books, 1998.

Stories of Thucydides. Retold by H. L. Havell. Indy-
Publish, 2004.

Works about Thucydides

Lapham, Lewis. *Theater of War: In Which the Republic
Becomes an Empire.* New York: The New Press,
2003.

Palmer, Michael. *Love of Glory and the Common
Good: Aspects of the Political Thought of Thucydides.* Lanham, Md.: Rowman & Littlefield, 2001.

Rood, Tim. *Thucydides: Narrative and Explanation.*
Oxford: Oxford University Press, 1998.

Stahl, Hans-Peter. *Thucydides: Man's Place in History.*
Cardiff: The Classical Press of Wales, 2002.

Titus Livius

See LIVY.

Titus Lucretius Carus

See LUCRETIUS.

Tristan and Iseult (*Tristam and Iseut*)
(1100s–1200s)

Tristan and Iseult are a fictional pair of lovers who
dominated the Western European medieval imagination. The story of their adulterous love even became part of the King Arthur story cycle.

Tristan (also rendered as Tristam or Tristram) is
the favored nephew of King Mark of Cornwall, and
he is sent to accompany the king's new bride, the
Irish princess Iseult (also rendered as Iseut, Isolt,
Isolde, Ysolt, etc.), on her boat ride to her new husband in Cornwall. On the voyage, Tristan and
Iseult mistakenly drink a love potion that was intended for her and King Mark; consequently, they
fall passionately in love. Once they arrive at court,
they continue to conduct their affair in secret. King
Mark loves both his nephew and his wife, so when
some of his knights and courtiers tell him they suspect Tristan and Iseult, he initially refuses to believe them. Finally, the king finds out about their

affair, and the pair are sent off in exile, where they
continue to meet.

In several versions of the story, Tristan marries
a princess of Brittany named Iseult of the White
Hands; even though he performs the marriage in
an attempt to forget his one love, he is still so ob-
sessed with Iseult that he marries the princess only
because she has the same name. Tristan is mortally
wounded, and he sends word to Queen Iseult to
come to him. Iseult sets out to meet her lover and
heal him, but she arrives after his death, and she
dies of grief. The two are buried side by side.

The origins of the Tristan and Iseult story may be
Celtic; the place- and character names derive from
Cornish and Welsh, and references to King Mark
and Tristan appear in Welsh bards' story collections
of the 11th century. But two 12th-century French
romances are the earliest surviving sources. One is
by a poet called Béroul, and the other is by a man
who calls himself Thomas à Angleterre (Thomas of
England). Both versions are unfinished, but an Old
Norse translation of Thomas's version is complete.
A French prose version of the story dates from the
mid-13th century, and this is the version that incorporates Tristan into the world of King Arthur
and the quest for the HOLY GRAIL. This extremely
popular version was translated into Italian, Spanish,
and even Russian and Polish, spreading the
Arthurian tales into Southern and Eastern Europe.

German medieval literature, however, not only
produced the earliest complete version of *Tristan
and Iseult* (1170–90), but also one of the great
works of medieval literature, the *Tristan* of GOTT-
FRIED VON STRASSBURG (1200). Gottfried's poem is
incomplete, but it is masterful in its exploration of
the characters' psychological states. Gottfried uses
the fatal love potion as a metaphor for "love at first
sight." Even though he focuses on the joy that their
love brings them, Gottfried does not neglect the
pain and betrayal that the affair causes every character involved. This version of the Tristan and
Iseult legend was enormously popular and influential, inspiring Richard Wagner's great 19th-
century opera *Tristan und Isolde.*

The Tristan and Iseult story inspired other writers not usually associated with the Arthurian cycle. MARIE DE FRANCE wrote a *lai,* or short song, called *"Chevrefoil"* ("Honeysuckle") about Tristan and Iseult, arranging one of their rendezvous in the woods. Other short works or fragments from longer ones depict episodes based on the famous lovers. Several surviving short poems in French describe incidents in which Tristan pretends madness or disguises himself as a wandering minstrel or beggar in order to visit Iseult while he is in exile. The story was so popular that it even appeared in the tapestries and textiles that decorated medieval castles.

Part of the appeal of the Tristan and Iseult legend stems from its time period and the culture that produced it; Tristan is the knight as courtly lover, while Iseult combines fidelity to her lover with resourcefulness in meeting him. The overwhelming power of their attraction to each other, as well as the painful consequences of their love, overrides any moral or ethical problem that their affair poses to readers, and their troubled passion has set the tone for literary depictions of romantic love for most of Western world literature.

Critical Analysis

The earliest French versions of the Tristan and Iseult story differ in tone and emphasis. Medievalists have called the Béroul version the "common version" because it takes a commonsensical and action-oriented approach to the narrative. When it focuses on the lovers' duplicity, it seems to regard their cleverness as admirable rather than despicable. When Iseult pleads her innocence before King Marc and King Arthur, she and Tristan plot for him to disguise himself as a leper and help carry her across a marshy brook. Thus, when she swears that the only men who have been between her thighs are her husband and the leper who carried her over the marsh, she technically tells the truth. Finally, the Béroul version contains earthy moments that are both humorous and disturbing. When King Mark tries to punish Iseult and Tristan the first time, he initially plans to burn them alive. When a leper proposes that a better punishment would be to give Iseult to the leper colony, Béroul spares no detail in describing why this would be worse than death:

> *No lady in the world could tolerate*
> *A single day of relations with us!*
> *Our ragged clothes stick to our bodies; . . .*
> *When she sees our squalid hovels*
> *And shares our dishes*
> *And has to sleep with us,*
> *And when, instead of your fine food, sir,*
> *She has only the scraps and crumbs*
> *That are given to us at the gates. . . .*

Marc agrees this is a fate worse than death and hands Iseult to the lepers.

Thomas à Angleterre's narrative does not focus on the main characters' trickery and action as much as it does on their psychological states and the effects the adulterous relationship has on other characters. This version, called the "courtly" version, is not simply more refined but more concerned with how the two main characters' passion has consequences for themselves and others. Tristan chooses to marry Iseult of the White Hands in Brittany because he imagines that marriage will offer him a release from physical frustration since he is separated from Queen Iseult. Yet as Thomas describes his thought process, this is not a simple problem that can be solved by substituting one woman for another:

> *When they cannot have their desire*
> *Or what they love most,*
> *They do what is in their power to do;*
> *Out of desperation they will do something*
> *Which often increases their pain twofold,*
> *And, seeking to be free,*
> *They yet cannot break the bond.*

Instead of finding peace within his marriage, Tristan feels little attraction toward his wife and guilt for betraying his true love and causing Iseult of the White Hands to feel rejected and bitter. Iseult, on the other hand, does not enjoy any pleasure with her husband, Marc, because he is not Tristan. To contradict the old saying, all cats are not gray in the dark, and probably the greatest innovation in the Tristan and Iseult story is the insistence that individuals cannot be commanded to love because of social institutions or codes of loyalty. Love becomes a wild force that threatens the social order: Tristan loses his standing in court and the protection of his closest kinsman, Iseult loses her husband's trust, and King Mark loses respect from his court because of his lenient dealings with the pair. Yet the doomed lovers are portrayed sympathetically in all versions of the story, and their struggle between social obligations and individual desires continues to inspire the Western imagination.

See also ABÉLARD AND HÉLOÏSE; MEDIEVAL ROMANCE.

English Versions of *Tristan and Iseult*

Béroul. *The Romance of Tristan and the Tale of Tristan's Madness.* Translated by Alan S. Fedrick. New York: Penguin, 1978.

Early French Tristan Poems. 2 vols. Edited by Norris J. Lacy. Cambridge, U.K.: D.S. Brewer, 1998.

The Romance of Tristan: The Thirteenth-Century Old French "Prose Tristan." Translated by Renee L. Curtis. New York: Oxford University Press, 1994.

Works about *Tristan and Iseult*

Eisner, Sigmund. *The Tristan Legend: A Study in Sources.* Evanston, Ill.: Northwestern University Press, 1969.

Grimbert, Joan Tasker, ed. *Tristan and Isolde: A Casebook.* New York: Garland, 1995.

Lacy, Norris J. and Geoffrey Ashe with Debra N. Mancoff. *The Arthurian Handbook.* New York: Garland, 1997.

Varvaro, Alberto. *Beroul's Romance of Tristran.* New York: Barnes & Noble, 1972.

troubadours (12th–13th centuries)

The troubadours were poets and musicians who became common in the south of France during the early 12th century. Like the medieval *jongleur,* or minstrel, troubadours traveled widely, but unlike the minstrels, troubadours composed and performed their own work. They wrote in a medieval language called Provençal, today called Occitan, and their lyrics resembled modern song lyrics in that they were meant to be sung to musical accompaniment. While most of the poets known to us were male, there were also female troubadours called *trobairitz.* The trouvères, the northern French counterparts of the troubadours, borrowed their ideas and techniques from the southern troubadours.

The troubadour style flourished over a span of about 200 years. The early troubadours first appeared in the first half of the 12th century in the province of Poitiers. From 1150 to 1180, they prospered under the patronage of Eleanor of Aquitaine, and in the years 1180–1209, the troubadour fashion reached courts in Italy, Spain, Hungary, and even Malta. With the beginning of the Albigensian CRUSADE (1208), however, the interest in courtly poetry began to decline, especially when troubadours lost their wealthy patrons, and religious fervor began to supplant earthly love as the popular theme for poetry. By the late 13th century, devotional songs addressed the Virgin Mary rather than mortal women, and the troubadours effectively disappeared.

The most important contribution the troubadours and *trobairitz* made to Western literature was their evolution of the concept of courtly love, or *fin' amor* ("fine love"). Courtly love, part of the code of CHIVALRY, concerned the worship of a noble woman by a poet who made himself a servant to love. This concept profoundly affected later MEDIEVAL ROMANCE, as seen in the works of such authors as CHRÉTIEN DE TROYES, MARIE DE FRANCE, and JEAN DE MEUN, as well as in stories about King Arthur and the HOLY GRAIL. While the style of troubadour poetry might be either light and courtly or brooding and reflective, the poems frequently use and reuse certain images, devices, and conventions to describe the poet's experience of love and life.

Many of the troubadour manuscripts contain short sections called *vidas* (from the Latin *vita* "life") that serve as a brief biography prefacing the poet's songs. Troubadours could be of any class, from noble to peasant, and in the 13th century troubadours frequented courts all over western Europe, from Portugal to the Holy Land. Since it is difficult to know whether the poet or another authored the *vidas,* it is virtually impossible to determine how much is factually true and how much was added to create interest. Several of the *vidas* serve as touching narratives that could stand as separate pieces of literature.

Critical Analysis

Troubadour poetry could address a variety of topics or take on any number of forms. The *vers* was often a moralizing poem, and the *sirventes* was a poem of blame or praise, frequently about deeds of war. The *tenso* was a debate poem that staged an argument between two or more parties; the *alba* was a song addressed to the dawn; the *pastorela,* based on the Greek pastoral image, involved the love affairs of shepherds and shepherdesses; and the *planh* was a lament on the death of a king or other important personage.

By far the most prevalent and influential of the genres was the *canso,* the song about love. In their treatments of love, troubadours often drew on biblical sources but also borrowed classical tropes from love poets such as OVID. From this they developed a concept of courtly love with very specific rules. The poet is invariably in love with a noble lady or *domna,* a situation innovated by William IX, Count of Poitiers and Duke of Aquitaine (born 1071), the earliest recorded troubadour. The lady is portrayed as possessing refined manners and speech and surpassing beauty. William writes, "[f]or the sweetness of her welcome, for her beautiful and gentle look . . . a man who wins to the joy of her love will live a hundred years." To love the lady is the chief joy of the poet's life. As William says:

"The joy of her can make the sick man well
again, her wrath can make a well man die. . . ."

The French troubadour Marcabru (fl. ca. 1130–56), supports this notion that love is the pursuit of the poet's life, singing: "He whom noble Love singles out lives gay, courtly and wise; and he whom it rejects, it confounds, and commits to total destruction." And Arnaut Daniel declares that he prefers his lady's love to any of earth's highest honors: "I'd not have the empire of Rome, nor be made pope of it, if thereby I might not return to her for whom my heart burns and crackles."

But the lady whom the poet adores is married, so the lover can only long for her from a distance, which produces an understandable state of distress. Equally distressing to the lover is the lady's behavior, which according to the rules of courtly love may be gracious or distant by turns. Sometimes she will treat him with warm affection, sometimes with icy disdain, and she may destroy his heart by faithlessly giving herself to another. Additionally, the lover may suffer from competitors' slanders, all of which add a tone of lament to the poetry. As Peire VIDAL complains, "No more than the fish can live without water, love-service cannot be without slanderers, hence lovers pay dearly for their joy."

When not complaining of the lady's coldness or infidelity, the lover in the poem frequently begs for her attention and love, as in these lines by Italian troubadour Sordello (ca. 1200–ca. 1269): "For Pity's sake I pray you, fair beloved, that with some little crumb of love's joy you come to my help, swiftly. . . . For otherwise I can have no joy, unless pity and mercy take you." In any circumstance, the pursuit of his lady causes the poet to suffer. Thus, love is the highest and most astonishing experience of which the human being is capable.

The female *trobairitz,* though addressing male lovers, use the same stylistic techniques and express the same sentiments of courtly love. For example, the Countess of Dia sings of her fidelity to her lover and her joy in love:

. . . my love for him has never strayed,
nor is my heart the straying kind.

I'm very happy, for the man
whose love I seek's so fine.

In another verse, she expresses a bitter lament over her lover's coldness and lack of faith:

. . . I feel your heart turn adamant
toward me, friend: it's not right another
love
take you away from me, no matter what she
says.

The clear style, pitch of feeling, and complexity of emotion achieved in troubadour lyrics helps explain why, when blended with skillful melodies, these songs pleased audiences for so long and gained the poet noble favor above all other entertainers at court.

Though the early troubadour poetry reveals inventive experimentation with topics and images, later troubadour poetry became rather formulaic in its adherence to certain devices, such as the love triangle, the feeling that there is no joy above that of loving another, and the lover's long suffering marked by periodic bursts of happiness. Though troubadours eventually disappeared, their code of courtly love persisted in medieval literature through the late MIDDLE AGES into the Renaissance and beyond, appearing in such works as Ludovico Ariosto's *Orlando Furioso,* Geoffrey Chaucer's *The Book of the Duchess,* Sir Thomas Malory's *Le Morte d'Arthur,* and Edmund Spenser's *The Faerie Queene.* Writers of later ages and nationalities continued to elaborate on and improve the tradition of lyric love poetry: the Italians DANTE and Petrarch, the French François Villon and Pierre de Ronsard, the Spanish Miguel Cervantes and Luis de Góngora, the German minnesingers, and English poets from William Shakespeare to John Donne, to name only a few. As translator Alan Press says, "the work of the troubadours lies at the origin of a centuries-long tradition of high lyric poetry in western Europe." In effect, the troubadours created and communicated to the rest of Europe an original way of composing poetry and talking about love whose forms and language have survived in Western culture to the present day.

English Versions of Works by Troubadours
Anthology of Troubadour Lyric Poetry. Translated and edited by Alan R. Press. Austin: University of Texas Press, 1971.
Bogin, Meg. *The Women Troubadours.* Scarborough, U.K.: Paddington Press Ltd., 1976.

Works about Troubadours
Gaunt, Simon and Sarah Kay, eds. *The Troubadours: An Introduction.* Cambridge, Mass.: Cambridge University Press, 1999.
Paterson, Linda A. *The World of the Troubadours: Medieval Occitan Society ca. 1100–ca. 1300.* Cambridge, Mass.: Cambridge University Press, 1995.

Troyes, Chrétien de
See CHRÉTIEN DE TROYES.

tuuwutsi narratives   *Hopi storytelling*
Tuuwutsi represent the principal narrative genre of Hopi traditional literature. In the custom of Native American storytelling, these oral narratives have a strong aural component. Among the Hopi, *tuuwutsi* are stories that a storyteller has heard secondhand. The context is secular, and the subjects are make-believe things. The Hopi distinguish *tuuwutsi* fantasy stories from *ka'atsa* ("not false") stories, which have preserved events in Hopi history. COYOTE TALES, called *istutuwutsi,* comprise a subgenre of the *tuuwutsi* narratives.

Hopi storytellers typically set off the *tuuwutsi* fictional narratives from normal discourse by using special phrases that provide formulaic beginnings and endings. For example, *Aliksaii* is the Hopi counterpart of "once upon a time," and *paigakpola* translates as "now to where it ends." The audience replies in expected ways at key places as the narratives are told.

Some of the Hopi *tuuwutsi* include "The White Dawn of the Hopi," a story of how the Hopi came to be; "The Hopi Boy and the Sun," a tale about a boy who travels with the Sun, his father, learns how to treat people rightly, and then returns to his own people to teach them the same; "Son of Light Kills the Monster," a story about how the Son of Light retrieves his kidnapped wife by conquering the monster Man-Eagle in a series of contests; "The Revenge of Blue Corn Ear Maiden," a tale of rivalry between two friends; and "A Journey to the Skeleton House," a story of a young boy's learning what became of the dead, his journey to the Otherworld, and how the living and the dead began to work together.

Both the *tuuwutsi* and *ka'atsa* are used by the Hopi, as are stories in other Native American nations, to recount tribal history, continue the ORAL LITERATURE/TRADITION, explain the creation of the world and its occupants, teach morals or lessons, entertain, and preserve cultural traditions and knowledge.

English Versions of *Tuuwutsi* Narratives

Hopi Coyote Tales: Istutuwutsi. Translated by Michael Lomatuway'ma. Edited by Ekkehart Malotki. Lincoln: University of Nebraska Press, 1990.

Malotki, Ekkehart, and Ken Gary. *Hopi Stories of Witchcraft, Shamanism, and Magic.* Lincoln: University of Nebraska Press, 2001.

A Work about *Tuuwutsi* Narratives

Shaul, David Leedom. *Hopi Traditional Literature.* Albuquerque: University of Mexico Press, 2002.

Valmiki, Maharshi (fl. ca. 550 B.C.) *poet*

Valmiki is the Indian seer, or *rishi*, credited with creating the epic *Ramayana*. Because of his long practice of penance and seclusion in his retreat by the river Tamasa, Valmiki earned the title of Maharshi, "maha" meaning great. He is celebrated as the first poet to compose in Sanskrit, and his *Ramayana* is considered the first real poem of India.

Legend surrounds Valmiki and the creation of his EPIC work. Some stories have it that he started life as a robber but saw the error of his ways and became spiritually devout. According to tradition, Valmiki was walking along the river Tamasa one day and watched a pair of lovebirds nesting together in a tree. When a hunter approached and killed one of the birds, Valmiki was so shocked and distressed that he cried out, cursing the hunter, "Thou shalt never command any respect in society for years to come as you have shot dead one of the innocent birds engrossed in love." Upon considering his statement, Valmiki realized that, in the Sanskrit tongue, he had spoken four rhythmic lines of eight syllables each, which closely resembled the meter of Vedic literature. He decided to call this poetic meter the *sloka* and use it as the form in which to tell an epic tale of love, devotion, separation, and sacrifice. Inspired by the god Brahma and

the sage Narada, who first told him the story of Rama as a model of humanity and kingship, Valmiki composed the first and most beloved poem of Indian history.

In the tradition of Sanskrit literature, the *Ramayana* is thought to closely follow the Vedas and thus is of an earlier date than the PURANA or the MAHABHARATA, the longest and most ornate of epics. Like other ancient poems, the *Ramayana* most likely first existed as a collection of stories passed along by storytellers who recited the poem by heart. Valmiki, though considered the poet, may never have put his work into written form. Scholars of Indian literature have debated at length about the date of composition, and no firm consensus has yet been reached. Tradition places the poet at the dawn of history, shortly after the Aryans began to migrate into what is now India. The majority of *Ramayana* scholars believe from various archaeological and other literary evidence that Valmiki, and Rama, lived sometime between the seventh and 11th centuries B.C. A genealogy of kings, which exists in the *Purana*, cites Rama as an actual prince of the Ikshavaku dynasty, but no dates are given.

The poem has been so extensively revised, extended, and transcribed that distinguishing the original subject matter devised by Valmiki from the later additions becomes simply an argument of style. Scholar C. V. Vaidya believes that sometime in the first century B.C., the poem was rewritten and recompiled into the form in which it exists today. Originally the poem celebrated Rama as a great man and the best of kings. The first-century additions and adaptations reflect the evolving beliefs concerning the avatars, or incarnations, of the god Vishnu. In Hindu tradition, the gods incarnated in human form to provide models for right living and intervene in certain affairs. In the *Mahabharata,* the god Vishnu incarnated as Krishna to help Arjuna win his great battle. After the composition of the *Mahabharata,* it was seen that Rama had been the god Vishnu in a different, previous form that had come to earth expressly to conquer the demonic tyrant Ravana. Scribes embellished the text of the *Ramayana* to reflect that belief.

Most critics accept the attribution of the *Ramayana* to Valmiki because the poet appears in two places in the action of the epic itself. In the first, during their exile in the forest, Rama, his wife Sita, and his brother Lakshmana visit Valmiki in his remote hermitage and converse with him. Later, after Rama has been restored to the throne but has had to banish Sita on suspicion of infidelity, Valmiki brings two young boys, Lava and Kusha, to court. The boys sing the story of Rama, and Valmiki then reveals that these two are the sons of Rama and Sita. Both of these instances, however, create confusion when compared to the rest of the poem. If Sita and Rama visited Valmiki in the woods, then he presumably already knew their story and would not need Narada to explain it to him. Also, the revelation of Rama's sons and Sita's final trial take place in the last portion of the work, which some scholars believe is a later addition or appendix and not the work of Valmiki himself. Similar contradictions and confusions appear throughout the poem, most likely due to its age and the number of people who have contributed to its retelling. As an example of poetic literature, the *Ramayana*

nevertheless stands as a work of great beauty and extraordinary influence.

Critical Analysis

Though the *Ramayana* can be appreciated as simply an epic story, along the lines of the SHAHNAMEH of Persia or the German NIBELUNGENLIED, it is, as scholar V. Sitaramiah says, "a great literary and poetical document." More than just the life or adventures (*ayana*) of Rama, the *Ramayana* documents philosophical insights and human truths. Like the *Mahabharata,* the *Ramayana* is concerned with the Hindu concept of dharma, which means not only duty but also right conduct. The conduct of Rama is considered an excellent example of following dharma because Rama embodies all of the virtues of the ideal man: He is modest of nature, physically able, intellectually brilliant, and spiritually aware. He shows compassion and consideration for all beings, is balanced in his emotions, accepts any challenge that will benefit the general good, and demonstrates complete reverence for and obedience to his elders. A fitting companion, his wife Sita, in her turn, embodies all the virtues of the ideal woman. She is described as "proud and peerless," surpassingly beautiful, and steadfastly faithful. Rama wins her in true epic fashion by performing a mighty feat: He breaks a bow that no other suitor had been able to bend, thus showing himself worthy of her hand.

The adventures of Rama and Sita commence with his willing exile into the forest. Rama is the son of King Dasarath and destined to become the next ruler of Kosala and its capital city, Ayodhya. One of the king's wives, Kaikeyi, convinces Dasarath that her son Bharata should rule. Though all are distressed by the king's decision, Rama cheerfully obliges the will of his father and prepares to go into exile. Sita and Lakshmana insist on going with him. For 10 years they live peacefully and idyllically, until the demon Ravana decides to capture Sita. Through a series of deceits, he manages to fly away with her to his island country of Lanka, where he holds her prisoner. Rama is joined in his search by the creatures of the forest. He and his army of forest dwellers attack Ravana, and the poem recounts in detail every blow of the battle that follows. In the end, Rama vanquishes Ravana, and Sita undergoes a trial by fire to prove that she was faithful to her husband throughout her imprisonment. The original portion of the *Ramayana* concludes with Rama and Sita returning to Adodhya and ascending the throne in triumph:

> Fourteen years of woe were ended, Rama
>   now assumed his own,
> And they placed the weary wand'rer on his
>   father's ancient throne.

Some modern translations include the last chapter, though it is considered spurious, where Sita is banished once more and bears her children in exile. Valmiki brings them to court, where they sing the epic, and in the dramatic confrontation between Sita and her husband, the earth opens and swallows Sita as the final proof of her innocence. Thereafter, Rama, who remains unmarried, has a golden image of Sita made, which he places beside him on her throne.

The *Ramayana* of India appears in other literatures of Southeast Asia, including the Buddhist *Dasartha* JATAKA and the *Ramakien* of Thailand. The *Raghuvamsa* of KALIDASA and the *Ramcharitmanas* of Tulsidas both draw from the *Ramayana*. Professor Wardiman Djojonegoro of Indonesia concludes that the *Ramayana* manages to cross many borders and many centuries because the essence of the story remains a "universal source of inspiration." He writes: "The Rama story articulates and projects a set of moral and ethical values, against which we can evaluate our own human existence. . . . It opens vistas that enable us to enrich our own lives."

English Versions of a Work by Maharshi Valmiki

Ramayana. Translated by William Buck. Berkeley: University of California Press, 2000.

Ramayana: A Modern Retelling of the Great Indian Epic. Translated by Ramesh Menon. New York: North Point Press, 2004.

Ramayana: India's Immortal Tale of Love, Adventure, and Wisdom. Translated by Krishna Dharma. Los Angeles: Torchlight Publishing, 2000.

Works about Maharshi Valmiki

Blank, Jonah. *Arrow of the Blue-Skinned God: Tracing the Ramayana Through India.* New York: Grove Press, 2000.

Rao, I. Panduranga. *Valmiki.* New Delhi: Sahitya Akademi, 1994.

Vatsyayana Mallanga

See KAMA SUTRA.

Veldeke, Heinrich von

See HEINRICH VON VELDEKE.

Venerable Bede

See BEDE.

Ventadour, Bernard de

See BERNARD DE VENTADOUR.

Vidal, Peire (Piere Vidal) (ca. 1183– ca. 1204) *poet*

Vidal, a Provençal TROUBADOUR who combined elegant simplicity with technically demanding metrical forms, was born in Toulouse, France, the son of a furrier. He began his troubadour career in Marseilles and also spent time at the court of King Alfonso II of Aragon. Vidal spent most of his life traveling between the courts of Marseilles, Aragon, and Toulouse. In 1196, after Alfonso of Aragon died, Vidal visited the court of King Emmerich of Hungary. He may or may not have joined Marquis Boniface of Montferrat on a CRUSADE in 1202, but he was at the Island of Malta in 1204. He probably died in Provence between 1208 and 1210.

The hallmark of Vidal's poetic style is his clarity and simplicity of expression, a characteristic he shares with BERNARD DE VENTADOUR. Unlike ARNAUT DANIEL, who combined technical mastery with obscure vocabulary and metaphor, Vidal strove to make his work melodious and accessible to his audience. He specialized in the *canso-sirventes*, a Provençal poetic form that mingles the ethos of courtly love (*see* CHIVALRY AND COURTLY LOVE) with contemporary political references. This form gives Vidal's readers a sense of his restless, brilliant personality. He boasts of his prowess in court tourneys and especially with the ladies:

> I am such an one that a thousand greetings come to me every day from Catalonia and from Lombardy, for every day my value mounts and increases, wherefore the King nearly dies of envy, for I have my fun and pleasure with ladies.

Vidal's claims need to be taken with a grain of salt. According to the rather fantastic biography that precedes his poetry in several manuscripts, he traveled to Cyprus and married a Greek woman, whom he claimed was a niece of the emperor in Constantinople. He was also given to extravagant behavior; when one of his patrons, Count Raimon of Toulouse, died, Vidal mourned him by not only donning black clothing but also by cropping and docking his horses' ears and tails and shaving his and his servants' heads. When Vidal loved a woman named Loba (which means "she-wolf" in Provençal), he made the wolf his heraldic emblem and even put on a wolf skin to be the prey of a mock wolf hunt to gain her pity and attention. Surprisingly, this eccentric man's poetry reveals a directness and elegance in language that makes him one of the era's most accessible and honored troubadours.

An English Version of Works by Peire Vidal

Trobador Poets: Selections from the Poems of Eight Trobadors. Translated by Barbara Smythe. London: Chatto & Windus, 1911.

Vigne, Pier delle (Pier della Vigna, Pietro della Vigna, Petrus de Vineis) (ca. 1190–1249) *poet*

Pier delle Vigne was born in the Italian city of Capua. He studied law at Bologna and became a notary at the court of Emperor Frederick II of Swabia (in southwest Germany), who was also king of Sicily. Vigne helped to draw up Swabia's law codes, and in 1220 he became secretary of the imperial chancellery. His rank, wealth, and power only grew exponentially.

It is believed that in 1244, Frederick II sent Vigne to help THOMAS AQUINAS's family forcibly retrieve young Thomas, who had recently become a monk against their wishes. By 1247, Vigne was a key member of the emperor's inner circle. In 1249, however, he fell from power, possibly because he had been falsely accused of treason. Frederick ordered that Vigne be blinded and led before the public in chains. Disgraced, Vigne died shortly thereafter. Some sources say that he died accidentally, others that he deliberately hit his head against a wall. In his *Inferno*, DANTE depicts Vigne as innocent of treason but guilty of committing suicide.

Vigne was a member of the Sicilian school of poetry, which translator Frede Jensen describes as "the first truly national literary movement in Italy." The school, which flourished at Frederick II's court between 1230 and 1250, included at least 25 poets who wrote poems of CHIVALRY and COURTLY LOVE in the Sicilian dialect. Its members drew inspiration from earlier Provençal TROUBADOURS like BERNARD DE VENTADOUR and JAUFRÉ RUDEL. Unlike the hired troubadours, however, the "Sicilians" were civil servants and nobles.

Vigne's surviving works include several letters written in Latin and a few poems, including two love poems. In "'Twas Love, whom I desire as well as trust," the poet assures his love that he "would speak well, and not be shy, / in telling you I have long loved you, more / than Pyramus his Thisbe could adore."

Unlike troubadours' works, Pier delle Vigne's poems are meant to be read rather than sung. They are not lively, but they are elegantly crafted.

An English Version of a Work by Pier delle Vigne

"'Twas Love, whom I desire as well as trust." In *The Age of Dante: An Anthology of Early Italian Poetry.* Translated by Joseph Tusiani. New York: Baroque Press, 1974.

A Work about Pier delle Vigne

Jensen, Frede, ed. and trans. *The Poetry of the Sicilian School.* New York and London: Garland, 1986.

Villehardouin, Geoffroi de (ca. 1150– ca. 1212) *historian*

Geoffroi de Villehardouin, considered to be the first French historian who wrote in his native tongue, was born into a noble family in Champagne, France. In 1185, he became Champagne's marshal, an important administrative position in the hierarchy of feudalism. Marshals were responsible for making and overseeing military preparations and also served as deputies to their lords in governing their provinces. Villehardouin must have had excellent organizational and communication skills for such a position. From 1198 to 1207, he was involved in the Fourth CRUSADE and was also made marshal of Romania (presently Thrace, in Greece) and given a fiefdom there. This firsthand experience made him well suited to write an account of the crusade.

The Fourth Crusade began in 1198, when Pope Innocent III called for a crusade against the Mus-lims in Egypt. Initially, his call was ignored, but French nobles finally gathered together in Champagne in 1199 to declare and organize the Crusade. After enlisting the help of the Venetians, the crusaders quickly became split by differing political goals. Some decided to go into Syria, but others, led by the Venetians and Philip of Swabia, decided that they first needed to restore the rightful heir, Alexius Angelus, to the Byzantine Empire to the throne of Constantinople. This group, led by Boniface of Montferrat, who was also the patron of the troubadour Peire VIDAL, was the one Villehardouin accompanied to Constantinople. Byzantines did not particularly like or want Alexius Angelus as their emperor, but in 1203, the crusaders conquered Constantinople, and he was made Emperor Alexius IV. The crusaders found themselves to be an unpopular occupying force, putting down pockets of rebellion throughout Constantinople and the neighboring countryside. When Alexius IV died in 1204, the Venetians and French were convinced he had been murdered and once more attacked the city. Constantinople fell, and for four days, the Western forces sacked the city. The Byzantine Empire was divided among the Venetians, the French, and other European rulers, and a Latin Empire was established in the region, with Baldwin of Flanders elected as the new emperor.

Villehardouin's history of the Fourth Crusade, *La Conquête de Constantinople* (The Conquest of Constantinople) is significant as a historical and literary document. A valuable eyewitness account of the important meetings and decisions that motivated the crusaders, it is also the first history written in French. In relating the events of the Fourth Crusade with exactitude and precision, Villehardouin pleads in good faith in favor of the Crusaders' high command and creates a valuable historical and literary document. Villehardouin's style is clear, concise, and well organized, and his account of the Fourth Crusade influenced the style of French historians beyond the Renaissance. Villehardouin disappeared from the political limelight in 1207 and died without ever having returned home.

An English Version of a Work by Geoffroi de Villehardouin

Joinville and Villehardouin: Chronicles of the Crusades.
Translated by M. R. B. Shaw. Baltimore: Penguin Books, 1963.

A Work about Geoffroi de Villehardouin

Beer, Jeanette M. A. *Villehardouin: Epic Historian.* Geneva: Librairie Droz, 1968.

Virgil (Publius Virgilius Maro, P. Vergilius Maro, Vergil) (70–19 B.C.) *poet*

Virgil's birthplace was the village of Andes near the northern Italian city of Mantua in the ancient Roman province known as Cisalpine Gaul, on the Roman side of the Alps. His father, who seems to have been a cattle farmer, beekeeper, and manufacturer of earthenware, once worked as a servant for a man whose daughter he married and must have become fairly prosperous, since he could afford to educate his son for an elite career.

Virgil attended schools in several cities. When he was approximately 11 years old, he was sent to Cremona, about 75 miles from Milan, to study grammar and literature. At the time, Julius CAESAR was governor of Cisalpine Gaul and advocated full citizenship and self-government for the Cisalpines. Virgil developed an enduring admiration for Caesar and for AUGUSTUS, his successor, that would last a lifetime. In 55 B.C., Virgil continued his schooling in Milan, then moved to Rome when he was around 18 to put the finishing touches on his education. He was lectured on Latin and Greek prose style, including forms of expression, literary devices and conventions, and rules of composition. Bored with the rigidity of these topics, he studied rhetoric with a popular instructor as preparation for a career in law or politics, but this discipline, too, he found restrictive and technical. In any case, he proved he had no knack for public speaking. He was, however, interested in writing verse, and he cultivated friendships with a group of writers known as the "New Poets," who were experiment-

ing in Latin with classical Greek poetic techniques. While in Rome, he enjoyed the patronage of men of wealth and influence, as he would for virtually his entire career.

LUCRETIUS's *On the Nature of Things* was an enormous inspiration to Virgil, who copied the poet's use of hexameter and emulated his faith in the wisdom of the Greek philosopher EPICURUS and his followers. The Epicureans blended an interest in nature, including human nature, with scientific analysis and made the pursuit of pleasure a legitimate way of life. "The effect of Lucretius on Virgil was tremendous," writes scholar Olivia Coolidge in *Lives of Famous Romans.* Virgil's "artistry, more subtle than that of Lucretius, is only possible because of the earlier poet's work." Indeed, Virgil spent most of his adult life in an Epicurean colony in Naples. (Despite his inclinations, Virgil was an unsophisticated man, diffident, physically awkward, perhaps embarrassed by his provincial accent, and of a delicate constitution. He never married.)

In 42 B.C., Augustus (then Octavian), seeking to settle 200,000 discharged troops, ruthlessly confiscated entire districts in Cisalpine Gaul, including, probably, Virgil's boyhood home. The family's estate was restored, possibly due to the intervention of a powerful friend, but Virgil was deeply moved by the suffering around the countryside and the misery of those who had been evicted from their homes. Beyond these borders was a collective weariness and disillusionment among a population that had just experienced the wrenching transition from a Roman republic to an empire.

Virgil purportedly wrote in his own epitaph, "I sang of pastures, of cultivated fields, and of rulers." These three subjects correspond chronologically to his works: *Eclogues, Georgics,* and the *Aeneid.* The *Eclogues* are pastoral poems patterned as dialogue sung by shepherds. They represent Virgil's response to the misery he witnessed in contrast to the pastoral splendor and time of tranquillity that preceded it. His themes are the death and renewal inherent in nature, and the work suggests past travails and a redemptive future. They are unique in the way Virgil combines the pastoral genre with contemporary issues. The *Eclogues* were published in 37 B.C., upon which Virgil became a famous man, an enormously successful and highly regarded poet, and the beneficiary of the patronage of Maecenas, a chief adviser to Augustus. Maecenas was also patron to Virgil's good friend and fellow poet HORACE, whom Virgil had introduced to Maecenas.

With Maecenas's encouragement, Virgil went to work on his next composition, the *Georgics*. Again, he presents the cycles of nature central to a farmer's life and shows how those who wrest a living from the land must toil assiduously to bring forth fertility and rebirth. The *Georgics* is didactic in nature, but in this work, as in the *Eclogues,* Virgil transforms the genre in his praise of Roman rural values and in the pathos he shows for the lack of peace in recent years. He views peace as the only condition under which agriculture and animal husbandry can thrive, yet he describes how the land has been desiccated by a century of warfare. Virgil took seven years to write the *Georgics,* completing it in 29 B.C. The finished work comprises four books on farming and cultivating corn, cultivating olives and vines, raising livestock, and beekeeping, respectively.

Virgil spent the rest of his life crafting his EPIC masterpiece, the *Aeneid*. Before completing it, he became ill while traveling with Augustus and never recovered. While he was dying, he pleaded with his executors to destroy the unfinished manuscript, since he feared it did not live up to his exacting standards. Augustus, who had heard excerpts of the work in progress and recognized its value, countermanded the order and had it published after the poet's death.

Critical Analysis

The *Aeneid* recounts in iambic pentameter the epic adventures of Aeneas, a Trojan warrior and the son of a goddess. Aeneas sorrowfully leaves his ruined homeland after it is sacked by the Greeks and founds the city that is Rome's predecessor. Virgil summarizes the story in the opening lines, rendered here in a prose translation:

> I sing of arms and of the man, fated to be an exile, who long since left the land of Troy and came to Italy to the shores of Lavinium; and a great pounding he took by land and sea at the hands of the heavenly gods because of the fierce and unforgetting anger of Juno. Great too were his sufferings in war before he could found his city and carry his gods into Latium. This was the beginning of the Latin race, the Alban fathers and the high walls of Rome.

Juno is queen of the gods and wife of Jupiter (corresponding to the Greek Hera and Zeus). She is Aeneas's persistent adversary throughout the 12 books of the *Aeneid*. Juno maintains a furious grudge against the Trojans, in part because of the mythic "Judgment of Paris." Paris, son of the king of Troy, was commanded to decide which of three goddesses was most beautiful: Hera, Athena, or Aphrodite. He chose the third, incurring the wrath of the other two.

In the *Aeneid,* Juno uses her powers to inflict a succession of disasters upon the hero as he wanders with his band of Trojan War survivors through Sicily and Africa en route to fulfilling his destiny. One of the most well-known incidents takes place when the refugees are shipwrecked on Carthage (now Tunisia), where Aeneas arouses the ardor of Queen Dido. Ultimately he honors his fate and sense of duty and leaves her. Tragically, she throws herself on a funeral pyre.

Aeneas finally reaches Italy, where, after bitter conflict, he establishes his city and founds the new race that will unite Italy with a common language, culture, and sense of nationality and ultimately give rise to the Roman Empire.

As in his earlier works, Virgil's themes in the *Aeneid* are those of peace and order, the devastation of war, and a destructive past giving way to a promising future. The work is also an eloquent hymn celebrating Rome's glory and its imperial destiny. In subject matter, it is like a blend of HOMER's *Odyssey* and *Iliad;* it is an epic adventure combined with violence and warfare presented in an original, almost novel style of poetry designed to create an epic for Rome as Homer did for Greece.

The *Eclogues* and *Georgics* became classroom texts during Virgil's lifetime, and quotations from the *Aeneid* dating from a few years after its publication have been discovered in bathhouses and streets in Rome and Pompeii. His impact on literature is ongoing, but it was especially influential on the development of medieval and Renaissance epics, such as Ariosto's *Orlando Furioso,* D'Aubigné's *Les Tragiques,* Dante's *Divine Comedy,* Chaucer's *House of Fame,* and Spenser's *The Faerie Queen.* Echoes of his work also can be seen in the works of Edmund Spencer, John Milton, DANTE, William Wordsworth, Lord Tennyson, John Dryden, Alexander Pope, Victor Hugo, William Shakespeare, Jorge Luis Borges, T. S. Eliot, and more.

English Versions of Works by Virgil

The Aeneid. Edited by Philip Hardie et al. New York: Cambridge University Press, 1994.

The Aeneid. Translated by David West. London: Penguin, 1990.

Virgil: Eclogues, Georgics, Aeneid 1–6, Vol. 1. Cambridge, Mass.: Harvard University Press, 1999.

Virgil: Selections from the Aeneid. Translated by Graham Tingay. New York: Cambridge University Press, 1999.

Works about Virgil

Baswell, Christopher. *Virgil in Medieval England: Figuring The Aeneid from the Twelfth Century to Chaucer.* Edited by Alastair Minnis. New York: Cambridge University Press, 1995.

Grandsden, K. W. and S. J. Harrison. *Virgil: The Aeneid.* New York: Cambridge University Press, 2003.

Levi, Peter. *Virgil: His Life and Times.* New York: St. Martin's Press, 1998.

Rossi, Andreola. *Contexts of War: Manipulation of Genre in Virgilian Battle Narrative.* Ann Arbor: University of Michigan Press, 2003.

Spargo, John Webster. *Virgil the Necromancer: Studies in Virgilian Legends.* Whitefish, Mont.: Kessinger Publishing, 2004.

Visnu Sarma
See PANCHATANTRA.

Vogelweide, Walther von der
See WALTHER VON DER VOGELWEIDE.

W

waikan (waikâ narratives) *Winnebago folklore*

Waikan narratives are a distinct category of Winnebago prose stories, the other being WORAK NARRATIVES. The literal translation of *waika* is "what is old;" *waikan* translates as "what is sacred." As part of the ORAL LITERATURE/TRADITION of the Winnebago, the waikan narratives preserve part of the Winnebago history and culture. They are considered the myth-proper literary form of Winnebago mythology. They are set in a primordial past, a time in which animals talked and spirits were commonly encountered on earth.

In Winnebago culture, waikan stories are considered private property and are owned by a particular person or family. Myths that are very sacred or long can possess a high monetary value and are often purchased in installments. As a *waikan* passes from one owner to another, the storytellers skilled in relating anecdotes add their own personal styles and interests to the traditional stories. The liberties taken in delivery are secondary, however, to the traditional stories, plots, themes, and characters.

Waikan possess distinct literary characteristics, and traditional *waikan* can be told only during the winter, when snakes no longer dwell above the ground; those who tell *waikan* when snakes are aboveground risk supernatural retribution and the wrath of their people. The action always takes place in a past mystical era, and characters are always of divine origin. The heroes are either spirits or deities such as the Thunderbird, Waterspirit, and Sun; or animal deities such as the Hare, Turtle, or Bear. Waikan cannot end tragically, so heroes are always depicted as immortal; they cannot die or permanently be killed unless they are evil.

Some *waikan* narratives include "The Adventures of Redhorn's Sons," a tale about Redhorn's revenge against murderers; "The Animal Who Would Eat Men," a tale explaining why elk have no front teeth; and "The Baldness of the Buzzard," which explains how the Trickster takes revenge on a buzzard for mistreating him.

These sacred stories are of special importance to the Winnebago tribe and to world literature. They are told by elders with high prestige and preserve the rich history of Winnebago culture as it has been passed down through the ages.

An English Version of *Waikan* Narratives
Smith, David Lee. *Folklore of the Winnebago Tribe.* Norman: University of Oklahoma Press, 1997.

A Work about *Waikan* Narratives
Radin, Paul. *The Trickster: A Study in American Indian Mythology.* New York: Philosophical Library, 1956.

Walther von der Vogelweide (ca. 1170–ca. 1230) *poet, songwriter*

Little is known about Walther von der Vogelweide's parentage, childhood, or later life. He was born and grew up in Austria but later left the country to seek patronage in the courts of Germany. Though it is not clear into which social class the poet was born, he was probably of noble birth and thus received a classical education, which in turn served as the basis for his poetry.

After the death of his first patron in Vienna, Walther established himself at the Hohenstaufen court in Germany. From there he traveled around the surrounding countryside as a kind of itinerant musician (called a *Minnesinger*), entertaining aristocratic and royal families with his singing and recitation. Later in life he settled at the court in Würzburg in southeastern Germany, where he ultimately died and was buried.

Probably the most important poet of his era in the German language, Walther was greatly admired by audiences, peers, and patrons. His body of work consists of two crusaders' songs (called *Kreuzlieder*), a choir song (called a *Leich*), as well as more than 100 poems consisting of chivalric love poetry in the *Minnesang* tradition, lyric poetry expressing the respect and homage owed by a knight to his mistress.

Walther von der Vogelweide's most accomplished works are his *Minnelieder,* or love songs, which he brought to an unrivaled level of artistic refinement. His lasting importance as a poet lies perhaps in his visions of love and women. Walther's concept of love was not one of one-sided servile devotion but of mutual affection, and for him feminine beauty consisted as much of inner qualities as of outward appearances.

Walther's collection of lyric poems is usually divided into three groups: his earliest and most conventional poems, reminiscent of court poet Reinmar der Alte; poems in which courtly love and all the trappings therein are cast off and replaced with abandon and spontaneity; and the most mature of his poems, those called *Sprüche* poems to denote the aged poet's responses to personal and political events.

Scholar Günther Schweikle has written of Walther von der Vogelweide, "He is the unparalleled master of medieval German poetry." The influence of Walther's work continues to be felt today, and he is considered the first in a long line of great Austrian poets.

English Versions of Works by Walther von der Vogelweide

Selected poems of Walther von der Vogelweide. Edited by Margaret Fitzgerald Richey. Oxford: Blackwell, 1965.

Songs and Sayings of Walther Von Der Vogelweide, Minnesaenger. Murieta, Calif.: Classic Books, 2001.

Walther von der Vogelweide: The Single-Stanza Lyrics. Routledge Medieval Texts Series. Edited and translated by Frederick Goldin. London: Taylor & Francis, Inc., 2002.

A Work about Walther von der Vogelweide

Jones, George Fenwick. *Walther von der Vogelweide.* New York: Twayne, 1968.

Wang Anshi (Wang An-Shih) (1021–1086) *poet, essayist*

Wang Anshi was born in Linchuan (Lin-ch'uan), Fu Prefecture (present-day Jiangxi [Jiangsu] Province). His father was a magistrate of the Song (Sung) court, and he spent most of his youth traveling with his family. They finally settled in Jiangning (Chiangning; present-day Nanjing [Nanking]). At age 21, Wang became a local assistant district magistrate after earning the "Presented Scholar" degree. He distinguished himself as an administrator and reformer, and in 1067 he was summoned to the capital as a Hanlin academician. The Hanlin Academy was a national academy of scholars within the imperial bureaucracy. In 1070 the emperor promoted Wang to the position of prime minister, but he did not enjoy the ruler's favor for long, and in 1074 he was forced to resign and return to Jiangning. It was during this time that Wang became increasingly interested in literary pursuits and Buddhist philosophy. Twelve years later, he died embittered after discovering that all his proposed reform policies were dismantled by the regent of the Song court.

Wang wrote more than 1,500 poems, many of which address the social issues and economic ills of Chinese society. He is best known for his essays in which he discusses various contemporary political and social problems, ideas concerning moral behavior, and historical issues. One such essay, "The Mountain Where Huibao [Hui-pao] Meditated" (1054), reveals the influence of thinkers such as WANG WEI and Buddhist philosophical thought. In the essay, Wang emphasizes the achievements of Hui-pao, a Buddhist monk who built a meditation retreat at the base of Mount Paochan. The essay serves as an allegory for Wang's own political career. His inability to advance far into the dark caves of the mountain represents his limited political advancement.

Despite his failed career, Wang's works are an important source of information on the political ideology and philosophical ideals of a man and the generation of scholars who influenced and were influenced by him. In *Inscribed Landscapes*, Richard Strassberg calls Wang a "major literary figure and influential poet" and "another of the Eight Masters of T'ang and Sung Prose."

Works about Wang Anshi

Freeman, Michael. *Lo-Yang and the Opposition to Wang An-Shih: The Rise of Confucian Conservatism, 1068–86.* Yale University Thesis. Ann Arbor: University Microfilms International, 1974.

Liu, James T. C. *Reform in Sung China: Wang An-Shih (1021–1086) and His New Policies.* Cambridge, Mass.: Harvard University Press, 1959.

Strassberg, Richard E., trans. *Inscribed Landscapes: Travel Writing from Imperial China.* Berkeley: University of California Press, 1994.

Wang Shifu (Wang Shih-Fu) (ca. 1250– 1337) *playwright*

Although Wang Shifu was the leading playwright of the Yuan dynasty in China, little is known of his personal life. He wrote in the popular *zaju* (*tsa-chü*), or comedy, genre and became one of the masters of the form. His work helped to popularize vernacular literature. Scholars have inferred from his plays that he received a good education in the Confucian classics and was also was well acquainted with the popular literature of the day. Fourteen plays have been attributed to Wang Shifu, but only three have survived to the present day. One of these is *Xixiangji* (*Hsi-hsiang-chi;* The Story of the Western Wing), one of the greatest early Chinese comedy-dramas, which remains popular even today.

Written in the late 13th century, *The Story of the Western Wing* tells the story of star-crossed lovers Zhang Gong (Chang Kung), an intelligent and handsome young student, and Cui Yingying (Ts'ui Ying-ying), or Oriole, a beautiful young girl from a wealthy family. The couple is forced to endure the meddling of Oriole's overbearing family, who choose another suitor for her to marry. In the end, with the help of Oriole's clever young servant, Crimson, Zhang Gong and Oriole are able to be married. The play established character types that would appear in China's vernacular literature for centuries to come: the brilliant student; the beautiful, thoughtful maiden; the forbidding, overprotective parent; and the clever maid.

Wang Shifu based his play on *The Tale of Oriole* by Yuan Zhen (Yuan Chen; 779–831), a Tang dynasty poet, and on *The Story of the Western Wing in All Keys and Modes* by Dong Jieyuan (Tung Chieh-Yuan), which included spoken dialogue and songs. Jieyuan's version was written in the "tell-and-sing" literary genre of the late 11th century. Wang Shifu continued this tradition, but adapted some of the lyrics and scenes to fit the *zaju* style of writing, a form of drama in which all the songs of a single act in the play were assigned to one role.

The Story of the Western Wing has been made into popular musicals and been rewritten by numerous playwrights. References to the play appear in many novels, including Cao Xueqin's (Ts'ao Hsueh-Ch'in's) *Dream of the Red Chamber* (or Dream of Red Mansions), a famous 18th-century novel about ill-fated lovers, and the anonymous 16th-century novel, *Chin Ping Mei*. The play was also a favorite during the Chinese Revolution of 1911, because Zhang and Oriole were seen as champions of freedom.

Wang Shifu's two other surviving plays are *The Hall of Beautiful Spring* and *The Story of the Dilapidated Kiln*. The first involves a political feud between two officials during the reign of Emperor Zhangzong (Chang-tsung) in the late 1100s. The second is a dramatic rendering of a popular story about a young student, Lu Mengzheng (Meng-Cheng), who overcomes a poor upbringing to make the top score on the civil service examination and to marry a beautiful young woman from a wealthy family. These plays, however, are not of the same caliber as *The Story of the Western Wing* and have received little attention over the years. However, all three plays established Wang Shifu's place in literary history for helping to popularize Chinese vernacular literature.

English Versions of a Work by Wang Shifu

The Moon and the Zither: Wang Shifu's Story of the Western Wing. Edited by Stephen H. West and Wilt L. Idema. Berkeley: University of California Press, 1991.

The Story of the Western Wing. Translated by Stephen H. West and Wilt L. Idema. Berkeley: University of California Press, 1995.

A Work about Wang Shifu

Zhang, Jing. "Peeping through the Wall: Reading Book III in *The Story of the Western Wing*." Available online. URL: http://cosa.uchicago.edu/shangjing 5htm. Downloaded on April 9, 2004.

Wang Wei (Mochi, Mo-ch'i) (699–759)
poet

Wang Wei lived in China during the Tang (T'ang) period, regarded as the height of Chinese civilization. He was born in Shanxi (Shansi) to a father who was a local official and a mother who came from a family distinguished in literature. At age 16

he moved to the capital with his brother Jin (Chin) and entered the social circle of princely society. After graduating from university, he was awarded a court appointment as assistant secretary of music. He bought an estate on the edge of the Wang River next to the Zhongnan (Chungnan) Mountains and lived there off and on for the rest of his life. After his wife died when he was a little over 30, he never remarried and continued with his official life, leading a long and undistinguished career in public service.

A passionate but reflective man, Wang Wei (known also as Mochi [Mo-ch'i]) poured his energy into poems, paintings, and music and was known in his time for all of these arts. Today, his poetic legacy is the only one that survives. Although in retrospect he is overshadowed by the creative genius of the other two major poets of the Tang dynasty, LI BAI and Du Fu, at the time that they lived, Wang Wei was the most prominent among them, famous for his delicate, detailed, and loving descriptions of natural landscapes. He was a devout, practicing Buddhist, and the quiet and mystical aspects of his religion are portrayed in the landscapes he evokes with words. His poems express tranquillity, purity, serenity, and a sense of control. They also emphasize his love of solitude and the sense that humankind is only part of a larger natural order. In the poem "Deer Park," for example, he writes, "Returning light enters the deep grove, / And again shines on the green moss."

The serene and simple imagery in Wang Wei's poetry was often meant to extend beyond its literal meaning. Four common elements of his poems are an empty mountain, rain, voice, and white clouds, all of which combine to create a feeling of something deeper than just a landscape. His poetry, however, was not formal religious poetry. A line in his poem "Return to Wang River," in a translation by Tony Barnstone, Willis Barnstone and Xu Hiaxin, illustrates the mystical and lyrical qualities of his imagery: "Far off in the mountains is twilight / Alone I come back to white clouds." The contemplative nature of his writing emphasizes its connection to his Buddhist identity and view of the world.

Wang Wei's combination of a spiritual feeling and sparse imagery appeals to today's readers. He has been translated more often than any other Chinese poet in the 20th century. Western audiences relate to the tension he sometimes depicts between the worldly and mystical sides of himself. In true Buddhist fashion, he kept himself detached from the materialistic world while holding his job in court. Wang Wei seems to have saved his reserves of emotion for his literary and other artistic activities. He expressed his deep spiritual concerns also by converting the house he had bought for his mother into a monastery after her death. The monastery housed seven monks, and although Wang Wei did not himself join them, he visited often and is buried on the grounds beside his mother. Accordingly, a theme of his work is a contrast between public life and seclusion, a topic that attracts modern Western audiences struggling to fulfill the demands of their hectic lives while retaining some sense of inner peace.

English Versions of Works by Wang Wei

Laughing Lost in the Mountains: Poems of Wang Wei. Translated by Tony Barnstone, Willis Barnstone, and Xu Haixin. Hanover, N.H.: University Press of New England, 1991.

Songs of the Woodcutter: Zen Poems of Wang Wei and Taigu Ryokan. Audio CD. Translated by Larry Smith. Huron, Ohio: Bottom Dog Press, 2003.

Three Chinese Poets: Translations of Poems by Wang Wei, Li Bai, and Du Fu. Translated by Vikram Seth. Boston: Faber and Faber, 1992.

Works about Wang Wei

Wagner, Marsha L. *Wang Wei.* Boston: Twayne Publishers, 1981.

Weinberger, Eliot and Octavio Paz. *Nineteen Ways of Looking at Wang Wei: How a Chinese Poem is Translated.* Kingston, R.I.: Moyer Bell, 1987.

Wei Zhuang (Wei Chuang) (ca. 834–910)
poet

Wei Zhuang was born in a town outside Chang'an, China, between 834 and 836. He spent much of his early life in Chang'an, the Tang dynasty capital, where he began to develop his literary ability by writing *ci (tz'u),* or lyric poems. Wei was one of the first poets to popularize the *ci* form and probably received much of his inspiration for his lyrics from the booming social life in the Chinese capital.

Wei left the capital in 877 to study under and work for a prefect in the Guozhou (Kuo-chou), Henan (Honan), Province. He returned to Chang'-an in 879 to prepare for the *jinshi (chin-shih)* civil service examination, which he failed the following year. Scholars have pointed out, however, that Wei's failure may have saved his life, because many government officials were singled out for execution when Chang'an was overrun by rebel bandits in 881.

During the fall of the capital, Wei escaped to the provinces, where he wrote his EPIC poem *The Lament of the Lady of Ch'in,* which brought him immediate fame. This poem describes the horrors of the sack of Chang'an, during which more than 80,000 people were executed. Wei also completed more than 1,000 poems and lyrics, though only about 375 remain.

Most of Wei Zhuang's early poetic and prose writings were destroyed when Chang'an was invaded. What little is known of his early life has been pieced together by scholars through analysis of his later poems.

A Work about Wei Zhuang

Yates, Robin D. S. *The Life and Selected Poetry of Wei Chuang (834?–910).* Cambridge, Mass.: Council on East Asian Studies, 1988.

White Mountain Apache myths and tales   *Native American folklore*

The White Mountain Apache tribe currently occupies a region in east-central Arizona of the United States. Before the White Mountain Apache Reservation was established in 1891, the White Mountain tribe, one of five groups belonging to the Western Apache, was largely nomadic. In the 1920s and 1930s, scholars Pliny Earle Goddard and Grenville Goodwin undertook efforts to record, translate, and preserve the myths and legends of the White Mountain Apache.

To the White Mountain Apache, as with the ZUNI NARRATIVE POETRY, storytelling is a practice that belongs to the winter months from November to February and should be done only at night, after dusk and before dawn. Telling stories in broad daylight is dangerous, especially in the spring, summer, and fall months, when all sorts of creatures are abroad; if snakes, insects, or even lightning hear stories about them that they do not like, they may seek to punish the narrator. This belief in the power of storytelling is shared among many cultures that preserve and transmit their histories, teachings, and cultural beliefs through an ORAL LITERATURE/TRADITION. To societies that largely depend on a spoken language to communicate, stories preserve memory, genealogy, identity, and understanding about how the world works.

Tales of the White Mountain Apache generally take one of two forms. Holy tales explain the origin of ceremonies and other religious practices; creation tales explain the creation of the earth, the emergence of its creatures, and slaying of monsters, and the foundation of Apache customs. While adventure stories about cultural heroes or fables about the doings of animals may be told for purposes of entertaining children, the holy tales are able to confer particular abilities or powers, and therefore the audience for specific tales was traditionally limited only to people who were ready for instruction. Altogether, the myths and tales contain a great deal of information about the material culture, economic life, social and familial organizations, and religious beliefs governing tribal life.

The White Mountain Apache myths also preserve a cycle of Coyote tales. While the creation tales convey ritual knowledge, the Coyote tales generally use an enjoyable story for a morally instructive purpose. Like the COYOTE TALES of the Hopi, the Coyote of the White Mountain Apache is a prankster, a ludicrous figure who tries to be cunning but who, more often than not, falls victim to his own gullibility. Coyote, however, can have an occasionally useful function. Big Owl, who has a minor cycle of stories, is usually depicted as slow and rather ignorant, causing only harm and destruction.

In the holy tales, the most important male figure, with the exception of the sun, is the hero Naiyenezgani. He is the benefactor of human beings who taught them important survival skills. The most important female figure is Isdzanadlehe, who taught humans how to plant and harvest crops. She is variously described as Naiyenezgani's mother or grandmother, in keeping with the Apache practice of tracing descent through the mother and organizing families around matriarchal groups. Other holy tales describe the *gan*, a class of beings who lived on earth before the White Mountain Apache and later went away. They are powerful spirits who, if properly invoked, can provide enormous benefits, but can also do great harm if offended.

Like the book of Genesis in the Hebrew BIBLE and also in the Sumerian poem *GILGAMESH*, the White Mountain Apache myths have a story about a flood, which itself contains many origin stories. This story explains why the tip of the turkey's tail is white, why the area where the White Mountain Apache live is sandy and flat rather than mountainous, and how corn was a gift of a turkey that distributed food to those who had survived the flood. As the story goes, the turkey provided gray, red, yellow, and blue corn, simply by shaking his feathers.

An indication that the White Mountain Apache folklore continued to evolve and grow as a tradition is seen in some stories, preserved in modern collections, that show the influence of the Spanish and later Europeans. Stories that include horses, firearms, and written documents all date from the period after the first European interactions. While certain stories preserve the origins and histories of clans or families within the tribe, most of the White Mountain myths are not clan-specific. Together the myths represent a rich and flexible literary tradition and provide a valuable cultural history of the White Mountain Apache tribe.

An English Version of White Mountain Apache Myths

Goodwin, Grenville. *Myths and Tales of the White Mountain Apache.* Tucson: University of Arizona Press, 1994.

A Work about White Mountain Apache Myths

Green, Bernard and Darlene Pienschke. *Stories of Faith: Among the White Mountain Apache.* London: Pen Press Publishers, 2001.

Wolfram von Eschenbach (ca. 1170– ca. 1225) *poet, songwriter*

Biographical information about Wolfram von Eschenbach is hazy at best. Though the precise span of his life is not known, he lived at the same time as his fellow poet GOTTFRIED VON STRASSBURG, who makes references to his competitor Wolfram in his works. Wolfram also lived at the same time as another famous German writer, HARTMANN VON AUE. He was probably born in the town of Eschenbach, in Bavaria, and achieved the rank of knighthood at a time when the both the Catholic Church and the German emperor were trying to consolidate their power into more centralized, hierarchical structures. This left a man trained for fighting, like Wolfram, on the fringes of society. He therefore took up writing as a career, and for most of his life the powerful Hermann of Thuringia was his patron and benefactor.

In his writings Wolfram sometimes refers to himself as illiterate, meaning he could not read and write Latin, the language of the clergy. He was, however, fluent in French as well as his native German. Wolfram's poems are clearly meant for oral performance and may have been composed orally as well; he could have hired a scribe to record the words for him. As a relatively impoverished nobleman, he would not have had access to the best education of his day, as he himself testifies. This was in no way a disadvantage in his writing, which shows a narrative talent that takes its strength from the message he seeks to communicate, not academic knowledge.

Along with his contemporaries, Wolfram lived in a society where politics were governed by the structure of feudalism and social codes were governed by CHIVALRY/COURTLY LOVE, ideals that infused the genre of the MEDIEVAL ROMANCE in which Wolfram was writing. His early verse lyrics show the influence of the TROUBADOURS of southern France, and Wolfram first gained recognition for his love songs (in German, *Minnelieder*). His greatest skill was with the *alba,* or song of dawn, which was highly cultivated by medieval French poets but relatively unknown to the Middle High German audience.

Wolfram's longer verse narratives are difficult to date, but his reference to his poem *Parzifal* (ca. 1210) in the opening to *Willehalm* (ca. 1217) may indicate that *Willehalm,* which tells of the earlier adventures of certain characters who appear in *Parzifal,* was actually written later. Scholars argue over whether *Willehalm* is complete or whether Wolfram intended further books. Upon his death, he left fragments of a work called *Titurel,* which he most likely began composing after *Parzifal* but never finished. His *lieder* (songs) cannot be dated but are most likely early works.

Critical Analysis

Wolfram's *Parzifal* is a complete work, which represents an achievement over the source he was using, *The Knight of the Grail* by the French romancer CHRÉTIEN DE TROYES. Chrétien's tale introduces the early adventures of the hero Percival and his quest for the HOLY GRAIL, but his tale strands the hero far away from his chosen quest and actually ends in the middle of the adventures of another Arthurian knight, Gawain. Wolfram adopts the characters of Parzifal and Gawain but completely reimagines them, turning the original tale of knightly battles into a deeply spiritual quest. Wolfram also draws on the epic tone of German heroic poetry, of which the NIBELUNGENLIED is a classic example. Translators Marion Gibbs and Sidney Johnson, in their introduction to *Willehalm,* call *Parzifal* "one of the great quests of world literature, acted out in the idealized world of the courtly romance." They add: "It is also a search for man's proper relationship to God, beginning in ignorance, and passing through disappointment, even antagonism, to the ultimate realization of Divine Love."

Written in rhyming verse, *Parzival* describes various episodes in the life of its hero, beginning with his birth and his youth as a laborer living in the forest, ignorant that he is truly a knight and destined to become a king. The story follows his chivalrous education and reception at Arthur's court, then turns to his noble deeds and failings as an Arthurian knight. Despite the numerous digressions and the fact that several chapters are devoted to the life and adventures of Gawain, another knight in King Arthur's court, at the heart of the novel is the story of Parzival's quest to find the Holy Grail and heal King Anfortas, who is also his uncle. Parzifal initially fails at his quest because, when he witnesses the magnificent Grail procession, he neglects to ask the most important question: Whom does the Grail serve?

To find the answer, he must take up a deeper and even more challenging quest, one that takes him to the very center of knightly ideals and moral conduct. In *Parzifal* a reader can clearly see Wolfram's faith in the ideals of "true" knighthood and his earnest belief that a harmonious world order can only rest on a return to these ideals. The quality that best describes Wolfram's ideal life is *triuwe,* or loyalty, which must underpin a knight's relationships with his lord and his fellow knights, his family, wife, and children, and his relationship to God. *Parzifal,* then, is less about the quest for the earthly Grail kingdom and more about the personal quest for understanding and devotion to the greater spiritual laws. The depth and artistry with which Wolfram portrays this quest make the 16 books of *Parzifal* one of the most astounding landmarks of medieval literature.

In *Parzifal* we find the narrative technique that most distinguishes Wolfram's prose: his direct address to the audience. Throughout the text, the narrator interjects personal commentaries and opinions into the story, which serve not only to leaven the dramatic tension and provide comic relief but also to give the reader insights into the characters, action, and the author's world vision. Also appealing is the lively and unpredictable way in which Wolfram relates the story. Ironic and comic passages are juxtaposed with serious discussions on religious and existential themes. Individual adventure scenes are described with great dramatic tension but also with much irony, as if Wolfram could not take the subject matter completely seriously. The following short passage from the fifth book in Edwin H. Zeydel's translation might be considered characteristic of the work and Wolfram's style:

> *Who fain would hear where he may stray*
> *Whom lust for deeds has lured away,*
> *Great acts of wondrous daring*
> *To them we shall be bearing.*

The originality and mastery of Wolfram's *Parzival* lies also in its poetic sophistication. Metaphors, similes, and hyperbole all come into play. The work is often humorous, but it is not a comedy, as its core is a harsh vision of the perplexing and horrifying aspects of human existence.

Willehalm is quite different from *Parzifal* in both tone and intent. The author retains his style of the direct address, speaking conversationally to his reader or listener. An early passage in the first book of *Willehalm* reveals this characteristic style as well as the author's ambitions, when after modestly pointing out his success with *Parzifal,* he claims:

> *I shall tell of love and other grief which in*
> *   consequence*
> *of their devotion men and women have*
> *   been suffering . . .*
> *No tale in German tongue can easily match*
> *   this whole work*
> *which I now have in mind. . . .*

The best Frenchmen are
agreed that no sweeter poem was ever composed in dignity
and truth. . . . They told it there: now listen
  to it
here. This story is true, though it may be
  amazing.

Willehalm recounts the struggles of the hero in battle against the invading Muslim forces from the south. In the tale, Wolfram continues with his use of fantastical names and hazy geography meant more to evoke exotic associations than to assume any genuine historicity. Scenes of vivid action, such as the battles of Alischanz, intermingle with scenes of contemplation or tenderness, as when Wolfram describes the love between Willehalm and Giburc. Though a different work than *Parzival, Willehalm* is imbued with no less spiritual awareness, Wolfram's contribution not only to his source material but also his lesson to his listeners.

Parzival has an assured place in the canon of the greatest Arthurian literature, next to the romances of Sir Thomas Malory and Alfred, Lord Tennyson. Richard Wagner turned Wolfram's *Parzival* into a famed opera, and the legend of the Holy Grail, with Percival as one of its chief knights, continues to inspire retellings in the forms of present-day novels and films.

English Versions of Works by Wolfram von Eschenbach

Parzival. Edited and translated by André Lefevere. New York: Continuum, 1991.
Parzival. Translated by A. T. Hatto. New York: Penguin, 1980.
Willehalm. Translated by Marion E. Gibbs and Sidney M. Johnson. New York: Penguin Books, 1984.

Works about Wolfram von Eschenbach

Poag, James F. *Wolfram von Eschenbach.* New York: Twayne Publishers, 1972.

Weigand, Hermann J. Wolfram's Parzival: *Five Essays.* Edited by Ursula Hoffman. Ithaca, N.Y.: Cornell University Press, 1969.

worak narratives *Winnebago folklore*

Worak narratives comprise one of two stylistically distinct forms of Winnebago Native American prose; the other is WAIKAN NARRATIVES. They are secular in nature in that their subject matter focuses on the real world and historical events. The *worak* (meaning "what is told or recounted") are treated less seriously than their *waikan* counterparts. Anyone in the tribe is allowed to relate a *worak,* and the stories can be told at any time of year. In addition, characters in the *worak* narratives are always human. Heroes are either human or divine beings who have thrown in their lot with man. The action in *woraks* always takes place within the memory of mankind, and the tales always end tragically.

Some *worak* stories include "The Annihilation of the Hotcâgara" (*Hotcâk* meaning "Winnebago"), a story about how yellow fever wiped out many Winnebago; "The Blessing of a Bear Clansman," a story in which a member of the Bear clan of the Winnebago is blessed by divine spirits to be successful in war; "The Great Fish," which explains why Lake Winnebago is full of sturgeon; and "Vita Springs," an account of a hot springs that the Winnebago believed to have healing powers. Like the *waikan* narratives, these and other *worak* stories have preserved much of the history, culture, and traditions of the Winnebago.

English Versions of *Worak* Narratives

Kieterle, Richard L., editor and compiler. *The Encyclopedia of Hotcâk (Winnebago) Mythology.* Available online. URL: http://www.hotcakencyclopedia. com/#anchor 1917766>. Downloaded on April 28, 2004.
Smith, David Lee. *Folklore of the Winnebago Tribe.* Norman: University of Oklahoma Press, 1997.

Xenophon (ca. 431–ca. 352 B.C.) *soldier, historian, biographer*

Xenophon was born in Athens; his father was a knight in the Athenian army. During his young years, Xenophon was one of SOCRATES' most successful students. He is said to be the first person to start recording his conversations with Socrates and noting down the great philosopher's sayings. These writings were collected in *Memorabilia* (relating Socrates' life story and his teachings) and *Symposium* (written as a dialogue in which Socrates is the main speaker).

The young historian's discipleship with Socrates did not last long, however. In 401, he decided to join Cyrus, the prince of Persia, in his campaign against his brother Artaxerxes II, king of Persia. He joined the prince in Sardis and followed him into Upper Asia, where Cyrus was killed in the decisive battle at Cunaxa. Left without a leader on the wide plains between the Tigris River and the Euphrates the Greek troops elected Xenophon their new general. He had not held an official position in Cyrus's army or ever served as a soldier, yet the soldiers' choice turned out to be a wise one. Xenophon successfully led the remaining 10,000 men on an epic 1,500-mile journey back to Greece.

Xenophon himself, however, did not go back to Athens at once. Instead, he joined the Spartans, served the Spartan king and general Agesilaus, and fought against Athenians in the Battle of Coronea (394 B.C.). When he returned to Athens a year later, he was banished for having fought against his own countrymen. The Spartans, however, rewarded him by giving him an estate at Scillus near Elis, where he moved with his wife and children.

For the next 24 years, Xenophon lived peacefully, writing, managing his slaves, hunting, and entertaining guests. But when Sparta was defeated in 371 B.C., he was expelled from his estate. Although his banishment had been lifted, he still did not return to Athens but spent his remaining years in Corinth. While there, he wrote some of his best works and spent much time contemplating the reasons for his banishment from Athens. In addition to having fought against his former countrymen, he also disagreed with the Athenian attitude concerning the war.

Xenophon believed that the happiest states are those that have the longest period of unbroken peace, and he considered Athens well suited to peace and happiness. Debating those who believed that war could benefit the city-state, Xenophon argued that the harshness of Athenian rulers would eventually strip it of its prestige and authority. Generosity and fairness, on the contrary, would gain Athens valuable alliances and power. Xenophon also believed that war would destroy the Athenian economy.

Critical Analysis

The most celebrated of Xenophon's works is *Anabasis*, which tells the story of Cyrus's military campaigns and the Spartans' heroic retreat, which Xenophon had engineered. The title *Anabasis* means "The March Up," although the majority of the work deals with the march away from the site of the disastrous battle at Cunaxa.

Anabasis was the first work that acquainted the Greeks with elements of the Persian Empire; it also revealed the army's weakness. Ironically, Xenophon's account of the Spartans' retreat through hostile lands is said to have influenced Greek pride and eventually resulted in Alexander's conquests in Asia. *Anabasis* also immortalized Xenophon as a gifted military leader and a hero of his people.

In addition to writing historical accounts, Xenophon also wrote biographies, making him a pioneer in the genre. One such work is *Agesilaus*, a panegyric on Agesilaus II, king of Sparta, who was one of Xenophon's close friends. His most famous biographical work, however, is *The Cyropaedia*, which tells the life story of Cyrus, the founder of the Persian monarchy, under whose command young Xenophon began his military adventures.

The title *The Cyropaedia* translates as "The Education of Cyrus," and the first of the eight books that make up the work deals with Cyrus's education, describing his hunting as preparation for fighting. Xenophon goes on to paint a highly romanticized portrait of Cyrus as an outstanding military leader and ruler. He relates Cyrus's talent in warfare, his generosity in forgiving defeated enemies, and his skill at turning former enemies into allies. Because of its romanticized nature, *The Cyropaedia* is considered by some critics to be a political romance rather than a biography.

The work also reveals Xenophon's admiration for Spartan ways, and his accounts of Persian history are mixed with details of Greek customs, with an emphasis on both military service (as influenced by Cyrus) and the importance of learning justice (as influenced by Socrates). In particular, Xenophon describes how boys in Spartan schools are punished for not returning favors, and how qualities such as self-control are valued and trained.

In general, Xenophon's works, even those structured as historical ones, serve to reflect his views on philosophy, life, adventure, history, economy, and politics. In *The Constitution of the Lacedaemonians*, for example, he expresses his admiration for the Spartans' disciplined life and values. In a later essay, "Ways and Means," he proposes methods to improve Athens's economy. He describes his adventurous life and provides vast historical details of life in ancient Persia and Greece in other essays, such as "On the Cavalry Commander," "On the Art of Horsemanship," and "On Hunting."

Xenophon's *Hellenica* is a historical account of Greece from 411 to 362 B.C. He is valued not only for the detailed information he provides in all his works, but also for the simple and clear way in which he provides it. He is one of the foremost historians of ancient Greece.

English Versions of Works by Xenophon

Anabasis. Translated by Carleton L. Brownson. Revised by John Dillery. Cambridge, Mass.: Harvard University Press, 1998.

The Education of Cyrus. Translated by Wayne Ambler. Ithaca, N.Y.: Cornell University Press, 2001.

Hiero: A New Translation. Translated by Ralph Doty. Lewiston, N.Y.: Edwin Mellen Press, 2003.

Xenophon's "Spartan Constitution": Introduction, Text, Commentary. Edited by Michael Lipka. Berlin: De Gruyter, 2002.

Works about Xenophon

Anderson, John Kinloch. *Xenophon*. London: Bristol Classical, 2002.

Hirsch, Steven W. *The Friendship of the Barbarians: Xenophon and the Persian Empire*. Lebanon, N.H.: University Press of New England, 1985.

Hutchinson, Godfrey. *Xenophon and the Art of Command*. Mechanicsburg, Pa.: Stackpole Books, 2000.

Prevas, John. *Xenophon's March: Into the Lair of the Persian Lion.* Cambridge, Mass.: Da Capo Press, 2002.

Xie Lingyun (Hsieh Ling-yün, Duke of K'ang-Lo) (385–433) *poet*

Xie Lingyun was a member of a prominent aristocratic Chinese family during the Qin (Ch'in) dynasty. He entered the government before he was 20 years old and spent the next 20 years engaged in politics. While the "barbarians" controlled the north, aristocratic factions battled for control over the Eastern Qin dynasty. After engaging in these power struggles for many years, Xie found himself on the losing side of a battle over the successor to the newly reigning Liu-Song dynasty. At age 37 he was exiled to Yung-chia on the southeast coast. During this period, he had time to contemplate his life and the natural world around him. He became reconnected to his long-held Taoist and Buddhist beliefs and began to write poetry.

Even after the exile was lifted, Xie did not return to court life but instead became a recluse at the family estate in the Shihning (Shih-ning) Mountains. In one of his long prose-poems, "Dwelling in the Mountains," he describes his choice: "I devoted myself to simplicity and returned to it all, / left that workaday life for this wisdom of wandering, / for this wilderness of rivers-and-mountains clarity."

For a Chinese aristocrat, however, the life of a recluse was not one of total isolation. Xie continued to live with his family and often entertained friends. In addition, the government ordered him to serve as a local governor at a far outpost. When he refused, he was banished to Nan-hai on the southern coast and later executed.

While Xie was prominent in government and a well-known calligrapher, he was most famous for his wilderness poetry. His poetry, greatly influenced by that of Xie Hun (Hsieh Hun), not only describes nature but also celebrates the mountain wilderness and rivers, revealing Xie's spiritual connection to his surroundings. Though few of his works survive, he is famous as the initiator of the "rivers-and-mountains" *(shan-shui)* tradition. As the Taoist hermit T'ao Hung-ching laments, "Here is the true Paradise of the Region of Earthly Desires. Yet, since the time of [Xie] K'ang-lo, no one has been able to feel at one with these wonders, as he did."

An English Version of a Work by Xie Lingyun

The Mountain Poems of Hsieh Ling-Yun. Translated by David Hinton. New York: New Directions, 2001.

Yang Wanli (Yang Wan-li) (1127–1206)
poet

Yang Wanli was born in southern China and grew up during a time of political turmoil in which the Jin (Chin) Tartars of northern China conquered the Sung dynasty. Yang lived in poverty in the southern Song (Sung) city of Zhu-sui (Chu-sui), away from the center of the conflict. Consequently, his childhood was relatively normal, and he received a classical education. He passed the civil service examination at age 28.

After three years of service at the Song capital, Hangzhou (Hang-chou), Yang was sent to Ling-ling in the Hunan Province in 1161. There he met and was mentored by a famous general, Zhang Zhun, who influenced Yang's views on the conflict between the Song and the Jin. Yang soon adopted the general's belief in strong resistance against the Jin and remained committed to that belief throughout his life. In the Confucian tradition, he was critical of the government when he saw corruption or weak policies.

Yang was also influenced by the poet Xiao Dezao (Hsiao Te-tsao), whom he also met in Ling-ling. After Xiao advised him on the style of his poetry, in 1162 Yang burned more than 1,000 of his poems because he believed they were poorly written.

Yang's later poetry, such as "Watching a Village Festival" and "Songs of Depression," was influenced by Zen Buddhism and combines the essence of a spiritual life with the events and concerns of everyday life. His collected works feature more than 3,200 poems and hundreds of pages of prose written during his time as a government official. When Yang died, he was considered to be one of the greatest poets of the Song dynasty.

An English Version of a Work by Yang Wanli
Heaven My Blanket, Earth My Pillow. Translated by Jonathan Chaves. New York: Weatherhill Press, 1975.

Works about Yang Wanli
Liu, James J. Y. *Major Lyricists of the Northern Sung.* Princeton, N.J.: Princeton University Press, 1974.
Schmidt, J. D. *Yang Wan-li.* New York: Twayne, 1976.

Yaqui deer songs *Native American ritual songs*

The Yaqui deer dancer is called the *saila maso,* "little brother deer." The deer songs, called *maso bwikam,* are traditional songs, usually performed by three men, that accompany the dance of the *saila maso.* To the Yaquis, the deer song is the oldest and most respected of their verbal arts. Authors Larry Evers and Felipe Molina describe them this way: "Highly conventionalized in their structure, their diction, their themes, and their mode of performance, deer songs describe a double world, both 'here' and 'over there,' a world in which all the actions of the deer dancer have a parallel in that mythic, primeval place called by Yaquis *sea ania,* flower world." The Yaqui deer songs reflect aspects of life practiced for centuries in the Sonoran desert, long before the appearance of Europeans.

Yaqui tribes occupied present-day Arizona and Sonora, northern Mexico. Their first European contact was the Spaniard Diego de Guzmán in 1533 and later the Jesuit missionaries, who arrived in 1617 and brought profound changes in community organization and belief systems. Yaqui folk literature contains mythical histories of the region prior to Spanish influence, describing the spirits thought to inhabit the land and the magic powers sometimes possessed by animals. These myths were part of the cycle of religious ritual and belief practiced by the Yaqui prior to the Jesuit missionaries, which the deer songs record and celebrate.

Aside from their agriculture, the Yaqui depended on deer as a food source. Dancing and songs were performed prior to the hunt to ensure success. The Yaqui deer songs reflect a worldview where all parts of the *huya ania,* the "wilderness world," live in an integrated community. Birds and insects, plants and animals, even the rocks and springs of the desert are intimately connected. The language of the deer songs, called *bwika noki,* or "song talk," is the language of this carefully interconnected, beautifully balanced community.

While the deer singers may know as many as 300 songs, at any given performance they will perform only a fraction of these. The first songs set the stage or purify the space in which the dance will be performed. A formal speech and often a procession follow, and then the musicians perform a sequence of songs. Usually the instruments include a violin, a harp, a flute, and drums, and songs may be repeated several times. The sequences are designed to symbolize the elapse of night and the coming of morning, which parallel the symbolic preparation, hunting, and killing of the deer. These lines from "The Fawn Will Not Make Flowers," translated by Evers and Molina in *Yaqui Deer Songs,* are part of an *alva bwikam,* a morning service song:

> This flower-covered dawn world rises up
> > brightly,
> here where they divide
> the enchanted earth with light.

The last songs of the cycle typically celebrate the roasting and eating of the deer, whose body is symbolized again with the imagery of flowers, as in these lines:

> My enchanted flower body,
> fire, above the fire,
> side by side is hung.

The rhythmic repetition of sounds, lines, and songs, and the images of death paired with the images of dawn and rebirth, give to the performance a mythic quality that parallels the natural cycle in which the Yaqui people lived their lives for centuries.

The Yaqui deer song is a living tradition that continues to this day. While performances of the deer songs are no longer connected to the hunt, they serve as more than a means of entertainment. The context in which the deer song is performed is vital to its enjoyment; the smoke from the fires, the chatter of the audience, the antics of the masked clown, and the noise of the dancers all complement the poetry of the songs. Moreover, the performances offer a way to celebrate, forge community bonds, and preserve an ancient cultural heritage.

English Versions of Yaqui Deer Songs

Endrezze, Anita. *Throwing Fire at the Sun, Water at the Moon.* Tucson: University of Arizona Press, 2000.

Evers, Larry and Felipe S. Molina. *Yaqui Deer Songs, Maso Bwikam: A Native American Poetry* Sun Tracks. Tucson: University of Arizona Press, 1987.

Padilla, Stan. *Deer Dance: Yaqui Legends of Life.* Lincoln, Neb.: Book Publishing Company, 1998.

Works about Yaqui Deer Songs

Painter, Muriel Thayer. *With Good Heart: Yaqui Beliefs and Ceremonies in Pascua Village.* Edited by Edward Spicer and Wilma Kaemlein. Tucson: University of Arizona Press, 1986.

Savala, Refugio. *The Autobiography of a Yaqui Poet.* Edited by Kathleen M. Sands. Tucson: University of Arizona Press, 1980.

Spicer, Edward H. *The Yaquis: A Cultural History.* Tucson: University of Arizona Press, 1980.

Yoshida Kenkō (1283–1352) *poet, essayist*

Yoshida Kenkō was born into a family of Japanese Shinto priests around the year 1283. He distinguished himself at a young age through his literary abilities and served in the Japanese court under the emperor Go-Uda. While his early poetry is traditional and conservative, he was regarded as a fine poet during his lifetime.

In 1324, Yoshida became a Buddhist priest. His most famous work, *Tsurezuregusa* (Essays in Idleness, 1330), a series of 243 short chapters or essays, reflects the Buddhist view of the world, especially the transience of all things and the cycle of life, growth, death, and rebirth. The essays are unified by Yoshida's belief that the world and everything in it was steadily declining, but this was not a negative view. As Yoshida says in "Essay 7," "If man were never to fade away . . . but lingered on forever in the world, how things would lose their power to move us."

While *Essays in Idleness* was not widely read during Yoshida's lifetime, it has become a standard work in Japanese education. It has also posthumously established Yoshida's reputation as an insightful and gifted essayist.

English Versions of Works by Yoshida Kenkō

Essays in Idleness. Translated by Donald Keene. New York: Columbia University Press, 1967.

Miscellany of a Japanese Priest. Translated by William H. Porter. Rutland, Vt.: Charles E. Tuttle Co., 1973.

A Work about Yoshida Kenkō

Chance, Linda H. *Formless in Form: Kenko, Tsurezuregusa and the Rhetoric of Japanese Fragmentary Prose.* Palo Alto, Calif.: Stanford University Press, 1997.

Yu Xin (Yü Hsin) (513–581) *poet*

Yu Xin was born in Chiang-ling, China, in 513. His father, Yu Jianwu, worked directly for two sons of the Liang dynasty's Emperor Wu and was able to provide Yu Xin with an excellent education; it is likely that some studies were at the Imperial Library. When he was 14, Yu Xin also attended classes taught by one of Emperor Wu's sons.

After Yu Xin passed the governmental examinations, he began a career in the imperial service. He spent most of his early career working for one of the Wu princes, Xiao Gang, in the Liang dynasty capital, Jiankang (Chien-k'ang; modern-day Nanjing [Nanking]). In 548, after a series of political and military miscalculations by Emperor Wu, Jiankang was attacked and conquered, and Yu Xin was forced to flee the city.

Despite the political turmoil that continued for years, Yu Xin remained affiliated with the Liang dynasty. In 554, he was sent as an ambassador to Chang'an, the capital of the Western Wei dynasty in the North, with the purpose of preventing an invasion of Liang territory. While there, he was held under house arrest for three years and not allowed to return to southern China for the rest of his life. Despite this, Yu Xin was well respected by the Western Wei and had numerous honorary titles bestowed upon him. He was recognized as the greatest poet of his century and treated as a cultural icon.

One of Yu Xin's most famous works is "The Lament for the South," which was written (ca. 578 A.D.) during his time in Chang'an, where he held mostly symbolic posts while devoting his life to writing. He helped compose the Zhou (Chou) ritual hymns and was the author of the congratulatory memorial on their completion. The "Lament for the South," a long rhapsodic poem, or *fu*, provides a historical commentary on the wars and political upheavals of the Liang dynasty. The work also expresses Yu's sorrow in the North and his wish to return to his native region. In relating the events of a decade ending with the fall of the Liang dynasty, Yu's poem is brimming with historical allusions. His own homesickness while in exile in the North, however, permeates the final verses of the lament:

As an honored guest . . .
I see bells and cauldrons . . .
I hear servings and song . . .
But how can they know that . . .
Among the commoners of Hsien—
Yang, not only the prince
Longs for home.

An English Version of a Work by Yu Xin

"The Lament for the South": Yü Hsin's "Ai Chiang-nan Fu." Edited and translated by William T. Graham, Jr. Cambridge, U.K.: Cambridge University Press, 1980.

Z

Zen parables (Buddha parables)

(ca. 528 B.C.) *fiction*

Zen Buddhism is a Buddhist school of thought that originated in India and came to China during the Tang dynasty (618–906) and Japan in 1191. The nature of Zen Buddhism is purposely illogical, because satori, a state of total understanding, cannot be achieved through traditional meditative methods. Understanding requires viewing the world through a "third eye."

Zen masters helped their students along the path to satori through the use of parables and koan, short dialogues or statements meant to engage the students' thinking. In one of the most famous koan, the Zen master Hakuin asks his students to hear the sound of one hand clapping. The question is designed to get the students to stop thinking in a traditional logical sense and to start reordering their thoughts based on their inner experiences. Zen parables work in the same fashion.

Parables are allegorical stories that help teach a moral lesson. However, unlike the famous parables of Jesus in the New Testament, Zen parables are often paradoxical, and despite their use as educational tools, they rarely explicitly define a moral; rather, they hint at possible ways of viewing situations. For example, in one parable, a student asks his teacher, "What is enlightenment?" The teacher replies, "When hungry, eat. When tired, sleep." Such a response might lead the student to learn or "see" that much of what we do is based on survival, yet there might also be 100 other interpretations of the teacher's response. In this way, Zen parables lead toward "enlightenment" by allowing students or listeners to interpret the parables as their conscious or subconscious leads them.

Zen Buddhism has influenced such prominent figures as Australian philosopher Ludwig Wittgenstein (1889–1951); German philosopher Martin Heidegger (1889–1976); and the poets Gary Snyder (1930–   ), Jean-Louis (Jack) Kerouac (1922–69), and Allen Ginsberg (1926–97). The effect of Zen still lingers. Not only have the parables and Zen meditative thought influenced every aspect of ancient and medieval Japanese society, they also continue to influence many aspects of modern world culture around the globe.

English Versions of Zen Parables

100 Parables of Zen. Translated by Joyce Lim. Singapore: Asiapac Books, 1997.

Wada, Stephanie, with translations by Gen. P. Sakamoto. *The Oxherder: A Zen Parable Illustrated.* New York: George Braziller, 2002.

Works about Zen Parables

Freke, Timothy. *Zen Made Easy: An Introduction to the Basics of the Ancient Art of Zen.* New York: Sterling Publishing, 1999.

McRae, John R. *Seeing through Zen: Encounter, Transformation, and Genealogy in Chinese Chan Buddhism.* Berkeley: University of California Press, 2004.

Sudo, Philip Toshio. *Zen 24/7: All Zen, All the Time.* San Francisco: HarperSanFrancisco, 2001.

Wu, John C. H. *The Golden Age of Zen: Zen Masters of the T'ang Dynasty.* Bloomington, Ind.: World Wisdom, 2003.

Zhang Heng (Chang Heng) (78–139)
poet, scientist, mathematician

Zhang Heng was born in Henan (Honan), China. He was sent to the capital, Loyang, to receive his education in Confucian philosophy. Zhang Heng showed an early aptitude for literary pursuits and achieved fame for his poetry in his 20s. His work *To Live in Seclusion* is considered a masterpiece of the late Han dynasty, and his poem "Rhapsody on contemplating the Mystery" is a good example of *fu*, rhapsodic poetry.

While most educated young men in China at the time sought to obtain government posts, Zhang Heng spent many years learning mathematics and astronomy instead. His accomplishments in these fields are extremely noteworthy and rival his literary fame. He was able to create an accurate chart of the stars, which assisted in keeping the imperial calendar accurate. He also invented a rudimentary flying machine, which was able to leave the ground, though only for a few moments. In 132, he invented the first seismograph, which traced the direction of earthquakes and their seismic waves. The device could detect shocks from earthquakes across China days before the reports filtered in from the site of the earthquake.

It was only later in his life that Zhang Heng held a series of important government positions in the capital and outlying regions, beginning in 116 and continuing until his death. He is remembered for his literary talents, his abilities in mathematics, and his strong moral code.

Works about Zhang Heng

Hughes, E. R. *Two Chinese Poets: Vignettes on Han Life and Thought.* Westport, Conn.: Greenwood Press, 1977.

Tong, Xiao, ed. *Wen xuan, or Selections of Refined Literature: Volume Three: Rhapsodies on Natural Phenomena, Birds and Animals, Aspirations and Feelings, Sorrowful Laments, Literature, Music, and Passions.* Princeton, N.J.: Princeton University Press, 1996.

Zuni narrative poetry   Native American folklore

The Zuni tribe, inhabiting a region of west-central New Mexico before European contact, preserved their religion, history, and cultural practices in a lively and textured tradition of verse narrative. Like other traditions of ORAL LITERATURE, Zuni stories are anonymous in origin and were meant to be performed. They were remembered and retold in Shi-wi'ma, the Zuni language. Storytellers frequently acted out the dialogue and other conversations within the story, requiring inventive techniques to represent a range of voices. Changes in volume, pitch, and rhythm were used to give emphasis. The tale-teller might use pauses or silence to punctuate a line; at other times he or she might chant or burst into song.

Zuni tales, because of their twining nature, were associated with snakes. Telling a tale out in the open might attract the "smile of a snake" (snakebite). Therefore, tales were reserved for the cold winter months, after the meeting of the medicine society sent all the snakes, especially the rattlesnakes, into their homes under the ground. Since no one wanted to speed along the brief bit of light available during the winter day, tale-telling took place after dark, to help fill the long evenings. Someone in the audience would address the storyteller with "*telaapi,*" meaning "take out a tale." The storyteller would respond with "*so'nahchi!,*" something to the effect of, "so it begins." Listener responses encouraged the tale-teller to continue, indicating that they were paying close attention, and no one was allowed to fall asleep until the story was over. The storyteller typically ended by reminding listeners that the events in the story happened long ago, in a mythical sort of time where things had different meanings than they do in the present world. This suspension of time allowed animals to talk, spirits to circulate, and magical events to take place side by side with daily living without evoking any sort of suspicion or surprise. In the absence of a written means of communication, the recitation of story and verse carried tribal memories, histories, and instructions on how to behave in the world.

Many of the Zuni narratives are origin tales, explaining the beginnings of religious practices or of a natural state. The story of "Coyote and Junco," for example, explains why coyotes have bad teeth, while the story of "The Girl and the Little Ahayuuta" explains why the Ahayuuta twins and their grandmother are worshipped at three separate shrines. The stories contain the Zuni's mythology, such as a description of the creation of the world by the All-Father, Awonawílona, as well as distant memories of tribal founders and migrations in search of favorable places to live. The narratives also portray values and practices in which the Zuni believed. For instance, the story of the boy hunter who never sacrificed the deer he killed carries a moral point, while the story of the boy who was raised by deer shows humans living in harmony with other creatures of the world.

The narratives also describe important religious practices and beliefs, such as the tale "The Sun Priest and the Witch-Woman." This narrative, which builds dramatic tension around the plans of the witches to kill the sun priest, makes clear the importance of the sun priest as the highest-ranking of all Zuni priests and the one responsible for greeting the Sun Father every morning with offerings and prayers. It records the practices of the medicine societies, such as the Saniyakya Society; or the Coyote Society, whose members cared for hunters and, at festivals such as Good Night, the winter solstice, held ceremonies wherein they cured, for free, anyone who came to them with an illness or complaint. It also emphasizes the importance of family or clanship and the beliefs that would guide one down the Pollen Way, the path of life.

Like any folktales, the stories recorded in Zuni narrative poetry have a deeper symbolic meaning, and the interactions of the characters convey valuable cultural information about Zuni beliefs, practices, and ways of life.

English Versions of Zuni Narrative Poetry

Cushing, Frank Hamilton. *The Mythic World of the Zuni.* Edited by Barton Wright. Albuquerque: University of New Mexico Press, 1988.

Finding the Center: The Art of the Zuni Storyteller. Translated by Dennis Tedlock. Lincoln: University of Nebraska Press, 1999.

The Zunis: Self-Portrayals by the Zuni People. Translated by Alvina Quam. Albuquerque: University of New Mexico Press, 1972.

Works about Zuni Narrative Poetry

Murray, David. *Forked Tongues: Speech, Writing, and Representation in North American Indian Texts.* Bloomington: Indiana University Press, 1991.

Tedlock, Barbara. *The Beautiful and the Dangerous: Encounters with the Zuni Indians.* New York: Viking, 1980.

Tedlock, Dennis. *The Spoken Word and the Work of Interpretation.* Philadelphia: University of Pennsylvania Press, 1983.

SELECTED BIBLIOGRAPHY

'Abd, Tarafah ibn al-. "The Ode of Tarafah." In *The Seven Odes: The First Chapter in Arabic Literature.* Translated by A. J. Arberry. London: George Allen & Unwin, 1957.

Ali, Abdullah Yusuf. *The Meaning of the Holy Qu'an.* Beltsville, Md.: Amana Publications, 2004.

Abegg, Martin, Jr., Peter Fint, and Eugene Ulrich, eds. *The Dead Sea Scrolls Bible: The Oldest Known Bible Translated for the First Time into English.* San Francisco: HarperSanFrancisco, 1999.

Abélard, Peter. *Ethical Writings.* Translated by Paul Vincent Spade. Indianapolis, Ind.: Hackett Publishing Company, 1995.

Abélard and Héloïse. *The Letters of Abélard and Héloïse.* Translated by Betty Radice. New York: Penguin, 1974.

Acker, Paul, and Carolyne Larrington. *The Poetic Edda: Essays on Old Norse Mythology.* New York: Garland Publishing, 2001.

Acosta-Hughes, Benjamin. *Polyeideia: The Iambi of Callimachus and the Archaic Iambic Tradition.* Berkeley: University of California Press, 2002.

Adam de la Halle. *Le Jeu de Robin et Marion.* Translated by Shira I. Schwam-Baird. New York: Garland, 1994.

Aeschines. *Aeschines: Speeches.* Translated by C. D. Adams. Cambridge, Mass.: Harvard University Press, 1992.

Aeschylus. *Aeschylus I: Oresteia.* Edited by David Grene and Richmond Lattimore. Chicago: University of Chicago Press, 1947.

———. *Aeschylus II: The Complete Greek Tragedies.* Edited by David Grene and Richmond Lattimore. Chicago: University of Chicago Press, 1956.

———. *Orestes Plays of Aeschylus.* Translated by Paul Roche. New York: New American Library, 1962.

———. *Aeschylus: Prometheus Bound.* Translated by Paul Roche. Wauconda, Ill.: Bolchazy-Carducci, 1997.

Aesop. *Aesop: The Complete Fables.* Translated by Olivia and Robert Temple. New York: Penguin, 1998.

———. *Aesop's Fables.* Edited by Jack Zipes. Illustrated by J. J. Grandville. New York: New American Library, 1992.

Ahl, F. *Lucan: An Introduction.* Ithaca, N.Y.: Cornell University Press, 1976.

Ahmad, Abdul Basit. *Ali Bin Ali Talib: The Fourth Caliph of Islam.* Houston, Tex.: Dar-Us-Salam Publications, n.d.

Albis, Robert. *Poet and Audience in the Argonautica of Apollonius.* Lanham, Md.: Rowman and Littlefield Publishers, 1996.

Alcaeus. *Alkaiou Mele. The Fragments of the Lyrical Poems of Alcaeus.* Edited by Edgar Lobel. Oxford, U.K.: The Clarendon Press, 1927.

Alcock, Susan E., John F. Cherry, and Jajs Elsner, eds. *Pausanias: Travel and Memory in Roman Greece.* Edited by Lysiacum. Oxford, U.K.: Oxford University Press, 2001.

Alexander, Doris. *Creating Literature Out of Life: The Making of Four Masterpieces.* University Park: Penn State University Press, 1996.

Alfie, Fabian. *Comedy and Culture: Cecco Angiolieri's Poetry and Late Medieval Society.* Leeds, U.K.: Northern Universities Press, 2001.

Allen, Peter L. *The Art of Love: Amatory Fiction from Ovid to* Romance of the Rose. Philadelphia: University of Pennsylvania Press, 1992.

Allen, Roger. *An Introduction to Arabic Literature.* Cambridge, U.K.: Cambridge University Press, 2000.

Allen, S. J., and Emilie Amt, eds. *Crusades: A Reader.* Peterborough, Ontario: Broadview Press, 2003.

Allinson, Francis G. *Lucian, Satirist and Artist.* New York: Cooper Square, 1963.

Alon, Hagit, et al. *The Mystery of the Dead Sea Scrolls.* Philadelphia: Jewish Publication Society, 2004.

Alter, Robert. *The Art of Biblical Poetry.* New York: Basic Books, 1985.

Ambrose, Saint. *De Officiis.* Edited with introduction, translation, and commentary by Ivor J. Davidson. Oxford, U.K.: Oxford University Press, 2001.

———. *On Abraham.* Translated by Theodosia Tomkinson. Chrysostomos of Etna, Calif.: Center for Traditionalist Orthodox Studies, 2000.

Amore, R. C., and L. D. Shinn. *Lustful Maidens and Ascetic Kings: Buddhist and Hindu Stories of Life.* New York: Oxford University Press, 1981.

Anacreon. *Greek Songs in the Manner of Anacreon.* Translated by Richard Aldington. London: The Egoist Ltd., 1919.

———. "If you can count the number" and other untitled poems in *The Norton Book of Classical Literature.* Edited by Bernard Knox. New York: W. W. Norton, 1993, 243–246.

Anderson, Graham. *Studies in Lucian's Comic Fiction.* Leiden, Netherlands: E. J. Brill, 1976.

Anderson, Johannes C. *Myths and Legends of the Polynesians.* Rutland, Vt.: Charles E. Tuttle, 1969.

Anderson, John Kinloch. *Xenophon.* London: Bristol Classical, 2002.

Anderson, William Scovil, ed. *Why Horace? A Collection of Interpretations.* Wauconda, Ill.: Bolchazy-Carducci Publishers, 2001.

Andersson, Theodore M. *A Preface to the Niebelungenlied.* Stanford, Calif.: Stanford University Press, 1987.

Andocides. *On the Mysteries.* Edited by Douglas M. MacDowell. Oxford, U.K.: Oxford University Press, 1989.

Andrews, Carol, ed. *The Ancient Egyptian Book of the Dead.* Translated by R. O. Faulkner. New York: Macmillan, 1985.

Angiolieri, Cecco. *Cecco, As I Am and Was: The Poems of Cecco Angiolieri.* Translated by Tracy Barrett. Boston: Branden, 1994.

Apollodorus. *Apollodorus: Library, Volume 1, Books 1 & 3 (9).* Loeb Classical Library. Translated by J. G. Frazer. Cambridge, Mass.: Harvard University Press, 1992.

———. *The Library of Greek Mythology.* Translated by Keith Aldrich. Lawrence, Kans.: Coronado Press, 1974.

Apollonius of Rhodes. *The Argonautika.* Translated by Peter Green. Berkeley: University of California Press, 1997.

———. *Jason and the Golden Fleece (The Argonautica).* Translated by Richard Hunter. Oxford, U.K.: Oxford University Press, 1993.

Apuleius. *Apuleius: The Golden Ass.* Translated by P. G. Walsh. Oxford, U.K.: Clarendon Press, 1994.

Aquinas, Thomas, Saint. *Aquinas: Selected Philosophical Writings.* Edited by Timothy McDermott. New York: Oxford University Press, 1998.

———. *St. Thomas Aquinas on Politics and Ethics: A New Translation, Backgrounds, Interpretations.* Translated by Paul E. Sigmund. New York: W. W. Norton, 1988.

———. *A Shorter Summa: The Essential Philosophical Passages of Saint Thomas Aquinas'* Summa Theologica. Edited by Peter Kreeft. San Francisco: Ignatius Press, 1993.

Arberry, A. J. "II. From the Beginnings to Firdausi." In *Classical Persian Literature.* London: Taylor & Francis, 1994, 42–52.

————, trans. *The Seven Odes: The First Chapter in Arabic Literature.* 61–66. New York: Macmillan, 1957.

————, ed. *Arabic Poetry: A Primer for Students.* Cambridge, U.K.: Cambridge University Press, 1965.

Arieti, James A., and John M. Crossett. *On the Sublime: Longinus.* New York: Edward Mellen Press, 1985.

Aripa, Lawrence, Tom Yellowtail, and Rodney Frey, eds. *Stories That Make the World: Oral Literature of the Indian Peoples of the Inland Northwest.* Norman: University of Oklahoma Press, 1999.

Aristophanes. *Aristophanes.* 3 vols. Edited by David R. Slavitt and Palmer Bovie. Philadelphia: University of Pennsylvania Press, 1998.

————. *Four Plays by Aristophanes: Clouds, Birds, Lysistrata, Frogs.* Translated by William Arrowsmith, Richmond Lattimore, and Douglass Parker. New York: New American Library, 1984.

Aristotle. *Aristotle's Poetics.* Translated by Hippocrates, G. Apostle, Elizabeth A. Dobbs, and Morris A. Parslow. Grinnell, Iowa: The Peripatetic Press, 1990.

————. *Nicomachean Ethics.* Translated by Martin Ostwald. New York: Macmillan, 1962.

Armstrong, Karen. *Muhammad: A Biography of the Prophet.* San Francisco: HarperSanFrancisco, 1992.

Armstrong, Regis J., J. Wayne Hellman, William J. Short. *Francis of Assisi: Early Documents.* Vol. 1, *The Saint.* New York: New City Press, 1999.

Arnaut, Daniel. *The Poetry of Arnaut Daniel.* Translated by James J. Wilhelm. London: Taylor & Francis, 1983.

Artmann, Benno. *Euclid: The Creation of Mathematics.* New York: Springer-Verlag, 1999.

Asser, John. *The Medieval Life of King Alfred the Great.* Translated by Alfred P. Smythe. London: Palgrave Macmillan, 2001.

'Attar, Farid od-Din. *Attar Stories for Young Adults.* Translated by Muhammad Nur Salam. Chicago: Kazi Publications, 2000.

————. *Conference of the Birds: The Selected Sufi Poetry of Farid Ud-Din Attar.* Translated by Raficq Abdulla. Northampton, Mass.: Interlink Publishing Group, 2003.

Aue, Hartmann von. *Arthurian Romances, Tales and Lyric Poetry: The Complete Works of Hartmann Von Aue.* Translated by Frank Tobin, Kim Vivian, and Richard Lawson. Philadelphia: Pennsylvania State University Press, 2001.

Auerbach, Erich. *Dante: Poet of the Secular World.* Chicago: University of Chicago Press, 1961.

Augustine, Saint. *City of God.* Translated by Marcus Dods. New York: Random House, 2000.

————. *Confessions.* Translated by R. S. Pine-Coffin. Middlesex, U.K.: Penguin Books, 1961.

————. *Monastic Rules.* Commentaries by Gerald Bonner. Foreword by George Lawless. New York: New City Press, 2004.

Augustus. *Res Gestae Divi Augusti: English and Latin.* Translated by P. A. Brunt and J. M. Moore. London: Oxford University Press, 1967.

Aurelius, Marcus Antoninus. *Marcus Aurelius.* Loeb Classical Library. Translated by C. G. Haines. Edited by G. P. Goold. Cambridge, Mass.: Harvard University Press, 1988.

————. *The Meditations.* Everyman's Library. Translated by A. S. L. Farquharson. Introduction by D. A. Rees. New York: Alfred A. Knopf, 2003.

————. *Thoughts of the Emperor Marcus Aurelius Antoninus.* Translated by George Long. Watchung, N.J.: Albert Saifer, 1995.

Austen, Ralph A., ed. *In Search of Sunjata: The Mande Oral Epic as History, Literature, and Performance.* Indianapolis: Indiana University Press, 1999.

Averroës. *Averroës' De substantia orbis: Critical Edition of the Hebrew Text.* Translated and edited by Arthur Hyman. Cambridge, Mass.: Medieval Academy of America, 1986.

————. *Averroës on Plato's* Republic. Translated and edited by Ralph Lerner. Ithaca, N.Y.: Cornell University Press, 1974.

————. *Averroës' Three Short Commentaries on Aristotle's "Topics", "Rhetoric", and "Poetics".* Translated and edited by Charles E. Butterworth. Albany: State University of New York Press, 1977.

————. *Book of the Decisive Treatise Determining the Connection between the Law and Wisdom, and Epistle Dedicatory.* Translated and edited by Charles E.

Butterworth. Provo, Utah: Brigham Young University Press, 2001.

Avicenna. *Avicenna's Poem on Medicine.* Edited by Haven C. Krueger. Springfield, Ill.: Charles C. Thomas, 1963.

———. *Ibn Sina and Mysticism: Remarks and Admonitions, Part Four.* Edited by Shams Constantine Inati. New York: Kegan Paul International, 1996.

———. *A Treatise on the Canon of Medicine of Avicenna, Incorporating a Translation of the First Book.* Translated by O. Cameron Gruner. London: Luzac & Co., 1930.

Axton, Richard, and John Stevens, trans. *Medieval French Plays.* New York: Barnes & Noble, 1971.

Babbit, Ellen C., trans. *Jataka Tales: Animal Stories.* New York: Appleton-Century-Crofts, 1940.

Bacchylides. *Bacchylides: A Selection.* Edited by Herwig Maekler. New York: Cambridge University Press, 2004.

———. *Complete Poems.* Translated by Robert Fagles. New Haven, Conn.: Yale University Press, 1961.

Bagge, Sverre. *Society and Politics in Snorri Sturluson's Heimskringla.* Berkeley: University of California Press, 1991.

Bahr, Donald, et al., eds. *The Short Swift Time of Gods on Earth: The Hohokam Chronicles.* Berkeley: University of California Press, 1994.

Bai Juyi. *Po Chü-i: Selected Poems.* Translated by Burton Watson. New York: Columbia University Press, 2000.

———. *The Selected Poems of Po Chü-I.* Translated by David Hinton. New York: New Directions, 1999.

Bailey, Alan. *Sextus Empiricus and Pyrrhonian Skepticism.* Oxford, U.K.: Clarendon Press, 2002.

Baldwin, Barry. *Studies in Lucian.* Toronto: Hakkert, 1973.

Baltussen, Han. *Theophrastus against the Presocratics and Plato.* Boston: Brill Academic Publishers, 2000.

Baltzer, Rebecca A., Thomas Cable, and James I. Wimsatt, eds. *The Union of Words and Music in Medieval Poetry.* Austin: University of Texas Press, 1991.

Barazangi, Nimat Hafez. *Woman's Identity and the Qu'ran.* Gainesville: University Press of Florida, 2004.

Barron, W. R. J. *English Medieval Romance.* New York: Longman, 1987.

Barrow, R. H. *Plutarch and His Times.* Bloomington: Indiana University Press, 1967.

Barry, Sister M. *St. Augustine, the Orator: A Study of the Rhetorical Qualities of St. Augustine's Sermons Ad Populum (1924).* Whitefish, Mont.: Kessinger Publishing, 2003.

Baswell, Christopher. *Virgil in Medieval England: Figuring The Aeneid from the Twelfth Century to Chaucer.* Edited by Alastair Minnis. New York: Cambridge University Press, 1995.

Batts, Michael S. *Gottfried von Strassburg.* New York: Twayne, 1971.

Baxter, Ron. *Bestiaries and their Users in the Middle Ages.* Phoenix Mill, U.K.: Sutton Publishing, 1998.

Beadle, Richard, and Pamela M. King, eds. *York Mystery Plays: A Selection in Modern Spelling.* Oxford, U.K.: Oxford University Press, 1999.

Beagon, Mary. *Roman Nature: The Thought of Pliny the Elder.* Oxford, U.K.: Clarendon Press, 1992.

Beckwith, Martha Warren. *Hawaiian Mythology.* Introduction by Katharine Luomala. Honolulu: University of Hawaii Press, 1977.

Beckwith, Martha, ed. *The Kumulipo, A Hawaiian Creation Chant.* Honolulu: University of Hawaii Press, 1981.

Bede. *De natura rerum liber (On Nature).* Edited by C. W. Jones. Turnhout, Belgium: Brepols, 1975.

———. *The Ecclesiastical History of the English People.* Translated and edited by B. Colgrave and R. A. B. Mynors. Oxford, U.K.: Clarendon Press, 1969.

———. *Historia abbatum (The Lives of the Holy Abbots of Wearmouth and Jarrow).* Translated by J. A. Giles. London: J. M. Dent, 1910.

Beer, Jeanette M. A. *Villehardouin: Epic Historian.* Geneva: Librairie Droz, 1968.

Beer, Josh. *Sophocles and the Tragedy of Athenian Democracy.* Oxford, U.K.: Greenwood Publishing, 2004.

Bell, Albert A., Jr. *All Roads Lead to Murder: A Case from the Notebooks of Pliny the Younger.* Boone, N.C.: High Country Publishers, 2002.

Bellow, Saul. *Seize the Day.* New York: Penguin, 1996.

Bendick, Jeanne. *Galen and the Gateway to Medicine.* Bathgate, N.Dak.: Bethlehem Books, 2002.

Benedict, Ruth. *Zuni Mythology.* New York: Columbia University Press, 1935.

Benediktson, D. Thomas. *Propertius: Modernist Poet of Antiquity.* Carbondale: Southern Illinois University Press, 1989.

Bernard, Catherine. *Celtic Mythology.* Berkeley Heights, N.J.: Enslow Publishers, 2003.

Béroul. *The Romance of Tristan and the Tale of Tristan's Madness.* Translated by Alan S. Fedrick. New York: Penguin, 1978.

Beswick, Ethel, trans. *Jataka Tales, Birth Stories of the Buddha.* London: J. Murray, 1956.

Beye, Charles Rowan. *Epic and Romance in the Argonautica of Apollonius.* Carbondale: Southern Illinois University Press, 1982.

Bierhorst, John, ed. and trans. *Black Rainbow: Legends of the Incas and Myths of Ancient Peru.* New York: Farrar, Straus & Giroux, 1976.

———. *Cantares Mexicanos: Songs of the Aztecs.* Palo Alto, Calif.: Stanford University Press, 1985.

Bingen, Hildegard von. *Hildegard von Bingen's Mystical Visions.* Translated from *Scivias* by Bruce Hozeski. Introduced by Matthew Fox. Santa Fe, N.Mex.: Bear & Co., 1986.

———. *Mystical Writings.* Edited and introduction by Fiona Bowie & Oliver Davies with new translations by Robert Carver. New York: Crossroad, 1990.

Binyon, Laurence. *The Poems of Nizami, Described by Laurence Binyon.* London: The Studio Limited, 1928.

Birley, Anthony. *Marcus Aurelius: A Biography.* New York: Barnes and Noble, 1999.

Bjerregaard, C. H. *Sufi Interpretations of the Quatrains of Omar Khayyam and Fitzgerald (1902).* Whitefish, Mont.: Kessinger Publishing, 2003.

Bjork, Robert E., and John D. Niles, eds. *A Beowulf Handbook.* Lincoln: University of Nebraska Press, 1998.

Blair, Peter Hunter. *The World of Bede.* New York: St. Martin's Press, 1970.

Blank, Jonah. *Arrow of the Blue-Skinned God: Tracing the Ramayana Through India.* Berkeley, Calif.: Grove Press, 2000.

Blensdorf, Jan. *My Name is Sei Shōnagon.* New York: Overlook Press, 2003.

Boase, Roger. *The Origin and Meaning of Courtly Love: A Critical Study of European Scholarship.* Manchester, U.K.: Manchester University Press, 1977.

Boenig, Robert, trans. *Anglo-Saxon Spirituality: Selected Writings.* Mahwah, N.J.: Paulist Press, 2001.

Boethius. *The Consolation of Philosophy.* Translated by Victor Watts. New York: Penguin, 2000.

Bogin, Meg. *The Women Troubadours.* Scarborough, U.K.: Paddington Press Ltd., 1976.

Bokser, Ben Zion. *The Wisdom of the Talmud.* New York: Kensington, 2001.

Bonner, Stanley. *The Literary Treatises of Dionysius of Halicarnassus: A Study in the Development of Critical Method.* Amsterdam: Adolf M. Hakkert, 1969.

Boron, Robert de. *Merlin and the Grail.* Translated by Nigel Bryant. Cambridge, U.K.: D. S. Brewer, 2001.

Bos, Egbert P., and P. A. Meijer, eds. *On Proclus and His Influence in Medieval Philosophy.* Leiden, Netherlands: Brill Academic Publishers, 1991.

Bosley, Keith. *The Kalevala: An Epic After Oral Tradition.* New York: Oxford University Press, 1989.

Bowen, Richard, and Iassen Ghiuselev. *Socrates: Greek Philosopher.* Broomall, Pa.: Mason Crest Publishers, 2002.

Bowie, Fiona, ed. *Beguine Spirituality: Mystical Writings of Mechthild of Magdeburg, Beatrice of Nazareth, and Hadewijch of Brabant.* Translated by Oliver Davies. New York: Spiritual Classics, 1990.

Bowring, Richard. *Murasaki Shikibu: The Tale of Genji.* New York: Cambridge University Press, 1988.

Boyle, A. J., and J. P. Sullivan, eds. *Martial in English.* New York: Penguin Books, 1996.

Bradshaw, David. *Aristotle East and West: Metaphysics and the Division of Christendom.* New York: Cambridge University Press, 2004.

Brann, Eva. *The Music of the Republic: Essays on Socrates' Conversations and Plato's Writings.* Philadelphia: Paul Dry Books, 2004.

Bredehoft, Thomas A. *Textual Histories: Readings in the Anglo-Saxon Chronicle.* Toronto: University of Toronto Press, 2001.

Bright, William. *A Coyote Reader.* Berkeley: University of California Press, 1993.

Briscoe, John. *A Commentary on Livy.* Oxford, U.K.: Clarendon Press, 1981.

Brody, Alan. *The English Mummers and Their Plays: Traces of Ancient Mystery.* Philadelphia: University of Pennsylvania Press, 1970.

Broker, Ignatia. *Nightflying Woman: An Ojibway Narrative.* St. Paul: Minnesota Historical Society, 1983.

Brooks, Miguel F. *A Brief History of the Kebra Nagast.* Lawrenceville, N.J.: Red Sea Press, 1996.

Brown, Brian, ed. *The Story of Confucius: His Life and Sayings (1927).* Introduction by Ly Yu Sang. Whitefish, Mont.: Kessinger Publishing, 2003.

Brown, Cheever MacKenzie. *The Triumph of the Goddess.* New York: State University of New York Press, 1990.

Brown, George Hardin. *Bede the Venerable.* Boston: Twayne, 1987.

Brown, Joseph Epes and Emily Cousins. *Teaching Spirits: Understanding Native American Religious Traditions.* Oxford, U.K.: Oxford University Press, 2001.

Brownlee, John S. *Political Thought in Japanese Historical Writing from Kojiki 712 to Tokushi Yoron 1712.* Waterloo, Ontario, Canada: Wilfrid Laurier University Press, 1991.

Brownlee, Kevin, and Sylvia Huot, eds. *Rethinking the Romance of the Rose: Text, Image, Reception.* Philadelphia: University of Pennsylvania Press, 1992.

Buck, William, ed. and trans. *The Mahabharata.* Berkeley: University of California Press, 2000.

Budge, E. A. Wallis. *The Queen of Sheba and Her Only Son Menyelek (I).* London: Oxford University Press, 1932.

———, trans. *The Book of the Dead.* Mineola, N.Y.: Dover Publications, 1996.

Buitenen, J. A. B. van. *Ramanuja on the Bhagavadgita.* Delhi, India: Motilal Banarsidass, 1968.

———, ed. and trans. *The Mahabharata.* 3 vols. Chicago: University of Chicago Press, 1973–78.

Budelmann, Felix. *Language of Sophocles: Communality, Communication and Involvement.* Cambridge, U.K.: Cambridge University Press, 2000.

Burgess, Glyn, trans. *Lais of Marie de France.* New York: Penguin, 1999.

———. *The Song of Roland.* New York: Penguin, 1990.

Burnett, Anne Pippin. *The Art of Bacchylides.* Cambridge, Mass.: Harvard University Press, 1985.

Burrell, David B. *Knowing the Unknowable God: Ibn-Sina, Maimonides, Aquinas.* Notre Dame, Ind.: University of Notre Dame Press, 1986.

Burton, Richard, trans. *Arabian Nights: Tales from a Thousand and One Nights.* New York: The Modern Library, 2001.

Buxton, Richard. *The Complete World of Greek Mythology.* London: Thames & Hudson, 2004.

Byock, Jesse L. *Feud in the Icelandic Saga.* Berkeley: University of California Press, 1993.

———. *Medieval Iceland: Society, Sagas, and Power.* Berkeley: University of California Press, 1988.

———, trans. *The Saga of the Volsungs.* New York: Penguin Classics, 2002.

Caesar, Julius. *Caesar.* Translated by A. G. Peskett. Cambridge, Mass.: Harvard University Press, 1984.

———. *Caesar's Gallic War.* Translated by W. A. McDevite and W. S. Bohn. Harper's New Classical Library. New York: Harper & Brothers, 1869.

———. *The Civil War.* Translated by Jane F. Gardner. New York: Viking Press, 1976.

———. *The Conquest of Gaul.* Translated by S. A. Hanford. New York: Viking Press, 1983.

———. *The Gallic War.* Translated by Carolyn Hammond. Oxford, U.K.: Oxford Press, 1999.

Callimachus. *Callimachus (Musaeus: Aetia, Iambi, Lyric Poems, Hecale, Minor Epic & Elegiac Poems & Other Fragments).* Loeb Classical Library. Translated by C. A. Trypanis. Edited by Thomas Gelzer and Cedric Whitman. Cambridge, Mass.: Harvard University Press, 1992.

———. *Callimachus: Hymn to Demeter.* Edited by Neil Hopkinson. Cambridge, Mass.: Cambridge University Press, 2004.

————. *The Poems of Callimachus.* Translated by Frank Nisetich. Oxford, U.K.: Oxford University Press, 2001.

Campbell, Gordon. *Lucretius on Creation and Evolution: A Commentary on de Rerum Natura 5.772–1104.* Oxford, U.K.: Oxford University Press, 2003.

Campbell, Joseph. *The Power of Myth.* New York: Anchor Books, 1988.

Canseco, María Rostworowski de Deiz. *History of the Inca Realm.* Translated by Harry B. Iceland. Cambridge, U.K.: Cambridge University Press, 1999.

Cantor, Norman F. *The Civilization of the Middle Ages.* New York: HarperPerennial, 1994.

Cappelanus, Andreas. *The Art of Courtly Love.* Translated by John Jay Parry. New York: Columbia University Press, 1941.

Caracciolo, Peter L., ed. *The Arabian Night in English Literature: Studies in the Reception of Thousand and One Nights into British Culture.* New York: St. Martin's Press, 1988.

Carey, Christopher. *Greek Orators: Apollodorus against Nesira,* Vol. 6. Oakville, Conn.: David Brown Book Co., 1992.

Carney, James, trans. *Medieval Irish Lyrics.* Dublin: Dolmen Press, 1999.

Carrier, Constance. *The Poems of Propertius.* Bloomington: Indiana University Press, 1963.

Carrière, Jean-Claude. *The Mahabharata: A Play Based upon the Indian Classic Epic.* Translated by Peter Brook. New York: Harper & Row, 1987.

Catullus, Gaius Valerius. *Catullus.* Translated by Charles Martin. New Haven, Conn.: Yale University Press, 1992.

————. *Catullus: A Commentary.* Edited by C. J. Fordyce. Oxford, U.K.: Oxford University Press, 1990.

Caxton, William, trans. *The History of Reynard the Fox.* Edited by N. F. Blake. Rochester, N.Y.: Boydell and Brewer, 1970.

Chadwick, Henry. *Boethius, the Consolations of Music, Logic, Theology, and Philosophy.* Oxford, U.K.: Clarendon Press, 1990.

————. *Saint Augustine, Bishop of Hippo.* Oxford, U.K.: Oxford University Press, 1986.

Chaitanya, Krishna. *The Mahabharata: A Literary Study.* New Delhi: Clarion Books; Flushing, N.Y.: Asia Book Corp. of America, 1985.

Chamberlain, Basil Hall, trans. *Kojiki: Records of Ancient Matters.* Rutland, Vt.: Charles E. Tuttle, 1982.

Chance, Linda H. *Formless in Form: Kenko, Tsurezuregusa, and the Rhetoric of Japanese Fragmentary Prose.* Palo Alto, Calif.: Stanford University Press, 1997.

Chaplin, Jane D. *Livy's Exemplary History.* Oxford, U.K.: Oxford University Press, 2000.

Check Teck Foo and Peter Grinyer. *Organizing Strategy: Sun Tzu's Business Warcraft.* Boston and Singapore: B-H. Asia.

Chesterton, G. K. *St. Francis of Assisi; The Everlasting Man; St. Thomas Aquinas.* San Francisco: Ignatius Press, 1986.

Chickering, Howell D., Jr., trans. *Beowulf.* New York: Doubleday, 1977.

Chirri, Mohamad Jawad. *The Brother of the Prophet Mohammad (the Imam Ali).* Qum, Iran: Ansariyan Publications, 1996.

Chishti, Hakim G. M. *The Traditional Healer's Handbook: A Classic Guide to the Medicine of Avicenna.* Rochester, Vt.: Healing Arts Press, 1991.

Chrétien de Troyes. *Arthurian Romances.* Translated by D. D. R. Owen. Rutland, Vt.: Charles E. Tuttle, 1997.

————. *Arthurian Romances.* Translated by William W. Kibler and Carleton W. Carroll. New York: Penguin, 1991.

————. *The Complete Romances of Chrétien de Troyes.* Translated by David Staines. Bloomington: Indiana University Press, 1990.

Church, Alfred Jr., ed. *Stories from the Greek Comedians: Aristophanes, Philenon, Diphilus, Menander and Apollodorus.* Chesire, Conn.: Biblo and Tanner Booksellers, 1998.

Cicero, Marcus Tullius. *Cicero. Volume XXVIII. Letters to Quintus and Brutus.* Translated by D. R. Shackleton Bailey. Cambridge, Mass.: Harvard University Press, 2002.

————. *Cicero: The Speeches.* Translated by Louis E. Lord. Cambridge, Mass.: Harvard University Press, 1959.

Cid, El. *Poem of the Cid.* Translated by Paul Blackburn. Norman: University of Oklahoma Press, 1998.

———. *The Poem of the Cid.* Translated by Rita Hamilton and Janet Perry. Introduction by Ian Michael. New York: Penguin, 1984.

———. *The World of El Cid: Chronicles of the Spanish Reconquest.* Edited by Simon Barton and Richard Fletcher. Manchester, U.K.: Manchester University Press, 2001.

Clanchy, M. T. *Abelard: A Medieval Life.* Oxford, U.K.: Blackwell Publishers, 1999.

Clari, Robert de. *The Conquest of Constantinople.* Translated by Edgar Holmes McNeal. Medieval Academy Reprints for Teaching, 36. Toronto: University of Toronto Press, 1996.

Clayton, Barbara. *A Penelopean Poetics: Reweaving the Feminine in Homer's Odyssey.* Lanham, Md.: Rowman & Littlefield, 2004.

Cleary, Thomas, trans. *The Essential Koran: The Heart of Islam.* Edison, N.J.: Castle, 1998.

Clinton, Jerome W., trans. *The Tragedy of Sohrab and Rostam from the Persian National Epic, the Shahname of Abol-Qasem Ferdowsi.* Seattle: University of Washington Press, 1996.

Clissold, Stephen. *In Search of the Cid.* New York: Barnes & Noble, 1994.

Cobby, Anne Elizabeth. *Ambivalent Conventions: Formula and Parody in Old French.* Amsterdam: Rodopi BV Editions, 1995.

Coffta, David Joseph. *Influences of Callimachean Aesthetics on the Satires and Odes of Horace.* Lewiston, N.Y.: Edwin Mellen, 2002.

Cohen, Norman J. *The Way into Torah.* Woodstock, Vt.: Jewish Lights Publishing, 2004.

Colautti, Federico M. *Passover in the Works of Josephus.* Boston: Brill, 2002.

Collins, John F. *Introduction to the Hebrew Bible with CD-ROM.* Minneapolis, Minn.: Augsburg Fortress Publishers, 2004.

Colton, Robert E. *Juvenal's Use of Martial's Epigrams: A Study of Literary Influence.* Amsterdam: Benjamins, John Publishing, 1991.

Comnena, Anna. *The Alexiad of Anna Comnena.* Translated by E. R. A. Sewter. Baltimore, Md.: Penguin, 1969.

Conacher, D. J. *Euripidean Drama: Myth, Theme, and Structure.* Toronto: University of Toronto Press, 1967.

Confucius. *The Analects.* Translated and edited by Raymond Dawson. New York: Oxford University Press, 1993.

———. *Wisdom of Confucius.* New York: Kensington Publishing, 2001.

Conte, Gian Biagio. *The Hidden Author: An Interpretation of Petronius' Satyricon.* Translated by Elaine Fantham. Berkeley: University of California Press, 1996.

———. "Ennius." In *Latin Literature: A History.* Translated by Joseph B. Solodow. Baltimore: Johns Hopkins University Press, 1999.

Cook, Albert Stanburrough. *The Possible Begetter of the Old English Beowulf and Widsith.* New York: M.S.G. Haskell House, 1970.

Cook, Robert, trans. *Njal's Saga.* New York: Penguin Classics, 2002.

Cook, Robert Francis. *The Sense of the Song of Roland.* Ithaca, N.Y.: Cornell University Press, 1987.

Coolidge, Olivia. *Lives of Famous Romans.* Boston: Houghton Mifflin, 1965.

Cooper, Helen. *Romance in Time: Transforming Motifs from Geoffrey of Monmouth to the Death of Shakespeare.* Oxford, U.K.: Oxford University Press, 2004.

Cosman, Carol, ed. *The Penguin Book of Women Poets.* New York: Viking Press, 1986.

Courlander, Harold. *A Treasury of Afro-American Folklore.* New York: Marlowe & Company, 2002.

Courtney, Edward. *A Companion to Petronius.* New York: Oxford University Press, 2001.

Coward, David. *A History of French Literature: From Chanson de Geste to Cinema.* Oxford, U.K.: Blackwell, 2002.

Cowen, Agnes, trans. *Cherokee Folk Tales and Myths.* Park Hill, Okla.: Cross-Cultural Educational Center, 1984.

Craik, Elizabeth M. *Hippocrates: Places in Man.* Oxford, U.K.: Oxford University Press, 1998.

Creed, J. L., and A. E. Wardman, trans. *The Philosophy of Aristotle.* Commentaries by Renford Bambrough. New York: Signet Classics, 2003.

Creel, H. G. *Confucius and the Chinese Way.* New York: Harper & Row, 1975.

Crossley-Holland, Kevin, ed. *The Norse Myths.* New York: Pantheon, 1980.

———, trans. *The Anglo-Saxon World: An Anthology.* Oxford University Press, 1999.

Cummings, Mary. *The Lives of the Buddha in the Art and Literature of Asia.* Ann Arbor: University of Michigan, Center for South and Southeast Asian Studies, 1992.

Curley, Michael J. *Geoffrey of Monmouth.* New York: Macmillan Library Reference, 1994.

Curtin, Jeremiah. *Creation Myths of Primitive America.* Whitefish, Mont.: Kessinger Publishing Company, 2003.

Curtis, Renee L., trans. *The Romance of Tristan: The Thirteenth-Century Old French "Prose Tristan."* New York: Oxford University Press, 1994.

Cushing, Frank Hamilton. *The Mythic World of the Zuni.* Edited by Barton Wright. Albuquerque: University of New Mexico Press, 1988.

———. *Outlines of Zuni Creation Myths.* New York: AMS Press, 1996.

———. *Zuni Folk Tales.* New York: G. P. Putnam's Sons, 1901.

Daibu, Lady. *The Poetic Memoirs of Lady Daibu.* Translated and edited by Phillip Tudor Harries. Stanford, Calif.: Stanford University Press, 1980.

Dalven, Rae. *Anna Comnena.* New York: Twayne, 1972.

Dane, Joseph A. *Res/Verba: A Study in Medieval French Drama.* Leiden, Netherlands: E. J. Brill, 1985.

Daniélou, Alain, trans. *The Complete Kama Sutra: The First Unabridged Modern Translation of the Classic Indian Text by Vatsyayana.* Rochester, Vt.: Park Street Press, 1994.

Dante, Alighieri. *Dante Alighieri's Divine Comedy.* 6 vols. Translated by Mark Musa. Bloomington: Indiana University Press, 1997–2003.

———. *The Divine Comedy: The Inferno, The Purgatorio, The Paradiso.* Translated by John Ciardi. New York: New American Library, 2003.

———. *The Portable Dante.* Edited by Paolo Milano. New York: Penguin, 1975.

Dauenhauer, Nora, ed. *Haa Shuka, Our Ancestor: Tlingit Oral Narratives.* Seattle: University of Washington Press, 1987.

Davidson, Charles. *Studies in the English Mystery Play.* Brooklyn, N.Y.: M.S.G. Haskell House, 1969.

Davidson, H. R. Ellis. *Gods and Myths of Northern Europe.* Baltimore: Penguin, 1964.

Davidson, Herbert A. *Moses Maimonides: The Man and His Works.* Oxford, U.K.: Oxford University Press, 2004.

Davidson, Olga M. *Poet and Hero in the Persian Book of Kings.* Ithaca, N.Y.: Cornell University Press, 1994.

Davies, Eryl W. *The Dissenting Reader: Feminist Approaches to the Hebrew Bible.* Aldershot, Hampshire, U.K.: Ashgate Publishing, 2003.

Davis, Dick. *Epic and Sedition: The Case of Firdawzi's Shahname.* Fayetteville: University of Arkansas Press, 1992.

Davis, Norman. *"Notes on the Middle English Bestiary." In Medium Aevum,* vol. 19. Oxford, U.K.: The Society for the Study of Medieval Languages and Literature, 1950: 56–59.

Dawson, Raymond. *Confucius.* Oxford, U.K.: Oxford University Press, 1981.

DeGanck, Roger. *Beatrice of Nazareth in Her Context.* 3 vols. Kalamazoo, Mich.: Cistercian Publications, 1991.

———. *The Life of Beatrice of Nazareth.* Kalamazoo, Mich.: Cistercian Publications, 1991.

DeWitt, N. W. *Epicurus and His Philosophy.* Minneapolis: University of Minnesota Press, 1954.

Demosthenes. *Demosthenes: On the Crown.* Edited by Harvey E. Yunis. New York: Cambridge University Press, 2001.

———. *On the Crown.* Edited by Harvey Yunis. Cambridge, U.K.: Cambridge University Press, 2001.

———. *On the False Embassy (Oration 19).* Edited by Douglas M. MacDowell. Oxford, U.K.: Oxford University Press, 2000.

Dickinson, G. Lowes. *Plato and His Dialogues.* La Vergne, Tenn.: University Press of the Pacific, 2003.

Diller, Hans-Jürgen. *The Middle English Mystery Play: A Study in Dramatic Speech and Form.* Cambridge, U.K.: Cambridge University Press, 1992.

Diodorus. *Antiquities of Egypt: A Translation, with Notes, of Book I of the Library of History of Diodorus Siculus.* Translated by Edwin W. Murphy. Somerset, N.J.: Transaction Publishers, 1990.

———. *Diodorus Siculus: The Reign of Philip.* Translated by E. I. McQueen. London: Bristol Classical Press, 1995.

Dionysius of Halicarnassus. *Dionysius of Halicarnassus: Critical Essays.* Translated by Stephen Usher. Cambridge, Mass.: Harvard University Press, 1976.

———. *On Thucydides.* Translated by Kendrick Pritchett. Berkeley: University of California Press, 1975.

———. *The Roman Antiquities.* Translated by Earnest Cary. Cambridge, Mass.: Harvard University Press, 1974.

Doe, Paula. *A Warbler's Song in the Dusk: The Life and Work of Otomo Yakamochi (718–785).* Berkeley: University of California Press, 1982.

Doniger, Wendy and Sudhir Kakar, trans. *Kamasutra: The Acclaimed New Translation.* Philadelphia: Running Press, 2003.

Donzella, Compiuta. "In the season when the world puts out leaves and flowers." In *An Anthology of Ancient and Medieval Woman's Song.* Edited by Anne L. Klinck. New York: Palgrave Macmillan, 2004. 113.

Dover, Kenneth James. *Aristophanic Comedy.* Berkeley: University of California Press, 1972.

———. *Lysias and the Corpus Lysiacum.* Vol. 39. Berkeley: University of California Press, 1968.

Dueck, Daniela. *Strabo of Amasia: A Greek Man of Letters in Augustan Rome.* London: Routledge, 2000.

Duncan, Barbara R., and Davey Arch, eds. *Living Stories of the Cherokee.* Raleigh: University of North Carolina Press, 1998.

Dunn, Hugh. *Cao Zhi: The Life of a Princely Chinese Poet.* La Vergne, Tenn.: University Press of the Pacific, 2000.

Easwaran, Eknath, trans. *The Bhagavad Gita.* New York: Vintage Books, 2000.

Edgerton, Franklin. *The Panchatantra Reconstructed, I: Text and Critical Apparatus.* American Oriental Series 2. New Haven, Conn.: American Oriental Society, 1924.

———, trans. *The Bhagavad-Gita: Translated and Interpreted.* 2 vols. Cambridge, Mass.: Harvard University Press, 1952.

Edinger, Edward F., and Deborah A. Wesley, eds. *Eternal Drama: The Inner Meaning of Greek Mythology.* Boston: Shambhala Publications, 2001.

Edwards, Mark J., trans. *Neoplatonic Saints: The Lives of Plotinus and Proclus by Their Students.* Liverpool, U.K.: Liverpool University Press, 2001.

Edwards, Michael. *The Attic Orators.* London: Bristol Classical Press, 1994.

Egan, Ronald C. *The Literary Works of Ou-yang Hsiu (1007–72).* Cambridge, U.K.: Cambridge University Press, 1984.

———. *Word, Image, and Deed in the Life of Su Shi.* Cambridge, Mass.: Harvard University Press, 1994.

Eisner, Sigmund. *The Tristan Legend: A Study in Sources.* Evanston, Ill.: Northwestern University Press, 1969.

Ellis, Peter Berresford. *The Chronicles of the Celts: New Tellings of Their Myths and Legends.* New York: Carroll & Graf Publishers, 1999.

Endrezze, Anita. *Throwing Fire at the Sun, Water at the Moon.* Tucson: University of Arizona Press, 2000.

Ennius, Quintus. *Annals of Quintus Ennius.* Edited by Otto Skutch. Oxford, U.K.: Oxford University Press, 1985.

———. *The Tragedies of Ennius: The Fragments.* Edited by H. D. Jocelyn. London: Cambridge University Press, 1967.

Epictetus. *The Art of Living: The Classic Manual on Virtue, Happiness, and Effectiveness.* Translated by Sharon Lebell. New York: HarperCollins, 2004.

———. *Discourses. Book I.* Translated by Robert F. Dobbin. Oxford, U.K.: Oxford University Press, 1998.

———. *Enchiridion.* Translated by George Long. Buffalo, N.Y.: Prometheus Books, 1991.

———. *Virtue and Happiness: The Manual of Epictetus.* Claude Mediavilla, calligraphy. New York: Random House, 2003.

Epicurus. *The Epicurus Reader: Selected Writings and Testimonia.* Edited by Brad Inwood and Lloyd P. Gerson. Introduction by D. S. Hutchinson. Indianapolis, Ind.: Hackett Publishing, 1997.

————. *Fragments*. Buffalo, N.Y.: Prometheus Books, 1992.

Erdoes, Richard, and Alfonso Ortiz, eds. *American Indian Myths and Legends*. New York: Pantheon Books, 1985.

Ervast, Pekka. *The Keys to the Kalevala*. Nevada City, Calif.: Blue Dolphin Publishing, 1999.

Euclid. *Euclid's Phenomenon: A Translation and Study of a Hellenistic Treatise in Spherical Astronomy*. Translated by Robert S. Thomas. Edited by J. L. Berggren. New York: Garland, 1996.

————. *Euclid: The Thirteen Books of the Elements*. Translated by Sir Thomas L. Heath. Mineola, N.Y.: Dover Publications, 1908.

Euripides. *Euripides*. Translated by Anne Marie Albertazzi. Edited by Harold Bloom. Langhorne, Pa.: Chelsea House Publishers, 2002.

————. *Euripides I*. Translated by Richmond Lattimore, et al. Edited by David Grene and Richmond Lattimore. Chicago: University of Chicago Press, 1955.

————. *Euripides' Alcestis*. Notes by H. M. Roisman and C. A. Luschnig. Norman: University of Oklahoma Press, 2003.

————. *Medea and Other Plays*. Translated by John Davie. Introduction by Richard Rutherford. New York: Penguin Classics, 2003.

Everitt, Anthony. *Cicero: The Life and Times of Rome's Greatest Politician*. New York: Random House, 2002.

Evers, Larry, and Felipe S. Molina. *Yaqui Deer Songs, Maso Bwikam: A Native American Poetry*. Tucson: Sun Tracks and University of Arizona Press, 1987.

Exum, J. Cheryl, and H. G. M. Williamson, eds. *Reading from Right to Left: Essays on the Hebrew Bible in Honor of David J. A. Clines*. London: Continuum International Publishing Group, 2003.

Fan Zheng Da. *Four Seasons of Field and Garden: Sixty Impromptu Poems*. Translated by Lois Baker. Pueblo, Colo.: Passeggiata Press, 1997.

————. *The Golden Year of Fan Chengda*. Translated by Gerald Bullett. Cambridge, U.K.: Cambridge University Press, 1946.

————. *Stone Lake: The Poetry of Fan Chengda*. Translated and edited by J. D. Schmidt. Cambridge: Cambridge University Press, 1992.

Farazdaq, Hammam ibn Ghalib al-. *The Naqaith of Jarir and al-Farazdaq*. Translated by Arthur Wormholdt. Oskaloosa, Iowa: William Penn College, 1974.

Faris, James. *The Nightway: A History and a History of Documentation of the Navajo Ceremonies*. Albuquerque: University of New Mexico Press, 1990.

Farquharson, A. S. L. *Marcus Aurelius, His Life and His World*. Oxford, U.K.: Greenwood Publishing, 1975.

Feeney, Denis, and Tony Woodman, eds. *Traditions and Contexts in the Poetry of Horace*. New York: Cambridge University Press, 2002.

Feeney, Kathy. *Marco Polo: Explorer of China*. Berkeley Heights, N.J.: Enslow Publishers, 2004.

Feldherr, Andrew. *Spectacle and Society in Livy's History*. Berkeley: University of California Press, 1998.

Feldman, Louis H. *Studies in Josephus' Rewritten Bible*. Boston: Brill, 1998.

Feldmann, Susan, ed. *The Storytelling Stone: Traditional Native American Myths and Tales*. New York: Delta, 1999.

Ferguson, Diana. *Tales of the Plumed Serpent: Aztec, Inca and Mayan Myths*. New York: Sterling, 2000.

Ferguson, Thomas S. *Visita Nos: Reception, Rhetoric, and Prayer in a North African Monastery*, Vol. 203. New York: Peter Lang, 1999.

Ferry, David. *Gilgamesh: A New Rendering in English Verse*. New York: Farrar, Straus & Giroux, 1992.

Field, Norma. *The Splendor of Longing in "The Tale of Genji."* Princeton, N.J.: Princeton University Press, 1987.

Finnegan, Ruth. "Proverbs in Africa." In *The Wisdom of Many: Essays on the Proverb*. Edited by Wolfgang Mieder and Alan Dundes, 10–42. New York: Garland, 1981.

Fisher, Rodney W. *Heinrich von Veldeke: Eneas: A Comparison with the "Roman d'Eneas" and a Translation into English*. Bern, Switzerland: Peter Lang, 1992.

Fitzgerald, William. *Catullan Provocations: Lyric Poetry and the Drama of Position.* Berkeley: University of California Press, 1996.

Flanagan, Sabina. *Hildegard of Bingen, 1098–1179: A Visionary Life.* London, New York: Routledge, 1998.

Flannery, Thomas L. *Acts Amid Precepts: The Aristotelian Logical Structure of Thomas Aquinas's Moral Theory.* Washington, D.C.: Catholic University of America Press, 2001.

Floridi, Luciano. *Sextus Empiricus: The Transmission and Recovery of Pyrrhonism.* Oxford, U.K.: Oxford University Press, 2002.

Fontes, Manuel de Costa. *Folklore and Literature: Studies in the Portuguese, Brazilian, Sephardic, and Hispanic Oral Traditions.* New York: State University of New York Press, 2000.

Forsyth, Fiona. *Augustus: The First Emperor.* New York: Rosen Publishing Group, 2003.

Fortini, Arnaldo. *Francis of Assisi.* New York: Crossroad, 1992.

Forward, Martin. *Muhammad: A Short Biography.* Oxford, U.K.: One World, 1997.

Foster, Benjamin, ed. and trans. *The Epic of Gilgamesh.* New York: W. W. Norton, 2001.

Frappier, Jean. *Chrétien de Troyes: The Man and His Work.* Translated by Raymond J. Cormier. Athens: Ohio University Press, 1982.

Freeman, Michael. *Lo-Yang and the Opposition to Wang An-Shih: The Rise of Confucian Conservatism, 1068–86.* Yale University Thesis. Ann Arbor, Mich.: University Microfilms International, 1974.

Freke, Timothy. *Zen Made Easy: An Introduction to the Basics of the Ancient Art of Zen.* New York: Sterling Publishing, 1999.

Friberg, Eino, trans. *The Kalevala: Epic of the Finnish People.* Helsinki: Otava Publishing, 1988.

Friedlander, Shems. *Rumi and the Whirling Dervishes.* New York: Parabola Books, 2003.

Friedman, Richard Elliott. *Who Wrote the Bible?* San Francisco: Harper, 1997.

Fujiwara no Teika. *Fujiwara Teika's Superior Poems of Our Time.* Translated by Robert H. Brower and Earl Miner. Stanford, Calif.: Stanford University Press, 1967.

———. *The Tale of Matsura: Fujiwara Teika's Experiment in Fiction.* Translated by Wayne P. Lammers. Ann Arbor, Mich.: Center for Japanese Studies, 1992.

Fulgentius, Saint. *Fulgentius: Selected Works.* Translated by Robert B. Eno. Washington, D.C.: Catholic University of America Press, 1997.

Fung-Yu Lan. *A History of Chinese Philosophy.* Translated by Derk Bodde. Princeton, N.J.: Princeton University Press, 1952.

Fusheng Wu. *The Poetics of Decadence: Chinese Poetry of the Southern Dynasties and Late Tang Periods.* Albany: State University of New York Press, 1998.

Gabba, Emilio. *Dionysius and the History of Archaic Rome.* Berkeley: University of California Press, 1991.

Gabrieli, Francesco, ed. *Arab Historians of the Crusades.* Berkeley: University of California Press, 1984.

Gagarin, Michael. *Antiphon the Athenian: Oratory, Law, and Justice in the Age of the Sophists.* Austin: University of Texas Press, 2002.

Gagarin, Michael, and Douglass M. MacDowell, trans. *Antiphon and Andocides.* Austin: University of Texas Press, 1998.

Galen. *Galen on Food and Diet.* Translated by Mark Grant. New York: Routledge, 2000.

Gamberini, Federico. *Stylistic Theory and Practice in the Younger Pliny.* Hildesheim, Germany: Georg Olms Publishers, 1983.

Gantz, Jeffrey, trans. *Early Irish Myths and Sagas.* New York: Penguin, 1982.

Gao Ming. *The Lute: Kao Ming's P'i-p'a chi.* Translated by Jean Mulligan. New York: Columbia University Press, 1980.

Gardner, John, and John Maier, *trans. Gilgamesh: Translated from the Sin-leqi-unninni Version.* New York: Knopf, 1984.

Gaskin, Robert T. *Caedmon: The First English Poet.* New York: M. S. G. Haskell House, 1990.

Gaunt, Simon and Sarah Kay, eds. *The Troubadours: An Introduction.* Cambridge, Mass.: Cambridge University Press, 1999.

Gelzer, Matthias. *Caesar: Politician and Statesman.* Translated by Peter Needham. Cambridge, Mass.: Harvard University Press, 1985.

Genner, E. E., ed. *Selections from the Attic Orators.* Oxford, U.K.: Clarendon Press, 1955.

Geoffrey of Monmouth. *The Historia Regum Brittanie of Geoffrey of Monmouth: Gesta Regum Britannie.* Vol. 5. Edited by Neil Wright. Rochester, N.Y.: Boydell & Brewer, 1985.

———. *The History of the Kings of Britain.* Translated by Lewis Thorpe. New York: Penguin Classics, 1977.

Gibson, Graig. *Interpreting a Classic: Demosthenes and His Ancient Commentators.* Berkeley: University of California Press, 2002.

Gies, Frances, and Joseph Gies. *Daily Life in Medieval Times.* New York: Black Dog & Leventhal, 1999.

Glassie, Henry. *Irish Folk History: Texts from the North.* Philadelphia: University of Pennsylvania Press, 1982.

Godolphin, F. R. B., ed. *Great Classical Myths.* New York: Random House, 1964.

Gohlman, William E., trans. and ed. *The Life of Ibn Sina: A Critical Edition and Annotated Translation.* Albany: State University of New York Press, 1974.

Goldin, Frederick, ed. *German and Italian Lyrics of the Middles Ages.* Garden City, N.Y.: Doubleday, 1973.

Goldstein, David, trans. *Hebrew Poems from Spain.* New York: Schocken, 1966.

Gonda, Jan. *Vedic Literature (Samhita and Brahmanas).* Wiesbaden, Germany: Harassowitz, 1975.

González Reimann, Luis. *The Mahabharata and the Yugas: India's Great Epic Poem and the Hindu System of World Ages.* New York: Peter Lang, 2002.

Goodman, Lenn Evan. *Avicenna.* New York: Routledge, 1992.

Goodwin, Grenville. *Myths and Tales of the White Mountain Apache.* Tucson: University of Arizona Press, 1994.

Gowan, Donald E. *When Man Becomes God: Humanism and Hubris in the Old Testament.* San José, Calif.: Pickwick Publications, 1975.

Grandsden, K. W., and S. J. Harrison. *Virgil: The Aeneid.* New York: Cambridge University Press, 2003.

Granger, Herbert. *Aristotle's Idea of the Soul.* Hingham, Mass.: Kluwer Academic Publishers, 2004.

Greeley, Andrew M. *Emerald Magic.* New York: Tor Books, 2004.

Green, Bernard, and Darlene Pienschke. *Stories of Faith: Among the White Mountain Apache.* London: Pen Press Publishers, 2001.

Green, Miranda Jane. *Celtic Myths.* London: The Trustees of the British Museum, 1993.

Griffith, Ralph T. H., trans. *The Hymns of the Rig Veda,* 3rd ed., complete in two volumes. Benares: E.J. Lazarus and Co., 1920–26.

Grimbert, Joan Tasker, ed. *Tristan and Isolde: A Casebook.* New York: Garland, 1995.

Grishaver, Joel Lurie. *Talmud with Training Wheels: Courtyards and Classrooms.* Los Angeles: Torah Aura Productions, 2004.

Guggenheimer, Heinrich W., ed. *The Jerusalem Talmud.* Berlin: Walter de Gruyter, 2000.

Gurney, Robert, ed. *Bardic Heritage: A Selection of Welsh Poetry in Free English Translation.* London: Chatto & Windus, 1969.

Gurteen, Stephen H. V. *Epic of the Fall of Man: A Comparative Study of Caedmon, Dante, and Milton.* Murieta, Calif.: Classic Books, 1996.

Gutzwiller, Kathryn J. *Poetic Garlands: Hellenistic Epigrams in Context.* Berkeley: University of California Press, 1998.

Haddawy, Husain, trans. *The Arabian Nights.* New York: Everyman, 1990.

Hadewijch. *Hadewijch: The Complete Works.* Translated and edited by Mother Columba Hart. New York: Paulist Press, 1980.

Hadot, Pierre. *Plotinus or the Simplicity of Vision.* Translated by Michael Chase. Chicago: University of Chicago Press, 1998.

Haile, Berard, O.F.M. *Navajo Coyote Tales.* Edited by Karl W. Luckert. Lincoln: University of Nebraska Press, 1984.

Halevi, Judah. *Book of Kuzari.* Translated by Harwig Hirschfeld. Whitefish, Mont.: Kessinger, 2003.

Halkin, Abraham S. "Judeo-Arabic Literature." In Finkelstein, Louis, *The Jews: Their Religion and Culture.* New York: Schocken, 1971.

Hallbeck, Einar S. *The Language of the Middle English Bestiary*. Cristianstad, Virg. Is.: Länstidning Press, 1905.

Hallie, Philip P., ed. *Sextus Empiricus: Selections from the Major Writings on Scepticism, Man, and God*. Indianapolis, Ind.: Hackett, 1985.

Halliwell, Stephen, et al., eds. *Poetics: Longinus on the Sublime, Demetrius on Style*. Cambridge, Mass.: Harvard University Press, 1996.

Ham, Edward Billings. *Rutebeuf and Louis IX*. Chapel Hill: University of North Carolina Press, 1962.

Hamilton, Edith. *The Greek Way*. New York: W. W. Norton, 1983.

Hamilton, John T. *Soliciting Darkness: Pindar, Obscurity, and the Classical Tradition*. Cambridge, Mass.: Harvard University Press, 2004.

Hamilton, Richard. *Architecture of Hesiodic Poetry*. Baltimore, Md.: Johns Hopkins University Press, 1976.

Hamori, Andras. *The Composition of Mutanabbi's Panegyrics to Sayf al-Dawla*. New York: E. J. Brill, 1992.

Han-Shan. *Cold Mountain: 100 Poems by the T'ang Poet Han-Shan*. Translated by Burton Watson. New York: Columbia University Press, 1970.

———. *The Poetry of Han-Shan*. Translated by Robert Hendricks. Albany: State University of New York Press, 1990.

Han Yü. *Growing Old Alive: Poems*. Translated by Kenneth O. Hanson. Port Townsend, Wash.: Copper Canyon Press, 1978.

Hanning, Robert and Joan Ferrante. *The Lais of Marie de France*. Durham, N.C.: Labyrinth Press, 1982.

Happe, Peter, ed. *English Mystery Plays: A Selection*. New York: Viking Press, 1979.

Harder, M. A., R. F. Regtuit, and G. C. Wakker, eds. *Apollonius Rhodius*. Sterling, Va.: Peeters, 2000.

Harris, Edward Monroe. *Aeschines and Athenian Politics*. Oxford, U.K.: Oxford University Press, 1994.

Harrison, Frederick. *The Writings of King Alfred*. New York: M.S.G. Haskell House, 1970.

Hartman, Charles. *Han Yü and the T'ang Search for Unity*. Princeton, N.J.: Princeton University Press, 1986.

Haruo Shirane. *The Bridge of Dreams: A Poetics of "The Tale of Genji."* Stanford, Calif.: Stanford University Press, 1987.

Hasty, Will. *Adventures in Interpretation: The Works of Hartmann von Aue and Their Critical Reception*. Columbia, S.C.: Camden House, 1996.

Hatto, A. T., trans. *Nibelungenlied*. New York: Penguin, 1965.

Hawke, D. M., trans. *The Life and Works of Jahiz*. Berkeley: University of California Press, 1969.

Hawkes, David, trans. *Ch'u Tz'u, The Songs of the South: An Ancient Chinese Anthology*. Taipei: Tun Huang Publications, 1968.

Hay, Jeff, ed. *The Middle Ages*. Vol 3. San Diego: Greenhaven Press, Inc., 2002.

Haymes, Edward. *The Nibelungenlied: History and Interpretation*. Urbana: University of Illinois Press, 1986.

Haynes, Holly. *The History of Make-Believe: Tacitus on Imperial Rome*. Berkeley: University of California Press, 2003.

Healy, John F. *Pliny the Elder on Science and Technology*. Oxford, U.K.: Oxford University Press, 2000.

Heaney, Seamus, trans. *Beowulf*. New York: W. W. Norton, 2000.

Heath, Malcolm. *Menander: A Rhetor in Context*. Oxford, U.K.: Oxford University Press, 2004.

Hedayetullah, Muhammad. *Kabir: The Apostle of Hindu-Muslim Unity*. Delhi: Motilal Banarsidass, 1977.

Heidegger, Martin. *Essence of Truth: On Plato's Parable of the Cave and the Theaetetus*. Translated by Ted Sadler. London: Continuum International Publishing, 2002.

Heinrich von Veldeke. *Heinrich von Veldeke: Eneit*. Translated by J. W. Thomas. New York: Garland Publishing, 1985.

Helgason, Jon Karl. *Rewriting of Njal's Saga: Translation, Ideology, and Icelandic Sagas*. Clevedon, U.K.: Multilingual Matters, 1999.

Heller-Roazen, Daniel. *Fortune's Faces: The Roman de la Rose and the Poetics of Contingency*. Edited by Stephen G. Nichols and Gerald Prince. Baltimore: John Hopkins University Press, 2003.

Helm, Alex. *The English Mummers' Play.* Cambridge, U.K.: D.S. Brewer, 1981.

Hemming, John. *The Conquest of the Incas.* Fort Washington, Pa.: Harvest Books, 2003.

Henderson, John. *Morals and Villas in Seneca's Letters: Places to Dwell.* Cambridge, U.K.: Cambridge University Press, 2004.

———. *Telling Tales on Caesar: Roman Stories from Phaedrus.* New York: Oxford University Press, 2001.

Henkenius, Mary Catherine, ed. *Kokinshu: A Collection of Poems Ancient and Modern.* Translated by Laurel Rasplica Rodd and Mary Catherine Henkenius. Boston: Cheng & Tsui, 1999.

Herodotus. *Herodotus: The Wars of Greece and Persia.* Translated by W. D. Lowe. Wauconda, Ill.: Bolchazy-Carducci Publishers, 1999.

———. *The Histories.* Translated by Aubrey De Selincourt. Introduction by John M. Marincola. New York: Penguin Classics, 2003.

———. *The Histories.* Translated by Robin A. Waterfield. Translated by Carolyn Dewald. Oxford, U.K.: Oxford University Press, 1999.

Hesiod. *Hesiod.* Translated by Richmond Lattimore. Ann Arbor: University of Michigan Press, 1959.

———. *Hesiod: Theogony, Works and Days, Shield.* Translated by Apostolos N. Athanassakis. Baltimore: Johns Hopkins University Press, 2004.

———. *Hesiod's Ascra.* Translated by Anthony T. Edwards. Berkeley: University of California Press, 2004.

Hightower, James R., and Florence Chia-Ying Yeh. *Studies in Chinese Poetry.* Cambridge, Mass.: Harvard University Press, 1998.

Hill, Jillian M. L. *Medieval Debate on Jean de Meun's Roman de la Rose: Morality Versus Art.* Lewiston, N.Y.: Edwin Mellen Press, 1992.

Hillebrandt, Alfred. *Vedic Mythology.* Translated by Sreeramula Rajeswara Sarma. Delhi, India: Motilal Banarsidass Publishers, 1980.

Hillenbrand, Robert. *Shahnama: The Visual Language of the Persian Book of Kings.* Aldershot, Hampshire, U.K.: Ashgate, 2003.

Hintikka, Jaakko. *Analyses of Aristotle.* Hingham, Mass.: Kluwer Academic Publishers, 2004.

Hippocrates. *Ancient Medicine, Airs, Waters, Places, Epidemics 1–2, Oath, Precepts, Nutriment.* Vol. 1. Loeb Classical Library. Translated by W. H. Jones. Cambridge, Mass.: Harvard University Press, 1992.

———. *Places in Man, General Nature of Glands, Fleshes, Use of Liquids, Ulcers, Fistulas, Haemorrhoids.* Vol. 8. Loeb Classical Library. Edited by Paul Potter. Oxford, U.K.: Oxford University Press, 1994.

Hirsch, Steven W. *The Friendship of the Barbarians: Xenophon and the Persian Empire.* Lebanon, N.H.: University Press of New England, 1985.

Hirshfield, Jane and Mariko Aratani, trans. *The Ink Dark Moon: Love Poems by Ono No Komachi and Izumi Shikibu, Women of the Ancient Court of Japan.* New York: Vintage Books, 1990.

Ho, Lucy Chao. *A Study of Li Ch'ing-chao, Her Life and Works.* South Orange, N.J.: Seton Hall University, 1965.

Hodges, Margaret. *St. Jerome and the Lion.* London: Orchard Books, 1991.

Hoffer, Stanley E. *Anxieties of Pliny the Younger.* Oxford, U.K.: Oxford University Press, 1999.

Hollander, Robert. *Dante: A Life in Works.* New Haven, Conn.: Yale University Press, 2001.

Holloway, Julia Bolton. *Twice-Told Tales: Brunetto Latino and Dante Alighieri.* New York: Peter Lang, 1993.

Holzberg, Niklas. *Ovid: The Poet and His Work.* Translated by G. M. Goshgarian. Ithaca, N.Y.: Cornell University Press, 2002.

Holzman, Donald. *Poetry and Politics: The Life and Works of Juan Chi, A.D. 210–263.* Cambridge, U.K.: Cambridge University Press, 1976.

Homer. *The Anger of Achilles: Homer's Iliad.* Translated by Robert Graves. Garden City, N.Y.: Doubleday & Company, 1959.

———. *The Iliad.* Translated by Richmond Lattimore. Chicago: University of Chicago Press, 1951.

———. *The Odyssey.* Translated by Robert Fagles. Introduction and notes by Bernard Knox. New York: Penguin, 1996.

———. *The Poetry of Homer.* Translated by S. E. Bassett. Edited by Bruce Heiden. Lanham, Md.: Rowman & Littlefield, 2003.

Horace. *Odes and Epodes.* Translated by C. E. Bennett. Cambridge, Mass.: Harvard University Press; London: William Heinemann Ltd., 1964.

———. *The Odes and Epodes.* Translated by C. E. Bennett. Cambridge, Mass.: Harvard University Press, 1964.

———. *The Odes and Epodes.* Translated by Niall Rudd. Cambridge, Mass.: Harvard University Press, 2004.

———. *The Satires, Epistles, and Art of Poetry.* IndyPublish.com, 2004.

Horne, Charles F. *Sacred Books and Early Literature of the East: Ancient Arabia, The Hanged Poems, The Koran.* Vol. 5. Whitefish, Mont: Kessinger Publishing, 1997.

Housman, Laurence, trans. *Of Aucassin and Nicolette: A Translation in Prose and Verse from the Old French.* New York: Dial Press, 1930.

Hovannisian, Richard and Georges Sabagh. *The Thousand and One Nights in Arabic Literature and Society.* Cambridge, U.K.: Cambridge University Press, 1997.

Hu Pin-Ching. *Li Ch'ing-chao.* New York: Twayne, 1966.

Huart, Clement. *A History of Arabic Literature.* Beirut: Khayats, 1966.

Hubbard, Margaret. *Propertius.* London: Bristol Classical Press, 2001.

Huby, Pamela and William W. Fortenbraugh. *Theophrastus of Eresus: Sources for His Life, Writings, Thought and Influence.* Boston: Brill Academic Publishers, 1999.

Hughes, E. R. *Two Chinese Poets: Vignettes on Han Life and Thought.* Westport, Conn.: Greenwood Press, 1977.

Hull, K. W. D., ed. *Martial and His Times.* London: Bell, 1967.

Huot, Sylvia Jean. *Romance of the Rose and Its Medieval Readers: Interpretation, Reception, Manuscript Transmission.* Cambridge, Mass.: Cambridge University Press, 1993.

Hutchinson, Godfrey. *Xenophon and the Art of Command.* Mechanicsburg, Pa.: Stackpole Books, 2000.

Ibekwe, Patrick, ed. *Wit and Wisdom of Africa: Proverbs from Africa and the Caribbean.* Trenton, N.J.: Africa World Press, 1999.

Ibn Gabirol, Solomon. *The Fountain of Life: Fons Vitae by Solomon Ibn Gabirol (Avicebron).* Translated by Harry E. Wedeck. New York: Philosophical Library, 1962.

———. *Keter Malkhut: A Crown for the King by Solomon Ibn Gabirol.* Translated by David R. Slavitt. New York: Oxford University Press, 1998.

———. *Selected Poems of Solomon Ibn Gabirol.* Translated by Peter Cole. Princeton, N.J.: Princeton University Press, 2001.

Ireland, S., ed. *Apollodorus: "Argonauts and Heracles."* London: Bristol Classical Press, 1992.

Irwin, Robert. *The Arabian Nights: A Companion.* New York: Penguin Books, 1994.

———, ed. *Night and Horses and the Desert.* Woodstock, N.Y.: Overlook Press, 2000.

Isocrates I. Translated by David Mirhady and Yun Lee Too. Austin: University of Texas Press, 2000.

Izumi Shikibu. *The Izumi Shikibu Diary: A Romance of the Heian Court.* Translated by Edwin A. Cranston. Cambridge, Mass.: Harvard University Press, 1969.

Jackson, William H. *Chivalry in Twelfth-Century Germany: The Works of Hartmann Von Aue.* Rochester, N.Y.: Boydell & Brewer, 1995.

Jacobs, Melville, trans. *Content and Style of an Oral Literature: Clackamas Chinook Myths and Tales.* Chicago: University of Chicago Press, 1959.

Jahiz, Abu Uthman 'Amr ibn Bahr al-. *Nine Essays of al-Jahiz.* Translated by William M. Hutchins. New York: Peter Lang, 1989.

James, Vanessa. *The Genealogy of Greek Mythology: An Illustrated Family Tree of Greek Mythology from the First Gods to the Founders of Rome.* New York: Gotham Books, 2003.

Jebb, Richard Claverhouse. *The Attic Orators from Antiphon to Isaeus.* Chicago: University of Chicago Press, 2003.

Jensen, Frede, ed. and trans. *The Poetry of the Sicilian School.* New York and London: Garland, 1986.

Jerome, Saint. *Select Letters of St. Jerome.* Translated by Frederick Adam Wright. Cambridge, Mass.: Harvard University Press, 1999.

Johansen, Thomas. *Plato's Natural Philosophy: A Study of the Timaeus-Critias.* Cambridge, Mass.: Cambridge University Press, 2004.

Johnson, John William, trans. *The Epic of Son-Jara: A West African Tradition.* Edited by Fa-Digi Sisoko. Bloomington: Indiana University Press, 1992.

Johnson, Will. *Rumi: Gazing at the Beloved: The Radical Practice of Beholding the Divine.* Rochester, Vt.: Inner Traditions International, 2003.

Johnston, Basil H. *The Manitous: The Supernatural World of the Ojibway.* New York: HarperCollins, 1996.

———. *Tale of the Anishinaubaek.* Toronto: Royal Ontario Museum, 1993.

Johnstone, Christopher Lyle, ed. *Theory, Text, Context: Issues in Greek Rhetoric and Oratory.* Albany: State University of New York Press, 1996.

Jones, Alan. *Early Arabic Poetry, Vol. 2, Select Odes.* Reading, N.Y.: Garnet Publishing, 1996.

Jones, George Fenwick. *Walther von der Vogelweide.* New York: Twayne, 1968.

Jones, Gwyn. *A History of the Vikings.* Oxford, U.K.: Oxford University Press, 2001.

Jones, Howard. *The Epicurean Tradition.* New York: Routledge, 1989.

Josephus, Flavius. *Life of Josephus: Translation and Commentary.* Translated by Steve Mason. Boston: Brill, 2003.

———. *The Jewish War.* Translated by H. St. J. Thackeray. Cambridge, Mass.: Harvard University Press, 1997.

Jouanna, Jacques. *Hippocrates.* Translated by M. B. Debevoise. Baltimore, Md.: Johns Hopkins University Press, 2001.

JPS Hebrew-English Tanakh. Pocket Edition. Philadelphia: Jewish Publication Society, 2003.

Judson, Katharine Berry, ed. *Myths and Legends of the Pacific Northwest.* Introduction by Jay Miller. Lincoln: University of Nebraska Press, 1997. 93–95, 102–104.

Juvenal. *Juvenal in English.* Edited by Martin M. Winkler. New York: Penguin Books, 2001.

———. *The Sixteen Satires.* Translated by Peter Green. New York: Penguin, 1999.

Kabir. *The Kabir Book: Forty-Four of the Ecstatic Poems of Kabir.* Edited by Robert Bly. Boston: Beacon Press, 1993.

———. *Love Songs of Kabir.* Translated by G. N. Das. New Delhi: Abhinav Publications, 1992.

———. *Songs of Kabir from the Adi Granth.* Translated by Nirmal Dass. New York: State University of New York Press, 1991.

Kalidasa. *Kalidasa: Shakuntala and Other Writings.* Translated by Arthur W. Ryder. New York: Dutton, 1959.

———. *Malavikagnimitram of Kalidasa.* Translated by M. R. Kale. Delhi: Motilal Banarsidass, 1985.

———. *The Recognition of Sakuntala: A Play in Seven Acts.* Translated by W. J. Johnson. Oxford, U.K.: Oxford University Press, 2001.

———. *The Seasons: Kalidasa's Ritusamhara.* Translated by John T. Roberts. Tempe: Center for Asian Studies, Arizona State University, 1990.

Kamo no Chomei. *Hojoki: Visions of a Torn World.* Translated by Yasuhiko Morigushi and David Jenkins. Berkeley, Calif.: Stone Bridge Press, 1996.

———. *The Ten-Foot-Square Hut and Tales of the Heike.* Translated by A. L. Sadler. Westport, Conn.: Greenwood Press, 1970.

Karenga, Maulana. *The Book of Coming Forth by Day: The Ethics of the Declarations of Innocence.* Los Angeles: University of Sankore Press, 1990.

Kay, Sarah. *The Romance of the Rose.* London: Grant & Cutler, 1995.

Kazhdan, A.P. and Ann Wharton Epstein. *Change in Byzantine Culture in the Eleventh and Twelfth Centuries.* Berkeley: University of California Press, 1985.

Keene, Donald. "The Tale of the Gengi," in *Seeds in the Heart: Japanese Literature from Earliest Times to the Late Sixteenth Century.* New York: Henry Holt & Co., 1993, 477–514.

———. "The Izumi Shikibu Diary," in *Travelers of a Hundred Ages: The Japanese as Revealed Through 1,000 Years of Diaries.* New York: Columbia University Press, 1999, 36–39.

Kellogg, Robert, ed. *The Sagas of the Icelanders.* New York: Penguin 2001.

———. *The Sagas of the Icelanders: A Selection.* Preface by Jane Smiley. New York: Viking, 2000.

Kelly, Douglas. *Internal Difference and the Meanings in the Roman de la Rose.* Madison: University of Wisconsin Press, 1995.

Kennedy, Duncan F. *Rethinking Reality: Lucretius and the Textualization of Nature.* Ann Arbor: University of Michigan Press, 2002.

Kennedy, Elspeth. *Lancelot and the Grail: A Study of the Prose "Lancelot."* Oxford, U.K.: Clarendon Press, 1986.

Kennedy, George. *Quintilian.* New York: Twayne, 1969.

Kennedy, Philip F. *The Wine Song in Classical Arabic Poetry.* Oxford, U.K.: Oxford University Press, 1997.

Khansa', al-. *Selections from the Diwan of al Khansa'.* Translated by Arthur Wormhoudt. Oskaloosa, Iowa: William Penn College, 1977.

Khayyám, Omar. *Rubáiyát of Omar Khayyám.* Translated by Edward Fitzgerald. Edited by Christopher Decker. Charlottesville: University Press of Virginia, 1997.

———. *Rubáiyát of Omar Khayyám.* Edited and translated by Peter W. Avery and John Heath-Stubbs. Hammondsworth, U.K.: Penguin Books, 1981.

———. *Rubáiyát of Omar Khayyám: A Critical Edition.* Translated by Edward Fitzgerald. Edited by Christopher Decker. Charlottesville: University Press of Virginia, 1997.

Ki no Tsurayuki. *The Tosa Diary.* Translated by William N. Porter. Rutland, Vt.: Tuttle, 1981.

Kilpatrick, Jack F. and Anna G. *Friends of Thunder: Folktales of the Oklahoma Cherokees.* Norman: University of Oklahoma Press, 1995.

Kissam, Edward and Michael Schmidt, trans. *Poems of the Aztec Peoples.* Ypsilanti, Mich.: Bilingual Press, 1983.

Klinck, Anne L. *The Old English Elegies.* Buffalo, N.Y.: McGill–Queen's University Press, 1992.

Knapp, Bettina L. *Images of Japanese Women: A Westerner's View.* Troy, N.Y.: Whitston Publishing, 1992.

Knappert, Jan. *Survey of Swahili Islamic Epic Sagas.* New York: Edwin Mellen Press, 1999.

Kolatch, Alfred J. *Masters of the Talmud: Their Lives and Views.* Middle Village, N.Y.: Jonathan David Publishers, 2001.

Kovacs, Maureen Gallery, trans. *The Epic of Gilgamesh.* Stanford, Calif.: Stanford University Press, 1989.

Kreeft, Peter. *Philosophy 101 by Socrates: An Introduction to Philosophy.* Fort Collins, Colo.: Ignatius Press, 2002.

Krueger, Roberta L., ed. *The Cambridge Companion to Medieval Romance.* Cambridge, U.K.: Cambridge University Press, 2000.

Kulthum, Amr ibn. "Untitled Ode." In *The Seven Odes: The First Chapter in Arabic Literature.* Translated by A. J. Arberry. New York: Macmillan, 1957.

Kumiko Yamamoto. *Oral Background of Persian Epics: Storytelling and Poetry.* Leiden, Netherlands: Brill Academic Publishers, 2003.

Kunkel, John H. *Winged Soul: Plato's Autobiography.* Philadelphia: Xlibris, 2003.

Kuo-ch'ing Tu. *Li Ho.* Boston: Twayne, 1979.

Lacy, Norris J., ed. *Early French Tristan Poems.* 2 vols. Cambridge, U.K.: D. S. Brewer, 1998.

Lacy, Norris J. and Geoffrey Ashe with Debra N. Mancoff. *The Arthurian Handbook.* New York: Garland, 1997.

Lambdin, Laura Cooper and Robert Thomas. *Companion to Old and Middle English Literature.* Westport, Conn.: Greenwood Press, 2002.

Lankevich, George J., ed. *Wit and Wisdom of the Talmud: Proverbs, Sayings, and Parables for the Ages.* Garden City Park, N.Y.: Square One Publishers, 2001.

Laozi. *Lao Tzu Tao Te Ching.* Translated with an introduction by D. C. Lau. Middlesex, U.K.: Penguin Books, 1963.

———. *Tao Te Ching.* Foreword and notes by Stephen Mitchell. London: Macmillan, 1988.

Lapham, Lewis. *Theater of War: In Which the Republic Becomes an Empire.* New York: The New Press, 2003.

Larner, John. *Marco Polo and the Discovery of the World.* New Haven, Conn.: Yale University Press, 2001.

Larrington, Carolyne, trans. *The Poetic Edda.* Oxford, U.K.: Oxford University Press, 1999.

―――. *Il Tesoretto (The Little Treasure).* Translated and edited by Julia Bolton Holloway. New York: Garland, 1981.

Latini, Brunetto. *The Book of the Treasure (Li Livres dou Tresor).* Translated by Paul Barrette and Spurgeon Baldwin. New York: Garland, 1993.

Leaman, Oliver. *Averroës and His Philosophy.* Richmond, U.K.: Curzon, 1998.

Lefkowitz, Mary R. *The Lives of the Greek Poets.* Baltimore, Md.: Johns Hopkins University Press, 1981.

Le Gentil, Pierre. *The Chanson de Roland.* Translated by Frances F. Beer. Cambridge, Mass.: Harvard University Press, 1969.

Legge, James. *The Chinese Classics, with a translation, critical and exegetical notes, prolegomena, and copious indexes.* Hong Kong: Hong Kong University Press, 1960.

―――. *The Texts of Taoism. Sacred Books of the East.* Vol. 40. Mineola, N.Y.: Dover, 1962.

Leigh, Matthew. *Comedy and the Rise of Rome.* Oxford: Oxford University Press, 2004.

León-Portilla, Miguel. *Aztec Thought and Culture: A Study of the Ancient Nahuatl Mind.* Translated by Jack Emory Davis. Norman: University of Oklahoma Press, 1990.

―――. *Pre-Columbian Literatures of Mexico.* Translated by Grace Lobanov. Norman: University of Oklahoma Press, 1986.

―――, ed. *Fifteen Poets of the Aztec World.* Norman: University of Oklahoma Press, 1992.

Levi, Peter. *Virgil: His Life and Times.* New York: St. Martin's Press, 1998.

Levy, Ian Hideo, trans. *The Ten Thousand Leaves.* Princeton, N.J.: Princeton University Press, 1981.

Levy, Jerrold E. *In the Beginning: The Navajo Genesis.* Berkeley: University of California Press, 1998.

Levy, Reuben. *An Introduction to Persian Literature.* New York: Columbia University Press, 1969.

―――, trans. *The Epic of the Kings; Shah-nama, the National Epic of Persia.* Chicago: University of Chicago Press, 1967.

Lewis, Franklin D. *Rumi—Past and Present, East and West: The Life, Teachings and Poetry of Jalâl al-Din Rumi.* Oxford, U.K.: Oneworld Publications, 2004.

Li Bai. *Li Pai: 200 Selected Poems.* Translated by Rewi Alley. Hong Kong: Joint Publishing Co., 1980.

―――. *Selected Poems of Li Bo.* Translated by David Hinton. New York: New Directions, 1996.

Li He. *Goddesses, Ghosts, and Demons: The Collected Poems of Li He.* Translated by J. G. Frodsham. San Francisco: North Point Press, 1983.

―――. *Poems of the Late Tang.* Translated by A. C. Graham. New York: Penguin, 1977.

Li Qingzhao. *Li Ch'ing-chao: Complete Poems.* Translated by Kenneth Rexroth and Ling Chung. New York: New Directions, 1979.

―――. *The Lotus Lovers: Poems and Songs.* Translated by Sam Hamill. St. Paul, Minn.: Coffee House Press, 1985.

―――. *Plum Blossom: Poems of Li Ching-chao.* Translated by James Cryer. Chapel Hill, N.C.: Carolina Wren Press, 1984.

Li Shang-yin. *The Poetry of Li Shang-yin, Ninth-Century Baroque Chinese Poet.* James J. Y. Liu. Chicago: University of Chicago Press, 1969.

Lichtenstadter, Ilse. *Introduction to Classical Arabic Literature.* New York: Twayne, 1974.

Lillegard, Norman. *On Epictetus.* Florence, Ky.: Wadsworth Publishers, 2001.

Lim, Joyce, trans. *100 Parables of Zen.* Singapore: Asiapac Books, 1997.

Lindheim, Sara H., ed. *Mail and Female: Epistolary Narrative and Desire in Ovid's Heroides.* Madison: University of Wisconsin Press, 2003.

Lindow, John. *Norse Mythology: A Guide to the Gods, Heroes, Rituals, and Beliefs.* Oxford, U.K.: Oxford University Press, 2002.

Lings, Martin. *Muhammad: His Life Based on the Earliest Sources.* New York: Inner Traditions International, 1983.

Liu, James J. Y. *Major Lyricists of the Northern Sung.* Princeton, N.J.: Princeton University Press, 1974.

Liu, James T. C. *Reform in Sung China: Wang An-Shih (1021–1086) and His New Policies.* Cambridge, Mass.: Harvard University Press, 1959.

Livy. *The Early History of Rome.* Translated by Aubrey De Selincourt. Introduction by R. M. Ogilvie. New York: Penguin Classics, 2000.

———. *Rome and the Mediterranean. Books XXXI–XLV of "The History of Rome from Its Foundation."* Translated by Henry Bettenson. Introduction by A. H. McDonald. Hammondsworth, U.K.: Penguin, 1976.

Lloyd, G. E. R. *Early Greek Science: Thales to Aristotle.* New York: W. W. Norton, 1970.

Loc Dinh Pham. *A Glimpse of Vietnamese Oral Literature: Mythology, Tales, Folklore.* Philadelphia: Xlibris, 2002.

Locke, Frederick W. *The Quest for the Holy Grail: A Literary Study of a Thirteenth-Century French Romance.* New York: AMS Press, 1967.

Lodge, Anthony and Kenneth Varty. *Earliest Branches of the Roman de Renart.* New Alyth, Scotland: Lochee Publications, 1989.

Loewe, Raphael. *Ibn Gabirol.* London: Weidenfeld & Nicholson, 1989.

Lofmark, Carl. *Bards and Heroes: An Introduction to Bardic Poetry.* Cribyn, Wales: Llanerch Press, 1989.

Long, A. A. *Epictetus: A Stoic and Socratic Guide to Life.* Oxford, U.K.: Oxford University Press, 2002.

Longinus. *On Great Writing (On the Sublime).* Translated by G. M. A. Grube. Indianapolis, Ind.: Hackett, 1991.

Longus. *Daphnis and Chloe.* Translated by Paul Turner. New York: Penguin Books, 1989.

Lorris, Guillaume de. *The Romance of the Rose: Guillaume de Lorris and Jean de Meun.* Translated by Frances Horgan. Oxford, U.K.: Oxford University Press, 1999.

———. *The Romance of the Rose.* Translated by Harry W. Robbins. Edited by Charles W. Dunn. Syracuse, N.Y.: Syracuse University Press, 2002.

Lorris, Guillaume de, and Jean de Meun. *The Romance of the Rose.* Translated by Charles Dahlberg. Princeton, N.J.: Princeton University Press, 1995.

Lucan. *Civil War.* Translated by Susan H. Braud. Oxford, U.K.: Oxford University Press, 1992.

Lucian. *Lucian: A Selection.* Edited by M. D. MacLeod. Warminster, U.K.: Aris & Phillips, 1991.

———. *Selected Satires of Lucian.* Translated by Lionel Casson. New York: W. W. Norton, 1968.

———. *True History.* Translated by Paul Turner. Bloomington: University of Indiana Press, 1958.

Lucretius. *De Rerum Natura: The Poem on Nature.* Translated by C. H. Sisson. London: Routledge, 2003.

———. *On the Nature of Things.* Translated by W. E. Leonard. Mineola, N.Y.: Dover Publications, 2004.

Luomala, Katherine. *Voices on the Wind: Polynesian Myths and Chants.* Honolulu: Bishop Museum Press, 1955.

Luria, Maxwell. *A Reader's Guide to the Roman de la Rose.* Hamden, Conn.: Archon Books, 1982.

Lynn, Richard J. *Guide to Chinese Poetry and Drama.* Boston: G. K. Hall, 1984.

Lysias. *Lysias.* (The Oratory of Classical Greece Series, 2). Translated by S. C. Todd. Austin: University of Texas Press, 1999.

———. *Lysias Orations I, III.* Commentary by Ruth Scodel. Bryn Mawr, Pa.: Thomas Library, Bryn Mawr College, 1986.

———. *Selected Speeches.* Edited by C. Carey. Cambridge, U.K.: Cambridge University Press, 1989.

Maalouf, Amin. *The Crusades through Arab Eyes.* New York: Schocken Books, 1989.

MacDowell, Douglas M. *Aristophanes and Athens.* Oxford, U.K.: Oxford University Press, 1995.

Machiavelli, Niccolò. *Discourses on Livy.* Oxford's World Classics Series. Translated by Julia Conaway Bondanella and Peter Bondanella. Oxford, U.K.: Oxford University Press, 2003.

MacKie, Hillary Susan. *Graceful Errors: Pindar and the Performance of Praise.* Ann Arbor: University of Michigan Press, 2003.

MacQueen, Bruce D. *Myth, Rhetoric, and Fiction: A Reading of Longus's Daphnis and Chloë.* Lincoln: University of Nebraska Press, 1991.

Macrone, Michael. *By Jove! Brush Up Your Mythology.* New York: HarperCollins, 1992.

Madden, Thomas F. *A Concise History of the Crusades.* Lanham, Md.: Rowman & Littlefield Publishing, 1999.

Maddox, Donald. *The Arthurian Romances of Chrétien de Troyes: Once and Future Fictions.* Cambridge, U.K.: Cambridge University Press, 1991.

Maier, John, ed. *Gilgamesh: A Reader.* Wauconda, Ill.: Bolchazy-Carducci, 1997.

Maimonides, Moses. *Codex Maimuni: Moses Maimonides' Code of Law: The Illuminated Pages of the Kaufmann Mishneh Torah.* Budapest: Corniva, 1984.

———. *The Guide to the Perplexed.* Vols. One and Two. Translated by Shlomo Pines. Chicago: University of Chicago Press, 1974.

———. *Rambam, Readings in the Philosophy of Moses Maimonides.* Translated by Lenn E. Goodman. Los Angeles: Gee Tee Bee, 1985.

Malotki, Ekkehart. *Gullible Coyote: Una'ihu.* Tucson: University of Arizona Press, 1985.

———. *Hopi Animal Stories.* Lincoln: University of Nebraska Press, 2001.

———, ed. *Hopi Coyote Tales: Istutuwutsi.* Translated by Michael Lomatuway'ma. Lincoln: University of Nebraska Press, 1990.

Malotki, Ekkehart and Ken Gary. *Hopi Stories of Witchcraft, Shamanism, and Magic.* Lincoln: University of Nebraska Press, 2001.

Malotki, Ekkehart and Michael Lomatuway'ma. *Hopi Coyote Tales: Istutuwutsi.* Lincoln: University of Nebraska Press, 1984.

Mann, Mary Anneeta. *Construction of Tragedy: Hubris.* Bloomington, Ind.: AuthorHouse, 2004.

Mann, Robert. *Lances Sing: A Study of the Igor Tale.* Columbus, Ohio: Slavica, 1990.

Marenbon, John. *Boethius.* Oxford, U.K.: Oxford University Press, 2003.

———. *The Philosophy of Peter Abelard.* Cambridge, U.K.: Cambridge University Press, 1999.

Marie de France. *The Lais of Marie de France.* Translated by Glyn Burgess. New York: Penguin, 1999.

Marsilio, Maria S. *Farming and Poetry in Hesiod's Works and Days.* Lanham, Md.: University Press of America, 2000.

Martial. *The Epigrams.* Translated by James Michie. New York: Penguin Books, 1973.

———. *Select Epigrams.* Translated by Lindsay Watson, et al. New York: Cambridge University Press, 2003.

Martin, Hubert. *Alcaeus.* New York: Twayne Publishers, 1972.

Mason, Herbert, trans. *Gilgamesh: A Verse Narrative.* Boston: Houghton Mifflin, 2003.

Mathers, E. P. and J. C. Mardrus, eds. *The Book of Thousand Nights and One Night.* 4 vols. New York: Routledge, 1994.

Matilal, Bimal Krishna. *Moral Dilemmas in the Mahabharata.* Shimla: Indian Institute of Advanced Study, 1989.

Matthews, Caitlin. *The Celtic Tradition.* Shaftesbury, Dorset, U.K.: Element, 1995.

Matthews, John. *Taliesin: Shamanism and the Bardic Mysteries in Britain and Ireland.* Rochester, Vt.: Inner Traditions International, 2002.

———, ed. *The Bardic Source Book: Inspirational Legacy and Teachings of the Ancient Celts.* Poole, Dorset, U.K.: Blandford Press, 1999.

Mayer, Roland. *Seneca: Phaedra.* London: Gerald Duckworth, 2003.

McCulloch, Florence, trans. *Bestiaries in Mediaeval Latin and French.* Chapel Hill: University of North Carolina, 1956.

———. *Medieval Latin and French Bestiaries.* Chapel Hill: University of North Carolina, 1962.

McCulloh, William E. *Longus.* New York: Twayne, 1970.

McCullough, William and Helen C. McCullough, trans. *A Tale of Flowering Fortunes: Annals of Japanese Aristocratic Life in the Heian Period [Eiga monogatari].* 2 vols. Stanford, Calif.: Stanford University Press, 1980.

McInerny, Ralph. *A First Glance at Thomas Aquinas: Handbook for Peeping Thomists.* Notre Dame, Ind.: University of Notre Dame Press, 1990.

McIntyre, Ann. *Culture and Society in Lucian.* Cambridge, Mass.: Harvard University Press, 1986.

McLynn, Neil B. *Ambrose of Milan: Church and Court in a Christian Capital.* Berkeley: University of California Press, 1994.

McNeese, Tim, ed. *Myths of Native America.* New York: Four Walls Eight Windows, 2003.

McNeilly, Mark. *Sun Tzu and the Art of Business: Six Strategic Principles for Managers.* Washington, D.C.: National Defense University Press, 1997.

———. *Sun Tzu and the Art of Modern Warfare.* New York: Oxford University Press, 2001.

McRae, John R. *Seeing through Zen: Encounter, Transformation, and Genealogy in Chinese Chan Buddhism.* Berkeley: University of California Press, 2004.

Meade, Marion. *Stealing Heaven: The Love Story of Heloise and Abelard.* New York: Soho Press, 1994.

Meier, Christian. *Caesar: A Biography.* Translated by David McLintock. New York: Basic Books, 1982.

Meisami, Julie S. *Medieval Persian Court Poetry.* Princeton, N.J.: Princeton University Press, 1987.

Mellor. Ronald. *Tacitus.* London: Routledge, 1994.

Menander. *The Bad-Tempered Man (Dyskolos).* Translated by Stanley Ireland. Warminster, U.K.: Aris & Phillips Ltd., 1995.

———. *Four Plays of Menander: The Hero, Epitrepontes, Periceiromene, Samia.* Edited by Edward Capps. Berlin: Melissa Media, 1981.

———. *Menander: The Grouch, Desperately Seeking Justice, Closely Cropped Locks, the Girl from Samos, the Shield.* Edited by Palmer Bovie, et al. Philadelphia: University of Pennsylvania Press, 1998.

———. *Menander: The Plays and Fragments.* Translated by Maurice Balme. Oxford, U.K.: Oxford University Press, 2002.

Mendell, Clarence W. *Latin Poetry: The New Poets and The Augustans.* New Haven, Conn., and London: Yale University Press, 1965.

Mendelsohn, Daniel. *Gender and the City in Euripides' Political Plays.* Oxford, U.K.: Oxford University Press, 2003.

Merwin, W. S. *The Mays of Ventadorn.* Washington, D.C.: National Geographic Society, 2002.

Michelini, Ann N., ed. *Plato as Author: The Rhetoric of Philosophy.* Leiden, Netherlands: Brill Academic Publishers, 2003.

Mickel, Emanuel J., Jr. *Marie de France.* New York: Twayne, 1974.

Mikalson, Jon D. *Herodotus and Religion in the Persian Wars.* Chapel Hill: University of North Carolina Press, 2003.

Miles, Margaret Ruth. *Plotinus on Body and Beauty: Society, Philosophy, and Religion in Third-Century Rome.* Oxford, U.K.: Blackwell Publishers, 1999.

Milhaven, John Giles. *Hadewijch and Her Sisters: Other Ways of Loving and Knowing.* Albany: State University of New York Press, 1993.

Miller, Barbara Stoler, trans. *The Bhagavad-Gita: Krishna's Counsel in Time of War.* New York: Bantam Books, 1986.

Miller, Dean A. *Epic Hero.* Baltimore, Md.: Johns Hopkins University Press, 2002.

Miller, Katherine. *St. George, A Christmas Mummer's Play.* New York: Houghton Mifflin, 1967.

Mills, Maldwyn, Jennifer Fellows and Carol M. Meale. *Romance in Medieval England.* Cambridge, U.K.: D. S. Brewer, 1991.

Mills, Mary Vandegrift. *Pligrimage Motif in the Works of the Medieval German Author Hartmann Von Aue.* Lewiston, N.Y.: Edwin Mellen Press, 1996.

Minor, Robert N. *Bhagavad-Gita: An Exegetical Commentary.* Columbia, Mo.: South Asia Books, 1982.

Mlodinow, Leonard. *Euclid's Window: The Story of Geometry from Parallel Lines to Hyperspace.* New York: Simon & Schuster, 2002.

Monaghan, Patricia. *The Red-Haired Girl from the Bog: Celtic Spirituality and the Goddess in Ireland.* Novato, Calif.: New World Library, 2003.

Mooney, James. *Cherokee Animal Tales.* Edited by George F. Scheer. New York: Holiday House, 1968.

———. *History, Myths, and Sacred Formulas of the Cherokees.* Asheville, N.C.: Bright Mountain Books, 1992.

———. *Myths of the Cherokee.* Mineola: N.Y.: Dover Publications, 1995.

Moore, Timothy J. "Terence and Roman New Comedy." In *Greek and Roman Comedy: Translations and Interpretations of Four Representative Plays.* Translated by George F. Franko, et al. Edited by Shawn O'Bryhim. Austin: University of Texas Press, 2001.

———. *The Theater of Plautus: Playing to the Audience.* Austin: University of Texas Press, 1998.

Morehouse, Ward, and Gregory A. Minahan. *The Caedmon School: An Anecdotal History and Appreciation.* Philadelphia: Xlibris, 2003.

Moser, Charles, ed. *The Cambridge History of Russian Literature.* Cambridge, U.K.: Cambridge University Press, 1992.

Mossman, Judith, ed. *Plutarch and His Intellectual World.* London: Duckworth, 1997.

Mother of Fujiwara Michitsuna. *The Kagero Diary: A Woman's Autobiographical Text from Tenth-Century Japan.* Translated by Sonja Arntzen. Ann Arbor, Mich.: Center for Japanese Studies, 1997.

Motto, Anna Lydia. *Seneca.* New York: Twayne, 1973.

Mowatt, D. G., trans. *The Nibelungenlied.* London: Dover Publications, 2001.

Muhammad. *The Koran.* Translated by J. M. Rodwell. London: J. M. Dent, 1994.

Murasaki Shikibu. *The Diary of Lady Murasaki.* Translation and introduction by Richard Bowring. New York: Penguin, 1996.

———. *Murasaki Shikibu, Her Diary and Poetic Memoirs: A Translation and Study.* Translated by Richard Bowring. Princeton, N.J.: Princeton University Press, 1982.

———. *The Tale of Genji.* Translated by Edward G. Seidensticker. New York: Knopf, 1978.

Murray, David. *Forked Tongues: Speech, Writing, and Representation in North American Indian Texts.* Bloomington: Indiana University Press, 1991.

Mutanabbi, al-. *The Diwan of Abu Tayyib Ahmad ibn al Husain al Mutannabi.* Translated by Arthur Wormholdt. Oskaloosa, Iowa: William Penn College, 1995.

———. *Poems of al-Mutanabbi.* Translated by A. J. Arberry. Cambridge, U.K.: Cambridge University Press, 1967.

Nabokov, Vladimir, trans. *The Song of Igor's Campaign: An Epic of the Twelfth Century.* New York: Ardis, 1989.

Niane, D. T. *Sundiata: An Epic of Old Mali.* Translated by G. D. Pickett. London: Longman, 1969.

Nichols, Aidan. *Discovering Aquinas: An Introduction to His Life, Work, and Influence.* Grand Rapids, Mich.: Eerdmans, 2003.

Nicholson, Reynold A. *A Literary History of the Arabs.* New York: Kegan Paul International, 1998.

Nizami. *The Haft Paykar: A Medieval Persian Romance.* Translated by Julie S. Meisami. Oxford, U.K.: Oxford University Press, 1995.

———. *Lailai and Majnuan: A Poem from the Original Persian of Nizami.* Translated by James Atkinson. New Delhi: Asian Publication Services, 2001.

———. *Layla and Majnun.* Translated by Colin Turner. London: Blake Publishing, 1997.

———. *Story of the Seven Princesses.* Translated by G. Hill. Edited by R. Gelpke. Mystic, Conn.: Verry, Lawrence, Inc., 1976.

Norinaga, Motoori. *Kojiki-Den.* Translated by Ann Wehmeyer. Ithaca, N.Y.: Cornell University Press, 1997.

O'Cuilleanain, Cormac, ed., et al. *Patterns in Dante.* Dublin: Four Courts Press, 2004.

O'Donoghue, Bernard. *The Courtly Love Tradition.* Manchester: Manchester University Press, 1982.

O'Flaherty, Wendy Doniger, trans. *The Rig Veda: An Anthology.* New York: Penguin, 1981.

O'Gorman, Ellen. *Irony and Misreading in the Annals of Tacitus.* New York: Cambridge University Press, 2000.

O'Grady, Desmond. *The Seven Arab Odes.* London: Agenda & Editions Charitable Trust, 1990.

O'Keefe, Katherine O'Brien, ed. *Old English Shorter Poems: Basic Readings.* New York: Garland Publishing Inc., 1994.

Okpewo, Isidore. *African Oral Literature: Backgrounds, Character, and Continuity.* Indianapolis: Indiana University Press, 1992.

Olivelle, Patrick, trans. *The Panchatantra: The Book of India's Folk Wisdom.* Oxford, U.K.: Oxford University Press, 1997.

Olschki, Leonardo. *Marco Polo's Asia: An Introduction to His "Description of the World" called "Il milione."* Translated by John A. Scott. Berkeley: University of California Press, 1960.

O'Meara, John Joseph. *The Young Augustine: The Growth of St. Augustine's Mind Up to His Conversion.* Revised ed. Staten Island, N.Y.: Alba House, 2001.

Ono no Komachi. *Japan's Poetess of Love Dream and Longing, Ono no Komachi: 117 poems.* Translated by Howard S. Levy. Yokohama, Japan: Warm-Soft Village Press, 1984.

———. *Ono No Komachi: Poems, Stories, and Noh Plays.* Translated by Roy E. Teele. Edited by James J. Wilhelm. London: Taylor & Francis, 1993.

Ophuijsen, Johannes M. Van and Marlein Van Raalte, eds. *Theophrastus: Reappraising the Sources.* Somerset, N.J.: Transaction, 1998.

Otomo Yakamochi. *Written on Water: Five Hundred Poems from the Man'yoshu.* Translated by Takashi Kojima. Rutland, Vt.: Charles E. Tuttle, 1995.

Ouyang Xiu. *A Lute of Jade.* Translated by L. Cranmer-Byng. IndyPublish.com, 2003.

Ovid. *The Art of Love.* Translated by James Michie. Introduction by David Malouf. London: Random House, 2002.

———. *Fasti.* Edited by A. J. Boyle and R. D. Woodard. New York: Penguin Classics, 2000.

———. *Metamorphoses.* Translated by A. D. Melville. Oxford, U.K.: Oxford University Press, 1998.

———. *The Metamorphoses.* Translated by Horace Gregory. New York: The Viking Press, 1958.

———. *Metamorphoses.* Translated by Rolfe Humphries. Bloomington: Indiana University Press, 1955.

———. *Ovid: Selections from Ars Amatoria, Remedia Amoris.* Edited by Graves Haydon Thompson. Wauconda, Ill.: Bolchazy-Carducci, 1999.

———. *Ovid: Selected Poems.* London: Phoenix House, 2004.

Owen, D. D. R., trans. *The Romance of Reynard the Fox.* Oxford, U.K.: Oxford University Press, 1994.

Owen, Stephen. *The Poetry of Meng Chiao and Han Yü.* New Haven, Conn.: Yale University Press, 1975.

Pachocinski, Ryszard. *Proverbs of Africa: Human Nature in the Nigerian Oral Tradition.* St. Paul, Minn.: Professors World Peace Academy, 1996.

Padilla, Stan. *Deer Dance: Yaqui Legends of Life.* Lincoln, Neb.: Book Publishing Company, 1998.

Page, Jake, and David Adams Leeming. *The Mythology of Native North America.* Norman: University of Oklahoma Press, 2000.

Painter, Muriel Thayer. *With Good Heart: Yaqui Beliefs and Ceremonies in Pascua Village.* Edited by Edward Spicer and Wilma Kaemlein. Tucson: University of Arizona Press, 1986.

Palmer, Michael. *Love of Glory and the Common Good: Aspects of the Political Thought of Thucydides.* Lanham, Md.: Rowman & Littlefield, 2001.

Palsson, Hermann, and Paul Edwards, trans. *Egil's Saga.* New York: Penguin Classics, 1977.

———. *Seven Viking Romances.* New York: Penguin Classics, 1985.

Palumbo, Arthur E., Jr. *The Dead Sea Scrolls and the Personages of Early Christianity.* New York: Algora Publishing, 2004.

Pandey, Rajyashree. *Writing and Renunciation in Medieval Japan: The Works of the Poet-Priest Kamo No Chomei.* Ann Arbor: University of Michigan Center for Japanese Studies, 1997.

Parry, Donald W., Jr., and Emmanuel Tov, eds. *Dead Sea Scrolls Reader: Exegetical Texts.* Boston: Brill Academic Publishers, 2004.

Parry, John J., and Robert A. Caldwell. "Geoffrey of Monmouth." In *Arthurian Literature in the Middle Ages: A Collaborative History.* Edited by Roger S. Loomis. Oxford, U.K.: Oxford University Press, 1985.

Parviz, Morewedge. *The Mystical Philosophy of Avicenna.* Binghamton, N.Y.: Global Publications, 2001.

Paterson, Linda A. *The World of the Troubadours: Medieval Occitan Society ca. 1100–ca. 1300.* Cambridge, U.K.: Cambridge University Press, 1995.

Pausanias. *Pausanias' Guide to Ancient Greece.* Translated by Christopher Habicht. Berkeley: University of California Press, 1985.

———. *Pausanias' Description of Greece.* Translated with a commentary by J. G. Frazer. New York: Biblo and Tannen, 1965.

Peabody, Berkeley. *Winged Word: A Study in the Technique of Ancient Greek Oral Composition as Seen Principally through Hesiod's Works and Days.* Albany: State University of New York Press, 1975.

Peck, George T. *The Fool of God: Jacopone da Todi.* Tuscaloosa: University of Alabama Press, 1980.

Peddie, John. *Alfred: Warrior King.* Gloucestershire: Sutton Publishing, 2001.

Pelling, Christopher B. *Plutarch and History.* Cardiff: The Classical Press of Wales, 2002.

Pensom, Roger. *Aucassin et Nicolette: The Poetry of Gender and Growing Up in the French Middle Ages.* New York: Peter Lang, 1999.

Perry, Ben Edwin. *Babrius and Phaedrus.* Cambridge, Mass.: Harvard University Press, 1965.

Peters, Edward M., ed. *The First Crusade.* Philadelphia: University of Pennsylvania Press, 1998.

Petroff, Elizabeth, ed. *Medieval Women's Visionary Literature.* New York: Oxford University Press, 1986.

Petronius, Gaius. *The Satyricon.* Translated by P. G. Walsh. New York: Oxford University Press, 1996.

Peynetsa, Andrew, and Walter Sanchez. *Finding the Center: The Art of Zuni Storytelling.* Translated by Dennis Tedlock. Lincoln: University of Nebraska Press, 1999.

Pfeijffer, Ilja Leonard, and Simon R. Slings, eds. *One Hundred Years of Bacchylides: Proceedings of a Colloquim Held at the Virje Universeieit Amsterdam.* Amsterdam: VU Boekhandel/Uitgeverij, 2004.

Phaedrus. *The Fables of Phaedrus.* Translated by P. F. Widdows. Austin: University of Texas Press, 1992.

———. *The Poetical Works of Christopher Smart: A Poetical Translation of the Fables of Phaedrus.* Vol 6. Edited by Karina Williamson. Oxford, U.K.: Clarendon Press, 1996.

Philippi, Donald L., trans. *Kojiki.* New York: Columbia University Press, 1982.

Pickthall, Mohammed Marmaduke, trans. *The Glorious Koran.* Elmhurst, N.Y.: Tahrike Tarsile Qu'ran, 2000.

Pindar. *The Odes of Pindar.* Translated by Sir John Sandys. Cambridge, Mass.: Harvard University Press, 1957.

———. *Pindar: Olympian Odes, Pythian Odes.* Edited and translated by William H. Race. Cambridge, Mass.: Harvard University Press, 1997.

———. *Pindar's Victory Songs.* Translated by Frank J. Nisetich. Baltimore, Md.: Johns Hopkins University Press, 1980.

Plato. *Apology.* Edited by James J. Helm. Wauconda, Ill.: Bolchazy-Carducci, 1997.

———. *The Complete Works of Plato.* Edited by John M. Cooper and D. S. Hutchinson. Indianapolis, Ind.: Hackett Publishing, 1997.

———. *Phaedo.* Translated by G. M. A. Grube. Indianapolis, Ind.: Hackett, 1976.

———. *The Republic of Plato.* Translated by Allan Bloom. New York: HarperCollins, 1991.

Plautus, Titus Maccius. *Plautus: Amphitruo.* Edited by David M. Christenson. Cambridge, U.K.: Cambridge University Press, 2000.

———. *Four Comedies.* Translated by Erich Segal. New York: Oxford University Press, 1996.

Pliny the Elder. *Natural History: A Selection.* Translated by John F. Healy. New York: Penguin Books, 1991.

Pliny the Younger. *Letters of the Younger Pliny.* Translated by Betty Radice. New York: Penguin Classics, 1990.

Plotinus. *The Enneads.* Translated by Stephen MacKenna. Edited by John Dillon. New York: Penguin Books, 1991.

Plummer, Charles. *The Life and Times of Alfred the Great.* New York: Haskell House, 1970.

Plutarch. *Essays.* Edited by Ian Kidd. New York: Penguin Classics, 1993.

———. *The Life of Alexander the Great.* Translated by John Dryden. Introduction by Victor Davis Hanson. New York: Random House, 2004.

———. *Plutarch: The Lives of the Noble Grecians and Romans.* Translated by John Dryden. Edited by Arthur Hugh Clough. New York: Random House, 1992.

Poag, James F. *Wolfram von Eschenbach.* New York: Twayne, 1972.

Poignant, Roslyn. *Oceanic Mythology: The Myths of Polynesia, Micronesia, Melanesia, Australia.* London: Paul Hamlyn, 1967.

Polano, H., trans. *Talmud.* Whitefish, Mont.: Kessinger, 2003.

Pollard, D. E., ed. *Translation and Creation: Readings of Western Literature in Early Modern China.* Amsterdam: Benjamins, 1988.

Polo, Marco. *Travels.* New York: Konemann Publishers, 2000.

———. *The Travels of Marco Polo.* Edited by Manuel Komroff. New York: Liveright Publishing, 2003.

———. *The Travels of Marco Polo: The Complete Yule-Cordier Edition.* Vol. 1. Edited by Henry Yule and Henri Cordier. Mineola, N.Y.: Dover, 1993.

Porphyry. *Porphyry's Against the Christians: The Literary Remains.* Translated by R. Joseph Hauffmann. Buffalo, N.Y.: Prometheus Books, 1994.

———. *Porphyry's Launching-Points to the Realm of the Mind: An Introduction to the Neoplatonic Philosophy of Plotinus.* Translated by Kenneth Sylvan Guthrie. Grand Rapids, Mich.: Phanes Press, 1989.

Porter, John R. *Studies in Euripides' Orestes.* Leiden, Netherlands: Brill Academic Publishers, 1994.

Poulakos, Takis and David J. Depew. *Isocrates and Civic Education.* Austin: University of Texas Press, 2004.

Powell, Barry. *Homer.* Oxford, U.K.: Blackwell, 2003.

Pratt, Norman T. *Seneca's Drama.* Chapel Hill: University of North Carolina Press, 2001.

Press, Alan R., ed. and trans. *Anthology of Troubadour Lyric Poetry.* Austin: University of Texas Press, 1971.

Prevas, John. *Xenophon's March: Into the Lair of the Persian Lion.* Cambridge, Mass.: Da Capo Press, 2002.

Proclus. *Fragments That Remain of the Lost Writings of Proclus.* Translated by Thomas Taylor. Whitefish, Mont.: Kessinger Publishing, 2003.

———. *Proclus of Constantinople and the Cult of the Virgin in the Late Antiquity: Homilies 1–5, Texts and Translations.* Translated by Nicholas Constas. Leiden, Netherlands: Brill Academic Publishers, 2003.

Propertius, Sextus. *Propertius: Elegies.* Edited by G. P. Goold. Cambridge, Mass.: Harvard University Press, 1990.

———. *Propertius: Elegies.* Translated by R. I. V. Hodge and R. A. Buttimore. London: Bristol Classical Press, 2002.

Prosser, Eleanor. *Drama and Religion in the English Mystery Plays: A Re-Evaluation.* Palo Alto, Calif.: Stanford University Press, 1961.

Qu Yuan. *Li Sao, A Poem on Relieving Sorrows.* Translated by Jerah Johnson. Miami, Fla.: Olivant Press, 1959.

———. *Tian Wen: A Chinese Book of Origins.* Translated by Stephen Field. New York: New Directions, 1986.

Quam, Alvina, trans. *The Zunis: Self-Portrayals by the Zuni People.* Albuquerque: University of New Mexico Press, 1972.

Quinones, Ricardo J. *Dante Alighieri.* Boston: Twayne, 1979.

Quintilian. *Quintilian on the Teaching of Speaking and Writing.* Edited by James J. Murphy. Carbondale: Southern Illinois University Press, 1987.

———. *Quintilian: The Orator's Education, Books 3–5.* Edited by Jeffrey Henderson and D. A. Russell. Cambridge, Mass.: Harvard University Press, 2002.

Radin, Paul. *The Trickster: A Study in American Indian Mythology.* New York: Philosophical Library, 1956.

Rajan, Chandra, trans. *The Panchatantra.* London: Penguin Books, 1993.

Ramirez, Susan Berry Brill de. *Contemporary American Indian Literatures and the Oral Tradition.* Tucson: University of Arizona Press, 1999.

Rao, I. Panduranga. *Valmiki.* New Delhi, India: Sahitya Akademi, 1994.

Regalado, Nancy Freeman. *Poetic Patterns in Rutebeuf: A Study in Noncourtly Poetic Modes of the Thirteenth Century.* New Haven, Conn.: Yale University Press, 1970.

Reiss, Edmund. *Boethius.* Boston: Twayne, 1982.

Reynaert, J. "Hadewijch: Mystic Poetry and Courtly Love." In *Medieval Dutch Literature in Its European Context.* Edited by Erik Kooper, 208–225. Cambridge, U.K.: Cambridge University Press, 1994.

Reynolds, Margaret. *The Sappho History.* New York: St. Martin's Press, 2003.

Richard, Jean. *The Crusades, ca. 1071–ca. 1291.* Translated by Jean Birrell. Cambridge, U.K.: Cambridge University Press, 1999.

Riehle, Wolfgang. *Shakespeare, Plautus and the Humanist Tradition.* Rochester, N.Y.: Boydell & Brewer, 1991.

Ritter, Hellmut. *The Ocean of the Soul: Men, the World and God in the Stories of Farid al-Din 'Attar.* Leiden, Netherlands: Brill Academic Publishers, 2003.

Roberts, David and Jon Krakauer. *Iceland: Land of the Sagas.* New York: Villard, 1998.

Roberts, W. Rhys. *Dionysius of Halicarnassus: The Three Literary Letters.* New York: Garland Publishers, 1988.

Robinson, B. W. *Persian Book of Kings: An Epitome of the Shahnama of Firdawsi.* London: Taylor & Francis, 2002.

Robinson, Charles Alexander. *The Tropes and Figures of Isaeus: A Study of His Rhetorical Art.* Princeton, N.J.: C.S. Robinson & Co., 1901.

Robinson, Ira and Lawrence Kaplan. *The Thought of Moses Maimonides: Philosophical and Legal Studies.* Studies in the History of Philosophy, vol. 17. Lewiston, N.Y.: Edwin Mellen Press, 1991.

Rodinson, Maxime. *Muhammad.* New York: The New Press, 1980.

Rood, Tim. *Thucydides: Narrative and Explanation.* Oxford, U.K.: Oxford University Press, 1998.

Rose, Martial, ed. *The Wakefield Mystery Plays.* New York: W. W. Norton & Co., 1969.

Rosenmeyer, Patricia. *The Poetics of Imitation: Anacreon and the Anacreontic Tradition.* Cambridge, U.K.: Cambridge University Press, 1992.

Rosner, Fred, and Samuel S. Kottek, eds. *Moses Maimonides: Physician, Scientist, and Philosopher.* Northvale, N.J.: Jason Aronson, 1993.

Rossi, Andreola. *Contexts of War: Manipulation of Genre in Virgilian Battle Narrative.* Ann Arbor, Mich.: University of Michigan Press, 2003.

Rougemont, Denis de. *Love in the Western World.* Translated by Wendy Doniger and Montgomery Belgion. New York: Pantheon Books, 1956.

Rubenstein, Jeffrey L. *The Culture of the Babylonian Talmud.* Baltimore, Md.: Johns Hopkins University Press, 2003.

Rubeinstein, Richard E. *Aristotle's Children: How Christians, Muslims, and Jews Rediscovered Ancient Wisdom and Illuminated the Dark Ages.* New York: Harcourt, 2003.

Rudel, Jaufré. *The Poetry of Cercamon and Jaufré Rudel.* Translated and edited by George Wolf and Roy Rosenstein. New York: Garland, 1983.

———. *Songs of Jaufré Rudel, Vol. 41.* Translated by Rupert T. Pickens. Toronto: Pontifical Institute of Mediaeval Studies, 1978.

Rumi, Jalaloddin. *The Book of Love: Poems of Ecstasy and Longing.* Translated by Coleman Barks. New York: HarperCollins, 2003.

———. *Mathnawi.* Translated by E. H. Whinfield. London: Watkins Publishing, 2002.

———. *The Soul of Rumi: A New Collection of Ecstatic Poems.* Translated by Coleman Barks. San Francisco: HarperSanFrancisco, 2001.

Russell, D. A. *Longinus on the Sublime.* Oxford, U.K.: Clarendon Press, 1964.

Rutherford, R. B. *The Meditations of Marcus Aurelius: A Study.* Oxford, U.K.: Oxford University Press, 1989.

Rutherford, Ward. *Celtic Mythology.* New York: Sterling, 1990.

Ryder, Frank G., trans. *Song of the Nibelungs: A Verse Translation.* Detroit, Mich.: Wayne State University Press, 1982.

Saadi. *The Bostan of Saadi: (The Orchard).* Translated by Barlas M. Aqil-Hossain. London: Octagon Press, 1998.

———. *Morals Pointed and Tales Adorned: The Bustan of Saadi.* Translated by G. M. Wickens. Toronto: University of Toronto Press, 1974.

Sacker, Hugh D. *An Introduction to Wolfram's "Parzival."* Cambridge, U.K.: Cambridge University Press, 1963.

Sacks, Kenneth S. *Diodorus Siculs and the First Century.* Princeton, N.J.: Princeton University Press, 1990.

Sallust. *Histories.* Edited by Patrick McGushin. Oxford, U.K.: Oxford University Press, 1992.

———. *The Jugurthine War and the Conspiracy of Catiline*. Translated by S. A. Hanford. New York: Penguin Classics, 1978.

Sappho of Lesbos. *If Not, Winter: Fragments of Sappho*. Translated by Anne Carson. New York: Alfred A. Knopf, 2003.

———. *Sappho's Lyre: Archaic Lyric and Women Poets of Ancient Greece*. Translated by Diane Rayor. Berkeley: University of California Press, 1991.

Sarra, Edith. *Fictions of Femininity: Literary Inventions of Gender in Japanese Court Women's Memoirs*. Stanford, Calif.: Stanford University Press, 1996.

Sarton, George. *Galen of Pergamon*. Lawrence: University of Kansas Press, 1954.

Savala, Refugio. *The Autobiography of a Yaqui Poet*. Edited by Kathleen M. Sands. Tucson: University of Arizona Press, 1980.

Saxton, Dean, and Lucille, trans. *O'otham Hoho'ok A'agitha: Legends and Lore of the Papago and Pima Indians*. Tucson: University of Arizona Press, 1973.

Schalow, Paul Gordon, and Janet A. Walker, eds. *The Woman's Hand: Gender and Theory in Japanese Women's Writing*. Stanford, Calif.: Stanford University Press, 1996.

Schiffman, Lawrence H. *Reclaiming the Dead Sea Scrolls: The History of Judaism, the Background of Christianity, and the Lost Library of Qumran*. Philadelphia: Jewish Publication Society, 1994.

Schlamm, Carl C. *The Metamorphoses of Apuleius: On Making an Ass of Oneself*. Chapel Hill: University of North Carolina Press, 1992.

Schmidt, J. D. *Yang Wan-li*. New York: Twayne, 1976.

Schoolcraft, Henry Rowe. *The Myth of Hiawatha and Other Oral Legends, Mythologic and Allegoric, of the North American Indians*. Philadelphia: J.B. Lippincott, 1856.

Schreiber, Carolin, trans. *King Alfred's Old English Translation of Pope Gregory the Great's Regula Pastoralis and Its Cultural Context*. New York: Peter Lang, 2003.

Schwartz, B. I. *The World of Thought in Ancient China*. Cambridge, Mass.: Harvard University Press, 1985.

Schwartz-Barcott, Timothy P. *War, Terror & Peace in the Qur'an and in Islam*. Carlisle, Pa.: Army War College Foundation Press, 2004.

Scodel, Ruth. *Sophocles*. Boston: Twayne, 1984.

Scott, David C. *Kabir's Mythology*. Delhi, India: Bhavatiya Vidya Prakashan, 1985.

Segal, Charles. *Pindar's Mythmaking: The Fourth Pythian Ode*. Princeton, N.J.: Princeton University Press, 1986.

Segal, Erich. *Roman Laughter: The Comedy of Plautus*. Oxford: Oxford University Press, 1987.

Sei Shonagon. *The Pillow Book of Sei Shonagon*. Translated by Arthur Waley. New York: HarperCollins, 1979.

———. *The Pillow Book of Sei Shonagon*. Translated by Ivan Morris. New York: Columbia University Press, 1991.

Seleem, Ramses. *Egyptian Book of the Dead*. New York: Sterling, 2001.

Selincourt, Aubrey de. *Phoenix: The World of Herodotus*. London: Phoenix Press, 2001.

Sells, Michael. *Approaching the Koran: The Early Revelations*. Ashland, Oreg.: White Cloud Press, 1999.

Seneca. *Hercules*. Translated by Ranjit Bolt. New York: Theatre Communications Group, 1997.

———. *Moral and Political Essays*. Translated by John M. Cooper. Cambridge, U.K.: Cambridge University Press, 1995.

———. *Oedipus of Lucius Annaeus Seneca*. Translated by Michael Elliot Rutenberg. Wauconda, Ill.: Bolchazy-Carducci Publishers, 2001.

———. *Seneca: Tragedies: Hercules, Trojan Women, Phoenician Women, Medea, Phaedra*. Vol. 1. Edited by John G. Fitch. Cambridge, Mass.: Harvard University Press, 2002.

Sethi, V. K. *Kabir: The Weaver of God's Name*. Punjab, India: Radha Soami Satsang Beas, 1984.

Severy, Beth. *Augustus and the Family at the Birth of the Roman Empire*. New York: Routledge, 2003.

Sextus Empiricus. *Against the Ethicists*. Translated by Richard Bett. Oxford, U.K.: Oxford University Press, 2000.

———. *Against the Grammarians.* Translated by David L. Blank. Oxford, U.K.: Oxford University Press, 1998.

———. *Outlines of Pyrrhonism: Sextus Empiricus.* Translated by R. G. Bury. Amherst, N.Y.: Prometheus Books, 1990.

Shakespeare, William. *The Complete Sonnets and Poems.* Edited Colin Burrow. Oxford, U.K.: Oxford University Press, 2002.

———. *The Tragedy of Julius Caesar.* New York: Washington Square Press, 2004.

Shalian, Artin K. *David of Sassoun: The Armenian Folk Epic in Four Cycles.* Athens: Ohio University Press, 1964.

Sharrock, Alison and Rhiannon Ash, eds. *Fifty Key Classical Authors (Fifty Key Thinkers).* London: Routledge, 2002.

Shaul, David Leedom. *Hopi Traditional Literature.* Albuquerque: University of Mexico Press, 2002.

Shaw, M. R. B., trans. *Joinville and Villehardouin: Chronicles of the Crusades.* Baltimore, Md.: Penguin, 1963.

Shell, Marc. *American Babel: Literatures of the United States from Abnaki to Zuni.* Cambridge, Mass.: Harvard University Press, 2002.

Sherman, Nossn, ed. *Tanach: The Torah/Prophets/Writings.* Brooklyn, N.Y.: Mesorah Publications, 1996.

Shikishi, Princess. *String of Beads: Complete Poems of Princess Shikishi.* Translated and edited by Hiroaki Sato. Honolulu: University of Hawaii Press, 1993.

Shoi Nihon, and W. G. Aston. *Nihongi: Chronicles of Japan from the Earliest Times to A.D. 697.* Rutland, Vt.: Charles E. Tuttle Co., 1972.

Silman, Yochanan. *Philosopher and Prophet: Judah Halevi, the Kuzari, and the Evolution of His Thought.* Translated by Lenn J. Shramm. Albany: State University of New York Press, 1995.

Singer, Kurt. *The Life of Ancient Japan.* New York: Routledge, 2002.

Singh, A. D., ed. *Kalidasa: A Critical Study.* Columbia, Mo.: South Asia Books, 1977.

Siorvanes, Lucas. *Proclus: Neo-Platonic Philosophy and Science.* New Haven, Conn.: Yale University Press, 1996.

Siraisi, Nancy G. *Avicenna in Renaissance Italy: The Canon and Medical Teaching in Italian Universities after 1500.* Princeton, N.J.: Princeton University Press, 1987.

Sisoko, Fa-Digi. *The Epic of Son-Jara: A West African Tradition.* Translated by John William Johnson. Bloomington: Indiana University Press, 1992.

Smith, Andrew. *Porphyry's Place in the Neoplatonic Tradition: A Study in Postplotinian Neoplatonism.* New York: Kluwer Academic Press, 1975.

Smith, Colin. *The Making of the Poema de mio Cid.* Cambridge, U.K.: Cambridge University Press, 1983.

Smith, David Lee. *Folklore of the Winnebago Tribe.* Norman: University of Oklahoma Press, 1997.

Smyth, Alfred P. *King Alfred the Great.* Oxford, U.K.: Oxford University Press, 1995.

Smythe, Barbara, trans. *Trobador Poets: Selections from the Poems of Eight Trobadors.* London: Chatto & Windus, 1911.

Sophocles. *The Oedipus Plays of Sophocles: Oedipus the King, Oedipus at Kolonos, and Antigone.* Translated by Robert Bagg. Introduction by Mary Bagg. Boston: University of Massachusetts Press, 2004.

———. *Sophocles I.* Translated by David Grene. Chicago: University of Chicago Press, 1991.

———. *Theban Plays.* Translated by Peter Meineck and Paul Woodruff. Oxford, U.K.: Oxford University Press, 2004.

Southern, Pat. *Augustus.* New York: Routledge, 1998.

Spargo, John Webster. *Virgil the Necromancer: Studies in Virgilian Legends.* Whitefish, Mont.: Kessinger Publishing, 2004.

Spatz, Lois. *Aeschylus.* Boston: Twayne, 1982.

———. *Aristophanes.* Boston: Twayne, 1978.

Spentzou, Efrossini. *Readers and Wrtiers in Ovid's Heroides: Transgressions of Genre and Gender.* Oxford, U.K.: Oxford University Press, 2003.

Spicer, Edward H. *The Yaquis: A Cultural History.* Tucson: University of Arizona Press, 1980.

Stahl, Hans-Peter. *Thucydides: Man's Place in History.* Cardiff: The Classical Press of Wales, 2002.

Stedman, Edmund Clarence. "Aucassin and Nicolette." In *Yale Book of American Verse.* Edited by

Thomas Lounsbury. New Haven, Conn.: Yale University Press, 1912.

Steinberg, Theodore L. *Reading the Middle Ages: An Introduction to Medieval Literature.* New York: McFarland & Company, 2003.

Stetkevych, Suzanne Pinckney. *Abu Tammam and the Poetics of the Abasid Age.* Boston: Brill Academic Publishers, 1991.

———. *Mute Immortals Speak: Pre-Islamic Poetry and the Poetics of Ritual.* Ithaca, N.Y.: Cornell University Press, 1993.

Stevens-Cox, James. *Mumming and the Mummers' Plays of St. George.* Beddington, Surrey, U.K.: Toucan Press, 1970.

Stone, I. F. *The Trial of Socrates.* New York: Doubleday, 1989.

Stover, Leon. *Imperial China and the State Cult of Confucius.* Jefferson, N.C.: McFarland & Co., 2004.

Strabo. *The Geography of Strabo.* Translated by Horace Leonard Jones. Cambridge, Mass.: Harvard University Press, 1967.

———. *Isaeus.* Loeb Classical Library. Translated by Edward S. Forster. Cambridge, Mass.: Harvard University Press, 1992.

Strassberg, Richard E., trans. *Inscribed Landscapes: Travel Writing from Imperial China.* Berkeley: University of California Press, 1994.

Strassburg, Gottfried von. *Tristan.* Translated by A. T. Hatto. New York: Penguin, 1960.

Streight, David. *Averroës: A Rationalist in Islam.* Notre Dame, Ind.: University of Notre Dame Press, 2000.

Sturluson, Snorri. *Edda.* Translated by Anthony Faulkes. Rutland, Vt.: Charles E. Tuttle, 2002.

———. *Heimskringla: History of the Kings of Norway.* Translated by Lee M. Hollander. Austin: University of Texas Press, 1991.

———. *King Harald's Saga: Harald Hardradi of Norway.* Translation and introduction by Magnus Magnusson and Hermann Palsson. New York: Penguin, 1966.

———. *The Prose Edda: Tales from Norse Mythology.* Translated by Jean I. Young. Berkeley: University of California Press, 2002.

Stylianou, P. J. *Historical Commentary on Diodorus Siculus: Book 15.* Oxford, U.K., Oxford University Press, 1999.

Su Shih. *The Prose-Poetry of Su Tung-p'o.* Translated by Cyril Drummond Le Gros Clark. New York: Paragon, 1964.

———. *Su Tung-p'o: Selections from a Sung Dynasty Poet.* Translated by Burton Watson. New York: Columbia University Press, 1965.

Sudo, Philip Toshio. *Zen 24/7: All Zen, All the Time.* San Francisco: HarperSanFrancisco, 2001.

Suetonius. *The Twelve Caesars.* Translated by Robert Graves. New York: Penguin, 2003.

Sullivan, Bruce M. *Krsna Dvaipayana Vyasa and the Mahabharata: A New Interpretation.* New York: E. J. Brill, 1990.

Sullivan, Thelma D., trans. *A Scattering of Jades: Stories, Poems, and Prayers of the Aztecs.* Edited by Timothy J. Knab. Tucson: University of Arizona Press, 2003.

Sunzi. *The Art of War.* Translated by Lionel Giles. Singapore: Graham Brash, 1988.

Surmelian, Leon. *Daredevils of Sassoun.* Denver, Colo.: Alan Swallow 1964.

Swain, Tony, and Garry Trompf. *The Religions of Oceania.* Library of Religious Beliefs and Practices. London: Routledge, 1995.

Swanton, M. J., ed. and trans. *The Anglo-Saxon Chronicle.* London: J. M. Dent, 1996.

Swanton, Michael. *English Poetry before Chaucer.* Exeter: University of Exeter Press, 2002.

Syme, Ronald. *Anatolica: Studies in Strabo.* Edited by Anthony R. Birley. Oxford, U.K.: Oxford University Press, 1995.

———. *Sallust.* Foreword by Ronald Mellor. Berkeley: University of California Press, 2002.

Tacitus, Cornelius. *Agricola and Germany.* Translated by Anthony Birley. Oxford, U.K.: Oxford University Press, 1999.

———. *Annals and the Histories.* Translated by Alfred J. Church and William J. Brodribb. New York: Random House, 2003.

———. *Histories. Book I.* Edited by Cynthia Damon, et al. Cambridge, U.K.: Cambridge University Press, 2003.

———. *Tacitus: Dialogus de Oratoribus.* Edited by Roland Mayer, et al. New York: Cambridge University Press, 2001.

Tagare, G. V. *Bhagavata Purana.* Columbia, Mo.: South Asia Books, 1989.

Talattof, Kamran, K. Allin Luther, and Jerome W. Clinton, eds. *The Poetry of Nizami Ganjavi: Knowledge, Love, and Rhetoric.* New York: Palgrave Macmillan, 2001.

Talib, Ali ibn Abi. *Peak of Eloquence: Nahjul Balagha.* Translated by Askari Jafery. New York: Tahrike Tarsile Qur'an, 1996.

Tao Yuanming. *The Selected Poems of T'ao Ch'ien.* Translated by David Hinton. Port Townsend, Wash.: Copper Canyon Press, 1993.

Tedlock, Barbara. *The Beautiful and the Dangerous: Encounters with the Zuni Indians.* Albuquerque: University of New Mexico Press, 2001.

Tedlock, Dennis. *The Spoken Word and the Work of Interpretation.* Philadelphia: University of Pennsylvania Press, 1983.

———, trans. *Finding the Center: The Art of the Zuni Storyteller.* Lincoln: University of Nebraska Press, 1999.

Tellegan-Couperus, Olga, ed. *Quintilian and the Law: The Art of Persuasion in Law and Politics.* Leuven, Belgium: Leuven University Press, 2003.

Temkin, Owsei. *Hippocrates in a World of Pagans and Chrstians.* Baltimore, Md.: Johns Hopkins University Press, 1995.

Terence. *The First Comedy of Pub. Terentius, Called Andria.* Translated by Joseph Webbe. London: Scolar Press, 1972.

———. *Plautus and Terence: Five Comedies.* Translated by Deena Berg and Douglass Parker. Indianapolis, Ind.: Hackett, 1999.

———. *Terence. Vol. 1: Eunuchus.* Edited by John Barsby. New York: Cambridge University Press, 1999.

———. *Terence.* Vol. 1. *The Woman of Andros, The Self-Tormentor, The Eunuch.* Translated by John Barsby. Cambridge, Mass.: Harvard University Press, 2001.

Terry, Patricia, trans. *Poems of the Elder Edda.* Introduction by Charles W. Dunn. Philadelphia: University of Pennsylvania Press, 1990.

———. *Renard the Fox.* Boston: Northeastern University Press, 1983.

Thackston, Wheeler M. *A Millennium of Classical Persian Poetry.* Bethesda, Md.: Iranbooks, 1994.

Thapar, Romila. *Sakuntala: Texts, Readings, Histories.* London: Anthem Press, 2002.

Theophrastus. *Theophrastus: Characters.* Edited by James Diggle, et al. New York: Cambridge University Press, 2004.

———. *Theophrastus: Enquiry into Plants.* Translated by Arthur F. Hort. Cambridge, Mass.: Harvard University Press, 1989.

Theresa, Sister M. *Nature-Imagery in the Works of Saint Ambrose (1931).* Whitefish, Mont: Kessinger Publishing, 2003.

Thiede, Carsten Peter. *The Dead Sea Scrolls and the Jewish Origins of Christianity.* New York: Palgrave, 2000.

Thomas, Rosalind. *Herodotus in Context: Ethnography, Science and the Art of Persuasion.* New York: Cambridge University Press, 2002.

Thompson, Eben Francis. *Wisdom of Omar Khayyám.* New York: Kensington Publishing, 2001.

Thucydides. *On Justice, Power, and Human Nature: Selections from History of the Peloponnesian War.* Translated by Paul Woodruff. Indianapolis, Ind.: Hackett, 1998.

———. *The Peloponnesian War: The Complete Hobbes Translation.* Translated by Benjamin Jowett. Buffalo, N.Y.: Prometheus Books, 1998.

———. *Stories of Thucydides.* Retold by H. L. Havell. IndyPublish.com, 2004.

Tigay, Jeffrey H. *The Evolution of the Gilgamesh Epic.* Philadelphia: University of Pennsylvania Press, 1982.

Tilakasiri, J. *Kalidasa's Imagery and the Theory of Poetics.* New Delhi, India: Navrang Publishers, 1988.

Tissol, Garth. *The Face of Nature: Wit, Narrative, and Cosmic Origins in Ovid's Metamorphoses.* Princeton, N.J.: Princeton University Press, 1996.

Todi, Jacopone da. *Jacopone da Todi: The Lauds.* Translated by Serge and Elizabeth Hughes. New York: Paulist Press, 1982.

Tolegian, Aram. *David of Sassoun: Armenian Folk Epic.* New York: Bookman Associates, 1961.

Tolkien, J. R. R. *Beowulf and the Critics.* Edited by Michael Drout. Phoenix: Arizona State University, 2002.

Topsfield, L. T. *Troubadors and Love.* London: Cambridge University Press, 1975.

Topsfield, L.T. *Chrétien de Troyes: A Study of the Arthurian Romances.* Cambridge, U.K.: Cambridge University Press, 1981.

Tuchman, Barbara W. *A Distant Mirror: The Calamitous Fourteenth Century.* New York: Ballantine Books, 1987.

Turville-Petre, E. O. G. *Myth and Religion of the North: The Religion of Ancient Scandinavia.* New York: Holt, Rinehart and Winston, 1964.

Twersky, Isadore. *Introduction to the Code of Maimonides (Mishneh Torah).* New Haven, Conn.: Yale University Press, 1982.

Underhill, Evelyn. *Jacopone da Todi: A Spiritual Biography.* New York: Books for Libraries Press, 1972.

Underhill, Ruth M. *Papago Indian Religion.* New York: Columbia University Press, 1946.

Urton, Gary. *Inca Myths: Legendary Past.* Austin: University of Texas Press, 1999.

Vallejo, Yli Remo. *The Crusades.* Edited by Thor Johnson. Great Falls, Va.: AeroArt International, Inc., 2002.

Valmiki, Maharshi. *Ramayana.* Translated by William Buck. Berkeley: University of California Press, 2000.

———. *The Ramayana: A Modern Retelling of the Great Indian Epic.* Translated by Ramesh Menon. New York: North Point Press, 2004.

———. *Ramayana: India's Immortal Tale of Love, Adventure, and Wisdom.* Translated by Khrisna Dharma. Los Angeles: Torchlight Publishing, 2000.

VanderKam, James C., and Peter Flinit. *The Meaning of the Dead Sea Scrolls: Their Significance for Understanding the Bible, Judaism, and Christianity.* San Francisco: HarperSanFrancisco, 2002.

Varsano, Paul M. *Tracking the Vanished Mortal: The Poetry of Li Bo and its Criticism.* Honolulu: University of Hawaii Press, 2003.

Varty, Kenneth, ed. *Reynard the Fox.* New York: Berghahn Books, 2000.

Varvaro, Alberto. *Beroul's Romance of Tristran.* New York: Barnes & Noble, 1972.

Vasey, Vincent R. *The Social Ideas in the Works of St. Ambrose: A Study on De Nabuthe.* Rome, Italy: Institutum Patristicum "Augustinianum," 1982.

Ventadour, Bernard de. *Bilingual Edition of the Love Songs of Bernart de Ventadorn in Occitan and English: Sugar and Salt.* Translated by Ronnie Apter and Mark Herman. Lewiston, N.Y.: Edwin Mellen, 1999.

Verma, Vinod. *The Kamasutra for Women: The Modern Woman's Way to Sensual Fulfillment and Health.* Tokyo, Japan: Kodansha International, 1997.

Vermes, Geza, trans. *The Complete Dead Sea Scrolls in English.* New York: Penguin, 1998.

Veyne, Paul. *Seneca: The Life of a Stoic.* Translated by David Sullivan. London: Taylor & Francis, 2002.

Villehardouin, Geoffrey de, and Jean de Joinville. *Joinville and Villehardouin: Chronicles of the Crusades.* Translated by Margaret R. Shaw. New York: Viking Press, 1963.

Virgil. *The Aeneid.* Edited by Philip Hardie. New York: Cambridge University Press, 1994.

———. *The Aeneid.* Translated by David West. London: Penguin, 1990.

———. *Virgil: Eclogues, Georgics, Aeneid 1–6,* Vol. 1. Cambridge, Mass.: Harvard University Press, 1999.

———. *Virgil: Selections from the Aeneid.* Translated by Graham Tingay. New York: Cambridge University Press, 1999.

Wada, Stephanie. *The Oxherder: A Zen Parable Illustrated.* Translated by Gen P. Sakamoto. New York: George Braziller, 2002.

Waite, Greg, trans. *Old English Prose Translations of King Alfred's Reign.* Suffolk, U.K.: Boydell & Brewer, 2000.

Waley, Arthur. *The Life and Times of Po Chü-i.* London: Allen & Unwin, 1949.

————, trans. *The Book of Songs.* New York: Grove Press, 1996.

Walther von der Vogelweide. *Selected Poems of Walther von der Vogelweide.* Edited by Margaret Fitzgerald Richey. Oxford, U.K.: Blackwell, 1965.

————. *Songs and Sayings of Walther von der Vogelweide, Minnesaenger.* Murieta, Calif.: Classic Books, 2001.

————. *Walther von der Vogelweide: The Single-Stanza Lyrics.* Routledge Medieval Texts Series. Edited and translated by Frederick Goldin. London: Taylor & Francis, Inc., 2002.

Walton, J. Michael and Peter D. Arnott. *Menander and the Making of Comedy.* Westport, Conn.: Greenwood Press, 1996.

Wang Shifu. *The Moon and the Zither: Wang Shifu's Story of the Western Wing.* Edited by Stephen H. West and Wilt L. Idema. Berkeley: University of California Press, 1991.

————. *The Story of the Western Wing.* Translated by Stephen H. West and Wilt L. Idema. Berkeley: University of California Press, 1995.

Wang Wei. *Laughing Lost in the Mountains: Poems of Wang Wei.* Translated by Tony Barnstone, Willis Barnstone, and Xu Haixin. Hanover, N.H.: University Press of New England, 1991.

Wang, C. H. *From Ritual to Allegory: Seven Essays in Early Chinese Poetry.* Hong Kong: Chinese University Press, 1988.

Warner, Keith Q. *Kaiso! The Trinidad Calypso: A Study of Calypso as Oral Literature.* Pueblo, Colo.: Passeggiata Press, 1999.

Waters, Frank and Oswald White Bear Fredericks. *Book of the Hopi.* New York: Viking Press, 1977.

Waters, Geoffrey. *Three Elegies of Ch'u: An Introduction to the Traditional Interpretation of the Ch'u Tz'u.* Madison: University of Wisconsin Press, 1985.

Watson, Lindsay C. *Commentary on Horace's Epodes.* Oxford, U.K.: Oxford University Press, 2003.

Wawn, Andrew. *Northern Antiquity: The Post-Medieval Reception of Edda and Saga.* London: Hisarlik Press, 1994.

Wehrle, William T. *Satiric Voice: Program, Form, and Meaning in Persius and Juvenal.* Hildesheim, Germany: Georg Olms Publishing, 1992.

Weigand, Hermann J. *Wolfram's Parzival: Five Essays.* Edited by Ursula Hoffman. Ithaca, N.Y.: Cornell University Press, 1969.

Weston, Jessie. L. *The Quest of the Holy Grail.* New York: Barnes & Noble, 1964.

Whaley, Diana, trans. *Sagas of Warrior-Poets.* New York: Penguin Classics, 2002.

White, Helen C., et al., eds. *Seventeenth-Century Verse and Prose.* Vol 1. 2d ed. New York: The Macmillian Company, 1971.

White, T. H., ed. *The Book of Beasts: Being a Translation from a Latin Bestiary of the Twelfth Century.* Mineola, N.Y.: Dover, 1984.

Wiget, Andrew, ed. *Handbook of Native American Literature.* New York: Garland Publishing, 1996.

Wilhelm, James J. *Miglior Fabbro: The Cult of the Difficult in Daniel, Dante, and Pound.* Orono, Maine: National Poetry Foundation, 1982.

————. *Seven Troubadours: The Creators of Modern Verse.* University Park: Pennsylvania State University Press, 1970.

Wilkins, Ann Thomas. *Villain or Hero: Sallust's Portrayal of Catiline.* New York: Peter Lang, Publishing Group, 1994.

Williams. Daniel H. *Ambrose of Milan and the End of the Nicene-Arian Conflicts.* Oxford, U.K.: Oxford University Press, 1995.

Wilson, Donna F. *Ransom, Revenge, and Heroic Identity in the* Iliad. New York: Cambridge University Press, 2002.

Wing-Tsit Chan. *A Sourcebook in Chinese Philosophy.* Princeton, N.J.: Princeton University Press, 1969.

Winternitz, Maurice. *History of Indian Literature.* Vol. 1: *Introduction, Veda, Epics, Puranas and Tantras.* Columbia, Mo.: South Asia Books, 1981.

Wiseman, T. P. *Catullus and His World: A Reappraisal.* Cambridge, U.K.: Cambridge University Press, 1986.

Wisnovsky, Robert, ed. *Aspects of Avicenna.* Princeton, N.J.: Markus Wiener, 2001.

Wolfram von Eschenbach. *Parzival.* Translated by A. T. Hatto. New York: Penguin, 1980.

————. *Parzival.* Translated and edited by André Lefevere. New York: Continuum, 1991.

———. *Willehalm.* Translated by Marion E. Gibbs and Sidney M. Johnson. New York: Penguin Books, 1984.

Wood, Frances. *Did Marco Polo Go to China?* London: Secker & Warburg, 1995.

Worthington, Ian, ed. *Demosthenes: Statesman and Orator.* London and New York: Routledge, 2000.

Worthington, Ian. *Historical Commentary on Dinarchus.* Ann Arbor: University of Michigan Press, 1993.

——— et al., trans. *Dinarchus, Hyperides, and Lycurgus.* Austin: University of Texas Press, 2001.

Wu, John C. H. *The Golden Age of Zen: Zen Masters of the T'ang Dynasty.* Bloomington, Ind.: World Wisdom, 2003.

Xenophon. *Anabasis.* Translated by Carleton L. Brownson. Revised by John Dillery. Cambridge, Mass.: Harvard University Press, 1998.

———. *Conversations of Socrates.* Translated by Hugh Trednnick. New York: Penguin Classics, 1990.

———. *The Education of Cyrus.* Translated by Wayne Ambler. Ithaca, N.Y.: Cornell University Press, 2001.

———. *Hiero: A New Translation.* Translated by Ralph Doty. Lewiston, N.Y.: Edwin Mellen Press, 2003.

———. *Xenophon's Spartan Constitution: Introduction, Text, Commentary.* Edited by Michael Lipka. Berlin, Germany: De Gruyter, 2002.

Xiao Tong, ed. *Wen xuan or Selections of Refined Literature: Volume Three: Rhapsodies on Natural Phenomena, Birds and Animals, Aspirations and Feelings, Sorrowful Laments, Literature, Music, and Passions.* Princeton, N.J.: Princeton University Press, 1996.

Xie Lingyun. *The Mountain Poems of Hsieh Ling-Yun.* Translated by David Hinton. New York: New Directions, 2001.

Yadin, Yigael. *The Temple Scroll.* New York: Random House, 1985.

Yang Wanli. *Heaven My Blanket, Earth My Pillow.* Translated by Jonathan Chaves. New York: Weatherhill Press, 1975.

Yates, Robin D. S. *The Life and Selected Poetry of Wei Chuang (834?–910).* Cambridge, Mass.: Council on East Asian Studies, 1988.

Yogananda, Paramahansa. *Rubáiyát of Omar Khayyam Explained.* Nevada City, Calif.: Crystal Clarity Publishers, 1994.

———. *Wine of the Mystic: The Rubáiyát of Omar Khayyám: A Spiritual Interpretation, from Edward Fitzgerald's Translation of the Rubáiyát.* Los Angeles, Calif.: Self-Realization Fellowship Publishers, 1996.

Yoshida Kenkō. *Essays in Idleness.* Translated by Donald Keene. New York: Columbia University Press, 1967.

———. *Miscellany of a Japanese Priest.* Translated by William H. Porter. Rutland, Vt.: Charles E. Tuttle, 1973.

Young, David, trans. *Five T'ang Poets: Field Translation Series.* Oberlin, Ohio: Oberlin College Press, 1990.

Yu Xin. *"The Lament for the South": Yü Hsin's "Ai Chiang-nan Fu."* Translated and edited by William T. Graham, Jr. Cambridge: Cambridge University Press, 1980.

Yun Lee Too. *Rhetoric of Identity in Isocrates: Text, Power, Pedagogy.* New York: Cambridge University Press, 1995.

Zacharia, Katerina. *Converging Truths: Euripides' Ion and the Athenian Quest for Self-Definition.* Leiden, Netherlands: Brill Academic Publishers, 2003.

Zaehner, R. C. *The Bhagavad-Gita: With Commentary Based on the Original Sources.* London: Oxford University Press, 1969.

Zagagi, Netta. *The Comedy of Menander: Convention, Variation, and Originality.* Bloomington: Indiana University Press, 1995.

Zepeda, Ofelia, ed. *When It Rains: Papago and Pima Poetry.* Tucson: University of Arizona Press, 1982.

Zi Chang Tang. *Principles of Conflict: Recompilation and New English Translation with Annotation on Sunzi's Art of War.* San Rafael, Calif.: T. C. Press, 1969.

Zona, Guy, ed. *The House of the Heart Is Never Full and Other Proverbs of Africa.* New York: Touchstone, 1993.

Zong-qi Cai. *The Matrix of Lyric Transformation: Poetic Modes and Self-Presentation in Early Chinese Pentasyllabic Poetry.* Ann Arbor, Mich.: Center for Chinese Studies, 1996.

INDEX

Boldface page references refer to main entries in the encyclopedia.

A

Abad, Per 72
Abélard, Pierre **1–2**
   translations of 147
      influence of 118
      influences on 229
      language of 189
Abū al-`Alā` al-Ma`arrī 2
Abu al-Qāsim. *See* Muhammad
Abū Firās, Tammām ibn Ghalib. *See* Farazdaq, al-
Abu Talib. *See* `Alī ibn Abī Tālib
Abū Tammām **2–3**
An Account of My Hut (Kamo) 157
Acharnians (Aristophanes) 20
Achilles 133
Acts of the Divine Augustus (Augustus) *See Des Gestae Divi Augusti*
adab 145
Adam de la Halle **3–4**
Addictus and Saturio (Plautus) 240
Adelphi (Terence) 300
Ad Helviam Matrem de Consolatione (Seneca) 275
Ad Monimum (Fulgentius) 109
Admonitions (Francis of Assisi) 107
Adonis Garcia (Zapata) 233
"Adon Olam" (Ibn Gabirol) 139
Ad Polybium (Seneca) 275
"The Adventures of Redhorn's Sons" 323
The Aeneid (Virgil)
   adaptations of 124–125
   composition of 32

as epic 97
influence of 172
influences on 18, 202
themes and structure of 93, 132, 320–322
Aeschines 27, 90
Aeschylus **4–6**
   contemporaries of 236, 286
   influence of 6
   literary criticism on 5–6
   themes in 136
   works by 280
   works on 21
Aesop **6–8**
   influence of 234, 262
   influences on 9
   literary criticism on 7–8, 76
   parallels to 230, 265
   translations of 185
Aethelred I (king of England) 11
Aetia (Callimachus) 60
Afer, Domitius 253
Afer, Publius Terentius. *See* Terence
African proverbs **8–9**
"After Being in Love" (Rumi) 265
Against Alcibiades (Andocides) 26–27
Against Apatourius (Demosthenes) 90
Against Apion (Josephus) 149
Against Aristocrates (Demosthenes) 90
Against Ctesiphon (Aeschines) 27
Against Eratosthenes (Lysias) 179
Against Polycles (Demosthenes) 90
Against the Christians (Porphyry) 248
Against the Dogmatists (Sextus Empiricus) 277
"Against the God of the Wind" (Han Yu) 123

Against the Logicians (Sextus Empiricus) 277
Against the Mathematicians (Sextus Empiricus) 277
Against the Physicists (Sextus Empiricus) 277
Against the Professors (Sextus Empiricus) 277
Against the Skeptics (Augustine) 29
Against Timarchus (Aeschines) 27
Agamemnon (Aeschylus) 5
Agamemnon (Seneca) 276
Agesilaus (Xenophon) 333
Agesilaus II (king of Sparta) 332, 333
Agni 256–257
Agricola 293
Agricolae De Vita Iulii (Tacitus) 293
Agrippa, Enrique Cornelio 158
Agrippina (empress of Rome) 275
Ahohas, Jaakko 153
Aitia (Callimachus) 60
Ajax (Sophocles) 286
Akiko (empress of Japan) 141
Alan of Lille 147, 260
alba 329
Albert the Great, Saint 303
Albertus Magnus 303
al-Būsīrī. *See* Būsírí, al-
Alcaeus **10**
   influence of 10
   themes of 61
Alcestis (Euripides) 91, 102
Alembert, Jean d' 80
Alexander IV (pope) 266
Alexander of Pharae 102

Alexander the Great
    contemporaries of 22, 100, 300
    impact of 17, 26
    influences on 333
    works on 92, 210, 257, 278
Alexandrianism 63
Alexiad (Anna Comnena) 16
Alexius I (emperor of Byzantium)
    15–16, 79
Alexius IV (emperor of Byzantium)
    319
Alf Layla wa-Layla. See The Thousand
    and One Nights
Alfonso II (king of Aragon) 317–318
Alfonso VI (king of Castile) 71, 72–73
Alfonso X (king of Spain) 72, 167
Alfred the Great (king of England)
    10–11, 15
Alighieri, Dante. *See* Dante Alighieri
`Alī ibn Abī Ṭālib **11–12,** 105, 145, 192
The Allegory of Love (Lewis) 65
allegory of the cave 239
Allen, Rosamund 258
Alley, Rewi 168
Almeida, Manuel 158
al-Mutanabbi. *See* Mutanabbi, al-
Alte, Reinmar der 324
Amara-sakti, King 230
Ambrose, Saint **12–13**
    influence of 29, 30, 168
    influences on 244
`Amiri, Diwan Labid ibn Rabi`a al-. *See*
    Labid
Ammonius Saccas 244, 245
"Amor de caritate" (Jacopone da Todi)
    144
Amores (Ovid) 227
"Amorium" (Abū Tammām) 2–3
Amr ibn Hind (king of al-Hirah) 13,
    297–298
`Amr ibn Kulthum **13,** 120, 298
Amyntas II (king of Macedonia) 22
Amyot, Jacques 175, 245
Anabasis (Xenophon) 333
Anacreon **13–14**
Analects 74–75
Ancient Spanish Ballads (Scott) 72
Ancient Spider 206
"ancient style" movement 122
"Anc ieu non l'aic, mas elha m'a"
    (Arnaut) 24–25
Andalusian School 120, 138
Andocides 26–27
Andria (Terence) 299
Anerin 39
Angelus, Alexius 319
Angiolieri, Cecco **14–15**
Anglo-Saxon Chronicle 11, **15,** 218
"The Animal Who Would Eat Men"
    323

Anishinaubaek. *See* Ojibway myths and
    legends
Anna Comnena **15–16**
Anna Dalassena 16
Annals (Ennius) 96
Annals (Tacitus) 233, 293–294
"The Annihilation of the Hotcâgara" 331
anno Domini dating, origins of 41
Anselm of Laon 1
Anticato (Caesar) 58
Antigone (Sophocles) 286
Antigonus 92
Antiphon 26
anti-Semitism 150–151
Antony, Mark
    contemporaries of 92
    political struggles of 31, 130
    works on 69
Apache myths and tales **327–329**
Aphrodite 202
Apion 149
Apocolocyntosis divi Claudii (Seneca)
    276
Apollo 202
Apollodorus **16–17,** 300
Apollonius of Rhodes **17–18**
    contemporaries of 60
    influence of 18
Apologia (Apuleius) 18
Apology (Plato) 282
The Apophoreta (Martial) 186
Aprokos Gospel 225
Apuleius **18–19**
Aquinas, Saint Thomas. *See* Thomas
    Aquinas, Saint
Aquitaine, William of Poitou, duke of
    257
Arabian Nights. See The Thousand and
    One Nights
The Arabian Nights: A Companion
    (Irwin) 304
Arabian Nights and Days (Mahfouz) 306
Arberry, A. J. 298
The Arbitrators (Menander) 188
Arcadia (Sidney) 175
Archelaus 286
Archelaus of Macedon 102
Archias 70
Archimedes 101
Ares 202–203
Argonautica (Apollonius of Rhodes)
    17–18, 60
Ariosto, Lodovico
    influences on 285, 313, 322
    medieval romance and 258
Aristarchus 17
Aristophanes **20–22**
    contemporaries of 59, 238, 280,
       281
    influence of 174, 302

literary criticism on 21–22
works by 101–102, 188, 281–282
works on 238
Aristotle **22–24**
    contemporaries of 187, 300
    influence of 1, 21, 23, 32–33, 35,
       111, 167, 183–184, 244, 245,
       248, 301, 302, 303
    literary criticism by 91, 102, 136,
       286
    literary criticism on 23–24, 173,
       300–301
    philosophical method of 277
    translations of 50
    works by 7, 281–282
    works on 32–33, 248
Armstrong, H. A. 244–245
Arnaut Daniel **24–25,** 312, 318
Arnold, Matthew 99, 185
The Arrangement of Words (Dionysius
    of Halicarnassus) 93
Arrian 99
Arrowsmith, William 103
Ars amatoria (Ovid) 227–228
Artaxerxes II (king of Persia) 332
Artemis 202
artha 231
Artha Shastra 155, 231
Arthurian legend
    courtly love and 311
    Holy Grail in. *See* Holy Grail
    medieval literature and 190
    origins of 67, 201, 217
    themes in 65–66
    Tristan and Iseult in 309
    works on 39, 67–69, 112, 115–116,
       124, 257, 258, 329–331
Arthurian Romances (Chrétien de
    Troyes) 67, 258
The Art of Chivalry (Vegetius) 147
The Art of Courtly Love (Capellanus) 65
The Art of Love (Ovid) 65, 116, 155,
    227–228
The Art of War (Sunzi) 290
Asceticism, in Middle Ages 108
as-Hamasa (Abū Tammām) 3
Ashurbanipal 113
Asser, John 11
ataraxia 277
Atchity, Kenneth 10, 276
Atea 206
Atea Rangi 206
Atharva-Veda 256
Athena 202
'Atiyya, Jarir ibn 105
Atlas 202
atman 46
Atrahasis 114
Atsumichi, Prince 141
Attalus the Stoic 275

`Attār, Faríd od-Dín **25–26**
Attic orators **26–28**, 179
Aucassin et Nicolette **28–29**
Aue, Hartmann von. *See* Hartmann von
    Aue
Auerbach, Erich 84
Augustine, Saint **29–31**
    as Doctor of the Church 12
    influence of 2, 31, 109, 168
    influences on 244
    life of 217
    literary criticism on 30–31
    translations of 11
    works by 189
    works on 118, 304
Augustus (emperor of Rome) **31–32**
    contemporaries of 92, 134, 135,
        172, 234, 320, 321
    reign of 227, 228
    works on 228, 235, 294
Aurelian (emperor of Rome) 173
Aurelius, Marcus. *See* Marcus Aurelius
autobiographies 32, 40, 149, 191–192
Autobiography (Josephus) 149
"Autumn" (Ouyang Xiu) 226–227
Avaiki 206
Averroës **32–34**
    influence of 32, 34, 303
    literary criticism on 33–34
    works on 304
Avianus 235
Avicebron. *See* Ibn Gabirol, Solomon
    ben Yehuda
Avicenna **34–36**
    influence of 303
    works on 304
Awiakta, Marilou 216–217
Aztecs
    creation myths 77
    poetry 208–209

B

Babrius 234
Babylonians (Aristophanes) 20
The Bacchae (Euripides) 102–103,
    137
Bacchylides **37**
badi 2
Baeda. *See* Bede
Bai Juyi **37–38**, 171
"The Baldness of the Buzzard" 323
Baldric, archbishop of Dol 80
Baldr the Beautiful 205
Baldry, H. C. 132, 308
Baldwin, Spurgeon 168
Baldwin of Flanders 319
Ballade (Villon) 190
Banquet (Dante) 83
Banqueters (Aristophanes) 20

bardic poetry **38–39**
    oral literature and 224
    parallels to 217
    sagas and 269
    themes of 190
Bar Kochba 88
Barnstone, Tony 326
Barnstone, Willis 326
Barrette, Paul 168
Basil, Saint 12
Bat 206
"Bath of Pallas" (Callimachus) 59
Battle of Maldon 218
Battus IV (king of Cyrene) 236
Beatrice of Nazareth **39–40**, 118
Becher, Anne 235
Bede **40–41**
    influence of 15, 112
    translations of 11
    works by 56–57, 189, 218
Beethoven, Ludwig von 203
Beguine communities 118
Bellon, Roger 263
Bellow, Saul 62
Bellum Alexandrinum (Caesar) 130
Benedict, Ruth 299
Bennett, C. E. 61, 135–136
Beowulf **41–43**
    as epic 97
    influences on 39, 270
    literary criticism on 15, 205, 283
    medieval literature and 190, 258
    Old English poetry and 217
Bergerac, Cyrano de 176
Bernard de Ventadour **43–44**
    influence of 318
    literary criticism on 318
Bernardino de Sahagún 209
Bernard of Clairvaux 118
Bernardone, Francesco de Pietro di. *See*
    Francis of Assisi, Saint
Béroul 258, 309, 310
Bestiare d'amour 44
bestiaries **44–45**, 167, 262
Bhagavad Gita **45–47**
    context of 182
    influence of 47
    literary criticism on 251
Bhagavata Purana 251
bhakti 46
Bible
    apocryphal books 49
    Christian 49
    Dead Sea Scrolls and 87–89
    Hebrew **47–50**, 77, 87–89
    influence of 2, 44, 108, 119, 149,
        167, 260, 269
    influences on 115
    vs. Koran 162, 163
    mystery plays and 197

    oral literature and 223
    parables, *vs.* Buddhist parables
        339
    printing press and 190
    Talmud and 294–296
    translations of 49, 148, 189
Bibliotheca Historica (Diodorus) 92
Bibliotheke (Apollodorus) 17
Bingen, Hildegard von. *See* Hildegard
    von Bingen
biographies
    of Greeks and Romans 245–246,
        333
    lives of Saints 266
Birds (Aristophanes) 21
Birrell, Jean 79
The Bitten Shoulder (Chrétien de
    Troyes) 67
Black Death 190
Blair, Peter Hunter 41
Blake, William 128
"The Blessing of a Bear Clansman" 331
"The Blinding of Tiresias"
    (Callimachus) 59–60
Bloom, Allan 238
Bloom, Harold 84–85
Boas, Franz 299
"Boat of Stars" (Li Qingzhao) 170
Boccaccio, Giovanni
    influences on 19, 232
    literary criticism on 305
    themes of 190
    works by 14–15
Boethius **50–51**
    influence of 1, 168
    influences on 244
    translations of 11, 147
    works by 189
Boethius (Reiss) 51
Bohemund of Antioch 80
Boiardo, Matteo Maria
    influences on 285
    medieval romance and 258
Boileau, Nicolas 174
Boniface of Montferrat 319
Boniface VIII (pope) 83, 143, 144
Book of Aeneid 124
Book of Affliction (`Attār) 26
The Book of Alexander 258
Book of Animals (Al-Jāhiz) 145
The Book of Apollonius 258
The Book of Directives and Remarks
    (Avicenna) 35
Book of Documents 74
The Book of Excellence and Rhetoric (Al-
    Jāhiz) 145
The Book of Healing (Avicenna) 35
The Book of Invasions 200
The Book of Marco Polo (Polo) 246–248
The Book of Marvels (Polo) 246–248

Book of Secrets (`Attār) 26
Book of Songs 51–52
    Confucius and 51, 52, 74
    influence of 253
    literary criticism on 252
The Book of Spectacles (Martial) 186
Book of the Dead 52–54
The Book of the Duchess (Chaucer) 313
The Book of the Dun Cow 201
*The Book of the Glory of the Kings of
    Ethopia. See* Kebra Nagast Chronicles
The Book of the Treasure (Latini) 167
Borges, Jorge Luis 322
"The Boy and the Deer" 299
Bradley, Marion Zimmer 68
The Braggart Soldier (Plautus) 240
Brandt, Sebastian 302
"Branwen, Daughter of Llyr" 201
Br'er Rabbit stories 232
Bricriu's Feast 200
British History (Nennius) 112
Britten, Benjamin 203
The Brothers (Terence) 300
Browning, Elizabeth Barrett 175
Browning, Robert 147
Bruce, James 158
Brut (Layamon) 219
Brutus 134
Brutus (Cicero) 70
Buddha 123
Buddha parables. *See* Zen parables
Buddhism
    influence of 38, 104, 122, 191, 195,
        222, 279, 291, 325, 327, 334, 335,
        337, 339
    Jataka tales 145–146
    Zen parables **339–340**
Budge, E. A. Wallis 158
Bunjil 206
Buri 204
Burrus 275, 276
Burton, Sir Richard 9, 156, 305, 306
Būsírí, al- **55**
Bustan (Saadī) 268
Byatt, A. S. 305
By Jove! (Macrone) 202
Byrhtnoth 218
Byron, George Gordon, Lord
    influences on 6
    literary criticism by 187
Byzantine Empire, collapse of 190

C

Caedmon **56–57**
    influence of 42
    works by 218
"Caedmon's Hymn" (Caedmon)
    56, 218
Caesar, Gaius Julius 31, 63

Caesar, Julius **57–59**
    contemporaries of 2, 62, 92, 130,
        134, 270, 320
    family of 31
    life of 69, 177
    literary criticism on 58–59
    works on 15, 41, 175, 228
Caius Marius 69
Caligula (emperor of Rome) 234, 275
Callimachus **59–60**
    contemporaries of 17, 18
    influence of 186, 250, 257
    translations of 62
The Canon of Medicine (Avicenna)
    34–35
canso 312
canso-sirventes 318
Cantar de mío Cid 72–73, 97
Canterbury Tales (Chaucer)
    influences on 68, 232, 263, 302
    literary criticism on 190, 305
Canticle of the Sun (Francis of Assisi)
    107
Cantos (Pound) 147
Cao Bi 60–61
Cao Cao 264
Cao Xueqin 325
Cao Zhi **60–61**
Capellanus, Andreas 65, 66
Captives (Plautus) 240
"Carmen Campidoctoris" 72
Carmen Saeculare (Horace) 135
Carmi, T. 138
carpe diem **61–62**, 220, 298
"Carpe Diem" (Horace) 135
Carrier, Constance 250
Carus, Titus Lucretius. *See* Lucretius
Casaubon, Isaac 302
Cassius Dio 308
Castro, Guillén de 72
Categories (Aristotle) 248
catharsis 23
Catiline, Lucius 69, 70–71, 270
Cato
    literary criticism on 174
    works on 58, 271
Cato the Elder 96
The Cattle Raid of Cooley 200
Catullus, Gaius Valerius **62–63**
    influence of 63, 186
    influences on 60, 250
    literary criticism on 249
Cavalcanti, Guido 85
cavalier poets, themes of 62
Caxton, William 190, 263
The Celestial Hierarchy (Dionysius the
    Areopagite) 249
Celestine V (pope) 143
Celtic mythology **199–202**, 257
Ceres 203

Cerquilini, Bernard 283
Cervantes, Miguel de
    influences on 302, 313
    themes of 66
Chaerephon 280–281
Chamberlain, B. H. 160
champu 231
Chandragupta II 153, 155
Chang Heng. *See* Zhang Heng
Chanson de Roland. See Song of Roland
chansons de geste
    characteristics of 65, 80
    influence of 107
    origins of 190
chantefable 28
Chao Ming-Cheng *See* Zhao Mingzheng
Chapman, George 99, 185
*The Chapters of Coming Forth by Day.
    See* Book of the Dead
Characters (Theophrastus) 301–302
Charlemagne (emperor of the West)
    65, 80, 189, 283–285
Charles d'Orléans 66
Charles of Anjou 167
Charmides (Plato) 238
Chaucer, Geoffrey
    contemporaries of 39
    influence of 305
    influences on 68, 229, 232, 261,
        263, 302, 313, 322
    literary criticism on 305
    themes of 66, 190
    works by 261
Check Teck Foo 290
Cheng Hou 290
Cherokee
    creation myths 78
    folktales **216–217**
"Chevrefoil" (Marie de France) 186, 310
Children of Heracles (Euripides) 102
Children of Lir 200
Children of Tuirenn 200
chimiky'ana'kowa 299
Chinook myths and tales **63–64**
Chin Ping Mei 325
chin-shih See jinshi
Chippewa. *See* Ojibway myths and
    legends
Chiu-ko [Jiuge] 252
chivalry **64–66**
    and Arthurian romance 65, 67
    Crusades and 80
    and Hold Grail 130
    influence of 107, 116, 124–125,
        269, 329
    in Middle Ages 189
    origins of 257
    troubadour songs and 146
    works on 112, 147, 212, 260, 285,
        318

The Choephori (Aeschylus) 5
Chopinel, Jean. *See* Jean de Meun
Chrétien de Troyes **67–69**
    influence of 68, 115, 124, 131, 329
    influences on 201, 311
    and medieval romance 190, 258
    works by 65–66, 130–131
Christ and Satan 217
Christianity
    converts to 29, 30–31
    critics of 248
    Crusades and 79–81
    Holy Grail and 130
    influence of 65, 124
    influences on 249
    Middle Ages and 189
    in Roman Empire 243
    spread of 79, 86, 109, 152, 157
Christine de Pisan
    influence of 190
    influences on 261
    on women 66
Chronicle (Apollodorus) 17
Chronicle (Jean de Joinville) 80
Chubb, Thomas Caldecot 14–15
Ch'u Elegies. See Qu Elegies
Ch'ü Yüan. *See* Qu Yuan
ci (poetry) 171, 291, 327
Cicero, Marcus Tullius **69–71**
    contemporaries of 130, 299
    influence of 29, 30, 167, 242, 293
    influences on 23, 101, 302
    literary criticism by 125
    literary criticism on 12
    opinions expressed by 173
    translations of 167
    works on 177, 245
Le Cid (Corneille) 72
Cid, El **71–73,** 190
Cid Campeador. *See* Cid, El
City of God (Augustine) 30, 31
City of Night (Rechy) 233
Civil War (Lucan) 175–176
Clare of Assisi, Saint 107
Clarissa (Richardson) 66
Clarke, Howard W. 133–134
classical epics 97
Claudius (emperor of Rome)
    contemporaries of 234
    influences on 172
    reign of 275
    works on 294
Clement of Alexandria 174
Cleon of Athens 20, 308
Cleopatra 92
Cligés (Chrétien de Troyes) 68
"The Cloud Messenger" (Kalidasa) 153–154
Clouds (Aristophanes) 20, 282

"The Cock and the Pearl" (Phaedrus) 235
Codicil of Jean de Meun (Jean de Meun) 147
Coffin Texts 53
Cohen, Abraham 295–296
"Cold is the North" (Li He) 169
Coleridge, Samuel Taylor
    influences on 6, 306
The Collection for Ten Thousand Ages 225–226
Collection of Old and New Japanese Poems 159
The Colliget (Averroës) 33
Columbus, Christopher 247
The Comedy of Errors (Shakespeare) 240
Commentaries on the Attic Orators (Dionysius of Halicarnassus) 93
Commentary on the Civil Wars (Caesar) 58, 59
Commentary on the Inca (La Vega) 199
Commentary on the Timaeus (Proclus) 249
Commentary on the War in Gaul (Caesar) 57, 58–59, 130
Commodus, Emperor 110
La Compiuta Donzella. *See* Donzella, Compiuta
Concerning the Origin and Location of the Germans (Tacitus) 293
Concerning the Ruin of Britain (Gildas) 112
Conchobar Mac Nessa (king of Ulster) 200
The Conference of the Birds (`Attār) 25–26
Confessio Amantis (Gower) 261
Confessions (Augustine) 29, 30–31
Confucius **73–75**
    Book of Songs and 51, 52, 74
    contemporaries of 165
    influence of 38, 74, 104, 122, 171, 297
    philosophy of 74–75
"A Congratulatory Ode on the Occasion of the Feast of Sacrifices" (al-Mutanabbi) 196
Conics (Euclid) 101
Conquest of Constantinople (Robert of Clari) 80
The Conquest of Gaul (Caesar). *See Commentary on the War in Gaul* (Caesar)
La Conquête de Constantinople (Villehardouin) 319
The Conscious Lovers (Steele) 300
The Consolation of Philosophy (Boethius) 11, 50–51, 147
Consolation to Helvia (Seneca) 275

The Conspiracy of Catiline (Sallust) 270–271
Constantine (prince of Byzantium) 15–16
The Constitution of the Lacedaemonians (Xenophon) 333
The Constraint of What Is Not Compulsory (Al-Ma`rrī) 181
Contares Mexicanos 209
Continuation of the History of Aufidius Bassas (Pliny the Elder) 241
Contra academicos (Augustine) 29
Contra Arianos liber unus (Fulgentius) 109
Convivio (Dante) 83
Cook, Robert 285
Coolidge, Olivia 71, 177, 320
Copley, Frank O. 178–179
Corinna 236
"Corinna's Going A Maying" (Herrick) 62
Corneille, Pierre 72, 203
correspondence 38, 70, 93, 104, 243, 293
Council of Clermont 79, 80
Countess of Dia 312–313
"The Country Mouse and the City Mouse" (Aesop) 8
courtly love **64–66**
    and Arthurian romance 65–66, 67, 68
    chivalry and 189
    influence of 116, 269, 313, 329
    influences on 229
    origins of 257
    troubadour songs and 146, 311, 318
    works on 43, 147, 259–261, 318
Coward, David 267
"Coyote and Junco" 341
Coyote tales
    Hopi **75–77,** 205, 313
    White Mountain Apache 328
    Zuni 299
Cranmer-Byng, L. 227
Crassus 57
"Craven" (Han Yu) 123
creation myths
    Finnish 152
    Indian 152
    Native-American 75, **77–79,** 223, 299, 314, 328, 341
    Oceanic 205–207
    oral tradition and 223
Creation Myths of Primitive America (Curtin) 78
Crispus, Gaius Sallustius. *See* Sallust
Cristóbal de Molina 199
Critical-Analytical Studies of Metal and Stone Inscriptions (Li and Zhao) 170

Croesus (king of Lydia) 6
Crónica de veinte reyes 72
Cronos 202, 203
Crow Indian creation myths 78
A Crown for the King (Ibn Gabirol) 139
Crusades **79–81**
    chivalric code and 65
    goals of 189
    impact of 257, 311
    participants in 107, 146, 318, 319
    works on 284
Ctesias 92
Ctesiphon 90
Cu Chulainn 200
cuicahuicque 208
cuicamatl 208
Cura Pastoralis (Gregory) 11
Curtin, Jeremiah 78
Curzon, Daniel 233
Cushing, Frank Hamilton 299
Cycle of Kings 199, 201
Cynddlew 39
Cynewulf 217
Cyril 225
The Cyropaedia (Xenophon) 333
Cyrus (prince of Persia) 332, 333

D

Daibu, Lady **82**
Dáire, Tadhg Mac 39
"The Dairy Maid and Her Milk Can"
    (Aesop) 7–8
Damasus (pope) 148
Daniel, Arnaut. *See* Arnaut Daniel
Daniélou, Alain 155, 156
Dante Alighieri **83–85**
    contemporaries of 14, 143, 167
    influence of 66, 190
    influences on 25, 85, 203, 229,
        235, 250, 313, 322
    literary criticism on 84–85, 128
    themes of 66
    works by 97, 318
    works on 14
Daodejing (Laozi) 165–166
Daoism
    founding of 165
    influence of 104, 122, 168, 264,
        291, 334
    tenets of 165–166
Daphnis and Chloë (Longus) 174–175
d'Arezzo, Guittone 85
Dark Age 190
Data (Euclid) 101
D'Aubigné, Agrippa 322
Davanzati, Chiaro 85, **85–86**
David of Sassoun **86–87**
Dawla, Sayfal al- 196
Dawlah, 'Ala' ad- 34

Dawlah, Shams ad- 34
Dawson, Raymond 75
da ya (ta ya) 52
Daye, Angell 175
Deacon Gregor 224
Dead Sea Scrolls **87–89**
    Bible and 49
    influences on 115
De Amicitia (Cicero) 70
De animae quantitate (Augustine) 29
The Death of Arthur (Malory) 68, 258
"The Death of Sohrab" (Firdawsī) 278
De beata vita (Augustine) 29
De Bello Gallico (Caesar) 130
Decameron (Boccaccio) 14–15, 190,
    232, 305
De Clementia (Seneca) 276
De consolatione philosophiae (Boethius)
    50–51
De Divinatione (Cicero) 70
The Deeds of the Franks 80
"The Deepest Essence of the Soul"
    (Hadewijch) 119
"Deer Park" (Wang Wei) 326
deer songs, Yaqui 78, **335–337**
"De Fide" (Fulgentius) 109
De immortalitate animae (Augustine)
    29
De institutione arithmetica (Boethius)
    50
De institutione musica (Boethius) 50
De Ira (Seneca) 276
De libero arbitrio (Augustine) 29–30
De magistro (Augustine) 30
Demeter 203
Demetrius of Phaelerum 234
democracy, origins of 26
Demosthenes **89–91**
    contemporaries of 27, 140, 141
    literary criticism on 173
    works on 90, 245
Demosthenes: Statesman and Orator
    (Worthington) 90
De musica (Augustine) 29
De Mysteriis (Ambrose) 12
De natura Deorum (Cicero) 70
De natura rerum liber (Jones) 41
Denby, David 133, 239, 281
de Officiis (Cicero) 70
De Officiis ministrorum (Ambrose) 12
de oratore (Cicero) 70
De ordine (Augustine) 29
De Providentia (Seneca) 276
de re Militaria (Vegetius) 147
De re Publica (Cicero) 70
De Rerum Natura (Lucretius) 99,
    177–179
Descartes, René 277
Description of Greece (Pausanias)
    232–233

The Description of the World (Polo)
    246–248
De Senectute (Cicero) 70
"The Deserted Camp" (Labid) 164
Desire Under the Elms (O'Neill) 203
Detti (Jacopone da Todi) 144
Il Detto d'Amore 261
deus ex machina 24, **91–92**, 102, 286
Devi Bhagavata 250
De vulgari eloquentia (Dante) 84
dharma 46, 231, 316
Dharma Shastra 155, 231
Dialectic (Abélard) 1
*Dialogue between a Philosopher, a
    Christian, and a Jew* (Abélard) 1
"Dialogue in the Mountains" (Li Bai)
    168
Dialogue on Orators (Tacitus) 254
Dialogues of the Gods (Lucian) 176
Dialogus de Oratoribus (Tacitus) 293
Diana 202
diarists 141–142, 191–192, 194–196
Díaz de Vivar, Rodrigo. *See* Cid, El
Dickens, Charles 302, 306
Didactic Poems (Hadewijch) 118
Diderot, Denis 80
Diego (count of Oviedo) 71
Diego de Guzmán 336
Dinarchus 27
Diodorus **92–93**
Dionysius II (king of Syracuse) 238
Dionysius of Halicarnassus **93,** 173
Dionysius the Areopagite 249
Discourses of Epictetus (Epictetus) 99
Discourses on Livy (Machiavelli) 172
Disputationes Tusculanae (Cicero) 70
Divan (al-Farazdaq) 105
Divani Shamsi Tabriz (Rumi) 265
The Divine Comedy (Dante)
    composition of 83
    content and themes 25, 84–85
    as epic 97
    influence of 190
    influences on 203, 322
The Divine Names (Dionysius the
    Areopagite) 249
diwans 3, 140
Djojonegoro, Wardiman 317
Doctor Faustus (Marlowe) 203
Doe, Paula 226
dolce stil nuovo 85
Domitian (emperor of Rome) 99, 150,
    242, 294
Donati, Gemma 83
Dong Jieyuan 325
Doniger, Wendy 156
Donne, John 313
Don Quixote (Cervantes) 66
Donzella, Compiuta **93–94**
The Dove's Necklace (Ibn Hazm) 65

drama. *See also* playwrights
   in Middle Ages 190
   miracle plays 190, 194, 198
   morality plays 190, 194, 198
   mummers' plays **193–194**
   mystery plays 190, 194, **197–198**
   tragedy
      Aristotle on 23–24
      development of genre 4
"Drawing Close to Love" (Hadewijch)
   119
Dream of Red Mansions (Cao Xueqin)
   325
Dream of the Red Chamber (Cao
   Xueqin) 325
The Dream of the Rood 217
Dryden, John 99, 128, 237, 240, 246,
   322
Dudley, Donald R. 178
Du Fu
   contemporaries of 326
   influence of 38
   influences on 297
   literary criticism by 168
   literary criticism on 169
Dunham, William 101
"The Dust Is Blown Over His Beauties"
   (Al-Khansā') 159
du-wen movement 122
"Dwelling in the Mountains" (Xie Ling-
   yun) 334
Dyskolos (Menander) 188

E

"The Eagle and the Beetle" (Aesop) 7
Easwaran, Eknath 45
"The Ebony Horse" 305–306
*Ecclesiastical History of the English
   People* (Bede)
   contents of 56–57, 218
   influence of 15, 41, 112
   language of 189
   translations of 11
Eclogues (Virgil) 320–321, 322
Edda **95–96**
   Elder 95, 204–205
   influence of 211
   themes of 190
   Younger Edda (Snorri Sturluson)
      95, 204, 269, 280
Edgerton, Franklin 232
education, in ancient Rome 253–254
Edward I (king of England) 79,
   189–190
Egill Skallagrimsson 279
Egil's Saga 269, 279
Eight Masters 325
Einhard *283*
Elahinama ('Attār) 26

El Cid. *See* Cid, El
Elder Edda 95
Eleanor of Aquitaine 43, 67, 257, 311
Electra (Euripides) 91, 102
Electra (Sophocles) 286
elegies 218–219
Elegies (Propertius) 249–250
*Elegies of Qu (Elegies of Ch'u) See Qu
   Elegies* 100–101
Elements (Euclid) 100–101
Elements of Music (Euclid) 101
Elements of Platonic Theology (Proclus)
   249
Eliot, George 302
Eliot, T. S. 6, 25, 131, 322
Eloquence in the Vernacular (Dante) 84
*Eloquent Testimony of the Great
   Calamity* (Ibn 'Alqama) 72
Emmerich (king of Hungary) 318
Encheiridion (Epictetus) 99
Encountering Sorrow (Lisao, Qu Yuan)
   252–253, 255
Encyclopédie (Diderot, ed.) 80–81
Eneit (Eneas; Heinrich von Veldeke)
   124–125
England, mythology of 199–202. *See
   also* Arthurian legend
"Enjoy the Passing Hour" (Horace) 61
Enlightenment, influences on 244
Enneads (Plotinus) 244, 248
Ennius, Quintus 96
"An Enquiry into Slander" (Han Yu)
   122–123
Ephorus 92
epic(s) **96–98**
   African 98–99
   Armenian 86–87
   Chinese 327
   classical 97
   Crusades and 80
   English 39, 41–43, 217
   Finnish 152–153
   folk 97
   French 283–285
   Germanic 124–125, 211–212
   Greek 60, 127, 131–134
   Indian 181, 315
   influence of 67
   literary criticism on 23, 186
   medieval literature and 190, 258
   oral literature and 223
   Persian 277–278
   Roman 96, 228, 321–322
   Russian 283
   satires of 28
   Spanish 72
   Sumerian 113
   themes in 136
   types of 97
Epic of Gilgamesh. See Gilgamesh

Epic of Son-Jara 9, **98–99**, 223, 289
The Epic of the Kings (Levy, trans.) 278
Epictetus **99**
Epicureanism 99–100, 177, 277
Epicurus **99–100**
   contemporaries of 187, 301
   influence of 57, 177, 320
   themes of 61
Epigrams (Martial) 186–187
Epimetheus 203
Epinician Odes (Pindar) 236
"The Epistle of Forgiveness" (Al-Ma'rrī)
   180
Epistles (Horace) 135
Epistulae ex Ponto (Ovid) 228
Epistulae morales (Seneca) 275–276
"Epithalamia" (Sappho) 272
Epodes (Horace) 135
Epstein, Isidore 295
Erasmus, Desiderius 254, 302
Erec (Hartmann von Aue) 124
Erec and Enide (Chrétien de Troyes)
   65–66, 67
Ervast, Pekka 153
Eschenbach, Wolfram von. *See* Wolfram
   von Eschenbach
Essays in Idleness (Yoshida Kenkō) 337
Estoria del Cid 72
Ethics, or Know Thyself (Abélard) 1–2
Eu, Jean de Brienne, count of 147
Euclid **100–101**
Eumenes 92
The Eumenides (Aeschylus) 5–6
Eunapius 173
The Eunuch (Terence) 300
Euripides **101–103**
   contemporaries of 101, 102, 280,
      286
   and deus ex machina 91–92, 102
   influence of 174
   literary criticism on 24, 102–103,
      173
   themes in 136, 137
   works by 91–92, 137, 177
   works on 21
Euthyphro (Plato) 238
Evers, Larry 336
*Examination of the Methods of Proof
   Concerning the Doctrines of Religion*
   (Averroës) 33
Exeter Book 217, 219
Eyrbyggia Saga 269–270
Ezra 295

F

Fables (La Fontaine) 232
Fables (Phaedrus) 234–235
"Fables of Bidpai" 235
fabliau 267

Fabulae Aesopiae (Phaedrus) 234–235
The Faerie Queene (Spenser)
   as epic 97
   influences on 68, 203, 313, 322
fakhr 13, 298
Fallacies (Euclid) 101
The Family Reunion (Eliot) 6
Fan Chengda **104–105**
Fan Ch'eng-t'a. *See* Fan Chengda
Farazdaq, al- **105**
Farīd od-Dīn. *See* 'Attār, Farīd od-Dín
The Far-off Journey 252
Fasti (Ovid) 228
"The Father of Indian Corn" 215
Father Sky 206
Favolello (Latini) 167
"The Fawn Will Not Make Flowers" 336
Fellini, Federico 233
feng 51–52
Fenian Cycle 199, 200–201
Fenrir 205
Fernando I (king of Castile) 71
feudalism
   and chivalry 64
   Middle Ages and 189
Fielding, Henry 175
Fifteen Poets of the Aztec World (León-
   Portilla, trans.) 209
Figures (Euclid) 101
file 39
fin'amor 43, 311
Finley, John H., Jr. 308
Finn 190
Finnegan, Ruth 9
Finnegan's Wake (Joyce) 201
Finnish national epic 152–153
Fionn, Gofraidh 39
il Fiore 261
Firdawsī, Abū ol-Qāsem Mansūr
   106–107, 277–278
Firdousi, Abū ol-Qāsem Mansūr. *See*
   Firdawsī, (Abū ol-Qāsem Mansūr)
Fisher King 130–131
"The Fisherman and the Genie" 305
"The Fishes and the Frying Pan"
   (Aesop) 8
Fitzgerald, Edward 220
The Five Treasures (Nezāmī) 210
Flaccus, Lucius 70
Flaccus, Quintus Horatius. *See* Horace
Flatha, Fear 39
Floire et Blancheflor 28
flood myths 77, 114, 115, 328
Florentine Codex 209
Florida (Apuleius) 19
folk epics 97
Fons Vitae (Ibn Gabirol) 138–139
"The Foolish Girls" 215
"For Her Brother" (Al-Khansā') 159
"The Former Cloud" (Kalidasa) 153–154

"The Four Branches of the
   Mabinogian" 201
Four Doctors of the Church 12
Fox, Matthew 128
"The Fox and the Grapes" (Aesop) 7
"The Fox and the Stork" (Phaedrus) 234
Frampton, John 247
Francés, Bruno 62
Franciscan Order 107
Francis of Assisi, Saint **107–108**
   influence of 143
   works by 189
Frappier, Jean 67, 68
Frederick II (Holy Roman Emperor)
   318
Freud, Sigmund 203
Freyja 205
Friberg, Eino 153
Frogs (Aristophanes) 21
Froissart, Jean 66, 190
Frost, Robert 62
fu (poetry) 253, 291, 338, 340
Fujiwara Michinaga 108, 194
Fujiwara no Kaneie 191
Fujiwara no Kinto 221
Fujiwara no Teika **108**
Fujiwara no Yasumasa 14
Fujiwara Sadaie. *See* Fujiwara no Teika
Fujiwara Shunzei 108
Fulcher of Chartes 80
Fulgentius, Saint **108–109**
Fulgentius of Ruspe. *See* Fulgentius, Saint

G

Gaius Octavius. *See* Augustus
Galba (emperor of Rome) 253
Galen **110–111**
   influence of 35
   influences on 129
Galland, Antoine 304–305
Gallienus (emperor of Rome) 244
Gallus, Cornelius 250
Gamboa, Pedro Sarmiento 199
Gandhi, Mahatma 46
Ganjāvī, Elyās Yūsof Nezami. *See* Nezāmī
Gao Ming **111–112**
"The Garden" (Ibn Gabirol) 138–139
Gaufridus Monemutensis 112
Gemara 295–296
Gemmei (empress of Japan) 160
Genesis poem 219
Gentry, Francis 211
Geoffrey of Monmouth **112**
   influence of 219
   influences on 201
   works by 67, 189
Geographical Relation of Tezcoco
   (Pomar) 209
Geographical Studies (Strabo) 288

The Geography (Strabo) 288
George, Arthur 278
Georgics (Virgil) 127, 320–321, 322
German Epic Poetry (Gentry, ed.) 211
Germania (Tacitus) 293
ghazal 298
Ghazali, al- 33
ghazal tradition 105
Gibbs, Marion 329–330
Gildas 112
Giles, J. A. 40–41
Giles, Lionel 290
Gilgamesh **113–115**
   as epic 97
   flood myth in 77, 114, 115
   influence of 115
   literary criticism on 113–115
   oral literature and 223
   themes of 61
Gilgamesh of Uruk 113
Ginsberg, Allen 339
"The Girl and the Little Ahayuuta" 341
"The Girl Who Took Care of the
   Turkeys" 299
Glosses on Logic (Abélard) 1
Goddard, Pliny Earle 327–328
Godfrey of Bouillon 80
Godfrey of Lagny 68
Godinho, P. N. 158
"Gododdin" (Anerin) 39
*The God of Socrates, Plato and his
   Doctrines* (Apuleius) 19
Gods and Heroes of the Celts (Sjoestedt)
   201
Goethe, Johann Wolfgang von
   influences on 154, 203, 263
   literary criticism by 175
   works by 250
Go-Kuden (Go-Toba) 279
The Golden Ass (Apuleius) 18–19
"Golden Bells" (Bai) 38
Golden Legend (Longfellow) 124
Golden Odes. *See* Hanged Poems
Golestan (Saadī) 268
Góngora, Luis de 313
Goodwin, Grenville 327–328
"The Goose with the Golden Eggs"
   (Aesop) 8
Gordian III (emperor of Rome) 244
Go-Shirakawa (emperor of Japan) 279
Goshuishu (1086) 142
Go-Toba (emperor of Japan) 108, 279
Gottfried von Strassburg **115–116**
   contemporaries of 329
   literary criticism by 125
   literary criticism on 309
   medieval romance and 258
   works by 65
Go-Uda (emperor of Japan) 337
Gower, John 229, 261

Gray, Thomas 237
Great Assembly 295
The Great Dionysia 20–21
"The Great Fish" 331
Greek mythology **202–204,** 228, 260
The Greek Way (Hamilton) 6
Green, Peter 17
Gregor, Deacon 224
Gregory, Horace 229
Gregory, Saint
    as Doctor of the Church 12
    translations of 11
Gregory of Nyssa 244
Gregory VII (pope) 189
Gregory VIII (pope) 79
Griffin, Jasper 69
Grimm, Jacob 116
Grimm brothers
    influences on 124, 232
    works comparable to 76
Grinyer, Peter 290
griots 98
The Guide to the Perplexed
    (Maimonides) 183
Guillame de Dôle 147
Guillaume de Lorris **116–117**
    influence of 147
    medieval romance and 258
    themes of 65
    works by 259–261
Guinizelli, Guido 85
Gulliver's Travels (Swift) 176
"A Gust of Wind" 215
Gutenberg, Johannes 190
Gutzwiller, Kathryn J. 60
Guyer, Foster 258
Gwalchmai 39
Gwilym, Dafydd ap 39

H

Haakon IV (king of Norway) 269, 280
Habakkuk, commentaries on 89
Hades 202, 203
Hadewijch 40, **118–119**
hadith 162, 192
Hadrian (emperor of Rome) 150, 184
Hafiz 220
Haft Paykar (Nezāmī) 210
haiku 296
Hakim, "Mad" Caliph 79
Hakuin 339
Halevi, Judah **120,** 139
Halevi, Yehuda Benjamin Samuel. *See*
    Halevi, Judah
Halle, Adam de la. *See* Adam de la Halle
The Hall of Beautiful Spring (Wang
    Shifu) 326
hamartia 23, 24, 136
Hamilton, Edith 4, 6, 128

Hamlet (Shakespeare) 204
HaNagid, Samuel 138
Handel, George Frideric 203
Hanford, S. A. 58
Hanged Poems (*Mu'alaqāt;* Seven Odes;
    Golden Odes) **120–121**
    history of 298
    poets included in 13, 140, 164,
        297, 298
Han Hsin 290
Han Shan **121–122,** 297
Han Xin 290
Han Yu (Han Yü) **122–123**
    contemporaries of 169
    influence of 226
"The Hare and the Tortoise" (Aesop) 7
Harith, al- 120, 298
Harold (king of England) 189
Haroun and the Sea of Stories (Rushdie)
    306
Hartmann von Aue **123–124,** 329
Le Haut Livre de Graal 131
Heavenly Questions 253
Hebrew Bible **47–50**
    creation story in 77
    Dead Sea Scrolls and 87–89
Hecale (Callimachus) 60
Hecataeus of Abdera 92
Hecuba (Euripides) 102
Hecyra (Terence) 300
hegira 193
Heidegger, Martin 339
Heike Monogatari (Kamo) 157
Heinrich von Veldeke **124–125**
Hel 205
Heliodorus 174
Hellados Periegesis (Pausanias) 232–233
Hellenica (Xenophon) 333
Héloïse **1–2**
    influences on 229
    language of 189
    translations of 147
He Lu (king of Wu) 289–290
Hen, Llywarch 39
Henry II (king of England) 15, 43, 186
Henry IV (emperor of Germany) 189
hEoghusa, Eochaidh Ó 39
Hephaestus 203
Hera 202
Hercules Enraged (Seneca) 276
Hermann of Thuringia 329
Hermes 202
Hermias 22
Herodotus **125–127**
    contemporaries of 125, 286
    influences on 17
    literary criticism on 92, 307
    works by 14, 280
Heroides (Ovid) 227

Herrick, Robert
    influences on 14
    themes of 62
Hesiod **127–128**
    literary criticism on 173
    themes in 137, 202
    works by 203
Hestia 203
Hicks, R. D. 99
Hieron of Syracuse 4, 37
Hieronymus, Sophronius Eusebius. *See*
    Jerome, Saint
Hieronymus of Cardia 92
hija (lampooning) 105
hijra. See hegira
Hildegard von Bingen **128–129**
    language of 189
    works on 118
Hildegard von Bingen's Mystical Visions
    (Fox) 128
Hina-of-the-moon 206
Hinduism 154. *See also Bhagavad Gita;*
    Mahabharata; Panchatantra; purana;
    Ramayana
Hippocrates 110, **129–130**
Hippocratic Corpus 129
Hippocratic Oath 129
Hippolytus (Euripides) 102
Hiroaki Sato 279
Hirtius, Aulus 58, **130**
Historia abbatum (Bede) 41
Historia General de Etiopia Alta (Teilez)
    158
Historia naturalis (Pliny the Elder)
    241–242
Historia Regum Britanniae (Geoffrey of
    Monmouth) 67, 112
Historia Roderici 72
Historical Sketches (Strabo) 288
Historic Cycle. *See* Cycle of Kings
histories
    of Africa 158
    of ancient civilizations 92
    of ancient Greece 125–127,
        307–308
    of Byzantium 16
    of China 226
    of classical world 93
    of Crusades 80, 319
    of England 15, 67, 112, 189, 219
    of English religious history 41
    of Greece 17, 307–308, 333
    of the Jews 149
    of Native Americans 81
    of Rome 96, 172, 241, 270–271,
        288, 293–294
Histories (Tacitus) 293–294
History (Herodotus) 125–127, 136
History of Ethiopia (Almeida)
    158

A History of Finnish Literature (Ahohas) 153

History of Jerusalem (Robert and Monk) 80

History of My Calamities (Abélard) 2

History of Reynard the Fox (Caxton) 263

The History of Rome from Its Foundation (Livy) 172

A History of Sanskrit Literature (Keith) 154

History of the Crusades (Runciman) 81

History of the Germanic Wars (Pliny the Elder) 241

History of the Incas (Gamboa) 199

History of the Jugurthine War (Sallust) 271

History of the Kings of Britain (Geoffrey of Monmouth) 67, 112, 189, 219

History of the Kings of Ethiopia (Agrippa) 158

History of the Peloponnesian War (Thucydides) 307–308

History of the Persian Wars (Herodotus). *See History* (Herodotus)

History of the Roman Republic (Sallust) 270

Hobbes, Thomas 308

The Hobbit (Tolkien) 95

Hodges, David 169

Hohokam Indians 222

Hojoki (Kamo) 157

Holland, Philemon 245

Hollander, Robert 84

Holloway, Julia Bolton 167

Holmes, Urban 68

Holy Grail **130–131**
    and Arthurian legend 65, 68
    courtly love and 311
    influence of 331
    Tristan and Iseult and 309
    works on 115, 190, 258, 329–330

Homage to Sectus Propertius (Pound) 250

Homer **131–134**
    contemporaries of 127
    influence of 16, 17, 108, 132, 174, 236, 269
    influences on 115, 203
    literary criticism on 10, 23–24, 84, 97, 133–134, 173, 176, 322
    oral literature and 223
    themes in 61, 136, 202
    views on 227

homosexuality, in ancient Rome 233

"Honeysuckle" (Marie de France) 186, 310

Hopi
    Coyote Tales **75–77**, 205, 313
    tuuwutsi narratives **313–314**

"The Hopi Boy and the Sun" 314

Hopi Coyote Tales (Malotki and Lomatuway'ma) 76

"The Hopis and the Famine" 299

Horace **134–136**
    contemporaries of 32, 134, 172, 249, 299
    influence of 61–62, 63, 168
    influences on 10, 60, 237, 302
    life of 234
    literary criticism on 135–136, 227, 235
    themes of 61, 172

Hortensius (Cicero) 30

House of Fame (Chaucer) 322

Hovnan of Khout 86

"How Dog Came to the Indians" 215

Howell, Peter 186, 187

"How the Deer Got His Horns" 216

Hroswitha of Gandersheim 300

hsiao ya 52

Hsieh Ling-yün. *See* Xie Ling-Yun

Hsi-hsiang-chi (Wang Shifu) 325–326

Hsüan-tsung. *See* Xuanzhong

Huai (king of Qu) 254

Hubbard, Margaret 250

hubris 23, **136–137**

Hugo, Victor 322

Hui-pao 325

humanist movement, influences on 254

Humphries, Rolfe 229

hyakushu-uta 279

Hyperides 27, 141

I

Iambi (Callimachus) 60

Ibis (Callimachus) 60

Ibn 'Alqama 72

Ibn Bassam 72

Ibn Ezra, Moshe 138

Ibn Gabirol, Solomon ben Yehuda **138–139**, 304

Ibn Hasan, Yequtiel 138

Ibn Hazm 65

Ibn Hujr. *See* Imru' al-Qays

Ibn Jabirul, Abu Ayyub Sulaiman Ibn Yahya. *See* Ibn Gabirol, Solomon ben Yehuda

Ibn Shaddad, Antara 120–121, 298

Ibn Sīnā. *See* Avicenna

Icelandic sagas 212–213, 269

Ida of Nivelles 40

Idylls of the King (Tennyson) 68, 131

The Iliad (Homer)
    contents and themes of 97, 131–134, 136
    influence of 16, 97, 322
    influences on 202

Imam 'Alí. *See* 'Alí ibn Abí Talíb

Impartial Judgements in the Garden of Literature (Zheng Hou) 290

Imperial Poetry Bureau 157

Impromptu Verses on the Four Seasons of the Countryside (Fan Chengda) 104

Imru' al-Qays 120–121, **139–140**, 298

Incas
    creation myths 77
    myth of Manco Capac 77, **198–199**, 223

In Catilinam (Cicero) 70–71

The Incoherence of the Incoherence (Averroës) 33

The Incoherence of the Philosophers (al-Ghazali) 33

Indra 256

Inferno (Dante) 84

Innocent III (pope) 107, 319

"In Praise of God" (Ibn Gabirol) 139

Inscribed Landscapes (Strassberg) 252, 325

"The *Interest without the Capital*" (Rumi) 265

Introduction to Theology (Abélard) 1

Ion of Chios 286

Iphigenia at Aulis (Euripides) 177

Ireland, mythology of 199–202

Irene (empress of Byzantium) 16

Irwin, James 206

Irwin, Robert 304

Isaeus **140**
    contemporaries of 140, 141
    influence of 27
    influences on 27

Iseult. *See Tristan and Iseult*

Iskandar-Nama (Nezāmī) 210

Islam. *See also* Koran
    converts to 2, 159, 164
    Crusades and 79–81
    founding of 192
    influence of 298
    influences on 244
    major figures in 11–12, 25–26
    spread of 79, 189
    works on 285, 331

Islamic law 162, 193

Isocrates **141**
    contemporaries of 140, 141
    influence of 27

Israel Antiquities Authority 87

Italos, John 16

Iwein (Hartmann von Aue) 124

Ixtlilxóchitl, Alva 209

Izumi Shikibu **141–142**
    influences on 222
    works by 296

Izumi Shikibu Nikki (Izumi Shikibu) 142

J

Jackson Knight, W. F. 97
Jacobs, Joseph 263
Jacopo dei Benedetti. *See* Jacopone da
   Todi
Jacopone da Todi **143–144**
Jāḥiz, `Abu `Uthmān `Amr ibn Bahr ibn
   Mahbūb al-Jāḥiz **144–145**
Jaroslav of Kiev 225
Jataka **145–146**
   influences on 317
   parallels to 230, 235
Jaufré Rudel 43, 44, **146–147,** 318
Jean de Joinville 80
Jean de Meun **147–148**
   influences on 2, 311
   themes of 65
   works by 116–117, 258, 259–261
Jensen, Frede 146, 318
Jerome, Saint **148**
   as Doctor of the Church 12, 148
   influence of 168
   influences on 254
   works by 177, 189
Jerusalem Delivered (Tasso) 80
Jewish Antiquities (Josephus) 149
Jewish War (Josephus) 149
jinshi 104, 111, 122, 291, 327
Jiuge (Chiu-ko) 252
jnana 46
John II (emperor of Byzantium) 16
John of Hexham 40
Johnson, John William 98–99
Johnson, Sidney 329–330
Jones, C. W. 41
jongleur 311
Jonson, Ben 14, 17, 245, 254, 302
Joseph of Arimathea 130, 131
Josephus, Flavius **149**
Journey through Genius (Dunham) 101
"A Journey to the Skeleton House" 314
Joyce, James 201
Juan Chi. *See* Ruan Ji
Judaism. *See* Hebrew Bible
Judith, Juliana, and Elene 218
Julian of Norwich 40, 189
Julius Caesar (Shakespeare) 245–246
Jung, Carl 203–204
Junius manuscript 217
Juno 202, 321
Jupiter 202, 321
Justinian (emperor of Byzantium) 140
Justinian (emperor of Rome) 121
"just war" concept 80
Juvenal **150–151**
   contemporaries of 150, 186, 254
   influence of 168
   influences on 302
Juvenalis, Decimus Junius. *See* Juvenal
Juzjani 35

K

Ka`aba 120, 121
ka'atsa narratives 313, 314
Kafur 196
Kagero Diary (Mother of Fujiwara
   Michitsuna) 191
kakekotoba 222
Kalevala **152–153**
   as epic 97
   oral literature and 223
Kalidasa **153–154,** 181, 317
Kalidasakavyasambhavam (Pandey)
   154
kama 231
Kama Sutra **154–156,** 231
Kamo no Chomei **156–157**
Kana'ti 216
Kane 206
K`ang-Lo, Duke of. *See* Xie Ling-yun
Kao Ming. *See* Gao Ming
karma 46
Katsuragi (prince of Japan) 213
Kawashima, Terry 222
Kay, Sarah 260
Keats, John 19
Kebra Nagast Chronicles **157–158**
Keith, Arthur Berriedale 154
Kennedy, Philip 298
kennings 95, 204, 218
Kenreimon-in Ukyo no Daibu. *See*
   Daibu, Lady
Kenrei Mon'in Ukyo no Daibu shu
   (Daibu) 82
Kerouac, Jack 339
Keter Malkhut (Ibn Gabirol) 139
The Keys to the Kalevala (Ervast) 153
Khadija 192
Khamse (Nezāmī) 210
Khansā`, al- **158–159,** 180
Khayyāmī Gheyā od-Dīn Abū ol-fath
   `Omar ebn Ebrāhīm al-. *See* Omar
   Khayyám
Khosrow and Shīrīn (Nezāmī) 210
King Harald's Saga (Snorri Sturluson)
   280
King Mark and Iseult the White
   (Chrétien de Troyes) 67
Ki no Tsurayuki **159–160,** 221
Kitab al-Bayan wa al-tabayyun (Al-
   Jāḥiz) 145
Kitab al-Hayawan (Al-Jāḥiz) 145
The Knight of the Grail (Chrétien de
   Troyes) 329
Knights (Aristophanes) 20
koan 339
Kobun (emperor of Japan) 213
Kojiki **160,** 214
Kokinshu 159, 221
Komachi, Ono no. *See* Ono no Komachi
Komachishu (Ono no Komachi) 221

Konde, Sogolon 98
Kongfuzi. *See* Confucius
Kong Qiu. *See* Confucius
Koran **161–163**
   authority of 145
   authorship of 192
   v. Bible 162, 163
   influence of 34, 164, 180, 193, 265
   literary criticism on 161–163
Krohn Rüdiger 116
Krsna Vyasa 182
Ku 206
Kulthum, `Amr ibn. *See* `Amr ibn
   Kulthum
Kumulipo 206, 223
K`ung Ch'iu. *See* Confucius
K`ung Fu-tzu. *See* Confucius

L

Labid 120, **164,** 298
"Lady of Heaven" (Jacopone da Todi)
   144
Laertius, Diogenes 301
La Fontaine, Jean de
   influences on 232, 235
   works by 8
lais 185
Lakota creation myths 77
"The Lament for the South" (Yu Xin)
   338
The Lament (Lisao Qu Yuan) 252–253,
   255
The Lament of the Lady of Ch'in (Wei
   Zhuang) 327
Lamprus 286
Lancelot, or The Knight of the Cart
   (Chrétien de Troyes) 66, 67, 68
Lane, Edward 305
Langland, William 190, 219, 302
"The Language of Poetry" (Snorri
   Sturluson) 95
Lan-p'ei lu (Fan Chengda) 104
Lao Tsu. *See* Laozi
Laozi **164–167**
   contemporaries of 74, 165
Lapham, Lewis 308
Larbaud, Valery 148
Latini, Brunetto 83, **167–168**
"The Latter Cloud" (Kalidasa) 153–154
Lattimore, Richard 5, 127
Laude (Jacopone da Todi) 143–144
Laxdaela Saga 270
Layamon 219
Layli and Majnun (Nezāmī) 210–211
Lay of Volund 205
Lebor Gabala 200
*The Legends and Lands of Native North
   Americans* (Martinez) 77
Le Gentil, Pierre 285

Leo III (pope) 189
León-Portilla, Miguel 209
Leo XIII (pope) 40
Lerner, Alan Jay 203
Lerner, John 247
Lessing, Gotthold 203, 240
Letters (Hadewijch) 118
Letters (Pliny the Younger) 243
"Letters of a Horse and Mule" (Al-Ma`rrī) 181
Letter to Herodotus (Epicurus) 99
Letter to Menoeceus (Epicurus) 99
Letter to Pythocles (Epicurus) 99
Lévi-Strauss, Claude 204
Levy, Reuben 278
Lewis, C. S. 65, 66, 259
Li Bai **168**
    contemporaries of 326
    influence of 104
    influences on 297
    literary criticism on 169
The Libation Bearers (Aeschylus) 5
"Liber ad Scarilam de Incarnatione" (Fulgentius) 109
"Liber ad Victorem" (Fulgentius) 109
Li Bo. *See* Li Bai
Li Erh. *See* Laozi
Life (Josephus) 149
"Life Is Brief" (Horace) 135
The Life of Avicenna (Juzjani) 35
Life of Beatrice (Beatrice of Nazareth) 40
Life of Charlemagne (Einhard) 283
Life of Merlin (Geoffrey of Monmouth) 112
Life of Plotinus (Porphyry) 173, 244
Life of Plutarch (Dryden) 246
Life of Pythagoras (Porphyry) 248
Li Gefei 170
Li He **169–170**
Lincoln, Abraham 101
Lineaje del Cid 72
Li Pai. *See* Li Bai
Li Po. *See* Li Bai
Li Qingzhao **170–171**
Li Sao (Qu Yuan) 252–253, 255
Li Shangyin **171–172**
"List of Verse Forms" (Snorri Sturluson) 95
Li T`ai Po. *See* Li Bai
A Literary History of the Arabs (Nicholson) 298
"Little Flowers of St. Francis of Assisi" 108
Lives of Eminent Philosophers (Hicks) 99
Lives of Famous Romans (Coolidge) 71, 320
Livy **172–173**
    contemporaries of 32, 172
    influence of 175
Llywelyn, Morgan 201

Lobo, Jerónimo 158
Loewe, Frederick 203
Loki 205
Lomatuway'ma, Michael 76
Longfellow, Henry Wadsworth 124, 215
Longinus **173–174**
    contemporaries of 173, 248
    influence of 293
Longinus, Cassius 173
Longus **174–175**
Lönnrot, Elias 152
Lono 206
Loptsson, Jon 279
Lord, Louis E. 70
"Lord, Where Shall I Find You" (Halevi) 120
The Lord of the Rings (Tolkien) 95, 201, 204, 270
Lorris, Guillaume de. *See* Guillaume de Lorris
Louis IV (king of France) 80
"Love Is the Master" (Rumi) 265
Lovelace, Richard 14
The Lover's Confession (Gower) 261
"Love's Maturity" (Hadewijch) 119
Lowa 206
Lucan **175–176**
    contemporaries of 93
    influence of 167
    life of 186
Lu Chiu-Yin 121–122
Lucian **176**
    influence of 19
    influences on 302
    works by 174
Lucius, or the Ass (Lucian) 19
Lucius Apuleis. *See* Apuleius
Lucretius **177–179**
    influence of 320
    influences on 96
    literary criticism on 177–179
    works by 99
Lucretius (Dudley) 178
Ludwig III (king of Thuringia) 124
Lu Jiuyin 121–122
"Luminous Stars in Praise of the Best of Mankind" (al-Būsírí) 55
Lun Yu 74–75
Luria, Maxwell 261
The Lute (Gao Ming) 111
A Lute of Jade (Cranmer-Byng) 227
Lute Song (musical) 112
Luther, Martin 254
Lu Yu 104
Lycurgus 27
Lygdamis 125
lyric poetry 37
Lysias 27, **179**
Lysis (Plato) 238
Lysistrata (Aristophanes) 21

M
Ma`arrī, Abū al-`Alā`, al- **180–181**
The Mabinogian 201
Macedonius 92
Machiavelli, Niccolò 172
Macrobius 244
Macrone, Michael 202, 203
Maecenas 134–135, 249, 321
Magna Carta 189–190
Magnusson, Magnus 280
Mahabharata **181–183**
    authorship of 251
    composition of 315
    contents and themes of 45, 46, 231, 316
    as epic 97
    influence of 154
mahapurana 250
Mahfouz, Naguib 306
Mahmud of Hgazna 106
The Maid from Andros (Terence) 299
Maigetsusho (Fujiwara) 108
Maimonides, Moses **183–184**
    works by 295
    works on 304
Makeda (queen of Sheba) 157–158
Makemake 206
Makura no Soshi (Sei Sho⁻nagon) 273–274
Malavika and Agnimitra (Kalidasa) 154
Malavikagnimitra (Kalidasa) 154
Mallanga, Vatsyayana 155
Malory, Thomas
    influences on 68, 131, 313
    literary criticism on 331
    medieval romance and 258
    themes of 66
    works by 190
Malotki, Ekkehart 76
Mama Huaco 198, 199
Ma'mun, al- 2
Manabazho 215
Manco Capac, myth of **198–199**
Mandeville, Sir John 247
Manfred of Sicily 167
The Man from Sicyon (Menander) 188
Mango Sapaca 199
Mankiller, Wilma 216–217
Manon Lescaut (Prévost) 66
Mansur, Nuh Ibn 34
Mansūr, al- 33
mantras 256
Manuel I (emperor of Byzantium) 16
"Manwydan, Son of Llyr" 201
Man'yōshū 225–226
Manyoshu (The Ten Thousand Leaves; Otomo, ed.) 214
Marcabru 44, 312
Marco Polo and the Discovery of the World (Lerner) 247

Marcus Annaeus Lucanis. *See* Lucan
Marcus Aurelius Antoninus (emperor
  of Rome) 110, **184–185**
Margareta, countess of Cleve 124
Maria Stuart (Schiller) 154
Marie de Champagne 67
Marie de France **185–186**
  influence of 190
  influences on 235, 311
  medieval romance and 258
  themes of 65, 67
  works by 310
Marlowe, Christopher 203, 229
Maro, Publius Virgilius. *See* Virgil
Mars 202–203
Marsden, W. 247
Martial **186–187**
  contemporaries of 150
  influence of 168
  influences on 302
  life of 253
  literary criticism by 63
Martialis, Marcus Valerius. *See* Martial
Martinez, David 77
Marvell, Andrew 62
Marzials, Frank 80
Masefield, John 263
Master Lao. *See* Laozi
"Master of the Universe" (Ibn Gabirol)
  139
"Math, Son of Mathonwy" 201
Mathnawi (Rumi) 265–266
Matisse, Henri 203
Mattathias, Joseph ben. *See* Josephus,
  Flavius
Matter of Britain 257, 258
Matter of Charlemagne 257
Matter of Rome 257, 258
Maui 207
McCarthy, Terence 258
McCulloh, William 174
McKenzie, Kenneth 86
McNeilly, Mark 290
Mechthild of Magdeburg 40
Medb (queen of Connacht) 200
Medea (Euripides) 91, 102
Medea (Ovid) 227
Medea (Seneca) 276
medicine. *See* science and medicine
medieval literature
  characteristics of 167
  drama 197–198
  epic poetry 283, 285
  influences on 11, 41, 51, 181, 187,
    189–190, 217, 235, 241, 300, 322
  literary criticism on 190
  literary genres 44
  romance **257–259**
    characteristics of 211–212
    development of 67

influence of 43
influences on 147, 259, 311,
  329
literary criticism on 258–259
origins of 190, 257
themes of 65
themes of 61, 71, 115–116, 229,
  262, 309
Tristan and Iseult in 186
medieval philosophy, influences on 11,
  19, 23, 244, 248, 249
Meditations (Aurelius) 184–185
Megasthenes 92
"Megha Duuta" (Kalidasa) 153–154
Meilyr 39
Melanchthon, Philip 254
Melmoth, Sebastian 233
Memmius 62
Memorabilia (Xenophon) 282, 332
Menaechmi (Plautus) 240
Menander **187–188**
  influence of 21, 174, 240, 299
  influences on 302
  translations of 299
Mencius 74
Mendelsohn, Daniel 102, 273
Mendez, Alfonson 158
Meng Chiao 122
Meng Jiao 122
Menyelek 158
Mercury 202
Mertens, Volker 124
Messalina (empress of Rome) 275
Metamorphoses (Apuleius) 18–19
Metamorphoses (Ovid)
  contents and themes of 228–229
  influences on 60, 202
  literary criticism on 305
Metaphysics (Aristotle) 23
Methodius 225
metics 179
Meun, Jean de. *See* Jean de Meun
Mexican Songs 209
Michael, Ian 73
Michael VII (emperor of Byzantium) 15
Michie, James 187
Middle Ages **188–191**. *See also*
  Medieval
    asceticism in 108
    courtly love tradition and 313
    Doctors of the Church in 148
    hymns of 144
    literary criticism in 176
    mythology in 199
    Neoplatonism in 139
    periods in 188
    social concepts of 64–66, 116
    women in 66, 94, 119, 129, 190,
      258
Midrash 163, 295–296

Midsummer Night's Dream
  (Shakespeare) 19
Miles Gloriosus (Plautus) 240
Il milione (Polo) 246–248
Miller, Barbara Stoler 47
Milton, John
  influence of 68
  influences on 17, 128, 203, 322
  works by 97
Mimnermus 249
Minerva 202
Minnelieder 324, 329
Minnesang tradition 324
minstrels 311
Le Miracle de Théophile (Rutebeuf)
  266–267
miracle plays 190, 194, 198
The Misadventures of Tim McPick
  (Curzon) 233
The Misanthrope (Menander) 188
The Miser (Molière) 240
Mishnah 295–296
Mishnah Torah (Maimonides) 183, 295
The Mists of Avalon (Bradley) 68
Mitchell, Stephen 166
Mocedades del Cid (Castro) 72
Mochi. *See* Wang Wei
Mo-ch`i. *See* Wang Wei
Mohammed. *See* Muhammad
moksha 46
Molière (Jean-Baptiste Poquelin) 240,
  245, 300
Molina, Felipe 336
Monarchia (Dante) 83
Monarchy (Dante) 83
Mone, F. J. 118
Montaigne, Michel de 185, 245, 277, 302
Montferrat, Marquis Boniface of 318
Monthly Notes (Fujiwara) 108
Montreuil, Jean de 261
Mooney, James 216
Moore, Thomas 14
Mór, Donnchadh 39
Moral Essays (Plutarch) 245
Moralia (Plutarch) 245
morality plays 190, 194, 198
Le Morte D'Arthur (Malory) 131, 190,
  258, 313
Mother Earth 206
The Mother-in-Law (Terence) 300
Mother of Fujiwara Michitsuna **191–192**
Motosuke 273
Motto, Anna Lydia 276
"The Mountain Where Hui-pao
  Meditated" (Wang Anshi) 325
Mourning Becomes Electra (O'Neill) 6
Mozart, Wolfgang Amadeus 203
Mu`alaqat. See Hanged Poems
Mu`ayyad, Abu Muhammad Ilyas ibn
  Yūsuf ibn Zaki. *See* Nezāmī

Muhalhil, al- 13
Muhammad **192–193**
    contemporaries of 159, 164
    family of 11–12, 145
    influence of 298, 306
    Koran and 161, 162
    literary criticism by 140, 159
    and spread of Islam 189
    works on 33, 55, 98
mummers' plays **193–194**
munazara 145
Murasaki Shikibu **194–196**
    contemporaries of 141, 273
    literary criticism by 273, 274
    literary criticism on 82
Murena, Lucius 70
musicians and composers 3–4, 128–129
Muslim Saints and Mystics (`Attār) 26
Mussin-Puschkin, Count 283
Mutalammis 297–298
Mutanabbi, al- **196–197**
Mu'tasim, al- 2
My Fair Lady (Lerner and Loewe) 203
"My Heart Is in the East" (Halevi) 120
mystery plays 190, 194, **197–198**
Mystical Poems of Rumi (Rumi) 265
myth of Manco Capac 77, **198–199**,
    223
Mythological Cycle 199, 200
mythology. *See also* creation myths;
    Holy Grail
    Celtic **199–202**, 257
    flood myths 77, 114, 115, 328
    Greek and Roman **202–204**, 228,
        260
    in Middle Ages 199
    Native-American. *See* Native
        American literature
    Norse **204–205**
        Eddas and 95
        influence of 211
        themes in 183, 206
        works on 280
    Oceanic 204–205, **205–207**
Myths and Rites of the Inca (Cristóbal de
    Molina) 199
Myths of the Cherokee (Mooney) 216

N

Nahj al Balagha (al-Sharif) 12
Nahuatl poetry 77, **208–209**
Napoleon 101
Naqaith of Jarir and al Farazdaq (al
    Farazdaq and ibn 'Atiyya) 105
Narada 315
Native American literature
    Aztecs
        creation myths 77
        poetry 208–209

Chinook myths **63–64**
creation myths 75, 77–79, **77–79**,
    223, 229, 314, 328, 341
Hopi
        Coyote tales **75–77**, 205, 313
        tuuwutsi narratives **313–314**
Incas
        creation myths 77
        myth of Manco Capac 77,
        198–199, 223
Nahuatl poetry 77, **208–209**
Navajo Nightway Ceremony songs
    78, **209–210**
Ojibway myths and legends
    215–216
Oklahoma Cherokee
        creation myths 78
        folktales **216–217**
O`othham Hoho`ok A`agitha
    222–223
telapnaawe narratives **299**
White Mountain Apache myths
    and tales 224, **327–329**
Winnebago
        waikan narratives 299, **323**,
        331
        worak narratives 299, 323, **331**
Yaqui deer songs 78, **335–337**
Zuni
        creation myths 78, 299, 341
        narrative poetry 78, 328,
        340–341
        telapnaawe narratives **299**
Naturales quaestiones (Seneca) 276
Natural History (Pliny the Elder)
    241–242
Natural Questions (Seneca) 276
The Nature of the Gods (Cicero) 70
Navajo
    creation myths 77
    Nightway Ceremony songs 78,
    209–210
Nennius 112
Neo-Confucianism 74, 122
Neoplatonism
    exponents of 248, 249
    influence of 244
    in Middle Ages 139
neoteric poets 62
Neptune 202
Nero (emperor of Rome)
    contemporaries of 175, 186, 233,
    275
    reign of 149, 241
    works on 294
Nerva (emperor of Rome) 242
New Ballads 38
New Comedy 21, 188, 240, 302
New History of the Five Dynasties
    (Ouyang Xiu) 226

New History of the T'ang Dynasty
    (Ouyang Xiu) 226
New Life (Dante) 14, 83, 190
new sweet style 85
Newton, Isaac 101
New York Review of Books 69
Nezahualcoyotl 208
Nezāmī **210–211**
Niane, D. T. 289
Nibelungenlied **211–212**
    as epic 97
    literary criticism on 95, 205, 283,
        316, 329–330
    medieval literature and 190
    versions of 269
Nicholson, Reynold 298
Nicomachean Ethics (Aristotle) 23, 302
Nightway Ceremony songs 78
Nihon shoki 160
nine gems 153
Nine Songs 252
Nizāmī. *See* Nezāmī
Njal's Saga **212–213**, 269
Norse mythology **204–205**
    Eddas and 95
    influence of 211
    themes in 183, 206
    works on 280
novels
    ancient Greek 174
    picaresque 233
    Roman 18–19
Nukada, Princess **213–214**
Nukata Okimi. *See* Nukada, Princess
Numbakulla brothers 206
Nun's Priest's Tale (Chaucer) 263

O

Oceanic mythology 204–205, **205–207**
Odes (Horace) 61, 134–135
Odes of Anacreon (Moore) 14
"Ode to Psyche" (Keats) 19
"Ode to the Mantle" (al-Būsírí) 55
Odin 204, 205, 280
Odo of Deuil 80
Odovacar (king of Rome) 50
The Odyssey (Homer) 23–24, 97,
    131–134, 202, 322
Oedipus (Seneca) 276
Oedipus at Colonus (Sophocles) 286
Oedipus the King (Sophocles) 286,
    287–288
Of the Fox and of the Wolf 262
"Of the Gods" (Protagoras)
    101
Óg, Fearghal 39
The Ogre (Menander) 188
Ojibway myths and legends
    215–216

Oklahoma Cherokee
     creation myths 78
     folktales **216–217**
Old Comedy 20, 21, 188
"The Old Dog and the Hunter"
     (Phaedrus) 235
Old English poetry 42, **217–219**
     influences on 270
     themes of 190
"The Old Man and the Hind" 305
Oliver of Paderborn 80
Olschki, Leonardo 247
Omar Khayyám **219–221**
O'Meara, Dominic 244
On Anger (Seneca) 276
"On Believing and Not Believing"
     (Phaedrus) 235
The Once and Future King (White) 68,
     131
On Coats of Mail (Al-Maʿrrī) 181
On Divination (Cicero) 70
On Duties (Cicero) 70
O'Neill, Eugene
     influences on 6, 203
     works by 21–22
On Fortune (Seneca) 276
On Free Will (Augustine) 29–30
On Friendship (Cicero) 70
On His Return (Andocides) 26–27
"On Hunting" (Xenophon) 333
On Imitation (Dionysius of
     Halicarnassus) 93
On Mercy (Seneca) 276
On Music (Augustine) 29
Ono 206
On Old Age (Cicero) 70
Ono no Komachi **221–222**
On Order (Augustine) 29
Oꞌ no Yasumaro 160
On Platonic Theology (Proclus) 249
"On the Art of Horsemanship"
     (Xenophon) 333
On the Causes of Corrupted Eloquence
     (Quintilian) 253
"On the Cavalry Commander"
     (Xenophon) 333
On the Commonwealth (Cicero) 70
On the Crown (Demosthenes) 90
On the Education of the Orator
     (Quintilian) 253–254
On the Embassy (Aeschines) 27
On the Greatness of the Soul (Augustine)
     29
On the Happy Life (Augustine) 29
*On the Harmony of Religion and
     Philosophy* (Averroës) 33
On the Immortality of the Soul
     (Augustine) 29
*On the Improvement of the Moral
     Qualities* (Ibn Gabirol) 138, 139

On the Murder of Eratosthenes (Lysias)
     27, 179
On the Mysteries (Andocides) 26–27
On the Nature of Things (Lucretius) 99,
     177–179, 320
On the Orator (Cicero) 70
On the Peace with Sparta (Andocides)
     26–27
On the Sublime (Longinus) 173–174
*On the Uses of the Parts of the Body of
     Man* (Galen) 110
On the World (Apuleius) 19
"On Virgins" (Ambrose) 12
Oꞌothham Hohoꞌok Aꞌagitha **222–223**
Opo no Yasumoro. *See* Oꞌ no Yasumaro
Optics (Euclid) 101
oral literature **223–224**. *See also* sagas
     of Armenia 86–87
     characteristics of 305, 328
     epics and 97, 98, 211
     functions of 78
     Icelandic 280
     Indian 230, 315
     Native American. *See* Native
          American literature
     Old English poetry and 217
     of Persia 278
     proverbs as 8, 9
     Russian 283
     Vedas and 256
Oral Torah 294–295
orators 69–71, 89–91, 140, 141, 179,
     242, 253, 274, 275, 300–301
     Attic **26–28**
Order of the Poor Clares 107
Ordo (Hildegard von Bingen) 128
Oresteia (Aeschylus) 5–6
Organizing Strategy (Check and
     Grinyer) 290
Oriental Philosophy (Avicenna) 35
Origen
     contemporaries of 174
     influence of 248
     literary criticism on 12
Orlando Furioso (Ariosto) 285, 313, 322
Orlando Innamorato (Boiardo) 285
Ossianic Cycle. *See* Fenian Cycle
Ostromir Gospel (Deacon Gregor)
     224–225
Otomo Yakamochi 214, **225–226**
Outlines of Pyrrhonism (Sextus
     Empiricus) 277
Ou-yang Hsiu. *See* Ouyang Xiu
Ouyang Xiu **226–227**
Ovid **227–229**
     influence of 2, 65, 116, 125, 167,
          189, 229, 312
     influences on 60, 202, 203
     literary criticism on 155, 176,
          228–229, 235, 249

themes of 66, 137
translations of 67
works by 249, 305
Owain (prince of Powys) 39
Owen, D. D. R. 67

P

Palladius 168
Palsson, Hermann 280
Panaetius 17
Panchatantra **230–232**
     influence of 232
     literary criticism on 76, 305
     parallels to 235
     themes in 231–232
Panchatantra Reconstructed (Edgerton)
     232
Pandey, Shri Mathura Datt 154
Pandora 203
Panegyricus (Isocrates) 141
Panegyricus Trajani (Pliny the Younger)
     242
"The Panther" 44
Panyassis 125
Papago Indians 222–223
Papatuanuku 206
Papyrus of Ani 53
The Papyrus of Hunefer 53
Paradise Lost (Milton)
     composition of 68
     as epic 97
     influences on 203
Paradiso (Dante) 84
Paragraphs and Periods (Al-Maʿrrī) 180
Parallel Lives (Plutarch) 245–246
Parsifal (Wagner) 131
Parzival (Wolfram von Eschenbach)
     131, 329–331
Pausanias **232–233,** 237
Pax Romana 31, 150, 175, 242,
     243, 294
Peace (Aristophanes) 20–21
Peak of Eloquence (al-Sharif) 12
Pearl 219
Peck, George 144
Peirre of Amiens 80
Pele 206
Perceval, or the Story of the Grail
     (Chrétien de Troyes) 67, 68,
     130–131
Pericles 237, 307
Perlesvaus 131
Perotti, Nicholas 235
Persephone 203
The Persians (Aeschylus) 4–5,
     136
The Persian Wars (Herodotus). *See
     History* (Herodotus)
Peter of Beauvais 67

Petrarch
  influence of 66
  influences on 2, 25, 147, 185, 229,
    250, 254, 313
  themes of 66
Petronius **233–234**
  translations of 233
  works by 174
Phaedo (Plato) 238, 281
Phaedra (Seneca) 276
Phaedrus **234–236**
  literary criticism on 234–235
  parallels to 230
Pharsalia (Lucan) 175–176
Phenomena (Euclid) 101
Philinus 92
Philip (count of Flanders) 67
Philip (Isocrates) 27, 141
Philip II (king of Macedonia) 22, 27,
  90, 141, 300
Philip of Swabia 319
Philippe of Novare 263
Philippi, Donald 160
Philippics (Cicero) 69
Philippics (Demosthenes) 27, 90
Philip the Fair (king of France) 147
Philistus 92
Philoctetes (Sophocles) 286
The Phormio (Terence) 300
Physics (Aristotle) 23
Physiologus 44
picaresque novels 233
Pidal, Menéndez 72
Pierre de Ronsard 66
Pierre de Saint-Cloud 262
Piers Plowman (Langland) 190, 219,
  302
Pillow Talk (Sei Sho̅nagon) 273–274
Pilpay 235
Pima Indians 222–223
Pinakes 59
Pindar **236–237**
  contemporaries of 4, 37
  influences on 17
Pine-Coffin, R. S. 31
Ping-fa (Sunzi) 290
Pistoia, Cino da 85
"Pitiful Captive" (Ibn Gabirol) 139
Pizarro, Francisco 199
The Place of Sweet Scents (Saadī) 268
plague 190
Plato **237–239**
  contemporaries of 20, 141, 238,
    281, 300
  influence of 1, 18, 19, 22, 27, 29,
    33, 100, 167, 244, 245, 270, 301
  literary criticism by 173, 273
  literary criticism on 173, 238–239
  philosophical method of 277
  translations of 50, 238

works by 281, 282
works on 33, 70, 248
Plautus, Titus Maccius **239–241**
  influences on 188
  literary criticism on 299–300
The Play of Madness (Adam de la Halle)
  3–4
The Play of Robin and Marion (Adam
  de la Halle) 3
playwrights 3–4, 4–6, 20–22, 96,
  111–112, 153–154, 187–188,
  221–222, 239–240, 266–267,
  286–289, 325–326
Pliny the Elder **241–242**
Pliny the Younger **242–243**
  contemporaries of 172, 186, 242,
    254, 293
  on Pliny the Elder 241
Plotinus **244–245**
  contemporaries of 248
  influence of 244, 248, 249
  works on 173
"Plum Blossoms" (Li Qingzhao) 170
Plutarch **245–246**
  contemporaries of 93
  influences on 302
  works by 127
Pluto 202
Po Chü-i. *See* Bai Juyi
Poe, Edgar Allan 306
Poema e mío Cid 72–73, 97
The Poem of the Cid 72–73, 97
Poem on Hidden Meaning (Rumi)
  265–266
Poems in Stanzas (Hadewijch) 118
Poetic Edda 95, 204–205
Poetics (Aristotle) 21, 23–24, 91, 136,
  173
poetry. *See also* Bardic poetry; Nahuatl
  poetry; Old English poetry; *Purana;*
  Tanka; troubadours; Zuni, narrative
  poetry
    Aztec 208–209
    ci poetry 171, 327
    fu poetry 253, 338, 340
    lyric 37
    neoteric poets 62
    shi poetry 171
    Zuni narrative poetry 78, 328,
      340–341
Politics (Aristotle) 23
Polo, Marco **246–248**
  Crusades and 81
  influence of 190
  translations of 247
Polybius 308
Polycrates (king of Samos) 14
Pompey 57–58, 175
Poor Heinrich (Hartmann)
  124

Pope, Alexander
  influences on 237, 254, 322
  literary criticism by 174
Porphyry **248**
  contemporaries of 248
  influence of 248, 249
  works by 173, 244
Porter, William 159
Portinari, Beatrice 83
Poseidon 202
Posidonius 92
Pound, Ezra 25, 147
"Prayer to Aphrodite" (Sappho) 272
Press, Alan 313
Prévost, Abbe 66
Primera Crónica General 72
The Princes of Ireland (Rutherford) 201
Principles of Arithmetic (Boethius) 50
Principles of Music (Boethius) 50
printing press, impact of 190
Pro Archia (Cicero) 70
Problems in Grammar (Pliny the Elder)
  241
Problems of Arithmetic (Omar
  Khayyám) 219
Proclus **249**
Pro Flacco (Cicero) 70
Prometheus 137, 202, 203
Prometheus Bound (Aeschylus) 5
Pro Murena (Cicero) 70
Propertius, Sextus 60, **249–250**
Prophecies of Merlin (Geoffrey of
  Monmouth) 112
Prose Edda (Snorri Sturluson) 95, 204,
  269, 280
Prose Lancelot 68
Pro Sulla (Cicero) 70
Protagoras 101
Proust, Marcel 306
proverbs, African **8–9**
"Pruning Trees" (Bai) 38
Psellus, Michael 244
Ptolemy
  influence of 118, 167
  works on 92
Ptolemy I (pharaoh of Egypt) 100,
  187–188
Ptolemy II (pharaoh of Egypt) 59,
  60
*The Pumpkinification of the Divine
  Claudius* (Seneca) 276
purana **250–251**
  composition of 182, 315
  oral literature and 224
Puranatna 251
Purgatorio (Dante) 84
"Pwyll, Lord of Dyfed" 201
Pygmalion (Shaw) 203
Pyramid texts 53
Pyrrho 277

Pythagoras 248
Pythian IV (Pindar) 236

Q

qasidah 13, 120, 298
"Qasidat al-Burda" (al-Būsírí) 55
Qāsim, Abu al-. *See* Muhammad
Qat 207
Qu Elegies **252–253**
La Queste del Saint Graal 131
Quetzalcoatl 208–209
Quintilian **253–254**
    influence of 254
    influences on 10, 23, 302
    life of 186
    literary criticism by 172, 249
    opinions expressed by 173
    works by 241
Quintilianus, Marcus Fabius. *See*
    Quintilian
The Quintuplet (Nezāmī) 210
Qur`an. *See* Koran
Qu Yuan 252–253, **254–255**

R

Rabelais, François
    influence of 305
    influences on 176, 245, 302
Racine, Jean 203, 245
Raghuvamsa (Kalidasa) 317
Ragnarok 205
Raimon (count of Toulouse) 318
Rainardo 262
Rakhsh 106
Rama 316–317
Ramakien 317
Ramayana
    composition of 45, 315–316
    influence of 317
    literary criticism on 181
RaMBaM 183
Ramcharitmanas (Tulsidas) 317
Rangi 206
Ranginui 206
Rata 207
"The Rat and the Frog" (Aesop) 7
Rāwiyah, Hammād al- 298
Rawlinson, George 126–127
Raymond of Aguilers 80
Raymond V of Toulouse 43
Rechy, John 233
recluse poets (China) 297
The Recognition of Sakuntala (Kalidasa)
    154
Red Book of Hergest 201
The Red Branch (Llywelyn) 201
The Region of the Summer Stars
    (Williams) 131

Register of Grasping the Carriage Reins
    (Fan Chengda) 104
Reinecke Fuchs (Goethe) 263
Reiss, Edmund 51
Religious Holidays (Ovid) 228
Remedia Amoris (Ovid) 228, 249
Remedies for Love (Ovid) 228, 249
ren 74–75
Renaissance
    courtly love tradition and 313
    foundations of 190
    influences on 19, 23, 51, 187, 229,
        240, 244, 300, 302, 322
    literary criticism in 176, 219
    themes in 61–62, 66
Renart le Bestourné 267
The Republic (Plato) 33, 70,
    238–239
Res Gestae Divi Augusti (Augustus) 32
"The Return" (Tao Yuanming) 297
"Returning to the Farm to Dwell" (Tao
    Yuanming) 297
"Return to Wang River" (Wang Wei)
    326
"The Revenge of Blue Corn Ear
    Maiden" 314
Reynaert, J. 119
Reynard the Fox 262
Reynard the Fox (Masefield) 263
"Rhapsody on contemplating the
    Mystery" (Zhang Heng) 340
Rhea 202, 203
rhetoric. *See* orators
Rhetoric (Aristotle) 7, 23
Richard, Jean 79–80
Richard I Coeur de Lion (king of
    England) 24, 186
Richard of Lison 262
Richardson, Samuel 66, 175
Richard the Pilgrim 80
Rig-Veda **256–257**
Riiki 206
Ring of the Nibelung (Wagner)
    95, 212
ritha 158–159
Ritusamhara (Kalidasa) 153
"rivers-and-mountains" tradition
    334
Robert II (count of Artois) 3
Robert de Boron 68, 131, 258
Robert of Clari 80
Rokkasen 221
Roland. *See* Song of Roland
The Roman Antiquities (Dionysius of
    Halicarnassus) 93
romance, medieval. *See* medieval
    literature
The Romance of Aeneas 258
Romance of Reynard **262–264**
Romance of Thebes 258

Romance of the Rose (Guillaume de
    Lorris and Jean de Meun) **259–261**
    composition of 116, 147–148, 258
    content and themes in 65, 66,
        116–117
    influence of 167, 261
    literary criticism on 260–261
    and medieval romance 190
The Romance of Troy 258
"Romances of New Spain" (Pomar, *ed.*)
    209
*Le Roman de la Rose. See Romance of the
    Rose*
Roman d'Eneas 124
Roman de Renart 190, 235, **262–264,**
    267
Le Roman du Graal (Robert de Boron)
    131
Roman Elegies (Goethe) 250
Roman mythology **202–204,** 260
Roman Odes (Horace) 135
romantic literature, influences on 51
Rome, fall of 189
Rongo 206
Ronsard, Pierre de 62, 313
The Rose Garden (Saadī) 268
"Rose Oser Sero Eros" (Shoaf) 261
Rougemont, Denis de 65
Ruan Ji **264**
Rubáiyát (Omar Khayyám) 62,
    219–220
Rubens, Peter Paul 203
Rudel, Jaufré. *See* Jaufré Rudel
"Rudel to the Lady of Tripoli"
    (Browning) 147
The Rule of the Community 89
Rumi, Jalaloddin 26, 196,
    264–266
Rūmī, Jalāl ad-Dīn ar. *See* Rumi,
    Jalaloddin
Runciman, Steven 81
runes 152–153
Rushd, Abū al-Walíd Muhammad ibn
    Ahmad ibn Muhammad ibn. *See*
    Averroës
Rushdie, Salman 306
Russell, D. A. 173–174
Russell, Rinaldina 94
Rustichello 246
Rutebeuf 263, **266–267**
Rutherford, Edward 201
Ruusbroec, Jan van 40

S

Saadī **268–269**
Sa'adia Gaon 138
Sadako (empress of Japan) 273
Sadī. *See* Saadī
Saga of Thidrek of Bern 269

sagas **269–270**
  influence of 211
  King Harald's Saga (Snorri
    Sturluson) 280
  mythology and 204
  Njal's Saga **212–213,** 269
  themes of 190, 217
  Volsunga saga 95, 269
Saidi, Ahmad 62
Saint-Gilles, baron 284
saints. *See also* Ambrose; Augustine;
  Francis of Assisi; Jerome; Thomas
  Aquinas
    Albert the Great 303
    Basil 12
    Clare of Assisi 107
    Fulgentius **108–109**
    Gregory, Saint 11, 12
    hagiographies 266
Saladin 79, 183
Sallust 167, **270–271**
Salonina (empress of Rome) 244
Sama-Veda 256
Samuel of Taima 140
Sancho II of Castile 71
Sanhājí, Sharaf ad-Dín Muhammad ibn
  Sa`íd al-Búsírí as-. *See* Búsírí, al-
Sanpoil Indian creation myths 78
Sappho of Lesbos **271–273**
  life of 174
  literary criticism on 272–273
  themes of 61
  translations of 62
Satire I (Juvenal) 150
Satires (Horace) 135
satori 339
Saturn 202
Satyricon (Petronius) 233–234
Saxo Grammaticus 204
Scaldic poetry 204
Schiller, J. C. Friedrich von 154, 203
Schlamm, Carl 19
The Scholar (Pliny the Elder) 241
Schoolcraft, Henry Rowe 215
Schweikle, Günther 324
science and medicine, writers on
  20–21, 33, 34–35, 110–111, 129–130,
  219–220, 276, 340
Scipio Africanus 96
Scivias (Hildegard von Bingen) 128
Scodel, Ruth 288
scops 217
Scott, Lockhart 72
Scott, Sir Walter 72
The Seafarer 218
The Seasons (Kalidasa) 153
Secundus, Gaius Plinius. *See* Pliny the
  Elder
Secundus, Gaius Plinius Caecilius. *See*
  Pliny the Younger

Segal, Erich 102
Sei Sho¯nagon 273, **273–274**
Sejanus 234, 235
Selu 216
Selu: Seeking the Corn-Mother's Wisdom
  (Awiakta) 216–217
Seneca **274–277**
  family of 175
  influence of 168, 276
  influences on 302
  life of 186, 253
  opinions expressed by 173
Seneca the Elder 274
Senzaishu (1183) 108
Septuagint 49
Servatius, Bishop of Tongeren 124
Seth, Symeon 235
Seti I (pharaoh of Egypt) 53
Seven Against Thebes (Aeschylus) 5
Seven Beauties (Nezāmī) 210
Seven Famous Greek Plays (O'Neill)
  21–22
Seven Modes of Sacred Love (Beatrice of
  Nazareth) 40
Seven Odes. *See* Hanged Poems
Sextus Empiricus **277**
Shah-nama. See Shahnameh
Shahnameh (Firdawsí) **277–278**
  composition of 106
  literary criticism on 316
  oral literature and 223
Shakespeare, William
  influence of 2
  influences on 19, 58, 203, 204,
    229, 240, 245–246, 313, 322
  literary criticism on 84–85
  themes of 62, 66
Shamsuddin of Tabriz 265
shan-shui tradition 334
Sharif ar-Radi, al-Sayyid al- 12
Shastra, Narsingha 155
Shastri, Devadatta 155
Shaw, George Bernard 203
Shelley, Percy Bysshe 6
shi (poetry) 171, 253, 291
Shi-chi 290
Shi-De 121–122
shih. See shi
Shih Jing. *See Book of Songs*
Shih-te 121–122
Shiji 290
Shijing. See Book of Songs
Shikishi (princess of Japan) **279**
Shinchokusenshu (1232) 82
Shinkokinshu (1201) 108
Shinto
  influence of 191
  sacred texts of 160
Ship of Fools (Brandt) 302
Shiva 256

Shoaf, R. Allen 261
Shonyoho 279
Shoshi (empress of Japan) 194–195
Sic et Non (Abélard) 1
Sicilian school 318
Sidney, Sir Philip
  influences on 175
  themes of 66
Siegfried 212
Sigrun 205
Sima I (emperor of China) 264
Sima Qian 74, 164–165, 290
Simonides 37
Sinchi Roca 199
Sin-Leqi-Uninni 113
Sir Gawain and the Green Knight
  content and themes of 66, 190,
    258
  influences on 68, 200, 219
Sita 316–317
Sitaramiah, V. 316
Six Poetic Genuises 221
Sjoestedt, Marie-Louise 201
Skandagupta 153
skepticism, as philosophy 277
slavery, views on 23, 102
slokas 251, 315
Smart, Christopher 235
Smith, Colin 72
Snorri Sturluson 95, 204, 269, **279–280**
Snyder, Gary 339
Socrates **280–282**
  contemporaries of 101, 179,
    281–282, 286, 332
  influence of 167, 237
  life of 74
  literary criticism on 174
  philosophical method of 277
  works on 20, 27, 237–239
Socratic Method 237–238, 281
Soliloquies (St. Augustine) 11
Solomon (king of Jerusalem) 157–158
Solon 237
soma 256–257
song (sung) 51–52
Song of Antioch (Richard the Pilgrim)
  80
The Song of Hiawatha (Longfellow) 215
The Song of Igor **283**
Song of Jerusalem 80
Song of Roland **283–285**
  content and themes of 65, 80
  as epic 97
  influence of 72, 107, 285
  literary criticism on 73, 283,
    284–285
  medieval romance and 190,
    257–258
"Song of the Campeador" 72
"Song of the Jade-hunter" (Li He) 169

Song of the Volsungs. See Volsunga saga
A Song on the Sorrows of Departure
[Lisao] (Qu Yuan) 252–253, 255
Songs of Ch`u. *See Qu Elegies*
"Songs of Depression" (Yang Wanli)
335
Songs of Sorrow (Ovid) 228
Songs of the Fringed Mouth Gods 210
Songs of the Highest Mountains 210
Songs of the Killer Enemies 210
Songs of the Navajo Canyon 210
Songs of the Sand Painting 210
Songs of the South. See Qu Elegies
"Songs of the Wedding Bed" (Sappho)
271–272
Son-Jara. *See Epic of Son-Jara; Sundiata,*
an Epic of Old Mali
Sonnet 73 (Shakespeare) 62
"Son of Light Kills the Monster"
314
Sophocles **286–289**
    contemporaries of 102, 125, 280,
    286
    influence of 203
    literary criticism on 24, 287–288
    themes in 136, 137
    works by 137
    works on 21
Sordello 312
The Spark from the Fire-stick (Al-
Ma`rrī) 181
Spenser, Edmund
    influences on 68, 128, 229, 313,
    322
    themes of 66
    works by 97, 203
Spinoza, Benedict 184
"Spiritual Couplets" (Rumi) 265
"Spring's Return" (Horace) 135
Sprüche poems 324
Srimad Bhagavatam 251
Ssu-ma Ch'ien *See* Sima Qian
Ssu-ma I *See* Sima I 264
Stabat Mater (hymn) 144
Staines, David 68, 258
Steele, Richard 300
Stephen (king of England) 15
Stesichorus 127
Stevens, John 258
Stoicheia (Euclid) 100–101
Stoicism
    adherents of 175, 184, 241
    goals of 277
    influence of 244
    origins of 301
    tenets of 99–100, 275
    works on 275–276
Stone, I. F. 281, 282
"The Story of Sohrab and Rostam"
(Firdawsī) 278

The Story of the Dilapidated Kiln (Wang
Shifu) 326
The Story of the Western Wing (Wang
Shifu) 325–326
The Story of the Western Wing in All
Keys and Modes (Dong Jieyuan) 325
Strabo **288–289**
    influences on 17
    literary criticism by 300
Strassberg, Richard 252, 325
"The Streets" (Fan Chengda) 104
Sturluson, Storri. *See* Snorri Sturluson
Subandhu 155
sublime 173
Suetonius 241
Sulla, Publius 70
Sullivan, Bruce 181, 182
Sulma, Zuhayr ibn Abi 120–121, 298
Sumerian civilization 113
Summa Theologica (Aquinas) 303–304
Sundiata 98, 289
Sundiata, an Epic of Old Mali **289**
"The Sun Priest and the Witch Woman"
341
Sun Sunt-zu. *See* Sunzi
Sun Tsu and the Art of Business
(McNeilly) 290
Sun Tzu. *See* Sunzi
Sunzi **289–291**
The Suppliant Maidens (Aeschylus) 5
Suppliant Women (Euripides) 102
surahs 161, 162
Surface-loci (Euclid) 101
Su Shi 104, 290, **291–292**
Su Shih. *See* Su Shi
Sutra Vritti (Shastra) 155
Su Tung-po. *See* Su Shi
Su Xun 290
Swanton, M. J. 15
Swift, Jonathan
    influences on 176
    literary criticism by 174
    literary criticism on 150, 176
The Sword in the Stone (White) 131
Symphonia armonie celestium
revelationum (Hildegard von Bingen)
128
The Symphony of the Harmony of
Celestial Revelations (Hildegard von
Bingen) 128
The Symposium (Plato) 20, 238
Symposium (Xenophon) 282, 332

T

Tachibana no Norimitsu 273
Tacitus, Cornelius **293–294**
    contemporaries of 242, 243, 293
    influences on 241, 254, 271
    literary criticism by 233

literary criticism on 59, 293–394
    works by 204
Tain Bo Cuailnge 200
Taira no Sukemori 82
Takia Haymanot (king of Gondar) 158
The Tale of Genji (Murasaki) 82, 141,
194–196
The Tale of Izumi Shikibu (Izumi
Shikibu) 142
The Tale of the Oriole (Yuan Zhen) 325
Taliesin 39, 199
Taliessin through Logres (Williams) 131
Talmud **294–296**
    Dead Sea Scrolls and 88
    origins of 48
    works on 183
Tametaka, Prince 141
Tanach 47
Tane 206
Tangaroa 206
Tanka *(uta; waka)* **296–297**
    characteristics of 213, 222
    practitioners of 108, 142,
    213–214, 221, 279
    uta 279
    waka 222
T`ao Ch`ien. *See* Tao Yuanming
T`ao Hung-ching 334
Taoism. *See* Daoism
Tao Te Ching (Laozi) 165–166
Tao Yuanming **297**
    influence of 38, 297
Tarafah ibn 'Amr al-'Abd **297–298**
    influence of 181
    Mu'allaqāt and 120, 298
Tasso, Torquato
    medieval romance and 258
    themes in 80
Tawhaki 207
The Teacher (Augustine) 30
Tedlock, Dennis 299
Tehuty 53
Teilez, Baltazar 158
telaapi 299
telapnaawe narratives **299**
Temmu (emperor of Japan) 160, 213
Temple scroll 89
Tenchi (emperor of Japan) 213
Tennyson, Alfred, Lord
    influences on 68, 131, 322
    literary criticism on 331
Te Po 206
Terence **299–300**
    influence of 300
    influences on 188
Terentianus 173
Terry, Patricia 205
terza rima 84
Tesoretto (Latini) 167
Testament (Francis of Assisi) 107

The Testament (Villon) 190
Testament of Jean de Meun (Jean de Meun) 147
Tetrologies (Antiphon) 26
Thabit, Zayd Ibn 161
Theatetus (Plato) 238
Theban Plays (Sophocles) 286–287
Theobald, Archbishop 112
Theodoric (king of the Ostrogoths) 50
Theogony (Hesiod) 127–128, 202, 203
Theologica Christiana (Abélard) 1
Theologica Summi Boni (Abélard) 1
"Theology of Aristotle" (Plotinus) 244
Theophrastus 187, **300–303**
Thesaurus Antiquitatum Sacrarum (Ugolino) 295
The Thesmophoriazousai (Aristophanes) 101–102
Thirty Tyrants 179, 281
Thomas, J. W. 125
Thomas à Angleterre 309, 310
Thomas Aquinas, Saint **303–304**
    contemporaries of 318
    influences on 184
    literary criticism on 303–304
Thor 205
The Thousand and One Nights 232, **304–306**
Thucydides **306–309**
    contemporaries of 280
    influence of 270
    literary criticism on 92, 307–308
Thyestes (Seneca) 276
Tian Wen 253
Tiberius (emperor of Rome) 234, 294
Tibullus 249, 250
Tien Wen 253
Timaeus 92
Timotheus 141
Tipitaka 230
Titans 202
Titurel (Wolfram von Eschenbach) 329
Titus (emperor of Rome) 186
Titus Livius. *See* Livy
Titus Lucretius Carus. *See* Lucretius
"To Anaktoria" (Sappho) 272
"To Atthis" (Sappho) 272
"To His Coy Mistress" (Marvell) 62
Toichi (princess of Japan) 213
To Kabinana 206
To Karvuvu 206–207
To Live in Seclusion (Zhang Heng) 340
Tolkien, J.R.R. 95, 201, 204, 270
Toltecs 208–209
Topelius, Zacharius 152
Torah 47–48
    oral 294–295
    written 294–295
Torrigiano, Maestro 94

Tosa nikki (*The Tosa Diary*; Tsurayuki) 159–160
"To Sayf al-Dawla on His Recovery from an Illness" (al-Mutanabbi) 196
"To the Baseborn Tyrant" (Alcaeus) 10
"To the Virgins, to Make Much of Time" (Herrick) 62
tragedy
    Aristotle on 23–24
    development of genre 4
The Tragedy of Julius Caesar (Shakespeare) 58
Les Tragiques (D'Aubigné) 322
Trail of Tears 216
Trajan (emperor of Rome) 242, 243, 245
translators 10–11, 50–51, 147–148, 167–168
Il Tratatto (Jacopone da Todi) 144
Travels in Search of the Sources of the Nile (Bruce) 158
The Travels of Marco Polo (Polo) 246–248
travel writers 104, 232–233, 246–248
Treasury of the Excellencies of the Spaniards (Ibn Bassam) 72
Treatise on Understandings (Abélard) 1
The Trial of Socrates (Stone) 282
The Trickeries of Scapin (Molière) 300
"The Tricking of Gylfi" (Sturluson) 95
Tristan (Béroul) 258
Tristan (Gottfried von Strassburg) 115, 309
Tristan and Iseult **309–311**
    and Arthurian legend 65, 67
    influence of 257
    works on 115–116, 186, 190
Tristan und Isolde (Wagner) 309
Tristia (Ovid) 228
Tristram. *See* Tristan
"Triumph of Love" (Petrarch) 147
trobairitz 93–94, 311, 312–313
trobar clus 25
Troilus and Criseyde (Chaucer) 261
The Trojan Women (Euripides) 102
troubadours **311–313**
    and courtly love 65, 189
    development of 67
    examples of 24–25, 43–44, 146, 317–318
    female 93–94
    influence of 85, 107, 118, 119, 144, 318, 329
    influences on 250, 262
    origins of 257
True History (Lucian) 176
Tsao Chih. *See* Cao Zhi
Ts'ao Hsueh-Ch'in 325
Tsao Tsao. *See* Cao Cao 264

Tsurayuki Shu (Tsurayuki) 159
Tsurezuregusa (Yoshida Kenkō) 337
Tu 206
Tuatha Dé Danann 200
Tu Fu. *See* Du Fu
Tulsidas 317
Tune: The Charms of Nien-nu" (Su Shi) 291
Tung Chieh-Yuan 325
Turoldus 283–284
Turville-Petre, E. O. G. 204
tuuwutsi narratives **313–314**
"'Twas Love, whom I desire as well as trust" (Vigne) 319
Twelfth Night (Shakespeare) 62
The Twin Brothers (Plautus) 240
"Two Poems on the Bianzhou Rebellion" (Han Yu) 123
Tyramus. *See* Theophrastus
tz'u (poetry). *See* ci

U

ubi sunt motif 219
Ugolino, Blasio 295
'Uke 206
Ulster Cycle 199, 200
Underhill, Evelyn 144
upapurana 250
Urban II (pope) 79, 80
Urvashi Conquered by Valor (Kalidasa) 154
uta. See Tanka
'Uthman, Caliph 161

V

Vaidya, C. V. 316
Valentinian (emperor of Rome) 12
Valerius 29
Valhalla 205, 269
valkyries 205, 269
Valmiki, Maharshi **315–317**
Van Buitenen, J. A. B. 181, 183
Vari 206
Varuna 256
Vatsyayana Mallanga 155, 156
Ve 204
Vedas 256
    comparable texts 152
    composition of 315
    oral literature and 224
    puranas and 251
    Rig-Veda **256–257**
Vega, Garcilaso de la 199
Vegetius 147
Veldeke, Heinrich von. *See* Heinrich von Veldeke
Venerable Bede. *See* Bede

Venus 202
Venus and Adonis (Shakespeare) 203
Vercelli Book 217
Vespasian (emperor of Rome) 149, 241, 253
Vessantara, Prince 146
Vesta 203
Victory Odes (Pindar) 236
Vidal, Peire **317–318**
    contemporaries of 319
    literary criticism on 318
    on love 312
Viga Glum's Saga 269–270
Vigna, Peitro della. *See* Vigne, Pier delle
Vigne, Pier delle 167, **318–319**
Vikings, characteristics of 269
Vikramorvashe (Kalidasa) 154
Vili 204
Villehardouin, Geoffroi de 80, 190, **319–320**
Villon, François 190, 263, 267, 313
Vineis, Petrus de. *See* Vigne, Pier delle
Viracocha 199
Virgil **320–322**
    adaptations of 124–125
    contemporaries of 32, 134, 172, 249
    influence of 168, 172, 174, 175, 189, 229, 269, 320
    influences on 18, 63, 96, 127, 202, 203
    literary criticism on 12, 176, 227, 235
    themes of 93, 172
    works by 97, 132
    works on 84, 135
Vishnu 256, 316
Vishnu Purana 251
Visions (Hadewijch) 118
Visnu Sarma 230
La vita nuova (Dante) 83
"Vita Springs" 331
"The Vixen and the Hedgehog" (Aesop) 7
Vogelweide, Walther von der. *See* Walther von der Vogelweide
Volsunga Saga 95, 269
Voltaire (François-Marie Arouet)
    on Crusades 81
    literary criticism on 150, 176
"The Voyage of the Argo" (Apollonius of Rhodes) 17–18
Voyages to the Sun and Moon (Bergerac) 176
Vulcan 203
Vyasa 251

W

Wace (Norman-French poet) 67, 219
Wagner, Richard 95, 131, 203, 212, 270, 309, 331
waikan narratives 299, **323,** 331
waka. See Tanka
Wakefield Master 197
Wales, mythology of 199–202
Walther von der Vogelweide **324**
The Wanderer 219
Wang Anshi 74, 291, **324–325**
Wang Maoyuan 171
Wang Shifu **325–326**
Wang Wei 325, **326–327**
War against Jugurtha (Sallust) 271
Warner, Edmond 278
The War of the Sons of Light against the Sons of Darkness 89
"The Washing Stream" (Li Qingzhao) 170
Wasps (Aristophanes) 20
The Waste Land (Eliot) 131
"Watching a Village Festival" (Yang Wanli) 335
"Watching the Reapers" (Bai) 38
"Water Music Prelude" (Su Shi) 291
Watson, Burton 122, 292
"Ways and Means" (Xenophon) 333
"The Way Things Are" (Lucretius) 177–179
Wei Chuang. *See* Wei Zhuang
Wei Zhuang 297, **327**
The Well of Life (Ibn Gabirol) 138–139
Wenebajo 215
Wenis (pharoah of Egypt) 53
Weston, Jessie 130
"The Whale" 44
"When the Days Are Long in May" (Jaufré Rudel) 146
Whiston, William 149
White, T. H. 68, 131
White Book of Rhydderch 201
"The White Dawn of the Hopi" 314
Whitehead, Alfred North 239
White Mountain Apache myths and tales 224, **327–329**
"The Wife of Bath's Tale" (Chaucer) 68
The Wife's Lament 219
Wilde, Oscar 233
Wilhelm, James 43–44, 147
Willehalm (Wolfram von Eschenbach) 329–331
William (duke of Normandy) 189
William IX (count of Poitiers and duke of Aquitaine) 312
William of England (Chrétien de Troyes) 67
Williams, Charles 131
"Willow Branch" (Li Shangyin) 171

The Wine Song in Classical Arabic Poetry (Kennedy) 298
Winnebago
    waikan narratives 299, **323,** 331
    worak narratives 299, 323, **331**
"Winter Evening" (Alcaeus) 10
Wit and Wisdom from West Africa (Burton) 9
Wittgenstein, Ludwig 339
Wolfram von Eschenbach **329–331**
    contemporaries of 329
    influence of 131
    influences on 68, 115, 131
    literary criticism on 329–331
    medieval romance and 258
    works by 65, 131
The Woman of Samos (Menander) 188
women
    in Norse mythology 205
    role and status of
        in ancient Arab culture 33, 159
        in ancient China 170
        in ancient India 156
        in ancient Japan 194–195
        in Byzantium 16
        in classical Greece 102
        in Middle Ages 66, 94, 119, 129, 190, 258
        in 19th-century Britain 156
    trobaritz 93–94
The Women of Trachis (Sophocles) 286
Wooing of Étaín 200
worak narratives 299, 323, **331**
Wordsworth, William 306, 322
Works and days (Hesiod) 127
The World of Bede (Blair) 41
Worthington, Ian 90
Written Torah 294–295
"Written While Traveling through the Western Suburbs" (Li Shangyin) 171
Wu (emperor of China) 337
Wulf and Eadwacer 219
wuwei 165

X

Xanthippe 281
The Xenia (Martial) 186
Xenophon **332–334**
    contemporaries of 332
    influences on 308
    literary criticism on 173, 174, 333
    works by 281–282
Xiao Dezao 335
Xie Ling-yun **334**
Xixiangji (Wang Shifu) 325–326
Xuanzhong (emperor of China) 168
Xu Hiaxin 326

Y

ya 51–52
Yajur-Veda 256
Yang Wanli 104, **335**
Yaqui
    creation myths 78
    deer songs 78, **335–337**
Yasodhara 155
Yazdegerd III (shah of Persia) 278
Yeats, W. B.
    influences on 201
    themes of 62
Yigdal prayer 184
yoga 46
York Realist 197
Yoshida Kenkō **337**
Younger Edda (Sturluson) 95, 269, 280
Ysengrinus 262

Yuan Chen 325
Yuanyu 252
Yuan Zhen 38, 325
Yue Fei 290
Yueh Fei 290
Yueh Fu (Li Bai) 168
Yule, Sir Henry 247
Yusuf, Abu Yaqub 32–33
Yusuf, Salah ad-Din. *See* Saladin
Yu Xin **337–338**
Yvain, or the Knight with the Lion
    (Chrétien de Troyes) 67, 68

Z

zaju genre 325
Zapata, Luis 233
Zeno 99, 301

Zenobia, Queen 173
Zen parables **339–340**
Zeus 202
Zeydel, Edwin H. 330
Zhang Heng **340**
Zhang Zhun 335
Zhangzong (emperor of China) 326
Zhao Mingzheng 170
Zheng Hou 290
Zitner, Sheldon P. 24
Zoroastrianism 106, 257
zuihitsu 274
Zuni
    creation myths 78, 299, 341
    narrative poetry 78, 328, **340–341**
    telapnaawe narratives **299**